DATE DUE

sweet tea

black gay men of the south

sweet tea

DISCARDED

E. PATRICK JOHNSON

The University of North Carolina Press CHAPEL HILL

This book was published with the assistance of the Z. Smith Reynolds Fund of the University of North Carolina Press.

© 2008 The University of North Carolina Press
Set in Arnhem and Monotype Grotesque
by Keystone Typesetting, Inc.
Manufactured in the United States of America

The paper in this book meets the guidelines for
permanence and durability of the Committee on
Production Guidelines for Book Longevity of the
Council on Library Resources.

The University of North Carolina Press has been a
member of the Green Press Initiative since 2003.

Library of Congress Cataloging-in-Publication Data
Johnson, E. Patrick, 1967–
Sweet tea : Black gay men of the South / E. Patrick
Johnson.
       p. cm.
Includes bibliographical references and index.
ISBN 978-0-8078-3209-7 (cloth : alk. paper)
1. African American gay men—Southern States—Social
conditions. 2. Southern States—Social conditions. I. Title.
HQ76.27.A37J64 2008
306.76′6208996073075—dc22   2008005617

A Caravan book. For information, visit
www.caravanbooks.org.

12 11 10 09 08   5 4 3 2 1

University of North Carolina Press books may be
purchased at a discount for educational, business, or
sales promotional use. For information, please visit
www.uncpress.unc.edu or write to UNC Press, attention:
Sales Department, 116 South Boundary Street,
Chapel Hill, NC 27514-3808.

In Memory of

Curt Blackman,

Dean Hashaway,

and Jeff Smith

contents

map & illustrations

acknowledgments

A book such as *Sweet Tea* really does not happen without the help of others. While I had the vision to begin this project and see it through, many people rolled up their sleeves and asked, "How can I help?" And for that, I will be forever grateful. Especially, I want to thank friends and colleagues who put me in touch with men they thought would be great narrators for this book. My dear friend Ian Barrett, formerly of Atlanta, was the first to put me in touch with men in the Atlanta area and in towns around the South. His contacts account for about a third of those interviewed. I cannot imagine how *Sweet Tea* would have happened without his assistance. Duncan Teague also provided contacts in Atlanta, Tennessee, Mississippi, and Louisiana. He really is fierce! Trudier Harris, Ann McCarthy, and Marsha Houston were extraordinarily helpful in finding men in Alabama, and Ann and Marsha hosted me during my trips. I want to thank both of them for their southern hospitality, good humor, and good food! In North Carolina, my dear departed friend Curt Blackman found most of the narrators in the Research Triangle. He looms large in these pages. I want to thank Johari Jabir for telling me about, and Carlton Rutherford for introducing me to, Jeff Smith. I recorded his story just in the nick of time. Gregg Redmon also gave me names of folks in North Carolina. In Tennessee, I want to thank Dwayne Jenkins and Tony Horne for asking folks to talk to me. In Louisiana, Greg Osborne, Ed, and Roderick gave me names of people to speak with and provided a place to lay my head. In Virginia, thanks goes to Roosevelt Cain, Tom Cunningham, Marlon Ross, Ian Grandison, and Keith Clark for hosting my visits and providing contacts. In Texas, I want to thank Njoki McElroy for hosting me and helping me find narrators.

Transcribing hours of interviews is not only time consuming, but also tedious. Without the assistance of younger and fresher ears and eyes, I would not have been able to get these interviews down on paper. I want to thank my two undergraduate assistants, Adrian Frandle and Megan Rosati, for their diligence. My graduate research assistants—Lori Baptista, Javon Johnson, Chloe Johnston, James Moreno, and Munjulika Rahman—put in overtime to make sure that each and every word of the narrators was accounted for and the index was thorough. Their work on this book will not be forgotten.

This book also would not have been possible without the financial support of Northwestern University, which awarded me two faculty research grants. The School of Communication also gave me a research leave during the 2004–5 academic year and a grant to complete the transcriptions of the interviews. The Martin Duberman Fellowship from the Center for Lesbian and Gay Studies provided resources with which to conduct the final interviews.

Various students and colleagues at Northwestern and at other universities in the Chicagoland area provided support—both emotional and professional—throughout the making of this book. They include Dwight McBride, Sandra Richards, Jennifer DeVere Brody, Sharon Holland, D. Soyini Madison, Ramon Rivera-Servera, Richard Iton, Darlene Clark Hine, Tracy Vaughn, Martha Biondi, Margaret Drewal, Carol Simpson Stern, Tracy Davis, John Keene, Lynn Spigel, Barbara O'Keefe, Jane Saks, Paul Edwards, Mario La-Mothe, Javon Johnson, Tamara Roberts, Jeffrey McCune, Marlon Bailey, Molly Schneider, and Joanna Thapa. John Howard and several anonymous readers helped to fine-tune *Sweet Tea* and push it toward having an even greater impact. Colleagues around the country who invited me to give talks or performances based on my interviews include Joe Roach, George Chauncey, Daphne Brooks, Bill Leap, Marlon Bailey, Francesca Royster, John Jackson, Torin Moore, Kim Singletary, Vicki Ruiz, Vicki Patraka, Lisa Flores, Patrick Finnessy, Bruce Burgett, and Ernest Daily. I want to thank the participants at the 2006 Black Performance Studies symposium at Northwestern, where I first debuted the performance based on the stories in *Sweet Tea*. Their appreciation of the narrators' stories encouraged me to keep performing them. The following institutions invited me to give performances: Northwestern, Princeton, Yale, Berkeley, the University of Pennsylvania, Lewis and Clark, Amherst, Mt. Holyoke, Stanford, Purdue, the University of Georgia, Hofstra, the University of Michigan, the University of Maryland, Bowling Green State, UCLA, the University of Illinois at Chicago, Emerson, Colgate, the University of Utah, DePaul, and the University of Washington.

Special thanks to my family back home in Hickory, North Carolina. You not only keep me lifted in prayer, but also grounded when I forget my "roots." I always get support on my projects from my "brister," Cedric Brown. Thanks for helping me push this one on through. My soul sister, Stacie Hewett, is always a fan on the side, whether she can understand what I am talking about or not. Keep on showing the love.

My partner, Stephen Lewis, is simply amazing. I do not know why he tolerates me, but he does, with all the love that he can muster. His willingness to let me go away from home for so long to collect these stories is a testament to his love.

To all the narrators of *Sweet Tea*, both those whose lives are chronicled herein and those that are not, I say thank you for opening up your homes and your lives—indeed, for pouring your tea. I hope that I have done your stories justice.

Thanks to the staff at the University of North Carolina Press, who worked diligently to copyedit, design, produce, and market this book, so it could get into the hands of readers. Finally, thanks to my editor, Sian Hunter, who believed in me long before this project. Her patience, integrity, and support will not be forgotten. This is our baby.

introduction

. . . .

The South, like all regions of the country, is a site of contradictions. The central role once played there by America's "peculiar institution," however, perhaps makes its social and cultural inner workings more complex. Race relations in the South are literally the stuff television shows, movies, and novels are made of, and they have directly affected the lives of most of its inhabitants. The region's long history of grotesque racial violence—slavery, lynching, cross burnings, etc.—is etched in the American imagination, laid bare like a freshly laundered sheet hung out to dry on a clothesline, a sheet that, after sundown, might glow blood orange before a torched home, car, or body. Yes, these images of insidious race hatred pervade the physical landscape and cultural backdrop of the land of Dixie.

But for every yin, there is a yang. Complementing the tortured past of the South is the gentility, civility, and general "good manners" of folk. The right to co-exist as neighbors across racial and class lines has been hard won on the very soil that was once taken from indigenous Americans and tilled by enslaved Americans. The past haunts the air, but one does not choke on the stench of flesh as before. The scent of magnolia is not spoiled by ashen bodies, but rather broken by the savory scent of collards, cornbread, and cobbler. Also wafting past most visitors are the local colloquialisms and diphthongs that can try the patience of the untrained ear. By and by, however, all of the senses "raise up" a harmonious hymn to take in all the South has to offer, not the least of which is a glass of sweetened iced tea.

What neither of these views of the South reveals, however, is the sexual other who is implicated in both the region's guts and its glory, its horrific past and its present graciousness. And yet, black gay southerners have co-existed in communities throughout the region for as long as there has been a "South." Beyond playing the stereotypical roles of florist, interior designer, musician, teacher, retail salesperson, and hairdresser, they have also served as doctors, dentists, entrepreneurs, lawyers, policemen, pastors, and pimps. They were reared in the same country kitchens and on the same front porches as their heterosexual siblings, cousins, and extended family. They speak the same colorful language, eat the same artery-constricting food, and deploy the same passive-aggressive techniques to circumvent unwelcome or seemingly inappropriate questions by addressing everything but what was asked. Indeed, black queers are a part of the patchwork quilt that is the diverse (and perverse) social fabric of southern living. And contrary to popular belief, not all southern homosexuals are silent about their sexual orientation. In fact, in some cases the more flamboyant one is about his sexuality, the more respect he garners, as is the case with several of the narrators in this book. For example, one narrator in Atlanta shared his view that really "self-possessed, street queens" are less likely to be harassed by a homophobe or to be gay bashed than he is when he goes to clubs because "a street queen will fuck you up. Everybody knows they carry blades, so people who might otherwise mess with a gay person won't mess with them out of respect." Then there is the story told to me by Ann McCarthy, one of the women in Tuscaloosa, Alabama, who helped me locate men for the research that went into this book, who told me, among other things, about a deacon in her church who used to cross-dress all throughout her childhood; her mother forbade her and her siblings to poke fun at this man because it was "disrespectful." And in "her" autobiography, The Lady Chablis, the black transgendered performer made famous by the book and film *Midnight in the Garden of Good and Evil*, writes: "My family has always been open to whatever anybody does or is—all 'cept for Mama. But the rest of 'em are pretty much all round loving people: if y'poor, love you; if y'black, love you; if y'white, love you."[1] These stories seem to corroborate Pete Daniel's assertion that "Southerners often accepted (or forgave) almost any eccentricity so long as it posed no threat to the established order."[2] But when gay men are still murdered in the South—as were my friends Curt Blackman and Dean Hashaway—we are reminded that there are exceptions to that acceptance and forgiveness.

Despite the South's history of racial segregation and religious fundamentalism, black gay men have carved out a space in which to live productive and fulfilling lives. While they may feel that some things about living where they do are not ideal, they nonetheless have made a conscious choice to remain in the South even in the face of great migrations of many gay men to urban spaces in the North, Midwest, and West and even in light of southerners' continued conservative attitudes toward racial and sexual minorities. The life histories of the narrators in this book provide insight into why men who are black and gay have chosen to remain in a region that has such a fraught racial past and a seemingly conservative view of dissident sexuality. If, in the South, public declarations of one's homosexuality or political activism are not the norm, then what other, more covert ways have these men found to resist oppression and to build community? One answer lies in the ways in which black gay southern men draw upon the performance of "southernness"—for example, politeness, coded speech, religiosity—to instantiate themselves as "legitimate" members of southern and black culture while, at the same time, deploying these very codes to establish and build friendship networks and find life and/or sexual partners. Participation in the church choir, for example, allows them to adhere to the religiosity of southern culture, but also provides a way to meet other black gay men and express their creativity. This is one instance in which a seemingly repressive sacred space actually becomes a vehicle for the expression of sexual desire. Instances such as these complicate gay histories that suggest that gay subcultures flourished best in northern, secular, urban spaces. Not only does the history of southern black gay men demand a reconsideration of what constitutes a "vital" subculture; it also necessitates a reconsideration of the South as "backward" and "repressive," when clearly gay community-building and desire emerge simultaneously within and against southern culture. Finally, the narratives presented here might offer other explanations for why so many black gay men remain in the South—explanations that have to do with cultural loyalty, a class status that prohibits physical mobility, and an affirming gay community.

Sweet Tea focuses on the life histories of African American gay men who were born and raised in the South and continue to reside there. Oral histories have proven to be an invaluable resource for documenting and theorizing the cultural norms, practices, beliefs, and attitudes of a particular historical period; the oral narratives of the particular men presented here simultaneously illuminate multiple identities—racial, sexual, gender, class— within a country where identity nonconformity has historically positioned one on the margins of society. As narrators of their own life experiences, however, these black gay men critique power relations as well as potentially legitimate them. Thus, their oral narratives provide insight into the complicated relationships between seemingly disparate communities of people. The narrators experience homophobia in black communities, yet they are an integral part of black community and church life. They experience homophobia and racism in white heterosexual and gay communities, yet they work among and have friendships with members of these same groups. Blackness and gayness are rendered alternately visible and invisible depending on the social context. The oral narratives of the subjects of this study evince larger questions regarding identity formation, community building, and power relations as they are negotiated within the context of southern history. Thus, the aim of *Sweet Tea* is manifold: to fill a void in the historical accounts of racialized sexual minorities in the South; to call into question the construction of the South as inhospitable to African American gay men; to account for the ways that black gay men negotiate their sexual and racial identity with their southern cultural and religious identity; and to highlight the ways in which black gay men build and maintain community through southern cultural forms that, on the surface, appear to be antigay.

The point here is that the social mores of the South dictate a passive-aggressive stance toward any transgressive behavior, especially the activities, behaviors, and indulgences that undermine its religious philosophies—drinking, gambling, adultery, and homosexuality, to name a few. So rather than "disrespect" the women of the house, men gather to drink outside on the back porch and have the alcohol concealed in a paper bag or disguised in a soft drink can or bottle; instead of doing "hard-core" gambling like poker or the slot machine, many southerners, especially women, will go to bingo night or surreptitiously buy a lotto ticket; men and women who have a "friend" on the side are careful not to bring any offspring from extramarital affairs around the legitimate children so as not to "embarrass" the family; and homosexual liaisons between supposedly straight men and known gay ones are treated similarly to heterosexual extramarital affairs: it's allowable as long as the indiscretion is not flaunted. During one of my visits to Tuscaloosa, Ann McCarthy actually called one of her neighbors who has been married to the same woman for close to forty years and who has four sons, to inquire if he would be interviewed for this book. His protestations (I could hear his raised voice through the phone while I sat three feet away at Ann's kitchen table finishing up my fried chicken) that he is not gay did not faze Ann as she nonchalantly reminded him: "Johnny,[3] why are you acting like you ain't gay? Everybody know that you and June Bug been carryin' on[4] for years, including Betty Sue. You know you need to come on over here and talk to this child. He's writin' a book on gay men in the South." The click on the other end of the line did not faze her either, as she continued to go through the phone book to find men whom she, and apparently the entire community, "knew" were "that way."

Ann outing Johnny would transgress the boundaries set between him, his lover, his wife, and the community that establish a complicity of silence about his and June Bug's carryin' on. The gentility, acts of politesse, and complicity of silence that form around taboo issues in southern tradition often take precedence over an individual's need to name that identity or flaunt that transgression. On the one hand, this kind of willful denial upholds institutionalized forms of oppression. On the other, it provides a space in which to peacefully co-exist and/or sometimes, in a paradoxical way, affirm one's identity or relationship. In other words, gays may transform those codes of gentility into queer codes of desire, gender, and class performance, or creative expression. As we will see in Chapter 3, this is particularly true for black gay men who are involved in the church, where their silence about their sexuality actually opens a space to "speak in tongues" about their identity in more nuanced ways. As James T. Sears reminds us, "Southern history is never simple and seldom straight."[5] Indeed, as the stories herein detail, the South is always already queer.

And yet many of the stories of black queer life have gone undocumented. Neglect on the part of historians of the South, black sexual dissidents' complicity of silence around issues of sexuality, and southerners' habitual taciturnity on things of a "private nature," all collude to keep the stories of southern black gay men's lives, like most taboo things in the South, "hidden in plain sight." With few exceptions, until recently histories of gay life in the United States have focused on urban spaces on the East and West Coasts—especially New York and San Francisco. I agree with Brett Beemyn's assessment that "a subtle elitism that views all but a few major metropolises as backward and entirely inhospitable to gays also contributes to this oversight."[6] Moreover, the general perception of the South as inhospitable has kept some scholars of gay history from excavating what, to my mind, is a more complicated space in which to negotiate one's (homo)sexuality. I argue, like Robert McRuer in another context, for a reexamination of the queer possibilities in the South and am "interested in what (perhaps more radical) cultural work can be done when . . . 'everywhere' includes such an apparently marginal and inhospitable place."[7]

A few historians of southern gays have attempted to correct this oversight by producing a number of very important texts on southern queer history. Chief among them are James T. Sears, John Howard, Carlos L. Dews, and Carolyn Leste Law. These scholars' texts fill a critical gap in the historical record by documenting the lives of the lesbian, gay, bisexual, and transgendered (LGBT) community in southern and rural communities. They have also been invaluable resources for the research for *Sweet Tea*, paving the way for scholars like me to contribute to this growing body of knowledge. While these books are crucial to the understanding of the queer South, none of them focuses exclusively on race or documents histories from the entire South, including states that were not part of the Confederacy, such as Oklahoma and Missouri. *Sweet Tea* also covers a broader range of age, class, gender, and educational demographics than has heretofore been discussed in histories of queer southerners.

While white and black folks in the South share a common history, it should go without saying that they didn't experience that history in the same way. Therefore, black folks' relationship to and perspective on the South—still marked by ambivalence—diverge in important ways from those of their white counterparts. Because black queers experience their race and sexuality (and class and gender) in a southern context, their relationships and experiences also diverge from those of white southern queers. This is why it is important to account for these particular histories. As suggested above, previous historians have detailed southern queer life, but none has focused exclusively on race as a category of analysis. And while many of the histories they have written include one or two queers of color as narrators of their experience, the overarching theme of these histories is one of region rather than region *and* race. The risk of these studies, then—their authors' intentions aside—is one that Donna Jo Smith voices: "If we allow 'southern queer' to mean 'white southern queer,' if we do not fully 'race' ourselves and our subjects, we will not decenter the white southern subject as 'norm' and will end up reifying the myth that the South is white."[8] The documentation of "raced" southern queer histories is also important for getting a different perspective on race relations in southern queer cultures. While Tennessee Williams and Carson McCullers may have joked about returning to the South "to renew the sense of horror," as Smith has pointed out, "a black queer southerner of Williams's and McCullers's generation" might not have such a desire "since that horror was all too real."[9] That "horror" is not just the ubiquitous and random racial violence directed toward black people, but also the racism within white gay communities in the South, as exemplified in the response a white informant in David Knapp Whittier's study on race and sexuality in a small southern rural town provided when asked if people mix by race and gender at house parties: "Afro Sheen is a poisonous grease that floats up to the surface of the water and makes you sick."[10] Such racism within white gay communities is merely a reflection of that found in the larger white community, and that racism is not limited to the South. Alternatively, *Sweet Tea* attempts to debunk the common myth that the South is a place where it is *more* difficult to be a black gay man, in part because—according to another common myth—black folks, in general, are more homophobic than whites, southern or otherwise. As some of the narratives in this book detail, many black communities around the South, and especially those in rural towns, accommodated sexual dissidents in ways unimaginable. The story related by the preoperative transgendered person from my hometown in rural western North Carolina is a case in point. For these and other reasons, the life histories of black gay men of the South provide not only different perspectives on the relationships between race and region, gender and geography, and sexuality and southernness;

they also serve as an intervention in the prevailing histories of homosexuality in the South and in the nation.

The idea for this book came to me in the summer of 1995 while attending a summer picnic hosted by the black gay organization US HELPING US, People Into Living, INC, in Washington, D.C. This organization "specializes in HIV/AIDS prevention and support services for black gay and bisexual men." Seated at a picnic table under a tent just a few feet from me was a group of "old-timers"—black gay men whose average age was around 65—who were talking about their gay lives "back in the day." Between the laughs and lies, grins and guffaws, tears and testimonies, were glimpses into remarkable lives: these were living archives of faces, places, events, deaths, births, past sins, and sex. I was spellbound, captivated by these stories in the same way I had been when I was a child listening to the stories of my grandmother. The difference, however, was that unlike my grandmother's stories, which validated my family and *black* history, the stories that these men told validated my black and *queer* history. At that moment, I knew that I would someday write a book that documented these stories. Unfortunately, none of the men who were present at that picnic is still alive, except in my mind's eye. But the echoes of their withered voices and the image of their shiny gold teeth, colorful clothing, and weathered faces are embroidered across the landscape of the history gathered between the pages of this book. Now, thirteen years later, I have been afforded the opportunity to document this part of history while other men are still here to tell their stories.

Rather than approach this project by employing a traditional text-based historiography, I felt it was important to employ oral histories as the key methodology. As a southerner, I have the gift of gab and of graciousness, to say nothing of the southern Baptist Christian ethos that guides my every move—despite my desire, at times, to have it otherwise. Therefore, I knew that I would be comfortable interacting with these men, and I knew that I could get them to open up to me in a way they might not open up to a nonsoutherner, a nonblack, or even a self-identified non-Christian. Like Zora Neale Hurston, I knew that "[black gay men] are most reluctant at times to reveal that which the soul lives by."[11] Moreover, oral histories, as John Howard has noted, in some ways provide an easier route into the lives of sexual dissidents, especially in the face of archivists, families of deceased queers, and other holders of queer history who are reluctant or unwilling to allow access to materials. Referring specifically to doing research on gay life in the South after World War II, Howard writes:

Difficulties in researching and uncovering the history of lesbians, gay men, and bisexuals in the United States are compounded when the inquiry is focused on a section that has been particularly hostile to sexual difference—the American South. Archivists and university administrators often express reservations about the validity of the field; families seeking to preserve the "good name" of their relatives routinely deny access to materials; and, as in any other part of the country, traditional historical sources remain largely silent with regard to homosexuality prior to the 1960s. Thus, oral history serves a vital role in reclaiming the lesbian, gay, and bisexual past, especially in the South.[12]

Howard's commentary echoes my instinct to approach the living—to interact with these men in their own environs to provide a fuller picture of the lives they performatively narrated.

Unlike Howard, I am not a historian by training and therefore I am not interested in asking the same questions that a historian might ask. Nell Painter suggests, "Making sense of the past is the work of historians, who create *historical narrative*."[13] But I am less interested in creating such a historical narrative, placing a priority on my interpretations, than in understanding the meanings and symbols embedded in the act of storytelling—of bearing witness to one's life and then co-performatively[14] interpreting the significance of that story. To construe this research as co-performance means not only acknowledging that both the researcher and the narrators are performing for one another; it also entails "paying attention" in a way that engages the bodily presence of both the researcher and the researched in the moment of the narrative event. This methodology, according to D. Soyini Madison, requires that "you not only do what the subject does, but you are intellectually, relationally, and emotionally invested in their symbol making practices and social strategies as you experience with them a range of yearnings and desires—coperformance is a doing with deep attention to and with others."[15] Thus, it was also important to me that I conduct an oral history project that would take advantage of my training in performance studies and ethnography, for the sensuousness of performance ethnography —the smell, taste, touch, sight, and sounds of the cultural space of the other—is also a part of the southern way.

Critical performance ethnography alters the traditional relationship between researcher and subject, demanding an ethical response from the researcher in witnessing and validating the narrative of the interviewee. Their relationship becomes reciprocal, and the importance of dialogue cannot be overestimated. Instead of interviewer and interviewee occupying the traditional hierarchical positions, their encounter is analogous to an invitation to dinner in a southern home in which the researcher is the guest and is asked to help by shelling peas, chopping onions, or setting the table. I was the invited dinner guest (in some instances quite literally) of these black gay male southerners who wished to share their life histories. I did more than attentively listen to their narrative performances—my presence actually validated and affirmed their stories. This was a conversation, not a one-way exchange, which is why, unlike other oral histories in which the interviewer's voice has been excised to create a sense of an uninterrupted story, in these narratives, I, in many instances, retain the questions I asked that prompted the narrators' comments. I also retain many of the narrators' stutters, pauses, and tangents to capture their voices in a way that does not render their speech "sterile" and to capture the performative nature of southern speech in general and of black gay vernacular speech specifically. Their stories also validated my own life story as a southern-born and -raised black gay man. These stories filled the air of living rooms, dining rooms, sunrooms, hotels, bars, and coffee shops, the pregnant pauses filled only by the sounds of ticking clocks or turned-down television sets or stereos as what words to say next or what question to ask was stifled by an indelible reverie. To be sure, not all of our communions were sentimental expeditions. Tears, contempt, condescension, and indifference also arose in that space we call performance. But it is the dialogic experience of co-performative critical ethnography that makes it such a valuable tool in engaging the lives of the other, the self, and the self and other in each other's eyes.

Employing oral histories and critical performance ethnography as methods for this particular project also seemed apropos given the importance of the oral tradition in African American culture, and especially of African American culture in the South. As classic ethnographies of black folks like Hurston's *Mules and Men* and John Langston Gwaltney's *Drylongso* demonstrate, the interaction between the researcher and informants is crucial to providing a multitextured perspective. Therefore, it's not just the words of the narrators that are important, but also the words and performances of those around him as well. For example, many of my contacts for this book were black women who solicited men to talk to me. My conversations with them, especially people like Ann McCarthy in Tuscaloosa, her sister Trudier Harris in Chapel Hill, and Marsha Houston in Atlanta and Tuscaloosa, were invaluable. Indeed, their recollections of black gay men in their communities helped contextualize many of the narratives in the book. These women's stories as well as the "gossip" about others imparted by the narrators are what John Howard refers to as "twice-told stories" or "hearsay." He writes: "This hearsay evidence—inadmissible in court, unacceptable to some historians—is essential to the recuperation of queer histories. The age-old squelching of our words and desires can be replicated over time when we adhere to ill-suited and unbending standards of historical methodology."[16] As an ethnographer, I want to capture the fullest picture of the lives I am portraying; to that end, I rely not just on the five senses, but also on my intuition and what southerners refer to as "motherwit."

An ethnographic approach allows for a more honest, self-reflexive rendering of these oral histories. While self-reflexivity within performance ethnography seems, at this point, commonplace or taken for granted, it is important to note that there are still ethnographic studies in which the researcher upholds a colonial gaze. My conducting this research was not, however, motivated by a need to exploit or imperially gaze upon the lives of these men. Indeed, a critical performative ethnographic approach demands that the researcher not only be conscious of his or her privilege (in my case, class and institutional affiliation), but also uphold an ethos of social responsibility toward the people being studied.[17] I want to validate these men's stories by sharing them with a wider audience, but I also have an ethical responsibility to assist those who desire my help. Self-reflexivity also means putting my own body on the line—that is, sharing my own history as a black gay man born in the South. Where appropriate, therefore, I share parts of my own queer southern history alongside that of the narrators.

Finally, framing these narratives and the ethnographic process as performance destabilizes notions of *the* truth and focuses more on "truth" as experienced in the moment of the storytelling event. In this way, the narrator's "experience" of his life is acknowledged and validated, but also corroborated by the presence of the ethnographer. Both are aware, however, that they are performing for the other—that this social interaction, however "real"—is nonetheless a "fragile fiction."[18] Walter Benjamin captures this process when he writes: "The storyteller takes what he tells from experience —his own or that reported by others. And he in turn makes it the experience of those who are listening to his tale."[19] Here again, we are pointed to the co-performative witnessing inherent in critical ethnography that disavows a static representation of the other or the self, as both journey on a collaboration toward making meaning of the social and cultural world around them. These narrative performances, according to Kristin Langellier and Eric E. Peterson, have "the potential to disrupt material constraints and discourse conventions."[20] For the men in this study and for me, those material constraints are multiple and in some cases include poverty, lack of education, lack of access to health care, and social and racial inequality—material constraints not easily disrupted through storytelling. But, as Michel de Certeau aptly reminds us, "What the map cuts up, the story cuts across."[21] Therefore, the oral narratives included here cut across generations, states, classes, religious affiliations, educational levels, and gender identities, giving name to the narrators' specific plights in history in ways that may impact their material conditions.

The 63 men whose stories appear in this book range in age from 19 to 93, but a preponderance of them (42) are between the ages of 26 and 45, while the second-largest group (20) is between the ages of 46 and 65. They hail from 15 different states—Maryland, Virginia, North Carolina, South Carolina, Kentucky, Tennessee, Arkansas, Oklahoma, Missouri, Texas, Louisiana, Mississippi, Alabama, Georgia, and Florida—plus the District of Columbia. They are lawyers, corporate executives, hairdressers, ministers, students, actors, professors, tailors, artists, administrators, architects, and realtors (or, in some cases, they are unemployed or retired).

When I began to do research for this book, my initial thought was to seek men out over the Internet, especially in chat rooms. But then I thought better of this for two reasons. First, I did not want people to mistake my intentions. When I was single, I frequented chat rooms often and was familiar with any number of pick-up lines—seeking out someone for "research" was one of them. Better to avoid giving someone the wrong impression or having to work my way out of an awkward situation. Second, I had to consider my own safety. I was going to be meeting most of these men for the first time, and I had no idea what situation I would stumble upon. Thus, I thought it better to be no more than one person removed from those I interviewed. The word-of-mouth method was effective because it kept at bay fears I may have had about approaching strangers, while it also eased the anxieties of the narrators because at least we had someone in common whom they trusted, and therefore they trusted me.[22] Accordingly, I began interviewing friends in North Carolina in the Triangle area (Chapel Hill, Durham, and Raleigh). These friends contacted other friends who contacted their friends to see if anyone was interested. The same snowball effect occurred in Atlanta, D.C., and Baton Rouge, until I had at least one contact in all of the southern states. In all, I conducted interviews with seventy-two men. All of the interviews took place between August 2004 and October 2006—significant to the extent that the presidential election and George W. Bush's return to office were on some interviewees' minds. I conducted all interviews face-to-face and recorded and transcribed them. While I had a general set of questions that I asked, I allowed the men to talk about

Narrators' Hometowns

anything they wanted. Because of that, some interviews lasted forty-five minutes, while others were over three and a half hours. The majority of the men wished to remain anonymous, and when that was the case, they came up with, or allowed me to create, pseudonyms; their need for anonymity in regard to their names did not usually extend to the place they were born, however. Many of the men did not mind if I revealed their birthplace or their current place of residence. They simply did not want to use their real names. Therefore, I did not change all of the names of people and places the anonymous narrators mentioned unless they explicitly asked me to. I have indicated the use of pseudonyms by placing quotation marks around the narrator's name and by excluding the last names of people and changing the names of places that narrators did not want identified. In cases where I do use the narrator's real name, I use only his first name unless the narrator insisted on a full name, which was sometimes the case. I also include biographical sketches of each narrator the first time he appears in the book. Sometimes these sketches are short, though at other times I use them as occasions to tell pertinent stories about my relationship with the narrator or to share a particularly insightful anecdote that might help contextualize the narrator's story. When a narrator appears subsequently, I provide his date and place of birth parenthetically after his name to remind the reader who is speaking.

Many of the narrators welcomed the invitation to be interviewed and were eager to tell their stories, especially older men or transgendered persons—perhaps because they were at an age or so flamboyant that they were less concerned about what others thought. A few of them even welcomed me into their homes overnight or at the very least prepared me a meal. Others agreed to be interviewed, but never showed up for the meeting. I can only imagine that they were afraid of exposing their identity to a stranger. As a researcher, this was frustrating not only because of the expense of travel, but also because many of those who stood me up had indicated that they had interesting stories to tell. On a few occasions, I rescheduled a missed interview. One such occasion was prompted by Ann McCarthy chastising one of her neighbors for not showing up. She was particularly peeved because she had prepared Sunday dinner for all of us, as the interview was to take place at her home. After waiting thirty minutes for Gerome to show up, Ann called him and read him the riot act. He gave her an excuse about why he couldn't make it, but it later became clear that he had gotten cold feet and had had to "pray on it [doing the interview]." After a subsequent phone conversation with me, however, he agreed to reschedule and I made yet another trip to Tuscaloosa to speak with him.

To be fair, I understand some of these men's reluctance to share their stories, especially given the current political and social climate not only in the South, but also around the country. With the conservative Bush administration setting the tone and several states passing antigay laws, the queer community is experiencing a backlash throughout the United States. Black religious leaders in particular are siding with white antigay conservatives in a way heretofore unseen in the black church—an institution that would, as one of my informants put it, "shut down if all of the sissies exited."[23] The Reverend Gregory Daniels of Chicago gave voice to the extreme side of this antigay sentiment and alignment with political conservatives when he said, as quoted in a February 2004 *New York Times* article, "If the KKK opposes gay marriage, I would ride with them."[24] On December 11, 2004, in Atlanta, a group of southern black ministers, led by Bishop Eddie Long of New Birth Missionary Baptist Church and the Reverend Bernice King, eldest daughter of Martin Luther King Jr., led a "Re-Ignite the Legacy" march in front of the King Center in protest of gay marriage, hiding behind a "sheet" of a different kind.

Naturally, these incidents and the rhetoric of hate surrounding them don't inspire those who might be struggling with their sexual identity to believe that a stranger can protect them from retaliation. John Howard encountered similar reticence when trying to secure black Mississippian oral history narrators for his research on gay men in the South. According to Howard, however, it was his whiteness and class status that seemed to deter some blacks from talking to or trusting him: "Generally speaking, African Americans seemed reluctant to participate in my project, cautious about revealing the names of other persons (regardless of assurances of anonymity), less likely to invite me into their homes, less likely to speak to me at length. For reasons well exemplified by the historical events chronicled here . . . many African Americans rightly are wary of white middle- and upper-class interlocutors."[25] The men in *Sweet Tea* often did, in fact, express relief or feel more comfortable when they discovered that I was black and myself a southerner; however, my being so openly gay sometimes mitigated this comfort in much the same way that Howard's whiteness denied him access to people and information. Thus, it was important for some narrators that we meet on neutral territory for the interview, like my hotel room or a mutual friend's home, rather than at their place of residence. It appeared that my presence could be explained—to family members, to nongay friends, etc.—because I am black (while Howard's could not since he is white), but at the same time, my perceived gayness—my effeminacy and my openness about my sexuality—could implicate the men by association.

As someone born in a black community in the rural South, I know first-hand the ways in which one internalizes the notion that "it's harder to be queer in the South than in the rest of the nation."[26] I don't mean to suggest that there is no merit to this notion, for many of the stories in *Sweet Tea* speak to the difficulty of being gay in the South, but the horror stories are counterbalanced by an equal number of encouraging and inspiring ones. Still, for all of my openness about my sexuality, I did have one experience in the field that reminded me of the ways in which notions of black respectability manifest internalized homophobia.

The experience came when I traveled home to Hickory, North Carolina, to interview Chaz, a preoperative transgendered person who lives "her" life as a woman Monday through Saturday night and "his" life as a man on Sunday in order to sing tenor in the mass choir at my home church. I'll allow Chaz to narrate her/his own story later in the book, but I describe him/her in order to set up the story of my own culpability in the code of silence around my homosexuality in the context of my hometown. While I suspect that most of the people in my hometown have figured out that I am gay, the topic has never come up in any discussions I have had with townspeople. And for all of my progressive politics, not once have I ever mentioned my (white) partner of ten years, even though he has accompanied me home on several occasions. I am not being self-aggrandizing when I say that my story represents the model black ascension narrative in the eyes of both the black and white folks in my hometown, especially given my single-parent, public-housing background. "See what happens if you work hard and get good grades?" they tell the younger black kids. "You too can get a Ph.D." To reinforce this belief, my hometown gave me my own day and celebration for being the first African American born in Hickory to receive a Ph.D. To buttress this bootstrap narrative, the wording on the cake at the celebration read, "From Zero to Hero."

What the townspeople and probably even my own family don't know is that it was partly my queerness that motivated my overachievement. It was the sense that, if I could only deflect attention away from my "high" butt, soprano voice, noticeable lisp, penchant for dolls and my mama's wigs—the things a homophobic bully's wet dreams are made of—if I could focus attention away from some of the fundamental parts of who I was coming to know as "me" by working extra hard for A's in school, by joining every possible high school club, by running for and winning senior class president, by working my soprano voice to outsing all of the girls in the soprano section in the church choir, by becoming a class clown and using my own overweight body as the "butt" of jokes, by being the "good" son who sends money home to help out when none of my siblings comes through, by agreeing to give speeches and lectures for the community to inspire young kids to stay in school and off drugs, then and only then, perhaps, when the unspoken, potentially devastating news that I am queer finally came, it wouldn't be so damn disappointing or might not matter at all. I do not mean to suggest here that all of the achievements over the course of my life have been motivated by my trying to circumvent my family and community's disappointment about my being gay. But I would be lying to them and to myself if I did not acknowledge that that has been a large part of what has driven my overachievement. It soon became part of the reason that when I went home I stayed only long enough to guarantee that I ran into just a few people, despite my mother's insistence that I call a hundred "play" aunts and god-mammas to let them "holla at me." *That way I could hope to avoid* having to lie in response to questions about when I'm getting married (*"I would have a long time ago if you hadn't voted for Bush, Sir"*) or when I'm going to have children (*"Well, most states have made it illegal, Ma'am"*). But, of course, if asked these questions, such rebuttals never pass my lips. Instead, I smile the polite, gracious smile that many of us queer southerners have learned to perfect, and ease some variation of the lie from my lips to the questioner's ears—the subtext of which says, "Kiss my ass, you low-down heifer. You know good and well that I'm a fag. How dare you ask me questions that you already know the answers to in an attempt to embarrass me in front of my mama?"— without anyone in the room flinching, but also understanding the signifying that has just transpired. Indeed, I was, and to some degree still am, invested in the facade of black respectability undergirded by a southern Christian ethos. It's my Achilles' heel, even after all of this time and even after living in a big city in a house with my partner. As black gay poet and activist Joseph Beam laments, "I cannot go home as who I am."[27]

And so, the upshot of this story is that I was embarrassed to be seen in public with Chaz because she undermined the reputation I had established as the "perfect" native (heterosexual) son. Hair coiffed, face beat back into her temples,[28] French manicured toenails, donning black leather pants and an off-the-shoulder pink mohair sweater, Chaz was fierce, and I was envious of her audacity to embody her "ass splitting truth."[29] As we sat in Chili's restaurant catching up on church and community gossip, drove around town, and ran errands for my mother, Chaz challenged all of my progressive politics by just being who she is in the world. Like Chaz, many of the narrators in *Sweet Tea* remind me and others who have traveled "the dirt-road-cum-boulevard to gay self-actualization—to identity, community, and political movement—[and who began] in the dark hinterlands of naïveté and deprivation, and [ended], happily, in the bustling corridors of wisdom and illumination,"[30] that if we think we have cornered the market on "liberation," we are sadly mistaken. The tea the "girls" of the southern tier are pouring these days is not only sweet, but also thirst quenching. ·

Speaking of tea, some readers may be curious about the title of this book as it relates to black gay men of the South, while others may take the relationship for granted. Well, in black gay vernacular, "tea" is not just a staple beverage of the South. Indeed, the word is often used as a euphemism for gossip, as in, "Chile, spill the tea" or "Pour the tea!" or "Chile, I have some SWEET tea to pour." Sometimes the word is not spelled out, but merely represented by the letter "T," as when The Lady Chablis says in her autobiography, "I was successful hiding my candy! Y'know, my T, my Truth."[31] Here, The Lady Chablis adds a nuanced version to "tea" by translating it as "truth," which suggests that, in the South, gossip is a form of truth! The word is also an adjective used to modify spaces, places, events, sex acts, and types of dissident sexual agents. "Tea dances," for example, are dances typically held in gay establishments on Sunday afternoons. "Tearooms" are public spaces such as bathrooms in hotels, theaters, and bars, or at roadside rest areas or gas stations that men frequent to engage in anonymous sex. "Tea bagging" refers to a man "dipping" his testicles in a sex partner's mouth, similar to the way one might dip a tea bag into a cup of hot water. "Tearoom trade" refers to a man who does not identify as homosexual but who trades sexual favors with other men (this usually amounts to self-identified homosexuals servicing the "trade") for money, cigarettes, a ride, or whatever is negotiated.[32]

How the word "tea" became a part of gay vernacular is debatable, but I suspect that it may have something to do with the gendered history of tea and sugar in Britain. Anthropologist and food historian Sidney W. Mintz argues that the history of sugar, especially in the early eighteenth century, is intimately connected to power and the differentiation of social status. He writes: "Whether as a medicine, a spice, or a preservative, and particularly in the public display epitomized by the subtleties, sugar uses were molded into declarative, hierarchical functions."[33] Mintz also theorizes that these "hierarchical functions" became associated with "tea as a social event," which according to P. Morton Shand, "a commentator on the English social scene," "was originally the prerogative of women, for the sexes were accustomed to separate at that epoch of an early dinner when the men began to take their wine seriously."[34] While Mintz dismisses Shand's theory of "teatime" as a gendered process in Britain, I find in his speculation a useful allegory for the ways in which "tea" and "sugar" circulate in southern gay culture. Shand notes: "Afternoon tea soon became an excuse for the indulgence of a woman's naturally sweet tooth. . . . Tea must not be regarded as another meal, a second breakfast. The bread and butter was camouflage, the little cakes were the real lure, the *pièce d'abandon*. . . . Tea is an excuse for eating something, rather than an avowed meal. It is a break, a challenge to the crawling hours, it 'makes a hole in the day.' . . . Another advantage is the extreme elasticity of its hour, so that one can order it at any time from 4 p.m., till half-past six."[35]

While Shand is clearly speaking within the sexist context of eighteenth-century British high society, the connections he makes between teatime and women's culture are worth pondering. For instance, the fact that gay men have appropriated a social event that is associated with high society is in keeping with the history of camp performance.[36] The Lady Chablis serves as an emblem of such mockery. Further, as gossip was undoubtedly a part of teatime hour, it makes sense that "pouring tea" or "spilling tea" among gay men means to share gossip or information. Shand makes note of the "4 p.m. till half-past six" teatime, and it just so happens that tea dances usually begin at 4:00 P.M., though at some bars and clubs they don't end until 7:00 or 8:00 P.M. While I cannot find a corollary between these British women's teatimes and gay tearooms for anonymous sex, perhaps their connection is to the fact that these women's teas took place in their own space, separate from the men in parlors consuming alcohol and tobacco. While this represents a form of segregation undergirded by sexism, one might argue that it also allowed a space for women to transgress or even subvert the social boundaries of their time. After all, no one really knows what those women were doing during their afternoon teas! The same can be true for the men who frequent the tearooms.

Regardless of its origins, sweetened iced tea has become the beverage of choice in the South. It is such a staple that South Carolina, for example, has adopted it as "the Official Hospitality Beverage by State Bill 3487, Act No. 31 of the 111th Session of the South Carolina General Assembly on April 10, 1995."[37] And in 2003, Georgia state representative John Noel and four co-sponsors introduced, apparently as an April Fools' Day joke, House Bill 819, proposing to require all Georgia restaurants that serve tea to serve sweet tea. Noel is said to have acknowledged that the bill was an attempt to bring humor to the legislature, but allowed as how he wouldn't mind if it became law. The text of the bill proposed: "(a) As used in this Code section, the term 'sweet tea' means iced tea which is sweetened with sugar at the time that it is brewed. (b) Any food service establishment which served iced tea must serve sweet tea. Such an establishment may serve unsweetened tea but in such case must also serve sweet tea. (c) Any person who violates this Code section shall be guilty of a misdemeanor of a high and aggravated nature."[38]

This preference for sweet tea transcends racial and class boundaries, and every family (and even different people within the same family) has its own recipe. My mother, for example, uses Lipton tea bags (about ten of them) and steeps them in about two cups of boiling water for about fifteen minutes. She then pours the steeped tea into a pitcher and squeezes the excess water from the tea bags. While the tea is still hot, she adds two and half cups of sugar to the pitcher and stirs it until it is dissolved. Next, she fills the pitcher with water until the tea turns the right color (I never knew what the "right" color was, but that's what she always said); she then slices a lemon (or, if she doesn't have a lemon, she uses reconstituted lemon juice) and puts it in. We children were forbidden to touch the tea before it had at least reached room temperature in the refrigerator. She serves it over ice. I used to love to eat the lemon slices after the tea was gone because they had absorbed all of the sugar that hadn't quite dissolved at the bottom of the pitcher. My aunt used three cups of sugar and always used real lemons—never store-bought lemon juice; my grandmother used instant Lipton mix (which contains sweetener), tea bags, *and* an additional cup of sugar! Any way it was served, it all "got gone." There are as many recipes as there are southern people.

The title of this book pays homage to the various ways in which "sweet tea" signifies in gay and straight cultures—whether in its most derisive manifestations in phrases like "sugar in his blood," "sugar in his tank," and "he's a little sweet" to indicate someone's homosexuality or in its more positive connotations related to desire, as in "he's sweet on you." The slippage between gay/straight, masculine/feminine, and out/closeted is precisely the site where the narrators in this book negotiate such multiple meanings and relationships. They employ southern culture itself, which produces its own codes and practices that mediate conflicting ideological positions, to speak to the complicated realities of their own lives. I take refuge in all of the multiple meanings of language and identity among these black gay narrators because they evince larger questions within the context of southern history.

While I offer critical analysis and interpretation of the narrators' stories, I, for the most part, allow them to speak in their own words. It is important to me that my "academic" voice be placed in the background in this regard. While I want to make the narrators' experiences accessible to my colleagues in academia, I don't want their life stories to be rendered in a way that makes them unrecognizable to the narrators themselves. I also want to capture the vernacular colloquialisms and cadences of southern speech. I should add, however, that while I allow the narrators to speak in their own voice, I have edited some of the narratives for clarity and continuity. For instance, I have deleted words and phrases such as "uhm" and "you know" when they were not a part of the narrator's typical speech pattern and were used as vocal fillers. I also edited stammers or incomplete thoughts. These deletions are indicated by ellipses in brackets, while unbracketed ellipses indicate a narrator's own pauses while thinking. Many of the excerpts from the narratives are presented straight through as they were told to me around a particular theme, while others are pieced together from various parts of the narrative, especially if the narrator discussed a topic in various parts of the interview. I indicate jumps in the narrative with a bracketed ellipsis on a line by itself. Such editing highlights how history, and the ethnographic process itself, is a fiction. Put another way, I, like Eric Wat in his oral history of Asian gay men in Los Angeles, "do not present this history as undistilled."[39] Accordingly, I want to be clear about the way in which I have framed these narratives to tell a particular story of black gay sexuality in the South.

Another "politics of representation" that I should address is my decision not to include the voices of black lesbians of the South. Gender politics in the South, and among black people in general, would render quite a different history for black lesbians than for black gay men—a tension that, admittedly, would be intriguing as a comparative study. Ultimately, however, a comparative study did not interest me as much as focusing on one community with which I was familiar. This conscious decision is not, of course, meant to suggest a devaluation of the lives of black lesbians of the South—whose rich history is crucial to any understanding of race, region, and sexuality—or to render a monolithic history of southern black homosexuality. It reflects my personal and scholarly interests, as well as a lack of time and financial resources to expand this project to include black southern lesbian narratives.

When I began conceptualizing the *how* of this project, my initial impulse was to organize the narratives/life histories according to the narrators' home states. My thinking behind that decision was to demonstrate that the South is not monolithic, each state having its own history, cultural codes, and ideas about sexuality. After I began the project, however, I discovered that there was more overlap among the stories than I had imagined there would be, and, on a practical level, organizing the book according to states would have resulted in some single-narrative chapters. What made more sense, then, was to organize chapters around themes that emerged across the narratives. While there are anomalous stories/narratives, the experiences these men chronicle more often overlap in ways that speak to many of their common material circumstances, their shared sense of cultural belonging (within and outside black communities), and their similar hopes and desires. Because the age range of the narrators spans more than seventy years, there are, as one would expect, some drastic differences in the ways narrators of different generations have dealt with certain issues; but, at the same time, some men generations apart narrate surprisingly similar stories and strategies for negotiating their sexuality. Where possible, I point out the similarities and cleavages between and among the narratives within the chapters, hoping to render a cogent, complex, and compelling portrait of these men's lives. To that end, *Sweet Tea* focuses on the *whole* lives of these men, not just on their sexuality. While their sexual identity is the overarching topic, it does not exist in a social or cultural vacuum. Indeed, these men's sexuality is but one identity around which many others may pivot and does not solely account for how race, class, gender, and region intersect in their lives.

I have included stories from most, but not all, of the narrators who talked to me. In any given chapter, the choice of which stories to include was based on which seemed to speak best to the topic being covered. When appropriate, I have sometimes included more than one excerpt from a narrator's story in a chapter.

Chapter 1, which focuses on growing up, highlights stories of family life in black communities and how the narrators integrated their sexuality into their upbringing. The chapter covers topics such as chores, sibling rivalry, extended family, segregated towns and racism, class status, and the role of education.

Chapter 2 challenges the whole notion of the "closet" as a trope for black homosexuality in the South. The stories chronicled in this chapter complicate the politics of the closet based on the ways in which the narrators negotiate their sexuality in various contexts. While some of the narrators employ the traditional "coming out" narrative to describe when they acknowledged their sexuality to themselves and announced it to family and friends, most of the narrators tell a more complicated and nuanced story. Indeed, some of the men do not self-identify as "gay" or are still conflicted about their sexuality, or at least about their identification with *a* sexuality or a particular label for it.

Chapter 3 discusses the very important role religion and the black church have played—and still play—in the lives of these men. From their earliest memories of going to church to their current participation in or disavowal of religious practice, the narrators speak about how they negotiate their sexuality and their spirituality. While the black church is undoubtedly a contradictory space—one that condemns homosexuality yet exploits the labor of its gay members, on the one hand, and affirms gay male talent and provides a sense of community and belonging, on the other—all but a few of the narrators indicate that their sexual expression has been influenced by their relationship to the church.

Chapter 4, which examines sexual activity, debunks the myth that homosexuality was always expressed clandestinely in the South. The narratives in this chapter graphically detail how sex between men was not only common, but prevalent in what might seem the unlikeliest of places, such as the athletic dorms of historically black colleges. This chapter is divided into subsections reflecting various topics that recurred in the narratives, among them first-time sexual experiences and later escapades, sex in the military and at historically black colleges, and HIV/AIDS.

Chapter 5 provides the full narratives of four non–gender conforming men. Their stories offer glimpses into living as a transgendered person, transvestite, or drag queen in small, rural towns and larger, metropolitan cities in the South.

Chapter 6 shares stories of love and loss. The chapter offers the love stories of couples who have been together for more than forty years, the stories of men whose partners have died, and the stories of those who long for love.

Chapter 7 reaches across generations to compare the narratives of the two eldest men in the book—one 93 and the other 86—with those of two of the youngest—one 23 and the other 21—highlighting their similarities and differences.

The Epilogue is a self-reflexive reverie on how doing this project has impacted my life and the lives of those whose stories are included here.

In addition to the chapters, I include an appendix, which provides a glossary of black gay vernacular terms, as defined by the narrators. Some of these terms are not specific to the South, let alone to black gay men, for their use can be documented in many white, Latino, and Asian American gay communities across the country. Other terms, however, are specific to a narrator's particular circle of friends or community and will not resonate beyond that context.

Since my move to Chicago from Durham, North Carolina, in 2000, I have had the good fortune to make many wonderful friends. And many of the friends that my partner and I have made over the past few years are also transplanted southerners who came "up South" because of a new job opportunity, as I did; to try out "city" life somewhere besides Atlanta; to attend college; or simply to "escape" the South. Whatever our reasons for leaving the South, the South never left us. Whether it's that alien accent that emerges when talking to our parents over the phone, those small "country ways" that we hang on to no matter how "citified" we become, or that longing for the soft-spoken gentility of elders that can take the edge off any stressful day, we are our region's children. No amount of migration will change that. I was reminded of this during each and every interview with the narrators in this book. Listening to their stories not only grounded me; it also took me back to divinely remembered places in my own history. They were telling *my* story while narrating their own—stories that take me back to the foothills of western North Carolina, sitting on the front porch of my family's public-housing apartment, watching the sun go down on a hot July evening. As the male cicadas would raise their mating call to Jesus, Mama and our neighbor Miss Isabelle would gather empty flower pots along the porch our apartments shared and stuff them with rags to burn to keep the mosquitoes away. When their gossip echoed the sound of the cicadas, that was my cue to put away the canning jar lids I used to create my mud pies and go into the house and "wash up," only to rejoin Mama and our neighbor for a nightcap of ice-cold sweet tea. It is this memory, and this memory alone, that keeps me longing for home again and again.

some bitter and some sweet
growing up black and gay in the south

In many ways, southern black gay men's lives are no different from other black southerners' lives. They are full of memories, both good and bad, that speak to the region's fraught history and its relation to the rest of the country. The narrators in this book speak with candor about being children of the South—of the joy of having open fields to run and play in; the comfort of southern food, family gatherings, and church functions; the onerous task of family chores and the strain of witnessing family dramas; dealing with homophobia and experiencing racism and segregation. The chapter title was suggested by the summation of his childhood offered by one narrator, Gerome, who seemed to be speaking for most of them: "When I stop now and look back at it . . . it's like some bitter and some sweet."

Among the most striking things recounted in these stories are the overwhelming recollections of racism. Nearly all of the narrators have a story about attending segregated schools or living in segregated neighborhoods or witnessing racial violence. One would not be surprised by such stories from men who were born before, say, 1970; but some of the younger men, born in the 1980s, also share such tales. While their responses to their experiences with racism vary widely, they were all affected by them in some way.

But those bitter experiences are paired with sweeter stories of childhood. In fact, some of the most humorous stories in *Sweet Tea* are found in these early childhood memories. From stories about getting in trouble and getting "whoopings," to tales of flamboyant queers in the neighborhood who served as role models, these narratives paint a vivid picture of how southern life accommodated what it wanted to while it policed and sometimes silenced other things.

The stories are presented in four groups, focusing on parenting and family dramas, education, racism and segregation, and gay members of the community. These categories are not rigid, however; they merely provide a general organization to themes that arose across stories when I asked men to talk about their early childhood memories.

PARENTING AND FAMILY DRAMAS

One of the most commonly held stereotypes about black families is that they are generally headed by single parents, and typically by the mother. This pathological view of the black family is belied by the men of *Sweet Tea*, whose family situations run the gamut. Many grew up in single-parent homes or with divorce. Others, however, were raised by two parents in one household, in addition to grandparents and extended family. For me, what is most compelling in these stories is how the men reacted to their parenting situation—whatever it might have been. Men who were reared in single-parent homes are very articulate in disavowing the notion that a "missing father" contributed to their being gay. Children of divorce describe the effects of being split between parents and in some instances how it made them more independent or distrustful or how it created abandonment issues in their adult relationships. Men raised by two parents who remain together to this day recall how their parents' relationship taught them lessons about love, life, and commitment. Not surprisingly, perhaps, no narrator's childhood was without contradictions, conflict, and complications.

. . . .
"C.C."

There's no way to describe C.C. but as a "character." He was born in 1961, one of six children, in Greenville, Mississippi. Greenville is a river port city that sits at the heart of the Lower Mississippi River, where Arkansas, Louisiana, and Mississippi come together. Of its 50,000 residents, roughly 70 percent are African American. C.C. now lives in Alabama and teaches dance at a large university. Outspoken and charming, C.C. is unorthodox in his approach to dealing with racism and homophobia, an approach that speaks to his unapologetic defiance of social norms and values. Eschewing identity politics, especially as they relate to "blackness" and "gayness," C.C. believes that we are all a part of what he calls a struggle in the "human condition." We met through a mutual friend who teaches at his university; since then, we have become fast friends. He serves as a mentor for many young gay men at his university who are struggling with their sexual identity. Two of those young men are narrators in this book. His mentoring style, like his philosophy of life, is direct and no holds barred.

Part of his doggedness, unfortunately, stems from his parents' constant fighting when he was young. The interview took place on November 4, 2004, in Tuscaloosa, Alabama.

My childhood was quite interesting. Wonderful, beautiful and dark, you know, that very Tennessee Williams or Chekhov. My grandparents owned their own grocery store. So being black and in the South where your grandparents own their own grocery store and property, that experience was a quite wonderful experience because you knew you were different. [. . .] The darker side was that my parents were very smart people but just had lots of problems. I mean, in terms of like my mother and father had their share of fights. My mother divorced my father, which was great for her. And I admit, at the moment when she divorced him, for some strange reason I thought, "I have to stay with him." And here I am a young man in like fourth grade or something like that. "Somebody's got to take care of him." You know. Because my father's also legally blind. So I can remember like staying at the house for a while and going from neighborhood to neighborhood, you know, all the neighborhood people, who was really taking care of me. And that just was the South. So it wasn't like I wasn't with many mothers. But of course my mother and my grandmother caught wind that that's what I was doing. And she's like, "You come down here and get this boy," 'cause my mom then had moved to Memphis.

So, yeah my childhood, when I think about it, was sort of like mixed up. I'd been exposed from like eight. What I mean by exposed [is] my mother was one of those people who really believed early on that you were going to get out of the house to go to tennis lessons or to band lessons, to go to theater lessons. She was a firm believer in that. She would wake us up on the weekend at a young age and say, "You're getting on the bus 'cause you're getting out of here. I'm not training people. You must learn to see what's available for you." So, my childhood was spent being very exposed to a lot of things right away.

My mother's first job I remember was at . . . What do you call those schools for young kids? Head Start. She was like the director of a lot of the Head Start programs, which now in retrospect I think affected me a lot. 'Cause that's when they were starting young kids, before preschool . . . You were being exposed and educated. And my father was one of those men who . . . I always tell people, it's interesting to watch a man who is legally blind be an incredible realtor. Yes, he took that test by tape and could walk in a house and tell you anything. He'd hit on those walls or walk around and say, "Yeah, okay." And he was good at it. Uhm hmm. 'Til the day he died.

It's really interesting to look back. Like when you hear all these catch phrases, like "It takes a village." You know, it was just like anybody who lived by you really took care of you. But I particularly remember these two families that were really poor, had huge, huge number of people living in their house. But those were the people I always wanted to be with. And so to this day, I feel indebted to them because they all remained in Greenwood, Mississippi, and pretty much probably [have] the same lives. But it's amazing how you can remember how instrumental those people were because they really weren't striving for nothing. And sometimes when you're not striving for anything. What I mean by not striving for anything, they didn't have any kind of like career goals. So, those people have so much love it's incredible that that's something that can just heal all wounds. And I felt very safe with those people because, early on they all knew I was gay. And in some ways some of the boys in those families began to protect me early on. And sort of growing up with that experience kind of altered my childhood, where there was this incredible need for some reason for men who really protected me. I even remember one of my brother's close friends who recently was telling funny stories how he remembered . . . "When you were in grade school, I was making sure that nobody was gonna mess with you." So I've always had that kind of protection.

But my parents fighting . . . When you start watching that stuff early . . . you get up out of that. It's like, ohhh! That domestic violence, down here, you might as well pop you some popcorn 'cause everybody's doing it. I mean it wasn't like you could leave. You'd go to the next house, it was just as common. People would just be like, "I'm gonna kick your bitch ass." And you'd go to your friend's house and their mama's getting her ass kicked, too. So it'd just become sort of like, "Oh. Okay." So that part was probably worst. Which I still think has a big problem. I didn't realize that until later. That really has a big problem with me and my issues with intimacy. 'Cause from that moment on, you start to protect yourself. So even when people was trying to be all nice to me, I was like, "Child." I ain't trying to hear that. I was protecting myself. [. . .] I started to protect myself in a way.

From day one when I got suspended from school . . . I always go back to that fourth-grade [experience] 'cause that was a pivotal point in my life. I decided, "No, unh unh. We're not gonna hear 'fag' every day." I remember picking up like a two-by-four, went down and just was like beating the children, Honey. Like, no, we ain't hearing this. So, I get home and police are there and they're knocking at the door and calling my father. And I'm sitting there, still feisty like, "No, no, I'm not hearing this no more. I'm not hearing this ever again." And I didn't because I was clearing this up. I'm not doing this every day. And that's one thing, you know, about the old school, they said, "You better go and kick that ass. 'Cause you kick that ass, it puts an end to it." [. . .] You just earn your props. So, there again, I just learned when you decide, "Unh unh. Unh unh." And when you live like that from that moment on, your life is different because, from the moment you walk in any door, people know, "Unh unh." There is no apology. And people pick up on that on count one. And it's the most frightening thing in the world. Like they still can't believe . . . I'm celebrating with my Bush-Cheney pin. I wear it everyday up there to say, "Now if you think you're going to steal my joy, then I'm joining your party." 'Cause you think I'm going to spend four years hating George Bush? No, I'm not. I've got too much creativity and energy that I need to be using some. If this is where the country is going, [whispering] we're going with them. [Chuckle]

And part of that is just I'm just a provocateur. It's like, "Oh no, you met the wrong one. I'm going with you on this one." I'm just going with you. Because if you don't, you wouldn't be able to get out of the bed if you really dealt with the shit that's thrown at you. The kind of hate and daily whatever. So you just have to find a way to say no. And that's that moment of going back to childhood where I've never apologized for anything.

· · · · · · · ·

ED
Ed was born in 1952 in New Orleans. Before the devastation of Katrina, he lived in the Ninth Ward and worked as a librarian at the New Orleans Historical Society. Ed is a gentle soul who is also very gracious. It is he who put me in touch with Countess Vivian, the oldest narrator in this book (see Chapter 7). On the day of the interview, I drove Ed to his favorite sandwich shop, where we both got catfish po' boys—a staple in New Orleans. The interview took place on January 22, 2005, at his home, after we finished our sandwiches. Since Katrina, I have not been able to contact him.

I think I had a well-balanced childhood. I had a mother and a father. They both lived in the home. I had one sister and I had two brothers that lived in the home with me. My father worked and my mother worked. I went to school at the normal age. Although I grew up in, from the age of three onward, we lived in a housing development, a housing project. But we never thought we were poor. We never visualized ourselves as being poor, even though [. . .] if you lived in a housing project, you were considered to be poor.

But my father and my mother both had values that they instilled in us, and one of the values was education. My mother only finished high school and my father [. . .] dropped out in his junior year in college, but he was fairly bright because both of his parents were educators, and he was skipped in his early years and he was only sixteen when he was in college. And his father was one of eight black CPAs in the country at that time. And he used to tell me that, and I kind of just didn't believe it. I used to say, "Oh yeah, you're right." But actually, when I did do my family genealogy, I looked on the 1920 census records for Louisiana, for New Orleans, and I found him and his two sisters, my aunts . . . one of them is deceased . . . and his brother, my uncle, who is also deceased, and his father and his mother. And it gave the occupation of my grandfather, my father's father, as being an accountant at an insurance company in 1920. So that is a CPA, all day long. So my daddy has been vindicated.

And my mom, although she only finished high school [. . .] she used to recite poetry to us, verbatim, by memory. And one of her favorite poems was "When Malindy Sings" by Paul Lawrence Dunbar, which is, you know, very difficult to recite, let alone remember, because it's in dialect. She would just chime it off like it was nothing, with proper voice inflection. Plus, she wrote poems herself and she wrote a song when she was a girl, about thirteen years old. And I'm still working on the research for this. She grew up in Mississippi, and she actually went to school part of her life with Richard Wright. She knew Richard Wright.

And my mother's still alive. My father's deceased. My mother is eighty-eight years old. [. . .] Unfortunately, because of her Alzheimer's, she doesn't remember anything now. But before that, she was quite lucid in terms of telling about family history. She wrote this poem one day when she was in school. She called it the "Happy Work Song," and there were these guys that used to come from town to town, buying poetry and lyrics for songs. And they bought her song. And I actually know that this is true because when I was a child she kept a scrapbook and she had the actual newspaper clipping of her winning a hundred dollar prize. . . . This would have been like in 1930 or something or so, because she was born in 1916. May 13th, 1916. They paid her a hundred dollars for her song, and it was written up in, I think, *The Jackson Daily News*, which was the black newspaper. And I haven't been able to find a copy yet. I'm still looking. And her song was renamed, kept the same lyrics, "Whistle While You Work," which unfortunately is the song used in the Disney movie, *Snow White*. And they've made millions off of it and my mother got a hundred bucks. But that's my mother's story altogether. But that's to just give you an idea what kind of parents I had. They encouraged me, you know, to be the best that I could be. And my father, at one point, worked three jobs I can recall. And my mother, when she did work, she worked mostly domestic work and food service work in cafeterias. But after the children came, she didn't work. My dad used to get all the work. But I don't know if I'm really explaining what my childhood was like through that.

Did you have chores?

Oh absolutely. All of us had chores. We had to wash dishes. We had to clean the floors. We had to keep our rooms clean. And we were disciplined mostly by my mother. We weren't disobedient children. And I don't feel as though we were ever abused. But my mother was the disciplinarian. She was somewhat of a drill sergeant–type. [Chuckle] When she said do something and you didn't answer her or do it, you might find a shoe or a pot flying past your head or something, you know, because she was gonna get you. And she may have not got you at that moment, but she would wait sometimes until you were asleep and surprise you with an attack. [Laughter]

And the only room that we could go in that had a lock on the door was the bathroom. But if you went in the bathroom, it was like going to a prison because you couldn't do anything in the bathroom but run the water, take a bath, you know. It's very boring in there. And she would tell you, "Okay you can stay in there, but the longer you stay in there, the worse your punishment's going to be when you get out. So you better come out now." [. . .] My brother, who is a year younger than I am, we shared a room so we had bunk beds. And when she used to get behind us with a belt, the first one under the bunk bed was sheltered because the bed was against the wall. So you had one and then the one that got second was sticking out. So she would grab the leg or arm and whip the arm or the leg or the part of the butt, whatever part she could reach. And you would just breathe a sigh of relief that, you know, she didn't get you. And you were safe to live another day. But it was never abusive because when she disciplined us, we were pretty bad at times and we deserved it. [Chuckle] And she laid down the law. My father seemed to be comfortable with that arrangement. After all, he was working all the time.

. . . .

FREDDIE

Among the men I met while collecting these stories, Freddie is one of the most memorable. He is a wonderful storyteller—being almost as talented at that art form as at his profession of painting. Although quite soft-spoken, Freddie has a captivating storytelling style that draws the listener in. One has to pay close attention to his use of words to catch the subtle humor and deft critiques of society and other characters in his stories. Freddie and his partner of over forty years (see Chapter 6) live in Atlanta in a home full of antiques. The house is also filled with Freddie's artwork. Although semi-

retired, he still takes commissions for paintings and works part-time at a gallery in downtown Atlanta. He also likes to garden. The interview took place at Freddie's home in Atlanta on October 30, 2004.

Freddie was born in 1944 in Madison, Georgia. Regionally referred to as "the town that Sherman refused to burn," Madison is located about sixty miles southeast of Atlanta. It is known for its beautifully preserved antebellum homes. Below Freddie recalls the painful story of learning that he was the product of a mother and father who did not want him.

How would you describe your childhood?

Oh, God. It was awful. I was an unwanted child—an unexpected child and an unwanted child. After four children, I think the doctors told [my mother] she couldn't conceive any more children. And then I came along, so I was sort of a surprise in that regard. But my father's mother was a very strong figure in my father's life. You saw the movie *Roots*? You know how they held the baby up? I kind of use that analogy. My grandmother held me up and declared that none of her blood was in me, which meant that her son was not my father. So my father, being the weakling that he was, I think, believed her. My mother's mother, my grandmother, lived here in Atlanta. And my mother would visit my grandmother in Atlanta. So my father's mother proclaimed that I was some—I won't use the "N" word—but some man in Atlanta's child—that I was not, in fact, his child. So that caused my grandmother and my father to treat me differently. My sister is just three years older than me. One of the more painful examples I can remember is us being on the school grounds at Bernie Street Elementary School. It's no longer there, but it was the colored school in Madison, Georgia. And us running out to the edge of the schoolyard, to my father and asking him for a nickel. And he pulled out a handful of change and would give my sister a nickel and wouldn't give me one, saying he didn't have any more. And I remember crying and that kind of thing.

And I think the most painful memory I have is my father's cousin A.C. and his wife, whose name was Maja [. . .] said to my mother one day, she said, "Bea, why don't you give Freddie to me since Aunt Evie and W.S. don't want him?" with me standing there.

And I remember starting to cry and hugging my mother around the legs. And I must have been very young because my mother was only five feet, two inches and I remember my head was about at her knee. So I was a very small child. And I remember crying and saying, "Mama, you gonna to give me away?" and she said, "No." There were other kinds of things, but those are the more painful memories I have of early childhood in Madison, Georgia.

Freddie smelling flowers in his garden. Photo by the author.

I do think that I was molested as a little kid in Madison, Georgia, possibly by more than one person. And I've been in counseling and cried through all of this stuff. But I think a part of that had to do with the fact that it was commonly known that I did not have kind of the protection of my fraternal grandmother and my father. Because my grandmother was a larger-than-life figure, and I think people respected her and some people might have even feared her because she was a *big* woman and she was very outspoken and just kind of a strong personality. I think that they knew that "It's open season on him because they don't want him so it's okay to do pretty much anything to him."

What did your parents do for work?

My father, in Madison, Georgia, worked for the planer mill, which was a processing mill for lumber. They would cut the lumber, and I guess they planed it into planks or boards or whatever. But my mother was always a domestic worker.

In 1952, when we left Madison, Georgia, my mother and my sister and I came to Atlanta. First of all, my mother came. My grandmother was ill so my mother came . . . probably in March or April of that year because it was before school was out . . . to take care of her mother who was ill. And she came back probably late April, early May and she said to my father . . . I heard her tell him this many times, that the two of them could not make it in Madison, Georgia, because there were too many external influences. She kept warning him that she would leave him. So when she came back, this was in 1952, she said to him that she was thinking of leaving him and she was going to move to Atlanta. She was going to take us and move to Atlanta, and she wanted him to join us because she had decided that they just could not have a life in Madison, Georgia, because there were too many external influences. And so it was about the time of my birthday, May 12th, we moved to Atlanta and my father was supposed to join us. [. . .] You're so young you wouldn't remember this, but there was a time when, if your father worked at a place, he could go to the boss man and say, "Oh, I've got a friend who needs a job," in many instances. And the man would say, "Bring him on." So, some of the men in the neighborhood here in Atlanta that my grandmother knew, had lined up a job for my father. And on the day he was supposed to come, he didn't come. I remember sitting out on the front steps, waiting kind of for him, much of the day. I knew the direction he would come from, and several times I saw a man who kind of looked like him and I got happy thinking that was him coming and it wasn't. So I remember how disappointed I was that he didn't come. And he never came. Instead, he moved to New Jersey with Lily Mae, one of the *problems* my mother had in Madison, Georgia. He moved to New Jersey with Lily Mae, and they have I'd say ten or eleven children. I had all these half siblings. They were in Jamesburg, New Jersey, and now I think some of them are in Jamesburg, and my father lives in Somerset with one of his daughters. And so my parents were never reunited. They never got back together. [. . .] You know, 'cause even though my father wasn't all he should have been, he's still my father. [. . .] And I keep saying that I'm going to ask him at which moment did he decide that he was, in fact, my father. Because I think he has, at some point, accepted that. I've been told many times by family members that I look a lot like my father's father. I didn't meet him. My grandfather died in February of the year that I was born, so he died in February and I was born in May. And I've had people tell me that, if he had been alive, my life would have been very different because he would have protected me from *them*. He would have been a kind of a more calming influence. And at some point, my father's mother changed her mind as well. I never did ask her before she died when she changed her mind, but I think at some point they could see some resemblances to people in the family and they changed their minds then. And certainly, here I am, sixty years old. I forgave them many years ago. I did. I don't know if you know this or not, but counseling is a scary process. You have to really be able to, I think, open those doors. And you also have to be able to, I think, admit or to give up on what I call a prevalent myth in the black community, this sainted mother myth. You have to kind of maybe see her for who she is, that just because she's your mother, she's not a saint. You can still love her, but you have to kind of see her for who she is—or either of your parents. Because in many instances, both the mother and the father, where they can do no wrong, you know. Well, I keep saying, "you know." But when I was in school, if you wanted to get a fight out of somebody, you'd say something about their mama. [Laughter] And I don't know if that's true today or not. I suspect that it probably is. And everything you could say . . . you might say might be true, but just the fact that you're saying something unpleasant about somebody's mama would get you a real fight. But if you're going into counseling, you have to kind of see all of these people for who they are and deal with the experiences you had with them.

[. . .] But at some point, I cut off all communications with my mother for several years. I didn't call her. If she called me, I was kind and gracious, but I didn't go to see her. I didn't call her. And this was a decision I made. My counselors were . . . thought I was very brave in making that decision. And my . . . I was in a group of ten other people in counseling. They were all just kind of amazed by the fact that I could do that. But I made the decision after years and years and years. Because the other part of the story is that my father and grandmother didn't want me, but neither did my mother. Well, she was determined to keep me because her mother didn't keep her. You see? It didn't matter how badly she abused us, her saving grace was always, "At least I didn't give you away." Because my mother was given away as an infant. The story I've heard is that my grandmother was very young when my mother was born, and her father gave my mother to some other people when my grandmother wasn't at home one day. And so my mother never forgave her mother for giving her away. But she was very angry and tormented and very abusive of my sister and I. And her saving grace . . . her defense always was, "At least I didn't give you away."

So, that was why she was determined to keep us, no matter what. But it didn't matter if she treated us like dirt. [Chuckle] So, that's the other part of the story. So I, for much of my life, have felt very much alone because in Madison, Georgia, I thought I had my mother. But once we moved here . . . Have you seen *The Exorcist?* I tell people that once she got us in Atlanta, her head did a 360 degree turn. And one of her favorite things to say was, "If it wasn't for you, my life would be wonderful." So, hearing that as a kid, I think, was why . . . I started to have thoughts of suicide. Because just think of it. If you're a little kid and your mother says, "If it wasn't for you, my life would be wonderful," you're going to think, "Well I hate making her life awful." And you start thinking about not being here. And for many years, I was suicidal and that was one of the issues I dealt with in counseling. And I think that those thoughts of suicide were kind of planted by my mother making that statement.

· · · · · · · ·

JAIME

Jaime is another great storyteller. That he has had such a colorful life, especially his years in the military (see Chapter 4), makes his stories that much more compelling. He is the older brother of Phil, another narrator in this book. The eighth of eleven children, Jaime was born in Covington, Kentucky, in 1961. Covington, the fifth-largest city in Kentucky, is separated from Cincinnati, Ohio, by the Ohio River. Jaime lives with his partner not far from the home where he grew up. The interview took place in Cincinnati at a mutual friend's home on July 24, 2005.

We used to laugh and joke that we kind of grew up in Mayberry. Because, you know, growing up in Covington, being this close to Cincinnati where, you know, there seemed to always be a lot going on. But over there it's a little bit slower, so we were kind of sheltered from a lot of the goings-on. Even now, the way things are, it's a lot different over there than over here. I would say I had a, you know, an average childhood. Normal, you know.

[. . .] There were eleven of us kids between my mother and father. And although my father he didn't complete his education, he wanted to make sure that we all had that option. Of the eleven kids, I think all of us went through Catholic schools throughout our whole, you know, from first to twelfth grade—those of us that wanted to. But the other side of that was we had to all go to work and help pay for it. As kids we, you know, we didn't really think we were poor I guess because we were not really denied anything basic that we needed. But, I mean you look back on it now you think, had your parents been born in a different time they probably could have been CEOs of a company, you know, being able to manage and run our family the way that they did. I think as opposed to the people, from my experience of the people that grew up around me, and as adults and talking to some of the people that I grew up with, we actually had it pretty good for our, you know, for that time and for that area.

Did you have chores when you were growing up?

Oh yeah. Oh yes. Our family pretty much . . . was like a company. My father, his saying was, "I don't care what you hear out there, there's no democracy in my house, what I say goes and if you can't abide by that, you have to leave. I've got too many kids to raise and I don't have time for any messing." He also managed one of those little tidbits like, like you have ingrained in your head like if you ever get in trouble or do something stupid that calls for you to have to go downtown and go to jail, then you might want to use that one phone call to call somebody that's going to help you, because there will be no help for you here at this house. And we all knew that right up front and everybody made it through without having to test that little rule, because my father was not one to say something and not mean it.

Did you and your siblings have a lot of friends in your neighborhood where you all played together and did things like that?

Yeah. We were that one neighborhood house that everybody hung at, you know, with there being so many kids, there was always a bunch of people there. And, especially dinnertime, there was always a couple of extra people at the table for whatever reason. And even, as I said, we weren't rich, but my mother just had a policy if someone is there and wanting to eat, then she'd find a way to feed them. You know, that's just the way it worked. Everybody pretty much hung at our house. A lot of, at that time a lot of people's parents didn't allow them to have company or hang at the house or that type—or we grew up in the era of plastic furniture, plastic covered furniture, so you know. It was kind of a whole street full of that. In our house it was too many of us for our parents to even be trying to worry about anything like that pretty much.

My mother took care of us. My father, his primary job he was an auto detailer. But we, as I said, from probably as far back as I can remember, probably at about five or six years old, my father always had anywhere from three to four part-time jobs in the evening cleaning different businesses around the city [with which we helped], and that was pretty much our life. We would come home from school; we would wait for him to get home from work, you know, [from] his primary job. We'd have dinner, and by that point, you made sure your homework and all that was done because he didn't want to hear you had to do homework after we come back from cleaning because it was usually pretty late in the evening. So, you know, other kids went out and played, we piled up in the station wagon and went and paid for our tuition. So that's basically, you know, that's how it worked. Everybody had a job at the different places that we went to, to clean or what have you, and everybody had a job at home. Well, it was pretty much you went by "the list," as we called it, on the refrigerator—the schedule—where, you know, if it was your week for dishes or help with the laundry or taking out the garbage, or whatever it was. Pretty much is how it worked.

· · · · · · · ·

"LARRY J."

Larry J. is one of the few narrators who barely came up for air during the interview. One question, and perhaps thirty minutes later I would be able to get in the next one! He is like many a southerner in that he just loves to story spin; he's a person who, in the middle of telling one story, has to tell several other stories as "context" for the main one. The result is sometimes something that resembles free associative speaking. A college friend of mine who knew that Larry J. had led an interesting life put me in touch with him. From the times we spoke on the phone before the interview, I realized that I was in for a treat.

Larry J. is a business professional and has a very successful career. He is also a poet who has self-published two books of verse, both volumes dealing with his painful childhood and his longing for romantic love. Regarding the former, he survived several abusive men in his mother's life. Regarding the latter, he's still looking for love, but has had lots of sexual escapades during that search (see Chapter 4). He was born in Camden, South Carolina, in 1959. The oldest inland town in South Carolina, Camden is located just thirty-five miles northeast of Columbia, the state capital. Larry J. is one of four children. The interview took place at his home in Charlotte, North Carolina, on January 7, 2004.

How would describe your childhood?

Probably a childhood of survival, because my mom and my dad were separated when I was very, very small. It's hard for me to remember exactly when, but I was not even in the first grade, so I would say I was probably three, four years old when my mom and my dad separated. At the time, when they separated, I had two other brothers. My mom was the person who pretty much raised me, for the most part. So I pretty much grew up in a single-parent home. But because my mom worked a lot, I ended up being pretty much raised by my grandmother. So think about Camden, which is a very rural area. My mom had another baby, probably before I was six. And I do remember that. And he got killed by her boyfriend who had shaken him to death. And I think they call it some kind of syndrome [. . .] today. So as a result of that, we ended up moving in . . . my grandmamma was pretty much, you know, "You all need to come stay with me." So we ended up staying with my grandmother in probably a six-room house, and there was probably twenty people in that house. I say twenty—and I may be exaggerating just a little bit—but I have a set of twin uncles . . . who are a year older than me. Then there was these other two males there, then my brothers. . . . I had two brothers at the time. And then my grandmother had another son of hers, plus at least two more daughters. She had ten kids. My grandma had ten kids, and the last two were, like I said, twins. So it was a houseful. Yeah, all of us in about a six-room house. So there was no such thing as a bedroom—I mean, a living room. Every room was a bedroom except for, you know, maybe the kitchen.

[. . .] I do remember having a paper route probably when I was in the fifth grade. Because my mom pretty much worked to try to maintain, 'cause my daddy did not provide child support, which continues to be a bone of contention. And I might be editorializing a little bit here, but I sort of wish I could go back and retroactively deposit those payments. Because you know now I don't understand why women didn't [demand child support], but back then they didn't. They didn't press the issue of child support, so look at the money we might have gotten from dear dad. But back then, you know, the Department of Social Services was certainly not enough to survive off of. I don't even know whether my mom even had the know-how to do that. She had like a ninth-grade education. You know back then folks didn't finish school. [. . .] As the years went by, my mom had a couple more kids. I now have three brothers and one sister. The sister's the youngest and she's thirty-five. My mom is sixty-four, so that kind of like gives you an idea.

So I pretty much raised my younger brother and my younger sister because, number one, I was, for lack of a better word, smart, I guess. Book smart. My oldest brother was always getting into trouble which, you know, that didn't pay off for him later on because he's still struggling a little bit. So it was pretty much between me and my brother who's like a year younger than me, who pretty much did everything. I was the one that pretty much was stuck with the raising of my younger brother and my sister. Because my brother that was a year younger than me, my granddaddy always took him hunting with him. So . . . they used to call me, way back then, "Professor" because I always was studying and all that. I think at a very early age I realized I wanted to make something of myself. And somehow I must have known that that was the way to do it. And so by raising my brother and my sister, I stayed home. I mean I was the one that was left to clean the diapers, you know, and to do all of that. Do all those chores. And as a result, I guess that it all paid off because I learned how to cook and everything. So, I'm pretty self-sufficient, even from the standpoint of just your basic day-to-day survival. Very self-sufficient at an early age, very independent.

You could walk to the country club in like fifteen minutes from my house. And I would do various chores over there, as they related to landscaping, you know, helping out. And I remember getting paid I think it was like two dollars an hour back then, during that time, to do that. And then on Sundays they used to have polo games, and we used to walk the horses after they would play a match or an inning. I think it's like six innings to a whole match, but after an inning, the horses had to be walked. I initially didn't do that. I ended up being the scorekeeper. [Chuckle] Because I was smart enough, I got to keep the score. And I also would set the ball up for the next time they got ready to play. So that was double pay. So instead of getting two dollars for that polo match, I was getting four dollars because I was really doing double duty. But yet my uncles and my brothers [. . .] we did the jobs that nobody else would do because we were not privileged as far as being schoolteachers' kids. Back then, if your mom or dad taught school, you know you were considered privileged and you didn't have to worry about going out to survive. But of course that money, you know, I was bringing in also helped with whatever household needs, so we'd give my mom probably half of what we made, you know. And so that's sort of like how that came up. And you know I worked at the country club for years. I think I worked there really pretty much until I got ready to go off to college, which was in 1977. They used to have a driving range, and I got to run that like one week out of the month because they could trust me. I worked there for a long, long, long time doing various odd jobs, and during the summer, I worked there. So in a roundabout way, I'd say a life of . . . a childhood of learning how to survive and becoming self-sufficient at a very, very early age.

[. . .] Our little neighborhood was sort of sandwiched . . . between the country club and a pretty . . . well the houses were brick homes, so pretty well-to-do back then, white neighborhood. So we were sort of like down in the valley. And so of course we used to go to those neighborhoods and rake yards and pick strawberries . . . not strawberries, blackberries, off those little sticky things and go and sell them. You could sell, my goodness, you could sell like a pint of blackberries for like a dollar. That was a lot back then 'cause the white folks would buy. So it wasn't just me who was trying to survive; we were all entrepreneurs at an early, early, early age. Except I think of all my cousins and uncles and brothers. I went on to school and got my bachelors and my MBA. My oldest brother is married, and he still stays in a little town outside of Camden called Lugoff, married to this minister. They have no kids. He pretty much has had a . . . for lack of a better word, a drinking problem all of his life. He's doing better, but it's still not . . . he left at an early age. I'll never forget. I was in the eighth grade, and he stayed back a year so he was in eighth grade too. But I remember him going up north to Jamaica [Queens, New York], which is where my dad stayed. He went up north for that summer so he could . . . you know, be with my daddy. And when he came back, he was corrupted. He already was smoking reefer. He was doing all this . . . and already started messing with women. And, you know, all that stuff, you know. And he's been corrupted ever since.

My brother who's a year younger than me now is retired from the Army. He stays in New Mexico. He's married, got three kids. The interesting thing about that is that they both married two sisters.

I've got my younger brother [who] stays in trouble. He's thirty-seven, thirty-eight now. He's constantly been in trouble. He doesn't have any kids that I know of, but he's in Camden, has lived off my mama for you know . . . just will not do right. I've tried to get him to do right and help him out as much as I can. But him and his girlfriend, they kind of stay from pillar to post. And they're still doing it. So you know, some people have to come to their own time, and it's just not his time. But then my younger sister, who's my one and only sister, is married and stays in Camden, has three kids. And she's been married like three . . . no, more than that. Her youngest son is fourteen. And she's thirty-five. And she just finished her associate's degree in pharmacy assistant, like a year or two ago. She was in medical technology and got pregnant in between that. And it's hard to get in that program once you get out. So that's what she's doing, but she's doing fine. Married to a man who was in the military, and he's out and he's working, and so she seems to be able to handle her own.

What did your mother do for work?

She did domestic work, and then she worked later in the factory for the last two years . . . two, three, four . . . no, for the last five years, she has not done anything, and a matter of fact, she is now staying with my sister because she has an apartment and all of that in government housing, but what had happened was she's developed early signs of Alzheimer's because she was physically abused, and which I saw some of that. And when you read some of my poetry, in some parts you'll see . . . you can see that in some of the poetry. Because as a small child, I remember we were not staying with my grandma at the time. She had moved in with this man and we were staying there. Again, I'm small so I don't really know what happened other than that I surmised that she was not at home and he was waiting on her to come home. She didn't come home or came home later than what was expected, and so when she walked in the door, you know, he started physically abusing her. And we were all standing there and didn't know what to do. And of course I remember, quite vividly, I picked up a chair and threw it. And I was probably like four, five, six years old. I may have been seven or eight at that time. And I remember throwing a chair and then, of course, running. And then somehow I ran down to the landlord's . . . wherever the landlord's place was, and told them what was happening.

Is this the same one that shook that baby to death?

No, no, no. That's my brother Stevie. He died when I was like four, and I think I was seven or eight when this happened. But my mama's been through a series of physical abuse . . . and back then, and that was a *common* occurrence, that men used to physically . . . and they still do it now, but I'm saying they used to *physically* abuse women. Now women are more standing up to it. But I recall vividly how he had beat her with . . . I remember it was like an orange hose, like a water hose. I remember so vividly 'cause my brother, the one who always stays in trouble, he was still a baby. I mean he was a baby. He was not even walking. But I remember, after he had beat her, I remember her holding him in her arms. I'll never forget that. And so you know, when you see stuff like that. My mom just had a life of abuse, so we think that's now coming back to haunt her. And it's through no fault of her own. So right now she's staying with my sister, so that has presented a lot of challenges for us, to try to deal with that. So we're still working through all of that. And the process, I'll tell you, of getting assistance . . . 'cause she's on Medicaid and so forth, but the process is . . . even for an educated person, which I consider me to be, it is a process. That is a process that will wear you down quickly. And so we're going through that. So that kind of like gives you probably more than what you were asking for, but . . .

. . . .

"ALEX"

Alex was introduced to me several years ago at my friend Ian Barrett's home in Atlanta. When I first met him—and every time since—he had me in stitches. He has a sharp wit and a quick tongue that will keep you entertained for hours. Although he is a business professional, he has a real talent as an events planner. Many of his friends in Atlanta ask him to plan their parties. So, not only is he the life of the party, he's its planner also! His narrative below reveals how his precociousness as a child shaped his personality today. He was born in Greenwood, South Carolina, in 1967. Greenwood is located in upstate South Carolina, about sixty miles southeast of Greenville. It is known for its annual Festival of Flowers in June. The interview took place in Atlanta on January 6, 2005.

Actually, I had a very emotional childhood, coming up in a single-parent home. I knew who my father was, as the efforts of my mother trying to make sure that I knew who my family was and that kind of stuff, to ensure that I had a well-balanced type of life. But I chose later on to distance myself from that side of the family at that particular time because it just wasn't working for me. The values, the views, weren't the same. And my mother was one to teach me to always go above and beyond. And every time I went down there to visit them, I felt like I was taking a step backwards. Not necessarily in time, but just in my mindset, you know? You know, she was, you know, instilling education. You know, go for, you know, the gusto. Do your best at whatever you do. And you get down there and, you know, they're drinking and . . . just a whole different type of environment. And so as a thirteen-year-old I decided that I didn't want to go back down there at that particular time. My mother didn't like the idea. And I can tell you a story about it.

[. . .] I had gone down there, and once again I was in this environment that I really didn't feel comfortable in. It wasn't, in my opinion, clean. I didn't feel safe. And I just didn't like the liquor and the drinking and the card playing and then the attitudes that come along with the effects of alcohol, which, of course, I didn't really understand what that meant. But I understood it enough to know that it made me uncomfortable.

Well, one particular night I was down there and I got into a huge altercation with one of my aunts who actually lived with my grandmother or grandparents. And she was just . . . oh, she had the filthiest mouth that any woman could ever have, or any person could ever have. And I mean she was just evil! And in conjunction with her being evil, I had an evil stepmother, who really resented me for being the firstborn child, firstborn grandchild. And I was named after my father. And then of course my older brother of the two half brothers that I have was also named after my father in an effort for her to, you know . . . try to make that connection, I guess, to him or whatever the case may be. So I woke up one morning about 5:30. I had my mother's little makeup kit. [Laughter] Ironically. [Laughter] This little red suitcase that's used for the makeup. And that's what I put my stuff in, you know, when I went down there. And it had the little mirror in the cover and what have you. And then there was this little red suitcase that went along with it. And I packed up my little bag. Didn't say a word to anyone. My mother worked about eight miles, nine miles from where my grandparents lived. It was pitch dark. And I got up before the crack of dawn and I broke out to where my mother was working because I was ready to go home. And my grandparents I guess woke up and they discovered that I was gone. They called my father. He lived right around the corner. Called my aunts. They all lived in the same like little neighborhood. Walking distance, pretty much, from everybody. And you know I was nowhere to be found, so they called my mother in a panic. And so she gets in the car and she drives, you know, to the location and meets me. I've been walking about two and a half hours now. So I was walking. My mother was very upset and threatened to whip my butt and all that kind of stuff, and took me back down there, took me back to my grandparents.

How far had you gotten?

I had been walking about two and a half hours, so I guess at least halfway. At least halfway. Just determined. [. . .] And so my great aunt was who I called Granny, she heard about the situation. Of course, I had gone back down to my grandparents to stay the rest of that weekend. And she called my mother and told her, she said, "You know, you've done the best that you can do. You've exposed him to his father's side of the family. Every time he goes down there, he doesn't want to go. He doesn't want to go. You know, you've done your part. Don't make him go back again. You know, he's made his decision. And when he's ready to bring them back into his life, he'll go bring them back in. But don't make him go because that's going to have more of a traumatic impact on him than him making the decision on his own that, you know, 'I want to include them in my life.' "

And your mother listened?

Yes. She didn't like it. But she listened. She did. [. . .] And I would always push the extra button just to see, you know. And I mean like for example, I was about maybe ten or eleven years old and my [. . .] family had a booth at the fair, the County Fair, you know. I can't remember exactly what the game was, but you know it was a balloon tossing and all that kind of stuff and whatever. And they had the bears and all that stuff for the prizes. And you know, on Tuesday was the night that all the students would go to the fair. And you had your discount and you got your tickets and what have you. Well, with us running the booth, I was at the fair maybe three or four days during the five or six days that it was there. Well, I'm a kid, so while I'm there I want to ride. I didn't want to sit behind the booth. And so my mother told me, you know, "You can't ride because I don't have any money." And I said, "Okay, fine." [Chuckle] You know, so I sat back there for a little bit and I thought about it. And I sat there, and they was taking in . . . they were taking in the money from the booth and they were setting it back there by me. [Chuckle] And I was just looking at it. I said, "Why shoot. Well, it won't hurt to take a couple of dollars [laughter] and go and buy me some tickets to ride a couple of rides, and then I'll come on back. It's no big deal." So I took a couple dollars and I went and I bought tickets and I was riding. Well, the fairgrounds were only so big and everybody knows everybody pretty much. Well, somebody came back and said, "Well [Alex] is . . . I just saw [Alex]. He's riding so and so and so and so." Well, they knew I was, you know, kind of roaming around and they knew I wasn't going to go out of the place. But my mother was trying to figure out, "Well how is he riding? He's got no money." And so she gave me the opportunity to tell her. I got back over there and she said, "Well how did you get tickets to ride?" And I said, "What are you talking about?" [Laughter] I can't remember who told her. One of her friends or one of my cousins or somebody said it. And she said, "Well where'd you get money to ride?" And I was like, "Well I don't know what you're talking about." And then she finally got me to admit that I was riding. And I said, "Oh well, I ran across one of my other, you know, friends and their parents bought the tickets because they didn't want them to ride by themselves so they asked me if I would ride with them. So they bought me the tickets too." And she didn't believe that. [Laughter] So she asked the person that I was talking about. I didn't think she'd go ask, but she did. Didn't say one word to me the rest of the evening about the situation. [Laughter] Not one word. [I] went on, you know. I was just as happy-go-lucky, having got my ride on, and I was back there, you know, with them, playing and doing what I do. The fair closed I think ten, ten-thirty. We got to the house. We got in the house. I guess they had counted the money. Back then, you know, you don't think they have an account . . . checks and balances. I don't know what they were selling, but anyway, they sold so much and they were taking in so much, so it should have balanced out. Well, they were short whatever those dollars were that I had taken. [Laughter] And I don't even remember how much it was. Maybe it was more like six or seven dollars. But she got me back to the house. She had me strip down, and she tore my behind up. [Laughter] Butt naked, with a belt. And actually, she started with a switch and the switch broke. And I had gotten into the hamper . . . trying to cover [laughter] . . . trying to protect myself under the clothes. And that just made her even madder. And she got that belt and oh she went . . . oh, she went to *town*. And I tell you, to this day, I betcha I'll never take anything again. And never have. Because it wasn't right. And I'll remember that whipping to this day.

EDUCATION

Most people outside of the South think of the region as undereducated. Never mind that some of this country's premier universities are located there—Duke, the University of North Carolina, and Emory, just to name a few. And for many folks, especially those of an older generation, riots over the integration of public schools—something many narrators will discuss later—also come to mind when they think about education in the South. What often isn't thought about, the stories that have not been told, are the stories about whites who, for good or naught, tried to help black students succeed in the midst of blatant racism and homophobia. Indeed, many of the men I spoke with shared stories about white teachers who saw something in them and went on to encourage them academically and who also sometimes supported them financially. This is one thing I have in common with these narrators, as I was the beneficiary of my first-grade teacher's philanthropy, though ours was a conflicted relationship, especially as I got older.[1] Like The Lady Chablis, who had a white teacher who "was the first person to open the door to the white world" to her, some of the men in *Sweet Tea* and I were, thanks to educators, afforded opportunities that, given our racial and economic status, we might otherwise not have had.[2]

Some of these narratives about the early years of education suggest that there is something about being queer that makes one more fastidious about learning. I realize that this statement is borderline essentialist (perhaps it *is* essentialist), but the theme of being "different," "artistic," "creative," "having a drive," and being a "bookworm" comes up too many times for it to be a mere coincidence. As with any totalizing argument, however, there are always exceptions that trouble these preconceived notions. For as many narrators as talk about being "loners" or not being interested in sports, there are an equal number who discuss playing football and basketball, dropping out of school, getting into trouble, or having a general disinterest in school. The contradictions among these narratives are what make them, collectively, so fascinating, and so human.

. . . .

CHARLES

Charles is a young activist and creative writer. At twenty-four, he had already garnered a reputation as an outspoken leader for the young black LGBT community in Atlanta and had published some of his nonfiction. Interestingly, Charles still dates women and considers himself to be "queer" more than "gay." At the time of the interview, he was a student at Georgia State University. An only child, he was born in Atlanta in 1980. The interview took place at my friend Ian Barrett's house in Atlanta on November 9, 2004.

Were your schools integrated?

Well, they were all-black schools. They might have had a few white people here and there but [. . .] it wasn't like, you know, we have to go there because you're black. We went there because that was the school you're zoned to. [. . .] We had what was called the magnet program, where you basically applied to the high school you wanted to go to. [. . .] And I chose Therrel because, well for a few reasons. You know, mostly because I didn't want to go to my zone high school. This is where it gets complicated. I didn't want to go to my zone high school because the kids that lived in my neighborhood were just, like, ruthless, like, I knew that it would have just been a really horrendous experience. [. . .] I didn't want to go to the feeder high schools because the middle school experience I had was really, really bad, too. Like, a lot of kids would pick on me and stuff, and I just didn't really have a pleasant middle school experience. Not so much because of the gay thing. Like that wasn't really it; it was more because, I mean I didn't talk like everyone else, you know. They said I sounded white, and I didn't really conform to the notions of masculinity that were really the most acceptable, just in terms of being kind of bookish, and speaking the way I spoke. [. . .] I think it's also in the, like, early '90s, when you started to see hip-hop culture defining black masculinity in a more rigid way. And I didn't really do a lot around hip-hop either. I mean, I did a lot around it to the extent that I listened to it, and I kind of knew what was going on, but it didn't define me. Like I didn't really use it as an identity marker. Like I didn't really dress that way, or really speak that way, not really—I didn't really use it to define me, like a lot of the other males in my school. I was just kind of into my own thing. And I paid a price for it, you know? I stood out. I was very different in terms of the way I spoke, the way I dressed, the way I kinda carried myself. And so I said all that to say, that I didn't want to go to the theater high school or the middle school because I was like, I want to go somewhere completely different and start over anew. And I went to Therrel, and even though Therrel still had a lot of the same stuff . . . I just didn't really get as much shit in high school. Well, for one thing, I was in the magnet program. And I think the magnet program is really about trying to like, concentrate. It was really about, like, okay, we're going to try to do the best we can to make sure you get the most out of this high school experience. And we're going to try to keep you, not so much keep you away from, but keep you sheltered from the rest of the high school environment, from the rest of the kids in the high school, because, you know, we're going to define you as kids that have potential, and kids that are probably going to go on to college. And so, you know, it was terribly sheltered, for like ninth and tenth grade. And then my junior year I started taking AP [i.e., advance placement] classes. [. . .] I'm very critical of tracking in schools, typical black kids. But I mean in a weird kind of way it was also something that kind of, I don't want to say saved me, but I think had I been around the other kids in school I would have continued to get a lot of shit, for being how I was. That isn't to say I didn't really get any shit in the magnet program, but [. . .] there was a way in the magnet program where you could be smart. When I was in middle school it was not okay to be a smart boy. Like, I also find interesting for like, conventional feminist arguments [. . .] second-wave feminists are arguing like, girls can't be smart in class, blah blah blah. My experience was one where, it was not okay for a boy to be smart, like you could be athletic, you can dance, you can dress well, but you can't be too smart. And, and certainly not be precocious. I was terribly precocious, you know, and so when I got to high school, I think there are ways in which, particularly in the magnet program, you can be smart and you weren't necessarily punished for it. [. . .] And it wasn't like, you know there's one peer group that's going to make everyone else's lives, everyone else's life hell; it was more like, everyone kind of find where they fit in, and you just kind of do the best you can. So, that was a very elaborate explanation as to my, my school experience.

. . . .

DUNCAN TEAGUE
My interview with Duncan was one of the most memorable because he has a wicked sense of humor. He is one of the few narrators in Sweet Tea *who insisted that I use his first and last name. He's just that fierce!*

Duncan, who lives in Atlanta, is a member of the black gay performance art/spoken word group, Adodi Muse. They've performed around the country and have produced a CD. Prominent themes in their work include black gay pride and self-respect, relationship dramas, and HIV/AIDS. Duncan is very much an activist, and most everyone in Atlanta's gay community knows him. Indeed, he helped me find men to be interviewed.

Duncan was born "sometime in the early '60s" in Kansas City, Missouri. The interview took place on November 1, 2004, at his home in Atlanta.

We went to Mary Harmon Weeks, which was a brand-new grade school. And it was in a black community and had a resource center instead of a library because it had more than books. I mean it was brand spanking new, and that's where I went for second grade through fourth grade. No. I'm sorry. I went there through fifth grade. Wow, yeah. I get confused because the school had a fire and they took the high-B students and the good readers who had excellent social skills because we had overcrowding and they took about a classroom of like ten of us and they put us back in the fourth-grade classroom, but we were doing fifth-grade work. And what I surmise is that it was one of those social educational experiments because you can't mess with your A students because they don't like change and they're spoiled brats. Yes I said it. [Chuckle] And you know they have to have everything just so. And you know the other students, you don't want to mess with their socialization or whatever because they're challenged enough. So they took the kids who they knew could handle being separated from their peer group and still do the work. And so we got our own teacher and we were in the fourth-grade classroom but we were a fifth-grade class. Because that was where there was room for us. So I get confused. But when we came home from the summer of the fifth grade and what was my brother's fourth-grade year, the school sent a letter home to my mother, saying that my brother was not really up to par to go to fifth grade. And I would have been going to sixth grade. And that they were going to allow him to pass so that he could stay with his social group, but he wasn't really doing the work. And my mother . . . I can still hear her yelling and screaming. Because she wanted to know that Phillip wasn't doing the work during the school year because she'd have gotten on him. And education was everything to my mother and my father. And when she called up there and she said, "Well if he isn't able to do fifth- grade work, he isn't going to the fifth grade. You put him back in the fourth grade." And they wouldn't do it back then. *Now* they would probably do it. But even at my mother's request, they weren't going to do it. So she said, "Y'all aren't going there no more." And my parents sacrificed. From that point through the end of high school, we went to private schools. Yeah. So some of those early neighborhood friends I sort of left in the early adolescence and went to private schools. And I went to the Lutheran grade school and then the Catholic high school. And my parents did not want me to go to the Catholic high school because we're Baptists. But there was no such thing as a Baptist high school. And I did not want to go to public high school. I just didn't. My mother thought that we would, but unh unh. I wanted to go with my friends to Bishop Hogan, and so I did. And I was . . . actually I think I was quite a success at high school.

There was a moment when my father was trying to butch me up . . . or get rid of the gayness. And so the Lord told him to send me to Tri-City Christian Academy. And it was about maybe fifteen miles from our home. And it was one of these fundamentalist Christian schools, non-affiliated with a major denomination that was ninety-something percent white. And it was horrid. And I started developing a spasm in my back that felt like I was having heart trouble. See, I had become a class leader and was recognized and all this, but I was also becoming a very gay young man. I guess my father was at his wit's end because what had been cute was no longer cute. And at the end of the first semester, given the muscle spasms and how much I hated the school and how inferior the education was compared to Bishop Hogan, I stood up to my father and I told him that I really didn't care what he or the Lord thought. I was not going back there. I was going to Bishop Hogan High School for my second semester of my junior year, and he and the Lord needed to work it out. And I considered that like a sort of coming out, in a way, because . . . and it wasn't about me saying, "I'm gay." It was about me standing up for myself against everything I'd been taught. And I really didn't give a damn. And so I have to be careful now because I have to remind myself that everybody wasn't me in high school. And everybody didn't stand up to their parents. And so when I hear the stories about gay men who wait until they're thirty, forty, fifty, whenever to come out, I really have to work at understanding them and understanding their turmoil, because that stepping up to my father was just a beginning.

. . . .

FREDDIE (B. 1944, MADISON, GA.)

In high school, even in elementary school there was one teacher in particular who would assign a girl to tell her if anybody bothered me when she went out of the room. I later found out that she was, in fact, a lesbian. And was a married lesbian. She had a husband and some children, but she was, in fact, a lesbian. And she would assign a girl to tell her, so along the way I was kind of protected by people. In high school, there was always a bigger boy or somebody who would kind of protect me. And the bigger boys, I never had sex with them, but they just kind of felt a sense that I needed protecting.

And something else happened. When I was in sixth grade, some boys were bothering me and the teacher kept us after school. And I would carry a single-edge razor blade in my pocket to sharpen my pencils, because if I went to the pencil sharpener they would bother me. Maybe somebody would put a tack in my seat or try to do something to me. Just little kid harassment. So after we were kept after school, the boys were going to line up to beat me up because they said it was my fault. So I would always say in the sweetest little voice—because you see I'm reasonably soft-spoken now—"Leave me alone. I'm minding my business. Don't bother me." So this boy ran up to hit me and I cut him across his shoulder with the razor blade. And by that time, the teacher came and said, "You boys better go home." So the last thing I heard him say was, "You're a mean sissy. I'm going to have your ass locked up." So I went home. I didn't say anything to my mother. And bravely the next day I went to school. And he came up to me and he had a hairline cut on his shoulder because I had cut through two or three layers of clothing. And he said, "You better be glad." I said, "Listen. Do not bother me. I keep telling you to leave me alone. I want to be left alone. I'm not bothering you. Don't bother me." But what always happened if anybody attacked me, they always ended up seeing some of their blood. Because I would bite them. Or I would hit them with a sharp object or something. But they always ended up seeing some of their blood. So because I was so supple, there was no way that they could twist my arm or do anything that I couldn't get out of. And I could run. I could outrun them if I had to run. So rumors spread. "Don't bother him. He's a mean little sissy and he's stronger than he looks." So that kind of followed me. Because I went to high school with a lot of the same kids, that kind of followed me. So I didn't really have many situations where I had altercations. And there were teachers who would protect me. I didn't take much physical education in high school because my homeroom teacher was the art teacher and she would get the physical education teacher to let me come to the art room. [Chuckle] And I would get, you know, a physical education grade. And I was always kind of treated like a girl, in a way. There was one teacher who only let girls ride in his car. And I always hung out mostly with girls, so one day my girlfriend said, "Come on, Freddie. Come on, you get a ride home with us." So I said, "What will he say? What will Mr. Hood say?" So I came and got in the car. And Mr. Hood looked at me and said, "Oh, it's you." [Laughter] So even if the girls were not there, Mr. Hood would give me a ride home. I later found out that he was having an inappropriate affair with one of the girls. But he would give me a ride home.

There were teachers . . . one teacher in particular . . . who was obviously trying to lure me into something, and even in front of people he was kind of inappropriate in a way. And everybody knew. My homeroom teacher would tell me, "I know who you're thinking about, Mister." And I'd say, "No I'm not." And she said, "Oh yes you are." He was a very handsome man. And had he approached me appropriately I would have probably . . . and probably not because I always had a sense that the teachers had power over me, that they were in a position of authority, that we were not equal. But like he would touch me kind of inappropriately. And there were a couple of others that would try to lure me to ballgames or what have you. But I always knew what they were up to, so I would never go. Because I always had a sense of their having authority over me, us not being equal. And so I didn't. I didn't. I had a rule that I didn't want to have sex with anybody at a place where I worked or went to school, at a place where I had to go. In case something happened and it went sour. Because I have observed relationships like that going sour because people didn't manage them well. And so I had a lot of these kind of wisdom and stuff at a young age. But the part of my life that was gay, basically was good. I was often protected by people and seen as special.

. . . .

KEVIN H.
Kevin H. teaches law, but he is also pursuing a Ph.D. at Duke University. We met in 2003 in Chicago while he was doing a visiting professor stint at Kent College of Law. Unlike most of the men in Sweet Tea, *Kevin is desperately trying to relocate out of the South. As a fortysomething single man, he feels that a larger urban space will provide him more opportunities—professionally and socially.*

Kevin H. was born in Texas City, Texas, in 1964. Texas City is located forty miles southeast of Houston and sits on the Gulf of Mexico. The United States's third-largest oil refinery, owned by BP, *is located there. The interview took place on October 28, 2004, in Carrboro, North Carolina.*

In elementary school, I don't really remember having friends so much. I mean I certainly remember people that I played with during recess and that sort of thing. But in terms of having, you know, sleepovers or stuff like that, no, not really very much. I mean there were kids in the neighborhood, you know, that I would consider myself having grown up with. But not really close friends. I had a couple of friends, you know, from middle school, and they're people, one in particular, my friend Dennis and I are still friends, you know, good friends today. And maybe a couple of people from high school. In high school in particular, I always felt like I was very different from everyone for lots of different reasons. I mean less so in terms of sexuality, I think. Not thinking about that. Though I certainly think that was part of it. And more . . . but more because I was really smart and I was really . . . you know, all I wanted to do was read and do stuff like that. I wasn't particularly athletic. I was in the band, you know, and that was kind of . . . that was fun, it was an activity. But I was the kind of kid in high school and junior high too I guess, that where you know I was always elected class president or some student council officer. But I really didn't have friends. I mean I didn't go to the high school dances, I didn't do, you know, any of that stuff because I really just felt, you know, so different from everyone and not having any of their interests. So I was just really wanting to get away, you know, graduate, leave, go to college. And it was really college when I first felt myself, you know, surrounded by people who were like me. I really became this incredibly social person that I had never been before. [. . .] I was completely a sort of closed-off kind of person before.

. . . .

SHOMARI

Shomari is a graduate student at Georgia State University. I met him at OutWrite Bookstore in Atlanta in 2003 during a book signing. We reconnected when I started contacting men to be interviewed for this book. He and Charles are good friends.

Born in New Orleans in 1977, Shomari is the oldest child of three. The interview took place on November 10, 2004, in Atlanta.

New Orleans is a Catholic town, so I actually went to Saint Gabriel the Archangel Elementary School, and I went there from pre-K to half of fifth grade. At the end, and when my fifth-grade year started, they decided Saint Gabriel was closing because enrollment was down, and the archdiocese had to close a lot of the smaller schools because they were running out of money, you know. At one point, in New Orleans, a lot of people sent their kids to Catholic school. Like even black people, like blacks sent a lot of their children to Catholic schools. There were tons and tons of Catholic elementary schools, sort of all over the place. But my school, they decided to close, and I went from being in a school that was primarily black to going to Saint James Pager, which even though it was right up the street, it was primarily white.

And I transferred in the middle of the year, so I was the new kid, the new fat kid, the new fat sissy sometimes, it just depends what day of the week it was, they decided to pick on me, for half of fifth grade and all of sixth grade. And then from seventh through twelfth grade I went to McMain Magnet. And they went from seventh through twelfth grade, and actually, in my eleventh-grade year, I went to the performing arts school, but it's not situated like most. Like here, in North Atlanta and Tri-City are usually sort of where the performing arts schools are in Georgia, and I'm using all these Georgia metaphors assuming you know what I'm talking about, but maybe not. But like here, what I've experienced is that, the performing arts schools are all-inclusive. Like you go to school for math and science as well as your theater classes, or your music classes, or your dance classes. In New Orleans it wasn't like that. We had this place called NOCCA, which is an acronym for New Orleans Center of the Creative Arts, and you go to NOCCA for half of a day, where you take all of your performing arts classes, and you go to your second school for math, science, English, and social studies. So, your day is split. And it's actually pretty cool. So I did that for my eleventh- and twelfth-grade year.

Do you remember any of the friendships that you made in elementary, middle school, high school, and are you still in touch with some of them?

It was primarily girls . . . it was, oh my God, Christelle, Chantelle, Cassandra, Jeanine, Glenisha, yeah. They all went to St. Gabriel's with me and I ended up seeing them in McMain. And we all went from seventh to twelfth grade there. Am I still in touch with a lot of them? From the younger grades, the people who I like, actually, not really, I'm not really in touch with, a significant portion of the people, that I went to high school with. My best friend, who I actually I met when I was in eleventh grade, you know we've stayed in touch. He lives in New York now, but we've been in touch, from, you know this whole time. Like and I'm like, I actually realized, god you're like one of my oldest friends, because a lot of those other people, I either just, grew apart, or we just, never, was never really, that close. Like I didn't really develop, like a significant group of friends until I went to NOCCA, until I went to the creative arts school, and, you know, here I had these other, like, and initially I didn't think of myself as an artsy freak, before, I was always very much a character. My family thought of me as a character because I was always running around, doing shit. And, I was always very dramatic. My mother calls me a drama queen, just very dramatic. Like I actually just thought of this thing, it was funny because when I was, like seven or eight, you know, you know how kids watch TV, we had just finished watching *Soul Train*. I just *loved Soul Train*. You know, the whole music and dancing thing, I just loved *Soul Train*. And I ran from in the other room, and it happened, I don't remember what group was on, but it was definitely a group that I was very into at the time, and I ran into the room and I was like, "Mama! Mama! Mama! Mama, my one ambition in life, is to dance in *Soul Train*." My mother had a fit. She had a fit, because she had just finished paying that Catholic school tuition. She was like, "If you're going to dance on *Soul Train*, I could send your ass to the free school," like, "you don't need to be able to read, to go," you know, "to dance on *Soul Train*." Yeah, I got whooped a lot as a child.

RACISM AND SEGREGATION

All of the narrators shared stories of racism and/or of living in segregated neighborhoods or attending segregated schools. In a few instances, some of the men witnessed or experienced racial violence firsthand, including visits from the Klan. While not all of the stories relate blatant acts of racial discrimination, many narrators detailed racial incidents that impacted their lives for years to come, such as being chased, being accused of stealing, or being treated differently in school. And not all of the men accuse whites of racism. Indeed, more than a few of them discuss racial prejudice among blacks—sometimes even within their own families.

On the topic of segregation, some narrators lament the integration of schools because, for them, it meant being bused across town away from their communities and into harm's way. Many are quick to note the racial tension and riots they witnessed or participated in during the slow integration of school systems in the South. Like my hometown of Hickory, North Carolina, many of these narrators' hometowns did not integrate their schools until fifteen to twenty years after *Brown vs. Board of Education*. Other narrators lament not only the integration of schools, but also the integration of society in general, which meant the end of an era when blacks supported and relied on one another. Integration, some argue, diluted the self-reliance fostered by all-black communities that had come to be taken for granted. With "white flight" to the suburbs in the wake of the civil rights movement, central cities declined, and many black communities were devastated by poverty, spiraling downward until recently, when they began to undergo gentrification, often, ironically, by white gay men.[3]

Roderick and "D.C.," in particular, note how certain black communities in their towns were named to reflect the value that whites placed on them— names like "The Bottom." Like the fictional town, The Bottom, in Toni Morrison's novel *Sula*, these black communities were the product of white

racism.[4] These neighborhoods were anything but fictional, however, embodying real, institutionalized racism that affected not only these black
men's lives, but black lives in general. The one thing more than a couple
of the narrators note as transcending race in their communities is sports.
Newly integrated high schools often meant blacks and whites playing side by
side on a team. Although the venue may still have been segregated, with black
fans and white fans seated in separate areas, as both Tim'm and Marlon note,
people came together across racial lines in order to root for their team.

But not all of the men in *Sweet Tea* express negative feelings about integration. Some feel that integration was absolutely necessary and provided
opportunities for blacks that would not have existed otherwise. Others believe that black communities have not done well because of black-on-black
crime, a general sense of black apathy, or what Cornel West would call
"black nihilism."[5] For the most part, generational differences explain the
varying attitudes about integration.

. . . .

HAROLD

Harold has become something of an uncle figure to me since we first met.
Of all of the men in Sweet Tea, *he is the only one who stays in touch on a*
regular basis. In fact, every time he sees a reference to my books, he'll copy
it and send it to me.

At seventy, Harold shows no sign of slowing down. He and his partner,
whose name is also Harold, have been together for over forty years (see
Chapter 6). They live in Washington, D.C., in the upscale northeast section.
Harold is an avid baseball fan and has promised me that he'll come to
Chicago to visit me and see a Cubs or White Sox game.

Harold was a member of the Boy Scouts of America for most of his youth,
an interesting fact given that organization's current stance on homosexuality.
He went on to become an Eagle Scout, which is the highest advancement
rank in the Boy Scouts, and, according to him, he is one of the few African
Americans to achieve that status. He is also a veteran of the Army, which
afforded him an opportunity to live in Korea and Japan. It was an experience,
he says, that changed his life.

Harold was born in 1936 in St. Louis, Missouri, and is the elder of
two children. The interview took place on May 4, 2005, at his home in
Washington, D.C.

For summer vacations for a period of time, after school was out, we went
with my grandmother back to her hometown, which was outside of Little

Harold held by his maternal grandmother in St. Louis, ca. 1936.
Courtesy of the narrator.

Rock, Arkansas. And my grandmother had relatives, and one of her relatives was a physician. But he practiced in this little small town. And when we visited, I had the opportunity of going with him on his rounds. And he provided the medical care to not just the poor African Americans, but even the poor white sharecroppers. Because he was the only doctor between this city and Little Rock. And I don't remember the miles, but it was quite some distance. And so we got a taste of rural American life. You had a little bit of a twist. We were still black in the American South, which was segregated. And one of the things that I have to tell you about is that two days a week, my grandmother and her cousin, who had married the doctor, would go into Little Rock to do shopping. And we would get dressed, and they'd put us into the car and they'd say, "Now you can't run and jump and scream and holler because it's not nice and blah, blah, blah." Because that's all we were doing for most of the week . . . was running and screaming out in this open country. And when we arrived in Little Rock, my cousin and my grandmother went to Pfeiffer's Department Store. And she parked and we got out and we rushed into the department store, and we were so excited to see the city again, and we ran to a water cooler and drank from it. Now mind you, St. Louis was not quite as segregated as Little Rock. They did not have water coolers for blacks and whites, but it was segregated. And before they could say, "No don't drink that water," we had jumped on a little stool and got up to the water fountain and we're drinking. And I guess the store personnel saw us. And then when they saw who we were with, it changed. It seems that my grandmother's cousin's husband was known in that area. She was known in that store. She could buy clothes, but she'd have to have them shipped to her because they had to be exact size, right size, because she couldn't try them on. So that was sort of a helpful thing. And that's when we started to learn the difference in races, really. Because we had been sort of kept away from it. Now on the trips to and from Little Rock . . . my grandfather was a Pullman porter, so we didn't pay too much attention to the fact that . . . because we did go into a Pullman car. But it would have to be the one that didn't have that many whites in it, or the whites would be at this end and you'd be at the other end. And they'd say, "Now don't go over into the middle of that car." Or in the chair cars on the railroads, they'd say, "Stay here." I don't know what was this attraction to water. Every time I found a water fountain, I was always heading for . . . and my grandma would tell me, "If you go back to that water fountain again, I'm gonna kill you." [Chuckle] Because I was constantly saying, "I want some water," you know. But those experiences were really . . . as a child, they could be frightening and then they're over with. And then later on, you get the full impact. But I did not get it until my aunt who worked for a company and they had picketing to let the people know that they were not getting fair pay. And that's when I began to see the differences. Then comes integration of schools. By this time, I'm out of the public schools but my sister, who still had years left in there . . . and she did not want to go. The school districts were broken up by where you lived. And by this time, we lived in an area that was right adjacent to . . . or we had white neighbors. My sister did not want [to go to school]. Oh she cried. She claimed she was going to move to Chicago. She did everything. And finally, when . . . the semester began, and my mother goes with her. And except for a little skirmishes that you have when new kids appear . . . not new black kids . . . where they're just new kids . . . but she soon got over it. And I think that it probably, with the fact that my parents would say, "Yes there are people who don't like you because of your color, but you cannot hate them for that."

When we moved that one particular time into this area, there was a park nearby and we got our baseball bats and gloves and headed straight over there. And I don't know how frank I should be about it, but there were a group of guys playing baseball. And we stood around, hoping that they'd say, "Come on, you want to play?" And finally somebody said, "Hey can we play?" And they said, "No, we don't play with niggers." And then again, even though we had newspaper stories and we heard our parents talk about what it was like in the South, we still did not . . . until it happened to us, okay? [. . .]

Were they [civic organizations] segregated when you were in the Boy Scouts?

Yes it was. Now the segregation didn't seem so obvious because, remember, organizations sponsored Boy Scouts and Girl Scouts. So your church or your school sponsored the Boy Scout unit that you were in, in your neighborhood. But there were times when you came together as Boy Scouts and Girl Scouts from a whole city. That was not segregated. I went to summer camp with scouts from other parts. My last Boy Scout chum died two years ago. And we started off when we were fifteen, sixteen, seventeen in the Senior Scouting program. That's where we met. And we met again twenty years later when we went to a reunion. And that's how we sort of became friends again after. But I do wish that churches, synagogues, would promote Boy Scouting, especially in the urban settings. In this city, the evening news is so filled with awful happenings. It's getting younger and younger that these events are happening, and especially to African American males. And now you must include girls. And it seems odd that, when I grew up as an African American, there was not that much money in my family or in the African American community. But they pulled together. They would not just say, "Oh we're praying for you." They did something.

My grandmother's church had various organizations. And I'll never forget it. They were called progressive circles. They helped the people in the community with anything that they possibly could. My grandmother would go back to visit her relatives, and she would take clothing that they had restyled, that were donated by her friends and her church, back to the poor people in that same city outside of Little Rock, and donate. They made quilts and they had care boxes before I guess it was CARE that they would ship back to these people in the hometowns of the church members who had migrated to the city of St. Louis and who had improved their status. Now improving the status was not that they went from perhaps a porter in their small town to the head of a company in St. Louis. But they did make more money and they shared. They took responsibility for the children in the neighborhood. If their parents were a little off about keeping an eye on them, somebody else saw it. And many a times we would slip to what would be kind of like the main boulevard area where the stores and whatnot . . . and they'd say, "Well I saw that boy run across the street the other day." And if I had not been sent there by my parents, then they'd want to know, "What were you doing over there?" And it would be only about five blocks. And I think that, when I hear of the horrible things that happen to boys and girls today by predators who are waiting for them . . . you know what I mean? If there were more eyes and ears. If there were more caring. And this idea of respect. I just realized it because about five weeks ago I turned sixty-nine. And I really have it in my mind now that I'm mature or older. But I have respect for youth at twenty-one, to begin with. Now I don't always get that same respect back, but I even get less of it now because nobody seems to pay any attention to who's next to them. I probably sound sort of cynical. But that's what unnerves me. And I think that each of us have a responsibility to ourselves and to our fellow man. And maybe, since we have equality to a degree, that we've lost some of the feeling for others. I don't mean others less fortunate. I mean all the others. I don't know how. When I was younger, when I first got out of school and I went to work, through the church I got involved with a youth program. And they were poor youth. They were youth from households with only one adult. And through the Boy Scout troop, which was what . . . by this time I was a Scout Master . . . we told them, "Okay you can't buy a brand-new uniform. But we can get a uniform for you. It will be used by another scout before you." But we would not give the uniform to him. He had to work for it. In other words, he had to join the unit and he had to stay in it and he had to do certain things. He had to attain a certain rank and then that uniform was actually his. And he had to take care of it. I went into homes in which there were eight to twelve children. And all of this, mind you, was in a neighborhood or a community. The last unit I had, I took twenty-seven Boy Scouts from poor, underprivileged homes, who were members of this unit, to the New York World's Fair in 1964. They paid all of their individual ways, even though our sponsoring institution was a church and put up the basic money. But we didn't tell them that. And we didn't tell their parents that. And we went to the New York World's Fair for four days and four nights, by train, and we stayed in a YMCA hotel and we went back and forth to the fair. We took out money on the sly and bought cameras for them. But we only said they could borrow them. It was only after we got back that we gave them the cameras. And we used that camera and their picture taking to be more involved in a Boy Scout program, which was a merit badge in photography. So those are some of the things I feel really excited about the fact that I had some involvement in giving back to another generation, I guess you could say.

You said that St. Louis was segregated. Was it segregated by some physical barrier, like people talk about railroad tracks or a street . . .

No. It was segregated by street. Okay. St. Louis sits on the banks of the Mississippi River. The oldest part is closest to the river. Most of the African American population lived in the old part of St. Louis. And this would be up until about 1949 or 1950. And then there was a movement by African Americans into other neighborhoods.

And what were the racial politics of your hometown? Were there interactions between blacks and whites, or did they not get along?

Yes. There was interaction between . . . good interaction, okay? The schools were segregated. The black schools . . . say in high school, they played their own black schools, okay? Now, if they became state winners, then of course you couldn't determine who they would play. It'd be another school. It could be a white school from another part of the state. But they found some way to cancel, okay? A friend and myself ran track, and we were fortunate enough to win some championships. When they held the track championships, they were in the southern part of the state of Missouri. And that was very, very segregated. We could not stay overnight there because there were very few blacks who had places you could sleep. So we had to go there, run the track meets, and then come back. And then later, that changes. Okay? The whole idea of eating out and going to the movies, all of this was segregated. And I remember when the movies integrated. At that time, there was a film that was in giant . . . oh what was that? It was a new technique and it was a biblical film. And my grandmother, who was not much of a moviegoer, wanted to see this movie. I don't . . . Was it *Ben-Hur*? [. . .] Okay, I take her to see this. And we dress up. She had her hat and the gloves, and I had my sport jacket and whatnot. And we go to a matinee. The movie house is integrated.

What year was this?

About '58, '59. And it was the most wonderful experience that she had. She went to movies, but because of her religious beliefs, she figured movies were a little [weird noise], okay? But this was something that she really wanted to see. I think it was *King of Kings* or . . . It was a Cecil B. DeMille. *Sampson and Delilah* or one of . . . Okay? Restaurants were still segregated. These are ones that are privately owned. But places such as the counters in the five and dime store, that had at one time been segregated, where you would go up there and sit down or buy a hamburger or hot dog and eat it there, okay? The neighborhoods slowly were integrating, but there was a lot of friction between the first ones to move in. There was an area in a part of the city . . . South St. Louis, that was totally Italian. And they were awful about families moving in. They would hold property if it didn't sell, before they would sell it to a black family. You could not rent an apartment, okay? Finally, with the help of the Catholic Church and the Urban League and the NAACP, with picketing and appealing through the ministers and the priests, they were finally able to break down these kinds of segregation in public places.

· · · · · · · ·

BOB

Although he does not describe himself this way, everyone I know refers to Bob as a self-made millionaire. He lives in one of the northwest suburbs of Atlanta in what is referred to in today's real estate parlance as a "McMansion." Bob is not pretentious, however. In fact, he is very generous with his home (there were guests staying there during our interview) and his possessions. During our interview, for example, he mentioned lending a friend his French crystal, Rosenthal china, and some family silver.

Bob is very clear about his views on most things, especially issues of race and religion. Those views have been clarified by time spent in therapy and by the life experiences of many years spent in the San Francisco Bay Area before moving back to Georgia after the death of his partner of twenty-seven years. "Alex" put me in contact with Bob because he said that he would be an "interesting case study" for my book. He was right.

Bob was born in Baxley, Georgia, in 1940. Baxley is located in southeast Georgia and has a population just under 5,000. Although a small town, Baxley is birthplace to two notable authors: Caroline Miller, who was the first Georgia resident to win the Pulitzer Prize, for her book Lamb in His Bosom *in 1934, and Janisse Ray, who won the American Book Award for her memoir,* Ecology of a Cracker Childhood. *The interview took place at Bob's home on May 14, 2005.*

The worst memories are racism, you know, being—and I didn't know it at the time, why I was feeling the hatred for my father, until I went through therapy. And that's another whole story. But having people come to your house and give you food, oh, that was debasing. Especially during the holidays, it was like a festive time of the year, and people having this, you know, dah, dah, dah. And all of a sudden this white man shows up with a turkey and some potatoes and he says, "This is for you." What? And I refused to eat it. And my mother couldn't understand why I would refuse to eat it. And I didn't know why I was refusing to eat it at the time. But later on in life, I realized that it was a reaction to something deep down in was saying, you know, how dare a person belittle me and my family by having to give me something that my father ought to be able to provide for us. But then knowing that at the time he couldn't do it, he had done the best he could do, and that's what my therapist helped me realize it; he did the best he could with what he had. And how many other people did any better than he did, you know, where are you coming from, you know? So I'm going like, oh, wow, I guess he did, so I can let that go. So I let it go, yeah. I finally found peace with that and have found some comfort in the fact that he did the best he could. But it was the racism. And to tell you the truth, there were white men in the community who would go with black women, and we knew about it, everybody knew about it. And there were folk who had babies for white men. And I got a cousin who had a baby for a white man.

When you say for a white man, do you mean that there was some kind of payment or arrangement?

They had sexual relations, and they probably were not willing participants. But because the person was white in a dominant role and then they acquiesced to their sexual advances, and they got pregnant. And they opted to have the baby because black women back then did not have abortions; they had their babies. And so there were children who were born who were— looked blue eyes and, you know, strange hair, to black girls. And everybody knew it. And then there were white men who would come to the black neighborhoods by night and we'd see these women going out and stuff. And so everybody knew. And I hated that as a child, knowing that, you know, here you are a black person, allowing yourself to be.

[. . . .]

Well, can you imagine the '40s and the Klan? And my father was very active—my father's brother was secretary of the NAACP back in 1951, I guess it was. No, 1948, because we had not moved from the rented property that we were occupying. And when the Klan came through and they had mistaken my father for my father's brother, who was a plumber and was middle class,

he was considered to be [an] uppity nigger because he had children in college and they had their own property and his wife's mother had property and
he was the only plumber in this town, so he could call the shots of, you know,
what he did, so he had money. And the Klan came looking for the [last
name]s. They thought that my father was [his brother]—and so that was very
scary, I remember that very vividly. My mother was horrified.

Did they come to your house?

They came—we lived on a dirt street, across from a tobacco warehouse.
And they were on the main highway. And my mother had never seen them
before, had never seen that parade. And so she thought it was a big night
parade because they all got out of their cars and with their lights on and
they were looking. And my mother said to the neighbor, "Oh, let's go look
at the parade. And see all those people in those uniforms," or whatever it
was. And the lady next door said, "Oh, my goodness, those are the Klans-
men." And somebody came running down the street, said, "They're looking
for York." That's my father, who was not at home. So my mother took my
sister and I and went to the railroad track. And we went down the railroad
track to escape the Klan in 1948. Um hmm. So it was very scary. So that was
very, very scary.

How many times did they come?

They only came once to us. But, of course, they were burning crosses in
other people's yards. So that was—so you knew, you know.

And were most of the white people in town that way?

Well, there were—the Jews were not—there were Jews in that town who
had, because of course now I look back on it, they were just as racist, I
suppose, as the southern whites, but because their history was tied more
closely to oppression, coming out of Germany, as our history, there was
some kinship to our suffering. So they had a way of providing jobs and other
kind of incentives to people of color. I had a cousin—not a cousin, it was—
well, it was a cousin, but she's so distant I don't know if you'd call her a
cousin or not, but who was away in college in 1950. I was ten. And she had
come back to that small town and was actually given a job as a salesperson in
a Jewish establishment. And all the other people who were not Jewish, all the
Wasps, they stopped shopping at—the only stores in town that were dry
goods stores, we called them then, where they sold clothing, were owned by
Jews and the jewelry stores were owned by Jews. So they had no other recourse but to go to those stores. But my cousin was a salesperson for the
summer. She came back and she worked there as a salesperson, so yeah.

Racially, I suppose in hindsight, we knew our place. And we were protected against the abuses because my mother worked for a family that for

years—this family, although they were racist and had racist attitudes, they took care of their coloreds. And so we were always—and now I hated it, as a child I hated it and I didn't know why I hated it, but now I know why I hated it. [Laughter] But they would give these little things to us and, you know, especially at the holiday times they would send these big packages and so. And then my father worked at this drug store for the most part. And they were benevolent and I don't like benevolence. I think it's a putdown. I mean, that's my own take on benevolence—maybe not in the sense of how I'm benevolent to the folk who are less fortunate, but I don't think that they're less than I am. I do it out of a sense of obligation and not out of a sense of you're less than and I have to do this. But I think in hindsight there were a lot of whites who were—except for the Jews, who gave us, who would give us books to read because we couldn't go to the library and they would slip us books and say, "Well, don't let anybody know that I've given you these books to read, you know," and that kind of stuff so, because we didn't have a library to go to in elementary school. In high school we did.

· · · · · · · ·

DAN

Dan was the first of his generation that I interviewed. He was born in Durham, North Carolina, in 1943. I have to admit that I found his willingness to speak to me surprising—mostly because I didn't know how willing older southern men would be to speak to me about being gay. Dan set a trend that would blow my theory about their reluctance out of the water. As I suggested in the Introduction, it was actually the older men who were most willing to speak about their lives as gay southerners.

Dan is of a generation of blacks who grew up in Durham during its heyday. Durham is the home of one of the first black-owned insurance companies in the country, North Carolina Mutual Life Insurance Company, founded in 1898 by seven black business, education, and medical professionals. In general, the city was a prosperous place for African Americans from Reconstruction on, giving rise to a vibrant black district called Hayti, where, according to W. E. B. Du Bois in 1920, the "social and economic development is perhaps more striking than that of any similar group in the nation."⁶ It is also home to North Carolina Central University, a historically black college. Dan was a beneficiary of this history before the black community's decline in the 1970s. He left Durham in 1961 to attend Morehouse College in Atlanta and then lived in New York, Puerto Rico, and Oakland before returning to Durham in 1992 with his partner of twenty-five years, who died in 1998.

Currently, he lives with his new partner in a historic neighborhood in Durham called Forest Park. He is a real estate agent and occasionally serves as a church organist. The day of our interview was a particularly warm August afternoon in 2004. After he showed me his collection of artifacts and paintings from around the world, we sat on his screened-in back porch and enjoyed a glass of—no, not sweetened iced tea—red wine.

When the neighborhood that you grew up in was segregated, was that reflective of the entire town?

I was born in the '40s, so I grew up in the '50s and '60s, and *Brown vs. Board* didn't happen until '54, and of course it didn't happen in the South until the '70s, you know, if it's happened yet. So I mean there was a major, there were black communities, you know. And there were white communities, and sometimes they would divide it by a street, I mean, on one side of the street could be black, and the other side of the street could be white, and so that was a sort of division, a dividing line between the communities.

How did that affect your racial identity?

This may sound crazy but it didn't affect it at all, you know? I mean, there were white people, there were black people. And we, I had everything I needed in my black community, and there was no reason for me to, I mean I never even thought about intermingling, or wanting to be with white people.

So you didn't feel like you were missing out on anything?

I didn't, you know. Because at that time Durham was probably the most progressive city in the South. You know, we had a fantastic educational system, we had a vibrant middle class and upper middle class of black community, and so we had our role models, we had vibrant churches, lots of social activities. . . . It was probably one of the few places where separate and equal actually coexisted. Because I mean, you know, like, we had, there were black swimming pools, there were black tennis courts, I mean you name it, we had it, you know. And so, you know, there was no looking over the other side of the fence, saying wow, wish we had this, wish we had that, you know, we had it, you know.

. . . .

FREDDIE (B. 1944, MADISON, GA.)

Certainly, I'm glad that things are integrated, but I think in a lot of ways . . . and this might sound awful putting this on tape . . . but looking back, I think in a lot of ways integration hurt the black community. Because what happened, a lot of black establishments dried up when there were options. I mean, in Atlanta, Auburn Avenue[7] was a lovely place to go when I was a teenager. And there were restaurants and there were kind of little clubs and things that were all black patronized. And many of those places just dried up. And something else happened. In my elementary and high school where there were all black people, until the day the superintendent or somebody white might have come, we could have kind of . . . Do you know that old saying that it takes a village? We kind of had that village, where the teachers were like parents and where the teachers could speak very frankly to you about the segregation and discrimination in the world and how you needed to be better, in many instances, than white people to get the same kind of jobs they got. And they could just speak very frankly about all kinds of things. That can't happen, I think, in an integrated setting. I think they taught us kind of a sense of pride in ourselves that I think is lacking. [. . .] My partner always argues that it's poverty. And I remind him they couldn't have been any worse off than we were. Because my mother could never get on Welfare because my father had an attorney in Madison write a letter to the Welfare Department here in Atlanta, that my mother left him on a farm to live . . . I don't know if he said the fast, hard, city life, but pretty much that she wanted to live the city life. So we could never get public assistance. And my mother was very sickly. She was ill a lot. And so we lived in some awful places. I don't know where I was going with this . . . Do you remember where I was? 'Cause I can get a little lost . . . I can ramble. [Chuckle]

You were talking about how integration . . .

Oh yeah. Integration hurt. I do think that. When I look around at how the black community was, in many instances, devastated in terms of businesses and organizations . . . certainly businesses are concerned.

Were living arrangements [in Madison] segregated as well?

They were segregated. I remember going to downtown Madison, Georgia, which is remarkably very much like it was then. I was a bright little kid, somewhere along the way . . . I guess I'm still bright, but somewhere along the way, I was not that interested in school. I didn't apply myself as much as I should have because I really had no goals. Like I just said, my goal was to finish high school and get a job washing dishes to help my mother. So I didn't do very well, but in Madison, Georgia, things were very segregated. And I remember as a little kid being good in arithmetic. We would go to the store and buy stuff; sometimes I would add up the merchandise and would tell the store clerk what the total was. And sometimes they would get angry. It was commonly practiced by white store clerks of overcharging black people. And because of the kind of segregation and other situations, you really kind of didn't speak out much against white folks. And sometimes the store clerks would overcharge black people and they would just accept it because to protest could have meant . . . like I never saw a lynching, but I've heard about them. I've heard people talking about them as . . . one of my grandmother's brothers was found on a railroad track, dead, and they're sure that the train didn't kill him.

My mother's biological father had to leave the South as a very young man because he had an altercation with a white man, so he had to leave or be killed. And he was unfortunately killed by pneumonia in New York, because a lot of southern blacks who went north couldn't stand the cold and they just . . . they just couldn't stand it because the tenements were drafty in many instances and they were just not acclimated to such weather. And he died as a very young man from pneumonia, we were told, in New York. But he did something to somebody. I think he might have had a Napoleon complex. I don't know this for a fact, but my mother was only 5'2". Her mother was probably 5'10". And I remember my mother's mother being probably my height. And I think my mother's father was a short man, so he might have had a Napoleon complex. [Chuckle]

· · · · · · · ·

"D.C."

D.C. is a retired high school teacher from the Baton Rouge, Louisiana, school system. From the time we first met, I knew that I would not have wanted to be a student who acted out in his class. Direct, brusque, and physically intimidating (he was a football star in college), D.C. has a serious edge, which is layered with a sweet gentleness.

On the day of our interview at his home in Baton Rouge, we were interrupted more than once by one of his neighbors, a young man who is the leader of a street gang in the neighborhood. Although this young man is married with kids, he also just happens to be D.C.'s occasional lover (see Chapter 4). D.C. revealed to me that he had forty-two of the "405" gang, a nickname he devised, in his home all at the same time. To say the least, this young man's presence and the backstory made my visit all the more interesting and provided more fodder for the interview.

After I heard about D.C.'s rocky childhood, his current personality began to make sense. According to him, his father beat his mother nearly to death and hit her in the head with a hatchet. This happened when he was seven months old. Later, he recalls: "When we became teenagers, he made an attempt to jump on my mother again but we were older. [. . .] I held him and my sisters beat the hell out of him. One of them stabbed the hell out of him with an ice pick, and the other one busted him in the head with some piece of iron or something, and left him for dead in the house. [. . .] And I feel they

got a chance to get him. And he died and I didn't. So I mean, I have no good
feelings about my father. None." This unresolved anger toward his deceased
father and the fact that he was a gang member as a child clarified for me the
feelings of distrust that he expressed about other people in his life. It may
also explain why he says, "I have a very bad temper, you know. I mean I can
explode like that [finger snap]." Just underneath that anger, however, are
flashes of tenderness, kindness, and a wicked sense of humor—all of which
I experienced during our interview. D.C. was born in 1951 in Shreveport,
Louisiana, the youngest of four. The interview took place on January 20,
2005.

Were the schools segregated?
They were. Yeah. Basically, all of my school years, all the way to high school. Like what I was saying is that at my senior year, they were beginning to attempt integration. 1969.

We had two white teachers at our school, and I thought that was the weirdest thing. I mean, the whole student body was black. You have to understand too, I went to school in what they considered one of the roughest areas, not just in Louisiana but in the country, period. It is bad to this day. So even when they did integrate, and they bused the whites in, the whites took them out of there. And the place is still basically predominantly black. [. . .] Even with integration. But there's one good thing about that, as far as I'm concerned. I'm more happy to have attended a segregated, all-black school situation than I would recommend for what I see today with kids. Because the teachers that we had wouldn't allow things that students get away with now. I mean I was a bad person. Okay I was. I was a gang member. I was a . . . I guess you'd call it like a thug. I used to have fights, basically every day. In junior high school, I jumped on at least thirteen teachers. I jumped on the principal, got kicked out of school for ten straight weeks. But at the same time, I was never dumb. So it did that to me. The predominantly black, segregated school is the best thing for black youth. And I believe that even today. Because I just retired as an educator myself in August. And it's pathetic how things are going in schools. And one reason I retired is because I got away with it for thirty years, and without repercussions. In other words, when kids do something out of line, I tell them at the beginning, "I'm not sending you to the office. This is the office, right here. And we're going to take care of that right here." And Mom and Daddy . . . I used to call them at the beginning of the school year to tell them exactly how I am, what I do. "And if you don't want this with your kid, you'll have to take them out of my classroom. Because it's only one grown person in the classroom." But now you've got kids that sit up and cuss you out like a soldier, and Mom and Dad will come back and reinforce it, you know. And I'm glad I'm out of it because I probably would have wound up going to jail and doing some real damage to somebody's child. So that's about it in a nutshell.

What were the racial dynamics of your time growing up?

You know, in my time, there were only two races. [Chuckle] I'm serious. In fact, in Shreveport, we didn't have nothing but blacks and whites. [. . .] I mean, I didn't know other people but blacks and whites in Shreveport.

And how did the blacks and whites get along?

They didn't. Well, you gotta understand too now, in my time when I was coming up, they were still siccing dogs on black folks. I grew up when they had colored water fountains, white fountains. When you'd go to the bus station, you had the colored section back in the back and the white folks section in another part. And I remember walking home from school . . . and see another thing is they'd come on buses. They'd bus white kids miles and miles, past our school. They came miles and miles and they'd pass our school and went miles and miles to other schools just to go to a white school, you know. And I remember one day, walking, and those kids threw something off and hit me with something and hurt me. And I'd be afraid. Growing up, I didn't care nothing at all for a white person because they were considered the enemy. And in most any situation, they'd act like an enemy. There was not a lot of interaction in my town, with blacks and whites, especially not students. Not at all. There was also this little thing that was still going around that, as a black young man, you were not supposed to look up at a white lady in the face. That was enough to get you put in jail. Okay. And so I basically always saw the white person as the evil spirit.

Did blacks and whites live on different sides of town?

Yes. Blacks had a little section of town, and that was it. Now the areas where I grew up, well they say it's the largest black community in the United States. It's called Clip Road. [. . .] It is all black. You understand what I'm saying? There are no other ethnicities in there. No Spanish, no Mexicans, no nothing. It's all black, one hundred and one percent. And it's almost ten by ten miles. I mean, you know, that big. So it's a big area. It's in Shreveport. Well, Shreveport now has annexed it. When I was a kid, it was not in Shreveport. In fact, we were kind of like . . . kind of felt like country. [. . .] We were like about six, seven miles outside of the city. But not being in the city, not having any kind of revenue and all this, the streets were poor, drainage was poor. And before they built the high school there, all the kids had to go to school in the city and they had to catch the bus . . . when they walked . . . you had to have two pair of shoes because you had to walk in the mud from your house, from the little muddy streets, to the bus. And when you get to the school, you take your muddy shoes off and put your good shoes on. You know. It was a lot of stuff like that. It was a lot of crazy things like that.

Was the black part of town separated by a railroad or any kind of marker or . . . ?

Not really. Now the Kansas City Southern Railroad is in the Clip Road area. And pretty much you could say on the other side of that part. But it's . . . well the lake is on one side, and then the homes around the lake, they were white homes. But it wasn't like, you know, in some cities, when you cross the tracks you're in the black neighborhood because the majority of Clip Road, there is not a railroad track. In fact, the Clip Road itself, there's no railroad track.

[. . .] We used to live in The Bottom. It's the bottom, where the worst part of the town is. It's adjacent to downtown Shreveport and it's downhill from it. It's down in the bottom, and it's The Bottom. That's where . . . on Friday and Saturday nights, you know, all the cutthroats, all the drinking and whores and prostitutes and everything like that, that was their territory. And we lived in an alley off The Bottom, one of the main streets of The Bottom. And it was horrible. I remember . . . I guess God takes care of fools, but we had to walk in that alley where there was all kinds of broken glass. We used to walk in there barefooted. And didn't cut our feet. [Chuckle] So I mean you know it was horrible.

Is it still there now?

They have renovated so much now. It's called Ledbetter, Led Belly, Ledbetter Square now down there. They fixed the houses up real well and it's a nice place to be now. But if you go in the archives and look at old Shreveport, you'll see what I'm talking about. Killings, murders, all that.

· · · · · · · ·

ED (B. 1952, NEW ORLEANS, LA.)

We lived in an area of the city called "The Ninth Ward." The city is divided up into wards. [. . .] But the Ninth Ward was the largest of all the wards in the city. And at the time that I was growing up, there was the Desire housing project and it was separated from the Florida housing project. And the Florida housing project was all white. And the Desire was all black. And they were separated by train tracks, a railroad and a canal, an industrial canal. And the train would come at odd times and block us off if we had to, you know, in order for us to catch the bus to get to downtown, we had to cross this track and go across the bridge that went across the canal. So it was an inconvenience for us, you know, but it didn't inconvenience the people on the white side because the bus stop and the bus were already on their side. But I remember little things like that.

I remember when Hurricane Betsy came in 1965, in September, how devastating it was and how I found out later that the mayor who was the mayor at that time, Victor Schiro, made a decision to close the locks that led to the canal. And while doing this, he caused the side where our development was to flood. But Betsy was so devastating, everybody in the entire city . . . we had a lot of damage on our side because . . . it didn't damage my family too much because we lived upstairs. But I remember the water was all the way up to the stairs and you had to go up a flight of stairs to get to the first floor of the building. And I'd say the water was almost about six feet high. I mean anywhere from waist deep, depending on how tall you were. And I remember people going by in boats and makeshift boats and doors that they had taken off and floating on the water. And it was horrible. And then there were all kinds of things in the water. And you saw snakes swimming in the water, you know, turtles, fish jumping in the air. Your back street was a lake. Our car floated down the street and was completely submerged. It was horrible. And of course, people were taking advantage of other people. They were gouging and selling ice for ten dollars—just cheating people, you know? And some people lost their lives because they had to be rescued. They were on their rooftops; it was so bad. I think I was about thirteen. Yeah, in '65 I was thirteen.[8]

What were the racial politics back then? Did blacks and whites interact at all?

Well, this was in the mid-'60s, and blacks and whites, we still had separation on the buses, separation of facilities. Even though *Brown vs. Board of Education* had been passed, it wasn't implemented in the South, at least not in New Orleans. So there was no integration of facilities. I do remember that there was a black beach that was called "Lincoln Beach." Why they couldn't think of a black man's name . . . whenever the black people got something, it was named after a white person who was considered sympathetic to blacks, like Abraham Lincoln. So it was Lincoln Beach. And it was a beach that was located in the eastern part of New Orleans, and it was a bus ride that took you about twenty to thirty minutes to get to it. It was about twenty miles away from the city. And it was a nice beach. It had a midway and a Ferris wheel, a roller coaster and everything. And the strange thing is that the beach was managed by the same family that managed the white beach, which was located on the lakefront, which is now where the University of New Orleans has property on the lakefront. And it was called "Pontchartrain Beach." But blacks were not able to go there until after 1964. But it didn't matter that much to me because I remember going to our beach. It was fine. We had rides. We had concessions. There were shows. James Brown, the Ink Spots, people like that would come and entertain. And dance contests, beauty contests, you know, all kinds of things were going on. There was a midway, and there were bumper cars and cotton candy. Everything kids liked when they went out to the beach. You know, Ferris wheel, roller coaster, haunted houses, all of that. And there were two pools. There was a large, Olympic size swimming pool and then there was a smaller size pool. And there was also a little kiddy pool for the children . . . for the toddlers. And then, beyond the beach was the sand and the lake. So if you didn't want to swim in the pool, you could go in the lake. On the way to the beach, they would have these fishing camps, these houses that were on stilts, and the people would live in them and fish and they would throw their waste right into the river. So after a certain amount of time, it was deemed unsafe to swim in the lake because of the fecal count in the water. And that was because the people in those houses were throwing their waste directly into the . . . they didn't care anyway because they knew it was right by the black beach. But I remember those times as good times. And I remember Lincoln Beach only stayed open ten years, from '54 until '64. It actually was dedicated in 1954, but blacks had been going on the site since 1939. It's one of my research projects. I'm trying to write something about the history of this beach. And it's just difficult to get information because a lot of the information has been obscured and the white press didn't give fair coverage to it. And you have to rely on black newspapers, and some of those things are sorely lacking. But I'm finding that, once it did integrate, all the blacks abandoned it and went to a white beach and it closed down because of the lack of business. But the strange thing is that the same family that managed the white beach also managed the black beach. And I think black people felt it was intrinsically better to go to the "white" beach because it was denied them. When something is denied you, and you can't have it and you finally get the opportunity to get it, you want it just because it's been denied you. It was found out that actually they spent as much or more money building the black beach than they did on the white beach. And I found the architectural plans for the beach, as well as the U.S. Army Corps of Engineers' aerial shot of what the beach looked like at that time. The pool alone was valued at a million dollars. And this would have been back in the '50s, and that's a lot of money. So I don't mean to keep harping on that one topic, but a lot of my growing up centered around that at the time [. . .] .

. . . .
"G.C."

*Marlon introduced me to G.C. and his partner during a visit to Charlottesville,
Virginia, in the spring of 2005. We hit it off immediately, and G.C. promised
that on my next trip he would not only allow me to interview him, but he would
also give me a tour of Charlottesville—and particularly the historic black parts
of town.*

*G.C. knows quite a bit about the history of black Charlottesville and the
surrounding areas. Part of this history has been passed down to him from his
parents, and part of it he has made a concerted effort to learn on his own. For
the most part, however, G.C. just enjoys storytelling—especially tales about
growing up in the South. G.C. was born in 1958 in Albemarle County, Virginia
(of which Charlottesville is the county seat), the youngest of five children. The
interview took place on August 11, 2005, in Charlottesville, at the home of
Marlon and his partner, Ian.*

*Do you remember some of the friends that you made in elementary, high
school? Have you stayed in touch with them?*

I remember them. I remember them quite well. In fact, I remember one
of the first white kids I met in second [grade]. In fact I saw his mother last
week at a neighborhood watch program. The county police office had a big
grand opening for everybody to see what they've done, and this woman was
there, and I looked up and I was like, oh, that's Steve's mother. It was kind of
interesting how all that happened because I can remember in second grade
when I first met Steve, it was sort of like, oh good, kid, you want to play,
you're kind of skittish about it at first. Then the first remarks that came out
of his mouth is like, hey I can play with you, but we can't play at each other's
houses. My dad will not allow this to happen. Fine. But we played at school.
And that was the beginning of the friendship in second grade and we were
friends throughout high school, college, after college. And we still stay in
contact. Not as much, but we see each other, and we still laugh and talk
about those days. In fact his mother, who I saw the other week, we were
talking about it as well; she since has divorced this guy and remarried as
well. There were a series of events with this guy; not only was he a bigot, he
was an abusive father and wife beater.

How would you describe the racial politics of the town that you grew up in?

It was very mixed. There were certain areas where it was accepted, the
mixture of blacks and whites, and I have to say blacks and whites because
that's predominantly what they looked at at that time. It was accepted. And

then there were other areas where you knew your place. You knew your place. You just did not go there. You just did not acknowledge, you didn't, you knew your place.

Were they physically segregated as well?

Physically segregated as well. And then there were areas such as the rural areas where there were blacks and whites who lived in houses, you know, up the street from each other. They weren't like gated communities, or neighborhoods like we see today. But then again there were neighborhoods, but those were just all whites and you knew that, like the Laurel Hills and the Park Road, that sort of thing, which was all white.

Railroad tracks always have played a major factor. In Crozet, the town that I grew up in, there was a railroad track that divided on one side, which was predominantly black, which was on the main highway. On the opposite side of the tracks, which got into the rural areas, if you were to drive through that area you would see all the homes that were pretty much right on the road, those were the black families. The homes that were further away with nice big yards, those were white families that had been there for a while. As you go out further area of rural, the farmlands, you didn't notice it as much. You didn't see it. A farm is a farm is a farm. The only way you would notice if you looked at the condition of the barns. The big red barns that you would see in catalogs and magazines with the nice silos, those were the white farmers. The nice big white picket fence. The old split rail fence and barbed wire and the barns with the flat tenders, those were pretty much your poor black families or the poor white.

What was your family's attitude about people who were different from you?

It was mixed. My grandparents, because of their upbringing, were not as liberal, I should say. They were accustomed to things being just that way. I can remember my great-grandmother fondly and her way, I guess we could say, she was pretty jaded in that every way was the white man's way. And I can still recall this, "Child, don't sit down like that, move your arms. The white folks won't like that." "Don't pick that glass up like that, hold your finger out because that's the way the white folks do it." And, "Girl, you better go in there and straighten that hair, don't you go out of here with that hair all napped up like that. The white folks don't do this." Now, mind you she was also very fair complected, and she was the first black midwife in the area. So she, everything was very proper because she had been taught to do this or else, and "else" could have been a number of things. My parents on the other hand were a little different. They were pretty much bent on that we were not going to endure what they had endured, seeing things. So it was not tolerated for us to say negative things about people of the opposite race.

· · · · · · · ·

GEROME

Gerome is one of the people I met through Ann McCarthy in Tuscaloosa,
Alabama. As I recounted in the Introduction, he is also one of the narrators
who stood me up for our first meeting—something for which Ann chastised
him later on. He shared with me later that he had to "pray on it" before he
spoke with me. His homosexuality is something that he hopes God will take
away from him (see Chapter 3), and therefore he was unsure whether he
wanted to discuss that aspect of his life.

Gerome is a diminutive, soft-spoken man who makes his living as a tailor.
He never completed high school and failed at attempts to obtain his GED.
Although he is functionally illiterate, he has managed to make a living
sewing. As his story below reveals, learning to sew was a saving grace.
Having lost his parents when he was very young, he quickly had to learn to
be somewhat independent. His older siblings were his primary caregivers
during his formative years. He was born in 1958 in Tuscaloosa and, except
for a short excursion to California, has lived there all his life. The interview
took place at Ann McCarthy's home in Tuscaloosa on January 9, 2005.

[. . .] I was just so disgusted with the black situation; blacks wasn't getting very good breaks in life. I went to work for this Korean family, Mr. and Mrs. Kwan that owned a boutique shop downtown. I went to work for them in their store, and they hired me to come in and to make sales on clothes, shoes, anything in the store. Wigs, belts, jewelry, whatever they had in the store. [. . .] They were downtown in the old Kresge's building. It's still down over there and turned into someplace now. This couple hired me to come in because I did alterations, you know. I could sew.

How did you learn how to sew?

It was more or less, I think, a gift from God, and my mother had that gift and my oldest sister could sew, you know. And my older sister kept the sewing machine. She had a portable Singer machine. She did a lot of beautiful personal tailoring. I mean, professionally. My mother was just a genius at it. She could make whatever, and it looked better than what came out of the store, to be honest, because I saw a lot of her work. And anyway, it was in me from birth I do believe. [. . .] I ended up leaving Mr. and Mrs. Kwan's after I worked there with them for a while. An incident took place there that I was devastated with. There was this guy that came into the store to steal. And I don't know if this guy had a gun on him or what, you know, but he came into the store. I was the only guy working in there, plus her. Her husband had left. This guy came in and he stole. Whatever it was he stole, he stole it and ran

Local club in Gerome's neighborhood, Tuscaloosa, Alabama.
Photo by the author.

Local store in Gerome's neighborhood. Photo by the author.

out of the store and went down the side and around the building. And this Korean lady, Mrs. Kwan, she goes after the man like a dodo. And she's looking at me like, "Get him, get him!" And I'm saying, "Oh no, darling. I was hired here not for your security, not your security guard. I'm the salesperson, so you go get him." And you know she ran behind him and I looked at this stupid woman. You know, we didn't know what this man had on him. So I *walked* out of the store behind her while she *running* and, you know. And I'm standing looking like, "Are you stupid enough to go down in that alley behind this place, behind a pair of shades or whatever it was he stole?" [Laughter] It wasn't like he stole the register or the money box or nothing, so I couldn't figure it out. But anyway, after then she was so upset over it, Mr. Kwan came back. Her husband, he came back to the store a little bit later and she told him about what the guy had done and everything, you know. And oh he was all upset over it and everything. But what got me was that the guy was black. And that was so embarrassing to me. So she and he both, you know, picked up on it because they came to me with it, you know, "That had nothing to do with you. He was not your friend, Gerome, and da-da-da-da-da." And I'm saying, "Okay." So I get up the next morning and go in to work and go in to work a few more days, and then I decided that I'm fixing to let this job go because I don't like this. That's frightening, someone coming in like that. What if he had had a gun and just shot up or something, you know. So I wanted to let it go, and then they talked me into working on with them for a while longer, and I did it. But then they found this place in Birmingham that they wanted to go because it would have been closer to . . . they would have been saving a lot of money on shipping stuff, you know, here to Tuscaloosa and all that. So they wanted me to relocate with them. And when I thought about it, you know, when the store moved . . . Young's Fashions was the name of it . . . Young's Fashions . . . When they moved to Birmingham, they wanted me to relocate with them because they knew of my situation. "He's a single guy, he has no spouse, no children, you know, he's single, he can go. He can come stay here," you know and all this. And they was nice to me. But I did not relocate, and that's when I think I made one of the first mistakes. Afraid to leave home, trusting these people when I should have been wise enough to know, "Okay Gerome this may be the door for you to go through." But I didn't. And I've regretted it since because they even told me, "Well when you decide that you want to come, let us know." And I didn't. Because I was doing great in the sales department, selling things that they couldn't sell, you know. You're talking about wigs, to the women, to them little ol' women. And I was selling wigs and shades, glasses, shoes, things that they weren't selling. And me being a black guy and most of the customers that came in there were blacks, you know, buying this stuff: makeup, powder, face powder, just whatever they had in the store.

I think I should have been brave enough to just go to Birmingham. But to me, at that time, Birmingham was like from here to New York. That's how southern I was, you know, stupid, you know. But then maybe it was meant and maybe it wasn't. I don't know.

So what did you do after that?

After they relocated, then I went and started working for this Ruth Fashions, this garment plant, factory. This white lady, very . . . now you're talking about the South and *racist* . . . I went to work for a blond-headed one. You know what I mean? [Chuckle] She was a way back sister from the old slavery time, and she felt like blacks were made to serve. And so I did it for not quite a year, for like seven months. I was on an assembly line, making his and her . . . she had like this garment factory and she had like I think about thirty-something people working for her. Thirty or a little less employees making like say women's dress coats and . . . she had these two black guys that were the spreaders.[9] [. . .] I could not take her hard racism. I just couldn't do it. And she *begged* me to stay. You know, she was willing to . . . for money, she was willing to come on down to earth and realize that this one is not going to bow. And I couldn't, for some reason.

What would she do?

She would come in and try to make more pressure. Okay, like for instance, she knew, "Okay he can turn over two hundred jackets a day." She needed someone to do that. You know, just sit there and run the commercial machine. She realized, "He could set two hundred collars a day. He could set two hundred sleeves. He could set a hundred and forty pockets," you know in jackets. And she saw, "Okay this nigger can do it." And you know behind our backs they were saying like, "niggers," you know.

Watch you?

Yeah. And they saw me being very productive. [. . .] At the time I'm just thinking it was just stuff telling me, "Do it, Gerome. You can do five-eighths seams. You can do half-inch seams. You can do quarter-inch seams. Do them and do them well. Do your best." And you know I did it. And this lady was sold on it. And she felt like, "Oh he wants to cut out of here now." So she decides to change her arrogant attitude to try to be more nicer, but I had already gotten the assurance within me, "You can leave now." But what she got out of it was that, "I just lost the one that was setting my collars and sleeves." So that meant she had to go back and retrain somebody, and she wasn't paying me that kind of money. If she had of came with the right *dollar*, I probably would have stayed there, but it wasn't enough money in it. So I told her. Her name was Bonnie. Bonnie *Ruth*. I told her, "Bonnie, listen. I don't mean no harm or anything like that, but I gotta go." I said, "I've done my last. I gave you my notice." And I didn't just up and quit now. But some part of me just wouldn't let me just be rude and just be nasty and just quit. Now don't you think now that it didn't cross my mind, because I was just that disgusted with her. I think it was like three dollars and thirty-five cents or something like that, back then. It wasn't enough money for me. Three thirty-five, you know? So I said, "No I'm not staying here for that." And when she did try to make an offer, I said, "That's awfully nice of you but I'm still going," you know. Did the notice. That lady stood there and watched me leave on my last day, you know. And later on in my life I said, "What was that for?" You know, was there something in there for me or for her? And I realized it was something in it for both of us. I found out, "Gerome you can do better, but you've got to learn to hold on until you can see your way through." And through that experience, I became better with my sewing. I got better at that. She came out with more money and she made, you know, she got paid for it ... for the work that we did or that I did. And then I left there and went to do another job. It was at food service at the university.

University of Alabama?

Uh huh, in the kitchen. And I just could not take that. So many big pots and pans and all of the banging, and it just wasn't me, you know. So I left that. And then I went to . . . I was requested at the university in the drama department to come into the drama department . . .

Costumes department?

Yes. And I went and did that. And the university just loved my work. You know, Dr. Moran and several of them on the committee there that was over the drama department, you know, said like, "We could give him . . ." what they did was they gave me a university package deal: full-coverage insurance, dental, hospital, a cost of living raise, just like on staff. Uneducated. Couldn't even hardly read. Still pitiful reading, you know. But I could work the devil out of that drama department, the costumes, making those costumes. And I mean these was like eccentric costumes and things. And we was doing some like for the *Wizard of Oz,* making costumes. And they couldn't understand how, "This guy here is barely reading and barely . . ." you know, "As slow as he is book wise, he can come in here and turn this thing out." And I was doing it, you know, in this whole drama department. And they got furious because I ended up leaving it. I stayed with it for like a year and a half, and then I left. And the reason I left was because this new quarter of students that was coming in, some of those students were . . . I don't know, they said they was northerners or whatever, but they were very prejudiced. Some of those white students were very . . . you know, doing nasty things. And I just said, "No I'm not going to let that rub off on me. I'm going to flee this environment," but I shouldn't have though, but I did. But I stayed there and I hate I left the benefits that I had because, had I stayed there with the university, I could have eventually got into study classes, reading and everything I needed. I could have been a student there and worked the drama . . . but that was something that was, like I would say it was nothing but the devil himself that made me get disgusted with it and say, "I'm not going to take that anymore. I'm just going to go." Because I was doing uniforms . . . not uniforms, costumes . . . for some of the students, and they were turning out perfect. I'd go back and come to find out they were doing spiteful things like picking the seams, you know. I mean racist stuff. You know, nasty stuff. And at that time, I wasn't aware of how low . . . and you probably have never seen it, but those people can do some nasty things. Things you'd never even think to do, to be low-down. But I found out these kids had been taught this, and now they are out of high school, they're like nineteen, twenty and twenty-one, twenty-two years of age and practicing how to be wicked. I knew that there were prejudices, but I'd never had a clue that they could be so spiteful. [. . .] So I left that. And they said, "Skipping sissy," but I was skipping my way to a little more sound peace. I just wasn't going to take it, and that was it.

· · · · · · · ·

GODFREY

Godfrey is one of many men that I met through my friend and student Curt, who was murdered (see the Epilogue). Curt had a wide social network, so he had a "reception" for me at our mutual friend "Rob's" home to introduce me to men who might be interviewed for Sweet Tea. *Godfrey was one of those men.*

An articulate and gentle man, Godfrey is what many southerners would call "cultured." His family was middle class and Episcopalian—something quite rare among southern blacks. He, like a few other middle-class men I interviewed, takes a lot of pride in the fact that he does not match most whites' stereotypical profile of black people—that is to say, that they grew up poor in single-parent homes. Godfrey was raised by both parents in a black middle-class community in Durham, where he was born in 1947. He is the older of two children. The interview took place on August 19, 2004, in his office at North Carolina Central University, where he is an administrator

Were all of your schools segregated?

Yes. Yes, definitely. I graduated from high school in 1965. By that time, a few pioneers had integrated the schools in Durham, but I wasn't one of them. And, very shortly after that, there was a concerted effort by the state to integrate schools, and so they started more active kind of busing in the city. The county schools were separate from the city schools, and so a lot of the white students actually migrated to the suburbs and to the county, and so integrating the county schools became a real big issue. When I was in school, however, there was one black high school in the city, and one black high school in the county, so that Hillside became the one place, mind you, we had several different junior high and elementary schools, but Hillside became the one place, if you were black, where, you know, the whole community kind of came together, which I think is part of the reason why it's so quote/unquote storied.

Did you feel like you missed out on anything because you went to a segregated school?

Oh no. Of course not. As a matter of fact, knowing what I know now, I think my education was far superior than if we had been in an integrated system, especially during that time period. I guess I was fortunate in that, with segregation, there weren't a lot of opportunities for blacks who were educated, so that, you know, people say that the mail system has never been the same since black Ph.D.s could find jobs elsewhere. The professors that I had at Hillside went on to teach college in the same subjects. You can't see the location on this tape obviously, but Hillside High School at one point was at the other end of the street, Brant Street, where the entrance to North Carolina Central was located. And there was a lot of interaction, at least academically, between the two. Some of the professors at the university came over to teach classes. A lot of the teachers, a lot of the students at North Carolina Central who were considering careers in education did their student teaching in the school system in Hillside. It was basically the only place they could go.

At any rate, we were talking about whether or not I felt like I missed anything. At any rate, I've had an extraordinary set of teachers. The school setting, I think, was much more supportive in that segregated environment than it would have been in an integrated environment where all the black administrators were replaced by white administrators, which happened so much in the South. So no, I felt that I was supported, that I got the best education I could get. When I went off to college, I found that my education was second to none, because we were fortunate enough to be in Durham, with the kind of resources we had, you know, universities, businesses, that sort of thing. And, quite frankly, you know, we were fortunate enough to have an opportunity to travel. We went places, we did things, we saw stuff, and we had, you know, a black library where, you know, the librarians tended to be neighbors, etc., etc. So you always got exposed, and, the world was yours. And, overtly during this time period, there was a consensus among, at least the black middle class, that you had to prepare your children to move forward, to move gracefully forward, and so they made sure that you were ready. You know, I remember that we used to have concerts by the North Carolina Symphony, and all of the black high schools in the area would be invited. Usually, to this university, North Carolina Central University, and, because they had a large gymnasium that could seat, you know, several hundred people. So they would all come there, and the symphony would perform. We would prepare for those symphonies, you know, everyone would, there'd be a sing-along, and then there would be two or three orchestral works, and so we were drilled. We had to know the song backwards and forwards, the song was put into context, we listened to the actual orchestral piece on recordings, we were told how to conduct ourselves, when to clap, etc., etc., you know. How you bathed, so that you would be presentable, etc., etc. So, you know, all of the tools you needed to succeed in life, I think, were given to you, as a matter of pride.

So was your neighborhood segregated, or the city segregated as well?

Yes, of course. I mean, even now Durham is divided by a set of railroad tracks. It's beginning to mean less, primarily because of the development of the Research Triangle Park, which was put in the southeast section of town, which used to be the black section of town, because land, quite frankly, in that area was cheaper. It also had the advantage of being right in the middle of a triangular landform that was between Durham, Chapel Hill, and Raleigh. As a result, the success of the Research Triangle Park has pushed development into that little corridor there at Durham, so you're finding, you know, white people moving into this neighborhood now, you know, mainly because it's still a black neighborhood and prices are cheaper, but it's also centrally located and close to everything that you'd want to be there. I mean, from where we're sitting now you could be in Raleigh, Chapel Hill, in half an hour, and downtown Durham in five minutes, and at least at this point, you know, all of the, the local points of, of interest, you know, whether that's Duke University, or the administration of any of those cities that I've mentioned, Research Triangle, or the University of North Carolina, you know, North Carolina State, all of those are within half an hour. So it's one of the best locations in town. Prices, as I've said, have not kept up with tonier neighborhoods, but that's coming.

"C.C." (B. 1961, GREENVILLE, MISS.)

When you were growing up, was your town segregated?

No and yes. [. . .] I just knew then it wasn't about black and white; it was just about people who had and people who didn't. Because I realized then we were different because we went from all-black neighborhoods to black and white neighborhoods because it was just clear to me it was about money. Like I realized working in my grandfather's store that poor white people had to come and buy their groceries on the notes 'til they got paid. So I knew then that, oh this ain't about race. It's just about people who've got something and who don't. And I've always been able to recognize that. Because of those early experiences, knowing . . . "What are you white people doing?" Because they would have to line up, 'cause like when they got their check, my grandfather would be standing there with those books and they actually would cash their checks. Well, he would cash the check 'cause he was going to take out their grocery money.

What would you say then were the racial politics of Greenville?

I really couldn't tell you because at that time, which is so disturbing to me now when I go back to those places, black people didn't think about white people. [Chuckle] At all. Black people . . . I mean we were like just all fabulous! I mean just, you know, every house you went to had that crystal. You know everybody was getting ready for to go to the Elks Club on Fridays. You were all going to the football game. And by the way, there may be some diva soprano [who] flew down to the South to give her concert. So you didn't even know. You didn't even talk about white people.

· · · · · · · ·

PATRICK

Patrick carries himself in a way that suggests that he's much older than he is. He reminded me of the older, distinguished middle-class black men in my hometown: he has a deep baritone voice, he's confident, but not cocky, a methodical thinker, and he has an aura of wisdom. He's what some would call a "man's man."

Before committing to do the interview, he made me promise that I would give him two copies of the book—one for himself and one for a friend who was struggling with his sexuality. I found this quite moving and think it says a lot about Patrick's character.

I did not know Patrick before the interview. I received his contact information from one of my contacts in Atlanta. We met at my friend Ian's house in Atlanta for the interview on Halloween of 2004. Patrick was born in

Vidalia, Georgia, in 1966. Vidalia, best known for onions of the same name grown there, is located in southeast Georgia and has a population of less than 15,000.

Was your town segregated?

Oh, very much so. Very much so. There's a railroad track that runs down the middle of my hometown, and black people lived on one side of that railroad track, and we had our churches and our grocery stores and our homes and everything that we needed to sustain us; and on the other side of the railroad track was just the polar opposite. That was the white. In my little town, there is a First Baptist Church, which is white, and there is a First African Baptist Church, which is black. So during the time that I grew up, almost everything was a white and a black. There was a white Methodist Church. Well, there's a black Methodist Church, you see. Even in high school, when we chose homecoming queens, there was a white homecoming queen and there was a black homecoming queen chosen at the same time. The proms were segregated. There was a white prom, there was a black prom. So it was—and the pop-, the black population at that time in my town was about 30 percent black. It was 70 percent white, 30 percent black. It was a place where time stood still. But in my opinion, everyone pretty much respected the other.

And I'll give you an example. Time stood still in the sense that we still had our Klan. I can recall vividly, as a child, minding my own business, playing in my own front yard, and my mother sitting on the porch and this car filled with young white boys driving by and throwing wet toilet paper at me in my front yard. And I remember my mother running down off the porch, grabbing me and running in the house. She never discussed what happened; she never said why she did it. All I knew was whatever they did she felt threatened her child. So she was removing me from harm's way. Several months after that, I recall waking up, hearing my parents talk, waking up and the house was completely dark, with the exception of this bright light that was coming from the front of my house. And I realized that that was the direction that my parents' voices were coming from. So I wandered into the living room, and my living room, which was about the size of the room that we're sitting in, was absolutely filled with light, but the light was coming from outside. And when I went to the window and looked out the window, there was a cross burning across the street from my house. Across the street from my house was the black elementary school. Someone had planted a cross on the property of the school and burned it, and our house just happened to be right in front of it. And so those are the types of memories. I clearly recall going to the doctor's office—there's a white waiting room, there's a black waiting room. I'm going to movie theaters—the black kids had to go around the back, up the stairs, and sit upstairs, while the white kids entered through the front door and sat closer to the screen downstairs. Other than those types of examples, everyone pretty much stayed to themselves. I don't recall a lot of racial tension, with the exception of those things that I've just mentioned. I remember growing up and going to school and having white kids very curious about the black kids. They wanted to know, "What do you eat, where do you live?" I even had a little white girl ask me, "What do you wash your hair with?" Those types of questions. But other than that, it was—I felt it was a very good place to grow up.

What it instilled in me was obviously a lot of pride about the community and the family and the place that I come from. Because whatever my parents and grandparents and elders had to live through in that part of Georgia was never once passed down to their children in the form of hatred. What was passed down to us was, you were born here but we don't expect for you to die here. There's a better world out there, there's a big world out there. We didn't have a chance to see it or experience it, but we want you to see and experience it. And the only way that you can do that is to get an education.

· · · · · · · ·

RODERICK

It's funny how people come in and out of your life. I first met Roderick in 1992 when I was a doctoral student in the Department of Speech Communication at LSU and he was a freshman majoring in voice. We met through another graduate student who worked part time at the black cultural center. Roderick was then, and still is now, an effervescent spirit. He has a knack for bringing people together.

After I left LSU in 1993, I did not keep in touch with Roderick but always wondered what had happened to him. Then, by sheer coincidence, we reconnected in 2002 in Chicago. A friend of Roderick's whom I had just met invited me to a brunch to meet some other black gay men in "Chi-town." Sitting at the table when I walked in was none other than Roderick. It was a joyous reunion. He had moved to Chicago and was working at a non-profit.

The reunion was short-lived, however, as he decided to move back to Baton Rouge to take a job in state government. The transition back to the South has been bittersweet for him, as he was happy to be closer to his family and old friends, but he misses city life and his larger black gay community.

Roderick's apartment was my hub during one of my research trips to Louisiana, and Roderick agreed to be one of my subjects, for which I am grateful. He was born in Baton Rouge, Louisiana, in 1974. The interview took place on January 23, 2005.

For me, it was simply you sort of knew where the black neighborhoods were. You knew where the white areas were. North Baton Rouge equated to blacks. South Baton Rouge sort of meant white, but there's also an old South Baton Rouge [that is] black. It's also called The Bottom. [. . .] The area by LSU, called The Bottom. It's old South Baton Rouge. Some of the streets slope down . . . like they have a slope down, and this is called The Bottom. In some communities, people refer to the bottom as like a real poor or low-down place. You know, "You're on The Bottom of the juke joint or something." The Bottom was actually a place where some very well known today black leaders came from in the community, or who did their thing and aren't around anymore or whatever. So it was a cool neighborhood actually. But now it's definitely economically depressed. Very, very, very much so. But you knew where the neighborhoods were. You just knew where the neighborhoods were. [. . .] In [the neighborhood of] Zachary [. . .] train tracks probably separated more of the blacks from the whites. There was definitely a train track and the blacks lived mostly up to the east of the train tracks and the whites lived mostly west of the train tracks. And there were some integrated areas too. It was interesting in Baton Rouge. And I think in Baton Rouge also, when it comes to race and neighborhoods like that, it may be unspoken, but you just know. Somehow you do know the neighborhoods you're going to. Where I lived it was saturated with black folks, so going to a white neighborhood involved getting in a vehicle and driving there. And there wasn't any interaction. Beyond the workplace, there was no interaction.

What were the racial politics in Baton Rouge? Did blacks and whites interact at all?

You may see me at work, but other than that, you know, you go your way, I'll go mine. Most of the churches, forget about it. I don't see much interaction. I think there's lots of separation in Baton Rouge. Then and now. And folks will try to be, you know, "We're not like that." Baton Rougers, I think, try to act like they're sophisticated when they're not. They take the fact that this is the capital city . . . they may take that with too much pride. And I really think that, you know, because it is a pretty forward-moving city. As of lately, it's proven that in a way by electing the first black mayor. But I think it's, it's here. There's racism. There's racial issues. People don't want to talk about it.

Roderick, age four, climbing a fence at the Baton Rouge Zoo.
Courtesy of the narrator.

Roderick sporting bell bottoms at age three.
Courtesy of the narrator.

People think that we're okay, but we're not. I think when it really comes down to the nitty-gritty, people show their true colors. Pun intended. I think we do have a ways to go when it comes to racial issues in Baton Rouge.

· · · · · · · ·

TIM'M

I met Tim'm in 1999 when he was a graduate student at Stanford. He decided not to finish his Ph.D. and instead to pursue a career as a spoken word artist and HIV/AIDS activist. He is a founding member of the black gay hip-hop group, Deep Dick Collective. Hailing from Little Rock, Arkansas, but reared in Taylor, Arkansas, Timothy (as he was christened) was born the son of a pastor in 1972. Taylor is a small town that sits on the border of Arkansas, just fifty miles northeast of Shreveport, Louisiana. The interview took place on September 24, 2005, at my home in Chicago. Tim'm currently lives in Atlanta.

Was [your town] integrated?

It was integrated. Like Taylor's an interesting town in that I don't know that any African Americans lived within the city limits, but there's a ring around Taylor. And that periphery is almost predominantly African American. It's one of those definite . . . I wouldn't say "other side of the tracks." But there's kind of that dynamic. And you know the black kids are essentially bused into town to go to school. And my graduating class was probably fifty-fifty. There were probably more whites in the school, overall. But it was pretty balanced.

What were the racial politics of Taylor?

Oh goodness. Racial politics of Taylor. Were there racial politics? It was definitely self-segregation. And one of the examples that sort of strikes me is, you know, one of the places where you had the most meaningful integration in my high school experience was through sports. Because you have one team and everybody plays, you know. But if you go to the basketball games at Taylor, at least it was this way when I was there, you have a black cheering section and a white cheering section. And the black parents and black families of the team sit in one section, and the white parents and students and whatever sit in another section. But mind you everyone's cheering for the same thing, but there's definitely that . . . It kind of reminds you of the reality that this is a town that wouldn't have integrated if it wasn't absolutely forced on them. And that dividing line was very clear. I mean in some ways, Taylor felt like an all-black school because, socially speaking and in some regards, the black students didn't really interact with whites. I was an exception because of academically, you know, I was in the upper level classes. And then because I knew that being involved on the campus and in school also bettered my chances of getting scholarships and other things, so I would force myself to interact with white students in other regards. I was president of Future Farmers of America, National Honor Society, a lot of other clubs. Not because, you know, I thought it was the coolest thing but just because, "This is my strategy for getting out of this place." You know, I think having an early awareness that this was not . . . And I think part of it was like coming from Little Rock and other cities, they may have been southern but it was definitely a sense that they were more progressive. Which I think is an interesting thing in the South. Like you know people say "the South," but there even is a distinction between urban South and rural South. So if you think Memphis is backwards, you know, go to some of those little towns out South where they're talking about how Memphis is like the bastion of, you know, liberalism and homosexuality and whatever, and it's like you're thinking, "Memphis? Huh? Are we talking about the same place?" But in relationship to some of these other places, it is. It's seen that way. So I think because we came to Taylor from Little Rock, we had a sense that like, "Okay Taylor's definitely backwards." Because Little Rock, even though it's a small city relatively speaking, and a southern city, because it's the main city in Arkansas, you do get these sparks of . . . a lot of people moved back from other places. I knew black lawyers and black doctors. Some of my peers in school were very wealthy African American people. Little Rock has a pretty substantial black upper middle class. And some of those kids were my classmates so I knew that there were black people who were well off. We just weren't one of them. [Chuckle] But I think that was an interesting thing to witness in a city that has a lot of African Americans . . . to actually get that class experience. Whereas when we moved to Taylor, it was pretty much like that. Pretty much all of the black people were poor, working-class, and that's pretty much it.

· *Describe some of your friendships in elementary, middle school, and high school. And are you in touch with any of those friends?*

Elementary school, probably not. Like I say, I think that moving around a lot really shaped my fear around developing close friendships. I can remember two people. It's kind of interesting. One was a young man named Craig Matthews. [. . .] We were really close. I think I had my first male fantasies about Craig. A white kid. He went to Terry and Franklin [elementary schools] with me. And there've been a few times when I'd Google him or try to look him up and then like "Nah, let me leave this alone." But I got invited to a party that his parents threw him, and then I got disinvited. Because they assumed that because whatever academic grouping I was in with him . . .

That you were white?

Right. And then when they discovered that I wasn't . . . and he was destroyed by it. And I remember him walking up to me on the playground one day and like just . . . almost like bawling and apologizing that he was so sorry, and I was telling him that it was okay and I knew it had nothing to do with him. But it was definitely one of those reality checks of, you know, like we're close and we're friends but this is still the South. It was also, I felt, like a reprimand against my love for him. I knew I liked him and I knew it wasn't just, "Oh he's my friend." And this was kind of leading up to like fifth, sixth grade. I mean I started to have a more developed notion of what relationship type stuff may have been. At that point, boys and girls were dating. They had girlfriends and boyfriends. And I knew I saw him in that regard. And so that racial thing, but also you know how class plays a role in that. So he was like the one friend I remember. The other was, interestingly enough, my elementary school–middle school girlfriend, Tracy [last name]. A wealthy African American. I think her father was a prominent lawyer. Her mother was a something like the Cosby family. And she was a paternal [fraternal] twin? And just wealthy. And I remember writing her a letter [chuckle]. That reference is in my book and on the CD. I wrote her a letter and she sent it back with all the corrections to my grammar. And I saw that as a class reprimand. Because you know Matthews the white boy, Tracy the black girl, but it was still like you know you're not just a nigger but you're a poor nigger. So you can't even hang with the rich niggers. And those are the only two people I think I can reference by name because their force in my life was pretty integral. The only other person I can think there was Alicia [last name] who graduated from Brown the same year I graduated from Duke. Her mother was a teacher at Terry. And I caught up with her because her brother Andre was in grad school at Duke while I was finishing my undergrad and I ran into him. He said, "I'm from Little Rock." And I'm like, "Oh do you know Alicia [last name]?" And he said, "That's my little sister." Ding, ding, connection. And Alicia and I kind of touched base at that point. It's "Oh wow!" like, you know. She was also a black student who was in the upper level classes, so we . . . It was kind of interesting to see that we had all . . . a few of us who were in that cluster had all gone on and continued to do some pretty interesting things. But I haven't really been in touch with anybody since then. High school is a little bit different. I was a part of what's called Upward Bound at Southern Arkansas University. I was a hugely popular person in that program in that . . . the way Upward Bound works in rural places like that, you get students from all these little small towns like Taylor. So it's not just one city's . . . it's like people from a vast body of places and at that point I knew I was leaving. I was very well aware I was gay by the time I was in there, although I was closeted. But I had a lot of friends. But most of my close friendships were not at Taylor. Most of my close friendships were through Upward Bound. And other students who probably had a lot more in common with me because they were academically accelerated, had hopes of going to college, you know, were probably a little bit more progressive in their thinking than maybe some other students because they saw themselves as wanting to leave the area and this Upward Bound was sort of this vehicle to this life outside of this place where a lot of people were dissatisfied with being for years and years and years.

How would you describe your family's feelings about difference?

My family didn't really trust white people. It was kind of a thing where in this world you had to interact with them, but if you could choose not to, it's best not to. It was very much, you know, if you could go to an all-black school and it was convenient, that would have been better. But since this is what works out, this is what you'll do. It was definitely this distrust for white people, which was marked by my mother in particular with like very specific incidences of being spat on, you know, walking to school when she was a kid in Taylor when the schools were segregated, you know. And just . . . I saw that develop. Like, as she started working at the school and seeing that I did have some sorts of connections to some of the white students that I considered my friends. You know, Upward Bound was a mixed-race kind of activity, but then we all had in common that we were all poor. Some of the differences were more class as opposed to . . . class was a bigger difference than race often was. So I mean definitely around . . . And that was really the only difference that got discussed. I mean when you live in Arkansas, race is kind of always present. It's like this . . . you know there were towns that were around with like . . . I believe up until the time I graduated from high school, like you know the KKK had a welcome sign on the town, you know, as people came through. And there were times that they were definitely recognized, "They have a huge KKK organization here" or if you're black and you're not supposed to be in town after a certain time. And this was still up until like . . . You know 1990 was when I graduated from high school and there were these places, when we would travel, just like we had to leave right after the game because, you know, it could get ugly. So almost a sense that like the sort of progress that would be made from '65 or whatever had not really affected my town and the parts in Arkansas where we lived. It was just kind of like it was a time warp. And the only reason whites and blacks interacted was because they were sort of federally enforced. Otherwise, people wouldn't have chose to, didn't want to. And there were exceptions to that. Like Upward Bound.

Like sort of institutional things that both people needed so they had to kind of do it together. But you still got the sense that like "No." One little, I think, noteworthy difference in my interactions around whiteness was I left my dad's church around twelve and started going to a Mormon church and so . . . a predominantly white church, very different religious experience than I grew up in. So I mean I had sort of a weekly interaction with white people who historically have a really negative understanding of black people and their rights to certain degrees of heaven and what have you. Other than that, it wasn't obvious to me. What was obvious to me among the Mormons that I went to church with on Sunday was that they were nice people. To me, they were nicer white people than the other white people. So to me it was kind of this really hopeful relationship to them because for the most part they didn't seem as racist as other white people I knew.

GAY MEMBERS OF THE COMMUNITY

I have often been in the company of white friends and/or colleagues who, at some point in a conversation about homophobia, suggest or express the belief that the black community (as if there is only one!) is more homophobic than white communities. And each time I hear this I cringe. I cringe not because black people aren't homophobic. Quite the contrary. Most of the black people I know hold or express homophobic views, including members of my own family. What troubles me is when people quantify the degree to which black people are homophobic because implicit in the "more" is the notion that black people also have more institutional power to enact their homophobia on the LGBT community, when that is simply not the case. Certainly, the black church is an institution that has recently gotten in bed with the government to spew hate and enact discrimination, but that relationship is still based on one less powerful institution (the black church) colluding with a more powerful one (a conservative White House) in order to curry favor. This indeed may make the public face of black folk appear to be more homophobic, but it does not account for what's actually happening on the ground in black communities around the country, and even in the South.[10]

In recalling their childhoods, the narrators in *Sweet Tea* reveal the full range of community reactions to people who were "funny," "that way," or had "a little sugar in their blood." Many such people were incorporated into the community without much fanfare, while others were ostracized and kept away from children. Others demanded the respect of their communities by going on the offensive—they took shit from no one. Finally, some of the narrators talk about their own gay family members who became role models or paved the way for them to deal with or accept their own budding homosexuality.

· · · · · · · ·

BOB (B. 1940, BAXLEY, GA.)

Were there other men in your community that people thought of as or knew were gay?

Oh, yes. We were told to stay away from them. Um-hmm. But you didn't know why. You were just told not to be—you just—well, now, don't go anyplace with Mr. So-and-So. No explanation was ever given. The musician at the Baptist church was married and had a big family, but he was a bisexual, now that I look back on it, because he approached me. I was in tenth grade. He approached me to go with him ten miles away to see some, I don't know, and I didn't do it. And I was told, "You don't do that." And then another man who belonged to that same church who was married and had children was openly—not openly, but everybody knew that he was very effeminate and we were told, you know, don't go near this person. And those were the only two men of African descent in my early experiences that were adults who were—who preyed on young boys. And I don't know anybody who ever had any experiences with them personally, but I know now in hindsight that—this is when I was a college person [. . .] and I had gone home with my cousin who I had maintained contact, who lives here in Atlanta now, this man who's now deceased came by my mother's house and he had these little pictures of naked boys and he was showing those to us. "Look at this. Look at this. Look at this." And I was embarrassed by that and so—because I didn't really like him. I was always offended by him somehow, I don't know. I suppose because we were—our family was always very neat and clean and orderly and his family was not. And it's sad to say that there was this caste—kind of a caste system. But, you know, we just didn't—and his mother was a seamstress but her place was junky. And people talked about it. And you could hear the older people talking about, you know, that. And so somehow I guess in the back of my mind, I just didn't really want to be associated with that person because it was outside of our caste, you know, so.

· · · · · · · ·

FREDDIE (B. 1944, MADISON, GA.)

Well, I guess the first real gay person I remember was in . . . I think I was in high school. His name was Billy. And [chuckle] it's funny. My grandmother was shacking up with a man. And I was going to visit my grandmother, and I heard a voice say, "Hey," and I said, "Hey." He said, "Come here." And so I went over. This guy was sitting on the steps. And he said, "You're Miss Evvie's grandson, aren't you?" and I said, "Yeah." "What's your name?" And I told him my name. He said, "Well I'm Billy." And so that was my first time meeting Billy. His name was Billy Hefflin. And so I started to visit Billy. He was kind of the first gay person I knew. And this started kind of a friendship until at some point I dumped him. [Chuckle]

And miraculously, the man my grandmother was shacking up with had a grandson, much younger than me. He was just the steamingest, hottest little sissy I ever met. [Laughter] And you know, I mean this was just a steaming-hot little sissy. And I won't call any names, but his mother wanted he and I to be friends, and we'd take him to the movies and stuff. And I did a bit of that with him, but all I can say is just a steaming-hot little sissy. And I did a few things with him. My grandmother, at some point, stopped shacking up with this man and moved on, and I lost touch with him. But the woman who married the grandfather had a granddaughter who was one of my girlfriends in high school. So one night I was visiting Gloria—her name was Gloria, and every year sort of at the beginning of a season, she would get out her clothing for the oncoming season. So she started opening shoeboxes and there were no shoes. Then she would look for dresses to go with the shoes, and the dresses were missing. And she said, "That goddamn Wooglie . . ." the little kid, they called him Wooglie. Was actually dancing in drag in Gloria's clothes. [Laughter]

There was a theater called "The 81 Theater" on Decatur Street here in Atlanta. It's been torn down a long time, and Georgia State University has a building on that site. But there was this guy, Snake, they called him. I don't know why they called him Snake because he was really kind of a fat, dark-skinned man. But they called it "Snake's Stage Show." There was live entertainment on Tuesday nights, where people danced, and some of them were drag queens and there would be homosexuals who would do what we call "shake dancing," exotic dancers. One called Miss Mary Jo and Madame Kilroy. Miss Mary Jo was the pretty one, a nice light-skinned guy who was really quite pretty when done-up, but had had no surgery or anything. And Madame Kilroy was not very attractive, but was very good at what he did. But Wooglie, this little guy, was dancing on Snake's Stage Show in Gloria's clothing and went on to have I think a total sex change, and now is a successful hairdresser in New York.

What time frame is this?

I think he's still alive now, but I'm trying to think. I finished high school in '52. I would say he was dancing in drag as early as . . . no, I finished high school in '62. So he was dancing in drag, I would say, in the early '60s, as a very young person. And I don't know at what point he moved to New York, changed his name a couple of times. I think he actually got married before he left Atlanta. But moved to New York and I think has a good life. I actually saw him on TV back in the early '80s. One of the shows was doing a special on black hair and he was a consultant. And has a name that sounds very phony. I will not call it because he . . . *she* . . . lives totally as a woman. Actually would come to Atlanta to model on the Bronner Brothers' fashion show and do hair. And she might still come to do hair. But went on to have the sex change and live a wonderful life.

And it was an interesting situation. I have a mutual friend, a friend who kept telling me about this girl. I knew that it was a girl who used to be a boy. And so after hearing about this girl several years, we were at a party one night and these two girls came in. And one of them looked at me and said, "Did you have a grandmother named Miss Essie or Effie or something like that?" And I mouthed, "Wooglie?" and she said, "Yeah." So that was how we kind of got reunited. We haven't kept in touch, but there she was, little Wooglie all grown up, with a different name. And was really quite pretty. Had some surgery done, I think to redo the nose. Nothing as extreme as Michael Jackson. [Chuckle] But it's kind of a success story because you know many of those stories are not successful. The girl she was with that night was a boy who entered Morris Brown College as a boy, finished Morris Brown College with a name change as a girl, was the son of an AME bishop, was the prettiest boy I've ever laid eyes on. To look at that boy, that wonderful skin and had wonderful shoulder length hair, was just a real pretty boy. And we didn't get to be really good friends, but he called me one day and said, "I want to talk to you since you seem levelheaded." And he came out here and said, "I have a decision to make. I can either go to grad school or I can complete my surgery." So I said, "I can only tell you what I think. I can't tell you what to do." I said, "But I have a question to ask you." I said, "If you don't go through and complete your surgery, are you going to wash that lipstick off your face, cut that hair and go back to wearing boys' clothes?" She said, "Oh never!" So I said, "Well if it were me, I would get the surgery so that I would be as much of what I look like as possible." And I said, "You can always go to . . . maybe get up some money and go to grad school, but I would hate to see you walking around looking like you're looking, living as a woman, and not being as much of a woman as you could possibly be." I said, "Now if it were me, that's what I would do. Or I would go back. Because look at me, I have no interest in having a sex change or living as a woman. I'm perfectly content living the life I live." I said, "But if you're not going to do that, I would have the surgery if I were you, if it were me." And so she did. Moved to New York and was totally destroyed by New York and is no longer with us. I mean even knowing he was a boy, he just had this wonderful skin. But just a beautiful boy. A beautiful boy.

I'm sure I've rambled way past the point. You asked me about gay people and role models. Billy was the first one I met, and people in the neighborhood talked about him. And I was with him one day . . . it was kind of funny but sad in a way. A little boy said, "Hey Sissy Billy." And Billy got all riled up. What occurred to me was that the little kid didn't mean any insult, but he had sat by his mother and seen Billy pass and she said, "There's old Sissy Billy." He thought that was Billy's name. Sissy Billy. Just an innocent sort of kid. And so I said, "His name is Billy. You don't want to call him Sissy Billy. That's not his name." And what I found was I always kind of carried myself in a way that made the neighborhood people distinguish me from the likes of Billy. I mean I was just a natural person. I never kind of put on. I mean what you see is what you get. I was always the same. My voice never changed. Well it changed some, but even now on the phone people still, "Yes ma'am" me. [Chuckle] There was a time I looked very androgynous. I didn't really have to shave until I was thirty. I never went in drag. I mean I might have gone to a costume ball or two. Well, I would buy sometimes things from the ladies department, a sweater or something if I like it. But basically I never went in drag. And oftentimes I was still, "Yes ma'am'ed" by people. They wouldn't mean any harm; it was just kind of a response. But Billy was the first one.

. . . .

DUNCAN TEAGUE (B. 1960S, KANSAS CITY, MO.)

When it came to gay folks, I'm very careful about this one because I don't buy the mythology that black folks are more homophobic than anybody else. And the reason I don't buy it is because I grew up knowing gay people whom my parents knew, and they were all in the church. And I'm not talking gay, I'm talking flaming queens who ran the choirs and sang the gospel music. And I met James Cleveland as a child. And the Troubadours, who were an all-male group, and none of them were butch. And I met the Hawkins Family. Yes, I'm gonna say it. And so I met Edwin and Walter Hawkins and their entourage and their family before they were out, some of them. I won't out all of them. But I will say those that are out now, I met them before they were out. And so there was this silence around their sexual orientation, but they were present. And the silence only got broken when there was some sort of controversy, and then folks would start whispering about the fact that they were gay or different.

And my mother hated it. She was very homophobic. And my father was, once again, more quiet about it—at least at that point. Because I think he was flabbergasted. He was just not ready to have not only a gay son, but a flaming queen son who was intelligent and articulate and a Christian and struggling with it. Nothing in Muscogee, Oklahoma, prepared him to have a son like this.

....

GEROME (B. 1958, TUSCALOOSA, ALA.)

There were two that were older than me. One lived like across the street. He was older but he was real feminine, sharp makeup. Okay, you see how smooth you keep your skin and everything? Okay, he would wear a little foundation to cover up the shading spots, but the eyelashes and the wigs and all that, no. If he did that, he left town to do it. But as far as being neat, very conservative, clean. His name was Oxford [last name]. He was very conservative with his limits. Now when he left town on his vacations to go to Ohio and places like that, I thought he was real discreet in his lifestyle. But he didn't care about anybody knowing about his feminine ways or what have you, you know. He was just a clean, clean, very particular person. So he was one. Then he had a brother that was little younger than him, named Evon. He was gay. Now, I and Evon became friends, you know. We were more or less on the same level. Evon may have been a year or two older than me, a couple years older than me. And then there was another gay guy that lived on the next street in back of us, James [last name]. He was gay. Very little, petite, feminine, you know. He was radiant.

Were they incorporated into the community or were they ostracized? How did people deal with . . .

I would say incorporated. They was not ostracized. They was just themselves, and who dealt with them dealt with them. It wasn't like, you know, being stoned or anything like that. None of that. It would have been a big riot, you know. But there were others in the city. But in that community, I could say that there were like three that was known, other than myself.

....

DEAN

Before he was murdered, Dean lived in Dallas, Texas (see Epilogue). He was an older student at Southern Methodist University. I met him at one of my book signings in Dallas in February of 2004. I was doing a reading/ performance with Njoki McElroy, a former colleague at Northwestern University who had performed as my grandmother in a show I directed. Njoki was on the faculty at SMU, and Dean was one of her students.

*Dean and I kept in touch after my visit, and he said that he would help
me secure other men to interview for* Sweet Tea. *At the time, I did not know
that Dean was conflicted about his own sexuality or that he suffered from
bipolar disorder. He also had other health problems and had surgery a few
times over the course of the year that we were in touch before my interview
with him.*

*Dean was born in Leesburg, Texas, in 1962, the fifth of seven children.
Leesburg is located just twenty miles east of Dallas and has a population
of less than 500. According to Dean his childhood was "Terrible. Terrible.
Alcoholic family, mother, father. Mother came from an alcoholic father,"
and he was a "Loner. Angry. Very creative though, very creative. Just never
knowing what was going to happen in the family." Dean's troubled family
background might explain why he had such a difficult time dealing with his
sexuality once he became an adult. The interview took place at Dean's
apartment in Dallas on January 11, 2005.*

There was an older man, he wasn't married. And they said that he messed
with men or raped little boys. You know, they would say that, you know, they
would say things like that. And even coming up as a teenager, my parents
was concerned about him raping me, thinking that he was going to rape me.
They would say stuff like, "Don't talk to him." Like one Sunday my sister,
older sister and her children and myself, we went for a country ride. And he
called me over to him. And I just went over. He says, "Do you want to go
drinking with me?" And I says, "No." I went home that evening and told my
mother. And my mother and father said, "Don't talk to him because he'll try
to rape you." And then they didn't want me to, because I was doing lawns
and stuff to earn money, they didn't want me to go to different places away,
saying that he would try to find me or something like that and rape me. And
the thing about it, this man had this reputation. And he even raped my great-
aunt, who was living alone, ill, and no children. And she had to be in her 70s
at that time. So when she moved here with my grandmother and my aunt,
well, my mother, she told my mother about how he would come there with
fruit and stuff because, you know, she would be there by herself, and just
how he would just rape her over and over. And so—and then to this day, this
same man is still living in that community. And he just has this reputation.
[. . .] So nobody in the community did anything about this man. And this
sister, this is a church member, and she would say that he doesn't rape
anybody, that women give him sex, you know, people give him sex, and that
people are lying, so the denial part was just amazing, how the community as
a whole. And one of my classmate's brother, he had I guess, you know, kind

of like had him as a sex slave. And his sister didn't know anything about it. So when we were in high school, people were just talking. And some of the community kids, you know, they said, "Well, you know, your brother lives—stays—goes over and stays with this man." And she didn't know anything about it, you know. And later, this guy died. He died, I think he had an asthma attack, swallowed his tongue or something like that. [. . .] So unless something was physically seen with their own eyes, nobody said anything in the community, you know.

· · · · · · · ·

"C.C." (B. 1961, GREENVILLE, MISS.)

It's funny. I just think my family always had a very interesting way. [. . .] I remember to this day, Sam. I mean . . . and Child, if you come in my house like the middle of the night, there'd be like drag queens . . . queens all over the house because they knew they could come to that place. And my step-father was a truck driver. And he'd come home and the queens would be in there playing spades and all that, so when I went to college, they continued to hang out there. [Laughter] Even 'til when he got sick with cancer, those queens was there taking care of him. So it's really interesting when you come up in a family like that. And they'd be there getting ready . . . we'd be like, "Hurry up ya'll," getting ready to shows. [Chuckle]

[. . .] When I was growing up, and this goes back to really what I know I can thank God for. Back in junior high school, I was going like to parties. I was going to grown folks' parties. Because there were gay men in the community that were very sophisticated. And this is something I tell everybody. I grew up around very sophisticated black gay men, and in some ways I didn't even know of any other thing. So that's why when I kind of started traveling and I would always think, "Well why are these rich men . . . ," be it Jewish, white or whatever, European, would be all over me. And I got it. I had the best education in terms of being well read, how to eat, how to have a wide palate. So when you're traveling, a young black man, and then meeting these people and going, "Oh this is different from even where I come from." So I think that was still that old school, where people were just not allowing you to be anything. They had a vested interest in your well-being.

· · · · · · · ·

GERALD

I first met Gerald in the mid-1990s in Amherst, Massachusetts, where he was a graduate student at the University of Massachusetts and I was a faculty member at Amherst College. He lived in Springfield, Massachusetts, for a while before meeting his current partner. They decided to move back south to Maryland.

Gerald was born in 1964 and grew up in New Bern, North Carolina, in the late 1960s and early 1970s in a single-parent household. New Bern is located in the eastern part of North Carolina, just thirty miles from the Atlantic Ocean and about fifty miles northeast of Camp Lejeune, one of the largest Marine bases in the country. The interview took place on May 5, 2005, at Gerald's home in the suburbs of Washington, D.C.

I had a cousin who was out and was a transgender. And, I had a great-uncle who was wasn't out, but he was out for his day. For his day, he was very out. You know? And, my grandfather used to make comments about taking an ax handle to him and that kind of stuff. You know? [. . .] He would become so mad. [. . .] My one cousin that used to come in, and he would come to visit my mother because my mother was more open and accepting, and um . . . he would be, you know, he would be dressed in women's clothing, and my grandfather would become so mad just when he walked in. And, he wanted to be called Latonya. [Laughter] And, you know, they called him Junior growing up. And, my grandfather refused. Everybody else in the family would call him Latonya, because he wanted to be called Latonya. And, he would correct you, but he didn't correct my grandfather, because my grandfather was very adamant about calling him Junior. He would always call him Junior. [Laughter] So, it was very clear early on that when it came to sexuality, that there was not that tolerance. The tolerance was not there.

I know you said that your grandparents had issues, but in general, did the community accept these people?

That was the interesting thing. Well, you know, they were just accepted. That's who they were. Even Junior, or I mean Latonya, who used to walk around in women's clothing and used to date Marines from the Marine Corp base [laughter], you know, because New Bern is you know Camp Lejeune and Cherry Point [a Marine air station] are there. And so even Latonya. I can't say everybody flocked to be their friends, but it wasn't like there were any hate crimes going on or any of that. I'm sure that they had their own personal struggles. My great-uncle came from a different experience, and you know, he was very religious, too. He had been in the military, very religious, and I remember there were always a lot of ministers around his house, and I didn't really understand the full significance of that until later years. He was dating a lot of the ministers in town. You know? [. . .] For me, that wasn't even a concept of who they were. And, he was known in town as the cake man because he made all the cakes, and he had sort of like a home bakery. You know? If you wanted a cake or a pie, you would go to Mr. Haywood. And, Mr. Haywood would make you a cake and a pie, and he would charge you for that. And, he was a cook at the local Holiday Inn. He did this on the side, the cakes and pies. And, my great-aunt actually does the same thing. She does cakes and pies and things like that. So, he was sort of accepted, because he was well known in the church as well, so people knew that Mr. Haywood was funny. [Laughter] They knew that Mr. Haywood was funny. Mr. Haywood was different. [Laughter] And, I guess they talked around him, probably about him behind his back, but I never really saw any real animosity directed towards him. You know, except for my grandma, who was really through with him most of the time. My grandmother was walking through a store one time, and this woman came up to my grandmother in Piggly Wiggly and said, "Mrs. Hazelton, would you please tell your brother to leave my husband alone." [Laughter] And, my grandmother would say, "Just get away from me with that common stuff." She used to call it that, "Get away from me with your common stuff." And, then she would go and say, "Haywood, I don't know why you have to have those men laying up on you." But, you know, she would really give him a hard time. But, as far as that, I never really saw any animosity directed toward him.

· · · · · · · ·

PHIL

I met Phil through another of my narrators, Bryant. Phil and Bryant dated years ago, and are now good friends. Phil is also Jaime's brother. It was interesting to hear two different takes on growing up gay in the same household.

Phil was born in Covington, Kentucky, in 1964, the tenth child in his family. Covington is just across the Ohio River from Cincinnati, Ohio. The interview took place on July 24, 2005, in Cincinnati.

Ohhhhhh, yeah. [Laughter] We had Miss Nelson, Miss Sandy. Miss Sandy was a semipro football player and looked like William "the Refrigerator" Perry in a wig. And then Miss Nelson was a former Golden Glove boxer. And she used to apparently indoctrinate several of the boys in the neighborhood, you know, pieces of trade and she'd turn 'em out. And nobody messed with them because they were huge guys. And then there was another guy named Ben [last name], who was just—to say "flame" is not even doing justice—I mean, he was the Statute of Liberty flame. [Laughter] Whoo! But, those were the kind of things that we saw. And he was like just real. He was real. He was interesting. He went to prison twice. And I think supposedly he killed one of his sister's husbands. And so, one had been beating on his sister, so it was never proven [. . .] but he went to prison for a while. And no one ever really messed with him. I mean, they kind of protected themselves, but people would say things when they'd go by, but they were just real. So that was our example of gay men and that was something you didn't want to be, you know.

· · · · · · · ·

BRYANT

Bryant has to be one of the most "country" gay men I know who also has bourgeois taste. He is a very successful corporate executive, who drives a Mercedes, lives in a beautiful home, and loves to travel. But just try to get him to eat something that hasn't been fried! Imagine trying to find KFC in Madrid, which he did on a trip to Spain with his partner.

I can say these things about Bryant because we are good friends. We met in 1999 after he had begun dating one of my good friends, Ian, in Atlanta. Bryant loves to tell stories and, as he notes in his narrative, he comes from a family of gossipers. When we get together, we often dish about celebrities, especially Whitney Houston.

Bryant was the very first person I interviewed for Sweet Tea, *so in many respects he was the guinea pig. He was born in Dublin, Georgia, in 1967 and is the eldest of four children. Dublin is located about fifty miles southeast of Macon and has a population of approximately 16,000. The interview took place in Atlanta on July 20, 2004.*

I remember them [his parents] talking about one person growing up who was a friend of my father's, and he was older. He was probably between my father's and my grandfather's age, maybe about 60-something now. But I remember them talking about him being gay. I don't know that he ever was, and he certainly doesn't have, he certainly, if he's gay now, I don't know anything about it. But I remember them talking about him. Everybody talked about him. If being gay came up at anybody's house, and it did sometimes, he was always the person that they pointed back to. He ran a barbershop in town, which sounds, because at the time men weren't doing women's hair in Dublin, so. But he was the, he was the town gay person, and if anything, we were told not to socialize with him, so we didn't go get our hair cut at that barbershop. But he was always at my grandfather's church because he was a friend of the family's; so they would be at church and they'd be nice to him, and then talk about him. Because after church every Sunday we always had to have a debriefing and dinner. Our dinners at home on Sunday happened immediately as soon as the service was over with, so we always ate about two o'clock, so we'd talk about everybody who had been in church. And he was . . . the only person, he's the only person I can really remember them talking about being gay. I don't remember them, I don't remember any other conversation about anyone else, not that, not to the extent, if they mentioned anyone else's name. I don't know that, I just remember him being the one. So there could've been a variety of people that they just didn't refer to, but he was the town black gay person that people talked about.

The general consensus about being gay was that it was very negative—hellfire and brimstone. We had sermons in, we had sermons in church, from both my grandfathers about mankind shall not lie with mankind. I think that was something, when I grew up and heard that later on. It was nothing new to me, because I had heard that as long as I can remember, that the worst thing that you could do was be like this man, be like this man. He spoke at my grandfather's funeral, and it's funny I can't think of his first name now; I can see his face as clear as I'm sitting here talking to you, but that was, you were not going to be, you're not supposed to be gay because you would be like this man. You're not supposed to be gay because my grand-father and grandfather, both my grandfathers preached against it. And I remember about the age of twelve, Dan Rather had a program on CBS, and he talked about gay men in a park, the sex, the public sex in a park. It was one of those *60 Minutes* programs, and I remember my parents sitting there watch-ing it with us, and I remember feeling uncomfortable about that because at twelve years old I already knew that I was probably going to be gay, and I remember wanting to watch the program but not wanting them to be in the room with me, but we only had one television. So we all had to sit there, we all had to have equal disgust at what was being shown, but I wanted to hear about it, because I didn't have, my only source of, even though that show was negative, because it wasn't showing anything positive, it was showing how men had sex in public in city parks; that was the first time I think I had ever heard that, or seen anything on television about it. And the first time I had heard conversations around anything gay outside of, "don't be like this man," and it was going on from what I had heard, from the pulpit.

....

RODERICK (B. 1974, BATON ROUGE, LA.)

I remember this one guy. We called him "Larry Harry." I'm assuming Larry was his official real name, but I don't know where the "Harry" came in at. [Laughter] He was a friend of my great grandmother. And he would come to visit. Her house was like a Dew Drop Inn. Everybody came to visit her. But yeah, definitely, we knew that Larry Harry was a "punk," as some of my cousins would say or you know, as my uncles would say. He would get his little daily walk in. He was effeminate. He would do his thing. The joke was, "You guys behave or we're gonna let Larry Harry come and getcha." Or, "We're gonna let you go home with Larry Harry." But no one ever bothered him. No one ever bothered him that I know of. Larry did his thing. Larry would come visit my grandmother, and that was that. The kids would giggle, "Oh that's Larry Harry." I remember that. I believe Larry's dead now. But I remember that.

I had an uncle who was gay. Well, I won't say he was gay, but he was really definitely bisexual because he had this girlfriend for years. Actually, what had happened was, one of my aunts got married . . . her second or third or whatever marriage . . . and at the wedding . . . her husband sang at this church—or what is it?—Greater King David. And the director of choirs there was this gentleman named Reginald [last name]. And Reginald sang at the wedding. And during the reception—it was at his mother's house because it had a big yard—during the reception, I saw Reginald. And at this point . . . I'm jumping all over the map here, so forgive me. I was definitely out of college when this happened. All I remember [is] being at the wedding and seeing Reginald talk and I knew Reginald was gay. I remember seeing Reginald talking to my Uncle Alonzo. And they're talking and I'm thinking to myself, "He's trying to work my uncle." And so at one point, there were some numbers exchanged. I think Reginald gave my uncle his number, and he took it, you know. And I was like, "Okay." So later on in the reception, I was like, "I saw what you did." He said, "What do you mean?" I said, "I saw you give my uncle your number." And he didn't know what to say. He was speechless. I was like, "Uhm hmm." And so he was looking at me like, "Damn. That little bitch." [Laughter] So he probably was thinking that about me, you know. So I said, "Uh huh." Well, Alonzo . . . Lonnie as we call him . . . Lonnie was killed. [. . .] And this happened in [. . .] 1994 or 5. But after he died, I was like, "Ma, did you ever think that Lonnie messed around?" And she said she had heard rumors and wasn't ever sure, but she had heard things, you know. So I said, "Oh okay." So she probably knew more than rumors, yeah.

I have an aunt, my mother's older sister, who actually lost two sons to AIDS. Definitely one of them was gay. We called him Junior. And he actually did prison time too. But I mean he was gay before he went to prison. It's not like he got turned out in jail. But he was definitely gay. It was one of those things that you know. You don't talk about it, but you know it's there. And there were other . . . probably some siblings in my biological father's family, too. You know he's gay but you don't need to talk about it. Like I know I've got a cousin . . . my aunt whom I had spoken about earlier, Aunt Yvonne, she's got a son that's definitely gay. And I know because, you know, we've hung out a few times. His name is . . . well it's spelled like "Roger," but she never would . . . it's pronounced "Ro-jé." [Chuckle] And we called him "Magoo." That's his nickname. So Magoo definitely is gay. [Laughter] He's cool. And it's one of those things; you know I've seen a lot of black families . . . maybe a lot of families in general. It's known about. It may not be talked about. But you know and you know that you know, as they say. [Laughter] And they're part of the family. What are you gonna do? So there's that acceptance too, there, where it's, "Okay yeah, you know." And that's that. It is what it is, you know. So there was some awareness of gay people.

. . . .
"KEVIN"
Kevin was born in Memphis, Tennessee, in 1981. He is one of the youngest men I interviewed. He is a "PK," or "preacher's kid." Later on in life, his mother also was called to preach and so was he. He is a minister of music for a local church. The interview took place on July 20, 2005, in Memphis.

There was this one guy who moved into the neighborhood when we were in elementary school, so probably about fourth or fifth grade. He used to come outside and dance in the driveway. Just turn on the radio and dance, I mean he was the same age. I'm like, what is the matter with this clown? And my dad, now he did come in the house one time and I remember this distinctively, he was like, who is this little gay boy across the street? He was like just always shaking and gyrating and all this stuff, and I was like I have no clue. So one day my younger sister and I, we were outside playing and we saw him dancing and he was on the phone and always talking wild and stuff. So we just went over there and introduced ourselves. We were like, "We are [Kevin] and Sandra." We were like, "Welcome to the neighborhood. We see you at school. Why do you dance like that?" So I think with that, he was the only one at that time, because even when we all were playing, it's like I, you might have gotten called sissy here and there, but that was the norm. I mean, we all called each other sissies, especially if we were playing the game hide-and-go-seek and somebody fell and started crying. Yeah, we're going to call you a sissy if you're a boy. He, on the other hand, that was the first time, when he moved into the neighborhood was the first time I heard the word "faggot." I was like, "oh my."
And who would be calling him that?
A few other kids in the neighborhood. Now, apparently some parents were calling him that too, because I remember this one girl, her name was

Sabrina and she stayed right next door to him, and she said, "Well my mama said you a faggot and you going to hell." And it was like, we were playing outside with him and we were like, okay. We used to hear him say little crazy things, but he said, "Your mama must be on crack." Just messing with her back. So it was like you could tell somebody's parents were talking, but for the most part, with the neighborhood we grew up in, everybody was still pretty much welcome in everybody's house, even though you didn't get a chance to come in, everybody was still welcome.

See in my dad's house, at our house nobody could come in that house but us. Even if he was there, no other kids because I think around that time, like the '80s and the early '90s, there was a lot of molestation was going on in a lot of homes around people who knew each other, so they were like, oh no, we're not going to play this game, you got to be going right on back to your house. Don't come here to get no water. Y'all come in the house, fine, but nobody else is able to come in the house. But with that they cut down a lot of junk, other than my dad, you know, making that comment at that time, we didn't really know of too much talking that went on, but I think it was so understood, as long as ain't nobody trying nothing now. I would say that my mom even actually was like, now there's nothing going on. Now she would ask things, and as we got older we learned that that meant is there anything going on out of the norm of what you've been accustomed to, or like what you've been accustomed to seeing. We were like, nah.

Do you think that guy was gay?

I mean I know he was. This is the crazy part now. He went to the same elementary school; we ended up going to the same middle school. By the time we got into high school, I think he transferred the last year. No, we ended up graduating together. So the year after we graduated, being that we still stayed in the same neighborhood, well I went off to college and I stayed on campus, but I would still come home, so he was still there. And one day I went over there and spoke to him, after we had graduated for about, after a year and a half, and he said he was getting ready to go and get ready for a show. I'm like, "a show? What kind of show?" He was like, you know, he has to perform. Okay, I understand that, but perform what? He was, "Oh just a little singing and dancing." I'm like, "oh okay." So he said, "Help me. I still need to get some stuff out of my trunk." So he opens up the trunk and all of a sudden all these gowns, wigs and . . . I'm like, "Are you a drag queen?" And he was like, "Well, you know this my little side gig." I'm like, "okay." So from there, I come to find out one of his boyfriends was a friend of my ex, and so that's how I knew that he was gay from that point.

coming out and turning
the closet inside out

2 "Coming out" is not always the best phrase to describe what people do when they acknowledge that they have same-sex attraction. In general, "putting one's business in the street" is something frowned upon in many black communities, including the communities in which many of the narrators grew up and currently live. As noted in the Introduction, most southerners avoid discussing topics such as sexuality in a direct manner. Thus, many of the men in *Sweet Tea* have not "come out"—as it were—to their families, even though, by their own acknowledgment, their family members "know." The open secret of these men's homosexuality, in most instances, complicates our common notions of what it means to be "out," especially in light of the white gay community's insistence on a politics of visibility. But as Marlon Ross has argued, "the closet" is not necessarily an apt metaphor for the place where black men who choose not to announce or visibly articulate their (homo)sexuality in a public way find themselves.[1]

The irony, of course, is that in many instances their homosexuality *is* public, for many of these men live with their partners or have brought their partners or men they were dating home to their families—and without incident. While this private acceptance without public acknowledgment may seem odd, or even an example of self-hatred, to some people, for these men and their families it becomes a way to accommodate taboo sexuality while still sustaining the veneer of southern religious mores, which in most instances is homophobic. In some ways, the "don't ask, don't tell" mentality of southern families and communities provides a space for these men to have more freedom to engage one another, for they employ the terms and codes of the South to co-exist with neighbors and family and still express their sexuality. Bringing So-and-So to the family reunion as a "friend" as opposed to "lover," for instance, is a way to circumvent the drama of introducing him as the latter.

This is not to suggest that every man with whom I spoke

embraces a gay identity. A few of them either don't like the term "gay" or "queer" because of its affiliation with white homosexuals or they consider themselves bisexual. Indeed, a few of the men in *Sweet Tea* have children and have been married or continue to sleep with women. The decision to disclose or not to disclose their sexuality with children and/or former wives is the topic of more than one narrative below. The narratives of these men in particular challenged my own fixed notions about what it means to live as a "black gay man," with all of the complexity that comes along with that nomenclature.

Contrary to what I thought I would find once I started interviewing, many of the men in *Sweet Tea* had announced their sexuality to their families and community. As is common in coming out narratives, the parents and family members of these men responded in a variety of ways, some of which varied over time. For instance, some parents moved from disgust and anger to mild tolerance to acceptance, while others never accepted their son's sexuality. Still others expressed unconditional acceptance from the beginning. One theme that emerged over and over again was the anger some family members expressed about not being told sooner. This sentiment had more to do with issues of trust than anything else. In general, the stories run the gamut of reactions. Some of the men express a reluctance to come out because they fear they will be rejected or banned from seeing their nieces and nephews, as was the fear of John and Kent—for whom the outcomes of revealing their sexuality within the family circle were dramatically different.

I got more than a chuckle from hearing the many different strategies that the men used to come out to their families. Like the family members' responses, they too, ran the gamut. One of my favorite ones was when a narrator chose to tell one family member who he knew would tell everybody else in the family so that he wouldn't have to. As southerners tend to be great bearers of gossip, this strategy was almost always foolproof. In fact, it was a strategy I employed when I came out to one of my brothers, who "volunteered" to share the news with my other siblings to "spare" me the pain of any backlash. Little did he know that I had already come out to my mother four years prior.

I was twenty-eight and teaching in Massachusetts at Amherst College. She had come to visit and we were watching the late evening news. After I took a deep breath, I turned to her and said, "Mom, I need to talk to you about something. There's something that I've wanted to talk to you about for some time now, but I haven't had the courage to say it." Because she always has a flare for the dramatic, she put her hand over her heart and said, "What have you done?" I said, "I haven't done anything. I'm gay." In her shrill, high-pitched voice and with a furrowed brow that always signifies a combination of confusion and disapproval, her first response was, "Pat, you mean to tell me that you like other men?" I said, "Yes, ma'am." She replied, "Why?" I knew then that I could only make her understand by providing her with some kind of anecdote or analogy. I asked her, "Mom, have you ever found yourself attracted to another woman?" She said, "No," drawing out the word while simultaneously shaking her head. I replied, "Neither have I," which was actually a lie, but I thought that it would help her to understand where I was coming from. At the end of that conversation, she said, "If that's the way you are, I just have to accept it. You're my son and I love you."

But that acceptance didn't really come for some years, as my mother went through a period of self-blame and shame about my being gay. She shared what I had told her with no one—not even her closest friends. And she was holding out hope that it was just "a phase." It finally hit home when I moved to Chicago with my partner, whom she had told everyone was my "roommate." That moniker didn't last long after we purchased a house together, to which my mother responded, "Pat, you're not going to buy a house with that *boy*, are you?" I had destroyed whatever hope she had of me marrying a woman, so she resigned herself to the fact that her baby son is gay. Now, she accepts Stephen, my partner, as a part of the family, and even walked in with me at our commitment ceremony. Indeed, our ceremony was the crowning moment of the ten-year period in which my mother wrestled with my homosexuality. At that event, she was given permission to accept and love me (and Stephen) unconditionally and without judgment not for what we do in bed but for how we love each other and how others love us. She now speaks the word "gay" freely, which never would have happened before.

While some of the narratives follow a similar positive trajectory, many don't. Some narrators share traumatic stories about their coming out to their parents, siblings, and extended family and the way it has shaped their current relationships with their families. More than one narrator speaks of telling his parents, getting a negative response or no response, and the subject never being broached again. Each in his own way, however, the narrators found a way to work through these negative responses by not internalizing the homophobia, accepting that it's not about them and it's something that their families and friends have to work through on their own.

· · · · · · · ·

ALBERT

Albert and I met in Chicago in 2005 at a conference on religion and sexuality at the University of Chicago. At the time, he was a student in the Divinity School at Vanderbilt University in Nashville, Tennessee. Albert was born in

Natchez, Mississippi, in 1981, the youngest and only boy child of five children. One of the oldest cities in, and the first capital of, Mississippi, Natchez is located in the southwest portion of the state along the Mississippi River. Cotton cultivation was pioneered in the Natchez area in the eighteenth century, leading to the city's prosperity as a river port before the Civil War. With a population of less than 20,000 today, Natchez is a popular tourist attraction, known for its preserved antebellum homes, slavery museums, and the birthplace of writer Richard Wright.

The interview took place on July 18, 2005, at Vanderbilt University.

Well, I came out to my father; he was the first person that I came out to, and my sister who was one of the twin sisters who happens to be a social worker. And then I was in conversation with my third older sister and we were talking about an experience that she had at a party and how all of the individuals that were there were lesbians and how it kind of freaked her out; and, I was kind of asking her questions about, well, how did she respond to it [. . .] and so forth and so on. And she got offended and she said, she raises the question, "Why are you taking up for them, are you gay?" And I said, "Well, what if I were?" And the conversation got really, really nasty and so I told her to call my social worker, my sister. And so she did and her twin sister found out because the sister that was at the event called the wrong twin, right. So the other twin, who wasn't the social worker, calls me and is angry at me because I didn't tell her. [. . .] So that's how my sisters found out. Now, my older sister doesn't know. And this is the sister who is like my mom. And my mom doesn't know. So I never made that connection with kind of withholding that information even from my oldest sister. But she doesn't know. I told my father because I had a trump card and that trump card was my father had gone out and had another child while married to my mom. [. . .] But that was the card that I was going to pull if he did not respond the way that I wanted him to respond.

What was his response?

My dad's response was very amazing to me. And this was just recent, like since I've been a student here. And I [. . .] called my dad. My dad was overseas, and I was crying and I just really wanted to tell him, or start the process of coming out to my family. [. . .] I remember specifically sitting on the floor in my apartment and saying I'm calling him first. And when I called him I was crying. He was like, "What's wrong, what's wrong?" And I was like, "I think I like guys." And he was like, "Huh? What are you saying, are you gay?" And I was like, "Yeah, but I'm trying to work through that, I'm going to counseling," and the whole reparative therapy deal came up of course, because I had been involved with a church who was, pushing us to do that kind of thing, so that was the only way out that I knew at that time. So I told him. He was like, "Okay well, I still love you. You're still my son," blah, blah, blah. "We'll get through this," blah, blah, blah. And that was the end of the conversation. Conversation closed. So I did not hear about this conversation, about this issue until recently when I decided that I was going to relocate from Nashville to Boston, or to California, and my dad was like, "Well, what about your problem?" And I was appalled. Okay, because I was like, oh now we get to have this conversation again. And he was like, "So where are you?" he said, "I thought you were in counseling," blah, blah, blah. I was like, "Well, guess what Dad, it's not going to change. And all of that other stuff, it's just not going to happen." So he was like, "Are you sure? What about God and praying?" blah, blah, blah. And I was just like, "It's not going to change." And then he said, "Well, you're going to do what you're going to do. Just be safe." [. . .] And I'm so very grateful that I came out to my father at an age when I was able to really understand or really decode in some respect some of the responses that he gave. And really situate him in the South as a man who has never had to deal with this issue before. When he made the comment in the first conversation about, "Well, we got to get you a girlfriend," I understood exactly why he made that, because he felt like, okay, it's like turn it on, so turn it off, or turn it off, so turn it on. And that a girlfriend would prove, would solve the issue. So this last conversation that I had with him, it was empowering for me. And it spoke to the character of my father. [. . .] And I'm just really grateful to have a father like that. You know, that despite being uninformed about the issue, [he] could really just say, "You're still my son and I still love you and we'll work through it," and blah, blah, blah. So, that's special to me, and I think that's been one of the major points in my development with my father and our relationship—that our relationship really took off in another direction. Because as a child, the interactions with my father were very limited in some respect, because he was always gone and providing for the family. My father was, is a good father. But, being a slave to "the man" kind of demands that he go and work, and so he did. But we never had a relationship, and it would seem that the only time that we had a relationship was when I was being compared to a cousin who played the sports and did the guy kind of things, and I was always good with my hands and crafts and things of that nature, and always doing things in the house and so forth and so on. So that was the only time that we really kind of spent with one another, and it was always a critique. But after that experience and sharing that story with him, our relationship developed for the good.

Do you think you'll come out to your mother?

I'm working on it. I am. I really, really am. You know, I had the weirdest dream last night, interestingly enough. A very, very, very vivid, vivid dream where I came out to my mom and her response was, she did not understand exactly what was going on. And of course parents go through the blaming of themselves and so she did that. And that conversation might have been sparked by a conversation that I had with my older, oldest nephew. I called and asked him if he still had his ears pierced, and he said yes. And I said, "Well, how is grandmamma responding to it?" And he said, "Well initially she did not want me to have it and blah, blah, blah, and then she said, 'Just don't be wearing those *big* earrings.' And then she was like, 'Well, we've got to get you some better earrings than that.'" And so she went and bought him a pair of earrings. So I think that that may have been one of the kind of undertones of that story, that dream that I had. Like, well maybe she's not there right now, but as time progresses maybe she'll be ready.

· · · · · · · ·

ANGELO

Angelo is the partner of a friend of my partner. He is soft-spoken and, on the surface, quite shy, until he gets to know you. After that he really opens up and can be quite funny. His various body piercings belie the initial impression of him as conservative.

Angelo was born the youngest of six children in Greenville, South Carolina, in 1976. He was raised in a single-parent home in a family that was highly religious. As his coming out story attests, his relationship with his family is a bit strained because of his homosexuality. Adding to this strain is the fact that he has a white partner with whom he has purchased a home. His coming out story is particularly interesting in that it coincided with the revelation of another big "secret" that his family had been keeping from him.

The interview took place on May 12, 2005, at the home of a mutual friend in the Greenville suburb of Simpsonville.

To what extent have you come out to your family?

Ever since I graduated [from high school]. I mean, she's [his mother] kind of already known [. . .].

And how did it go?

It didn't go too well [laughter] considering it was at church and when I graduated. And also finding out at that moment that my sister was my mother—that's when things just kind of all blew up, per se. I got a card from my sister, and she stated that, you know, "Congratulations, Son, on your venture into the world," and all that. And that's when I was like, "Why did you give me the wrong card? I mean, why does it say 'son' "? And that's when she started crying and let me know that she was my biological mother.

And so, you were raised with a woman who you thought was your sister, but who was actually your mother?

My mother, umm hmm.

Why did they keep it a secret?

I do not know. I mean, when I've asked her about it and I've asked my grandmother—which is my adopted mother—about it, she stated it was to keep me away from my dad's side of the family, because of their behaviors and criminal backgrounds and all that. They just wanted to more or less give me a clean slate to start from and not have that stigma of being a Harper or being associated with them. So therefore, the adoption had taken place.

So the woman that you thought was your mother was actually who?

My grandmother.

OK. And how old was your mother when she had you?

She was in the tenth or eleventh grade.

And did your father know that she was pregnant with you?

Yeah, he was there. He was there at that time. Well, I called him. I've only talked to him maybe two times throughout my twenty-eight years, and on those two occasions, first was basically "just to hear your voice" and the second time was trying to set a date [to meet], which his new wife does not want any of that to take place. So she's pretty much hesitant on the fact that it may do something to the kids—the kids that they have now. So, that's just been a work in progress.

Hmmm. So I'm still trying to understand about the answer that your . . . grandmother, who you thought was your mother, adopted you because she wanted to keep you from your father's side of the family. But why—if he didn't want to have anything to do with you . . .

He does. He told me that he did. He did put forth every effort to do what he could, but they shunned him away. So that's pretty much where that stands.

So who did they tell you your father was when you were a kid?

My grandfather, he died in the services. I mean, he came back home, but he died as a result of the injuries from the service. So I was about three years old, so I had like minimal knowledge of what he was, what he looked like, other than pictures.

But you thought he was your father?

Yeah. I mean, he's who I've always . . . I have his name.

So your grandmother legally adopted you?

Yeah. They both legally adopted me.

And what's your relationship now with your family in general?

It's OK, but it's distant. It's pretty much I'm doing things on my own because of who I am and what I choose to do with my life. I mean, I have contact with them periodically. Recently, as of about a year or so, things have just kind of changed due to sudden things that have happened in our family. My home—well, the home that I was raised in, it caught on fire, so that kind of tied things together and made everybody get closer and become aware and understand that I am gay. [His actual mother] accepted it *then*, and this has kind of like torn us apart *now*. And she just expressed to me that she's always had a fear that [I] may end up like other people—viruses or living the lifestyle in which it's destructive. And I was like, "Well, Mom, there's a different side of that." I mean, people are so stereotypical as far as they'll portray one side of it and everybody thinks it's that way. Not that I'm trying to prove to her that there's a good side to being gay versus a bad side—it's just that this is who I am. I mean, I've conveyed that to her and now I'm just letting her accept it. And let her just be Mom or either not be in my life.

· · · · · · · ·

BOB (B. 1940, BAXLEY, GA.)

To what extent did you come out to your parents?

Oh, much, much later. I had been through college and gone back to my hometown to work, to help pay my folks' house out of debt, because my last year in school they sort of mortgaged the house to put me through school. I sort of owed a debt to them, so I went back and helped them pay it off. And was sexually repressed that entire year, had no sexual experiences. But then there was high school students that—boys who I fell in love with then because I was very, very energetic and very caring and more than they had ever had experienced. And I don't know if they were in love with me for that or if that was something else, but I think it's probably because I was caring and nurturing other than in a sexual attraction to me. But I suppose that, yeah, my mother had come to California in the '70s and just asked me, because I was living with a partner there. And so she asked me and I said, "Well, yeah." She said, "Well, we've always known." But I think the way she asked it was, "Well, are you sleeping with Al?" And I said, "Yes." And she said, "You know what the Good Book says?" I said, "Well, yeah." And so later on in life, we started talking about things. And I said, you know, in the African Methodist Episcopal Church, they do something called a Decalogue, which is part of a ritual where they go through the commandments and the congregation respond in singing, "Lord have mercy upon us and incline our hearts to keep the law." You sing that response, but it never says, "Thou shall not be a homosexual." It says, "Thou Shall not kill." [Laughter] So later on in life, we were talking about that. And I said, "Well, you know, when we do the Decalogue," which is a law, the Decalogue means the law, you know, in Greek it's the law, and it's the commandments that were given to Moses. And so it's a bridge between the Old Testament and the New Testament and the parts is part of the ritual. So you do that before you enter into the New Testament, reading of the scriptures. And but nowhere where it says that thou shall not be a homosexual, but it does say, "Thou shall not kill" and "Thou shall not commit adultery." "Thou shall not steal." "Thou shall not bear false witnesses against thy neighbor." "Thou shall not covet thy neighbor's house nor thy neighbor's wife nor neighbor's ox nor his ass or anything that is thy neighbor's." All those things are there and then you respond, "Lord have mercy upon us and incline our hearts to keep this law within it." [. . .] So later on, my mother and I were talking. And I said, "I didn't make myself this way and you didn't make myself this way," because she said, "Where did we go wrong?" [. . .] My father never questioned me. Never, ever said anything to me. Ever. Never. It was my mother. And she said, "Well, where did your father and I go wrong?" And I said, "You didn't," because I was an adult then and I had been through college. [. . .] I had become read and widely read. [. . .] My father never, ever—he knew, I'm sure he always knew. But yet, he'd never even approached the subject with me at all. He passed away in '82. And had come to California, where my partner and I lived—I mean, he didn't stay but he came out there on many occasions and lived in the house with us. Interesting, my mother—we took—my father passed away and my partner and I said, well, my mother was very—in search for a reason, so we said, "Let's just take her to Europe." I had a cousin in Europe at the time. He said, "It may help her a little bit," so we took her to Europe. And so we were in France, I never shall forget, and the hotel we were in wasn't up to the standard that my partner really felt that we should be in. So we went to another hotel which had a larger room with a small bath which was not down the hallway, which a lot of the European hotels are, you know, back in the day, back in—most of them now have bathrooms in the rooms, but the rooms have been reduced in size because they put the bathrooms in there, so. But the room had to have a rollaway bed put in it because the bed was a two-quarter bed—three-quarter bed I guess you'd call it, yeah, a three-quarter bed. So we had made the arrangement that my mother and I would sleep together in that three-quarter bed and then my partner would sleep on the cot. And my mother said, "Well, wouldn't you all like to go down to the bar?" My mother was very liberal by then. She was open-minded because she knew and she accepted us. And we came back and she was on the cot. Because the room was so small, in order for her to get dressed for bed, we went out to allow her [to get dressed for bed] because the bathroom was this big [gestures to indicate the size of the room].

And your sister?

Oh, my sister's always known and she's very supportive. [. . .] I had a partner for twenty-something years. And when he passed away fifteen years ago, my mother came out to California and—because they didn't come for the funeral, they came after that, she and my sister came to support me and to go to the lawyer and stuff like that to get the will straightened out and everything. And my mother was just a total mess. She was crying. My sister was crying and the whole bit. And so they knew. And so my sister always supports me. She said, "You know, just always—I don't care who you sleep with, you can sleep with the dogs if you want, but you're still my brother. Just take care of yourself. And love one person at a time." [Laughter] So I just have one sister, so we get along very well.

....

BRYANT (B. 1967, DUBLIN, GA.)

I don't think I knew that I was supposed to come out to my parents. In September of '90 I went to the gay club for the first time. In November of 1990 I met the guy in there who would become my first relationship. And I think I had started buying the *Advocate* or the *Out* [which are magazines for a gay audience], or something like that. Once I came, once I went to the club, I was like okay now I've absorbed as much stuff about being gay as possible, because I was one of those people that would sneak in the library and look at the book about homosexuality and make sure nobody else was looking. So I had started reading the *Advocate* and the *Out* and it was 1990 and the people, there was more visibility around being gay, so I thought that once you acknowledged to yourself that you were gay, then the next thing to do was to tell your parents. So when I started dating the guy in November, we dated and then I would, I remember my mother asking me whether I was going to come home for Thanksgiving. And I said, "No, because I'm dating this older woman." And it was really this older man, this much older man. And she was like, "Oh, when are we going to meet them?" So then I decided I can't go through with this lie over and over and over again. Because I was spending you know, Thanksgiving with this man. And it was like, I kept going back, because there was still a whole bunch of religious stuff, going back and forth, back and forth, even though I had went to the gay club and was in this relationship, I was still very much conflicted religiously. And I remember reading in the *Advocate* or the *Out*, I couldn't tell you the Bible verse or whatever it was, but there were two, two verses that were quoted. One was, "Shall the pottery ask the potter why hast Thou made me this way?" And I remember thinking, hmm, that's interesting, that's like a square pot asking, "Why did you not make me round?" Because I'm made square. And I remember one was, the other one was, "I am what I am by the grace of God." And reading those two things, those two lines, in whichever one of those gay magazines, made everything okay with me. That was the thing I needed to see to balance my spirituality with my sexuality. Ever since that day I never had any, any feelings around, I'm gay so I must be doing something that's inappropriate, that is not compatible with my spirituality. That went away. But I remember then saying, "Well, how do I approach my parents?" Because in my case, I was the oldest child; I was the academic star; I was the one who had been on the honor roll, who had gone to college, and all this whole stuff. And by that time my youngest sister had gone to the service, got pregnant, then got married. My brother had had a child out of wedlock, so I was like well, surely to God I can't be the one to unload yet another bomb. And I could not imagine sitting like we're just sitting, and saying, letting the words fall out of my mouth: "I need to tell you all something." Although that's the way I had seen it portrayed on television.

So, the guy that I was dating in Atlanta had gone away for the weekend, and I got a legal-sized yellow notepad and started writing. And I just wrote and wrote and wrote, in long hand, and I wound up with twenty pages on this legal pad, back and front. Not ten pages that equaled twenty, but twenty pages that were back and front. So, announcing to them after like, this long preface of the first several pages, I'm gay. And then proceeding to explain how I knew I was gay, and then a few pages back and, I've met someone, and I don't live in Athens like you think I do, I really live in Atlanta. And by the way, this man is not young, he's forty-three, which was my mother's age at the time, forty-two years was my mother's age at that time. So, he's actually eight months older than my mother. So I remember writing that letter, putting it in the envelope, and I had a little blue Honda Civic at the time, a little three-door hatchback, and I remember riding around with it sitting in the car, in one of those big, brown manila envelopes, like one of those interoffice envelopes. And I rode around with that thing in the car, and I was like, do I drop it, because once I put it in this mailbox, I can't take it back. So it was like a Saturday afternoon and I drove up to one of those blue drops on the side of the street mailbox, and I sat there in front of the thing, it was an office park so there wasn't nobody there but me, and I sat in front of that blue thing, and I remember sitting in there looking at that, looking at that envelope, and I finally reached in the thing and I just layed it on the lid, and I was like, I can still take it back. I can still take it back. And I finally dropped it. And when I drove away from that thing, I started crying when I let it go, because I knew what that was going to mean. I couldn't, I couldn't get it back. I had then made this leap from not only being out to myself, but I was about to out myself to my parents. So I sat around and waited. And my father called me like, two days later, and said, "We got your letter." I said, "okay." He said, "So are you gonna come home and talk about it?" And I said, "Yeah, I'll come home in a couple of weeks and talk about it." And I was more afraid of how my father would react then how my mother would react. [. . .] My mother and I had had a really close relationship. I think it, I think it is because although I've denied every time somebody mentions it, I think it's because to some extent, your parents love all their kids, but I was my mother's shining star, I was her baby that could do no wrong. And my father was always, always seemed like he could be . . . he had a temper so I thought he could be, that would just set him off. So I went home like two weeks later. I sent the letter home the weekend of Easter. I went home, it must have been Mother's Day, because it was one of those years when Easter fell later in the year. And I went home like right around Mother's Day, and my father was outside in the front yard, raking leaves, raking up the ground; he had just cut the grass. And he asked me, he said, "So are you sure? You're sure you're gay?" And I said, "Yeah." I don't even think he used the word "gay," he just said, are you sure? And I said, "Yeah." And he said, "You think you can change?" And I said, "Nope." And he said, "Okay." And then as I was, as we were finishing that conversation, literally that fast, my mother pulled up in the yard with my younger sister. They were coming back from the grocery store. And she walked in the house, walked past me, and then she said, "Why did you have to tell me?" And the whole floodgates just started. Crying and crying and crying, you know, "You didn't have to tell me, I didn't know," she said, "I always thought you were, but why did you tell me?" It was like, why did I tell her. It was more so, she seemed more upset that I had confirmed it than she even knew anything about it. Because she said, "I always thought you were." And she said, I remember her word for it, she said, "How can you be gay? The doctor showed me your thing when you were born and I know you were a boy." And I said, "Well, being gay doesn't really have to do anything with my gender. I'm still a man. So, I'm still male." So . . . she was more concerned about what people were going to say, how it was going to impact my younger sister who was thirteen and still in high school, and would the people be picking on you and making fun of her in high school because her brother was gay, and all this whole laundry list of reasons to push me back in the closet. So she didn't, she had that little fit and then never mentioned anything again.

But I was supposed to stay the night that night and I was in my bedroom, and we had four old *Encyclopedia Britannicas* in our rooms, in my bedroom, like, A through L, M through whatever. And I remember picking up one of them. I think I was looking for the word "homosexuality" or something in the encyclopedia, and a letter fell out, a one-page letter, and it was a hand-written letter that my father was going to write back to me, I guess to re-spond back to my letter. And I don't remember all of the words, I just remember seeing him saying, I just remember reading the thing like, "I don't think I could ever drink behind you anymore because I don't know where your mouth has been now," and I got upset about that letter, and it must have been about two o'clock. I don't think I could sleep that night. It must have been around two or three o'clock in the morning, and I read the letter and I got up, in the middle of the night, packed my stuff up, and made sure I was tiptoeing out the house, closed the door, and got in my car, started crying, and drove all the way back to Atlanta. Didn't say that I was leaving, didn't give them any indication or whatever. I was hurt, having read that letter, and I just got in the car and drove back. And my daddy called me the next day and he said, "When you first got, when you first told me I didn't know how to respond." He said, "I didn't send this to you, but I didn't know how to take it."

So he knew you had seen the letter?

I told him why I had left when he called back the next day, when he called the next day. So he said, "You know, it's gonna take us some time to get used to it, just like you got hurt, we got hurt." My older brother and sister didn't care; the younger ones didn't care. My brother and sisters didn't care at all, period. My sister, Tammy, all she cared about was the sex. "Tell me what you did?" My brother didn't care, period. He mentioned nothing. And my younger sister, it rolled off her back [. . .]; all of my mother's drama about what would happen in high school never came to fruition, so. It just kind of like, stayed there unannounced until I'd mention it again. Although they knew then, they knew to call me in Atlanta. I think my father called one time and left some kind of a Bible verse on the guy's [answering machine] who I was staying with apartment in Atlanta, the guy who I was dating. And I called back and said, "If that's what you're going to say, then you can't call me anymore," and that never happened again. And like three years later my mother finally asked me about the guy that I was dating. It wasn't the same guy; it was somebody else. She said, "See I'm getting better now. I can talk about it." And that was like, 1994. I came out to them . . . I came out to myself in 1990 and to them in '91. I just gave you a really long, protracted story.

No, it's really, really interesting. So, now it's, what, ten years later?

Thirteen years later.

And what's your relationship now with your parents.

It is really good now. I think what they, the first time that I brought someone home, '95, maybe, I brought the guy that I was dating then home, they were really nice and sociable. I thought it went really well. Apparently, it didn't because they were just, it was the first time they got hit in the face with, he's gay and he's going to be bringing men to the house. And when I was going to come home that following Christmas, because I think I had gone home in April with that guy, my mother was like, "Well, you're welcome," and I was like, "Okay. I'm going to come home with the guy I'm dating." [And she said,] "Well, *you're* welcome." And I said, "You know, if he's not welcome, then I'm not welcome either so I'm not coming." So I went home, we had a talk and, I think they were concerned I would come home and do something inappropriate in the house. And I was like, "Well, I'm not going to be in a dress and in pumps, and this guy, and we're not going to be slobbering all over each other." Just like I would expect my brother and his wife not to be slobbering all over each other in front of the grandkids. So we had a, they didn't know what the expectation was, they had never seen two men, not only did they know that I was gay, now they had a picture to associate with the fact that I would be sitting with a man, I would be with a man. So the next person that I took home was this man who I'm in a relationship with now, and that was like 1999, four years later. And it was the difference between night and day. My mother hugged him when she saw him the first time, my father did, my sister did, they, when Ian got ready to leave, my sister said, I think he was trying to shake my sister's hand, she said, "You can't shake my hand now, you're part of the family, you have to give me a hug." So now it's like, they've gone a complete, I guess it's taken them eight years, eight, nine years later, eight years later they've gone a complete 180. And now, we're back to where we were prior to, they just know that I'm gay now [. . .] if they're still dealing with the fact that I'm gay, I don't know anything about it.

And I've always told everyone, I think, my mother I think is deeply religious, I don't think she would ever be the person to be a PFLAG [Parents and Friends of Lesbians and Gays] mother. I just don't think that. [. . .] This is her course of her belief: I think that she loves me because I'm her child. [. . .] She just would not be the person to be, being gay is right. And I don't think she really thinks that being gay is wrong; I think she has just done whatever she had to do to compartmentalize it all in some way and make it work for her. So, and in doing so, our relationship went back to the way it was prior to me sending that letter thirteen years ago. So she's fine with it. She embraces Ian like he's one of the family. She calls and asks for him instead of asking for me. So in Athens they now [they say], "When you all come home, don't get a hotel room, you just stay with us," which is surprising because she did say that, but they don't care. So they've come full circle now, whatever that full circle means for them, they're at that place. And my, my sisters and brother have always been fine with the whole thing. My aunts and uncles have always, I think. I've introduced them to the guys that, I've only brought home two people, and they're fine and the same way: hugging and, come over to eat, and walk down to my aunt house and go home and talk to her, so they're all fine with that. My grandparents were the last two people to come aboard because I think my grandmother, my mother's mother, although that's another one I hate to admit, I think that I was her favorite grandchild too. Because I was a sickly child when I was first born, I had spinal meningitis, and two weeks after I was first born, the doctor diagnosed me with spinal meningitis, and, apparently, according to my mother, had I not gone to the hospital that night I would have been dead by the next morning. So they thought that anywhere up until the age of twelve, it could be recurrent, and I might die still. [. . .] My mother and grandmother were the primary caregivers after I came out of the hospital. So that goes back to your question who has the most influence, my grandmother was always there. And I think she was always, my grandmother always thought that her grandbaby was gonna be the preacher, and the you know just the whole Dublin stuff, somebody was going to take on the family name and continue it going. So . . . although there's many other males in my family, and some of them are preachers, went on to become preachers locally in Dublin, I think she still wanted her baby to be the one. And she was never standoffish to Ian, she just never was— and even to this day I don't think. [. . .] She's eighty-five years old. My grandmother wouldn't use the term "gay" with me ever. My "friend," that's probably as far as she's ever gonna get. [. . .] My mother's father died in 1985, so I never got around to telling my grandfather because that's when I was in high school. And my other father, my father's father, I think he just kinda wound up putting things together, you know. [. . .] He was far more strict and stringent than my father but I know he knew the whole thing 'cause he met Ian, socialized with him, talked to him, but he wasn't ever, I think he, I think were he still living, he was the one who always used to ask me about the granddaughter, the daughter-in-law, when are you going to marry? He stopped that question once I started bringing Ian home. [. . .] I don't think he ever would have been embracing or at peace with the fact that his grandchild was gay—at all.

. . . .

"D.C." (B. 1951, SHREVEPORT, LA.)

You know that's very interesting because I know they know. But my family is like this. They don't discuss it. They never discuss it. My older sister, she and I get along best of all. She loves me to death. But she doesn't discuss it. And if someone tries to discuss it in a demeaning way or something, not about me but just about gay people, period, she will immediately attack or whatever. But no, they don't discuss that. [. . .]

Maybe I'm kind of whacky on this, but I just always sometimes wish and hope that I had a situation like I see some people where they have a family that don't like me because they found out I'm gay. Well, you know, my attitude on that is, if my family started . . . excuse my language, I'd say, "Fuck my family." Because my opinion is this: God made me, He made you. They say God doesn't make mistakes. So I'm not a mistake. And I get so sick and tired of people who call themselves heterosexuals, who think that because they're supposedly heterosexual that they are better or what . . . I think that they're the worst people, as far as I'm concerned, because they are critical. I mean being gay is just what it says, "happy." You know, it's not . . . I can pick up a paper every day and read about these heterosexual people are killing their wives or killing their husbands and doing this and all this kind of stuff. Most crime that gay people are guilty of is loving. And they want to love too much. And too many. [Laughter] You know?

And a thought about not letting them adopt. I have some gay friends who have kids. And you couldn't find any better parents. And I look at some of the jackasses and brats that I've taught, whose mammy and pappy are nothing but sperm donors. They should have crossed their damned legs when they . . . the baby come out, 'cause it's my feeling, "What you did with it after it got here was a sin." But you don't let a gay person have it because they're supposed to be gay. You know . . . I don't want to get in that . . . I get excited about certain things when I talk about them. But go ahead. [. . .] And my mom's gone and all, but my mom knew I was gay.

. . . .

FREDDIE (B. 1944, MADISON, GA.)

Indirectly, I would tell my family members. I remember my father's mother was visiting once [. . .] and I came home and she said, "You got a lot of phone calls. But not one of them was from a girl." So I said—I called her "Ma Book."

Her name was Eva Booker, but we called her "Ma Book." I said, "Ma Book, if you want some girls to call somebody at this number, maybe you should get some girls and have them call you." You know, stuff like that, I would say. And my nephews were two years apart, and at family gatherings sometimes I would call them out, "Chuck, Tommy, come here." And I would pat them on their heads and say, "You all see these [the two nephews]?" And I said, "If she doesn't give you any more, you won't be getting any." Pointing to my sister.

But when I was a teenager, I don't know how old I was, I was home alone and my sister's husband's stepfather . . . I guess my sister's stepfather-in-law or father-in-law because he was the only father my brother-in-law knew [came by]. He was like a Jekyll and Hyde kind of figure. During the week he was this meek, mild-mannered man who would go to the store for you and was very quiet—a real handsome man. He worked for the City of Decatur [Georgia]. And in those days, when you said someone worked for the city, it usually meant he was a garbage man. He worked for the City of Decatur and did yard work for people in Decatur. But during the weekend, when he would start drinking, he would become this other person. He would make his own music and dance to it. You could hear him coming. And I was home alone one day and he came and wanted to use the bathroom. [. . .] The house we lived in, you had to go through the bedrooms, through the kitchen, to the bathroom, which had been an afterthought, I think, on the house. So I was in the mirror, and he came and stood behind me. And so as I turned to ask him what was he doing, he kissed me. He grabbed me and kissed me on the mouth, and I pushed him away and said, "What are you doing?" And he said, "I know about you." I said, "You don't know anything about me." And he had an erection and he said, "I know about you." And I said, "You don't know" and I probably used some curse words. I said, "You don't know a goddamn thing about me." And he said, "Yes I do." And I said, "Well, so what?" So, he wanted me to have sex with him, which I refused to do, or give him two dollars because [chuckle] I think he needed a drink. [Laughter] Another drink. So I said, "No." And he said, "Well, I'm going to tell." And I said, "Well, tell them. I don't care." Because once I knew, or once I accepted or identified that I was homosexual, I decided that I didn't make this decision for me. I did not plant these feelings; they're there; and, I would not be threatened by it or certainly not be blackmailed by it. I didn't announce to everybody, but most people knew. So after that, I was very careful to not let him in the house. And I guess months or a year or so might have passed, and one day I accidentally opened the door and the same scenario repeated itself: either have sex with him or give him money, or he was going to tell. So that night, I refused. And that night, later on, he told my mother. So I heard him start to tell her, and I decided I'm going to go to bed because I had no idea what my mother would do. I wouldn't have been surprised if she had, as they say, "put me out," asked me to leave. So I went to bed. I thought, "If she's going to . . . whatever she's going to do, she's going to have to wake me up, 'cause I'm going to bed." But I heard him start to tell her things and I heard her . . . she didn't respond pleasantly to him. So the next day, she didn't say anything. But in a couple of days or so, my sister started wanting us to have these walks in the park. [Laughter] Something we had never done. But it was so classically my mother. My mother, in many instances, would abdicate . . . if that's the word. People thought my sister was my mother because my mother would send her, my sister, on my mother's behalf. My mother would make some excuse. And even though my sister was just three years older than me, she was heavier and looked considerably older. And so after a couple of invites to go walking in the park, I agreed because I knew my sister wanted to talk about it. So my sister said, "You know, Pete told mother something about you." And I said, "Well, yes, I know." She said, "You do?" I said, "Yes." I said, "First of all, didn't you know? Don't you know already?" And I think she started to cry and said, "No. We didn't know." And I said, "Well, listen, all your friends . . . everybody knows. I thought you knew." What Pete told Mother was that I approached him. And I said, "What he lied about was me approaching him." I said to her, "You know how he is when he's drinking." Because fortunately, Pete had kind of touched all of them inappropriately. I said, "Just the way he has touched you . . ." I might not have used the word "inappropriately," but I said, "Just like he has touched you and other folk. You know how he is when he's drinking." I said, "What he did was he wanted me to have sex with him or give him two dollars. And because I didn't, he told. But I did not approach him. He approached me just like he has approached you and other folk that we know about." Because it was commonly known that when he was drinking he was just a totally different person. So she said, "Well, you know, we didn't know. But we love you anyway. Is there anything that can be done?" And I said, "No. What I heard is that . . . this is the way I am. I am perfectly comfortable with it. This is how I feel. This is how I am. And I have heard that attempts to change it just makes it worse in many instances." So in a couple of days, my mother said, "You know I know, don't you?" And I said, "Yes." She said—and this is one of her crowning moments—she said, "I didn't make you and you didn't make yourself. All I can say is for you to try and be decent." And I said, "Mother, I've always tried to be decent. And I plan to continue." [Chuckle] So that was sort of . . . and you know certainly there were some conversations after that, at some point, about it. But there was a time that my mother and my sister would buy a pair of . . . a new pair of heels, and I would wear them around the house to break them in—at their request. Because our feet were the same size. And all kinds of things, you know, that I thought . . . I just kind of thought they knew. It just wasn't talked about.

So after that, I just continued with kind of an openness. Both of my nephews and my niece think of my partner as Uncle Leroy, because they don't remember when he wasn't there. A few family reunions ago, one of my half siblings from New Jersey . . . a couple of them visited . . . said, "Freddie, Leroy has been around forever, hasn't he?" And I said, "Well, yeah. Since 1965." And she said, "Well, I knew he was always there when we would come visit as little girls." And I said, "Well, yeah, he's always been there, you know."

. . . .

"G.C." (B. 1958, ALBEMARLE COUNTY, VA.)

I'm out to my parents. I came out to my parents thirteen years ago. I was thirty-four years old, and it was a very, very, very tough thing to deal with. I had to deal with the religious side of things because I knew that the deep roots with church was going to be tough for both my mother and father to battle with. But at the same token I've always been a rebel, and by that time it was like you do or you bust. By damn, this is my life, I'm thirty-four years old. I am not going to live a lie the rest of my life. I am going to be happy if it means, if I have to stand alone, I will stand alone, but I will be happy. And also I will not let my parents go to the grave and not know who their real son is.

So how did it go?

Oh, it was horrible. It was horrible. In fact the first day that I wanted to come out, I had had this thing all scraped out. I was going to take my mother out to lunch because I was very close to my mom. We were going to have lunch and at lunch, after we finished eating I was going to tell her. Well, the first time I took her out I swear she must have knew what was going on because she would not let me carry on a conversation, she just kept talking on and, okay, well it's time for you to go back to work and, oh she just manipulated the whole thing. So I choked on it and I said daggone, she must knew something was coming and she just didn't want to hear it. Well, the second time I planned it was about three, four weeks afterward. It was like no, we're going to discuss this. So we had lunch, we walked through the mall. We got back to her car and my car and she got in and I said, "Look, you know I asked you to come to lunch for a reason, and the reason is I needed to talk to you." I said, "As much as I love you and I know you love me, but it's time you know who your real son is." And I said, "I'm gay." And immediately she began to cry and she looked at me and she turned and she goes, "Oh my goodness. I've always had a feeling, but oh my." And she sat there for a while and she said, she began to talk about the religious side of things, "But you know this is just not right, it's not Christian like" and she chatted about that for a little bit, and she cried. She goes, "Well, we've got to talk to your dad." I said, "Well, I would appreciate if you let me tell dad." I said, "But if you so choose to do so, that's fine, you do what you have to do." And my last words before she drove off were, "The only thing I ask of you is not that you accept the fact or agree with it, but that you will continue to love me as your son, that's all I ask." And she drove off. Well, that night I got a phone call with the scriptures being quoted, and I don't remember which ones. I just held my breath and I said, "Okay whatever."

From your mother?

From my mother, yeah. Two days later I get the phone call and she's livid and she's screaming and yelling about something, and I took it and hung the phone up. And this went on for a while. And then she didn't want to talk about it. My dad yet still hadn't said anything, and I have yet to even say anything to him and been in his presence because I know my mom well enough that she's probably, has already talked to him. Well, it wasn't until two months after I came out to her, I went out to visit and she was not home but my father was out in the yard cutting grass, and he stops cutting grass, walks over to me, puts his hand on my shoulder and he goes, "Now, so what's this about you being gay?" And I looked him in the eye and I said, "Dad, it's true, I am." And he said, "Well, you know I really don't agree with it because that's just not what my Bible tells me." He said, "As far as religious side about it, I just can't agree with it. However," and he goes on and he throws his hand up, "we're not going to talk about this again, but you are my son and I love you, and yes I will support you in whatever way you need me to. Now that's the end of the conversation." And that was it. That was it.

Now to go back on this, as I said my mother and I had always had a very close relationship. My dad and I, we were close, but it was rocky. Typical, I'm his only child, his only son. My father was a very domineering person in that his way was the only way. And of course I bucked heads with that because I'm, no I'm not going to do it this way, that's just the way I am. But we got through it. Mom, on the other hand, was the one that blew up; he was the one who was calm. So just what, and I tell everybody this all the time when you're coming out, just what you expect it's going to be the exact opposite. If you expect them to be very calm, be prepared they're going to be outrageous. If you expect them to be outrageous, they're going to be calm. And vice versa with whomever you think of. And sometimes it may be, but it fell just opposite of what I thought. So for about a year, we went through some rocky roads with dealing with my mother before she really got her grips together and fortunately it worked out. But what really solidified my partner and myself and my parents as a unit was seven years ago, 1999, '98, '99, '99, my father had a very bad stroke and during that period of time he was able to really get to know my partner, who happened to be there with him through thick and thin. And who also was there for my mom. They developed a very, very close relationship. In fact, they're probably closer to him now than they are to me. In their eyes he does no wrong. And it's great, it's really great because they got to see him as a person, not as a gay person, but as a person first, then him as a person who happens to be gay, but also is our son-in-law, or our son. They will refer to him either "our son" and "our son-in-law." So it worked out. Sometimes you have to ride the storm, and if you sit there and lay low with it and ride it and don't push, which I was determined, and as I told them in the beginning, I don't expect you to agree, all I ask is you to love me as your son and continue and to give him the respect as a person. So we, and so it's there and I couldn't have asked for anything better.

What about your siblings?

My siblings were fine. The oldest one, of course she said, "I always knew it, I just knew it. That boy could twirl a baton better than any of us." As a kid I did it all. I played kickball. I played dodgeball. I played football, whatever. But I always had an aversion; I don't know why I was always captivated by the baton. I guess it's because I was so mystified because of the shiny thing, this stick that people could throw up in the air and do tricks with, that I was determined; I saw it more of something to do tricks with versus something that girls do. It wasn't so much of a majorette as in the traditional. I saw, I was more into the feature twirler, the one who did the acrobats, the one who could spin it off of a shoulder and wrap it around their neck and the mouth. So I would emulate those things and never took a formal lesson, but by the time I got to high school and tried out for drum major, of course I entered it into my act and a lot of the girls couldn't understand how I could do it better than they could and not do lessons and, yeah, enter contests and walk away with first place doing tricks that would take them six years to learn and I did it in less than a year. So yeah my oldest sister said, "Well, I knew it, but that's okay." My brother was, "Oh that's okay. It's cool, you know, no big deal." My middle sister, she was okay, didn't say a whole lot. She was like . . . I guess too because at that time me being thirty-four and they're all older, they've been there, seen that and all that, by that time they've all either encountered or even had friends who are gay. And my older sister, she had a couple of gay male friends who she just adored. My middle who lived in Richmond, of course she was used to it, she'd seen it all as well. My brother, he'd work with them, so it was no big deal.

....

JAIME (B. 1961, COVINGTON, KY.)

To what extent are you out to your family?

Oh it's, it is out there. [Laughter] [. . .] Rodney and I have been together, this December 17th will be seventeen years. I'm never one to throw what I do up in front of anybody's face. But you know, as I was telling you earlier, when I really came to terms with this, who I was, when I accepted the fact that this is how I was born, this wasn't going to change, I couldn't pray it away, I couldn't go to one of those religious organizations that pretend that it's not there. When I really came to that realization it was like [. . .] somebody being born again in the church. I was born again in my sexuality because at that point I decided I will not let anyone make me feel bad about it. I would not let anyone tell me that what I'm doing was wrong, family included, you know. And I pretty much have always danced to the beat of my own drum anyway. As my family goes, I was probably the rebel when it came to disobeying my parents and that type of thing. I initially left home. I quit high school and left home when I was fifteen. And everybody else kind of went on and did their own little thing. I took a little harder road.

What is your current relationship with your family?

My brothers and sisters know that I love them and their families, and I don't expect them to understand, although I think they all fully do. But the only thing I would ask is don't be disrespectful of me and I won't be disrespectful of you. But, you know, my younger nieces and nephews call my partner "uncle." His nieces and nephews call me "uncle." Just like I don't want to know what they're doing in the bedroom, they don't need to know what I'm doing. It's like I tell them all the time, we've been together seventeen years; we are not doing it just as much as anybody else of seventeen years has been. [Laughter] But I have to say that my family pretty much, as families go and hearing some of the stories of some of the other people's families, because you know it's not an easy thing for any family, and then when you have two people [Jaime's brother, Phil, is also gay (and was also interviewed for this book)]. And then, you know, my baby sister, you know, she goes from one year to the next, she's with a man, then a woman. And then I have a niece who's gay also. So, it's not anything new to them, you know, at this point. And granted I don't ever know how they do when they're not around me, but I do know that they've always been fiercely protective of me. And I've seen that to the point where one night, me and three of my sisters were out one night and I ran into an old friend of mine and she's with some guy who I knew to be a guy that dated drag queens and was messing around himself. I think I kissed her on the cheek or something, and we were at a club. I was maybe eighteen or nineteen, and he was out with her and he made the comment, "You know, don't be kissing on that fag" or something like that. And one of my sisters heard him say it, and the next thing I know the lights are on in the club and my sisters are standing there like, "You gonna call somebody out their name you punk ass, blah, blah, blah. And let's handle this right here and right now. You're not going to call my brother out." And we're not a violent family at all. They've always been that way, and I can't ever say that as far as my brothers and sisters are concerned I feel like I have a problem. Any problem I probably had in that area was more so probably within my own self, becoming outside, you know.

When you left home at fifteen, where did you go?

I moved in, my best friend had a cousin who had an apartment in the projects in Covington called Jacob Price and she had an apartment there, but she stayed with her boyfriend, so she was never there, so we moved into her apartment. And just stayed there.

Did you get a job?

I worked. I worked. What I was, I actually did, because see I never, as I said I quit school, but I always knew that that would not be the end for me, so in between that, at first I, you know, would do all those shifty things to survive because, I mean, I was. I had overstepped my bounds and me and my father had this really knock-down-drag-out where he told me, "You know, from now on with your smartass mouth," he said, "there ain't going to be no belt no more buddy, it's going to be these [cups his fists]." So I made up my mind that I would never raise my hand to my father, wasn't going to fight my father, but you're not going to be putting your knuckles up on me either, so I walked out. You know, it was touch and go there for a while. I was eating toast, dry toast and Snickers. [Laughter] Luckily enough, this girl, the girl who's apartment we were staying in, there was a convenience store down in Covington, and there was this guy that used to work there that liked her. So we would all go up to the convenience store and she would flirt with him and lean over the counter and shake her titties at him and we would be done carried half the store out. [Laughter] That's how I ate initially. And then I just did little things. I started just getting part-time, because I knew, I had a work history. I already knew how to work at that point. Find little odd jobs here and there, doing whatever it took. I mean I was not ashamed to do whatever.

But on the other hand, I was still going to the Covington Adult Learning Lab still trying to study and get my GED, because I knew I wanted to go on and take some college courses or whatever.

So your falling out with your father was more about you just not wanting to follow his rules than you being gay. Or was it a combination of both?

It was a combination of both, Patrick, but I think what it was, I had made up in my mind that, at that point I had told myself that the reason why my father was being so hard on me was because he did, I mean he suspected me. We had never talked about it, there had been little things said and quit acting like a girl. And any effeminate qualities that I have now, I take those and I cherish those and I honor those. And my sister Shirley, she taught me how to throw a football with a spiral; she taught me how to play baseball; she taught me how to fight. So it wasn't like it was all frou-frou feminine. But I was raised by women mostly, so you naturally pick up some characteristics of the people that you were raised by. So I didn't see that as a negative for me. I just felt that, some of my ways and the way I did my hands was because of the influence of the women around me. I didn't necessarily think that that made me weaker for it, because I didn't see the women in my family as being weak, you know? I don't know. I just never really worried about that side of it. Now I look back at a lot of the young guys that are coming out and seem like everybody wants to be a girl. It ain't like I'm just gay, I'm a man that loves a man, it's like everybody wants to put on the dress, and I never understood that. That was never my experience. I mean outside of the fact that I probably slept with men, my life would probably pretty much be considered a heterosexual life.

And how did your other siblings deal with you being gay? The older brothers?

Again, I would have to say that if there was ever a problem or if they ever had a problem with it they never expressed it to me. Four years ago and we had our Thanksgiving down at my mother's old church hall, because no one person's house can hold us all. Before we have our Thanksgiving dinner, which is a whole other story because we have the dinner but we also have a little intergenerational talent show and before dinner we say a blessing and then we all, we give the floor to any individual that wants to say a blessing or tell us what they're thankful for at this point, this, that, and the other. And my brother Wendell had made the comment that we are all family, and he mentioned my partner's name, Rodney, all of us are family and we're all one and just, you know, blah, blah, blah, blah. It was just really touching because we never even had talked about the subject at all. Ever. I mean they've always known.

For one thing they probably would be scared of what might come out of my mouth had they said something to me in the first place. Because I do remember my sister Robin, you know fifteen was a really rough time for me because I was just lashing out because you know, as I said, you go to bed Sunday night praying that you know something's wrong, that you're trying to pray it away, it's not going, you just have anger and I had anger. I was hanging with this guy; his name was William Gray. He probably had some kind of crush on me at some point or this, that, and the other. He had hit on me a couple of times, and I just rebuffed him and told him politely, "I'm sorry William, but I am in no way . . . ," and you know, I never played with him and all that, but he was a teacher at the time, plus he owned some property, and I was out on my own and I had to work, so I would do little odd jobs and help him and that kind of thing, so I don't know if he kind of got the wrong idea behind that. But I pretty much had to tell him there is never going to be a day, ever, that I'm going to be sexually attracted to you, ever. It just gets on your nerves after a while. But my sister had been home and told my family that it's all in the neighborhood that that's who I'm sleeping with. So I'm thinking, "No, this bitch didn't." So I go home, and it was one of them Sunday afternoons. Whatever went on during the week, usually on Sunday the committee was there, and they were discussing the transgression before the whole family, putting the vote before the family court to see if you was going to be ostracized or shunned or whatever for that week until the next week. And of course, you know, I was always before the family court. I always had something going on. But, yeah, Miss Baby [his sister] tried to root me in front of my whole family because I was talking about her boyfriend at the time, her fiancé; it was her kid's father. They were going through some drama and fighting and arguing and this, that, and the other. She said something smart aleck to me and I said something smart aleck back to her in reference to her boyfriend, and she made the comment that [in surly tone] "At least I'm sleeping with the right sex." And that was the first time I ever remember just getting mad because I was up to her clean in the eye in front of my mother, father, brothers and sisters, and everybody. I told her, I said, "Sweetheart," I said, [snaps his fingers two times] "The problem is you're just mad because I'm doing it right." And I said, "You're mad because that worthless man you got ain't doing nothing for you and at this point I can have my pick," because it just made me so mad, and it wasn't true. We weren't doing nothing. I didn't want him, but you know me, all you have to do is throw me a bone and I'll bite. And I did; I told her, I said, "If I am fucking him, you're just mad because as a man he's treating me better than your man should be treating you and that seems to bother you for some reason." And didn't nobody said a word to me after that. I guess they said, "This son of bitch is clean, straight up crazy now." When I finally said I was leaving home, I guess they said, "boohoo."

· · · · · · · ·

JERYL

Jeryl is one of several men I met through Duncan Teague. He was born in Americus, Georgia, in 1971, the youngest of four children. Americus is a small city in southwest Georgia, the birthplace of Habitat for Humanity. The interview took place on November 9, 2004, in Atlanta, where Jeryl now lives.

It was the night of my junior-senior prom, and my senior year in school and I had asked this young lady to go to the prom, and she turned me down. And I don't know why she turned me down; in my mind I came up with several reasons—maybe she knew I was gay, maybe she couldn't afford the dress, or whatever the reason—but I had made a few friends who also were experiencing some of these same sex feelings. And, I received a call, a few days before the, junior-senior prom, saying, hey, a group of us are going to Columbus, a neighboring town, to this bar, would you like to come along with us? So knowing that my parents would never agree to this, I said sure, and I had a car, when I was young, so I took my car and parked it somewhere there in town, and got in the car with one of the guys, and we went to Columbus, and we had a big time. And about midnight or one o'clock we thought, okay we should start getting back to Americus. And, about halfway there, there's this long stretch of road, the car broke down. And, you know, there we were, and we walked and tried to figure it out, and tried to fix the car and ask for help, and did everything we could do at that point in time. Of course, no one had cell phones then. About seven or eight o'clock in the morning, a hunter coming through town was going towards Americus and agreed to take us, if we would pay him. And, so I had a little money in my pocket, I don't know what I gave him, but I gave him a few dollars for taking us, and he dropped us off at my car and I took my friends home, and went, home. And, there were cars lined up and down the driveway, and down the street. In the house, there were relatives, there were teachers, there were neighbors, there were family friends, everybody got the phone call that Jeryl was missing. That was a pretty devastating experience. So I initially lied and told my parents that I went to the prom and that I went out with friends and had a little accident on the way home, and my father said. "Okay, come and show me, where you had the accident." And we rode around for a while. I couldn't find a suitable spot to say, this was it. So, we pulled over and he said,

"Okay, what's really going on here?" And I said, "Daddy, I'm gay." And that's how I told my father, and he cried. And we had very little conversation, you know, back and forth at that point. I think he asked me, why I felt that way, what the experiences were like. And I remember trying to explain it by saying that, "My homosexuality came to me, Dad, as naturally as your heterosexuality came to you." And we went home, and for some reason he told me to go back to their room. And I went back, and a few minutes later my mom walked in and said, "Your dad says that you have something to tell me." So I told her, and suddenly everyone knew. So that's how I came out to my parents.

. . . .

JOHN
I met John through my colleague Dwight McBride, who grew up with him in Belton, South Carolina, a small rural town (population less than 7,000) in the northwestern part of the state. John was born in Belton in 1966, one of two children. Although he goes by the name John, his family calls him Reggie. The interview took place on May 14, 2005, at his home in Clemson, South Carolina.

I came out to my mother and father. Before I graduated from Clemson years ago, he [his father] would come to pick me up on the weekends sometimes, to bring me home. And I remember one time specifically he said, "Reggie, you don't seem to ever say anything about any girls. Son, are you gay?" And I said, "Well, Daddy, you know I'm just so busy in school. I try to keep my grades up. There's just stuff I don't have time for, you know." So I lied to him to his face. And years later, one night I was at school, and my mother called on a Tuesday night . . . and I know it was a Tuesday night because I was watching *Thirtysomething* that used to come on. I used to love that show. And I said, "Who is calling me during my show?" [Laughter] So I answered the telephone, and my mother said . . . I don't know if she said people had been talking about me. She never said the word "gay." She said, "Well, is it true?" And I just knew when she said it. I knew what she meant. She didn't say "gay" or "homosexual" or anything like that. She just said, "Is it true?" And I said, "Yes." And I just heard the air, you know, leave her as she just [exhales]. So then she went into the little spiel about the Bible says this, that, and the other. And that's how I came out to my mother—over the telephone. And the funny thing is my father doesn't have to this day a problem with it. And I kind of got upset about that because, in my mind, him getting upset about his only son—well, I have a half brother, but the only son with his last name—about his only son not carrying on the family name that, to me, would have made him upset. But when I talked to him, when he didn't get upset, I thought he didn't care. You know. But he said, "You know it's your life. Live the way you want to live. I don't have a problem with it." That's ideal for everybody, except me. I just thought that he should have been involved enough, or he should have cared enough to get upset about it. And he didn't get upset. And I can't fault him for that, but I guess I just wasn't, you know . . . that's where my head was. But my mother, she had a problem with it, and that was the reason why I just dropped out of the picture for like years and years and years, and only came back into their lives when she was diagnosed with ALS. It's like Lou Gehrig's disease, where you lose most of your muscular functions. She was diagnosed with that. And the way I found out about that was that one day here, on a Saturday . . . If you notice I can tell you the days when things happen, but anyway, one Saturday, I was expecting a friend of mine from Simpsonville to call, but it was her instead. And I answered the telephone and . . . I don't know if she knew it was me, but when I heard it was her, when I heard her voice, I pretended like I wasn't who I was and I said, "I'll take a message for him and have him call you back." And I called her back later and then she told me about her condition, and then I went home shortly thereafter. And then from that point, I've been going home. And I got back with my family from that point forward.

So you came out to your mother in your senior year of college?

No, I came out to her in 1989. I took a whole lot of time out of school, so when you say, "senior year," what year is that? In 1989. And yes.

And then because of her reaction, you stopped going around all of your family? Or just your mother?

All of my family. I mean I didn't go to Belton for years. And that's not too far from here. I just divorced myself from Belton and everything about Belton.

Is that because your mother told other people in the family and they had issues with it?

No, she didn't. I think part of it was that I wasn't always close with my family and when this came up, it was something that just drove us apart further. And so I just said, "Well, I'm going to cut my losses now and go off on my own." Because I felt that at that time—I've since changed my opinion—that I hadn't lost much. And I just said, "Well, you know, I don't need this in my life, so I'll just get rid of it and start fresh." And basically that's what I did.

So it wasn't because they put you out or . . . You said, "I don't want to have anything to do with them"?

Yeah. I think it was largely my decision. I don't think I was ready to grapple with them. I think it was something that would have involved me assessing my love for my family, you know. I just wasn't emotionally mature to go through that. I thought [. . .] this is a hassle, emotionally. I'm not going to deal with that. I'll just deal with it on my own.

What's your current relationship with your family?

I'm back in the fold. [Laughter] I see my father. Well, he's a busy man so I don't see him that much. But I see my father and I go home occasionally and call and this, that, and the other.

And what is your relationship with your sister?

It's good. But it's strained. Maybe that's too strong a word for it. But there's a challenge to it. Last August—on a Saturday. [Laughter] They were coming from a cruise, a family cruise, and they had stopped at my parents' house in Belton on their way back up to D.C. And my sister's husband and two kids . . . Wayne is my sister's husband's name. I was saying goodbye to them because I wasn't going to be there the next day and they were leaving the day after that or something. So I was saying goodbye to them. And Evan is seven and Courtney, my niece, is eighteen. I was saying goodbye to both of them: "Bye, Courtney. Bye, Evan," you know, hug, squeeze, squeeze. [Mock hugs them] I later found out that my brother-in-law had a fit that I was touching his son, my nephew. As if to suggest that I was giving some type of sexual innuendos or, you know, molested him in full view of my family—I mean not that I would do it anyway, but would I be so stupid as to do that in front of my family? Well, when I found out that he said that, when my sister told me that . . . and she decided to tell me that because . . . you know it wasn't that her fears were affirmed. It was nothing like that. She feels as I do, as my father does. That this is totally Wayne's issue and he is totally off base with this reaction. She felt she had to let me know where he was coming from. And that's fair. That's fair. But you know that really hurt me. And you know I think he's big in the church too. He just drove a wedge between me and my sister. And I can't [tell her to] divorce him. That's a little bit overkill, but that's the challenge we have is that she has him as a husband. He doesn't feel comfortable with just me around Evan anymore. He says, that "Whenever you see him in the future, you just wave at him, just say 'hello.' " THAT'S EXTREME! I can't accept that. And so it's been my reaction to, you know, cut my nose off to spite my face. So well, he's out of my life. Evan included. I don't need that. And that's something . . . that's really tragic.

So you don't go around him at all?

No. I mean that just happened last August, and I haven't had the chance to, you know, with them living in D.C., you know, we don't get a chance to see each other that often. But this summer, well actually next week, my father's going to my niece's graduation from high school. It's not been presented to me that I should come. And actually my father told me that he was going. My sister told me that my father was coming. So it's just not been something that's been made known to me, and I just feel like it's almost by design, that I'm not welcome. And it's not from her perspective. She's in the middle and I recognize that. But if he wants to play this game and it's not a game because there are lives involved. If he wants to be that way, well then you know fine. That's your son. You raise him the way you see fit. But he doesn't realize how much he's limited Evan's behavior. And by that I mean the fact that he even suspects that Evan could be influenced like that. Any behavior outside of this narrow line that he must walk on is going to be construed as being gay. And I really hate that for him.

· · · · · · · ·

JONATHAN P.
Jonathan P. is an architect who lives in Durham, North Carolina. He is one of the many people I met through Curt, my friend who was murdered (see the Epilogue). Jonathan was one of the key organizers of the memorial for Curt and of the scholarship started at Duke in his honor.

Jonathan was born in Houston, Texas, in 1974. He is the younger of two children. The interview took place at his home on August 18, 2004.

I haven't. Well, I did with my sister back in '98 when I got out of school, which was an interesting time, that August, August 26, 1998, coming out of school, coming into Savannah, Georgia. In '93 when I left home to go to school I was running, mentally I think I was running away from home, simply because I had to go find myself. I couldn't do it at home, even if I found a school I could go to at home, I couldn't do it because the context of my home and my family and you know, church and whatever. So, I had to get away. I ran away. So, in doing so, being away from home about five, six years, and moving to Savannah, Georgia, I had to reconnect back to my family and the closest person that I could reconnect to was my sister. We were more alike than anything else. I called us two as thick as thieves. [. . .] She was struggling in school. She had to find money to pay for school, so she went into the reserve. And so she was doing her boot camp and she wrote me this touching letter, and we were trading letters back and forth, and one day I told her in a letter. But I think that she didn't get it until I came home one summer. She wasn't quite surprised because, like her, like everybody else, even if I were straight, I'm still strange. [Laughter] So, you accept my strangeness before you accept me being gay. So we were tight. We were tight when I was small. In fact, she was the only person I was close to when I was growing up, you know, when I talked about not having any friends. She would be the only person, I would bother occasionally, because my love and affection for her would show up as teasing her or getting on her nerves, or whatever, or moving into her room while she's out of the house or something. So she would be the first one. She would be the first one.

Eventually, I told my cousin Audrey, because we're more alike too. It's funny, my cousin Audrey and my sister could be on the same level as me, but they're coming from different, opposite directions in my life. So, it was her and Cousin Audrey, and then, it was just right there, that's all, I left it to those two people. Now, maybe throughout two, three years, when I lived in Georgia, I think maybe my brother had figured it out. I mean no one has come out and asked me, or said it. I only think my brother figured it out because my sister called me one day, she said, "You know Jerome called me one day when you was in college and asked if you was gay." I said, "Why did he do that?" She said, "He said because when he came in, when he called you when he was living in Hampton, that your roommate would pick up the phone and he would sound so feminine." So he asked me, this was you know, years before, if I was gay. I said, "What did you tell him?" She said, "I don't know."

Well, when I moved to Savannah, Georgia, in '98, I stayed with my brother for two years. I stayed with him for a couple of months, then moved out and stayed for two years in a townhouse, and I moved back in for about a couple of months before I left to come here. But my sister-in-law made the funniest comment when I told her I was moving to Raleigh, North Carolina. She was sitting on the stairs, she goes, "Oh you're moving to the, you moving to North Carolina, wow! That's the Bible Belt country. Do you think you can handle it?" My sister-in-law graduated from Columbia University; she's a lawyer, so she has plenty sense; so she was saying to me, without spelling it out. I was like, "Oh, yeah, yeah," and left it at that, you know.

Do you think you will come out to your mom at some point?

Okay. Like, after two years living in Savannah, Georgia, my ex at the time, we took a trip; we took two trips. He's from Chicago and I'm from Houston, so for my vacation we went to Chicago. He was out to his family. For Thanksgiving, we went down to Houston. [Chuckle] Went down to Houston, and so he came in, and I think that first night, we slept in separate bedrooms, but I wasn't all too quite comfortable having my boyfriend sleeping in my parents' house. As much as I thought it was okay, I didn't think it was comfortable. So the second, third night, I slept over my aunt's house. We slept over my aunt's house, for a couple nights. But I think when we left to go back to Georgia and I went to go visit my grandmother, my grandmother made a slight comment.

She says, "Yeah your cousin told me you was going to bring your partner down here." [Chuckle] You know how old folks put words together, just kind of slurring it all together. I said, "Yeah." And to this day, she keeps asking, "So how is your friend, Derrick?" Or my aunt would say, "So, how is your friend?" You know. Or my, other aunt, from Denver, I remember Curt and I went over to her son's house for a Superbowl party. This was like, two years ago. So, this is how I know I think my family knows. Word got back around to me through my cousin in Greensboro, she calls me and says, "You know your aunt Alice's asking about Curt, because she thought it was Derrick." I said, "How does she know Derrick's name first of all, and why is she asking who is Curt?" She says, "You know, I don't know, but she was asking because she knew, because she was asking about what he do for a living, and da da da." I said, "Well first of all, it's not Derrick" and I hadn't seen Derrick in two years. "Second, you know Curt is my friend." And she says, "I know all that but I'm just saying, I got a phone call from Aunt Alice." You know, stuff would come around like that, you know. But, to put the topping on the cake, my parents never asked me about marriage; they never asked me about kids; they never asked. And I think, to some degree, again, that word, "gay" is, still, I don't hear it. I don't hear it from my parents' mouth. So, I don't know. I think to some degree that I did come out, but not in the way that everybody else would come out. You know, who would bring their male friend over for a couple of days for Thanksgiving?

How would you describe your current relationship with your parents?

Good. [. . .] When I bought this house, pretty much I had weeks and months to prepare for my housewarming. And my housewarming was a turning point, literally and, as a symbol of my life, because, at that point, I invited everybody. I invited my gay friends; I invited church members; I invited my entire family—my aunts, uncles, first cousins, my grandmother, the young adults from church, people from work. This is who I am. I am here, living in Durham. I'm not saying, I'm not preaching to them that I'm gay. I'm saying this is who I am, that I'm living in Durham now. I bought this house, this lovely house, and this is where I live, all are welcome. All are loved. So, three weeks ago, when that happened, my mother, my father, my brother just, by a blessing, got back from Iraq, that same weekend, and they drove up here, him and his wife, and his children, and his mother-in-law, and his sister's niece and nephew, they all slept downstairs. My cousins from Tennessee and her husband and little child, one year birthday, my cousin from D.C.—my two cousins from both sides of my family, from D.C. my aunt and uncle from Denver, my other uncle from Denver, my ten, fifteen people from Houston. Yeah, so it was a big family, almost like a family reunion. And so, open house was that Friday night here, and then we had some activities in Greensboro, Saturday and Sunday. So when they arrived, I of course had church people already here. And my job was in the kitchen. And they arrived, I was like, "I'm here. Here I am." And when everybody started eating, before we started eating, they asked me to do a prayer. I was like, "I cooked the food." Then I asked my father to say the prayer, the blessing; once he said the blessing of the food, I felt complete. I felt complete, because my parents never came to any place where I stayed. I felt complete. I didn't have a good solid relationship with my mother and father only because I couldn't talk to them, personally. I can now, but I don't. I don't talk to them. I talk to my mom a bit, tell her if I'm depressed or something, but I won't tell them, "Oh, you know, my boyfriend . . ." I don't do that. Me and my sister does that, but there's no reason to do that with my parents, they already got problems between themselves.

. . . .

KEANAN

Keanan is one of the narrators I met through a mutual friend in Atlanta. Keanan's parenting parallels that of many narrators who were raised in single-parent homes. Surrounded by women, male role models were sometimes few and far between. Nonetheless, Keanan does not attribute his being gay to not having a father figure. Estranged from his biological father, Keanan did receive guidance from his stepfather during his teenage years after his mother remarried. Later in life he tried to establish a relationship with his biological father. He has a teenage daughter himself. An only child, Keanan was born in Griffin, Georgia, in 1967. Griffin is a small town located forty miles south of Atlanta. The interview took place at his home on October 31, 2004.

Strange enough, you know, I do have a daughter. I have a fourteen-year-old daughter; she'll be fifteen in February. And you say, wow, how did that come about? But it happened, and I'm glad that that happened. At one point in time, I kind of regretted it because—not because she's here, but the way in which the whole thing came about. And the timing just was not right. I was in college and it was like wow, I am just not prepared for this, what am I going to do? That type of thing and that type of responsibility as to I wish that I would have waited. But looking at it in hindsight, you know, if it didn't happen then, it would not have happened. And I have so many friends who are gay that part of them, you know, I won't say they envy me, but they're like, "Well, wow, you have a kid, you know, that's something I've always wanted," or "That's something I probably may not experience or get an opportunity to do unless I adopt or, you know, go through a whole big legal battle and artificial insemination and all of the above," and etc., etc., etc. And I value the relationship that I have with my daughter. I have not shared this aspect of my life with her. If and when it comes up, and it will come up, and when she gets to the point where I think she can deal with it and handle it, then of course I will let her know because I'm not going to live a lie or be in a closet or, you know, keep that away from her. But I don't think that—and even with my parents, they don't necessarily agree with my lifestyle but they, you know, love me in spite of. And that love is unconditional. And my mom clearly told me that, you know, "Well, what you're doing is wrong and I don't condone it and"—I mean "I don't agree with it, you know, I don't support it. But if that's the route you've chosen to go," and I think she knew early on anyway, so. She came and asked me one day if I, you know, if I liked men. [Laughter] And I'm like, "What do you mean, do I like men?" I was like, "Well, yeah, I like them. I don't dislike them. Why do you ask me?" She's like, "Boy, don't play with me. You know what I'm talking about," that type of thing. And so once she asked that question, that opened up a whole other can of worms. And we sat down and we had that conversation. And, you know, it was like here I am being cocky, you know, well, let's just go in and get this over with. "What is it you want to know? And let's just ask all these questions because I ain't"—this is me talking to her. "Because two weeks from now or a week from now, you see something on TV or you hear about something, I don't want you calling me, asking me all these questions and all this stuff." And she was like, "Boy, I'll call you when I want to and ask you what I want to ask you." So, you know, that whole thing, "I brought you into this world, I'll take you out." So that was that authority. But it was great. My mom is my best friend. We have a relationship. We talk two and three times a day, if not more than that. I'm very close to her. But we had that conversation and it was good. I have not brought a partner or a friend or anyone that I was dating home to meet the parents, if you will, because I don't want to put my parents through that. If I was in a relationship long-term and I knew that this was the person, the soul mate, or at least I had an inkling of an idea that this was going to be someone that I'm going to be with for a long period of time, then yes, he would meet my parents. But that has not happened yet.

You sort of answered this with regard to your mother, but to what extent are you out to other family members?

I'm not. I had an uncle—well, they know, because my mom has told them, you know. Her brothers and sisters, she can't hold water to some degree. [Laughter] But, you know, I have an uncle who is deceased, he knew. And he even talked to me about it. And, of course, I did not—I'm like, as I'm sitting here thinking, man, you must be crazy, you think I'm going to tell you, for you to run back and tell my mom. But I understood his position because he was there and he wanted to help me. And if I needed to talk to someone, I could talk to him. And, he even said, "Well, you know, if you think you may need counseling and want to talk to somebody, you can, you know, let me know." And I'm like, "Whatever." I'm not going there, I'll deal with this on my own. But, he's deceased, he knew. My aunt whom I lived with for a period of time knew. And that's how the whole thing came about. When I say the whole thing coming about, you know, she had a conversation with my mom and told my mom, you know, "All these guys keep calling here." Silly for me not to get separate phone lines. I was staying with my aunt at the time. And, you know, that stemmed the conversation with my mom asking me. And, of course, my aunt knew. And then, so, I mean, there were other family members that know or whatever. And it may be discussed among their immediate family but the extended family, it's one of those things, it's not discussed. And I didn't have to show up at anybody's wedding or funeral with a partner or what have you, so wasn't no big deal.

. . . .

"KEVIN" (B. 1981, MEMPHIS, TENN.)

Ooh. Put it this way: they know. I've explained it to them in this way. I said that I realize that I like men, you know. I've never gone into detail about sex with other men with them, oh my God, because I'd rather die. But with that, I told them don't look for me to invite anybody over; we're not going to dinner. I said, "I'm not trying to be a woman, so you don't have to look for me to be trying to dress up in women's clothes. I'm not trying to take whatever role you all think that women should have." I said, "I just like being with another man sexually. And I'm not attracted to all men." I [. . .] I said, "Well, and not to say I'd go for every man. I'm not the one that pursues them, they pursue me." I said, "But with that, you're not going to be shamed by it," is what I tell them. "I'm not going to make a fool out of you or myself all because I like being with another man. At the same time, I don't expect you to fully understand," I said, "but I also don't expect you to disrespect me, because I'm not going to disrespect you. I'm not going to bring anything up in your house." Nobody's ever come to the house with me. There's been no sex that has been had by me in the house ever. And I plan on keeping it like that as long as I'm there.

So you live at home?

Yeah, I currently live at home with my parents.

So you told both of your parents?

Yeah. How I ended up telling my dad—I mean they knew, you know they knew, growing up they knew about that. Or they at least sensed it, but that was the big taboo, once again especially in the black Baptist Church. And so with that, my dad I remember, when I moved back home after University of Memphis, moved back home and things were just so tense, all because at that point we weren't going to the same churches. By that time I was playing in my uncle's church. I had left my dad's church; he had been pastor for maybe two years at that point. So things were a little tense and the communication where it once used to be was not because we were growing up, and so I think we were all having issues, you know, trying to adapt to those changes. I remember one time my dad said, "Come on and go with me," because we had just had an argument at the house, which was totally rare and out of the normal. So it's like, I think that's why I probably didn't end up getting slapped like I should have, because it was out of the normal. So it's like okay well we see something is wrong somewhere, so somebody needs to talk. That was always me. So we left and we talked, and I remember one night I told him, "Well, there have been some things that I've been dealing with for years I felt that I could not share with you." I said, "Yet I don't want you to feel that what I'm about to tell you is your fault. It's not. You all had nothing to do with what happened in preschool. Absolutely nothing to do with it." I said, "It wasn't like I saw something that was here in the house." I mean, I saw a wonderful relationship between my parents, who've been married, I think it'll be twenty-four and twenty-five years this year. So I've seen a healthy and a wonderful relationship with what's supposed to be between a man and a woman. I said, "But when you get finished, my sexual desire did not come from you all. It came from another little boy touching me at school and that's, you know, only thing I knew about it." My dad, now he cried, he started crying because he said, "I just wish I could have protected you." And I'm like, "Well, Dad some things . . ." But then he said, "Well, this has happened for whatever reason and I just hope that you're able to take whatever it is and live your life to the fullest." So I'm like, "thanks." And with my mom it was like, because she and I are so much alike, I can sit here and like have a conversation with you now and not be so, I'm probably much more graphic or would be much more graphic, but sometimes I don't even have to say too many words for her to understand exactly what I'm talking about. With her, it hasn't been the same sit down, enter the conversation like I had with my dad, but with my mom, we haven't had to be so, I haven't had to be so detailed with her. But she knows and she's gotten the same spiel about ain't nobody going to be coming to the house and all that same stuff.

And your sisters? You came out to your older sister in high school?

Oldest sister, I came out to her in high school. Now my youngest sister, by the time I got to Christian Brothers and University of Memphis and I had my own place, I just sat her down and just broke it all down. I told her everything, though. There were a few limited things I told my older sister. My younger sister and I, we've always been close—but there was that area that we just didn't talk about. She and I played together the most. She and I shared bottles. We were just really cool as we got older, it's like we've just become closer. She's my best friend. I tell her everything. Same way she does too, so [. . .] it's like, I guess you could say father, son, holy ghost, and then Cassandra you know. But she knows just as much as they do.

· · · · · · · ·

KEVIN W.

Kevin W. and I met through Ian Barrett. He was born in 1962 in Washington, D.C., the youngest of three children. He currently lives with his son in Atlanta.

Everybody in my family knows. I shouldn't say everybody in my family knows. Everybody in my immediate family. So my mother, my brother, and my sister know. My father is deceased. And I didn't come out to him before he passed away.

And how did that experience go, the coming out to them?

It went fine. I told my sister first because I had just gotten out of my first relationship and I was hurting. And my sister had always been able to make me feel better. And so I had to tell her that I was gay first so that she could understand what I was then telling her about. And all she did was jump up and hug me and say, "Thanks for telling me." And then, it was probably three or four years later before I told my mother. And the delay wasn't that I thought that anything was going to be different. I really didn't think that anything was going to be different, because my mother and I, all of my family have always been close. I just wasn't sure that if telling her, what that was going to do, what that information of her knowing, how was that going to benefit her or not, you know, what was I going to do. And that was my primary reason for not telling. I just couldn't figure out. So I'm telling her now and so what. But the other thing that was nagging at me was I kept thinking if I get hit by a truck and all these friends are at my funeral, I didn't, wouldn't want her to feel like I didn't trust her enough to tell her this aspect of my life. And that's actually what it came down to. I really just felt like I was hiding. But not negatively hiding, but I just wasn't sharing a part of my life with her. If something happened [. . .] I thought that she would actually be mad at me because I didn't trust her enough to share that. And then I told her. Then she said, "You're over twenty-five, you're not married, what else was there to think." Just like that. She said, "You didn't really need to tell me, but if it makes you feel better telling me, then I'm glad you told me." And that was it. And literally the next day and every other day, nothing else had changed, which is just what my sister and I had discussed. Nothing was going to change because our mother loves us no matter what. And it was just, I like the same sex. That was it. And then when I told my brother, who's a Catholic priest. Because my brother's my brother first; he's what he does second. And his first question was, "Do you have anybody to share your life with?" And I said, "no." I said, "Not right now." He says, "Well, I hope you find that, if that's what you want."

Talk a little about your decision to adopt a child and to be a single parent.

Okay. I was living in Greensboro at the time, and it was getting close to my thirty-seventh birthday. I was in a post office line getting stamps, and I don't know what triggered in my head. I don't know if I saw a picture of a kid. I don't know if I saw a kid. I really don't know what the trigger was. No. I'm sorry. I was thirty-three at the time. I said four years from now, when I'm thirty-seven, if I don't have anybody significant in my life, I'm going to adopt. Because I can't imagine kids, I mean I know there are kids out there who have absolutely nobody to take care of them, or to provide for them. And I've had such a blessed life. I have such a rich life. My friend Phil says I have such a charmed life, that if I could make a difference in one, I will do that. Well, then I got to be thirty-seven and, you know, I was busy traveling and doing my own thing, and then a couple years later I was like, well you know, now's the time to do it. And so the decision for me has been real easy just because I have had such a blessed and rich life. And not rich in terms of money by any stretch of the imagination, but rich in terms of support, of friendship, of family, of faith, that that's what I wanted to do.

Do you have any concerns about raising your son as a single parent, as a black gay man in the South?

Yeah, no. My concern is that, and I always have to check myself, is that my frame of reference, my worldview is shaped from having a mother and a father. And so because of that sometimes I think, well what is he missing? Am I allowing him to miss something because he doesn't have a mother or he doesn't have more of a female presence, a daily presence in his life? And even though I couldn't change that even if I were straight, you know, I couldn't necessarily just change that, but I think of that in terms of well, should I move back home to D.C. where my mother and sister could see him more on a weekly basis instead of once or twice a month when they come down or we go up there? But that's really my, I don't really have concerns over being single, being black, or being a gay man. And the other thing I keep in mind is that he really had no one. So you're taking someone who really didn't have anybody to care for them, and you're giving them one parent who's like moving heaven and earth to make sure he's getting everything that he needs, so I think he's going to be okay. And there are lots of people I know who have one parent who are like the world's greatest people. So I really don't have any concerns. I don't have any concerns about us being in the South. I think anywhere I would choose to live be it South, North, East, or West, because of where I would choose to live, they would have the values that I would want, which would be community, which would be people that believe in something and people that believe in being supportive of you no matter what. So, I think that would be wherever I would choose to live. So we live here, and he's got his Uncle Jerry next door, who is clearly not his uncle. You know, he's got his Uncle Bryant, his Uncle Ian, his Uncle Don. He's got all those people that love him and will support him. And so I couldn't be in a better place.

When the time comes, how do you think you'll explain to him your sexual orientation?

Tell him like it is, that people love different people and they don't have to . . . it just doesn't have to be a man loving a woman, or a woman loving a man. I think it's going to be a little bit easier, that I'll be able to point to people and say, like your Uncle Bryant loves your Uncle Ian and they are a couple. That they live together, that they share their life together. That I'll be able to say your Aunt Amy and your Aunt Laura are the same thing. That he sees that. And right now he's not questioning it. And I mean I know there will come a day when he does, but I mean, you know, he sees them, not being intimate, but he'll see them kiss and, I mean he sees me kiss men and he sees me kiss women too. He hasn't ever questioned it. And when Joseph, my boyfriend at the time, I mean, when Monty came he would see us in bed. In the morning, he would come in and he never questioned. What he had a problem with was Joseph being in bed with me because he would get out of his bed and climb in bed with me. That's what he had the problem with. He had the problem with you're in my spot. Not and you're a man. You know? So that's what he had the problem with. So I'm sure there will come a time.

But it's just kind of interesting, you know, we don't talk about gender roles or anything else. But he gets these things literally from the cartoons and things like that. Like his pre-kindergarten teacher, pre-K teacher, he would say, "I'm going to marry Ms. Laurie so she can be a queen." I'm like,

"Well, ipso facto that makes you king," you know. And that's at four, you know; they get these things because to be queen you have to have a king. And because she wants to be a queen daddy. And I'm like, "Okay." [. . .] What concerns me is, I'm sure any parent is concerned by, is the people that he interacts with. What's going to be the impact on him from other people in school or, you know, "your dad's gay" or, you know, whatever they choose to call it. That's my concern. How the rest of the world affects what he thinks. So, you know, my job is to give him confidence enough for him to face anything and just know that he has got the best of all possible worlds.

· · · · · · · ·

KENNETH

Kenneth is one of several men I met through my friend Ian in Atlanta. Of all of those I interviewed in the Atlanta area, Kenneth was definitely the most charming—and hospitable. Although our meeting for the interview would be the first time we met, he insisted on cooking dinner for me: baked chicken, green beans, potatoes, and, of course, sweet tea. It was absolutely delicious.

Kenneth was born in Baltimore, Maryland, in 1965 to working-class parents who had migrated from Alabama. The interview took place in his home in Atlanta on November 10, 2004.

Oh, but I am out to them; they all know. I actually came out to them officially in 1993, right before the march on Washington. I came out to them because I felt that it was important to come out to them, affirmatively, so that they wouldn't just be sitting there watching TV one day and see me, you know, march down a street with a flag, you know. So I felt compelled, that I really needed to tell them.

What was their reaction?

My mother cried. She didn't cry necessarily because I told her I was gay. Listen to this. She was crying because I hadn't told her sooner. She felt like she had let me down or, because I hadn't been able to tell her before I did. And that hurt her. My father was kind of more matter of fact, like he said, "I just want you to be happy. And I may not know much about much more than that." But then [. . .] it was interesting [. . .]; we didn't kind of have any kind of game plan or anything afterwards, but, then they kind of in turn, outed me to the rest of the family, so to speak.

How did that go?

I guess it went well for them. [. . .] I'm glad they did, you know. And you know, both sides of the family have still been very much a part of my life, and very much my family, so, for all intents and purposes it went fine. You know, there wasn't any kind of big blowout, or anything. And actually what was very pleasant about it was that it stopped all those marriage questions. You know? I don't get those anymore. [Laughter]

What is your current relationship with your parents?

As of 5:30 this morning, we were still talking. [Laughter] Because, I talked to them this morning, called my father this morning, you know, so we're still very close. They'll be here in a couple of weeks. So yeah, I had to actually get a new cell phone, get a Verizon phone, because they have Verizon phones, so we can all talk, without using up minutes.

How do you feel about the life choices that you've made, in light of being a black gay man?

You know, I have had my stumbles, my falls. I think the biggest, and best choice I did make was to move, here. That was very much a turning point in my life. Coming out. Choosing to come out was a very important moment in my life. You know, those are choices, that you know, I don't regret. I can't say that I would have done it any differently. I can't even say that I should have come out sooner, because I came out when I needed to come out, when I was ready to. And I remember very clearly in my mind, I said, I'm going to come out to my parents, because at this point in my life, if they decide that they don't want me in their life, I can go on without them. I knew that, because I had built a life for myself. Fortunately, that didn't have to be the choice, but I knew that, if that's what it came down to, I could.

. . . .
KENT

Kent is one of my oldest and dearest friends. We met as freshmen at the University of North Carolina. Kent and I hit it off so well because we share a love for music. He is a gifted self-taught pianist who also loves to sing, and I just loved to sing. We spent hours in the dormitory lounge playing the piano and singing and "acting the fool," as we sometimes say in the South. We joined the gospel choir our freshman year, with Kent serving as one of the main musicians.

Kent was born in the small, rural town of Berea in 1967, the youngest of four children. Located thirty miles north of Durham and thirty miles south of the Virginia state line, Berea has a population of less than 5,000. Kent comes from a family of musicians, as his mother, father, and eldest brother all played the piano. His eldest brother died of complications due to AIDS and was a role model for him as a musician and as a self-actualized gay man. The interview took place at a mutual friend's home in Carrboro, North Carolina, on October 27, 2004.

My sister was the first family member I came out to. As I said, I was twenty-five, and at the time I had met my first long-term partner—my only long-term partner. And we're great friends today and still love each other quite a bit today. But coming out to him is coming out to me. [. . .] It was almost like a fairy tale in a sense. We had a hard time talking to each other about ourselves. And then once we came out to each other, he said to me, "Well, there's something else I have to tell you." And I said, "What is it?" And he said, "The first time I saw you, I felt very attracted to you." And I sort of laughed and said, "Well, I felt the same way." So we . . . everything was out on the table and we thought, "What do we do with this?" And I told him, "Before we move any further, there are some things I need to discuss about me." The first thing being the whole religious thing and reconciling that. But then I felt that if I told a family member that would feel really good and helping me gain some confidence about navigating my way through this. And so I told my sister. And I didn't think I would have a problem with my sister because of my brother, you know? So it paved the way, in a sense. And so I came out to my sister and my brother-in-law at the same time. And about that time, my partner and I had been dating and officially became a couple. And I asked her, I said, "Do you remember him?" And she said, "Yeah, I remember him. He's your best friend now. You're good friends." And I said, "We're more than friends." And at first it went over her head, and then it hit her and she said, "Oh! Okay." And my biggest fear with that was the possible denial of access to my nephew and niece. They are my heart. I know I never really had to worry about that. And then my brother-in-law, he said . . . "Well, I never knew you were gay but it doesn't matter to me." He said, "And as far as the kids go, we're wondering when you're going to take them off our hands so we can have some free time." So that made me feel good and it gave me a big confidence boost. My late brother-in-law never discussed it, but I think it was one of those things that we understood each other. I think my father knew, but I never told him. During that time, he became very ill and he was dying of cancer. That was a burden I didn't want to put on him, nor my mom at that time. I came out to a few friends, a couple of my relatives, some cousins. And then Labor Day weekend two years ago, at the ripe old age of thirty-five, I told my mom. When I talked to my sister years ago, she and I both agreed that Mom would go to her grave knowing . . . not knowing, rather. And you know, the older I got and the more I loved who I was . . . not that I had a problem with self-esteem, but you know? I just saw this as more as being somebody else's problem and not mine. The more confidence you gain, the more I say, "You know what? What if I die before she does? I would have spent my whole life not revealing to her who I am."

At this time, my partner and I were exes. We had split up but we still vacationed together, and I went up to where he lives and I spent some time with him just to get away from my scene. I called back home to check on Mom and see how she was doing. She forgot that I was flying up there. She asked where I was and I told her. And she said something that just really ticked me off. And so finally, without notice I just snapped. And I said, "Mom, you know what?" I said, "The average life expectancy for a black male now is about seventy years." I said, "I've spent thirty-five, half of that, pleasing everybody else." I said, "The next thirty-five are mine and anybody who doesn't like it, I really don't care." I said, "Do you hear me what I'm saying?" And there was silence on the phone. I said, "Do you hear me?" And she said, "Well, all I want is for all my children to be happy." I said, "Well, trust me. I am." I said, "And I'm going to be happy." I got off the phone with her, and I immediately called my sister and I wept. And I just said, "I can't take it anymore." And she said, "What's wrong?" She said, "Calm down." She calmed me down on the phone, and I just said, "I'm tired. I really can't do this. I can't." I said, "Mama's the last hurdle. She's got to know." And my sister said, "She's got to know what?" So I said, "I'm telling her. I've got to tell her." And she said, "Kent, are you sure?" "I've got to." She said, "Well, why don't you take a day or so, think about it, pray about it." She said, "You've still got a couple of days up there. When you fly back, if you still feel that way, you've got my full support, you know that." And that's what I needed to hear. I got back in that Monday. I called her. I took the afternoon off from work. I said, "Mom I'm coming up there. We need to talk." And that was the last . . . as far as I'm concerned, that was the last major hurdle for me.

What was your mother's reaction when you actually had that conversation?

She was in disbelief. She claimed she didn't know, but to me, I think mothers know. I just really do. And then a lot of it was from her actions. When my ex and I were a couple, we basically participated in a lot of our family functions. My ex is a white, Italian American midwesterner. So he didn't have any family down here. And so we did things with my family. Sometimes we went on holidays and even my sister's fortieth anniversary, he was right there with the rest of my family. And my Mom would make sweet potato pies. In my time in undergrad I probably got three or four in all. She made him one about every other week and would fuss at me, she'd say something like "That's his. Don't you eat it," you know? And I'm thinking to myself, "Okay is there something you want to tell me?" And there were times when she would say things that would make me think, "Okay, she knows." And I thought, "Well, maybe this will open the door." Then I got to the point where I thought, "Well, I won't say anything, but if she asks me I won't deny it, I will tell her." But she never did. And so like I said, it finally got to the point where I just couldn't take it anymore.

And so she knows, and do you talk about it or . . . ?

We haven't. We actually haven't talked about it in a while. I told her. When I told her we had a lot to discuss. Of course the Bible thing came up. Of course I'd done enough research too, you know; it was easy defending any of the claims, whether it be Old Testament, New Testament. I think I can hold my own with any preacher in the country. I've actually read Greek and Hebrew translations. And I know about the nuances of Greek and Hebrew words, what they mean in certain contexts, and what the social order was during those times and how different they are today. Case in point, she and I were talking about Leviticus, of course. My favorite. And I said, "Mom, you're a widow and you have two male sons left. Neither of your sons lives in the city limits like you do. You're considered an outcast, a social outcast by ancient biblical law because you don't have a male relative to take care of you." I said, "You and I both . . ." I said, "As many churches that you've sung and played in . . ." I said, "You are a pillar basically in this town. People know you and respect you." I said, "You're not supposed to have that kind of position, according to ancient Hebrew law." She sort of looked at me and then I said, "And if you want to be really literal, then I'll . . ." And she said, "Well, that was Old Testament." I said, "Let's look at David and Jonathan." I went there and I showed her the whole story of David and Jonathan, and read it to her, and how their souls were knit together. And even after David assumed the kingship and Jonathan and his father died in battle, the news got back to David that they had died. And David lamented, saying that Jonathan's love for him "surpassed the love of women." That's Samuel 2:1–26. I showed her those words. She was . . . she had nothing to say. And I left the conversation and I said, "Mom, I told you. The only reason I told you is so that you would know." And it's not that my mom ever actually did or said anything homophobic; it's just that she needed to know. And I said, "If there are any questions, any time that you want to ask me, or anything you want to say, ask me." I said, "I'm now an open book. I've got no secrets from you now." There were a couple of times in the course of a year that she might have mentioned one or two things. I took her to visit a friend of hers in a nearby town, a childhood friend, and her friend remembered me from when I was a kid playing the organ at the church and everything. Of course she saw me and she said, "Married yet?" That question came up and I said, "No, I'm not." "Well, why not?" I said, "Well, you know, some people just aren't the marrying kind." And I left it at that. This woman, who had recently lost her husband and was probably still in mourning, I guess she felt it was her duty to get the world married. [Laughter] And she was going to start with me. But I wasn't going down like that, and so finally my mom decided that she was going to jump into the conversation, which surprised me. And her friend said, "Well, you know what?" She said, "God just . . . you just can't give up. God just hasn't sent you the right one yet." And I said, "I'm pretty sure." I said, "In fact I know I won't be getting married." And she said, "Well, you never know what God has in store." And then my mom opened up her mouth and said, "Yeah that's right." And I looked at my mom with this look like, "No, you didn't just say that." And so I looked at her friend and said, "Excuse me." And I looked at my mom and said, "Mom, I'm not getting married. You know I'm not getting married. And we both know why." My mom said nothing else the rest of the visit. And on the way home, I took her back to her apartment, and I said, "Mom, this is very new to you. And I told you what I told you because I felt you needed to know." I said, "For future reference, I don't need you to defend me in a situation like that." I said, "Before I told you, I've had to deal with people like her, and whose intentions were good." And I said, "I've even had to deal with a couple of nasty people. But I know how to defend myself. And I don't have to come out to do it. I don't need you to make excuses for me." Well, that sort of opened the floodgates and I intended to take her back to her place and just leave and go back to Chapel Hill, and she instead kept me there. I didn't leave her place until like twelve midnight. She just had question after question. And they were earnest questions. They were questions that she was really interested in and she wanted my take on. So we've had those type of discussions. Right now we're at the point where, yeah she knows I'm different and she doesn't talk about it.

[. . .] Now as I've gotten older, my tolerance for stupidity and ignorance are less and less. So now somebody might say something and I might come out to them, and that depends on Number One if I think they're worthy of me coming out to them. If my telling them is merely for them to trivialize my identity, then I wouldn't tell them. If I think they want to know and it's a chance to educate them, then I'll tell them. Just like right now, where I work I'm not officially out to anyone. Of course when you know you see the choir director is thirty-seven, near forty and he isn't married and he's basically said no to every dinner invitation in that church, that's come in that church, two and two still equals four and I think some people can add. But also the church is famous for denial. So, I'm at the point in my life where, if anyone asks me in the church, I won't deny it. And if it means . . . I don't know if, you know, legally I could be fired. It's a shame to think that, but it's the reality of things. So those are sort of like my ways of being an activist, in a sense. Not really in your face or "Let's put a bumper sticker on my car." It's just living my life.

"KG"

KG was in his last year of law school at LSU when I met him. Roderick introduced him to me at a time when they were dating. KG describes himself as having the "gift of gab," which I found to be true. He's also quite conservative for someone so young.

The eldest of three children, KG was born in New Orleans in 1978. Both of his parents are professionals—his mother a banker and his father an accountant—and so brought their children up in a middle-class environment. After law school, KG moved back to Slidell, Louisiana, where his family currently lives, to practice law. The interview took place on January 20, 2005, at Roderick's apartment in Baton Rouge.

I told my dad that I was gay. [Laughter] That was a very interesting conversation that we had. He wasn't happy, of course, you know. Don't blame him. Because I'm named after him and the whole, from what I'm thinking a family life, I don't know what it's like to have a son, so I don't know what the expectations are or, you know. But he got quiet for a little bit. But funny enough, you know, he did his own rant and tirade and lit up a cigarette, which by the way he doesn't smoke now but he did that whole thing. And after about—we were in the car on our way to work. [Laughter] I know, funny enough, right?

How long ago was this?

This was the spring or the winter—spring. Okay. I say spring because I was still in school—the January term of 2002. So this was really three years ago, easily three years ago. After his entire spiel and, just he's not accepting it. He told me that he won't—don't expect him to accept it. But after that whole fifteen-minute tirade, he says, "Well, you know, there are gay guys out there who climb rocks and who play football and who are just," you know, so I just interpreted it that it was okay, as long as you don't come around me with a dress and some makeup, we going to be cool, you know, and that was fine. And then about maybe a month, month and a half after that, I normally listen to Christian radio. So I happen to have driven this particular day. And we're coming home from work and I don't know who it was on the station that day, but homosexuality just happened to have come up as one of the topics. Okay. If I'm ever with him or if I'm with any member of my immediate family, if that comes up, be we at church or if it's on TV, I mean *Ricky Lake*, whatever, I get hot. You know, I'm like, "Oh, God," because I don't know what to do, you know? He just kind of looked over and he says, "Have you been praying about what we talked about some minute ago?" And I was like,

"Yeah, you know I have." And he was like, "Okay." And that was the end of the conversation. And that was it. And he has not mentioned anything. I've not said anything since then.

My brother and my sister, we lived together my freshman year of law school. And last—this is when we were still living together, so this is last spring. So the January term of 2004, sometime between January and May, my sister—we have, you know, a computer in the spare bedroom, what have you. So she went on to do whatever it is she does. And apparently gay.com just happened to have popped up. Right? Of course, I was on gay.com, you know. So she was kind of upset. But she was more or less upset at the fact that I didn't tell her and not that I was gay. So she kind of took it in stride. She was just like, "I always thought, but I never knew." And she told me she even wanted to ask my best friend from home because she heard stuff, but she didn't know, what have you. I was more worried about my younger brother than her. But he was actually the coolest. Not that he was okay with it, because I know they're not. But he was more, I don't know, more or less—I can't even think of the right word. He wasn't as bad. It was not nearly as bad with him or with the two of them as I thought it was going to be. So I know they know, because we talked about it that night. But my mom, I haven't. And I just assume between my sister and my brother and my dad. But I just assume moms know, you know, because moms know their kids, you know what I mean? [. . .] But I really and truly believe my mother has been the one that has known from the jump. I do. And my dad even told me that day in the car. He told me that this is something that he and my mom had been concerned about since I was about twelve or thirteen. Because he told me, "We were concerned about this for like ten years." So at the time I was twenty-three. So yeah. So, of course, I'm thinking to myself, "Why the hell you all didn't tell me nothing?" You know? I mean, but that's just me, you know. "Why you all didn't tell me?" you know.

Did you ever have a conversation with your mother?

No, I haven't.

She hasn't brought it up?

She hasn't, you know. I remember we were watching the Miss Universe Pageant two years ago, I think. No, it was before I started law school. [. . .] No, this had to be before I started law school, so this was three years ago, before I was getting ready to go. She says, "That's the kind of girl I want you and your brother to bring home, you know, a nice, pretty, well-rounded girl," you know. So I didn't say anything. And then even recently she's been talking about my future wife and to make sure that whatever—whomever I bring has got to be somebody who doesn't come from a family with problems because we don't have any problems. We all love each other. We all get along, da, da, da. But she's still talking about a wife.

And my best friend, Bridget, in school—she's also my best friend—she's great. She's much older than I am, just what I needed when I got her. But she's just like, "You don't want to do this, KG, but you're going to have to. You're going to have to just be like, look." And she's right, because I don't want to do it. Oh, God, I would hate to do that because I know they have expectations, I know they do. You know, because I have expectations of them. So I'm sure, I'm more than sure they got certain things that they're looking for to come from me. So I don't—it's not so much that I don't want to burst their bubble, but it's like shit, fucking proverbial rock and hard place. So no, I haven't had a discussion with my mother. I haven't. And I want to but I don't really want to. My mom and my ex-girlfriend are in the same category. I kind of want them to just know.

. . . .

"LAMAR"

Lamar is one of the most fascinating men I interviewed. He is well known in both gay and straight communities in Atlanta. In fact, a friend of mine who now lives in Chicago but grew up in Atlanta put me in touch with him because he remembers Lamar's famous parties, where celebrities like Diana Ross have been seen.

Lamar is dark, tall, and lean and prides himself on being feminine. One of the more memorable lines from his interview is, "I'm from the generation when men were men, women were women, and sissies were women." He and another narrator in this book are good friends, and the other narrator told me that Lamar actually got that saying from him. Both of them say it with such elegance and conviction that the origin is not really important.

Lamar was born in Jacksonville, Florida, in 1945, the youngest of three boys. The interview took place on November 3, 2004, at his office in Atlanta.

You know, this is so strange. I'm extremely educated and my mother's not. But we have never had a conversation about my sexuality. I remember she wrote me a letter when I was a freshman in college about relationships. In her own way I guess that was her trying to tell me she understood or whatever. I can remember quite vividly, when I was in about ninth grade, I wanted to redecorate my room. And I painted it a lilac color, almost a light pink. And she had no knowledge I was gay. I went out and bought paint. The same guy that I was talking about earlier, he and two of my friends helped me to paint the room. When she came home it was painted that color, and she said she didn't like it and wanted to know why I painted it that color. I told her I liked it. It was pretty. She thought it should be blue or something else. You know, in hindsight.

And your brothers, do they know?

Yeah.

And what was their reaction?

Well, I think they always knew. You know it was never discussed. My older brother is three years older than I am, so I would tell you, you know, when we were in sixth or seventh grade, you know how brothers get into tussles or fights or at least skirmishes about whatever, if he got angry, he'd call me a faggot or sissy or something like that.

What's your current relationship like with your mother and your brothers?

My oldest brother is deceased. He died about four years ago. My mother, I have a good relationship with her now. Now I have a relationship. I have been in a relationship with a young man for twenty-two years. And whenever I'm at my mother's house, if he's there with me, we don't sleep together or share our bed. I will sleep on the couch and he will sleep someplace else. If my mother ever comes to visit me in my house, now we don't, we sleep together; we don't change and we just, we just never have had that discussion. You know, unfortunately I can't give you this great story that we had this confrontation, my mother and I, about my sexuality or any of that. I haven't. Whereas some of my friends have had, you know, great confrontations with their . . .

Drama.

Drama. Right. I've never had that kind of problem.

So you say you adopted a son or did you have a son?

I adopted a son.

What made you decide to adopt a child?

That motherly instinct. I always wanted to have a child. I knew I would never marry to have children. And I was one of the first black single men in the city to adopt a child, you know. At the time when I adopted my son I was really, everybody knew I was gay and didn't believe it. But my children, my son kind of changed me. I also raised a daughter. My lover has a biological daughter. And I raised her from the time she was less than a year old. And she's twenty-two now.

Do they live with you? Both of them live with you?

Uh huh.

And what were they, what were their experiences about the two of you; they knew you were a couple obviously—or did they not?

Yeah, they knew. I think—well they knew, they didn't know anything differently. I think when they were small, we had a smaller house, because we shared a bedroom. And as they got bigger we got a bigger house, and we don't have to share a bedroom as such, but we do share a bedroom. I would be curious at some point to know what they think. But I think children always know. But that doesn't have anything to do with their love for you.

Right. How old are they now?

My son is twenty-seven. My daughter is twenty-two. And I'm a grandfather now. I have a grandson.

. . . .

MARLON

Marlon is a friend and colleague who teaches African American literature and cultural studies. Before I met him in person, I was a big fan of his scholarship. We met in 2000 at a conference I organized at the University of North Carolina at Chapel Hill.

Having lived in Michigan for years, he and his partner moved to Virginia after they accepted teaching positions at the University of Virginia. I made two trips to Virginia and stayed with them on both occasions. I interviewed Marlon on the first trip on May 5, 2005. Marlon was born in 1956 in Cuero, Texas, and is one of seven children.

I remember going through this process and thinking and coming to the conclusion that this is who I am, and I have three options. I can tell everyone and make an issue of it. I can simply live my life, and if people ask, I'll say, "This is who I am." Or, I can try not to be this. And, trying not to be this is just not going to work. So, I chose the middle option, which is basically the option I've always known. I don't hide it. I've never told any of my family. I never said the words, "I'm gay," to any of my family except my younger brother. And, yet, they all know. My partner, we've been to visit. They come to visit us. And, it's just that way. I write about it all over the place. My students read my work.

What is your current relationship with your parents and your family?

My mother passed away in 1994. My relationship with my mother was very, very, intensely close. We talked constantly on the phone after I went to graduate school in Chicago and got my first job, and you know, throughout that, she came to visit. And, it was very close. That summer when I came home from my first year of college, I told my mother I was never getting married. And, she said, "I just want to know, is it because of the negative experiences that some of your older siblings have had with marriage?" I said, "No, it has nothing to do with that." And, basically she said, "That's your decision. That's fine. I understand. I just want you to be happy." That is what she said to me many different times, and she used to say things like, "Your friends take care of you, don't they?" And, when I said, "Yes," she would say, "I'm happy. I think you're happy." It was clearly a major concern of hers that I not be unhappy, which I guess, you know, for people of her generation, I think gays often lived unhappy.

I was not as close to my father. We had a difficult relationship that flared up when I was in high school, where I became arrogant, I would say, and disrespected him on some occasions, whereas before I had always feared him. I was to the point of, not shaking, but just being totally silent in his presence. And, it was because I didn't understand him, and I don't think he fully understood me. [. . .] My father has always been proud of me and all of us; he had always been very proud. And, only in later years did he begin to express that. But, when my mother died, he had assumed many of the qualities of my mother. For instance, my mother had a tradition of always sending all of us cookies and cakes at Christmas through the mail. When my mother died, from that first year to the present, my father took up that tradition and always does that. When I would call home, I would talk to my mother for, you know, it could go on for hours, and I would talk to my father for five minutes and then we would have nothing to say. It's still difficult to have a conversation, but it's a lot easier now, and I try to call him, and he certainly calls me. And, he came to visit here and we had a great time, but he and Ian got along very well. He met some of our friends. So, it's hard to characterize it. I really respect and admire him. I just think he is a remarkable person to have provided for seven children with seasonal work. Knowing now in terms of cost, what things cost and how difficult it is, I just really am astonished by what they were able to accomplish.

I'm close to my siblings. We are a very close family. And, we stay in touch. It's harder for me because I'm the one who's away, you know, further away, but we visit when we can. My younger brother comes to visit quite frequently. And, my older brother came to visit. They stayed at our apartment in D.C., and then they came here. They weren't so crazy about D.C., but they loved it here. They love the country. And, so we had a great time, and they want to come back. My other siblings want to come visit, but it's hard.

MICHAEL

Michael came to the reception that Curt held for me to meet people who might be interviewed. He is a diminutive man but carries himself in "grand" fashion. In fact, he described himself as "the favorite grandchild and favorite nephew" in his family. He is also very well connected in the black community in Raleigh, North Carolina, and has been president of various black political organizations.

He was born in Raleigh in 1968. The interview took place on October 28, 2004, in Raleigh.

Everybody in my family knows. And then of course, all my aunts and uncles know, my grandmothers know. It was not easy for me.

What were their reactions?

[Deep sigh] Oh, very mixed. For example, when I had this twenty-first birthday party, my father was the first person to ever say, he pulled me to the side and he told me, you know, happy birthday and whatever, he gave me money. He said, "Someone said X is gay," you know, this guy I was talking to. And I said, "Really?" [Laughter] And he said, "People will say cruel things." And that was it. Well, after we broke up and I had other relationships or whatever, I had friends who would call the house or whatever and my brother, who was in school, in high school or junior high school at the time, and my brother would say, "Michael, some fag is on the phone for you." [Laughter] You know, stuff like that. And I would say, "Give me the phone, boy," and whatever. [Laughter]

My mother's sorors, you know, would call. I'd see them at the mall. And before I could get home, my mother would say, "Well, Michael, such-and-such called and said you were at the mall with some gay boys or running around with some gay boys." And, you know, I would laugh and just go on. But I think the straw where it really hit them was when I was modeling for a major boutique-ish type of store here. And moved from that to one of my cousin's where she does hair. And I had this high top fade thing. And she asked me to do this hair show for her. And I said, "Yeah." She said, "Well, you going to let me perm your hair?" And I said, "Girl, whatever you want to do, long as you're going to pay me." Well, she permed it. And after it permed, it fell down here [points to his eyebrows]. And it was this really pretty long bang. And she said, "That's so pretty." And, you know, because this was cut off and I had this big slope thing. And when it fell, it was just here, so she just cut it. And she curled it; she curled this bang. And I went home to my parents. And my father was doing the hedges. [Laughter] And I got out and I'm walking, you know. And I just never pay any attention to my father, I really don't. And I'm going up the steps and he grabs my bang and he tries to cut my hair with these hedge clippers. And I'm hollering like a girl, "Daddy, Daddy, you know, what you doing? You're messing up my hair." [Laughter] And so my mother comes out and she says, you know, "Leave him alone," and, you know. And it ended. And, of course, you know me. I go right back to the salon and get my hair done again.

I would think, given that you had a gay uncle who was open about it, that it wouldn't have been a big deal to your parents.

My parents were very hurt in the fact that I had been engaged twice. They said my uncle, you know, "Your uncle has done this, you know, you're hanging out with him, it's his influence," and they were upset with him for a very long time. And realistically, my uncle played absolutely no role in this whatsoever. He didn't even know I was sleeping with men, and he was in D.C. So he played no role. And so for a long period of time—well, not for a long period of time, but for a few months they took my allowance from me, because I would say I'm going to D.C. They'd say, "You're not going to D.C. to spend my money going to no gay clubs," and this kind of thing. And they took my allowance from me and I was like, "fine." My grandmother gave me money. My uncle sent me money. So I still did whatever. But I think one of the great things about my parents is that being gay has never changed who I am. And at some point, and I don't know when this happened, I don't remember how many years after, but at some point I remember riding with my mother somewhere. We were coming or going to a funeral. And this lesbian pulled up beside us. And she said, "Look at that damn lesbian." And she said, "These lesbians and gays," and, you know, she just went on about them. And I said, "Yes, girl," you know. And at some point, they just forgot. They see me the way I saw my uncle, as I'm just their son and not their gay son. And at times, they really have to catch themselves because they're talking about gay people or gay issues and they forget that I'm gay.

· · · · · · · ·

KENYATTA

Kenyatta was born in Hampton, Virginia, in 1974, and is the fourth of five children. He was raised in a two-parent, middle-class family in a neighborhood that he describes as "Mayberry." In addition to his "day" job, he writes fiction. The interview took place on May 3, 2005, at his home in Maryland.

It happened always the way I thought it would, which was that it would be unplanned and that someone would say something, and in reaction, I would just do it. And that's exactly what happened. I was on the phone with my mother and she made some comment about gay people. Before I came out, there was a point in my life that it seemed like every single day, this was the topic of the day on TV. Like every episode of *Oprah*, every episode of *Donahue*, you know, the news, something—every day, I could not escape it on TV. And my mother called and we were talking on the phone and she made some comment, and it was just really negative, and I responded to her, "Well, Mom, I just don't think that's true." And she said, "Do you mean?" I said, "I mean, you can't say that about people. I mean, I know that doesn't apply to me, and you know, I'm gay." And she didn't say anything, but I heard all these wordless sounds. Tsk, tsk, tsk, oh, um-um-um-um-um-um-um. And, you know, [laughter] I was listening to her head kind of explode. And then there was a period of time—I don't know, three weeks, four weeks, I don't know how long it lasted—but I remember very clearly, she asked me not to tell my father. "I know how your father is and I don't want you to experience how he's going to react to you when you tell him this," is what she said. And so I didn't. I didn't say anything to him. But she started to go full court press on biblical responses. And so one day she calls me, and it's an early morning—I wanna say it was a Saturday morning. My boyfriend at the time is at my house, and actually we are laying in bed, and the phone rings and I answer the phone, it's my mother, and so she's—"I want you to turn to such and such a scripture and read." Chile, please. And the conversation must've been tense, but I don't remember how it ended, except that she got off the phone, said she was going to the track to jog. My father called back about ten minutes later and he said—and just because caller ID said it was a home call, I thought she was calling back. So I answered the phone, it was my father, and he's like, "What's going on between you and your mother?" I said, "What do you mean?" "Something's been going on for, like, two weeks now and she won't tell me what it is." And I'm like, "Oh, God." [Laughter] You know, like, am I gonna come out to my father while I have my boyfriend lying here next to me? So I said, "Well, you know, we've been having some debates about some issues that we don't agree about." He said, "What is it?" I said, "Daddy, don't ask me that question unless you want me to answer it." And he said, "I want you to answer it." And I said, "OK." I said, "Well, we're having issues because I have told her that I am gay." And he said, "Well, that's what I thought it was; I just didn't understand why nobody was gonna tell me." And I said, "That's it?" That was the big explosion? And he's like, "Well, I mean, you know, I think that's nasty." [Laughter] "If that's what you wanna do, I mean, that's up to you. That's your life, it's not mine. I mean, I don't think it's gonna lead to anything good, it's nothing but destruction and damnation coming towards you, but if that's what you wanna do, whatever." And we got off the phone. [Laughter] And I just sat shell-shocked, because in my head when I had imagined it happening it would always be in response to something someone said. But I thought that my mother would say, "Oh, Baby, Mama knows." And be OK with it. My father would say, "What the hell!" The exact opposite reactions, and I was not prepared for that at all. But that was how it happened. I never formally came out to any of my brothers or sisters; the conversation made it to them somehow and each of them, in their own way, kinda said something to let me know that they had been told. My older brother and I—who had a very tense relationship growing up—that seemed to be the stone that kind of—I don't know. Once that boulder was moved out of the way, our relationship has been phenomenal since then. I talk to a close friend of mine about this all the time. I think that straight black men have a huge problem with closeted black men. There's something about that that makes them very uncomfortable. And I don't know if it's because it makes them think about their own desires or, you know, whether or not they've ever checked somebody out and caught themselves doing it and so could they be a closeted black gay man? I don't know what the issue is, but time and time again, I have found that I've watched straight black men have very strong negative reactions to black men they perceive to be gay who would not say they were. And those same men had no problem with me and were, you know, we developed very tight relationships based on my openness. Yeah, so it seems like once that was now said, now we can be tight, now we can be brothers. But . . . all the way up until, oh, God, we had a terrible time, we had a terrible time growing up. It was horrible. But now, it's like everything's cool.

How would you describe your current relationship with your family?

Probably the best it's ever been. My mother passed about six years ago, six and a half years ago—unexpectedly—and she and I were very close. I think that her initial shock began to wear off and she began to—like, I would say things about who I am and what I want out of life and what I expect. And I would tell my parents all the time, you raised militant children, so this is just biting you in the ass. If you had not done that, then you wouldn't have to deal with an activist brotha about his sexual orientation. So we were very close and I didn't expect—her passing was very sudden. [. . .] But in any event, she went first, that was unexpected, and so the only positive of that has been that my father and I had to figure out how we were going to love each other. And I think we've negotiated that very well now. There's still sort of a "don't ask, don't tell" policy in the family, and I don't know if that's because in preparing for my outing, I very purposefully distanced myself from my family and I just didn't talk about my personal business and I didn't ask them about theirs. And so, if something was going on in one of my sister's marriages, I don't wanna know is what I would say. People call me up and wanna talk about it—nope, nope, nope, don't bring me that, I don't wanna know about it. And in return, I guess we kind of got trained and it worked very well, so that now, nobody ever asks me about anything. You know, if I'm dating somebody, they don't know. And they have never asked about it. There are days when I wanna get mad at them for that, you know, dammit, why don't you ask me if I'm coming with somebody or if I'm coming alone this year for Christmas? But I also know that I kind of designed that, and so I have to take some ownership for that.

· · · · · · · ·

"RICH"

Rich is a literature professor at a small liberal arts college in Maryland, but we met when he was a graduate student in New England in the mid-1990s. He was born in Pensacola, Florida, in 1962. The interview took place on May 4, 2005, at his home in Baltimore.

Okay. Except for my mother, it went well. I think it was the summer of '97. A pastor that I have in Atlanta recommended that I go see a counselor or a therapist to talk about it, because I had confided in him that I was predominantly homosexual. And I went to this counselor through the Lutheran Church and was shocked because, you know, from the beginning he didn't think there was anything wrong with it. And I later teased my pastor. I said, "Thank you for sending me to this man. You thought he was going to make me straight, but he didn't. He said nothing is wrong with me." . . . I would say five years, maybe ten years, before coming out, were always bittersweet, because I always hated going home and being faced with the question, "Who are you dating?" "When are you getting married?" And it made me very evil towards people looking back at it. So I knew that I needed to do this. And also, I never wanted someone else to tell the people who were the closest to me. I was working in Atlanta in the summer of '97. And I flew home to Pensacola. And I decided I didn't want to tell everybody, but I knew if I strategically told people, the word would get out to everybody. And it worked wonderfully. I'm never asked the question, "When are you getting married?" anymore. But I'm trying to say I flew home and my mother was working that Saturday and I paced like crazy until she got home. And then she got home and we sat down and we talked about it, and I think she was just in shock about me telling her. I think that she always knew, even though she will never admit to that, because I know it had been rumored in the family that I was and other people had mentioned it to her and she disagreed with them. But for the most part, her reaction when I was at home that weekend, which I flew in, I guess I flew there Friday night and I left Sunday. Also it was a short visit and she didn't really lose her mind until after I left. And she lost it more with other people. With me, we were, for the most part, civil. The main part of our dialogue was through letters, you know. I think part of me trying to sell it to her was saying that I was in therapy. She had hopes that the therapy would cure me. And I told her that the therapist didn't think that I needed to be cured. But she had hopes, and I think she really lost it when I refused to say that it was something that I could be cured of.

That weekend also I came out to my father. And we had been estranged because of the divorce, so I think my father, in his mind said, well, you know, if this is going to go on top of the way that we've already been estranged, this is going to be the end of our relationship. And it wasn't. I mean, you know, he cried a little bit, and I'm not 100 percent sure why that is. I have some theories. But he was very accepting. He said, you know, "You're my son and I love you. And, you know, if that's what you're attracted to, then, you know, that's what it is." I told him outside of a bar, and we went inside and had a drink. And actually in some ways it made our relationship even closer. And one of the things that he did, I wanted to do my parents and then go back to Atlanta and tell my sister, who I knew had always known and my brother-in-law. But my father, I think in some ways, thought that I had already discussed it with my sister. So he called and left a message that pretty much told my sister what was coming, you know. He said, "I had a talk with Rich and everything is fine and I love him and blah, blah, blah." So in some ways, my sister knew. And then that Monday, because my sister was working and had a little one, we had no alone time. So I had to just say, "Let me drive, I need to talk to you." And I told her on the way home from commuting from work. And she said that people had asked her for years and years. And she said she didn't know or to ask me. But she was not surprised at all. And my brother-in-law was the funniest. He said, "This is fine and well but I hope you don't think you're telling me anything I don't know." So he said he had known. He said he didn't know at the beginning when they were dating, but he said a year or two after they were married, he just thought that I was. And he said all of his brothers had asked him from the beginning. And he was like, "Ask him, don't ask me."

And then I called one or two friends who were like close, close. And one of them had some problems with it. I think she thought that it was going to like change our relationship. And when she got over that, the relationship is strong. She had a son, and her husband wanted to make sure that it was okay for her son—his son to come visit. And I said, "Of course it's fine for your son to come visit. I'm the same person that you all have known and, you know, we're good friends." And I think in some ways, one of the reasons I'm glad I did it was because some of the people, particularly people of older generations, they thought that, you know, homosexuals are like monsters. They didn't know that it could be somebody who was as smart and as nice and loving as I was. And I'm glad that I did that. Because I know the morning after I came out to my mother, we went for a walk. And she had a gay couple who lived down the street that she, for the most part, had never spoken [to]. She said, you know, "We laugh and talk about them." But the day that we passed their house, she spoke. And to me that said so much, you know. I don't know if that was like, "I guess I got to be nice to them now, I have one in my family," or whatever. But I was a little surprised because—but I guess—and my mother articulated it well, when people told her, "Why are you losing your mind? You're very supportive of your godson, who is gay. And you have friends who are gay and lesbian." And her answer was, "But that's my damn son." So even though she was welcoming and whatever of other people, it didn't hit *home*, home, until it was, you know, someone who, you know, who she had birthed. And I think our current relationship is pretty much don't ask, don't tell. I did a conference at my college a few years ago on James Baldwin and took her a program home. And she read the program and then she handed it back and said, "I can't, you know, show anybody this program." And in the program it mentioned that my dissertation was on African American male homosexuality. And I thought like, here we go again. So I put on my armor, and I was just like I'm out of here. I don't have time to deal with this stupid shit. And she said, "We're not going to do this; we're going to sit down and talk." And she goes, "Well, what is your dissertation about?" And I explained to her what the dissertation was about. I'll tell people she still didn't ask for that program back, but at least she knew she didn't have all these theories. But I think she's over me ever marrying. She knows that she's not going to have a daughter-in-law. My pastor at the time said that part of her depression was her mourning the loss of grandchildren from me and a daughter-in-law. And I think she has gotten over that mourning. Though I've heard, years and years after that, she did say, "Well, you know, Rich just needs to settle down and marry." And, that may still be in her heart, but I think that that's over. We both had cancer scares two summers ago and it really brought us very close. But the relationship was very close. I talked to my mother at least twice a week, every week, for the first twenty-five—first thirty years of my life. And then when the letter came out and we went back and forth, we maybe talked I would say maybe once every six months. And I know that she really missed me and was strained. And I was very—I was very—I guess evil would be a word. But I was very unapologetic, because I had lived a lie for so many years because of her. And I didn't have any sympathy for what she was going through. You know, I had put my life on hold, and I had to make a stand, a stand that I could never have made at eighteen. But at thirty-five and being self-supporting, I made that stand. And she saw that I could be, you know, as evil or more so as her and that I was not going to back down from this being who I was. So I think, that spoke volumes. But, I mean, I don't think that I could go home with a partner to her house. My father and stepmother said I could stay there, but I'm not one of these people who have to push it and make people uncomfortable. So, unless she broached it, I wouldn't ever bring up who I was dating with her. I think the relationship we have now is as far as it's going to go in relation to me dating men. I mean, it would be nice if she would go a little further, but I don't require that. [. . .] In the last two years I think we've gone another step.

Right after, I could tell that she didn't want to go places where I was. I don't know what the hell she thought was going to happen. I was going to show up in a dress or whatever. But I could tell that if I was going to visit a certain group of relatives, she wouldn't go. And I would love to know how among her friends how she's communicated it. Because I know right after, she couldn't even tell her own husband that I was gay. And my brother-in-law was like, "You need to tell." She did discuss it with her pastor but—and I know my stepfather knows; he's not an idiot. He may have known before, she even admitted it. But I don't think that she discusses it with her friends. Or if she does, I would love to know. [. . .] She's retiring in a year or two. I would love for her to do a book or to do an interview on what she went through because, I mean, I've talked to other friends about what their African American mothers have gone through and it seems to be a common bond. A lot of the mothers think that it's something that they did wrong. And I would love to maybe at one point in her life be able to discuss what she went through. I know to her it's an embarrassment to her. And I get a feeling that she thinks that it's something that she did wrong. And I think in some ways she was disappointed that my father was so loving because she was like, "Well, what did your father say?" And I said, "Oh, he didn't have a problem with it. He said he loved me." And I could just see her saying, "Damn. He's no help." And I think she was surprised that I got the unanimous love and unconditional love and support from other people. And I think in some ways, that helped her to make a little progress. But the people that I came out to initially on that weekend, everyone said, "It doesn't mean anything to me. I still love you, blah, blah, blah." She never said that. You know, I guess she didn't feel that. She refused to lie. And at that point she still had hopes of me being cured.

· · · · · · · ·

RODERICK (B. 1974, BATON ROUGE. LA.)

Mother knows. Stepfather probably knows. Father probably knows. My mother and my *new* stepfather, which she just married, they definitely know because we had a very in-depth conversation this last year about it. She even just said to me, "But It's wrong. The Bible says . . ." And I broke it down. I said, "Mama, I'm sick of that shit." And he was sitting there too, her husband . . . her fiancé at the time. And I just kind of said some of the things that I learned while in Chicago. These are things that came out of the pulpit where I was. I explained some things and I broke down certain scriptures, those special scriptures that people throw out. But she didn't do any of that, but she just kind of still had this thing of, you know, being very open about her two gay sons—loving them but still feeling like it's wrong. I shared some things with her about how I feel about it. And she was saying, "You know, I think you just gave your first sermon." Now that was a double-sided thing. That was a backhanded compliment. [Laughter] And she even said she always did hate to hear pastors say homophobic things. She always hated when pastors said things against the women preaching or negative things about women having certain roles, you know. She always had a problem with that. [. . .] So she knows. We really do have a beautiful relationship, and I'm happy to say that. And for me, that's really all I need. I'm like, "If Mama knows and Mama's cool and she loves me unconditionally," as she has said on several occasions, "fuck the rest." That's how I feel.

Are you and your brother out to each other?

Oh yeah. Oh yeah, yeah. Yeah, yeah, yeah. We are.

Did he come out to you first?

I came out to him when I found out somebody he had slept with . . . [Laughter] I was messy. I was a bad boy. I was a bad boy. Long story short, there was a young man that apparently my brother had slept with or had an encounter with when they were in college. The young man was trying to see him again. And my brother was ignoring him. He wouldn't return the phone calls. Ol' boy showed up at the house one day and I'm like, "What's really going on?" So through my investigation, I discovered that this man was gay and my brother and he had some connection and I let my brother know: "I know this because I had him too. And I found out that he was with you, so what's up?" [Laughter] And he didn't want to talk about it. [. . .] He had a lot of denial issues himself. He had a lot of issues period. [Chuckle] Just issues period. [. . .] He's paid for some of his choices in his life. And he's HIV positive and I don't mean that in the same context. In the context that he got, as some people say, "he got caught up in punking," you know. He was in school, doing well, National Guard or Army National Guard scholarship or whatever. But he got caught up in stuff, and he ended up dropping out of school, college. And at one point, he abruptly—this was how it all kind of came out in the open with my mother and my father—he abruptly moved out of the house to live with this older man who he was seeing. He was much older than him. He was a teacher and all that stuff. It was the summer of '93 or '94. She was like, "Look. I'm worried about my child's safety. I don't know any grown man that lives by himself that takes in boarders, who's a teacher. And I need to know." But that's the story that he [the brother] told. "But, what's going on? And if you know something, you need to tell me." I was like, "Sit down, Mama." We sat down on the couch and I poured the tea. [. . .] I said to myself, well, I'm not letting my brother go out by himself. "Mama, I have had relations with men too, but I think I'm bisexual." I had to sugarcoat mine. [Laughter] I sugarcoated mine. Oh God. Speaking of performance, THAT was a performance. That was a Golden Globe–worthy performance— not an Oscar—but a Golden Globe–worthy. I just broke it down and said, "Yes, he and the guy have been dating. They are a couple. He has moved in with him. And I've been knowing about this. And since you finally asked, that's why I'm telling you, but I'm not just going to put Tony out there by himself. I too have my things." And one of her reactions was, "Okay, now that I know . . ." one of her reactions was, "Well, I would have more so thought Tony than you. 'Cause I could see things in him when he was growing up." And I was kind of like [makes a face]. . . . "I didn't think so much so for you." I said, "Well, you know." And I think she held out hope that I would even-tually, you know, grow out of it and be with a woman. Even when I moved to Chicago, she came to me in 2001 and she was like, "Oh, yeah, your friend— Sandra?—she's a really pretty girl, son." "Yeah, Mom, she is." But she knows now, for a fact. That's not who I am.

I think that, at this point, my relatives know. There's a song, "If you don't know me by now, you'll never know me." I think they probably know. [. . .] I'm fitting into the whole southern mold. But don't ask and don't tell or I will exist and live my life and do things to the best of my ability, and they won't condemn me one way or another and we just won't talk about it. And also [. . .] my homosexuality probably was a driving factor for me being an overachiever by local standards, if you will. [Laughter] And that's also one of the things too that they can't deny. I don't hold the card, but if I ever have to use the card, I will. Whereas they can say I'm the one that's bragged on. I'm the one of the few of the siblings in my age range who finished high school and one of the only who finished college—on my mother's side of the family, definitely. And you know, I'm the one who's traveled around different parts of the world. I'm the one who lived in Chicago for three years. I'm the one who's now, you know, doing the job I have now. And I'm the one who's on TV. I'm the trophy in the family in the display case; one of the few [laughter] that's in the display case. So I have that collateral, if you will. And I know I've got that. And I think they know that too, probably. And they may not know it consciously, but they do kind of in a way. But I'm fine like it is. I am fine with it as it is. Because I don't feel like it's really any of their business, on the one hand. But I'm happy with who I am. And if the time ever comes . . . if I am blessed to find a partner, oh yeah, it's going to be like, [laughter] "He's coming to the Christmas party. He's coming to . . . you're going to meet him and this and that." That's how it's going to go down. That's just how I envision it anyway.

· · · · · · · ·

SEAN

I have known Sean for close to twenty years. We met when I was an undergraduate at UNC-Chapel Hill. Sean has always been, and continues to be, a "grand diva" in every sense of the word. He is well traveled, loves to entertain, and is the life of the party most everywhere he goes.

Although he is an architect, he now sells real estate in Atlanta. He was born in Durham, North Carolina, in 1970. He is the eldest of three. The interview took place on Election Day, November 2, 2004, in Atlanta. The results of the election were not in when we did the interview.

I actually came out to my mother and her husband when I was almost twenty-five years old. I had moved to Georgia at that time. And I had a girlfriend in college. And it was February 1995. And I had been to New York to visit my godbrother, actually. And my girlfriend from college was living in New York and I was hanging out with her. And came back to Georgia and was talking to my mother. And she was asking all sorts of questions about my girlfriend from college and what I got her for Christmas and what we did and blah, blah, blah, blah. And I said I got her nothing for Christmas. And then she said, "Oh? Why? Wasn't that your girlfriend?" And I was like, "Well, she *was*." I was like, "We broke up, and I told you that." And I'm thinking to myself, "Why you playing? You know this." [Laughter] And she sort of asked me, she said, "Well, do you have a girlfriend?" I was like, "No." "Do you want to have a girlfriend?" I said, "No." She said, "Well,"—she started asking me a series of questions. And she said, "Is there something wrong?" I said, "No." I said, "As a matter of fact, everything is right." And she said, "Okay. Well, you know, just wanted to know." And I was like taking a nap when she caught me on this particular Saturday, because I used to tutor kids on Saturday morning and that used to just wear me out. So when I would come home, I'd take a nap. And my mother and I are very close and we would talk like every Saturday. And I immediately like woke up out of that nap. I was like, "Oooh, Miss Ma'am is trying to come for me." So I called some friends of mine who had already come out to their parents and I talked to them and we did this big old conference call. This is like with my best friends. And so we were all talking about it. And then I just made a decision at that point that on or before my twenty-fifth birthday that I was going to have the discussion, and I did. And I'm grateful that I did. It was a wonderful coming out experience. And I realize that everyone does not have the same.

What was your mother's response?

It was . . . I had a meeting, I remember. And I came home. And I kept saying to myself, I'm going to tell, I'm going to tell, I'm going to tell, I'm going to tell. And she called me and we started talking. And I specifically remember for one entire hour, I am making conversation about nothingness, you know. And so she then says to me, "Why are you holding me on this phone?" And I gave some stupid excuse like, "Oh, I don't know, you know, I just want to talk," or whatever. And then she says, "Well, what's on your mind?" And then I said to her—she and I had that discussion, that first discussion in January. I remember it because I was back from New York in January. It was after New Year's. And now it is February, the month of my birthday. And I said, "Do you remember we had a discussion about a month ago?" And she cut me off and she says, "No, we didn't have a discussion. I asked you a series of questions." [Laughter] You know, so I blinked twice, you know, [laughter] thinking Miss Ma'am was coming for me again. So she obviously remembered it. And then I said, "Okay, well, yes. You asked me a series of questions." And I said, "Well, I just kind of wanted to talk about that." And then she said, "Okay." And I really didn't know how to come out to her. And then I said—I'm pausing and, you know, saying uh, uh, uh, you know, really stupid like. And then I said, "Well, is it okay?" And then she says, "Yes, it's okay." And then she says, "Now, is what okay?" And I was like, "Well, you know." And then she says, "No, I don't know. Is what okay? I want you to say it." I was like, "Well, like, is it okay?" And then she says, "Is what okay?" I was like, "Is it okay for me to be this way?" And then she says, "To be what way?" And I said, "Is it okay for me to be gay?" And then she says, "Yes, it is." And then she said, "I just have one question." And I'm thinking, oh, my God, she's going to ask me, well, I don't know if this is appropriate to say on the tape. [Laughter] She's going to ask me do I get it up the butt, okay. [Laughter] So that's what I'm thinking. I'm thinking, okay, she's going to ask me, do I get it up the butt. And then she said, "I just have one question." And I said, "Okay, what is it?" And she said, "Are you happy?" And I said, "Yes, I am." I said, "Actually, I'm very happy." And then she says, "Good, because we just want our children to be happy." And I thought that was just wonderful. [. . .] I was dating someone at the time and it was just that I was dating. And so about two weeks after we had that discussion, I am telling her about this guy I'm going out with and it's just silence. It's just silence on her end. So I stopped talking about that. And like the next week I talked to her about it. And she just said, "Well, I'm not ready to talk about those things yet." But that's all better now.

What was your stepfather's reaction?

Who cares, really? I mean, I'm an adult. It's not like he's really my step-father, he's my mother's husband. There's a difference.

So you didn't have that conversation with him?

I wouldn't say that I did not have that conversation with him. He was present in the conversation. I was speaking more to my mother than to him, but he was aware and a part of the conversation. But whether he accepted it or not really made me no never mind. So when I said who cares, it—that really didn't matter to me.

What about other family members?

I came out—well, we talked. Because at that time, I am almost twenty-five, so my youngest sister was only about eleven at the time. And my other sister was about twenty; she was in college. And we decided that I wouldn't tell my other sister right away or that my mother wouldn't tell, either way it went, and my youngest sister, we would let her grow into it. And I told the sister that's next to me. I guess I verbally said it to her two or three years after, two years maybe after that. And for whatever reason, she gave all this drama with tears and all this other kind of stuff. And I'm like, "Thing. Didn't you grow up with me?" [Laughter] And my other sister is, as a matter of fact, my other sister just this year called me on a Sunday morning to say, "I am tired of people saying that you're gay and I just wanted to ask you, are you gay?" [Laughter] And I said, "Yes, I am." "Okay, well, great. I heard it from you." [Laughter]

STANLEY

*Stanley and I met at LSU. Although we both graduated from the same
doctoral program, he came to the department a few years after I had left.
We share the same dissertation adviser. He was a member of black theater
groups in New Orleans for many years and taught theater before going back
to school to receive his Ph.D.*

*He now teaches at Nichols State University in Thibodeaux, Louisiana,
where he lives with his partner. While he was born in Port Arthur, Texas, in
1950, his mother raised him in Eunice, Louisiana. He has one half sister, a
stepsister, and a stepbrother. The interview took place on January 22, 2005,
at his home in Thibodeaux.*

One of the first experiences I had of accepting who I was, was brought
about by a woman who was in my class that I taught at LSU at Eunice, who is
still today probably my best woman friend. Barbara [last name], a white
woman. And she was into working with people with addictions and just all
kinds of things. And she sensed a heaviness on me in class one day. I was
teaching a beginning writers course in English. I was just doing it for LSUE. I
didn't have any interest in English, but my real teaching at LSUE was in
speech, which I had credentials for. But they wanted me to teach one class in
English, and she happened to be in that class. And she came to my office one
day and she said, "Mr. [last name], you really look unhappy." And I told her
the story. And then I told her, "I'm gay and I'm just having trouble accepting
who I am. I'm miserable." And she really empathized with me, sympathized
with me. And we sort of connected and we became close friends. And she
taught me a lot about accepting myself for who I was. And [begins to cry] . . . I
felt like I could never do enough to thank her for what she had done for me.
She was a lady who was having a hard time financially. She had been divorced
and her husband came from a very wealthy family. But she had actually, I
guess she'd gotten out of that divorce and she'd gotten out without much and
she was living off of Welfare and food stamps, and she was living in this apartment complex. And one day I decided I would go to a store and buy groceries
for her. And I brought them to her house. And I just couldn't do enough for her.

And while she sort of encouraged me to really accept who I was, I sort of
encouraged her to keep going to school and finish school, you know. And
this day she has a master's degree in counseling. And we're still very good
friends, and she really taught me to really accept myself, that there was
nothing wrong with me. I'd never heard anything like that before.

And I think something else she did for me that was really powerful was that she connected me with other gay people. It's very interesting. She had been an alcoholic and a drug addict. And she was recovering. She was in a kind of step program. And she said, "You need to come with me to one of our twelve-step meetings." She said, "I go to meetings in Jennings," which is like forty miles away from Eunice. And she said, "I go there once or twice a week" or something like that. And she said, "And a number of people there are gay." And so I did. And I didn't know what to say, you know, because I wanted to be a part of what was going on and they would always say like, "My name is Stanley and I'm an alcoholic," and I wasn't an alcoholic. [Laughter] I could leave from meetings and I could drink. I mean I was not an alcoholic, but that's the only thing I could do because my real purpose for being there was to sort of try to get an understanding of who I was.

And I was somebody whom I believe was trapped in an addiction, because I cruised quite heavily. The cruising had gotten me into the trouble that I'd been in, you know? And I'd lost money, lots and lots and lots of money. Guys robbed me. You know, I'd been stabbed a couple of times. I had my car stolen. I've had, you know, just from picking up guys. That even continued quite often until I went to Baton Rouge. And Barbara helped me to see that I was okay and there was nothing really wrong with me. And then like I said, I got introduced to these friends at AA and then I started connecting with other AA groups, and there was a group that met in Baton Rouge that was a gay AA. And so everybody there, practically, was gay. And I started hanging out with a lot of them after our meetings. And what happened to me was being in Baton Rouge in graduate school, working on my Ph.D., I met gay people in the department that I became friends with, who were in my program. And that excited me more than anything. And I think that changed my life.

Do you think that the years you spent cruising were your way of not dealing with your sexuality because you thought you couldn't be open about it, the only way you could express it was by . . . ?

That's right. I felt I had to hide to do it. To do whatever I was doing. I felt that I couldn't approach people I knew because then I could be outed by them. You know if they were not accepting. I couldn't approach them, so the best thing to do was to approach strangers or approach people who were looking for the same thing I was looking for. And I wasn't attracted to a lot the gay men, I was attracted to straight men. I found a sort of little small community of gay men right here that I associated with. And they taught me the cruising patterns. I went out there with them a couple times, so I knew the cruising patterns. And so, very often, what I'd end up with is I'd end up with hustlers. And again, you know, they were after the money. Very often I didn't get reciprocal sex. You know, I was left to manage on my own to get off the best way I could. But they were not interested in getting me off. They were interested in getting off. But for the money. I've met a guy, several times, who I wanted to have a little affair with, who would say, "I want the money up front." And I'd give him money and he'd leave. And I felt like I couldn't do anything about it because what could I do? You know, everybody would know if I complained. You know, if I called the cops, I felt like the cops would say, "Well you're doing this. Why don't you stop?" And I got myself into a number of bad, bad situations that I'm just surprised that I didn't get killed in a couple of those situations that I was in. And that's what my friend Barbara used to say all the time, "You're gonna get killed if you don't stop. You've got to get some help." And so I started seeing a counselor, really seeing a counselor. And he didn't really help me very much because he ascribed himself to the Christian religion. The first goal was, he felt like maybe I could change. And that wasn't working. And so then he decided that, you know, "Well okay. Let's work on the behavior that is hurting you." You know, going out cruising, picking up the wrong people. "Why don't you try to find a way to meet people in a more legitimate way?" You know, in a nicer way than what I was doing. And I could never really understand that. And I always go back and think that maybe it just is not meant to be for me, at that time. And maybe that was good because I often feel that, if I had been in the gay world, hooking up with gay people at the time that I was being so sexually promiscuous, I would have gotten AIDS and died.

To what extent are you out to your family?

I'm very out to my family. Now my mother is deceased. My father's deceased. And I was not out to them at all. [. . .] My stepfather died before I even came to an understanding of my sexuality. My mother died after I came to and accepted some understanding of my sexuality. But I never discussed it with her.

Do you think she knew?

Yes. You know, I was involved in an altercation in which I was entrapped by a policeman in a situation in Lafayette, Louisiana. And I was teaching school at the time. And I had to call my mother from jail. And she called my pastor. The first person she called was the pastor at our church. And he had to come and get me. And like I said, I was teaching school at the time, teaching high school. And he came and got me the next morning. And we went to the district attorney, and he pleaded with the district attorney not to press charges against me. And the district attorney agreed to drop the charges if I would agree to see a . . . well my preacher had told him that I would agree to see a counselor for my activities. And my preacher thought that I could just change. His suggestion to me was kind of cute at the time, kind of funny too, to think about it. His suggestion to me at the time was to date his niece. He said, "She is such a nice girl." And he said, "I think you should date her." And he said, "It'll just change you." And I said, "Well, maybe so. Maybe soon." I told him I'd give that some thought, but I never did. I never even thought about doing that. No. But anyway, so that situation sort of outed me to my mother in a way that she never, ever approached it. And the way I knew that she knew was . . . my room at the house was right off of the kitchen, and she and my sister got up for coffee one morning and I heard their conversation. And my sister said, "Well, Mama, you know if he is, he is. There's nothing you can really do about it." I don't remember the conversation really closely. But that told me enough to know, years later . . . like four years ago when I met Bill . . . that I could come out to my sister. And I had never been out to my sister either. She immediately accepted me. She had a number of gay friends. But she immediately accepted me. She had no problem with that. And she still has no problem with that. And all of her kids have no problem with that.

· · · · · · · ·

TIMOTHY

When I met Timothy for our interview, I thought he looked familiar. Then I realized that he and I had been in the Research Triangle in North Carolina around the same time in the mid-1980s, as he attended North Carolina Central University and I attended UNC–Chapel Hill. After more conversation, I discovered we had something else in common—his younger brother, Stacey, who was a classmate of mine at UNC. Stacey is also gay.

The fifth of six children, Timothy was born in Durham, North Carolina, in 1965. The interview took place in Atlanta, on January 6, 2005.

I came out directly to my mother, probably my junior year in college. That was the year I was living on campus, knew I'd be moving back home that summer, and I was dating someone that lived in Raleigh, going to school. I knew I'd probably be going back and forth a lot and she would probably question, "What are you going to Raleigh so much for?" So I just told her, "I want to talk to you about something this evening, no this weekend." She was a nurse, and instead of it happening like when she got off work on Sunday, [when I] got home Friday afternoon from work and [I] just said, "Hey, how you doing?" I went to her bedroom. "How you doing? La da da da da." One thing led to another and I came out. It was a beautiful conversation.

So there was no drama?

No. She questioned things. As I mentioned earlier, she questioned, "Well, do you think it was because you were rejected by Yvonne in eighth grade?" And I thought that was beautiful, first of all for her to remember that, and for her to try to answer some questions for herself and for me. She asked me about my brother. She said, "Well, how about your brother?" And I said, "Well, I don't feel it's my place to tell you that. If he wants to tell you he will." And I think, Stacey, when he was at Chapel Hill, he wouldn't come home much on the weekends. So what he was doing over there I don't, I didn't know for a while. But he dated more females in high school than I did and, I said that's for him to say. I had a friend who I reference as my cousin, because we grew up together through our church and our families were close. She said that Gregory's mom, Stella, and she had had the conversation about Gregory and I. I'm like, "Oh my God." But I remember Stella making comments about Gregory. If she ever found out one of her sons was gay she would abandon them and just hearing these negative comments, I thought, "oooh." But Greg was effeminate also.

And was he gay?

He was gay. Yes, he's gay. So that made me feel a little bit better. This was some years later in terms of she and Stella having a conversation, but they were both waiting for both of us to come out to them. She was supportive from that day forward.

And what about your siblings?

[Long pause] They had basically found out in subsequent years. My freshman year in college, for homecoming, I took a picture with my boyfriend and several of us at homecoming on someone's sofa or something. And I was sitting like this [demonstrates sitting gap legged on the couch], and I was up under—this is him and he was, I was here under his arm, and he gave me the portrait to keep because he didn't want to keep it in the dorm, or he didn't want his family to find it. And I had it in the top of my drawer, just up against the front of the drawer. And I came home one day from school, from college, and my mom said, "Hey, how you doing?" She was in the living room sewing. "Your sister left you a message in the bedroom." I was like, "Okay." I get to my bedroom and the picture's on my dresser with a note, "Tim, you're practically sitting up under this guy. What's up? Give me a call." This is my older sister. I didn't know if my mom had seen the note, read the note, if my sister said anything to her. But she taught high school in Durham, so I'm sure she was exposed to young guys with effeminate nature or whatever. So, I said I guess I better call her. I called her on the phone. She was around at my grandmother's. Small talk. "Alright, talk to you later." "Wait, wait, wait, wait, wait. What's up? What about that picture I found?" And I, rather than becoming defensive like, "What the hell you doing going through my drawers anyway?" That's what I was saying earlier, when I accepted who I was, I just wanted to finish school and move away. So, it was my freshman year and I'm like, how am I going to deal with this for four years? I'm not gonna tell you. So I denied it. I said the person taking the picture told everybody to get close on the sofa. Those were all of my buddies from school. So it was probably put in her mind early, but I never came out to them while in school. I moved here to Atlanta. When Stacey moved here, when my family would come to visit we would do what we called "de-fagging the house"—taking down pictures and that kind of thing. But we got to a certain point in our lives where we said we're just gonna stop doing that. So we'd leave pictures up, and then when they would come to visit over the years, they discovered it. We would bring our partners around and sometimes take them home on occasion—Stacey more so than me. So I say he outed me to my family. [Laughter] But, they've been supportive too. I mean, in the years that they've known, that's not been a problem. My father, he would often ask, "Why you don't have a girlfriend?" Because he lived right down the street from campus from North Carolina Central, and I would stop by to see him from time to time and, "You got any girls over there yet? Meet any girls?" That kind of thing. But, he finally stopped asking the questions. He asked my mom, "What's up with your son?" You know. And she says, "I don't know, why don't you ask him yourself." He never has directly asked me.

Really. Even now?

Even now. Even now. But he and my stepmother come here often, because she has relatives here and they're both retired. So Stacey has taken his friends home. When he came to visit, he met my partner that I was living with at the time, so yeah, I know he knows. But we never talked about it. But he just knows. "How is, what's your friend's name?" I say, "He's fine." That kind of thing.

· · · · · · · ·

TONY

Tony teaches directing and acting and has directed a number of shows in Memphis, Tennessee. He was raised in a middle-class home, one of five children of a physician and a stay-at-home mother. He was born in 1961 in Memphis. The interview took place on July 20, 2005, at his parents' home in Memphis.

Tony, age three. Courtesy of the narrator.

Oh, I'm out to my mother, and I'm not out to my father. It's one of those odd things. My mother and I talk about it openly and have, not forever, but since I was probably about maybe thirty-one or thirty-two. And I told all my siblings. My father knows that I am gay, but we don't talk about my being gay. I did not tell him I was gay; my sister told him. He asked her and she told him. And that was the extent of it. I think from the age of twenty-two on, I've tried to say—to tell him, and I just don't do it. And now he's eighty-two and I still haven't done it and I don't know if I ever will. I don't know. It's not something that he's—I don't feel like he really wants to discuss it. And I know he's not antigay. I mean, I'm sure he's treated gay patients over the years. I mean, he tries to be fair in his treatment of people, and he's seen all types of people from all walks of life. But dealing with me being gay ob-viously would be harder for him than dealing with a patient who might be gay. I know that when I worked in the HIV world, I felt like he never really wanted to hear about what I did for a living. And I sensed that he was not that clear about it, what I did, or comfortable with it. And I was very proud of what I was doing, and I don't think he could tell you to this day what I did when I worked in HIV, because I think HIV makes him nervous. And I know that treating HIV-infected patients made him nervous, so he wouldn't do it, as far as I can tell. My brother and he have a practice together; my brother still runs the practice. I know my brother would treat them but my father would not. And even though that's not necessarily a gay disease, I think in his mind it is or has some relationship to it, so it made me less comfortable even talking about that. But yet he knows, he knows I'm a dancer, he knows I'm a theater artist, he knows I worked at a whole bunch of AIDS agencies, and obviously our primary clientele was gay people. I mean, I do very gay things, if there are such things as gay things. I have very gay people that come over to visit [laughter] the house. So I don't know, it's just an odd thing. I think the one time I felt like he really kind of just dropped into it though, I had a boyfriend who moved here. And he never could remember the boy's name or who he was or where he was from when he used to come visit here. And then when he moved here, he was over here one day and he's much more butch than I am and he loves football and my father loves sports. So they ended up watching football together. I don't know where I was, but I was at work or something. Well, Lord have mercy, they bonded. He fell in love with him. And when we broke up, everybody knew but I didn't tell my father because I'm not out to my father. So one day I said something about his apartment downtown. He goes, "Oh, you all moved?" And I said, "You all?" I said, "I ain't moved nowhere. I still live up here and he lives down there." And he was aghast. I could just tell he was visibly shaken and upset by it. He was like, "When?" And I knew what he was saying, he was basically saying, "When did this split happen?" And it finally occurred to him that we were not a couple and it was very sad to him. He didn't ask and I didn't go any further with it, but those little moments that we have like that are kind of special. But I think I would like to come out to him, I just haven't done it.

church sissies
gayness and the black church

When people think of the South, after foodways and hospitality, religiosity is often what comes to mind. But not just any religiosity: the South is frequently associated with a virulent and unrelenting fundamentalism. Some believe it is a fundamentalism that sets moral standards even its followers cannot uphold, and certainly the scandals surrounding fallen televangelists like Jim Bakker and Jimmy Swaggart seem to provide evidence of this. Indeed, in the Bible Belt, the Ten Commandments are just the tip of the iceberg on a long list of "thou shalt not"s. It is hardly surprising, then, that many folks consider homosexuality incompatible with "righteous living."

While the black church has often upheld many fundamentalist tenets, the way those guidelines have been enforced or practiced has always been more nuanced—because they had to be. Black church parishioners have not always had the luxury of waiting on divine intervention when it comes to obtaining equal rights. In slave communities, for instance, religious gatherings sometimes became sites for plotting rebellions. And "stealing away" was code for heading North rather than going to heaven. As an institution, the black church historically has been the cornerstone of black thought, politics, spirituality, and morality in America. As C. Eric Lincoln and Lawrence H. Mamiya suggest, "The Black Church has no challenger as the cultural womb of the black community."[1] In the South, in particular, the black church has been a formidable presence in the struggle for racial equality, from slavery on through the civil rights movement. As in many institutions, however, its progressive public face has often camouflaged more problematic internal policies and attitudes—sexism and homophobia being just two. That is, until recently, when the camouflage has sometimes been discarded. As mentioned in the Introduction, the current leadership of the black church has been more explicit about its stance on homosexuality by openly opposing gay marriage and supporting other antigay legislation. Slowly shifting from a tolerant "don't ask, don't tell" policy to one of explicit condemnation, the black church, more than at any other time in its history, seems to be turning its back on many of its own: gays and lesbians.

Why, then, do so many black LGBT individuals remain in these religious spaces? The answers are complex. According to some of the men in *Sweet Tea*, despite the church's homophobia, it is a place of comfort—a place, ironically, where they were first accepted, where they first felt a sense of community and belonging. Ultimately, it is a contradictory space, one that exploits the creative talents of its gay members even as it condemns their gayness, while also providing a nurturing space to hone those same talents. It is contradictory in other respects as well. As more than one narrator attests from personal experience, for example, ministers who preach homophobic sermons are sometimes known to have had same-sex sex themselves. On one of my trips to South Carolina to conduct interviews, I discovered that a scandal had just erupted between two prominent black churches in Greenville. According to rumor, the ministers of these churches were having an affair and were caught having sex the Saturday night before church by one of their wives. The scorned "first lady" of the church reportedly proceeded to share what she had witnessed with the congregation the next morning during the announcements portion of the worship service! While such high drama may be unusual, many black churchgoers are familiar with ministers who preach homophobic sermons but are known to have dalliances with their male parishioners.

Other contradictions are manifested by gay church members themselves. Some of the narrators acknowledge the homophobia of their churches yet are committed to remaining members. Their explanations for remaining often center on how they have separated, at least psychologically, the minister's homophobic discourse from the space itself. In those instances, they claim to have distanced themselves from the "church" as represented by the preacher and other authority figures and to focus more on their "individual/personal" relationship with God—one that emphasizes the fact that God made them in His own image and therefore they are not an "abomination" in His sight, as some of their pastors suggest. Therefore, when a minister gay bashes in his or her sermon, these men don't internalize it or take it to heart because those words, in the way they have rationalized it, don't pertain to them. Indeed, "when their view differed from those of church leaders, they relied on their own reading and understanding."[2] Others suggest that when their ministers list homosexuality as a "sin," it's acceptable because they list it along with other sins, such as drinking, adultery, stealing, and cheating.

Finally, some men actually expressed that they had not totally reconciled their spirituality and sexuality, with one narrator, Gerome, going so far as to say that through prayer, God will take his homosexuality away.

But this is not the total picture. I was surprised, for instance, to find many men who disavow the black church, who renounce the homophobia and antigay rhetoric. Some of these men left the church altogether, while others found their way to alternative churches like the Metropolitan Community Church (MCC), a cross-racial denomination typically led by LGBT members, or Unity Fellowship of Christ (UFC) Church, a church founded by the Reverend Carl Bean of Los Angeles to cater specifically to the black LGBT community. The critique of these churches, from inside and outside, however, is that in the case of the MCC, the music isn't as good, the service isn't "black" enough, and it's more of a place to "hook up" than to worship; and, in the case of UFC, the spirit is there, but there are no "elders," which, according to some, are crucial to the black church service. Nonetheless, these two denominations have provided alternative sites of worship for those who feel uncomfortable in traditional black churches, especially in the current hostile political climate.

Despite the homophobia, both implicit and explicit, gay men are integral to most black church organizations. One of the most enduring stereotypes in the black church, for instance, and one not peculiar to the South, is that of the flamboyant choir director, musician, or soloist. The narrators of *Sweet Tea* speak to this stereotype in various ways and provide nuanced as well as unsurprising reasons for why gay men flock to the choir. One of the more humorous theories is the one provided by Freddie, who suggests it's because the choir robe resembles a dress! Then there is conjecture by many narrators that gay men are in the choir because they are naturally "creative," "artistic," or "talented." In addition to these, I would like to offer yet two other reasons why I believe the choir is so important. First, participation in the church choir provides a way to adhere to the religiosity of southern culture but also build a sense of community within what can sometimes be a hostile space. This is one instance in which a seemingly repressive sacred space actually affords a vehicle for the expression of sexual desire. Second, as some of the men suggest, the choir provides a medium to express one's sexuality through the theatricality already built into the church service. Freddie's joke about the choir robe is an example—an example that hits close to home.

In my youth, I was one of several budding queens in the church, and we all learned very quickly—subconsciously or not—how to express and affirm our queerness without ever naming our sexuality. To riff off the title of a song by the gospel group the Clark Sisters, we knew that "to name it is to claim it."

Thus, we used the choir as our sword and shield. In the children's choir, we baby church sissies would flame as bright as we wanted, and it was totally acceptable. For many years, the choir was my saving grace. The choir was where I felt free to express myself and where I felt appreciated. By the time I was twelve, I had made quite a reputation for myself as "the little fat boy with the high butt and high voice that could sing." I was the only male soprano, and I could outsing any of the girls in the soprano section. I got the church to shoutin' every Sunday by singing a solo originally sung by Yolanda Adams with the Southeastern Inspiration Choir out of Houston, Texas. The song is called "My Liberty"—how prophetic.

Grown folks marveled at, and some of my peers envied, my soaring melismas and general vocal theatrics. What I realize now, but didn't back then, was that I was a budding diva who was using the medium of gospel music to express not only my spirituality, but also my sexual and gender identity. I would catch the spirit at times, especially during my solos, and step down out of the choir stand and twirl down the aisle while my robe ballooned around by pudgy body—all the while holding a note and making sure that no one took the microphone out of my hand. The little queen in me was begging to show out, and I had a captive audience.

My stories of growing up and performing in the black church choir are similar to the ones the men of *Sweet Tea* share. As one of the narrators declared, "Where else but in the black church can a queen be a star whether she has talent or not? Baby, it ain't the army where you can be all that you can be, it's the church. Homophobic or not, church folk will give you your props." Black gay men have surmised that the church is a place to express their talents in performance sites that don't necessarily compensate for the church's homophobia but at least counter its effects.

The choir is just one of many church organizations in which narrators discuss being members. As children growing up in the church and even now as adults, many of these men serve on the Usher Board, the Deacon Board, or the Board of Trustees—or are ministers themselves, such as "OKC" from Oklahoma. Moreover, more than a few narrators share delightful stories about attending Vacation Bible School, surprising though it may seem that a child would enjoy spending the first few weeks of summer vacation in church every afternoon. Admittedly, I was one of them. And for poor kids, of whom I was also one, the free hot dogs, cookies, and Kool-Aid, as "Rob" suggests, was also an incentive. The point is that the church provided and continues to provide a site where, despite its contradictions, gay men can build community, exercise their creativity and leadership, and express their spirituality and sexuality.

I believed, when I began my research, that most of the men I would interview would be Baptist. This was not the case. As evidenced below, these men represent a whole host of faith communities: Baptist, Methodist, Episcopalian, Presbyterian, Catholic, Jehovah's Witness, Unitarian, Church of God in Christ, Pentecostal, Muslim, and nondenominational. Interestingly, many experiences related by the narrators transcend denominational boundaries, especially when it comes to the role and the importance of the church in their upbringing and in their communities in general. Moreover, their stories tell us something about the history of the black church in the South, particularly in rural areas. For instance, one common theme throughout the narratives is the fact that many churches only met twice a month because the congregations were so small that they could not afford to pay preachers a full-time salary. In some instances, preachers served two churches in the same town, but alternated Sundays.

The narrators' tales of race and region, sexuality and spirituality, complicate any preconceived notions about what it means to be a black southern gay churchgoer. In addition to the stories that one would expect to hear about being gay in the church, there are stories of affirmation, participation, and reconciliation. The "messiness" of these narratives is what makes them wonderful and heartbreaking at the same time. Admittedly, the challenge for me during some of these conversations was not imposing my own judgment on the men's beliefs. While I share in some of their experiences of growing up in the church in the South, my growing disdain for the church did not always allow me to connect with their stories because of what I perceived to be internalized homophobia. In those instances, I found myself probing deeper in some misguided attempt to "save" these men from self-hatred, only to realize, in the words of Janie Crawford, the protagonist of Zora Neale Hurston's *Their Eyes Were Watching God*: "Two things everybody's got tuh do fuh theyselves. They got tuh go tuh God, and they got tuh find out about livin' fur theyselves."[3]

. . . .

ALBERT (B. 1981, NATCHEZ, MISS.)

Well, I often recount the stories of going to church on the first and third Sunday, which is really familiar in Mississippi in particular because most pastors have two or three other churches and a job somewhere else, and they kind of stretched themselves in that respect. But very, very religious in some respects. Even if it wasn't just being, you know, not really participating in church, but just being there was something that was a priority in my family. I can recall [. . .] my father kind of urged me to become a junior deacon, and I can recall receiving the little junior deacon book and reading it and doing the duties of a deacon in the church and having that space to kind of express those types of practices. I sang in the choir, sang on Sundays, sang during family reunions. But religion was a very, very important thing in my family.

Were you raised Baptist? Methodist?

Baptist. Missionary Baptist. Yeah.

Did you enjoy church?

Well, I really did not come into full understanding of religion until I got to [Piney Woods] boarding school. I remember as a second-semester freshman at boarding school coming to know that Jesus was the Son of God. So while the religious component was primary in the household, the types of conversations were not being discussed, and it took me until I was a freshman in high school to realize that Jesus was the Son of God. But I had been in church all of my life.

So what were you learning?

I don't know. I don't know. I don't know. My memories are very vague in some respect about the church, and I don't know if it's because I maybe slept through it, or what the case might have been. In terms of discussing faith, I did not know about Jesus. So when I got to boarding school, it was really fascinating to come to know that information and to be in a community that was intentional about developing a consciousness about Christianity and other religious traditions and to see for the first time people shout and dance and speak in tongues and so forth, at boarding school. People got the spirit at my church, but it was running and screaming, but never the speaking in tongues and the laying of the hands. We had this one guy in my church, Shouting John, that's what they called him of course, and I can remember as a child he sat in the first pew in the church and as a child Shouting John would get up every Sunday and just run in front of the whole parish, you know. And I could just imagine what visitors were thinking. But it was nothing for us because we had become so accustomed to it. And then there was this other man who sat on the deacon bench, and that man cried every Sunday. And I never understood until I was much older what was going on with him. He was just crying, just wailing all the time. It was really interesting in that respect to see those dynamics, but to be exposed to those dynamics in a high school setting, you know, those were things that old people did. You know, young folks didn't run around and speak in tongues and be so expressive in their worship. So it was new, it was new. And [. . .] my experiences with it also deals a lot with having sang in the choir in boarding school and to be a part of an ensemble that traveled the world and worshipped together and to kind of experience the spiritual transformations that were taking place on an individual level and on a collective level. Even as we're on the stage performing, to see individuals really catch it and really begin to weep and to be expressive in their worship. My Piney Woods experience was really, really instrumental in helping me to understand who I am as a spiritual being.

It's in Piney Woods, Mississippi. It's probably about two and a half hours from my home, and it is one of four remaining African American boarding schools in the country. And I had peers from all over the country, and about five or six foreign countries there, so it was really an interesting environment to see and to witness and to learn from those individuals and to kind of exchange ideas. I was sharing with my mentor a few days ago, who is at Piney Woods, is now the interim president of Piney Woods, how Piney Woods was very interesting insofar as dealing with class and seeing how some of the poorest people could come to a boarding school and some of the wealthiest people come to a boarding school, and there was never a privileging of any sort that was taking place, and how our lives were changed, the poor people's lives were changed, and the wealthy people's lives were changed just by interacting with one another. It was an awesome experience. Much of who I am is very much so because of that experience.

What role does religion or church play in your life currently?

Well, I guess I'm an apostate. Because I am no longer a part of a church, but I am a part of the community of believers, community of faith. And how I go about experiencing God may be avant-garde, may be a bit different than the traditional way; when I am able to encourage that young man in the dorm, that's experiencing the holy for me. When I am out and people recognize that there has been some synthesis between being a spiritual individual and being a sexual individual, a sexual queer individual, where I have kind of shaped out of my experiences some method to the madness in some respect, I feel like I experienced the holy being. I mean, I don't have to be in a church, and part of me says I have to be in a church, but right now, at this moment now, I'm not in a church, because I feel like I'm doing more ministry outside of the church. When I am helping people understand and appreciate and embrace who they are, that's totally me. This goes for not only queer people but straight people also, okay. Helping people kind of synthesize those two ends that have seemed to be divergent in one way or another. So, I am still spiritual. I have been baptized and I love God. I love God. And every day I wake up being in this curious homosexual body, I thank God, because if God is the God of wrath and I am not to be, because God is powerful, God could have taken us out a long time ago. But because God allows me to exist here in this space, I know I'm in relationship with Him. And I know that God is real. And I know that God delights in me, in His creation. So that's how I rest at night. And I love, irrespective of difference. That's one thing that drives me. Every day I wake up, I say, "God how can I love just a little more, despite the adversities that may present themselves? How am I able to love the homophobic person? How am I able to love the racist individual more?" I've managed to have conversations with people who share totally opposite beliefs than I do, and I can walk away from them and say, "Thank you. The conversation has been rewarding in so many ways." And to know that they're walking away from me making a judgment.

Why do you think that there are so many black gay men in the church, especially in the choir?

Beyond the choir robes? [Laughter] And the drag, right? [Long pause] You know, there's something about music that's transcendent and to hear such beautiful voices come from such denigrated and debased bodies, something real about that. I think it was Paul that says, we will be persecuted about our bodies dying every day, you know, becoming the sacrificial lamb. I think that the bodies of all those homosexual men are the sacrificial lambs every Sunday, when they stand and they sing praises. And they bring together a community of believers. I don't know why it seems as if most gay men are in the choir. Maybe it's special. Maybe it was meant to be that way. Maybe that's the only connection for gay men. Maybe that's the only link that keeps us a part of the community of faith and God understood that. So maybe we were positioned there, intentionally, divinely.

. . . .

AL

AL was born in Nash County, North Carolina, in 1956, the second of three children. He now resides in Raleigh but has lived in various parts of North Carolina. AL and I share an interesting history in that from 1980 to 1981 he was my Sunday school teacher in Hickory. At the time, I had no idea that he was gay, but I do remember that we kids loved his Sunday school classes because he was so much younger than the other church members who taught the teen class. He used to have us over to his home for dinner and take us to cultural events around town. Although we were naïve teenagers, especially when it came to homosexuality, we did notice that he never hung around women and that there always seemed to be a host of out-of-town "buddies" who came to church with him. I would soon come to know some of these "buddies" when I enrolled at the University of North Carolina at Chapel

Hill. Oddly enough, AL and I never saw much of each other after he moved from Hickory. It wasn't until 1998, when I returned to UNC to begin a postdoctoral fellowship, that our paths crossed again.

Another postdoctoral fellow invited me to a gay Halloween party in Raleigh but never mentioned the name of the person hosting the party. Imagine my surprise when AL came to the door! The running joke that evening was that he used to be my Sunday school teacher, which gave his and my friends plenty of ammunition for ribbing us and making all kinds of innuendos about what he was teaching us in class. He confessed that he had known I was a "budding queen." I retorted, "Well, it takes one to know one."

The interview took place at AL's home in Raleigh on August 14, 2004.

What role does your religion, church, play in your life now?

A very strong role. I go to a MCC church, and funny enough, only within the past two or three years have I been comfortable telling people. [. . .] Cause I was in a Baptist church—a black Baptist church. And you know, I was involved in doing this and doing that, and da da da da da, and over time I began to realize who I am is really not working here. Because you'd hear those sermons every now and then, about homosexuality from the pulpit, and fire and brimstone, and all this kind of stuff. And then on top of that, every now and then there'd be kind of a rumor thing, a scandal thing, floating around—you know I hear, "So and So is gay," you know. My God, the world's coming to an end. [. . .] Plus, other things were happening, and I left that church, and I came to the MCC church, which I love. I love the pastor. The congregation is very warm, nice people. And so church plays a very big role for me, from a moral conscious standpoint. I know that Jesus Christ has saved my soul, so when people approach me—I was at the mall the other day and this lady approached, and she said, you know she said, "Jesus is coming back," and I said, "Yeah, I know." She said, "You better get ready," and I said, "Yeah, I am." And there would've been some time when I would have hesitated, you know, to say that, but church still plays a role in my life. I'm not as active as I used to be. I don't teach Sunday school like I used to, and do those kind of things, but church still plays a strong role. In helping me keep my values system, I guess, where it is.

Do you think church is important to the majority of black gay men in this area? In the South?

I think it's important to them, yes, but [. . .] I feel like it's still kind of disconnected. In other words, the church, the concept of God, of Christ, is important to us. And in many cases the activities of our church are important to us. But [. . .] it's almost like it's a one-way relationship. We give things, we do things in the church, but the support we get is oftentimes because of who they think we are, or what they think we are. And [. . .] if they were to find out we were gay, that support would no longer be there. And so that's why I kinda tend to think it's kinda one way.

Do you think that they really don't know? Or that they just don't say anything?

I think it's a combination of all of the above. One of the local churches here was recently on the front page because the minister was preaching against homosexuality. This was during the time when gay marriage was heating up with Massachusetts and San Francisco. And he got front-page coverage—black minister, black church, antigay marriage, antihomosexual, da da da da da, and the whole nine yards. And I think this was the same minister who at one point a couple of years ago stood up and said something [. . .] along the lines of, "I don't have any gay people, you know there are no gay people in my congregation, in my choir, in my . . ." [Laughs] Now that's when I said, "Chile, please. I know two or three!" So I think some of them don't know. I think some of them are just talking, 'cause some of them are really hypocritical, they're real hypocrites. So it's a mixture of all of the above. I don't know which one it's most of, but it's some of all of it.

Why do you think the choir is such an attractive space for gay men?

That's a good question. I've often thought about that, because I've always had this thing about choir directors and pianists. Some of the most talented people around, but I don't know many who either aren't gay or haven't played around. But at the same time when you step back and think about, okay this is part of the arts, and when you look at the arts you tend to think okay, the ballet dancers, the artists. I don't know. I can't explain it. If you figure that out, let me know.

Do you think that church is a place for gay men to meet other gay men?

Oh absolutely. When J. L. King [author of *On the Down Low: A Journey into the Lives of "Straight" Black Men Who Sleep with Men*] said that, when Oprah asked him, "Where do you go to meet men?" he said the same thing as you. I believe it. And I've heard, even though I haven't experienced it, I've heard too many people that I know talk about, you know, guys that they meet or have met in church who you know, walk up and make sure they greet, and some-times say things like, "Give me a call. Let's get together and have lunch," and so forth. And I hate to say that, but that's such a typical, you know, line kind of thing; we don't really do that in church, you know? A friend of mine came and visited from out of town, and he's you know, a handsome, sexy little guy;

he was in the foyer of the church and one of the guys from the church, you know walked by. I guess they were crossing, and stopped him, and had a conversation. And within two minutes, had given him his number. And I'm going, my friend is visiting from out of town, there ain't nothing, there's no, you know get together over lunch, you know, thing that can occur here, you're not new in the area. So that's nothing more than, you know, a pass. [Laughs] Anyway.

· · · · · · · ·

ANGELO (B. 1976, GREENVILLE, S.C.)

And what role did church or religion play in your upbringing?

In mine, it played an important role, to the point that I actually went to theological school. [. . .] It hasn't been completed due to [laughter] issues or whatever, but it still does play an important role in my life.

What denomination were you?

Holiness. Started out as Baptist, but it kind of changed when I went to school and taught under the Holiness. I actively participated in every function, participated in every service, even with the bishop, and the pastors—just highly involved. 'Cause I kind of looked up to them as mentors, and they kind of guided me as well as, considering the absence of a father. So, you know, my mom encouraged me to be around them.

What did you enjoy most about church?

Just the activity, the gatherings, being together amongst others—just basically the teaching. Just being enlightened of what it actually is and the Word and going in depth with it and basically the overall social part of it.

At what age did you start to realize that you have same-sex attraction, and what was your reaction to that realization?

Oh, it was early. [Laughter] Early to the extent that by being in church and being around the male figures, I would always be around the male figures, so I was pretty much under the impression that that was acceptable or that being around them and seeing what I saw—that was pretty much, not to say an arousal, but that's what kind of introduced me to the attraction for other males.

When you say "seeing what you saw," what did you see? [Laughter]

[Laughter] Just the activities of being around other men and quote/unquote some things that were [. . .] going on in the church that, you know, you look upon as being wrong, such as men doing things they shouldn't be doing, but you know, seeing if they're who I'm supposed to look up to and that's what they're doing, that that's what I'm supposed to be doing. Because

I observed two men, two preachers or church officials. They were [laughter] in the basement having sex. They were having sex.

And did you ever say anything?

Later on, and [. . .] that led to my being discharged from the church, [because] I spoke of it in an initial sermon. That's when [. . .] I was kind of discharged from it. I noticed it as a child and then as growing up, I thought that's, you know, normal. But throughout reading and being taught the Word, that's not what's supposed to be. And then, as I gradually grew up in the church, that just kind of led me to believe that if this is what two men are supposed to be doing, is this what two women are supposed to be doing? Not to say it kind of misconstrued my perceptions of what sex is supposed to be— it's just that that's my initial introduction to it.

And so you preached about it?

I initially preached about Adam and Eve and the beginning of the Bible, which is what you basically start out with. And just spoke of how people were doing things within the church and how did they expect it to grow if you're not doing what you're supposed to be doing? How do you expect for God to bless you [. . .] if you're misguiding other people? So as I spoke upon that, afterwards, things got quiet to the extent that, they knew about it. Some of the officials *knew* about it. And other people in church knew of what was going on but failed to say anything about it.

So they dismissed you and not the other ones?

Yes, because it was more or less my word against theirs and that it was inappropriate to say what I said . . . in front of guests and other visitors that came. That should've been an issue that I should've discussed with the pastor or with the bishop.

But if you didn't name names, what was the big deal?

But it's just that it was a known thing in the church and that they knew what I was talking about, and for fear that something else might be brought up. It's just that it shouldn't have been said.

. . . .

BOB (B. 1940, BAXLEY, GA.)

What role did religion or church play in your upbringing?

Well, of course, you know, it revolved around the church when I look back on it. And I have mixed feelings about that now that I'm widely read and I think that Christianity was imposed on the black man by the slave master and so there was something to be said about that whole experience. But now having said that, that experience and that community, for whatever reason, became a source of support for families because whenever families got into financial trouble or bereavement or even when I went away to college, they would take up little collections and help send little packages. It was always something to do every week because you went to church school and then the services twice on Sunday; you went in the morning and then you went in the evening. So it was the thing—you knew about nothing else because there was nothing else to do.

[. . .] I was an African Methodist Episcopal. And my grandparents had come from Jamaica, so they were Episcopalians. And so our orientation to the church was more Episcopal in terms of our belief systems, more traditional and very conservative, in the sense of rituals but not in the sense of judging other people. But very ritualistic in terms of, you know, you do this and you do that. [. . .] Although I was and my grandparents had been part of that faith community from the time that they had come from Jamaica early on, we still attended other denominations so that it was a community of people knew that you might be officially a member of that congregation but you still would go to other faith communities. [. . .] It was interesting because there were four major churches and then they all had their services once a month. So once a month, there was a Baptist service. And once a month, the next week was a Methodist and the next week was a Baptist, the next week was a Methodist. So the first Sunday, we went to the Baptist church. The second Sunday, all the Baptist people came to the Methodist church. The third Sunday, we all went to the Baptist church and the fourth Sunday we went to another Methodist church. So we all went to each other's churches.

Why was that?

Because it was small enough. And the congregations were very small. And the ministers had more charges to take care of. And they were itinerant ministers, they had very little, if any, formal education in terms of pastoral, you know, psychology and sociology and—but they had, I think, earth sense. And father wit. And their wives were always nurturing. And most of the wives were musicians, and they would do all of the pageants.

Were you active in the church as a child?

Um hmm, Yeah. Well, I was the Sunday school secretary for a while.

What does a Sunday school secretary do?

Well, you have to take the minutes of the Sunday school. And you assisted the superintendent in terms of making sure that everything was readied for the classes. And taking the roll. And then the attendance. And keeping up with what was the finances. And then making the report at the end of the session. And then it was expected that the secretary would also go to the

Sunday school convention, which was convened once a year. And so that was expected. And then so I did that. And then I was in the youth choir; that was expected. [Laughter] Whether you could sing or not, you had to be in that. And then [. . .] I was an acolyte. That was in that African Methodist Episcopal Church. They didn't have that in the other churches at all. But it was part of our ritual that you have acolytes. And so my cousin and I were both acolytes when I grew up, so that was a very interesting experience. And everybody on my street that I lived on were members of that church, everybody. It was a small street. I lived on a street called Third Street, but it was across the main highway, but then that was along St. James. [. . .] It was in 1901 when they organized that faith community. And the Episcopal Church, they met in homes. [. . .] Because there were only like two families that were Episcopalians, they decided not to send an Episcopal priest anymore because they were meeting in homes, they would do the mass in homes. So then the closest thing to the Episcopal Church was the African Methodist Episcopal Church because the ritual is almost the same. So then we became African Methodist Episcopalian.

What role does church or religion play in your life currently?

Not much. Not much at all. And I think it's because, you didn't ask the question but I'll expand on that. I believe that Christianity is a forced form of slavery on people of color. This is my own personal belief. In that people who came from the motherland had a different view of the world and that it was a respect for nature and the gifts that come to us from the Creator, whoever the Creator is. And [. . .] just for amusement I thumb through the religious channels here in Atlanta and I see all the racist ministers talking about all the stuff that goes on and the abortions and the war is right and Bush is right and hearing people say that if you don't believe in Bush, a vote for Bush is a vote for God, and all this kind of stuff. So then it makes you really wonder about this. And then looking at what's happening with the Catholic Church and especially the fact that a German person who helped to persecute Jews was elected Pope. And his father was a member of the—and he was a Brown Shirt when he was, you know, a youth. Not to say a person can't be reformed, but then you have people in Africa and the Third World who really could have made a big difference in terms of tolerance. And so my whole worldview is changed over a period of time. And so I don't believe that I need to have a belief system that is steeped in the traditional white man's Christian belief system, which was actually forced on us by the slave master. And I think that the reason black people beat their children is because it's a reaction to how they were beat by the slave master. And I react very violently when I hear . . .

because I was a nurse practitioner and I have taught parents about the harm that it causes when you whip a child because it's not love. Why would you say, "I love you" and you're inflicting pain? That's not love. And so I have a very, very different worldview. And so the reason I attend a faith community is not because of my belief in the power of what the worldview, especially white view, of Christianity is, and it's a Christian church that I go to—faith community that I go, but it's a very affirming community. It is nonjudgmental. It's very accepting. They have seminars on brothers on the DL [down low]. Brothers who are questioning. They have a ministry on singles. And the music is always—the anthems are very wonderful and they are prepared in such a way that it tells you that there's been training and work done. And they sing from the masters. And I like that.

It's a black church?

Yeah, um hmm. And it's an AME church, 10,000 members. And the woman who sits behind me has fallen in love with me and says I'm the most handsome man in the congregation, and so I said, "Oh, I don't know anything about that." And has called me and invited me to dinner and sends me all kinds of cards and stuff. So the woman who knows I'm gay wants to go to church with me one Sunday so the woman will get off my back. She said, "So I'll go with you one Sunday and I'll be on your shoulder and she'll leave you alone."

So my worldview of religion is more of a social support network because there are gay people in that congregation. I was invited to their home for Christmas parties. [. . .] And the Christmas party was all around bringing toys for tots. And so you went to their home, a beautiful home, they've been together for like twenty years, these boys, and one of them sings in the choir and one of them is in something else. And they're known in that congregation that they are partners. And they're affirmed and they're accepted. [. . .] So I participate to some level in that faith community because of the relationships. And they don't do a doctrine. Their doctrine is more liberal than where I've been before. Never have I ever heard them deliver a homily or a sermon where a person's sexuality is called into question. It's always very uplifting, about the need to be forgiving and accepting, and to challenge people to do the best they can with what they have.

Why do you think there are so many black gay men in the church, and especially in the choir?

Because the choir would not exist without them. [Laughter] And if they left the choir, the church would fold. Many ministers are gay or bisexual or— I've had [. . .] a transitory relationship with a young man since I've been here who is a church choirmaster. And although we no longer have a relationship, when I first came here, I met him, and he's a church musician. And he told me that his minister was his first lover. Um hmm. And so it's very common.

Is his minister also married?

He was married at the time, um hmm, yeah, um hmm, yeah.

But why do you think that, especially churches that have pastors that preach homophobic sermons, why would black gay men continue to attend?

You know, it's very, very puzzling, because I think it's a self-hate kind of thing. I mean, I've been in therapy [. . .] and I was a psych nurse also for six years on the weekends in San Francisco, so I'm able to sort of look at behavior and dissect it. I think that people are not learned. An emotional charge that people get out of hearing the rhetoric, even though it's self-debasing and it's derogatory to you, it's still the fact that you're in that mix makes you for that moment a little bit better than the person who's not there. [. . .] I was dating a man who is a church administrator for a very large Baptist church and I could no longer see him. I said, "You know, the man preaches homophobic sermons and admonishing people to vote for Bush. And he laughs about gay people in your presence. And how can you be the church administrator and you sit there and listen to that?" I said, "That's a bunch of bullshit. How can you do that?" And so I just said I won't allow myself to be associated with you anymore, so we just broke it off. That only lasted like two, three months anyway. [. . .]

But I think that there is that dichotomy going on with black men and this ambivalence. It goes back to I think the mentality that the slave master has put on black people that you have to believe in this power. And that somehow you're going to be saved in the end. But then if you are gay, you're going to be damned to Hell and you're going to go fire and they preach all this bullshit. And people still go. But I think they go because they want to be seen. I think they go because they dress well. I think they go because the women like the way they look because they become the fag hags. I use that word advisedly. The women who really like the men who are gay and they know they're gay, always compliment them on, "Oh, don't you look so well today." And then they invite them to dinner and then they cook all these meals and they invite these people over. And so it's as if there is a sense of community and they have positions of importance in those congregations. Many of them are choir members or choir directors or on boards and stuff like that, if they're not openly out of the closet. And in my faith community, most people who are all out of the closet; there are no closeted people there. Partners sit next to each other. And I know a woman who is a professor of theology at Emory and she is associate minister there and her partner sits in the third seat from the front and everybody knows.

....

BRYANT (B. 1967, DUBLIN, GA.)

Growing up, the church was very influential because both my parents were the children of preachers. I can't remember a Sunday other than if I was on my deathbed that we didn't get up and go to church. It wasn't optional. We would go to Sunday school, and because my mother's father was the preacher, she led the Sunday school, much like she does now, to this day. So we were there before anybody got there, at ten o'clock, to set the church up, turn the lights on, turn the power on.

I remember services being very long, but I also remember that as soon as they stopped I could carry a tune in a bucket. I was in the choir, in both churches, on the first and third Sundays my mother's church, on the second and fourth Sunday at my father's church. I remember going to every Vacation Bible School that ever happened. At my father's church, the church was literally less than 150 yards from the back door of my house, and it was across our backyard, so we didn't have to walk across the road; we stepped from our backyard into the church ground. So there was no separation from our house to the church, so we were there constantly. We went every Sunday, every Wednesday night, and then Friday night when they had prayer meetings, and then of course Saturday I went to choir practice for the Sunday performance at church.

My father and mother never played secular music in the house. We never played secular music. [. . .] We had an eight-track player in the car, an eight-track player in the house, and we had all of the gospel artists that you could think of. On Sunday mornings before we went to church a program used to come on on NBC, and it was like a gospel show. [. . .] My father was in the gospel group; he was like the backup singer in the group. I don't know why, because my father can't sing, but he was in a singing group, so when we weren't in church and he had to go to some gospel singing, we would go to that too. So Sunday evenings we'd be driving to whatever church, but he would play those gospel eight-tracks all the time. [. . .] I think sometimes that he probably was conflicted around his religion. [. . .] His father, my grandfather, was very strict. I think he wanted to attend church somewhere else but didn't and felt compelled to go there, so he was probably dealing with some of that. So we kinda got the feel to it that my father was enforcing his religion on us, so on Saturday morning when we were watching cartoons, he would come in, turn the television off and pop in an eight-track tape and sit there and make us listen to it. You couldn't go to the room, you had to sit in the living room and listen to the gospel tape. I remember him marching me out of my room and making me sing along to those gospel tapes as well.

Bryant, age twelve, standing in front of his father's Electra 225, on his way to Sunday school in Dublin, Georgia. Courtesy of the narrator.

When I relate this story everyone says, "Well, how could that possibly be?" But I remember in the summer of 1980, right before I went to high school, I was almost thirteen years old, sitting at the kitchen table with my mother and father asking them, what was the dial on the stereo system that said "AM/FM" because we had never turned on the radio. Ever. Period. And my mother said, "Get down there and turn it up, flip it over to FM, and turn the power on." And when I turned the power on, I remember the radio playing, and I was shocked, because I had never heard radio before, and I remember the song was the Pointer Sisters' "He's So Shy" was playing in the background. The first time ever, that I had ever heard radio. [. . .] We couldn't go to [. . .] any school-related functions. My cousins [whose home] we were going to weren't [. . .] playing secular music [. . .] We lived across the road, next to my aunt, and she wasn't playing secular music. So my neighbors until 1979 were my two aunts that lived together, one of them had a child, and my grandfather, my father's father. It was three houses on a dirt road, so we had no other neighbors, so I never heard any music other than what I heard in my own house.

So it was the summer of 1980, and I was thinking, "Oh, there's the radio." And that was the first time that I had ever heard music. And I can remember from that point, then, I bought a song hits book from the Piggly Wiggly that had all the words to the lyrics of the song. And I discovered, "He's So Shy" was actually in the countdown, the Kasey Kasem countdown, America's Top Forty, and I used to sit there in front of that radio once I discovered, from twelve to five o'clock, listening to Kasey Kasem count down all forty songs, singing along with them. I could tell you what song in what order in what place, because religion had dominated up until that point. I didn't know anything else. Religion was the main point, it dominated everything— everything that we did and everything, particularly until 1980. I was turning thirteen. Until that point I didn't know anything other than gospel music and going to church. We had never gone out. [. . .] Other than going to go visit my friend Gerald, who was my best friend, and even his parents were very staunchly religious, never heard anything there either.

I didn't know anything about disco music. I didn't know who Donna Summer was; I had never heard of Aretha Franklin or Natalie Cole; I didn't know who any of those people were until after 1980. That whole seventies era, I didn't know anything about any of that music, at all, or any of that culture. Because we were driven by bedtime and stuff so I was never up past nine o'clock. I didn't know what came on. So until thirteen, my bedtime was nine o'clock, and it was rigorously enforced.

Did you enjoy going to church?

I don't think that I enjoyed the sitting and listening to the sermons, because we were always going to my grandfather's, and grandfather's churches. And unlike today, where the minister had to prepare text, they thought about it and you might get a different message, you would get the same message over and over again. [. . .] Both churches were small, they had memberships of about 50, 60 people. So it was the same sermon that they would just preach whatever they felt, the term was "I preach whatever's laid on my heart." So you would get the same message repeatedly, and there was no really beginning and no end; they just stopped preaching when they got, when they felt like they had got tired of talking. So a sermon could be thirty minutes or it could be an hour and thirty minutes, or in some instances it could be two hours. So I remember my grandfather just sitting there [makes a gasping sound], sweating you know, breathing. You know how they get real high and start sweating, and I'm like, "You look like you 'bout ready to pass out." But I enjoyed [. . .] being in the choir, or doing stuff extraneous to just sitting there when I could be involved, involved a little bit more. Because I was always loud, I was always vocal. [. . .] And I knew all the songs anyway 'cause my daddy made us listen to them. So anything anybody ever came up with, I could always sing and sing at the top of my lungs, which, good, bad voice whatever, I didn't care. I knew the words and I was not shy about opening my mouth.

[. . .] Because we were the grandkids of the preacher, we always had to do the Easter program; you had to say something. If any of the kids were going on children's day, you were going to be in the program, which was fine by me because I wasn't really that shy. I would say you didn't have to coax me to do my Easter speech or to be an usher and let people in, passing out fans. I wasn't opposed to doing that, so I didn't mind going to church. I just didn't like being in church all day long.

And I can remember being a kid and having to go [. . .] wherever my grandfather was preaching, particularly those pastoral anniversaries at some other church. If he had to go somewhere else and preach, we were going. So church could last from ten o'clock in the morning Sunday school at our time, when we went for our own service, to five, six o'clock in the afternoon because we would go to two o'clock, eat at the church, and then get in the car and go to wherever my grandfather was preaching, and sit there for another two hours. [. . .] I think that's why I became a *60 Minutes* junkie, *60 Minutes* would be coming on at seven o'clock when we would be coming in. So then it just timed, like, *60 Minutes*, go take a bath, and go to bed, because *60 Minutes* went from seven to eight. We'd take a bath eight to nine, and we went to bed at nine o'clock, because it's time to go to school.

Did your parents make you read the Bible outside of church?

My father did that one time. It didn't go over well though, probably because maybe *he* hadn't read the Bible. [Laughter] So it wasn't like we were learning from someone who was a learned scholar. So [. . .] I remember him trying to pull out the Bible one time and having us sit down and read through it, and I think it probably bored him, and we never did that anymore. Of the two of them, I would say my mother's probably the much more spiritual person. And I think it's because my mother's family is much more embracing and easier to get along with, and [. . .] my mother's family was pretty well off in Dublin.

What about the church? Church was very much a part of your younger life, what about now? And what, is there a sense of community there as well, in the church?

I think probably, right as I was coming out maybe, because I was attending not a gay church, but a church that was one of the largest churches in Atlanta and there were lots of black gay men. I was back in the choir, and there was a community of black gay men in that church choir that I socialized with. I think later on, last, maybe, ten, twelve years, particularly attending the church that I attend now, I don't feel that same sense of any connection with black gay anything in the church [. . .] even the church that I attend now, I don't feel any sense of real connection to. Probably explains a lot of the reasons why I don't feel compelled to go that often, because I think that the reason I probably don't feel the sense of gay community is because I don't feel any real connection to that church itself. I think if I was attending somewhere else, maybe that would be different.

In the church that you joined, you said that when you first came out you were in the choir, and you felt a sense of community there. Was the choir a place where there were a lot of gay men?

Yes there was. There was the choir director. Always seems to be the case. Who is now, interestingly enough, the choir director at the church I would like to attend. There was probably the entire tenor section of the church. [. . .] It was gay friendly, not gay affirming, but it wasn't a gay bashing church, so I felt like I could be in the church without really having to make any, any effort to be hidden. Or any real changes around my personality, so I could be, I could attend the church and enjoy the service, and I did. And had this camaraderie with the other people that knew that I was gay, and I knew that they were gay, and they didn't feel any sense to being anything different than what they were when we were in choir rehearsal, or in the pulpit on Sunday morning. So, that to me was a different feeling than I had ever had. Maybe because that was the first church too, [. . .] that I attended after leaving home. [. . .] From about '85 to '91 I wasn't a regular attendee of any church. I started going there, and I was like, "Hmmm, this is nice, a different change. There's no bashing here, and I can bring the guy that I'm dating to the church, and he can sit in the same, the same pew out in the congregation with me. We can ride together, we can leave together, and come to the events and no-body's going to say anything negative." People were openly gay. And the church I would want to attend now is very much gay affirming, to the extent that the pastor wants to perform commitment ceremonies—is willing to.

And this is a black church?

Black Baptist church. And, it is really gay affirming. [. . .] We attended there off and on when we were down in Decatur. I would like to go there now because I think that, I think due to the influence that religion had on my life for so long, good, bad, or indifferent, I think that it's important for people to feel some sense of, for me anyway, to feel some sense of connection, to a physical, I know spirituality is like, you can do it all within yourself, but I feel a need to be in a church. But I don't feel like I'm getting [. . .] a lot out of the church I go to now. I go because I feel like a sense of obligation, whereas I would like to go and feel like I'm going to church because yes I need to be in church, but I enjoy coming and I look forward to being there and when I am there, I don't have to be someone different than who I am when I'm not there. And I think I'm certainly at the point in my life where the church has to be gay affirming. Gay friendly is nice, but we won't be doing no Leviticus 18 and 22.

. . . .

"C.C." (B. 1961, GREENVILLE, MISS.)

You know, my mother and them was interesting. My father really couldn't stand people who was in churches, 'cause he thought they were all ignorant. [. . .] And he believed in God. He believed in us going. And so later him and I would have these incredible conversations about, "Can you believe that shit?" I mean he just thought they were like ignorant 'cause, you know, for him it was like all these people who was irresponsible and, "Oh, the Lord's going to take care of the garden." He really had issues with that. And he attended church on a regular basis. So it's really interesting being exposed to all kinds of . . . I think I've been Catholic. Methodist. I've been sprinkled. I've been sanctified. [Laughter] I joined all of it. Dunked underwater, over the water, walked on water. [Laughter] So, those years were very formative for me and still remain.

Were you active in the church?

Yeah. Ushered. I was very active. Because the church also, especially for gay people, was like a safe haven, too. [. . .] Because people still try and deny. There are more gay people in church than at the bars. So even as a young child, you begin to like put two and two together. [Chuckle] So it's not like anyone would have any bad experiences up in churches.

Even if the preacher was gay bashing?

Oh, when I got old enough to understand what was being said, then yeah, I had to like let it go 'cause I never understood what I called those "church sissies." And what I mean by that is they're everywhere. And Atlanta and all is full of 'em. And mind you, I thank God they're there and so I don't want to say anything bad about them, but I never understood that concept of people going places where you were going to be *bashed*? How could you find Jesus up in there? So I, on purpose, I avoided what I called "church sissies." Like all those church sissies, I stayed away from them because that was a little too crazy for me. [Chuckle] Flippin' over all those benches and all that stuff and then, at the end of the night, you're gonna be like in bed with somebody in the name of hate? 'Cause you have to hate yourself. So, I ain't never want none of that bad hate sex at all, so I stayed away from churches. [Laughter]

What is your current religious church affiliation or your perspective on religion and church?

Mine is really church without walls. [Chuckle] Thank God I've found peace with it. You know you just have to know Jesus for yourself and leave it at that. I walk around this house every day and talk to God all the time and that *is* my church—my everyday life. Everything I do is church.

Why do you think there are so many black gay men in the church, and especially in the choir?

Right, and all that stuff. The thing that I keep talking about in this interview is most people never forgive themselves for being gay. It's just that simple. And that's why it has been the hardest thing, for me, to ever really truly deal with a black man. They n-e-v-e-r forgive themselves for being gay. [Long pause] And I think that no matter how painful or no matter how they could be bashed up in there, they still just feel like, "If I'm *there*, Jesus may not *really* see my other side, because I still think I'm a bad person." So, that's what that is.

DUNCAN TEAGUE (B. 1960S, KANSAS CITY, MO.)

You've talked about this some. But I want you to talk about what role
religion or church played in your upbringing.

Everything. [Chuckle] No, Honey, it didn't *play* in my upbringing. It *was* my
upbringing. There was 4105 South Benton and then there was 4733 Elmwood,
where Westminster Baptist Church was. That was the other place. [Chuckle]
There was no separation. When your father is the pastor and the church is less
than two hundred people, that is your extended family. Or when it's at its
boom, maybe two hundred plus. But that is your extended family. And my
mother's prominence in the church even before my father became a minister,
as a member of the choir, you know. And the church was just part of our life.
And I have tried. I have tried as an adult, you know, as an intellectual who is
trying to question belief systems and God and you know . . . I embraced exis-
tentialism for quite awhile, and still do to some degree as a Unitarian. And I
try to stay home on Sundays. And I can't do it. [Chuckle] You know it's like I
have to go somewhere on Sundays. I have to be a part of some sort of religious
thing or do something on Sundays. Now once I joined, it was easy to stay
home but you know, when I didn't have a church home for a while, it was crazy.

Do you enjoy going to church?

Yes. Yes, because I was a leader at church. And church was, at times, just a
little bit safer. And especially after my voice changed and I became quite a
good baritone singer at church. So not only was I gifted and rewarded for my
intelligence and my abilities at church, but I was loved and admired and I
got all the stuff that, you know, they claim we don't get as young black kids.
But I got it. And to this day, that's still an instant family. It's different now
but, you know.

What role does religion and church play in your life currently?

I'm a lay minister at my congregation.

And what congregation is that?

The Unitarian Universalist Congregation of Atlanta. You know, I tried.
God knows I tried just hanging out. Before I knew it, I was on the lay ministers committee. And then I started speaking regularly at the Marietta Congregation, which is predominantly white and predominantly straight. But let
me tell you, them liberal folks out there in West Cobb County, they love me.
And I love them, too. There are some beautiful people out there. And that
wasn't part of my mythology before.

Why do you think so many black gay men (a) are a part of the church and
(b) specifically in the choir?

Well, I don't agree that all of us are in the choir.

No, that many are.

Many are in the choir and in front of the choir. The pulpit. We're in church because everything is full of gay men. And maybe, as Andrew Ramer [author and gay spiritualist] would claim, because that's our calling. To be spiritual leaders. Not abominations, but the folk running the thing. Because in every denomination, if you look around and you look close enough, you'll say, "Oh my!" And it's not just Christians. I mean, the Indians and Hindus have the sect of transgender folk who roam from city to city. You can't get rid of us. You can't even have your faith without us. I mean of course the black church presence in the community is because it's ours. It's our institution. And prior to recently, it was ours without intrusion by white folks. I think that's changing. Sadly. And so if you're going to have an institution in the black community, you need educated, sensitive, articulate, bright young men running it. And guess who that just described? [Chuckle] You know James Baldwin said that we couldn't enter the twenty-first century without him, and he was so right because they're teaching his words in English classes—a black gay man who came out of church.

. . . .

ED (B. 1952, NEW ORLEANS, LA.)

Well, I came from a divided household, in that my father was a Catholic, but he wasn't a practicing Catholic, and my mother was a Baptist, raised as a Baptist. And when I was younger, my mom used to have us go to the Baptist church. I can remember going to Sunday school and then having to stay for the service, which to me seemed like it was so long. Like you're going to church all day long. And it scared me because the first time I saw a lady catch the spirit, she screamed and jumped up and her wig flew off and she just started trembling and vibrating, kicking . . . [chuckle]. And then the sisters in the white come and fan her and, you know. And then she goes into a complete limp and falls off. And I said, "Mama, is she dead?" And she's, "Shut up, shut up" [whispered] and "She's just gotten the spirit." I was thinking to myself, if that's what the spirit is, I don't want it. And I don't want to ever catch it, you know? [Laughter] And people, I think, don't look at it from the viewpoint of a child. You know, what that looks like. It looks like you're having a seizure, really. And it scared me. And so I said, "Well I hope I never get that." And that was one of the things that kind of turned me off to going to church, was seeing that. And plus it was so long, and then it just seemed like it was so theatrical and most of the ministers had this way of speaking where they would . . . well, they all have to shout. And some of them would make this noise in the microphone like, [makes wheezing sound] like they were gasping for breath. [Chuckle] There's such drama, you know?

[. . .] I went to public school from kindergarten to the third grade. And when I was entering the fourth grade, my parents enrolled us in Catholic school. At that time, it was me and my brother and my sister, I think. [. . .] It was a school in the neighborhood, St. Phillip the Apostle. It was run by the Sisters of Providence. This was an order of black nuns. I think they're from Baltimore; their order is from Baltimore, Maryland. And I guess they had a mission to the blacks. And they didn't say that we had to be converted, but somewhere along the line I became Catholic because we were force-fed catechism and I think my father and mother agreed that it would be best for the children to become Catholic. So I remember going through baptism and confirmation, confession and all those things that you do as a Catholic person. And in fact, I was even an altar boy, you know. And that was during the time when the mass was said in Latin and we had to reply in Latin. And we assisted the priests. The priests were pretty interesting. Well they have to drink all the wine at the end of the Eucharist, where the bread and wine is changed to the body and blood. After Communion is distributed, they're supposed to clean the vessels and drink everything, eat the leftover [. . .] But this one priest [. . .] would be drunk sometimes. We knew that. And then at certain rituals we would have to have the incense in the consorium [censer]. And I remember one time . . . I was standing next to the other altar boy. And this priest—he was a white priest, we all had white priests back then—he said, "Get that damned smoke out of my way." [Laughter] And he said, "Get that damned smoke out of my way" to the boy, but he said it, you know, just for people in his earshot. But the audience didn't hear it. But I was shocked! He cursed. A priest cursed. And I found out a lot of things about nuns and priests back then, you know. [Chuckle]

[. . .] I'm not really a Catholic anymore. This might seem strange, but I'm a Jehovah's Witness. Because those two things, homosexuality and Jehovah's Witness, are diametrically opposed. But I have my reasons for being this at this point in my life. I took my time. I studied it. And I chose it. It's my own choice, and I do believe the Bible is the Word of God. I do believe, you know, that Jesus Christ was sent here as God's Son. I do believe in that. And unfortunately, the Bible condemns homosexuality. Up until now, I had tried to reconcile those two things, you know, being a homosexual or having homosexual feelings for men, and my sense of spirituality because I felt I was a good person. I believed in God. I still do. And some of my friends and I, we are politically opposed because I have friends that are partners and they justify their relationship by saying that God wouldn't have created you in the first place, the way you are, if it wasn't okay. And to a certain degree, I can see that. But then you have other things to consider too. Like there's things in the Bible that say, "Don't do it," you know. Where I'm at right now in my life, it's going to always be a struggle. It's going to always be something that's with me. I don't deny that I'm this way. I still have feelings and I'm still very much alive. With certain things, sometimes you just have to learn how to control it.

Why do you think there are so many black gay men in the church, and especially in the choirs?

Because the black church is used as a vehicle to, not to be theatrical, but to unleash whatever it is you have inside you. You know, in the name of praise. And I think that gay people in general, whether they're black or white, we're just different and we are talented, for the most part. We are very talented. Because I know that I have the capacity, when I do a presentation before the class, I know that the students are looking at me and saying, "Well he sounds like a girl or he talks softly or his mannerisms are like a certain way." But whatever they're thinking, they have to listen to what I'm saying, and if they do listen, they stay in the game because I'm not there to give them a fashion show on me. I'm there to impart knowledge to them. [. . .] It has something to do with praise. A lot of us are gifted, talented in many ways. Vocally, we give our praise. And we inspire others through our voices. And I have met a lot of guys who go to church, but then they turn around and they're just sissies the next day after church. That's the thing that you have to reconcile. You can't be both things. It's really hard. I mean if you really believe what you read in the Bible, you can't have it both ways. You'd like to have it in your mind both ways, but you can't have it physically both ways.

· · · · · · · ·

ANTHONY "FIRST LADY" HARDAWAY

Anthony, or the "First Lady," as he is affectionately referred to, was born in Memphis, Tennessee, in 1969, the youngest of six children. He was reared by his paternal grandparents but was never told why his mother and father sent him to live with them. The nickname "First Lady," or alternately "First Lady Regional Mother," comes from his imitation of black church women whose "crowns" (hats) and furs were ostentatious and whose demeanor when they entered the church demanded respect. Indeed, they carried themselves as if they were the first lady of the church or even the United States. Anthony's deft imitation of these women in public—hats and furs included—garnered him a reputation within his circle of friends and later

*on in his larger church community as someone who also should be respected.
Part of this gendered aesthetic has to do with representing the South in
a positive way: as Anthony explains, "You couldn't go nowhere and not
represent the South looking good. And at the same time, you knew who you
are, meaning black, gay, churchy, and all of this."*

I heard about the First Lady before I began interviewing men for Sweet
Tea. *I tried to reach him for two years, but to no avail. Then, out of the blue,
he contacted me via e-mail to say that he was my "biggest southern fan." He
had read an essay that I wrote for a journal and was so pleased with it that
he wanted to contact me. Once we finally spoke on the phone, he realized
that the person who had been sending him e-mails about interviewing him
and I were one and the same. He immediately agreed to be interviewed.*

*Like Duncan Teague, Anthony is a community activist. He believes that
his calling is to educate the "children" about* HIV/AIDS, *on being successful,
on the value of black literature and literacy, and about black history. He
writes for a local gay magazine in Memphis and is involved in the planning
of black gay pride events. Also like Duncan Teague, he insisted that I use his
first and last names—and his "First Lady" moniker, too.*

*I was able to arrange an interview with Anthony during one of his visits
to Chicago. The interview took place at my home on October 13, 2006.*

How would you describe the influence of religion on your childhood?

Very extremely heavy. Religion made me who I am today. I can't take that
away from myself. Extremely heavy. When I was coming up, education and
religion was, and is still in Memphis, the key element to success. If you can
go to school and, maybe obtain your degrees, as well as be a preacher, you're
considered high, high, high, high on the scale. Because normally if you're
smart, if you're talented and educated and all that, and you can preach and
do all of this, they trained you for that. Actually, they trained us for that.
Actually, that was supposed to have been my route. But I guess knowing who
I am, I didn't want the norm, I couldn't accept the norm: get married, have
kids, build the church up, become somebody, die. I couldn't accept that. I
didn't want to accept it because I know it's a part of me, but it wasn't all of
me. And I would have been lying if I would have done that.

*Why was the preacher like held in such high esteem? Why was that the
trajectory for someone's life? Why was that the avenue to such high esteem?*

He [the preacher] was looked up to as a doctor, a lawyer. He was the one
that led us. He was the father of the community. And it's like a fraternity, so
to speak. Preachers are held in extremely high regard. And even in their
world, you can be elder, reverend; bishop is considered the highest of the

high to us. So in religion in my life, that means something down South. And it's tremendous. That's the way to go. That's the way we were taught, as men, as young males in our church. You actually wanted to be a deacon or something like that. It was an important factor in our life.

And you were raised Pentecostal?

I was raised around Pentecostalism. And for the record, I'm still on the records as a Baptist. I'm still on the record as that, but again, [because of] the education, the upbringing, the culture that was around me, I leaned very heavy toward Pentecostals simply because they fascinated me. Baptist was starch; it was fine, it was about the education. But Pentecostal was about the feelings, the emotions. And being an artist, even as a child, that meant a whole lot to me, because I was able to move while I was singing. I was able to express myself. I was able to do all of these things, and it was okay in the Pentecostal movement. In the Baptist movement, you could do it, but you had to do it under sort of strict regulations. Not strict, strict, but they were strict enough. You couldn't beat a tambourine in the *congregation* in the Baptist church. You were looked at. But in the *sanctified* church, that's fine. In fact, we expect you to do that. And that meant a lot to me; that meant that I was able to move around.

And were there other kids that found that freedom of expression as well?

Not really, because with that freedom of expression, you could be ostracized for that.

Oh, really?

Oh, God, yes, especially as a man. I mean, not as a man, but as a male child. Because you were not expected to shout, to express yourself.

In the Pentecostal church?

You could, but you still had to keep your masculinity in check, even as a child, because if you didn't, you were scorned for that.

By whom?

By the elders of the church. Okay. We used to hear this all the time, "You can sing, but you sing too much like a girl." I'll never forget in my church, there was a lady, she's still living to this day, she didn't mean any harm, but that's all she knew. My voice was too high. And she told me that, "Okay, you just sing too high. Can you sort of lower your voice?" And what she was telling me was, could you bring some type of masculinity to your voice—as a child now. So what I started doing was, okay, well, let me try to deepen it up or something. So I stopped practicing in my high-pitched voice, which was natural to me. And even to this day, when I look at her, I think about it. I'm not mad at her for it, but when I look at her, I think about that. Like, hmmm, okay, you stopped that, but that's cool. I think about that quite often in my life. I ask the question sometimes, if I was actually raised in another city, maybe in another condition, so to speak, where would I be now? Because I used to have a dream of wanting to play the piano. Again, I didn't do it because of my background. My mom and dad wasn't there to encourage me to do it, so why do it? And at this time in my life, I was still trying to shelter myself from the bruises and the hurt that came with being a very small, effeminate, black, male child [. . .] that had no protection around him. There was not a mother and father to protect you from the stares and the words and what people would say to you, because you probably had this gift that you didn't know came with ostracism, if that's the correct word for it, what I mean.

I remember in elementary school, every time we had a production or something, when it came to dancing, I would be selected for it as the head male dancer. But at the same time, I remember people saying, "Oh, yeah, he can dance. But he has these moves and these ways." I was never called a faggot. I would be called a sissy because I had my ways, and my mannerisms were so ladylike, so to speak, so little girl–like. I didn't want to get dirty and all this, that, and the other. And again, I didn't know this was something that was considered bad as a male child. So what I started doing, I started covering up things so I wouldn't be talked about. Let me throw a little dirt on my clothes or let me not comb my hair the way I would really like to comb my hair, things like that. So when it came down to the artistic part of it, I had to tone it down. I'll never forget when I heard [my mother] say, "You're going to church all the time and singing in the choir and doing all this." I'll never forget, she said, "I don't want no faggot singing child." The tone was so like that. So I stopped singing. And I wouldn't sing. And [. . .] the church was putting it out, get up there, do it, do it, do it. And all I'm thinking in the back of my mind is, but my mother wouldn't be pleased. So what I would start doing is I wouldn't perform in front of her at all. And if somebody told her, I just wouldn't show up for the performance. I would do it because I knew the repercussions. That stayed in my mind. So I stopped everything. But by the time I got to junior high and high school, they were cultivating this talent, and I wouldn't tell her. I wouldn't tell any other family members; I didn't want them to come. But what would happen is the community would go back and tell them, "Oh, your grandson really did this and really did that." My grandmother was okay with it, but it would get back to my mother. So I didn't want to do it, I didn't want to share this, because I remember what was said at a very young age. And it's something that still affects me today. I tend to close my eyes when I say it. And I do that so I can escape. You can't hurt me. I'm going to give you this gift, but you can't hurt me. You know what I mean? And before my mother made her transition, actually she never saw me perform on stage, ever. And I made sure of that. I think she heard me sing at my junior college, a solo, that was about it. But to perform on stage, to actually see me in a production, she never saw it. And sitting here now, I guess I realize that that came from that. And I really don't have any regrets about that. That might be harsh to say, but it's the truth.

So I'm trying to understand this: on one level you're saying that the Baptist church was a little more strict in terms of what you could do, but in the Pentecostal Holiness church you could be a little more expressive—it was encouraged, but only to a certain degree?

Right. I used to be good at imitating people, and I used to love to do it. The thing of it was while I was imitating people, I would get into the scene or into the song. So the older women in the church, I could mock them to a tee. Could hit the note, just everything. And again, this is something I was doing to make people laugh, to be friends and everything, but at the same time, people were responding to this music, to this sound. And they would say, "Okay, do this again." But when I would do it, the spirit would be ushered in, so to speak, so I couldn't play with it anymore. It became for real and serious. And once that started happening, then the invitations would start coming in. People would want you to do this, people would want you to do that. And that was fine with me, but I would like to keep it hush-hush, quiet-quiet. The Pentecostal church didn't mind it when I moved, when I did these little movements and stuff like that. And what I mean by the little movements, to me as an artist, you can't really—the full effect of it has to come out. And when it comes out of me, I have to move with it. And it reminds me somewhat of Mahalia [Jackson], Dorothy Lovecoat, and people like that. These people moved while they sang. And I understood that and I responded to that. But again, at the same time, I caught myself imitating them, and at the same time, I was running from myself. Because the singing and the performance were helping me to remove that hurt. That's why I would close my eyes. In fact, I remember in some of the teachings in my high school, my coach used to say, "If you keep closing your eyes, I'm going to get you," because when I closed my eyes, I would do what I need to do. I would probably start at one part of the church, but I'd end up in the back of the church, because of the singing and the movement that came with it for me. I couldn't just sing a line and if that line meant something to me, I couldn't just stand there and sing it, I had to share it with you. I knew what it meant to be hurt. I knew what it meant to be hungry. To not have the things that you really want to have. I knew what that line is, "When I was motherless, Lord, you took care of me." So to say that and to have lived it, how can you just stand there and say it? I had to share with you. And once I got to college, one of my professors, he used to tease me about it all the time, he said, "You're not going to just sing and just stay right there, you're going to come and get me." And he told me, he said, "And I like that." So it was the elders that was telling me to go for it, but at the same time I had to be mindful of my surroundings around me. Meaning family people. Because a lot of family were not really church-church people, at all. I had to have my aunt, that kept me in the church, and I had people that was in the church that were related, but the immediate family, not always so.

Did you enjoy church?

Oh, I loved it. I lived for it. Even today, I live for it. But I enjoy the old-school church more now than I do the modern day. I appreciate the modern day, but my coming up, I really enjoyed it because it was an institution of learning, of family values, of the village, so to speak. Because the church really didn't hurt me, per se. I haven't been hurt by the church; it was the surroundings once I left outside the church. I thought I was taught your family, they're your protectors. And sometimes family were actually protecting what I thought they should have been protecting. That's the difference. So yeah, I love the church. That's why, again, I say I can't deny that about me.

When you were singing in the choir, did you do other things, did you participate on the usher boards or—?

Yes, in fact, I was an usher first. I can tell you that story. I was an usher first, because I used to like helping people. I used to love doing that. I started singing when I went to the children's choir rehearsal, and I went there because I didn't have nothing to do that day. And while they were rehearsing, I would again be up there mimicking people, the older ones. I'm like, "Well, if Sister So-and-So sang this or if Mama So-and-So sang this, she'd do it like this," and the kids would start laughing. And so again, the mother of the church is like, "Baby, you need to go on up there and start singing." And I'll never forget the very first song. It scared me because the people started shouting. And I was like, okay, but I was very young at this time, maybe six or seven. And I share this with you, you're probably one of the only ones that I've probably shared it with. The first song was "One Day at a Time." I'll never forget as long as I live. In fact, I still have the piece of paper because back then, we used to write the words down and put it on paper and then go up there and sing. And I would sing this song and it's amazing because I understood the words, to a point, but I didn't—but when I first started doing it, it was at a choir day at my church. I'll never forget it as long as I live. When I opened my mouth and started singing, all of a sudden these people started hollering and screaming. And I was like, "What's going on?" I thought I had done something wrong. But I couldn't stop because I had started. So the second verse, I calmed myself down. Because I'm thinking, okay, well maybe I'm doing something wrong or whatnot. That's when it first started. Again, all this time when I was at home playing church, I was just imitating people. So when this happened in the children's choir, I was like, oh, God. And so when another friend of mine's explained to me what was going on, she's like, "No, no, no. They weren't disliking you. They liked you." And I was like, "really?" Okay. So she gave me the go ahead to go on and open up, and so before I realized it, when we started singing these other songs. From there, at the age of seven and eight, the elders of that church, when we had special events, I wouldn't just sing with the children's choir anymore, they were telling me to go over there with the big people. And here I am, this little, very small child, standing in front of these huge women, they were huge to me, and I would get hit on the back and all of this. And they were saying, "Sing it, child." Again, I'm thinking, okay, what is going on? So my friend was in the audience, she's like, "Yeah, keep on, keep on, go for it." So this performance came there. And I was getting confused about it. But then, once I realized what was going on, I understood it then. Because I knew about the spirit and all that, but I wasn't used to a microphone in my mouth at this early age. In fact, I think I stopped using the microphone once I got to college, because the microphone was a distraction to me, I didn't like holding something in my hand. I wasn't able to move freely. Now, education-wise they taught me that's country. "That's country singing, baby, when you don't use the micro-phone." But that's when the professors started saying, "Okay, we see what we need to do with you. You're a production person. You're a stage person. You can't stand to be limited to things to hold in your hands and stuff like that." So what started happening was I would just stand there and sing it. Real crazy. But down South, in Mississippi, you can do that and get away with it. Alabama, you can do that and get away with it. Because I didn't know it was call-and-response then. All I can say, these older people would really talk back to you on this. And again, that thing of, okay, you're preaching now. You're being a preacher. You're doing this. And again, all these labels start coming onto me. And I didn't understand it. And I was scared of the pulpit because again, this was this box. And if you got up in this, you had to do this. And I was like, "No, that's not me, because I like little boys." And that was still in the back of my mind at this time. I knew what I liked. So that was going. And like I said, I wasn't raised by my mother and father, so I'm feeling like I'm not up to par. I like boys, secretly. I don't feel like I'm up to par. These people over here are telling me to do this. These people over here are telling me to do this. What's going on? It's too much tugging going on with me. I don't know which way to go. I don't have anybody I can go to and ask them, "What's going on? What is this like?" I didn't know.

What role does the church or religion play in your life currently?

It's still important to me to commune with the divine. And what do I mean by that is I don't have to go to church all the time, even though I prefer to do that. The calling on my life now places me in places where I probably can't get to the church every Sunday, on Wednesday nights. But I make sure that the work that is being done would be the same as if I was in this quote/unquote place, this temple, this church, which means that I can do outreach in another city at someone's home, to me that's still church for me. And I still need to commune with the—and when I say this word, I don't mean a denomination, I mean the people—I still have to commune with the saints. In the South, in the black gay village, we call each other saints sometimes. "Hey, Saint, what you doing, Saint?" "Well, Saint, how are you?" And we say that because we were raised with that. We grew up and are still a part of that. So religion, the church, it's still very much a part of me. And I think that would never go away. It's just like when James Baldwin used to say it. It's just ingrained in me. I can't dismiss it, no matter how much I want to. So it's still there. Again, I may not be able to get there, to the house of prayer every Sunday, or to the annual events and all this stuff, but I promise you, my presence will be there because I'm going to make sure that I do what needs to be done. Now, if there's something that needs to be done, it's going to be done. I may not be able to be there, present-wise, but my love will be there, my spirit will be there. That's what I mean by that.

Why do you think there are so many black gay men in the church, and
particularly in the choir?

We have such a talent. Well, first let me use the word "gift." We have such a profound gift. And when I go back to Mother Africa, everything was ceremonial—beads, feathers, masks, movement, music, sound, drums, that the church is our haven and the black Mecca in the black world. That's our haven. If you don't have anything else, you got the church. So singing has always been a way for a lot of us to release. And again, to express ourselves. So, I mean, think about it, I'm a part of something that has a lot of sound to it. I'm making movement with it. I'm able to express myself. And in doing this, I'm helping to heal me. So I'm communing in a place that I've been taught is safe. It may not be safe for everybody or it may not be safe today, but I was taught it was safe, before I started getting ridiculed. So it's that I like to sing in this choir and make the people do this, that, and the other. Because we're a very moving people when it comes to music. And I think that's one of the reasons why we're in the choirs and different areas. And it gives us a chance to be in a production, so to speak. The bigger the choir, the better the choir, the more you can get away with certain things. And even in your home church. If this musician is wearing this piano or organ out and you're able to really direct this choir or sing this song, then everybody is in the spirit of rejoicing, so they're really not going to ridicule you for that, at that moment. Do you know what I mean? So I believe that's one of the reasons why so many of us, it gives us the opportunity to express ourselves in the church a little bit more than if you were in any other auxiliary of the church, if you know what I mean. If you're an usher, you can't do a whole lot, you just usher. If you're a Sunday school teacher, you just teach. If you're a minister, you still have to be poised and refined. But in that choir stand, I can get away with some stuff. I can see what I need to see. I can do what I need to do. And that's the truth what I'm saying. So it's all right to be in the choir because, first of all, this robe allows me to sometimes fantasize about some things. It can be a gown; it can be whatever. I remember doing that. I remember doing—this robe made me, I was able to flow. If I did certain things, maybe I wouldn't be ostracized, if I twirled a little bit and hit this note, because that was like a Sam Cooke to them, that was like a James Brown movement to them, so they could identify with that, and I can get away with it, because this robe is really going to hide this twist I got. So I believe that's one of the reasons why the choir has always been the glamour, to a point, of the church, to me.

. . . .

FREDDIE (B. 1944, MADISON, GA.)

I attended church regularly in Madison, Georgia, and even after moving to Atlanta. At some point, when I was old enough to make my own choices, I realized, just looking around, because I was always kind of a very observant little kid, I observed human behavior and a lot of it just didn't quite seem right. I would ask my mother [. . .] "Mother, if So-and-So did this and blah, blah, blah, is that right?" And she would say, "No, that's not right." And sometimes I'd say, "Well, Mother, you did that to me the other day." [Chuckle] And sometimes it was well received and sometimes not. But sometimes she'd say, "Oh, I did?" and I'd say, "Yeah, you did." And so I did that kind of thing. So I was a very keen observer. So when I was old enough to make my own decisions, I made the decision to stop attending the church I was attending. And I think I made the decision to kind of stop attending church altogether because I realized that I was in very bad company. I realized that I was in very bad company, and that these people were—I don't think I knew the word hypocrite then—but these people were hypocrites. But I realized that I was in very bad company because I observed their behavior. They would go to church and shout and carry on. And during the week, I would observe that they really weren't very good people. And I always thought that going to church was kind of where you kind of get a kind of an energy that would take you through the week or through life, on a certain kind of a path. And I noticed how they would talk about folk in an unkind way and how they weren't as kind or as giving as they could have been.

[. . .] But I have very basic rules about how I interact with people that I think were implanted in those early years in the church. And I don't know if I'm going to start going back or not. But if I do, there's a big church on the corner, St. Philip's AME church. Because it's convenient. [Laughter] I can walk. I don't drive. I can just walk up there in ten minutes and come on back home. So if I should start attending church, that's where it will be.

[. . .] And I hear all this about the church. There's a lot of hypocrisy because who do you think is directing the choirs, mostly singing in the choirs, and playing the piano? In most black churches that I am aware of, black gay men.

Why do you think that is? Why do you think there are so many gay men in choirs in churches?

Well, you know what I think some of it is? [Chuckle] This might sound really silly. That robe is very much like a dress. [Laughter] And they can carry on and shout in that sort of legitimate dress. I don't know. You know they say we're talented, but I think that people in all sexual persuasions are talented and can sing. But I've considered that because I have observed gay men really shouting and carrying on in these robes—working the robe. So, I don't know. That's just my own little silly kind of thought about it. But I've considered that. And it's like a performance. They can perform, you know. They can perform. They can be seen.

Does that take precedence over sometimes being gay bashed by the preacher or . . . ?

Well see, I don't know. I don't understand that because I personally would not sit in a congregation with one of these "Adam and Eve" and "Adam and Steve" sermons, more than once. I actually stopped attending the church service that we normally attended during our family reunion in Madison because they had the same ignorant preacher each time, and each time he would seem to get on that kind of subject matter. And I personally felt insulted by it; I'm not going to sit through that one more family reunion. So, the last couple of family reunions I have attended, I have not attended church service because I would not sit through that. I really wouldn't. And I don't understand gay people who routinely attend churches where they're constantly bashed. I don't understand that. I really don't. And I certainly don't understand it from the point of view of the preacher judging 'cause let's face it: many of these preachers who are doing that, are probably doing the choir director. Doing one of the choir members. I have certainly known that that was going on in some of those situations.

By the same token, years ago I had met this older preacher who . . . I was coming from somewhere and he offered me a ride. And I said, "All I want is a ride. I don't want nothing else." So he agreed that he would just give me a ride, but he certainly wanted more. And I think that first night, on the way home, he stopped the car before he got to my house. I said, "What are you doing?" He said, "I just wanted to look at you," because he thought I was so attractive. And at some point, we did start to have sex and he would try and get me to attend his church. And I said, "No. There's no way I'm going to sit out in the congregation of your church when we are, in fact, having an affair and you are, in fact, married. So at the very least, we're committing adultery. And I certainly wouldn't get anything from your sermon." [Laughter] "I wouldn't get anything from your sermon, so certainly no, no I'm not going to do that." And I wouldn't. I really would not. I think there's a lot of hypocrisy. I know there's a lot of hypocrisy in these churches, and I don't always understand.

Recently, a local minister led a march against gay marriage. And I've certainly heard, privately, that he is carrying on a most inappropriate friendship with a young man, and I heard this from Leroy. My partner attends the senior citizens center. And apparently the young man's grandmother shared with Leroy that this preacher is having what looks on the outside like a most inappropriate friendship with her grandson. Buying him clothing and . . . I don't know if he bought him a car or not, but spending money on him. But it looks most inappropriate.

. . . .

GEROME (B. 1958, TUSCALOOSA, ALA.)

Oh, until I got into like the ninth grade, that's when it became clear to me that there is a God. You know? I knew that there was something, but I couldn't quite put my finger on it because from a child up, I would always say, "God if you're real, do this or do that" or, you know, certain things. That sounds crazy, I guess. But I would, you know, try to give Him a test. And He didn't have to respond. He's the father and I'm the child. And stupid as I was, I didn't know it. And He waited until the right time to reveal Himself to me, and then that's when I caught on, "Oh You are there." And I would say it was like in the last year of high school I'll put it like that. And I didn't even complete it, you know, high school. I just gave up, quit, because I was going through a lot of anxiety, anger, bitterness, you know. Dealing with my sexuality and not understanding it and confused. No guidance, no parents, no one to give me no answers, you know? And like that. And these things you couldn't go to your older sister and talk to her about. Even my oldest brother, I couldn't talk to him about that. So it was just like *me.*

Were you going to church regularly?

Unh uh. Not regularly. I got in there strong, like I said, after my last year or so of high school and I quit. I ended up going. But I came up in the church, as a child, because my mother started that when we was kids. That was one thing she insisted on. She would drive us to her church down in Greens [i.e., Greene] County on Sundays. And I can remember that as a child. But after my mother passed, my sister did not pursue it. She wasn't, you know, that into that. But now she is, you know, studying more. We wasn't demanded to go to church as children because she didn't, you know, pressure. It was on us. If we wanted to go, we'd go. And me dealing with all the turmoil that I was dealing with at that time as a child, I had no idea that I needed to be in church. So I didn't just grow up in there every Sunday. I went when I wanted to, like holidays, Easter and that. But then after the end of high school, my last year of high school, I really started learning more and more and more. "Gerome this is important. You've got to get yourself fed spiritually. You need more insight on God, more understanding." [. . .] Now this may sound weird to you, but I think it was the Holy Spirit because I do believe that God is the Holy Spirit. I believe that He communicates with us through there. And that's what was drawing me, gradually. You know, "Go to worship. Listen. Hear what is there." And other thoughts would come through, and I'd wonder, "Am I going crazy here?" It would be like letting me know, "No. Listen. Find out what this means and that means." Certain things like praying. How do you pray? What is praying? What is giving tithes? What is giving offerings? What is Bible studies about? What is Sunday school about? Things that I had never even considered in my younger years, not having someone to teach me this. You know say a kid like yourself, you may have had parents there to encourage you along the way. I didn't. I had to kind of feel my way through the dark until God started turning on the lights for me.

Did you participate in the choir or usher board?

Unh uh. No guidance. Nobody to give me the . . . and to me, that's something that should have clicked in me as a child, even though I didn't have the parents there. It looked like, to me, that should have been one of my . . . you know, but it wasn't there. It was not there, so I didn't do it. I didn't know. Wasn't aware of it.

Is there any particular theory about homosexuality that you believe, about why people are gay? Is there some thought about that that you feel personally, you know, why people are gay?

Now, that's a deep one, 'cause I would like to share my opinion, but I don't want to throw you off.

No. It's what you, how you personally feel.

I think that it's a . . . I'm coming with it now. [Chuckle]

[Chuckle] Bring it.

Okay. I think that it's wrong, as far as right and wrong. I think that God loves the homosexual—the person—but He hates what they do. I don't think that He condones a man being with a man. And that's just my makeup, what I believe, you know from what I have learned from say, high school on out, that "Gerome it's not right." That it's just not right. He created male and female, and there is a way, there's a reason why He did it. Now, I think that there is a force that is against God, which I believe that there is a Satan. I believe that the devil exists. And he sets out to destroy what God has set out to do. Now, that may sound crazy to you, but that's my belief, biblical belief. I believe that it's wrong and to not be able to just turn it off [snaps his finger] like I would like to if I could. I don't want no wife. I know that. I know that I don't want no parts of no female as a sex partner. Other than my friend or my sister, you know, something like that, or a teacher as a female friend. You know, I could do that. But as far as the sexual thing, I think it's wrong and I hate that I did not come up with someone that was wise enough to cultivate me along the way so that I wouldn't be dealing with this now and wrestling with it now. You know, the sexual thing, now. You know? I think that, had I been dealt with earlier or taught as a child, I wouldn't have to deal with this now. [. . .] I don't believe that there is anywhere written that He said I have to have a wife. [. . .]

I believe in the Bible, and I believe that He said he would "rather you be as you are, but if you cannot contain yourself . . ."—I think He's talking about sexually—"it is better to marry than not." So I think that I would like to live my life single, you know, free of any sexual conduct, none of that. But not knowing what I was getting into when I was that young, that I would have the thoughts about it now, I never would have went that route.

So do you think that you can save yourself from being gay?

Oh yes. I found at a time in my life I was going through so much frustration, like, I would say like it had to be in my mid-twenties, which it was, before I turned thirty, I found myself getting into more Bible study classes and what have you, and learning more and being too inquisitive. I just couldn't take what the preacher said; I had to go back and find out "Is this in the

Bible, is this . . . ?" And not being able to read the Bible the way I wanted to and interpret it right, I had to go deeper into it and get more insight on it and find out what did this word mean, "celibacy," you know, what does this here mean? You know, different words.

I just found that I believe I can live a celibate life. I can live without it. I do believe that. And I found myself, doing it the times that I did within the past ten years, the times that I did it was to please another person. You know this guy that I had been with when I was young or something like that.

Do you think that you would still be gay, but you're just not acting on it?

Unh uh. You see, you either are or you aren't.

It's either or? In your estimation, if you pray hard enough then you will be cured?

Free of it. I would say free of it. But cured, yes.

Free of it.

Yes. And I don't think that you would even have that desire there. I think that through praying and trusting God and holding out, you know like I think He says somewhere in there, "If you resist, it will flee you. It will flee from you." And that's anything. If I resist smoking cigarettes. If I just fight that urge and continue to fight it. And He knows my heart. Crying, I don't mean crying, "God take me off these cigarettes! God get me off of this, get me off of that!" He knows our desires, and I believe that He will just, you know, "I think Gerome has wrestled with this long enough." And He will just move it. Same way with the sex thing. I think that if you lay it on the altar before God, go to God with it. And when I say "altar," I mean before him in prayer and secret, in your own prayer time, your prayer closet or wherever, lay it before God and make your request known to Him. "Lord I believe that Your Word is telling me that it's wrong. Okay, I'm with you on this. I want it to be gone. Now, you say I don't have this because I'm not asking for this. So I'm making it known to you God, I want this gone and when are you going to take this desire from me?" You know, "Come on now," you know. And talk to Him. I don't think I have to be on my knees in no certain position, just in my everyday cleaning around the house and at work, in my heart, in my mind, and in my thoughts. I think that, in time, it will fade away. Now, to *you* that may be, "No." And I believe that, that He will move it if you're *serious*. If you really want it gone. If you love Him enough, I believe that God will move it. And you will not have no problems with it, you know, that I will have no problems with it. But now we all have to go *through* whatever we have to go through. You know, some people, He may just wipe it [snaps his fingers] away like that, you know? And then there are some who have to go through some ups and downs until they finally come to the point and He'll know,

"Now okay, this one's ready to come out of the fire. He's serious. He's really wanna let that thing go now." 'Cause see, some of us go to God playing, you know. Like, "I really want to let go, Lord." Then He'll get you out of it, and then you end up backsliding. You ever heard of the word "backsliding"? Okay. That's what happened to me one time, you know, and I was too young and stupid to know what I was doing. But, after I've gone through, gone through, gone through, I do believe that it will be you know just like a thing of the past.

So in your words, are you serious now? Are you ready?

To come . . . be free of it?

Umm hum.

Oh yes! Well, I'm already, you know, I could see where . . . oooh, if you only knew where I come from, you know. So I would say that He's doing it in His time. Because I left it up to Him, you know, to deliver me out of this. I mean, ask yourself: Do you believe that it's pleasing to God? I mean any person with a drop of God in him would know it's unnatural, it's not right. And He didn't say you had to have a woman. Or whether you're a lesbian that you've got to have a man. You know? It's just that He's the main focus, and I think that He expects us to honor Him through his Word and what He says to do. And I do think that people can live free of sexual contact and all of that. I don't think we was put here to just wallow with each other and party to party. You know people go too far. I mean just think, say, if you've got two or three friends and their two or three friends got a friend and a friend, and they're just criss-crossing and all this, some sickness, something's gonna kick off in there wrong. And it's gonna cause emotional stress between you and the friends because they're with the person you're with.

Now, I think if we do it according to what I've learned, biblically, it won't be no frustration. You're with your spouse and you don't go any further. Now, if you've got to have sex, get you a spouse. Go to Him about who He wants you with, but don't just go out and grab somebody because of what they've got or what you think you can make out of it. Acknowledge Him, pray about it, be patient. It may take a day, a week, a month, a year, however—*years.* But He will reveal to you. But, if you love God, I believe that if you trust Him, you'll wait, you know. It's just like me coming out of this thing. No matter how lustful I may feel or whatever, "Fight the urge, Gerome." He's given me enough in His words to know that, "Oh you can overcome this. It's just up to you *individually* to use the tools that you have." And the first thing would be His Word. To resist the wrong crowds, you know, come from among the ones that you know are deliberately doing it. And I wasn't wise enough to know what was going on in my life at the time. He was moving in my life, and I didn't know God was moving in my life. He was bringing me away from that particular crowd. And to now, I'm free to them. [. . .] When I realized, it was like over a year later, that I don't even be with Oscar anymore, Gerald anymore, Michael anymore, Andre anymore. You know, old friends. We lost interest in the same things. We didn't do the same things. They more or less cling to each other, but for somehow or another, through some mysterious way, God slowly eased me out of the movie . . . out of the picture. [Chuckle] Until where now I go through a lot of lonely evenings at home. But I find better things to do like get off into my sewing or painting or something around the house to do. And even this new kick that He's got me on is doing this extra work, like out of the house you know. So it's okay, this occupies my mind and gives me something to do. And being forty-six years of age, I've got to admit, I had no idea that I would be going through this at this age. I thought I'd probably be relocated in a whole different world.

You've talked about this throughout the interview. What role does the church, religion, play in your life currently? Today.

Okay. Let me see if I can break this down to you very clear. Okay. Right now I'm a bit disappointed in the churches. Not God. Not the buildings. But people. They have just smeared . . . how can I put this . . . feces all over it. And that's a nasty word to use, but they have really just made it nasty, stinky. And I go now trying to do it out of obedience. Like I believe in my heart that I owe God 10 percent of what I earn, whatever he blesses me with. And I go. Like this morning, I did not want to go in the midst of the people. You know I dress up, go in there and try to get as close to the front as I can if I get in there in time. [Laughter] So they'll be to my back. So I don't have to deal with them. You know, I don't like this now, you know, having this feeling, but it's a beautiful place to go if you are in a Christian environment. But it's sad what preachers are doing now, getting in the pulpits and gay bashing. "God created Adam and Eve, not Adam and Steve." That's tacky. For a person to say that God called him, when God is so intelligent and so wise until He don't even ordain a person that hadn't grown past that level. To stand there and stab at some of His children that are wrestling with what gay people wrestle with. You understand what I'm saying? I don't think God put every one of these preachers in the pulpit. Some of these people think God told them to go preach, when I heard this old lady say, "No baby, He told you to go pee." [Laughter] Not preach. He didn't say, "Go preach." Like the old lady said, "No baby, he didn't tell you to go preach. He told you to go pee and you misunderstood Him. Where are the Q-tips?" So what I came up with was that I don't believe that God put [. . .] a lot of them there. There are a couple in the city out of all of the, maybe over 500 of them in the city, that say God called them. I don't think they were ready. They went on their own. So I think they are putting God to open shame. They are driving away the ones that I think God really called. Because He said He came for the sinners. He didn't come for the perfect, the uprighteous. He came for lesbians, homosexuals, murderers, thieves, you know, backbiters, liars, these are the ones that the Church, this building, is for. To come in and to commune with God, get to know Him better, to learn, to be distracted from everything and just go there. But when you've got crooked people in the pulpits saying that they've been called to preach and offending and making a mockery out of a gay person if they see them come in that church, and treating them like they are better than them, that's worse than in the Bible and the woman that was being stoned for being a prostitute. And we're looking at this right now. So that's why I said they have just smeared this . . . I hate that word, like I said earlier and I hate to say it again, but they just did it. They really just did it nasty, and it's out of ignorance because they don't know. And they've got the Bible right there before them. And for an illiterate person to be able to know when God is speaking to them, then you know something is wrong with this picture. This person can get it, but this one that's got this D.D.D. behind their name and all this Ph.D. can't figure *that* out? That is one thing you don't do. You don't judge these people like that. You pray *for* them. If you've got anything to say, if you're truly born again and you believe in God in your heart, you don't have to discuss it with your friends. In your prayer closet alone, you're going to stop and say, "God bless our so and so son down the street. You know that little boy or that little girl that's wrestling with that." Or it could be a kid that's a thief in the community. I don't think that it's such that God had more pity on homosexuals and lesbians than He do on a thief or a kid that is just low-down, a disobedient child. He loves all of us equally. Sin is sin in His eyes. So I look at it now as a whole picture, to say that society and hypocritical hypocrites have picked out gays to point at. And it's a nasty thing what they're doing. And I don't believe . . . I know it's . . . The Holy Spirit lets me know every day when I get up, "Gerome I'm with you. I love you." Something speaks to my heart, letting me know, "Get up and do another day. It looks cloudy today. It's going to be a little dreary, but go on regardless to what the old sissies are saying about you or what the young sissies are saying, what the church-hoppers are saying, what relatives are saying, what your neighbors are saying . . . Go forward, Gerome. Don't look left. Don't look right. Just go on. Keep your eyes on Me. Know how you treat your co-workers. Know how you treat your neighbors. Know how to treat these people. Be kind and I'll bless you." Now that's what I get in my heart. But what these churches are doing, I just throw it out in the trash. I don't even play with them. I go in there, you know . . . And a lot of times I like to get down front so I don't have to . . . Actually the good preacher ain't hittin' on too much of nothin' 'cause I see him . . . [Laughter] But I slip in there sometimes, at the last minute, running late and I have to sit in the back. And I don't like that 'cause I've got to watch all this false shouting and "AMEN." And Lord, don't let him say nothing about a gay or a sissy. Oh, these churches! And they really start carryin' on then, you know. That's the cutest thing to them. These hypocrites sitting up there don't even know that this is the place you come to get rid of those critical, judgmental spirits. But they don't know that. They don't know that it's not right. God don't want me judging your child for what your child is guilty of or have fell short of. He don't. If I can *help* that child, what can I do to be a help to this child, other than badmouthing or trying to make it hard for him or thinking that my child is too good to associate with that child? Like now all this gossip is going on about little boys shouldn't be playing too close together. I've listened to these so-called sisters, these women saying that, "No, child, whenever you see Randy playing too close to Paul like that, you separate them; they gonna come up funny." Now isn't that stupid? You know like little boys have to be brought up *rough*. And there are guys, men, that really felt like they had to be hard on their kids to make them boys. I mean, some of your best designers aren't gay but they were, you know, they sew. But then, if you sew, you're gay. If you cook, you're a sissy. You know? So I say, "How stupid can society be?" And I'm looking at this mess in the church now to where, like I said, I don't find anything cute about it. Now I have seen a couple of ministers that was on television that I liked. You know that did some pretty good sound teaching that I can say, "I trust them," you know, their teaching. But locally, unh unh. I'm just going to this church that I go to because I feel obligated to go to worship and to go pay my tithes and offering. Now what that preacher do with it, it's between him and God. Now, I should know, now, Gerome when you're putting money in a bag with a hole in it . . . [Laughter] Now, don't you think it's time for this one to end? Next question! 'Cause I have gone too far with that one.

Why do you think there are so many gay men in the church choir?

I'm not positive on this, but I think they feel more comfortable there than they do, say, out in society. Like say a lot of them would like to probably play baseball, you know, in their spare time. Or football. They could still be Christians, you know, and play baseball and go to church. But a lot of them are doing it because, I think, they get to express, to relieve a lot of what's going on in there. You know, what's in there, in them. You see what I'm saying? "If I just make the choir rehearsal, if I get to choir rehearsal or whatever, I can just sing it . . ." I think it's a sense of relief for them, you know, to look forward to going because they deal with this society that is so cruel. You've probably been, you know, isolated from it. But there are some cruel people out here. And I noticed that even in my church, the male choir, I noticed . . . I don't get in it, but I noticed there are quite a few, you know.

And I'm looking at this one young man now, and my heart just goes out to him when I see him. On the usher board. And you know it's obvious that it's there. But to think what he's wrestling with now, he should be able to go to church and to just be relaxed. But he go there and you can tell he still under stress, tense. And he's fighting it, you know. And I say, "Oh my goodness, this child is wrestling with something that could be so easily resolved." But he just don't have the knowledge to know that he don't have to worry about them. "Just lift your head up baby and go on." I've been down that road. It's not worth it.

And another thing, I think when I prayed about the fact of doing this book with you—now that we're on this subject, I'm fixin' to change it a second. But I said, "Lord am I to do this?" you know. And at the time I didn't get no response. And I didn't get a response, you know. And then I ended up *missing* you the first time. And I said, "Well, Lord maybe that wasn't . . ." Do you understand what I'm trying to say? Do you believe in God?

Oh absolutely!

Do you believe that He can respond to you in a way?

Absolutely.

Okay. That first time, I don't think I would have been as open as I am now, if we had met then. Now this has cost you another trip and all this here, but at that time, I don't think I would have been as relaxed as I am. And I had to feel your spirit more or less and talk with you on the phone. And when you called last night, I kind of felt even better about it. And I was beginning to think to myself back here about a week or so ago, "Okay Gerome, you can go now and speak what you've got to say."

· · · · · · · ·

KENT (B. 1967, BEREA, N.C.)

It's interesting. Like I said, I grew up in the Pentecostal Holiness Church. Our little community of Berea had a Baptist, Pentecostal Holiness, Church of God in Christ, Methodist. We had different factions of Christianity. But everybody knew each other because everybody . . . even though we were in separate churches, a lot of times we were all related. A bunch of us were all related, so it was like I could go to this church and worship pretty similarly. I mean, everything was pretty much the same. Not a lot of difference. There was one church that might not allow, say, female preachers. And my aunt was our assistant pastor of our church. I remember her going to another one of the churches, the Church of God in Christ, our local Church of God in Christ, and she was asked to speak at a women's day event. They wouldn't let her in the pulpit and they did not acknowledge her as a reverend, but they set a lectern on the side and she had to preach from the lectern. As a young kid watching this, I'm thinking, "Okay, aren't we all supposed to be God's children?" So that was a little confusing for me. But as I grew up to learn more about each other's doctrine, you know things made sense. [. . .] You talk about it especially among your own circle, but I guess in an unpretentious way, you would just accept that's just the way it is. People are going to be different about some things, and you still speak to them, you still go over to their house and eat, they spoke to you, you spoke back, and you catch up on the days gone by. So it's one of those things.

How would you describe the influence of church and religion on your childhood?

Oh wow! Where do we begin? The influence of church and religion on my childhood. As far back as I can remember, there was always church. I can't remember not being at church. Being a boy soprano . . . teaching . . . you know, I'm six years old and I'm teaching parts to the adult choir. Then at ten years old, teaching myself how to play and eventually playing [the piano]. And then there's just the lessons that you learn about how to treat your fellow man, how to set goals for yourself for life, to do unto others as you would have them do unto you. The Golden Rule is not just a cliché: it really has been valuable in my life. It's interesting because growing up in the United Holy Church we went into convocations, as a lot of African American churches have their big organizations and their regionals and a lot of times for our youth events . . . with all the youth in our little church, and all of us, we were related, we were the children or grandchildren of sisters and brothers, of which my mom was one of nine. But I was always the youth representing our church at Sunday school rallies, public speeches. . . . I remember one time writing a paper all on my own on Galatians, the fifth chapter, the "Fruits of the Spirit." And this particular Sunday school convention was held at our church, growing up. And the regional superintendent, I remember seeing him in tears because he said he had never heard anyone, adult or child, explain it that way. And he was very impressed and taken, and he was so moved that he just cried. He was just taken away by the spirit. And at that time, I just remember having a good feeling that something I did made somebody feel good. Those were some of the things that the church and religion meant to me.

Of course, those rules that were put early on helped guide my formative years. As I became older, of course, I was able to research things on my own and question things. A lot of times in your churches, most of your churches—I say "most," maybe "many" would be an appropriate word there—in many of your churches, you're not encouraged to think on your own. And in my tiny, little rural Pentecostal Holiness Church, our pastor, who was an older, very wise, settled man sort of bucked against the norm. He encouraged us to think for ourselves.

Did you enjoy going to church?

Yeah, I did. I did. There came the time, of course, when I hit those teenage years and I was like, "Okay Mom, how many services are we going to today?" And then being a musician at ten, I was expected to be in church when all the other kids weren't. Case in point, we'd be in church all day long from Sunday school on, and then we would leave. And back in that time, families took turns feeding the pastor, and the pastor's wife or family, if the family came with him. And so I remember you'd see people in church all day, and then because they were your family you would see them at your house right after church because they'd all come to eat with the pastor. After the pastor and his wife went on back to where they lived, the town where they lived, then my aunt who lived across the road from us, sometimes we would go over to my aunt's house just to fellowship. You know, that's how families did at the time. And then my aunt's son lived right down, like right behind their house. And we'd end up at my aunt's house. Well, she had a piano. Well, they would start up again right there in the house. So the kids and grandkids, we'd be out playing. The door would open and the next thing I'd hear was, "Okay y'all let's go. Let's come in. It's time to praise the Lord, time to worship." Well, I knew what that meant. Basically, it meant everybody else could keep playing and riding their bikes. It meant I had to go in and play music for the devotional service. And I remember that distinctly. I mean that will always stay with me. And it didn't seem fair at the time, as a child. And, in retrospect, it's those very things that have helped me form my spiritual tenets.

Do you think in general that the South and southern culture is about repressing things or not talking about, specifically, sexuality, or does it bleed into other things?

I think that, culturally speaking, it's from two aspects: Being southern and then the church. Again, I go back to the church because the church is in my experience. And I think having read John McNeill [*The Church and the Homosexual* (1976)] and [John] Boswell, with his treatise on homosexuality in the church and social acceptance [*Christianity, Social Tolerance, and Homosexuality* (1980)], the church has always had a hard time dealing with sex, period, much less sexual identity. I think even in this time, in this day, the reason we have a lot of what we have in the atmosphere, especially the political atmosphere, is because the church can't separate sexual acts from sexual identity. So sometimes people are demure about things, and pretending it doesn't exist is easier to deal with . . . it's easier to do that than deal with the issue at hand. I'm thinking right now, and I mentioned this to you earlier, if I had a twenty dollar bill for every pastor, every preacher that's ever propositioned me in twenty-seven years now of music ministry, I'd have a lot of money. Right now I know ministers who are married, but they're gay men. And, along the way, someone might have told them or they told themselves that, "Okay, if I just get married this will go away." Some of them found that it didn't go away and that they were miserable and had to get out of their situation. Some of them found out that it's not going away, "But I've made a decision to be a husband and now I have a child," and so they choose to be socially responsible in that regard. But ignoring stuff, I think, is just a heck of a lot easier than dealing with it. And I think that might not be just a southern thing. I think it could be a human thing.

Why do you think there are so many black gay men in the choir?

There's something about music. If you look at the music period . . . And if you look at the history of a period, we get some of the greatest stuff ever written . . . My favorite musical, *West Side Story*, was written by two gay men . . . the music and the lyrics by two gay men, Steven Sondheim and Leonard Bernstein. Good stuff, great stuff. You can't beat it. It's a way of expression and I think that, on a lot of levels . . . I think that on a lot of levels we're repressed in a lot of other areas of our lives. And that's a wonderful mode of expression. Music, it's not just a cliché, it is a universal language and it opens you up in ways unlike other vehicles. Writing is great. [. . .] For some people, that's their penchant and sort of go with it. Music is one of those things. And then being in the African American community, gospel music just is something liberating. . . . It transcends the soul. It does make you feel like shouting; it does make you feel like lifting up your hands and doing your dance. And that's the way also gay men can connect to their higher being, to their God. When other people deny them and their God, through their songs they can access their God. And it doesn't matter what anybody else says.

Do you think that there's something about what you've sort of described as— you didn't use this word, but it sounds like—ecstasy.

Umm hmmm.

Does the music become a vehicle for outward expression that reads as the spirit, but it's also reading something about gay identity? If that makes sense.

Hmmmm. I think I feel where you're going. I've been in plenty of services where someone will just start dancing in spirit. And you sort of look at them go, "Uhm hmm." [Laughter] Or even if they were to sing a song. Something about that voice and what they do with it and you're like, "Hmmm." So, I don't know, there might be something very metaphysical going on there. Who's to say? But I think there might be some unspoken energy there or something that's inexplicable. You know. You don't know why you know, but you just do.

Why do you think so many gay men stay in the church even though the preacher might be homophobic or the church in general might be homophobic?

The sixty-four thousand dollar question. Again, a lot of it is what's instilled in them from their youth. It's the one thing that they can look back to that has been a constant. It may change as they get older. I know for me there were things in embracing my sexual identity, there were things in the formative years that were taught to me in church that worked for me. And as I began to read on my own and embrace me, there were things that didn't work. And I had to ditch those and hold onto the ones that worked for me. And then sometimes I didn't even ditch those; I had to reinterpret them. So those things are still in me, although they're part of an institution that basically sees me as a second-class citizen. I don't put my focus so much on the institution as I do my relationship with God. That's more important to me than some ignorant homophobic preacher trying to tell me where he thinks I should be, in heaven or hell. I know what my creator made me to be.

Going back to the earlier question about the choir and ecstasy, do you feel that the church or the choir, or church culture, provides a place for people to hook up?

[Chuckle] I can answer that in one of two ways. [Laughter] There's the "no" answer. This is a "yes and no." The "no" is the obvious structure is rooted in what's accepted as good Christian behavior and etiquette. There are certain things you don't do. And you'll find that on the heterosexual side too. You know a young man sees a young lady in church but you're just not going to . . . you're going to step up correct, you know. And there are just certain things you won't do to bring shame onto you or her. So I think it's like that on both sides.

The "yes" is that when, considering that so much of our interaction as gay men is done undercover, for lack of a better expression, a lot in most churches you can't openly be who you are without suffering some kind of penalty, that yeah, you do look for those little subtle signs and when you see it, it's like water for the thirst. [Laughter] Beyond that structure of the church, you see it and you say, "Okay, this is too precious to let go" not to explore, if you will. This might be someone who might not even be gay, but the signs might be there. And then that person might be gay, but you might be no more than friends. And you know what? That's a good thing. It's not always about hooking up all the time. Just having a social circle of gay friends that are compatible, I think that's very valuable. So many times gay men get together and I guess a lot of them feel, "I've got to hook up." And the fact of the matter is that's what a lot of homophobic straight America has painted us as. And that's not to sound judgmental because by no means am I standing on a soapbox, but it's just to say that it's diverse. Even within that church structure. People get together, and "hook up" takes on a different meaning from situation to situation.

What role does church play in your life currently?

The church as a structure, as a social structure, I depend on it for . . . I think the most valuable thing I get out of it is the element of fellowship. That's very important. It is true, no man is an island. [. . .] When the service is over and I play the "Amen" and I turn the organ off, I go home. I don't want to see them after that. You know, I don't have that kind of after-church fellowship. But while I'm there and I'm in that room, they're wonderful people and there are some that I know would stand by my side if I ever needed them, and I would do the same. They're not necessarily in my inner circle, but they're good people. And there's a family-type atmosphere there. And I like that. But what's more important to me than the institution of church is my personal relationship with God. That means more to me than anything because the institution of church has killed people, has endorsed racism, misogyny, and of course, homophobia. Hitler thought he was killing the Jews because he was being a good Christian. And even the Bible says there's nothing new under the sun. All these things that have happened, we see it now with the intense homophobia, with our current political atmosphere, using the Bible to divide people and to get a certain political outcome. So those things are not my salvation. My personal relationship with God is important to me.

. . . .

"LARRY J." (B. 1959, CAMDEN, S.C.)

What role does religion or church play in your life currently?

That is a very interesting question, and I have struggled with that since college. You know I've been going to Baptist churches. Remember I told you my mother was United Methodist. I am now back to United Methodist. Found a nice little church. It's a small church and I used to go to these big churches, Baptist churches, two hundred people. Nice service, everything is nice. I don't know anybody there, except one guy I went to college with, and he's straight and married and got kids. But it's something that is missing, that I just don't feel connected to. So I have gone to Unity Fellowship, which is a gay church. Gay pastor. Predominantly black congregation. There's one or two whites that go there. But a lesbian is the minister. Enjoy the service. It was no different than any other service and other than it was a lot more emotion, a lot more. I felt comfortable. I mean, you know, I just felt comfortable with it. So I went once. I participated in a poetry reading there. Went to a play this past week, December 28th, a play called, *Black Like Us*. And my friend and I usually go to a Baptist church for New Year's Eve. And my friend is ten years older than me. I'm forty-five, he's fifty-five. And I said, "I want to do something different. Let's go." And he agreed to go. And we had an excellent time. [. . .] This is the church that I feel comfortable with, and I really think I'm leaning more towards joining.

Why do you think there are so many gay men in the choir?

I think because it's an avenue for open expression. I really do. I really do think that. And being in the church, you know, that's pretty much where they can find that. But let's not even talk about the church. Let's not even talk about the church. Let's just not talk about it because when you think about it—I mean, I'll never forget. I'll never forget this minister told me he had had some dream about me. He had some dream. And I'm like, okay. One of my frat brothers. Big Methodist church in South Carolina. And so as big, bold, and beautiful as I was then, I called him up and says, "What did you dream? What was the dream?" He says, "I dreamed that you and I were in the bed together." He just outright told me. I said, "Well, do you want to make that dream come true?" So here I go, rolling over from Rock Hill to York, South Carolina. We jumped into bed and I mean, a horse. I mean his dick was bigger than a horse's dick. And you know I asked him—and I got that poem in the book—I asked him, "How is it that you can do this and be a minister?" You know what he told me? "Simple. It's all state of mind." And so I think that for the folks that are in the choir, I really think they feel comfortable so that's who they associate more with. Most of us are in the choir, and who else is in the choir? Women. Women don't have no problem with gays. *Some* do. The ones who can't get a man do. But other than that, they don't. They love it because, oh gosh, they flock because we know the tricks of the trade. We can tell them tricks about makeup. We can. They'll come to you and, "Come decorate my house for me. You do such a good job." I'm just saying; we have the talents. We're able to take it a little bit further. You'd be amazed. And I think for the most part, we feel more secure around women 'cause we feel like, you know, we're not worried about them beating on us or saying ugly things.

MARLON (B. 1956, CUERO, TEX.)

You've hinted of this earlier about the role religion played in your life. Could you talk about that a little more in terms of the role religion played in your upbringing?

Oh, it was central, absolutely, it was. And, I would say in pretty much positive ways, for the most part, we were educated in the church. That is, we went to Sunday school. We went to church. We went to a small country church where my father was a head deacon. My mother was secretary, and we all had roles to play. I was church pianist. I was Sunday school pianist. I was a terrible pianist. My sister was in the choir. We all had roles to play. And, the preacher was an authority figure. And, our Sunday school teachers were authority figures and were friends of the family. That church turned out to be a traumatic experience later because there was an ordeal that happened at a particular moment with the selection of a preacher, which often happens in small churches. But, it ended up . . . I won't go into the details. It ended up basically ostracizing my family from the church. This was after I had gone away to college, but it was traumatic for my parents, who had devoted much labor and many contributions financially and otherwise to the church. There were jealousies about my parents and all kinds of wild, totally untrue accusations that led to a divorce from the church. And, my parents, it took them a while to join another church. But, they just attended church at various places for a while. I know it was really traumatic and something that my mother never quite got over because these were her best friends, supposedly, that engaged in this. So, you know, it was not a rosy picture this church. There were things going on that I wasn't aware of. But, my memories of the church are of this small wooden building on a slight hill in the country surrounded by thick, by trees, and just having worship services there and experiencing my father, you know, shout, and my mother's prayers, which were very heart-felt, and you know, the people I knew and worshipping, getting religion, and being baptized out in the country—a tank, basically—in the man-made pond. I went through that whole experience.

Did you enjoying going to church as a child?

No, I did not. [Laughter] I loved the singing of the choir. Church scared me; especially I would tense up during prayer service. [. . .] We only went to Sunday school up to a certain age, and then we started going to church. I mean that's my memory of it, and I think that's correct. We were certainly not taken to revival meetings until a certain age when they thought we were ready for it. But, I just remember having kinds of tense feelings because my father would really get the Holy Ghost, and he would run out of the church, and you would hear him shouting outside, and that was scary to me and even though I was supposed to understand. I didn't quite understand what was going on, though I was taught what it meant. My father did not show emotions, and that seemed the moment when emotions seemed out of control.

I did not like the sermons; especially on special days it seemed they could go on forever. I didn't understand the sermons until a certain age. And, I think that was the part of religion that frightened me, the hellfire. I mean it was supposed to frighten me. [Laughter] Fire and brimstone, I mean we really, you know, we got that. This was weird, because it was very contradictory because we were taught very strongly that God was a loving God, and that God was a personal friend and protector, so I was confused I think. I still am [laughter] about these theological concepts. But, I adopted religion. What's the word? I wholeheartedly participated in it and identified with it once I got religion and was saved, and that made it less frightening. I'm not articulating this very well because I think a certain element of fear is always there, but there is a kind of diminishing of it after a certain point when you begin to understand it more emotionally and conceptually.

What role does religion play in your life currently?

It's always there as kind of an almost unarticulated anchor for my values. There are certain things that I cherish deeply that I was taught growing up, and I think spiritually and emotionally and some ephemeral way, sort of the Protestantism that I was taught is always there. I don't subscribe to exactly the ways I was taught through theology, but it has influenced who I am, and there's no way of denying it. I don't attend church regularly. I used to when I was in Chicago. I used to go to an MCC church. Ian and I went to a very small emerging African American church that ministered to sexual others in D.C. We never went back mainly because Ian grew up Catholic, and I grew up Protestant, but not quite with the kind of intense, almost Pentecostal Protestantism that they were implying toward with individual testimonies and everything, which was too far for us. But, we liked the experience in other ways. It was a great sense of community. So, I would say religion is always there even if I am not a churched person.

I still have problems with the preaching, whether it is a white church, a black church, or a mixed church. And, I don't want to sound arrogant saying this, but I really don't feel that I learn a lot from the preaching. You know sometimes you have very thoughtful sermons, but I think it's a strange experience to just sit there and be talked to from a pulpit. I guess at Unitarian churches, they don't have the minister . . . the minister is on the same level as the congregation, which I kind of appreciate. But, still there's a separation.

I'm very skeptical and suspect of people who have been ordained because frequently it's a license to self-righteousness—not always, but frequently.

Why do you think there are so many black gay men in the church, especially in the church choir?

The church is undeniably a center, if not *the* center of African American community life. And, most black gay men, I would say, the vast majority of black gays—men and women—identify strongly with black community and have strong positive experiences along with strong negative experiences with the church, just as, you know, as Americans we've learned to just sort of deal with the worse part and still be Americans—almost against our wills. [Laughter] I think that the church is similar, that it is something we're not willing to give up on, or you know, that most are not willing to give up on. I don't know about the choir, or you know, music ministries. I don't know why, but it's there all over the place. It's really not a myth. It may be a stereotype, but it's a reality, too. And, I think it's part of black gay culture at this point, and that it's one way that people are mentored, to be in the church as a gay person, and to be in the church period. [. . .] Music is so highly valued in African American communities, I think, in both religious and secular music, and it's a place where gay men are highly appreciated even if in some places there may be a stigma or doctrine preached against homosexuality. Doctrine is interesting in the black church because it's so tempered necessarily by the realities of black life.

. . . .

MICHAEL (B. 1968, RALEIGH, N.C.)

As I said, my parents were Muslims and so there were extreme routines. We were very strict about how households were ran. We didn't eat pork. We always said "yes, sir" and "no, ma'am." Growing up, I wore a blue suit and a red tie, red bow tie every day, bald head. No cursing, no profanity, no—you know, I just had no idea that these things existed really, up until I was probably in junior high school. Because we were Muslims, my activities really centered around, you know, service, to that extent. In terms of my personal beliefs, I've always wanted to be a minister—a Christian minister at that, even before I knew exactly what that meant. I always thought I would be a minister and a teacher. And early on, as early as second grade. And my grandmother was heavily involved in the Baptist Church. Every second Sunday I spent with my grandmother. And I would go down on Friday. We would always have fish. [Laughter] On Saturday, we would go out and shop, we shopped every Saturday. And Sunday, we'd go to church and then go to a funeral. So whoever was dead, you know, I didn't know the person, she may not know the person, might be somebody's neighbor from fifteen houses down or something. And my grandmother lived in the country. But she believed in going to people's funerals.

So there was no conflict between your grandmother's Christianity and your parents' Muslimism, especially with regard to you and how you were being—?

It was never a conversation. My parents had the great foresight to allow me to make choices, to allow me to be involved in things that I wanted to be, and nothing was pushed on me. And I really had, now that I think about it, an ideal upbringing. You know, I started drinking when I was probably twelve. I'd go to the club with my aunts and uncles because I always was with them. And when you're in the country, everybody's related to you, so I'd go with my aunt and she'd say, "Sit on this stool, boy." And, you know, "Here, have a beer." And I'd sit there, you know, and watch, and when it was time to go, we'd go. So it was never an issue of what my age was or whatever. You know, she would just say, "This is my nephew," and that was that.

These were your father's siblings or your mother's or a mixture of both?

Both. Both.

So they weren't Muslim?

No, the only—well, my uncle in D.C., my gay uncle, he was a Muslim. And then I have an uncle that lives two doors down from my parents, and he is a Muslim. But I had other aunts and I have an uncle that's one year older than I am on my father's side and I spent—I just spent every weekend with a relative, you know, I never stayed home. And being the oldest grandchild or the favorite cousin, you know, everyone always said, "Where's Michael?" You know, "I'm coming to get Michael this weekend," or whatever.

What role does religion and church play in your life currently?

I could do nothing and I do mean absolutely nothing if I did not have a spiritual background. When I think about the things I've gone through in life, for example, I remember—I mean, thinking back to hanging out in college and so forth, I remember we would be so drunk from driving from Raleigh to Durham, and at that particular time, even though I lived in Raleigh, I didn't realize you could get on the Beltline to get to Durham. I only knew [Highway] 70. But we would be so drunk, we'd have to change drivers every 10 minutes on 70. And I remember smoking marijuana and I had this lover—I just loved marijuana, and I was, you know, one of these people, two tokes and I'd be done. But I had this lover who had cocaine in the marijuana and I didn't realize it until my cousin said—you know, I was smoking with my cousin. I said, "Girl, my lip is just so numb." She said, "It's that damn cocaine." And that's when I realized I'd been smoking cocaine for two years.

You know, and it's these little experiences. And when I think back, I said it is only for the grace of God. And when I look back in terms of my friendships or many of those friends who started out with me, most of them are dead. And I don't know why He saw fit or She saw fit, but I'm still here. I'm doing well. And life is good for the most part. You know, I haven't been perfect. I've made some mistakes. But yet still, I've always acknowledged a higher power. And I've always asked for strength in God.

Is church a place where gay men go to meet other gay men? Or is it just by chance?

For me personally, there is a difference in a gay church or what we would call the standard church. The gay church to me is the church I go to after I go to my regular church, where I'm really involved and take seriously. The gay church is the social.

Is that like an MCC?

Um hmm, it's an MCC where I leave my church and drive to Durham. And we get drunk or have cocktails prior to going to the church. And then we go to the church and we sit and look to see who we might want to talk to. And that's sad to say because oftentimes that's the only outlet that some folk feel they have, you know, the only place where they feel they're going to be accepted. But for me, I can't take it seriously.

Do you find the church accepting of your sexuality?

I think if you go to a church that is spiritually based, truly spiritually based, they are accepting of just about anything. I think African Americans, and I go to an African American church, so I guess I need to qualify that. African Americans are more accepting than anybody else in the world. You can have whatever, they will deal with it better than anybody else, you know, they'll take it on and drag it out or, you know, talk about you, but they'll still love you and be there more so than anything else. In terms of being gay, again I think they can accept you, pray for you, be there for you, but they don't necessarily want to know you're gay. They don't want you talking about it.

Sort of a willful denial?

No, I don't think it's a willful denial. I think if that's your business and if you do it and it applies to you, then that's between you and your God more so than saying, you know, pointing a finger and saying, "You gay boy, sittin' out there," and everybody's looking at you. You know, I think the church just preaches whatever, and if it applies to you, it applies to you, you know. In my church, it's no pointing fingers. But at the same time, I think a church is really—or my church is geared towards personality. My pastor knows if he says something I don't like, he's at risk of me standing up and cussing his ass out, either from the choir stand or walking to the pulpit or storming out.

So I think he knows, much like any other church, the boundaries, what's acceptable in that church. So every blue moon, he may touch upon gay this or alcoholism or whatever. But if he dwells on gay, I slam that damn hymnal and I be getting ready to get up because—and it's just personality and I realize that's not in every church. But I have a relationship with folk in my church and they know me.

········

PATRICK (B. 1966, VIDALIA, GA.)

I grew up in a very traditional Southern Baptist church—emphasis on Southern Baptist. I would go to church for the following reasons: I had the absolute best Sunday school teachers in the world. I loved the way that they presented themselves; I loved the way that they knew what they were talking about; I loved the way that when you asked them a question that was specific to the lessons that they were teaching, they had an answer and they didn't mind that you were asking. I loved the way that they stimulated my imagination when I listened to their lessons. After Sunday school, we would immediately move into church, and I loved the theatrics of the preacher. I loved how he would just work himself into a tizzy and be sweating by the end of the sermon. Did I listen to what he said? No. [Laughter] No. Did I really listen to anything that my Sunday school teachers said? Biblically speaking, no; it was their presentation, it was how they could command attention that grabbed my attention, and that's why I liked going to church as a child and as a young adult.

Now, translating and bridging that into my adulthood, what it allowed me to do as a child was to question what I was hearing, just as I was allowed to be inquisitive and question and gently challenge what I was being told and what I heard at home, I was encouraged to do the same at church. And as an adult, I felt that I had been given the seed to question spirituality, religion, and the courses that I was going to take in my life in those areas. And I would say, then, that the biggest role of church in my life was that it granted me the ability to question what I hear from a spiritual perspective and then make my own decisions, and give me the opportunity to then go on my own private journey.

What role does religion or church play in your life currently?

None.

Why?

None. [Sighs] I don't feel that I need an organized church, spiritually. I'm very disenchanted with what I see from a distance here in Atlanta. [. . .] It may happen in other places, but here in Atlanta, we have churches where in order to become a member, you have to turn over your tax forms. In order to go to church, there are those who feel the need to dress in the very best clothes and drive the most expensive automobiles and be seen. That disenchants me; it breaks my heart. I don't care to be a part of it. My spirituality is extremely important to me, and I have found other avenues to make that part of my life more complete. But an organized church is not the answer for me now. I don't think it's ever been an answer for me, not even as a child. I just liked the theatrics of church. I love it.

Yeah. This is a question that is sort of related to the theatrics of church. And I think once I ask it, you'll understand why. [Laughter] Why do so many black gay men join the church, become a part of the church, especially the church choir?

I don't understand the power of the church choir, do you? The church choir—the music, whomever controls the music in the church influences the church. Think about it. Whomever participates or controls the music within the church has a huge influence on the church. Preachers preach better when they've got good music behind them. You can be as flamboyant as you wanna be, but you know what? While they're watching you, they're not watching you—they're listening to the music that you're producing. It gives you an opportunity to feel and be a part of a basic foundation that is in your blood. You can walk in that church, walk into that music stand, direct that choir and, for the next hour to hour and a half, you are completely a part of a community. No questions asked. I think that also is another reason why so many black gay men are involved in music with their church.

Then what happens, then, when the music subsides and the homophobic sermon comes? How is that negotiated?

Well, I think that it requires that the gay person shut themselves down and deny a basic part of themselves. I can remember, as a child, listening to one of my mother's preachers [. . .] say mean things about homosexuals and the fact that they're gonna die. I went home and my mother sat down and we talked about that for a long time. What does he mean by that? Why did he say that? That's not very nice. He shouldn't have said that. My mother agreed with everything that I said—"No, he shouldn't have said that. A man of God really would not say that." So it depends on who you have to balance or bounce that off of. You know, you could really go home and just hear that all over again from someone who believes and supports what they're saying, or you can go home to someone that can—as a child, at least, go home and have to balance that. That is *his* opinion. That's not necessarily everybody else's opinion. That is the one man's opinion at that one moment in time that you just happened to hear. And that's the way that it was really handled when I was growing up.

Do you think that church is a place for gay men to hook up?

Oh, of course it is. [Laughter] Always has been. Of course it is. Always has been.

How does that happen?

Whatta you mean, how does it happen?

What are the rituals? I mean, how does one go about that? You know, does one, for instance, join the choir . . .

For the record, I've never picked a man up in church. [Laughter] Maybe after church, on church grounds, but never in church. How does it happen? I think it happens just the way it does in all other places. I just think that church is just a setting. Whether it's, you know, being in an office environment and you realize that there's another gay person in the office and you find ways to let them know that you're gay also—whether it's something that you're romantically interested in, or just the fact that hey, you're not alone, I'm over here. You find a way to make it known. And I think that church is just one of the many scenes and settings that it can happen in. And I think that you will find that it will replay itself across these various settings. The office is one that I've just used; I've had friends to tell me—again, this never happened to me—but I've had friends to tell me that, you know, if you're in the choir, you go to choir practice on Wednesday night, one of the deacons kinda hangs out long after the choir practice is over and you start to talk, can I give you a ride home. There're overtures. And again, the church is just one of the many scenes and settings that it can happen in. [Laughter]

. . . .

"OKC"

OKC was one of the more intriguing men I interviewed, because of his background. He is the pastor of a church and for several years lived in the church parsonage with his partner. It took me a while to wrap my brain around that one given that he presides over a church in Oklahoma City, Oklahoma. When I arrived to conduct the interview, he and his partner had recently moved out of the church parsonage into a home they had purchased.

In addition to being a pastor, OKC is an elementary school teacher and part-time caterer. He is, indeed, a jack-of-all-trades. I was the beneficiary of his cooking skills during my visit, as he cooked me a breakfast that included fried apples, bacon, eggs, and homemade biscuits. He also gave me a tour of town, which included driving down "church row," where there were twenty-six different black churches, from Baptist and Methodist to Buddhist and Holiness.

OKC was born in Oklahoma City in 1962, the fifth of six children. The interview took place on January 17, 2005, in Oklahoma City.

One of the churches on "church row" in Oklahoma City, Oklahoma.
Photo by the author.

I can almost say there wasn't a week go by that I wasn't in church at least three times a week. And on Sunday, all day. You know, we grew up COGIC [Church of God in Christ]. So we would leave the house at 8:00 in the morning, going to Sunday school, breakfast and Sunday school. And then went through morning service and stayed in the afternoon for YPWW [Young People Willing Workers] and they went right into evening service. So on Sundays we probably didn't get back home until 8:00, 9:00 at night.

Did you enjoy going to church?

Oh, yeah. Yeah, yeah. Very much. I sang in the Sunshine Band. [Laughter] That was our angel choir, so to speak. So it was the children's choir. [. . .] So we would sing every Sunday. I was active in the ushers. And I was active with the junior church, junior deacons coming up. [. . .] I went from the Sunshine Band, which was anywhere from five to the age of nine. And then went right into youth choir, right into the young adult choir, right into the assembly choir, right into the adult inspirational choir. And then in my later years, became youth director. And then later on, youth minister. Later on to youth pastor. So this has been very instrumental.

So why did you choose to go to seminary?

Just my upbringing, you know, couldn't get away from it. I knew I was different in two ways. That was my sexuality and my social. I knew that I was attracted to the same sex. But I also knew that I wasn't a party person. I wasn't a drug person. I wasn't a drinking person. So I was always attracted to the church realm.

Do you feel that you were called to preach?

Yes. Yes, definitely.

Do you have a call story?[4]

Well, I do. What it is, is that I had a feeling and I've always had a knack or the ability to draw people. Always had a loving spirit. So I ran for quite some time. It wasn't that I became ill or I was in jail or, you know, something I came close to losing my life or anything like that that I acknowledged the call. I knew that there was an anointing on my life. I knew that I had the ability to write fully and rightly divine the truth, the word of God. And my calling was first acknowledged in my singing. So, one day in church, this was in 1980 actually, it was in Houston, Texas, at a convention. And I just acknowledged the fact that no matter how I wanted to be rough, no matter [laughter] how I wanted to be with the gang bangers and go to the parties and stuff, I knew that it wasn't in me. And while doing the convention, the Lord just said, you know, "This is what you've been called to do," you know. "You have an apostolic call on your life. You're a people person. And I'm going to embed and implant the word." And there it was.

What role does religion and church play in your life currently?

Very much, very much. I pastor to over 300-member church. And it's not a quote/unquote "gay" church. So it plays a very, very, very, very heavy part of me.

What kind of church is it?

Fun-loving. It's a multicultural, very loving and supportive church. I mean, from the dope addict to the homosexual. From, you know, the loosed woman to the tight woman. So it's just loving.

What denomination?

Non.

Nondenomination. How did you come to pastor the church?

I actually started this church. I started the church, then we merged with another church, and I took over both churches and became the senior pastor of both.

Is the church accepting of your sexuality?

First of all, I don't know if they really know. They would have to know to be accepting or non [accepting]. It's not something that I wear on my forehead or on my sleeve. It's not something that I go out and say, "Oh, we're fighting for gay rights this week," you know. It's not something that I stand in the pulpit and declare that we need to, you know—I don't preach against it and I don't preach for it. I just preach Christ. And Christ being the center, that means compassionate and loving, for whoever. So if that's being taught, we don't see the gay or the lesbian, we see the person. And that's what I teach, the person, not their vices, not their addictions, but the person.

Have you been pastor of other churches?

Yes.

In the South or all over or . . . ?

Two in the South and two in the East.

And what were you experiences at those churches?

Same thing. Same thing, I mean, although I went to one church that was very much homophobic but now, you know, they're just as loving as the one I'm in now.

Why do you think there are so many gay men in the churches, particularly in the choir?

Because we love to sing. [Laughter] I think, you know, it's almost like a yearning. It's almost like a you just need to be—you just have a sense or want to be accepted. And you know how you challenge the ones who really are unwilling and you have to make a point. And you want to make a stand. So where are the most obstacles for the gay man or the lesbian woman? In the church. So they go to make a stand. And that's what I think. And given that, you know, then you have different branches and you have different ones where now, you know, they've just become, well, I'm going to go to an all-gay church because I'm not accepted here. But I think you ought to again challenge the fact and stay where you are. Be who you are and stay where you are, you know, because Christ is coming back for the spirit man. And we don't know, judgment is not ours. Condemnation is not ours. So although some theologians may argue the point that it's wrong, there are a whole lot of other things that are wrong, okay? So, whereas the theologian that will argue that it's wrong and try to speak against it and not accept the homosexual in the church, then you're not being compassionate or you're not teaching love. So again, I just think that they're in the church because they, too, want to be loved. They want to be accepted. And they want to make a difference. And they can.

Is the church a place to meet other gay men?

You can. [Laughter] Again, if you know the tell-tale signs. [Laughter] I wouldn't say the church is a place to meet. It's not a place to pick up trade. I mean, even if it was a heterosexual, I don't think that's the place where you go to meet and greet and hook up, get a hookup. I don't think so.

So, your church doesn't have a singles' ministry?

No. And we don't have a marriage ministry, either. [Laughter] So, I mean, we do things as a family. And the family can consist of those that are married and those that are single, you know, it's family. To me personally, when you start dividing, you know, division plays a heavy part. So when you start dividing, that leaves room for people to come up and have their own gender—they have their own agenda, is what I want to say. And so we're just one happy family. The only separating is that all the men go in for men's class on Sunday evening. All the women go to a women's class on Sunday evening. All the children go to a children's class. And then we all meet back and we have church. So, no, because when you start doing single ministries, you know, it's like you're trying to do a hookup. And I'm not trying to do a hookup. [Laughter]

So your church is really ecumenical and sort of more of an outreach and programming?

Yes.

How do you compare your church to other churches in town where you live?

We're different because [laughter], you know, some things that I won't tolerate. I won't tolerate gay bashing. I won't tolerate addiction bashing. So if that's the mentality that you have, then you need to move around. Any type of bashing is not tolerated. And yes, I will ask you to leave. [Laughter] If I find it to be that you're the source of that. There's too much and too little that we—

there's too much in a sense of there's too much to do and too little time to do it in. So we don't have time for that. And if you can't teach, preach, and exemplify love and tolerance in this church, you need to move on.

· · · · · · · ·
"ROB"

Rob was born in Eden, North Carolina, in 1965, the youngest of ten children. Eden is a small town that sits on the North Carolina–Virginia border. It's population is just under 20,000. Rob now lives in Raleigh with one of his older brothers. Although Rob and I sort of knew each other from our days at UNC-Chapel Hill, we didn't become close until Curt, my friend and former student who was murdered, befriended Rob. Since Curt's murder, we have become even closer.

Rob has worked in higher education administration since graduating from college. He is, by all accounts, one of the most generous people you could ever meet. He often opens up his home to friends in need and has been known to throw fabulous cocktail parties. Like many of the narrators in this book, Rob has not been able to find a companion, a fact that he suggests relates to some unresolved issues from his childhood. The interview took place at his home on August 15, 2004.

Very religious household, so that was sort of pretty much instilled. I don't know what you'd call us in terms of denomination, Baptist, yes. Some members of my family attended Methodist church; I would go with them to Methodist church, so I had sort of this interesting mix of experiences with organized religion per se in terms of the kinds of church services I would attend. I have a brother who attended and joined the Holiness church for a time and sort of broke away from the quote "family church," so I really don't classify myself in one particular way or another, in terms of religious affiliation. I guess I have an affinity toward Baptist, the Baptist experience.

In general how would you describe the influence of church or religion on your childhood?

My religious experience had a tremendous impact on my growing up and all of my childhood, because that was sort of the yardstick by which I measured myself in terms of doing the right thing, or doing the wrong thing and feeling guilt about it, which is, I guess, what?: Catholic, Baptist, and all kinds of other religions rolled into one. But I think early on, and even to this day as a black gay male approaching forty, I still grapple with homosexuality and the church and where I fit in to that, *how* I fit into it, or even if I *do* fit into it. And just reconciling all that's been instilled in me in terms of having sexual experience with a man and whether that's right or wrong. I've been taught it was wrong; I've also been taught not necessarily that it's wrong, but God doesn't make mistakes, so you know, you're okay whoever, however you turned out to be. I think it goes back to my comment about the endurance test, because I would always ask myself, "God, how long do I have to live in this little cocoon, this little shell, and keep this little secret that nobody else possibly can understand, or would've gone through?" An eight-year-old's thought, there. "And why did You allow this to happen if You're such a wonderful God?" So there was always that question, growing up.

Did you enjoy going to church?

Absolutely not. [Laughter] Going to church was, I guess another endurance test. I would dread Sundays, and it has not been until my later years, probably during college, that I really appreciated the ritual of going to church, and what that can do for one's spirit, and one's psyche. Because for me, it was a chore. It meant I had to go to bed early Saturday night, which I never did, I would always stay up and watch TV, and of course be pooped the next morning when time came to wake up for breakfast and get ready at eight o'clock. You know, it was a chore, so I didn't enjoy the experience, as a child. The only thing I enjoyed about church was summer Bible school, Vacation Bible School, because we got cookies and Kool-Aid. [Laughter] So, and that was actually at a Holiness church, that wasn't even at my family's home church, as we would say. And I think eventually as fate would have it, the more you hear phrases and things repeated of course the longer they stay with you, and that's sort of how I began to learn the Bible, and that kind of thing.

We had, in our neighborhood when I was, probably between the ages of six and ten, we had these two women who moved into our community from Philadelphia, Sister Anita G., and Sister, oh gosh, what's her name, we called her Mother Turner; I don't remember what her name was. Anyway, they were two evangelists, and they for some reason chose our community, and moved in. [. . .] Our community was a circle, sort of a cul-de-sac that we lived on, and so each house in the neighborhood would rotate having Bible study, or prayer meeting at our homes. So, I remember enjoying that more than church, and I thought, wouldn't this be great if we could just, you know, do church like this, you know, have it at six or seven o'clock at night, you don't have to worry about getting up early, disrupting your sleep pattern, all that stuff. I enjoyed that and felt like an adult because I got to participate, whereas in the formal, you know, 11 A.M. church service when I was growing up children did not participate; you sat and you listened, but you were never heard. And it wasn't a time when, as is the case today, they have a children's message, and they bring all the children forward; no, none of that. You sat there in your little suit or bow tie and sat up straight for three or four hours, and listened to the preacher yell, and the choir sing, and, you know, if you're fortunate enough to have a voluptuous mother, not that my mother was voluptuous, but she had, she was a good-sized woman, so it was a nice headrest for me to lay my head on and fall asleep. But otherwise you only had that hard church pew, and that became so uncomfortable as you would, you know, bob your head back and forth, trying to stay awake to get through this, you know, hour-long sermon. So, you know I very much did not like church, in terms of having to get up and prepare to go somewhere and sit and be uncomfortable for three, four hours. So that's why I liked the Methodist church, you were in and out in an hour, hour and ten minutes, so you didn't have time to fall asleep, really. And then of course, shifting to enjoying more than church, what I used to call night church, the prayer meetings that we would have in the community at everyone's home. It was just like church, there was singing, the evangelists would sort of preach, and anybody was welcome.

I think today in some church settings, there's this glaring at people who are different, even though the church is supposed to be this sanctuary for all who come, there are still churches I guess that you know, you're leered at because you look different, or you're not dressed in a certain way. Particularly in the black church, I find, you have to look a certain way. And that has changed, thank goodness I think, because you now find people going to church without ties, and women wearing slacks, or pantsuits, or whatever to service. Or jeans, or whatever, which, you know, when I was a child growing up, no, you had to have on a suit, and a dress, and a tie for the men, and all that, so.

[. . .] My mother came from a family of ten as well, and so did my father, ten children also, which is interesting that it's carried on for so many generations, but my aunts on my mother's side belonged to a Primitive Baptist church, and I remember going to that church, I think it was once a month— the third Sunday of the month. And that doesn't sound bad: church once a month, great. But it seemed like it rolled around so quickly, and it was the most boring church service, because one, there was no choir. They would sing from these little hymnals, and, oh gosh, what's it called, the guy who leads the chant, he would, you know recite a portion of it and lead the congregation, and they would [. . .] raise up a hymn.

I remember on many occasions—and I think this is why I have come to appreciate religion, but at that time, just despised it and dreaded it—they would follow literally the Bible in terms of washing the disciples' feet. So on, I don't know, communion Sunday, I forget, it may have been, and as a child, I was nine, ten years old, washing, quote/unquote "washing," these elderly people's feet, in a little basin that the church women would have. It was communion Sunday because the women had on white. Women would have on white dresses with white aprons, and they would go off and get these little basins, and bring back water, and towels, white towels, the cleanest, whitest towels I'd ever seen, and you'd tie a towel around your waist—the women were on one side of the church, and the men were on the other side of the church. There were two parallel rows with this center aisle, and the men would be on one side washing one another's feet, and you would be singing this hymn while you were doing it. And I would always peek over at the women to see why they couldn't come over and join us to wash feet because I wanted to go sit with my mother, [laughter] because I did not want to wash these people's feet. I didn't know these people. Many of whom were my cousins, I learned as I grew up. But, you know, you see these old men with hammertoes and bunions and corns and he's going to take off his sock and you gotta wash his foot. And you really didn't wash his foot, he would, he would sit and maybe cross his one leg over the other, and over the little wash basin, and you would cup your hands, and just, you know, get a little bit of water and sprinkle it over his feet and dab the towel and dry—that was all you had to do. The women, they would leave their, I would watch, they would leave their hose on them, but slip the little foot out of their shoe, they would sprinkle, just sort of spritz the water and dab the little toe. This was to make us appreciate what Christ did, I guess, with his disciples and all that, and make one humble, I think, in many ways. And it only served to alienate me from church, but I look back on that experience and realize, yeah, it really did make me understand, you know, what it is, not to boast, and not to, you know, think you're better than someone else, so much so that you couldn't, you know, wash their feet. Interesting experience, I never seen anything like it; never done anything like it since, but just sort of a very colorful life experience, and so I started looking at church as kind of this funny, weird thing I never could quite wrap my mind around, some of the experiences I had, like the foot washing, and the incantations. And you know, [. . .] there was no piano in this church, there was no organ in this church.

What role does religion or church play in your life now?

It's a far more significant role. I'm not a regular church attendee, but I, as a child, accepted that there is a higher being, joined the body of Christ as a child, very young child, was actually baptized, and come to appreciate the inner peace that a spiritual relationship with God, can give me, during times when things are going really well, and life is wonderful, as well as when things are not so wonderful. And knowing that there's an inner place I can go, because for me church is not so much about the organized outward,

Sunday, 10 A.M., 11 A.M., 9:45 service or whatever, as it is about one's own spiritual awakening, I guess, and acceptance of things spiritual. I don't feel that I have to have church in my life in order to have a relationship with God. And Mother's probably rolling over in her grave, because you have to have church: "Where there are two or more gathered in my name," blah, blah, blah, you know the verse. And I appreciate that, I was sort of force-fed all those kinds of adages as a child, and have adopted many of them as an adult, but can now look back on them with a little bit more information than I had as a child, to draw upon, and understand.

Do you think the black church in the South is accepting of homosexuality?

No, the black church as a whole in the South is not as accepting.

Then why are there so many gay men in the church?

Exactly. Because it's the South, and you don't talk about it. It can go on, but you don't talk about it. You can have any number of types of people, in church, but once their differences start to come out, you start to separate what is the wheat from the chaff, or whatever. And in a church that's supposed to be one united body you can't have that, so it's the South, it just wouldn't be southern to talk about, that kind of thing in church. So you don't bring it up, and you've got your choir director who's flaming, and the minister of music who's flaming, and you've got the preacher who's probably flaming but pretend not to on Sundays. So people will accept almost anything if you put a pretty smile on it, and not talk about the differences, or don't bring them to the forefront. You might acknowledge the fact that, okay, yeah, he shakes a little bit too much when he's directing the choir, or I wonder, I saw Pastor So-and-So with, you know, brother whoever, but as long as you don't talk about it, and don't bring it up, it really hadn't happened, it really doesn't exist.

Why do you think the choir is sort of this breeding ground or that black gay men in the church gravitate toward the choir, being director, or minister of music?

The same reason I was in choral ensemble in high school. [Laughter] It's fun. And you can sing, and be seen, and have all your cute clothes. I don't know why that happens so often. It's a creative, artistic pursuit, I guess, and, I don't know. I don't know why that happens.

. . . .

RODERICK (B. 1974, BATON ROUGE, LA.)

Faith was always a part of my upbringing. Religion was part of my upbringing. [. . .] We didn't go to church much when I was really little, I don't think. No. My mother kind of had gotten out of the church. Not like turned her back on it but just wasn't going. And that just came with, you know, having two kids in diapers and da, da, da . . . this crazy husband and whatever. But then it became so that it was like breathing, you know, you go to church on Sunday. You get involved. You sing in the choir. You go to Vacation Bible School. You go to this. You go to choir rehearsal. You join the youth choir—the junior choir, as it was called. So I sang in the junior choir, and my brother did too.

My parents were at separate churches for years, though. My stepdad went to a separate church. His church home was in St. Francisville. And my mother went to church in Zachary. So we were at New Light, the three of us, and Dad was at Mt. Pilgrim in St. Francisville. And years went by before he finally said, "Okay I'm going to come on and be a member here," 'cause my mom was like, "I ain't going up there." And I asked her, "Mom, why won't you go to church with Daddy?" I said, "Don't you know the family that prays together stays together?" I'm always asking these probing questions. And she was like, "I'm not raising my children up in that damned country church." [Laughter] That was her reaction. "I'm not raising y'all up there in that country church." Because she thought it was too backwards, a little too backwoods. And it was. They were old school. [. . .] They would sing those hymns and those meters, "Amazing Grace" lasted five minutes, in the first verse. I remember being in church, just going like "UGH." I did not know what they were saying, singing, because I was so little, for one. But I knew the [mocks the singing of the hymn in the church] AAAAAAMMMMAAAAAAAAZZZZZZZZZZZZZZIIIIIIIIIINNNNNNNGGG GRRRRAAAAAACE.[5] You know how it goes? That's fifteen seconds. And you're still standing there. I was like, "What are they saying?" And when we got to New Light, the church we were raised in, I was like, "Oh!" I remember the moment. I don't know what age I was. I remember the moment. I was like, "Oh that's what they sing at Daddy's church. We just sing it faster here." I didn't know. So she wanted us to be raised in a little bit more happening church. And then my dad finally came on board. And my dad was a head deacon also at the church. So it was a power thing too. He was a deacon. My mom was an usher. They wanted her to be a deaconess, and she never would be a deaconess. I don't think she wanted the responsibility. I don't know. Maybe she didn't feel she was worthy. I remember one of the pastors, I mean, he would be like, "Please, we need young women on this thing" and she was like, "Unh unh." I guess she didn't want the responsibility, or maybe she didn't feel that she was whatever. Maybe she thought it was an old lady's role because her grandmother was one. So maybe she was like, "My grandmother's deaconess. I don't wanna be no damn deaconess" [Chuckle] I don't know. She didn't say, "damn" probably. But church was always there.

Did you enjoy going to church?

Actually, yeah. I enjoyed going to church. It was good to be a part of something. I think my personality is such that I always want to be a part of something. Maybe not these days because I'm more independent now, but it was good. I loved singing in the choir, until the point I kind of got tired and left it alone. But I loved being there. I had good friends there. It was sort of the thing to do. I felt, you know, that's how you get to heaven. That's how I figured. I wanted to go to heaven. If I'm going to be saved, I got baptized at a young age. [. . .] So that's kind of how I looked at it; it was like that's what you're supposed to do. And as I got older, of course I got to look at things and evaluate things and sort of see for myself. Okay, there's certain things I will accept and there's certain things I won't accept about church. And that church also, I mean, there was no homophobia said in the church, from the pulpit in the church I grew up in, you know. That's another conversation, but to answer your question, the church experience was a part of our existence, you know.

[. . .] A preacher will say something negative in the pulpit. But he's got a choir full of sissies, one of which he may be doing himself, you know. You've got women who will say, "Oh So-and-So," and this and that and the other, but yet there's a gay man doing their hair or redecorating their house, you know. Or the man may say something negative or whatever. He might be like, "Oh no, I believe a marriage is between a man and a woman" and this and that, and yet he will patronize the flower shop owned by an obviously gay man and his partner, and bring roses home to his wife. But perhaps they don't think about it from that perspective. Some of them do, I think, perhaps.

Much of the South may be conservative and I say "pseudo-Christians." A lot of people get offended when I say that, but I say "pseudo-Christians" because I say, as for me, the essence of Christianity is embracing all people. And also, the essence of faith is acknowledging and representing all faiths. I'm sick of going to ecumenical services for the sake of going to ecumenical services. And yet you speak, and you have the Muslim guy, you have the Jew here or the rabbi here and whatever, whatever. Just that one event, and you don't see them again until the same time next year. What kind of shit is that? That offends me about being back in the South. I spent three wonderful years in Chicago, where I truly got to experience a tolerant and inclusive society—not always, but a very inclusive environment where all people were respected, you know. But in the South . . . I'm back in the South and it's like, you know, you're either Christian or you ain't. You know? [Chuckle]

My frustrations come in when it comes to church and faith. Personally, I haven't joined a church since I've been back, and that's been almost a year. I have been in churches and I've been at events where a person has said some negative things, some homophobic things, and where some people may say, "Well, I'm just going to take that for what it's worth." And I've heard it said, even in Chicago, "Well, that doesn't apply to me. I'll just let that go by because the other things that he says are great." I'm like, "No, that's bull-shit." Somebody made the comment, "Why would I go somewhere where I'm going to be torn down?" Because for me, I don't know how important it is to the next gay person, but to me, it is a part of my being, my existence. I don't wake up and just say, "Oooh, I'm going to do this." No. It's part of who I am. So I'm not going to go in my church, contribute to the ministry, drop my dime in the bucket when it's passed, to have you get up there and the minister say this homophobic thing. Unh unh. No.

And I was in a part of my experience that wasn't like that, and it was wonderful. So to come back here and be around these so-called Christian ministers and all that? I don't have time for that. And then I heard something recently by a guy who did some, just said some crazy shit. He talked about the DL [down low], he talked about this and that, black women can't find a man because they're either locked up or on probation, holding another man's hand, all that. He trashed gay marriage. He talked about this DL thing, the sexual immorality. He said, "Sexual immorality is destroying the black com-munity." I was reading this. And I found out a week later, he himself, there's a rumor that that preacher himself was caught with a man some years ago. And yet it happens all the time. I'm sorry for this whole tangent I'm on about these black preachers, but it's just so rampant, all these black preachers who are doing these homophobic things and is it miscegenistic, misogynistic, I don't know how the term goes, but talk about, you know, against women being in the pulpit, being, you know, preachers. But yet, you know, they'll be sleeping with every woman that'll open [her] legs. Or they'll pry them open. They're doing that. I'm like, you know, "Where is your moral value? What is your issue?" That's such hypocrisy, to me. And ignorance, too. True ignorance. I don't want to be part of that anymore.

· · · · · · · ·

TIM'M (B. 1972; RAISED IN TAYLOR, ARK.)

I think I always felt, growing up, that like, I guess being an inquisitive or questioning young child, I always wanted to know "why?" And I think when your father's a minister and your mother is heavily active in the church and you just come up in that intensely religious environment, there's a lot you can possibly take for granted. Like I think about what it means to be a PK and different interpretations of what that means. And for me it was kind of like you know, people say, "PKs are bad." We were bad as kids.

"PK" meaning "Preacher's Kid"?

Right. And there may be something to that in the sense that like you grew up being so much more aware and attuned to the contradiction between what's being said in church and the lives people are living and their own like vulnerabilities and hypocrisies. So yeah, you go to church on Sundays and there's this rhetoric and then you go home. And you know home may be a place where your dad's sleeping with more than one woman than your mom or there's physical or domestic abuse happening. So this ruse of like religion gets questioned very early. At least it did for me. And I think, to some extent, for some of my siblings as well. And I think that was always a major struggle for me that I think was intensified once I started to recognize that I had attraction for boys. Because it was like, okay, here are people that are saying the life that I might choose to want to live is wrong, but they're not even consistent with what they're saying. [. . .] It was kind of the spark of like maybe God doesn't hate me because there's so much other stuff that's not followed . . . that's not adding up anyway.

And I developed an intense love for religion and God, and an avid reader of the Bible. At one point people thought I would be a youth minister. And even as that translated from moving from say, Sunday school lessons at the Baptist church where my mom went after my parents separated, to the Mormon Church where I was like a student leader, did speeches at conventions. I was a very pious [pronounces it "pee-us"]. Is it pious (pi-us)?

Pious.

Pious. That's one of the other southern things, like how to pronounce words. Because if I don't hear it, it doesn't necessarily register for me. But, yeah I mean I was a virgin through high school. I mean I was a good Christian church boy.

Did you enjoy church?

No. No, I didn't enjoy church. I enjoyed certain aspects of it. I enjoyed the music. I enjoyed the singing. But because I had an early awareness of my sexuality, I was always skeptical and I was always fearing. I always saw religion and church through the lens of my sexuality—every aspect of it. So, you know when people talked about sinners, I felt talked about. Whether or not they were talking about homosexuality, I felt talked about. I identified with, you know, groups of people that may have been talked about. I found ways to relate to the lesson so that it did have some application for me. And at one point I literally did fight my sexuality. In my latter teens, you know, I went through periods where I would fast. You know, thinking that if I fasted and prayed that God would take this demon away that made me attracted to boys, that He would and I would just be normal like the other boys and like girls and do that. And then you know that led to lot of drama. You know, suicide attempts and ulcers and a lot of other stuff. But I didn't enjoy church. I enjoyed church in the way that I enjoyed when my family got home from church and we would sit around and sing songs together and harmonize and there was that sort of joyful, familial presence that was great. But it was less sort of about the religion than it was about the experience of coming together with people you like and almost celebrating. [. . .] The more dogma appeared in the church, the less I actually enjoyed it.

What role does church or religion play in your life, currently?

Church and religion. Interesting transitions with the church and religion in the sense that my current relationship has sort of brought me back to my roots in Christianity. My current partner is a very spiritual person. We sing a lot together. We sing in the car if there's a CD on or harmonizing, and there's a bit of a spiritual element to that. And more recently, I was invited to his church. I'm not sure if that's the church I will continue to go to. I have questions, despite how progressive the church seemed except in certain ways, about whether or not I could be his partner in that church. [. . .] If I want to reevaluate and embrace my Christianity, I want to be able to do so in a context where more than they don't say anything negative about gayness, but they actually do and can affirm that I have a relationship and that there's a creator that can bless that relationship. Because my current relationship is immensely spiritual. We pray together. We pray for the relationship. I ask for guidance about a lot of things. It's really interesting how, you know, at one time I felt like I had to divorce myself from Christianity because of my sexuality. And now I feel like it's my sexuality that has brought me back into conversation with my creator, with God, and wanting a spiritual connection, this spiritual relationship, and a spiritual life. And you know it is the relationship that has created that conversation for me and made it possible to have. Whereas before, it was like, "Okay I'm gay. Christianity has to leave. I can't do both." And now, I feel like I have to do both. I need God to help me through not just this relationship, but a lot of that. I guess being in a primary relationship has that focus, that it drives a lot of what you do and give you support in a lot of the things you do. So I definitely privilege it in that way. It's an intense thing to be reinvestigating at this point because I've gotten pretty comfortable with expecting that I wouldn't have a relationship with God anymore. But there are times now when I hear a gospel singer sing something . . . I remember I used to get really upset when I would go to churches and I would feel touched because I was like, "Wow! I know this feeling is in my blood." I mean, my dad was a preacher. I grew up in the church. And I understand what it's like to feel the Holy Spirit or whatever it is that moves you and it touches you. But for a long time I associated that feeling with "God hates you." And so what would it mean to be able to experience that feeling with a resolve and knowingness of a God that loves me and celebrates my relationship. And that's what I'm getting to now.

Why do you think there are so many black gay men in the church, particularly in the choirs?

That's a really good question. 'Cause I'm like, "Well do the straight boys just not sing?" [Chuckle] I mean when I was in the choir. I was in the choir at college. I was in gospel choirs. You know. I think that is a place. I think, you know, without sort of writing it as a rule, I think that has become sort of an accepted space for the black homosexual. And even if that space is about [. . .] what some people consider maybe the working through the sexuality through, you know, singing or through the ministry of music, it's still an accepted kind of space. Why do I think there are so many? I think black gay men are extremely talented, for one. I think we're very creative and talented. I think there's a certain flamboyance, you know, whether that comes across as masculine. There are a lot of deacons, too. People don't talk about the deacons, but there's a lot of gay deacons in churches as well. I mean, we point more easily to the sort of archetypical choir director or some of the piano players, but like I know gay drummers in churches and other musicians and deacons and even preachers. So I think that faith, in general, guides a lot of black gay experience because, on some level, for one to live their life as they do, I feel like there has to be some belief. It's like faith is the substance of things hoped for and the evidence of things not seen. And so with any lack of evidence that the way you choose to love is the sanctioned way, with all the societal evidence telling you that you're wrong, you're a sinner, you're bad, you know, there's a really close connection. And this is why I feel that my relationship has brought me back closer to God, because I feel like that faith that I had that this is as right as it is, is spiritual. It's the very essence of God. It's not "other," opposite of that. It's like it's the very essence. The faith I have, the courage I've dredged up to love him and to share that love with other people around me, in a society and a culture that says it's wrong and says it's bad and says that we're sick, is about faith. And it's the very essence of, I think, spiritual life and experience. And I think that, on a certain level, a lot of gay men get that in church. It seems contradictory when a lot of the dogma is saying otherwise. But I think on a lot of levels, black gay men are spiritual in that way because they're often searching for that affirmation of self and their experience. And when I went to church with Eric, I noticed that there were a lot of, you know, men I believed to be gay there. And I was like, "Oh wow!"

do you get down?
homosex in the south

4 In black vernacular speech, to "get down" has typically been associated with dancing or feeling the "soul" of the music.[1] Contemporarily, however, the phrase has emerged within black gay communities to signify one's same-sex desire, often posed through the question, "Do you get down?" This question is posed as a code between black men who have sex with other men, but who do not identify as "gay," or men who have come to be called "down low brothers."[2] While men on the down low are typically those who come to mind when the general population imagines same-sex sex among black men in the South, many of the narrators here dispel the myth that all "homosex"—a term I borrow from John Howard to signal "sexual activities of various sorts between two males"—is always of a clandestine nature.[3] On the contrary, the men of *Sweet Tea* recount sexual activity that was blatant and in plain sight as well as sex on the down low.

As one might imagine, asking these men to open up about their sexual activity was, at times, awkward, especially considering the fact that I was meeting many of them for the first time. Given the premise of the interviews, however, many men delved directly into their sexual history without my prompting, and some, like "D.C." and "Larry J.," took great delight in sharing stories about their sexual exploits. The most uncomfortable moments for me came when narrators told stories of sexual abuse. Not having gone through that experience myself, I could only imagine the difficulty of reliving those moments for a total stranger. And yet, at times I felt that because I was a stranger, the narrators who had been sexually abused used the interview as a cathartic moment—as a way to work through their feelings about this traumatic experience.

The stories are presented in five topical sections, devoted to first-time experiences, later sexual escapades, sex at historically black colleges, sex in the military, and HIV/AIDS. The first four topics are those that emerged over and over again across the narratives with regard to the types of homosex the narrators engaged in and the places and spaces where they engaged in sex. While the last section on HIV/AIDS does not necessarily pertain to sex acts per se, I felt it important to include this discussion because of how HIV/AIDS has influenced the way the narrators think about sexuality and because of the impact the disease has had on their personal lives, as well as to account for those men who are actually living with the disease.

MY FIRST TIME: EXPLORATION AND NONCONSENSUAL SEX

Like gay men of various races and regions, black gay southerners engage in homosexual exploration during their pubescent years. Some of the places where this exploration occurs are also typical of boys coming into their (homo)sexuality—school bathrooms and playgrounds, abandoned buildings, and tree houses. But the narrators also name spaces for their exploration that are peculiar to the landscape, cultural institutions, and class status they inhabited: cornfields, vacant lots, church pews, and outhouses. Given how much time many gay southerners spent in the church during their youth, it is not surprising to learn that one of the more prevalent sites for homosexual exploration was, and is, the church. While my own sexual history in the church does not include homosexual exploration, I can recall my first kiss and "dry humping" with a young girl occurring under a church pew during summer camp. One narrator recalls having had anal sex as a young boy with multiple boys in the church. Moreover, many of these homosexual exploratory incidents happened with relatives—the proverbial "cousin" or sometimes even a brother. Again, class status at times played a role in bringing male relatives in close contact with one another because of having to share the same bed or even a pallet on the floor.

Although most of the men suggest that they had some agency in their first homosexual encounter(s), more than a few relate stories of being forced or manipulated into having sex with an older person when they were emotionally, physically, or psychologically ill prepared. Despite this taking of innocence in their formative years, none of the narrators in question believes there is a corollary between the sexual assault or manipulation and their gayness, even though their parents might think otherwise. What is most interesting about the stories of nonconsensual sex is the number of narrators who never revealed to anyone that they had been sexually abused. And in those instances when they did reveal the fact, most often parents did not report it to the police—perhaps out of guilt or shame, or perhaps out of an allegiance to the general complicity of silence that is seldom transgressed when it comes to sexuality in the South.

. . . .

BOB (B. 1940, BAXLEY, GA.)

At what point did you act on these [homosexual] feelings?

I suppose it was around ninth grade maybe. Not sexually, but there was an attraction for an older person. I guess this person must have been in the tenth or eleventh grade. I always hung around with him, in order to be in his presence. And he would allow me to carry his books and stuff like that. And he was just always a nice person, I thought. And I had an unusual attraction to him, now that I think about it, but I don't know if it was sexual or not, but it was an attraction that was normal for me but, you know, abnormal for somebody else.

Right. Do you think he knew what was going on?

I don't think he did.

No?

It was a big brother. Oh, yeah, he was an only child. And so he didn't; I don't think he knew. But then, obviously when I got to be older, we started having the experiences.

With this same guy?

No, no. No, not with that person. With my own age group, um hmm, with two boys, my age group, yeah, in my age group. We started doing mutual masturbation. But it was a sin to touch, so you didn't touch each other. It was like, "I can't touch you."

Where was this occurring?

Well, we had our little house in the woods, you see, our little tree house. And we built up these little pasteboard boxes around it and had really built it all up. And so that's where we would meet to do our little games and stuff like that. We had BB guns and which now I think was a hideous thing to do. And we would kill birds and things like that. Played hide-and-seek and whatever, I don't know, war games, which is now hideous to think about, we did those. We didn't know any better. You were fed that, so that's what you did, so.

Did you ever talk about what you did afterwards?

Well, no. My first experience of having an erection with other boys in public was I'd go to pick berries with about four other boys. And the older boy was with us. And we were out in this field in an old abandoned farm. We walked out there. I must have been in ninth grade, I suppose. We walked out there to pick berries. And he went, so he jacked off in front of us. And I didn't know, I'd never done that before.

He just spontaneously . . . ? [Laughter]

He started talking about it and his girlfriends and whatever and he just pulled it out. So then I thought he had gotten ill because I never seen anybody do that and his face got all contorted. [Laughter] And I said, "I'm going to tell my mother that you got sick, you were playing with yourself and you got sick." He said, "Well, before you do that, you go home and try it. And after you try it, if you want to tell it, then you tell it." So I went home and tried it and I never told it. [Laughter] So then we did it every day after school.

· · · · · · · · ·

BRYANT (B. 1967, DUBLIN, GA.)

When did you first become aware of your sexual orientation?

That's a good word. I've thought about this a little bit. I can remember at the age of about six or seven, not knowing anything about being gay but I mentioned that my father's family that we used to go to Six Flags with [. . .] was my father's first cousin, so their kids were our second cousins. And [. . .] their son was a year younger than me, and they lived in what was a sharecropper house but they had [. . .] an outhouse for a bathroom. And I can remember going out to that outhouse with that cousin; it was two little cutout seats, and you would go in there and you just had to turn the little latch down to lock the door, and I remember sitting in that outhouse and we would both be sitting there looking at each other's penis, dick—whatever you want to call it—and [. . .] mine would get erect. I can remember being seven years old sitting in there and I'd be touching it, trying to push it down, and they would be getting hard and [. . .] that to me just seemed fascinating.

[. . .] When I was in the twelfth grade, I went to work for the fast food chain Captain D's, and the manager there, who was twenty-three, and I was seventeen at the time, he started flirting with me. And I didn't know that he was flirting with me. I sensed it, but I didn't know that it was flirting, because I didn't know what flirting was. And you know he would say things. And I still wasn't talking to him about it. But one night when we were closing, he asked me to drive someone to their house in his car. And I did, you know. I was still naïve, because I had never really kissed anybody or been with anybody or done anything. And I remember he kept making jokes, what would be now flirting. And he pulled the car off to the side of the road, back off this little dirt road, and pushed me in the middle of the seat of the car and just jumped on top of me. And what would be dry humping. I still didn't know what that was, so I was like, thinking he was playing, wrestling. I didn't even do any-

Bryant's senior class portrait, 1985.
Courtesy of the narrator.

thing, respond back, or kiss him, I didn't know what was he was trying. If he tried to kiss me, I don't remember that. So then I just remember him saying we're going to close one night together by ourselves, and I was like, "fine." And that's when I knew that there's something going on here, but I still wasn't going to tell anyone what was happening. So maybe a week later we did close the restaurant together late at night, eleven o'clock. I remember being very nervous, because I knew something was going to happen. On the way out of the front door he grabbed me back and pulled me back in his arm, and was holding me from behind, and was still doing this dry hump thing and somehow or another I was doing the "uhhh," you know, this struggle. And I got turned around so that we were facing and his beard, or stubble, rubbed against my face. And I think this is why I'm attracted to men with beards today. That just ended all of my struggle at that moment and I remember kissing him. That's all it ever went to, he'd just kiss me, he asked me did I want to go down on him. I didn't even know what that meant. So I just said, "umm unh" [nonverbal for "I don't know"]; I didn't answer the question. So about thirty minutes of that kissing. And I remember feeling very guilty, *extremely* guilty, very, very, extremely guilty.

. . . .

DAN (B. 1943, DURHAM, N.C.)

We belonged to Boy Scouts, and the boys would do things that boys do. And one of my neighbors told my mother that during the day in the summertime, all these people, these little boys would just be coming down and hanging out at our house. She didn't understand why, you know. And so my mother one night sat me down at the dining room table, and she said, you know, Mrs. [neighbor's name] had told her that—but the way she phrased it, I thought she knew what was going on. And so I just blurted out what we were doing.

How old were you?

This was in seventh grade. And I just told her, you know; not only did I tell her what I was doing, I tell her what we all were doing, and named names, and one of the names I named happened to be the son of the minister. And not only had we been doing this at my house and other people houses, but we had been doing it in the church parsonage. Well, needless to say, that created all kinds of stuff, and they called a meeting.

Who called the meeting? The parents?

The parents.

With the minister?

With the minister. That probably was the most traumatic, dramatic thing that ever happened to me.

How many boys were there?

Let me see . . . there had to be like ten of us.

And what were y'all doing exactly? Just sort of experimenting, or . . .

No, I mean we were having sex.

Oh, you were having sex. Anal intercourse?

Yeah.

Wow. In the seventh grade?

In the seventh grade. We were not having oral sex because at that time oral sex, I mean, that was like the worst thing someone could do.

Why was that?

I don't know. I think it may have just been in the black community, but sucking someone's dick, I mean, that, to be called a "cocksucker," was like, you know. But the rest of the stuff that we did. But I don't know if anyone who, at that stage in our lives, was having oral sex.

Wow. And so what happened?

What happened is that we, you know, I couldn't go anywhere. I was grounded for like two years. [Laughter] Seriously. The only place I could go was like to church.

But I guess it was, it had to be supervised, because . . .

Well, my parents would actually take me to church and pick me up, you know. Which, of course, they didn't realize what was going on at church, the fellows, you know, we were still carrying on.

Oh, so you were still carrying on in church?

Oh yeah, we didn't stop. We just were much more careful of what we did and where we did it.

What did your parents say to you about this revelation?

[. . .] They, they sort of freaked out initially. But again, my mother and I had a relationship where we could, because she was a nurse, we could talk about anything and everything, and we did, you know. And so, after I told her what was going on, that we were carrying on, that we were having sex, I didn't go into graphic details until later, when she asked me exactly what we were doing. And I told her, you know. Oh my God. Well, she just sort of wigged out after that. For about four or five months, you know, I had my own little dishes, my own silverware.

Oh really?

Oh yeah. That was just to punish me. My father's reaction was later on. Because I went through this two-year thing from seventh to ninth grade, and I think I mentioned earlier about my experience with the minister, and how that just turned me off, with him. There was a church convention that—you may be familiar with this—that they used to have in the summers, and you would go away for the revival during the summer. Well, I went as a representative of my church, and I'm playing the piano, and organ and stuff. And we all stayed at one of the member's houses down in the country. And the men had the beds, and the kids slept on the floor. Well, we were in the ninth grade or something. One of the guys was from Philadelphia, and we were attracted to each other. And so after everyone had gone to sleep, or so we thought, we started masturbating. Well, his father was the bishop, and that morning I was just asked to pack my stuff and I was brought home. So obviously someone had seen us, or heard us, or whatever. And this minister, he just [went] ballistic. And I lost all respect for him at that point. And my father's comment was, you know, "You are what you are, you can't, you know, we love you, the only thing that I ask is that you be discreet, because Durham is very small, and you know, if your grandmother found out it would kill her." And so, you know I said, "Okay." That's the only talk my father and I ever had about my being gay. And he said, you know, just be discreet. And it's ironic because when I graduated from college and went to New York, the last thing my grandmother said to me on the Sunday night before I left was be careful of the men that you meet. So I mean, she already knew.

. . . .

"D.C." (B. 1951, SHREVEPORT, LA.)

When I was in seventh grade, I remember, I think that's when I really got wind of that. Because I had this buddy of mine; I mean we were real tight. I used to play dominoes and cards at his house. And his mom and other folks, they didn't do that. And that was like entertainment. But she didn't want her boys with no girls at all. And she didn't let them go nowhere. She didn't let them do anything. And she had two boys; both of them were well endowed— *too* well endowed almost. And through some kind of wrestling with him and all this kind of stuff, he became erect and it felt good and we were rubbing or something and we did that kind of little junk for a while. [. . .] It was a whole year and something before any penetration happened. And I remember that, when that happened. And then I said, "Wow." I would say it started in seventh grade. Let's say all through middle . . . well, it wasn't no middle . . . junior high school in my day. And high school. I had sex with him and his brother mostly, and their cousin. And a few guys in the 'hood. Well, in the gang naturally. And that was about it.

You know, I was a very good looking guy, and a lot of the girls liked me and, you know, I was an athlete. I was a football player in high school, track and gymnastics and all that, singing in the choir. I had a band and stuff. I sang at the club on Wednesday nights and all. So I was real popular. And I played the girls and I played the boys too, you know.

So you had girlfriends as well?

Oh yeah. Yes indeed. In fact, my senior year, that's when my son was conceived. And I mean I felt kind of bad about that, but hell. Condoms were not a discussion in my day. In fact, hell, I don't even know if I knew what one was. I'm serious. I don't even remember seeing a condom when I was a kid coming up. It was a whole different time.

Oh, there's another thing. [Chuckle] There was this lady who used to babysit us and we used to have sex. The lady, yeah, that babysat. I mean she was an older lady because she was older than my mother. But I don't know if she just loved me, she screwed me. And I used to have sex, with her husband sitting out in the yard, you know. She'd be stooped over the window and I'd be behind her and you know . . . [Laughter] And I remember every Friday, when he got off work and got paid, he would bring home all these drinks and barbecued ribs and wine. And he would already be halfway messed up and finished getting messed up when he got there. And we'd be having sex and eating barbecue and drinking wine and that kind of thing.

· · · · · · · ·

FREDDIE (B. 1944, MADISON, GA.)

Well, I don't know about most kids, but I've come to think that very painful memories are sometimes remembered in ways that can be tolerated. I'll have flashes of memories. I have one memory of going to an outhouse. When I left Madison, Georgia, most black folk had outdoor toilets. I remember going to the outhouse and Cousin A. C. was in there and he said, "Oh come on in." And I remember this intense feeling of fear. There was a look in his eyes that I can still remember. And I remember being very much afraid of going in there with him. And I just think, normally a little boy would have gone in with a safe adult male. But I remember not going in there with him. And I remember kind of the look in his eyes that was very frightening to me, and this feeling of apprehension about going in there with him. So I suspect that maybe he might have been one of the people who did something to me.

[. . .] When I was in counseling, I shared with my counselor that the first time I had anal intercourse I was very young. But it was during a game of hide-and-seek with some neighborhood boys. And I noticed that one or two boys would always hide with me. And as the crowd thinned out, there was two bigger boys and me and another little boy. And so one of the bigger boys said, "You all want to do something?" and the other little boy said, "I will if you will." And I knew exactly what we were going to do. And like I say, a dab of spit and a half hour later, I had had sex for the first time I remember having sex.

And one of the more telling things is that it was a familiar experience and it wasn't painful. And a lot of my friends say their first time was very painful, how excruciating. But it wasn't. It was like a familiar experience. And even before then, like I knew what was going to happen. My counselor said, "Well, you know, at that age, you should not have known any of that. You should not. So something had to have happened to you to implant that information. You'd have to have had an experience for something to have that information in your head." Because I knew exactly what was going to happen. When the two of them were hiding with me, I could feel their bodies next to mine and I knew. I said, "This is going to be an interesting night." And it was. And that started it. And this was, oh, God, it was, I think it was the summer between fourth and fifth grade. I was really very young.

. . . .

KENT (B. 1967, BEREA, N.C.)

I did have an experience though, where I was molested. When I was probably seven. Actually, I might have been a little older. And this is something that went on for about a few months. I mentioned earlier that my mom and dad had a restaurant. And they hired a neighborhood boy who was in a single-parent home, in an abusive home. And they hired him to give him something, some work so he could make some money and try to make it on his own. He also moved into the house with us when his mom nearly, she tried to stab him, so he moved into the house with us. And that's where it began. It started as mutual exploration. There was something that was incredibly intoxicating about the experience. I wasn't repulsed by it. In fact, I was drawn to it. It was happening to me. It was the taking of a child's innocence, but as a child I didn't feel like I was being violated. And that might sound strange, but aside from the physical aspect of it, he was paying attention to me and that felt really nice.

How much older?

He was probably seventeen at the time, somewhere in that area.

Did you ever tell anyone?

I didn't have to. My dad put two and two together. And needless to say, he put him out of the house. He lost his job and, quite honestly, he's lucky that my dad let him live. I think one of the things I dealt with later on in my twenties was that I'd blocked a lot of that stuff out. And it came rushing back in my, by my mid-twenties. It came rushing back like a river and I could remember the sights, the sounds, even the smells. I think one reason I blocked it out (here I am trying to diagnose myself), is that after it happened my mom and dad did the best they could as far as trying to deal with the situation, but their way of dealing with it was to pretend it didn't happen. I had no one there to tell me, "It wasn't your fault. You're not responsible for this." I felt like something that, at one point felt natural and beautiful, suddenly I felt ashamed because I felt like my parents' love, I'm going to risk losing this. And so their way to deal with it was not to deal with it, and it offered none of us an opportunity for outlet, to express what anyone was feeling in the situation so that we could deal with it, heal and move on. And so a lot of stuff stayed repressed. My mom mentioned it when I came out to her a little over two years ago. And she thought maybe that was the reason why I was telling her I was gay. But I told her that I remember having these feelings before that happened. So his molesting me didn't make me gay.

Do you know where he is now?

When I was in my twenties and I was dealing with that whole scene with everything coming back, a lot of it was reaction to finding out things. I thought he had died. Someone said he was killed in a car accident. I found out that he was actually living in New Bern [North Carolina] somewhere and that he had married and had kids. And honestly, during that point, I was ready to find him and I wanted to confront him. And, a friend of mine convinced me to just let it go. Somehow I was able to. I think just having an outlet to talk about it, during that time, was what I needed.

· · · · · · · ·

JONATHAN S.

Jonathan S. was one of several college students I interviewed whose experiences of growing up gay varied drastically from those of older men. He was another person I met, in an indirect way, through Curt's network of friends in the Research Triangle Park in North Carolina. Jonathan was born a fraternal twin in Warrenton, North Carolina, in 1983. With a population just under 1,000, Warrenton is located in north central North Carolina, near the Virginia border. In addition to his twin sister, Jonathan has one older brother and two older sisters. The interview took place on October 29, 2004, on the campus of the University of North Carolina at Chapel Hill, where he was a student.

Freshman year [in high school], I was fourteen, which is actually when I met the first guy I would end up being with. He actually lived right down the road from me, and I didn't know him at that point. We had algebra or something like that together. I had taken all of my math in middle school, so when I got to high school, I jumped up to the upper math, which is why I was in there with him. And I remember there was some excuse he gave to get my phone number. I don't remember what it was. I was so oblivious to this whole thing. I had no idea what was going on until, like, I look back, you know. And like, when I was in the situation, I don't remember feeling like that was gonna end up happening. We started talking in December; we started talking on the phone. And then we started talking more frequently. And I didn't know what that meant necessarily, but I knew it wasn't necessarily normal. Like, I knew that for me to be thinking about him and wanna go home and call him, is a little odd, and to be wanting to go out with him was a little odd. But at this point, I still didn't necessarily realize what that was. And I was still oblivious, basically, to the whole thing until we kissed for the first time. I remember feeling like that's what this feeling is, because I had never been able to place it. I remember having this sort of inclination to be around males, but I never knew why. I didn't know what it was and I didn't necessarily look at it as abnormal. [. . .] Basically, after that first kiss, my grades fell, like, a lot. Because I was basically not doing any work. Now I look back on that, I was real bold. I used to just sneak out of the house, and I would go stay with him.

What do you mean, "stay with him"?

Like, I would go stay with him.

At his house?

Umm hmmm.

You were the same age?

I was fourteen; he was seventeen. The way his house was set up, all his doors had locks and his bedroom had a lock, and he was the only one with the key. So I would go in through the window, of course. Yeah, I was a little devious. But go in through the window and I'd stay over there and I'd get up at, like, 6 A.M. and then walk back home.

So you were in walking distance to his house?

Oh, yeah, yeah. I mean, to somebody in the city it was a long way, but to me, I mean, my whole life was spent, like, walking through the woods and stuff like that. So that little half a mile was nothing. But I'd go in through the window and I would be coming back in at, like, 6 A.M., getting right into bed and then get back up at 6:30 and go to school. So I was maybe operating on, like, two or three hours of sleep for a couple months, and I remember I used to just fall asleep in class. [Laughter] Like, I'll be sitting there, next thing you know I'm, like, out, just cold. And my grades fell, like, I remember I was ranked like eighth in my class first semester, and then, second semester, I was ranked forty-first because it was just like C's across the board that second semester. I didn't really care. I was so interested in trying to figure out what sort of all that meant for me. And we actually ended up having sex, which was interesting. It happened on January 28th, 1998. I don't know why I remember that date.

[. . .] So your first experience was with this seventeen-year-old?

Uh huh. That was my first sexual experience. That I think actually, in some ways, has sort of shaped me a little bit, because I mean, I liked it, so it was something that I pursued more so than I would have sex with a female, had I had sex at that point.

He was experienced, you said, and like, was it just sort of, you know, mutual masturbation or did you actually have anal sex?

No, it was sex, anal sex. But at first, it was, for a while, I was only comfortable kissing him, and even then, that took a little bit of—like, I couldn't just do it. It wasn't completely natural. I still felt like this is something I shouldn't do.

Did you feel like he was sort of teaching you? 'Cause when you were sneaking out of your house and going over, what were you doing then? Just sort of studying together or . . . ?

No, at first, we would just, like, sleep together, which I liked.

So it was just about sort of being with somebody?

Right, being with him. And I didn't feel like he was teaching me, which I guess could be 'cause he said he was inexperienced. [. . .] But to me, looking back, I thought he would've been, but who knows. But I didn't get the feeling that he was necessarily teaching me, because [. . .] when we did have sex, I didn't get the feeling that he knew what he was doing. I mean, [laughter] that's just me. 'Cause like, even when we would kiss, he would have the same hesitation that I did. So I didn't necessarily feel like he was teaching me—felt like we were sort of learning together, to an extent. And it was cool for a little while, because of the fact that his friends knew about us. So it was kind of like they knew me and I knew them and blah, blah, blah, and all this stuff. It was almost like, they're a couple. So that was good for me.

And the reason why I'm asking, because you were saying earlier that, you know, you didn't really know what these feelings were and you had no images of gay people or whatever. So I'm trying to figure out how you go from that kind of naïveté to actually, you know, having sex and knowing what to do, especially if he's not experienced, you're not experienced. You just decide, "Oh, he has a hole." [Laughter].

Yes. [Laughter] It was sort of like after we kissed, things just sort of progressed. Like, I knew the concept of heterosexual sex. So I could kind of figure, you know, "Oh, well, my mouth goes there," you know. [Laughter] Like I knew, I sort of knew what a woman and man did, so I could kind of figure out what a man and a man would do. And when it came to us actually having sex, there was a little bit of feeling that maybe he was teaching—not necessarily teaching me a little bit, but I just remember just laying there. [Laughter] And he was just like, this is all you have to do. So, I mean, I didn't like it the first few times, but I figured this is what he wants to do, whatever. But eventually, I sort of got used to it and I liked it better, and I started to be more attracted to him, which made it better, you know.

· · · · · · · ·

"ROB" (B. 1965, EDEN, N.C.)

As I grew toward the age of eight or nine I guess it was, that was probably the first time that I ever experienced anything sexual. So very early experience with quote/unquote sex, it really wasn't sex per se, because I didn't know what that was. But the usual childhood fooling around with other guys and other girls. Then it became quite a bit more serious for me, and I guess emotionally scarring in some ways, because we had, inevitably, the neighbor who actually molested me, and I never confessed that to anyone until, gosh, I was twenty-nine, I think, when I told my family. My mother knew, but she never told anyone else. I told her, so of course I was taken to the hospital. I wasn't physically hurt or harmed, or anything, but just I guess the emotional scarring that she wanted to get me checked out and all that. And that happened, I think, twice, and I don't know if I've suppressed, repressed, if there were other occasions, but I do remember two distinct occasions, where our neighbor across the street, I guess lured me over there. I still remember him saying, "Come on let's go play football or something." And I really don't remember how much older he was than I am, or than I was, but I would think he was probably a teenager, at that point probably in his late teens. And I think he's now, has joined the Army, I don't know where he is now, lost track of it. But that experience turned my, innocent endurance test into something a lot more serious for me. And then I, of course, didn't become a hermit but went into the whole shy, self-esteem or lack of self-esteem mode from that point forward.

Shifting gears a little bit, when did you first become aware of your same-sex orientation, and how would you describe your reaction to your awareness of that?

My awareness came fairly, relatively young. I didn't have a reaction to it, per se, I just thought, oh this is interesting and continued doing what I was doing. It came, I guess, in fourth grade. There was this guy in my class named Doug. And I used to do everything with Doug, I always wanted to spend time with Doug, I always sat next to Doug, wanted to get in the same reading group, whatever was going on, I had to be with Doug. So there was just this little bond, this little attachment that formed. And nothing ever, nothing of a sexual nature ever happened, but I always felt this, this connection to him. And I found out many years later, he was gay. I don't have any contact with him now, but, so, I mean, that was, that was the extent of it.

The first sexual experience didn't come until high school, when I was visiting my brother at college. And of course trying to be precocious I was trying to hang out with his friends and all this. And my brother was busy working on something for school, a project, or his thesis, I don't even remember. I was seventeen, and he left me with one of his friends, one of his classmates, to sort of quote "babysit" me until he was done with whatever he was doing. And as it turns out, I ended up in this guy's bed with him, and I don't remember how we ended up that way, other than my brother ended up not being able to pick me up, so just decided "Well, just spend the night and I'll come get you in the morning." So, this guy gave me a blow job, and you know, I was just paralyzed, lying there in bed I'm thinking, "Well, what am I supposed to do? Should I move? Am I supposed to say something?" I distinctly remember not pulling away, and just going with the flow, seeing what was going to happen. And he finished, I ejaculated, and that was it. Turned over, I went to sleep; he got up and went to his bedroom. And the next morning not a word was spoken. We had breakfast, and I was thinking, "Oh my God, I must be gay." This must be, you know, what happens, okay. So that was my reaction, was that seven, eight years later, to the realization that I might be different.

Did you ever tell anyone?

I told no one. I told absolutely no one. My brother passed away, and I don't think I ever told him.

[. . .] I didn't have my first sexual experience with another man until I was twenty-eight years old. [. . .] I had that experience at the same time my brother told us he was HIV positive. So I immediately jumped to the conclusion, okay, I'm gonna die now, because, you know, disaster comes in threes, and you know. And despite the fact that I had begun HIV testing, as a result of a project I had done in college, in '84 or '85, I'd been getting an HIV test every year, because we did this sexual survey thing, and all this stuff about college-age students' sexual activities. So I was getting tested, and despite negative tests, I still thought, okay, one day it's going to come up positive and it's going to be me, you know, all this stuff I've done: all this stuff, one blow job. You know, even harking back to the molestation I guess, as a seven-, eight-, or nine-year-old, thinking okay, this is it. So, for me that really curtailed my sexual activities. I would of course, look at other guys and all that kind of thing and flirt with them, but never, ever, did anything with them, until I was twenty-eight. And the sexual experience was much like the one I had at age seventeen, except it was very similar in terms of being frozen and not knowing what to do and just lying there. But I enjoyed that; it was a good experience for me. I wasn't ready for it, emotionally, but, you know, physiologically and physically it was a good experience for me. I met him at the Power Company, in Durham, of all places. Six [foot], three or four, big muscular guy, it was a white guy. And you know, just, you know after that I thought I was in love.

My experiences with friends and college, that was where I started to solidify my sexual identity because my freshman year roommate was just a dreamboat. I remember praying the summer before I got my housing letter telling me who was going to be my roommate and where I was gonna live, God please let him be gorgeous. I was starting to feel this, you know I had just had my blow job, in my junior year, or beginning of senior year, and you know, this was just great. The guy who did that was really good looking, so this, this was going to be great, we were going to be roommates, you know. My brother talked to me about his experiences in college and when I'd visit, all kinds of subtle things would come out between him and his roommate, guys coming to and fro from the shower, and I'd be sleeping on the floor, and that kind of thing. And so I started picking up on these little nuances and clues about what college and dorm life was really gonna be like, so I thought, this will be great to have a good-looking roommate, make this all the more fun. So I couldn't have asked for a better first year roommate. Gorgeous, intelligent, smart, funny, and oh so sexy. And this guy, to this day, he pretends he does not remember this, but of course, being a gay guy, you remember this kind of thing. He came in from the shower one day. I was sitting on the sofa. We had this loft in our dorm room, so we had a sofa underneath the loft and our beds were up on top of the loft. He came into the room from the bathroom, he had showered, and I was sitting there reading or doing something on the sofa. He came in, stood in front of me with his towel, dropped his towel, facing me, mind you, dropped his towel in front of me. And I knew he was testing me, trying to see if I would look up, because I'm sure he tried to pretend to be straight, Mr. Hetero. I guess he is. I don't know. I still don't know. I still have my doubts. A girl can wish, right? He dropped his towel in front of me, and I guess he was expecting me to stop what I was doing and look up. I didn't move. I didn't lift my eyes from the page. Wanted to, like all get out, but didn't, because I had seen the goods before anyways in the shower. So from that point on, I was like, this bastard is trying to feel me out and see what the deal is. I'm not gonna give him the satisfaction. So, that was when I started realizing, there are people out there who are going to test me and figure out what's going on. So, our roommate situation didn't change, we were friends to that point, but after that the friendship started to kind of change, and took on a different tenor. The guard went up. And the next year, we went our separate ways and got other roommates. But I'll never forget that experience.

....

RODERICK (B. 1974, BATON ROUGE, LA.)

I was sexually molested by an uncle, my biological father's younger brother, at my grandmother's house while I was being babysat. I was probably three or four. I remember that. And I didn't understand what was going on, but I knew what happened was not right. There was some oral sex involved. And I told my mother what happened, and then . . . oh she lost it! And she told my dad, and my dad wanted to kill my uncle. And it was a major uproar. I don't remember all. But I remember she did call the authorities. I do remember it being discussed and me talking to some investigator. I remember that conversation. My mother and I, we never talked about it again. It was up until I was maybe a teenager or maybe in college, I brought it up. I said, "Ma, I haven't forgotten about that. That happened." And she just burst into tears. I think she told me that the man said, "Ma'am, I believe your son is telling the truth." Who knows what the laws were like back then. This was '78, I guess, or '79. And molestation was such a taboo thing to talk about anyway in the black community. I don't know what even the rules were and how the laws worked in the state then. Maybe there had to be an admission. Of course, he denied it. I don't know what happened, but I know he was not arrested. I know there was not any recourse. And to this day I can't speak to him. I see him. I don't want to. I would never have. I have maybe two or three words to say to him. And I reminded my father maybe several years ago, I was like, I reminded him, "I haven't forgotten what happened. And that happened. And you know that happened." [. . .] But black folks don't want to talk about that. [Chuckle] I don't care where you are, the South, North, East, West, whatever. That was probably the most negative thing that happened to me.

....

TONY (B. 1961, MEMPHIS, TENN.)

I thought to be gay and to be sexual as a gay person, you had to be well versed in every sexual act possible. And in order to be accepted, that you had to have techniques, and I set about to have these techniques. Not that a lot of these things were things I wanted to do, but I thought if you're going to do it, you have to do it the way you're supposed to. And so I would even force myself to do things I didn't really want to do or I even have a friend at school who I recruited one time to be my sort of sex surrogate, you know.

Meaning what? What does that mean?

Because he could help me do things I wasn't good at, so I wouldn't have to be bad at it with somebody who I was trying to sleep with. So like I was not very good at being a bottom, you know, and so I thought I needed practice. I needed to have a sex surrogate, so here I recruited him one time to be that because I wanted to be good at that, so when I was ready to go and have sex with somebody, if that was something that came up, I could be, you know, good at that, too. I could be good at all these things. And it probably sounds absurd, I don't know, you know, but for eleventh graders.

So he was like your teacher, or I'm still trying to understand. So if you were trying to be a bottom, you were having him fucking you?

Basically, yes, yes. To help me to be comfortable with it. So it was just to experience it in a low-stress situation, as opposed to experiencing it when I would have performance anxiety, you know, where I've got some strange man who I don't know who's expecting me to be like some diva in the bed, you know. That was so important to me that I thought I had to be good at all this stuff that I'm practicing, I'm recruiting a surrogate to help me, that kind of stuff. And so that's the world I thought I had to try to fit myself into, because it was the only world I knew about was from that movie [*Cruising*], but from the books and from *After Dark* magazine [an entertainment magazine geared toward and popular among gays]. I still have all those *After Dark* magazines. It very much shaped who I was at that time.

Do you remember your first same-sex sexual encounter and how you felt afterwards?

Um hmm, um hmm. It was that boy I was telling you about that went to my high school when I was in public school. And it was the summer between tenth and eleventh grade. I went over, you know, under the ruse that he set up, which was to—because I like to play musical theater albums and he wanted to hear them because he liked theater, too. So I'm going to play my musical theater albums. How gay is that? We're going to play soundtracks, you know, from *A Chorus Line* and *Pippin*. Gay, gay, gay, gay, gay. But he had other plans, honey; it wasn't about no records. It was about trying to get in my pants. So, you know, we're sitting on the couch like this. And ultimately he tries to touch me and start kissing me. I remember feeling just scared to death. And then I remember once the kissing and whatever we did started, it just seemed like maybe a hundred years passed. It seemed to be that long.

Tony, age eighteen, in the musical talent review, "Feelings," at Winston-Salem State University, 1979. Courtesy of the narrator.

Everything was in slow motion, I remember that, it just seemed like it was hours and hours and it really wasn't. And I remember him taking me to his mother's bed, who was at work, because he really wanted to do more. And I had never had sex with anybody at this point, so kissing somebody and starting to take my clothes off with somebody, that was pretty exhilarating right there, you know, I didn't need to do anything else. And we didn't because my mother was coming to get me, because I couldn't drive at the time. I don't think I had my license, and if I did she sure wasn't going to let me drive her Cadillac. So I just knew that we had to stop this. And all I remember after that was feeling really excited about it and trying to find other opportunities to continue this exploration. I don't remember feeling really bad about it. I just thought it was really fun and exciting and I wanted to do more of it. I don't remember if he did this after I went away for the summer, because I went to dance camp that summer to the School of the Arts. I remember that whole summer wanting something to happen and trying to hang around people I thought were gay who could tell me about things or introduce me to things or do things to me or with me, which I don't—that never happened. But by the time I got away that fall in the eleventh grade, I was certainly open, fully open and ready to do that. So the next experience after that I was actually seduced by a boy I knew from here, who was an Italian white boy. We both studied ballet here together and he was at the school with me. He was a college freshman and I was a high school junior. So that was the first time I had sexual intercourse with a man. So the first time was just kissing. And then the second time, which was several months later, was, you know, [whispering] we went all the way.

CARRYIN' ON: SEXUAL ESCAPADES

It takes a lot to make me blush. After all, most of my research focuses on sexuality. Suffice it to say, I "clutched my pearls" on a number of occasions during interviews with some of the narrators while listening to their stories about sex. Many of them take "carryin' on" to a whole different level. I suppose that one of the reasons why the stories were shocking to me is because the narrators who were sharing them are so unassuming or did not fit the mold of the kind of person who, in my mind, would engage in some of the sexual activities they describe.

Despite my surprise at hearing some of these stories, I never passed judgment, which may be why the narrators were so free in sharing them. Admittedly, I enjoyed listening to these tales of ménage à trois, sex in the pews with the preacher, sex in the parked car of the driveway of the married man with the threat of the wife coming outside at any moment, sex in the middle of a golf course, etc. But my interest arose from more than prurient fascination. The tales were compelling because they expressed in a real way the sexual agency of these men, an agency not commonly associated with the South, and especially the rural South. Their sexual escapades contradict the image of the South as sexually "slow," boring, or clandestine. Indeed, the children are carryin' on.

. . . .

"D. BERRY"

Tony, a narrator in this book, introduced me to "D. Berry." We met for the first time for this interview. He was born in Memphis, Tennessee, in 1960, the elder of two children. The interview took place on July 20, 2005, in my hotel room in Memphis.

I guess that one of my wildest nights was three years ago, Gay Pride in Atlanta, Georgia. I was at Piedmont Park from 11:30 till 7:30 in the morning. That was the wildest thing.

Details. [Laughter]

Oh. I had sex with one guy, but the rest of the night, I was mainly just assisting and looking.

What do you mean by assisting?

Giving 'em lube, giving 'em condoms. And then one guy said, "You got . . ." And I said, "here's some." And I said, "here." And he said, "Lube me up, man." [Laughter] And of course, I did, and I watched them screw, and it was just—oooh, there were so many people. And this went on until 7:30 in the morning.

So did you go out to sort of be a, for the lack of a better word, a counselor or, you know, to give people protection? Was that your motivation for going there?

No. A friend of mine lived not far from the park. I went out to the club, and I was going to make my way through the park on the way home, and I went through and I met this guy and we talked and we did what we was gonna do. And he said, "Okay, bye," and I said, "What they doing?" And I went over there, and I said, "What're they doing over there?" And I was just trying to find out why everybody was just kind of walking through there and disappearing. So I kind of found a way down through the trails, and I seen it was a group over here and a group over there, and I just had them and I just give 'em to 'em cause I always have 'em on me.

'Cause they didn't have them themselves?

If I hadn't been there they probably wasn't gonna use 'em. That was like the wildest time. Like I said, 7:30, it was still sunup. [Laughter] There's a lake in the middle of the park; there's a swimming pool. And there was a guy from Memphis on his knees, just going all the way down this line of all these guys. I just went, okay, and then I went home. So that was one of the wildest nights I can remember. Now, you know that I ain't been back since.

· · · · · · · ·

FREDDIE (B. 1944, MADISON, GA.)

I know guys who would always want to give the trade money because they thought they should give the trade—Well, you know what trade is? And I said, "I'm not doing that. He enjoyed it as much as I did. And in many instances more." [Laughter] I'm not doing that, because during certainly a part of my life we were very poor. I'll never say I was a prostitute. Most of the men I've ever interacted with were older. And many of them would give me money because I was in school, I was a student, I needed money, and it wasn't like a clear exchange of sex for money. But many of them would give me money. [Chuckle] I just never had any money. But I just never thought that you should pay someone to have an enjoyable experience.

[. . .] I'll back up a bit. When I was in the old neighborhood, there were two attempts at gang rape. And I always had very keen senses. And it was the same boy, the same boy was the instigator. But after the second attempt . . . you know how you just kind of . . . there's this little voice in my head that kind of like says, "Be careful." So the first time, ironically, he and I had sex and he came by my house and wanted me to come and go with him. I was thinking we were going to have sex again. But you know how you walk at night and you can see the shadows in front of you? I was noticing that he would seem to reach for me. And I would look at him. And I said, "Okay there's something up here." So I knew where the most likely spot might be for people to hide. Because this was, I think, the second attempt. And so I started to run. And I think I went to his house, because his mother and I had become friends. I would almost always become friends with my friends' mothers because they always said I was wise and they would sit and talk to me. So I went to his house, and I think I told his mother that a dog was after me or something. The next time I saw him, I said, "You know, I'm going to tell your mama on you." And I never understood that. Why he would try and do that? But it happened twice with this same boy. And it was so frightening each time, that it would kind of scare me.

[. . . .]

Well, there was an era, I'll call it an era of my life that kind of basically any interaction with a man meant that it was going to be sex. I had to make an adjustment. [. . .] I mentioned the guy I cut across the shoulder. He and I did not attend the same high school. He attended the trade school, Carver Vocational School. I was walking home one night and he was driving by. This was years later. I might have been in college. And he picked me up; we ended up going somewhere and having sex. He had gotten married and had a family. And this is one of my more dangerous encounters. He parked in his driveway with his wife and his mother-in-law inside, and we pulled off all of our clothes and had sex in what he said was a 1939 Al Capone. It just was a big old car. The doors opened from the middle and the back seat was like a bed. And he went in and told them something, and we did that more than once. And when I think back, now when I look back at that, I shudder at what could have happened. I mean it was just amazing. [. . .]

One story I'll share with you. There was this little guy; he was very short. We went to elementary school together. We would ride the same school bus, but he didn't attend the same school. The bus passed Carver Vocational School on the way to Price High School. Boys would call me "sissy" or something, and he would put down his books and want to fight them. And then I would say, "Leave them alone." So at some point I noticed that he was very angry with me. I could see the anger in him. He wouldn't speak. And I worked in the corner store. So being the professional that I was, I would always go over and say, "Good afternoon. May I help you?" or whatever. So I noticed that his anger seemed to subside a bit. He didn't look as angry. And one night he started kind of hanging around the store a bit. So one night we were in the store alone, and I had given him his purchase and gone back to putting up stock or whatever. He was still there. So I said, "Can I get you something else?" And he said, "What time are you getting off?" And I said, "Oh, probably eleven, eleven-thirty. Why?" He said, "I have something for you." And I said, "What?" So he said, "This," and he kind of looked down. He was short. And we would walk on inverted drink crates in the back, so we were taller than the counter. So I made him come down to where I could see his body full length. And so when he said, "This" he had this enormous erection. [Chuckle] So I clutched my bosom in shock. [Laughter] At two things: at the size of his penis, and by the fact that he was wanting to talk to me again, wanting to be friendly. So I told him what time I was getting off. Even though I lived across the street from the store, we went in the opposite direction because we wanted to walk and talk. So the first thing I asked him, I said, "I don't understand. I'm confused." I said, "You've been walking around here for all this time not speaking to me, as if you were angry with me, and I hadn't done anything. What was your problem?" He said, "Well, I was angry." I said, "Well, why?" He said, "Well, I wanted some. I knew you were having sex with other people, and I wanted some." And I said, "But Honey, I'm not the Avon lady. I'm not going door to door. You didn't ask." [Laughter] So this started us having sex, and he wanted us to kind of have an open relationship. And here again I said, "I don't think we should do that." I said, I'm not going to call his name, I'll just say, "John." It's not John. I said, "John, you know how they treat me. How they've always treated me. It's like a label that, once it's on, it doesn't come off." I said, "And if you and I start going to movies and stuff openly, that label will get stuck on you. And I don't know if this is the life you want or not." I said, "This is my life. I've decided. This is how I am, this is how I'm going to be. This is not a phase I'm going through and I'm out of the phase." I said, "So I think we should just kind of . . . You can still speak to me, of course. But I think we should kind of be discreet in our kind of relationship until you make the decision that maybe this is what you really want. Because once that label gets stuck on, it doesn't come off." So unfortunately, I would notice kind of an intensity about him each time we would have sex. Because he wanted to kiss. He asked how would it be to kiss, and I said, "I guess it's like kissing a girl. Lips are lips." So when I kissed him, he said, "It's not like kissing a girl." I didn't ask him if it was different good or different bad. But I noticed that after we would have sex, sometimes he would caress me and there was kind of an intensity there that really started to concern me. I think once he told me he loved me, it concerned me because it was strange. And one of my regrets in life is that, in a very short time, my life changed drastically. I met Leroy, I moved out of the neighborhood, I got a job, and I didn't get to say goodbye to him. And I didn't want to call his house because all of his family members knew me, you know. We were right in the neighborhood and all of his family members knew me and I didn't want to cause him a problem. Maybe in retrospect I should have written him a letter or something. But I never got to say goodbye to him. And fairly recently, within the past few years, my friend I mentioned from the old neighborhood from high school saw him and mentioned my name and he said he didn't remember me. And I'm thinking that if he would get angry with me about having sex with other people, even though he had not asked, that me kind of disappearing out of his life might have hurt him very badly. I'm sure he probably remembers me, but he might have totally blocked it. That might have been more traumatic for him than I might have imagined. But my life changed drastically. I always felt that maybe it would have been easier for him to get in touch with me. And to this day, I have not seen him since. I have not seen him in forty years. He's still in Atlanta. Well, I don't stay up nights thinking about it, you know. [Chuckle] But, you know, we all have these regrets. We look back at situations where we wish we had done something differently. But, you know, nothing I can do about it now.

· · · · · · · ·

"LARRY J." (B. 1959, CAMDEN, S.C.)

Well, here I was a senior in high school and worked at the YMCA. Well, there's this guy that worked at the YMCA who was a football player for Camden High School. [. . .] And he must have been a sophomore. He may have even been a freshman. But he worked at the YMCA too that summer. Well, we were walking across the country club, and I'm down to the little shed area and we had stopped. For some reason, we stopped. I stayed in Kirkwood and he stayed in the neighborhood behind Kirkwood, like across the tracks. Now across the tracks, that's where most of the schoolteachers and the well-to-do stayed over there in that area. So anyway, we were walking together. And what usually happened is that his mom or somebody would come by and pick him up, but that day obviously they were not coming, so he had to walk home. So I'll never forget this. I'll never forget this. He said, "Motherfucker, suck my dick." You know, just like a boy would say. And [laughter] . . . I said, "I don't suck on anything that I ain't gonna get full off of. [Laughter] That's what I said [. . .] and he says, "Oh yeah." And so he pulled it out. [. . .] You know I didn't clutch pearls then. That's what they call it now. But I was like, "Wow." And so I said, "Well, you go around there." So he went around like on the backside of there. So I went around there and I started [makes gulping sound]. I had never done that before. And he had a big dick. I mean [laughter] he had a big piece. So I was gagging on it. I'm just saying. I didn't know what to do. I had no experience with doing that. And so he said, "Motherfucker, you don't know what you're doing." Something, something, something. And so we stopped. So nothing else happened and so he went on his way and I went on my way. And I didn't really think much of it. Well, now mind you, I had to see him tomorrow at work. And somehow we got in the basement of the YMCA. [. . .] We snuck down there and was trying different little things. He was trying to do some anal. He was trying to screw me and no lube or nothing, you know. I mean I didn't know a thing. I didn't know any of that.

Had he had experience? He sounds like he had had experience.

Yeah. Or he may have been just kind of like experimenting. I mean, like I said, he was a football player. Now he played on the football team. That's what I'm sitting here telling you. So you know that was just becoming too risky. So we arranged that we were gonna meet like later on that night at the country club. We was gonna meet back and then we were going to go on one of these what I call the greens and mess around on one of the greens. So we snuck out of the house, [and I] went [and] took my little bath. I took a bath and snuck a towel, 'cause back then I was like a senior, my mom, you know, as long as you come in at a decent hour. Now we're talking about after it got dark and this was during the summer, before fall happens. So I'd go and meet him on the green. And I think we had some Vaseline or something. And he was trying to, you know, penetrate. But I'm telling you, it was big. And I wasn't used to this kind of stuff here. And he was trying to force it, and of course I was moving away and all this stuff. And there was no such thing as no love, no kissing, no foreplay. Not that I'd know anything about all that. Well, he gets angry. And I'll never forget, he gets angry. [. . .] And he started holding me tight, squeezing me, and punching. Not punching real hard but, "Motherfucker," and I was running and he was catching me and running and hitting me. Not hard and not in my face, but just hitting me. And I'm, "Just leave me alone. Don't bother me no more." We just went through that. And so I made up my mind I wasn't gonna fool with him anymore. I wasn't gonna do it. I just couldn't. But you know, here we are still working together. And he'd make all these little snide remarks. "I know you want some more of this." What are you to do? Something to get your nature up. You know so like I said, we kind of fooled around a little bit and I'll never forget this fool never could get to the point of penetration and all of that kind of stuff, so we just kind of fooled around just a little bit more. And by that time, it was time to go off to school. I was glad to get away 'cause then I could leave that behind me and wouldn't have to deal with that anymore. So I go off to college, a little bit more wiser now.

[. . .] I was in my senior year [of college] and I was sort of not really doing a whole lot now, but wanting to. [. . .] And anyway there was this guy that was up there in summer school and he really was gorgeous. I just had to have some of him. I just had to. But he was clearly straight. Or, would play around—trade, for a lack of a better word. Well, I don't quite remember how it happened, but I made it known to him that I wanted him. And I'll never forget, I was sitting in the apartment one night and the phone rang and it was him. He had a girlfriend and he said there was this concert that he wanted to go to and if I would help him out he would let me suck his dick. That's what he told me on the phone. [Chuckle] Now, mind you, I'm staying in some apartments and he's staying in a dormitory. The apartments are on the other side of campus. I think I got to his dorm room in like fifteen, twenty minutes. I mean it usually would take thirty-five minutes. Of course, I get there and the room is just pitch black. I thought, "Oh shit. What have I got myself into? This guy's gonna beat the shit out of me." But I came on in there. He had the room all dark. I never will forget. And [he] was like laying on the bed. So I give him the money so he'd let me suck, suck for a little bit—wasn't long. So that was that.

And you had become better at it [giving blow jobs] by then?

[Laughs] Yeah. He was just doing that for the money. Literally, just for the money. And so I think that just happened that one time. [. . .] So I graduated, went back home, stayed at home. And of course that was the summer of my discontent because I ran upon this guy I knew once from high school. So we met one time. [. . .] We sort of met in some woods. Isn't that awful? And I'll never forget. By then he was probably getting ready to graduate or had graduated. Anyway, I will never forget that night. I'll never forget that 'cause I thought I was gonna die. So I'll never forget, I was giving him a blow job and I stopped. And you know he was cursing me out, "Why did you stop?" So he started ejaculating, I mean he started jacking his dick. He started and then he came. Well, by then he was real frustrated with me. And I'll never forget him putting his hands right here at my throat. And you know this was a football player and now, he was strong. I was a little small thing, you know. And he [makes gagging sound] I mean literally cut off my circulation, literally, seriously. He must have felt it, too, 'cause he stopped. He literally stopped. So I'll never forget that. And I knew then. I was really liking him. I never fooled with him again. And I think I may have seen him maybe once or twice, but I wised up and tended not to be bothered with him. So that summer was absolutely the summer of my discontent.

Anyway I ended up getting a job in Columbia [South Carolina] with the auditor's office like in July and commuted from Camden. But by then I had to have a little car. So from Camden, [I] commuted to Columbia. But didn't go out. [. . .] Well, then you know the desire was all there then. Oh man! And there was this cute—and looks aren't everything—but there was this guy in the neighborhood that would stand like on the corner. I would stop at a stoplight and I would have to turn, and he was there. And oh, he was just [sighs] so . . . mmmm . . . And he would always wave real friendly. And so I'll never forget, one day I said I'm gonna see what this is about and went and parked like on the side. And so he was over there talking to somebody. So the person left and I sort of motioned and said, "Could you come over here for a minute?" And so we kind of like just chatted for a little bit. And I kind of like asked him what did he get into. He said, "What you wanna do? What you wanna do?" He says, "I need some cigarettes." I said, "I'm looking for some meat." That's what I remember saying, "I'm looking for some meat." I was bold. Man he was a straight guy. And so he said, "Meet me back here in about fifteen minutes. You gonna give me some money for some cigarettes?" And I said, "Oh my, yes." And I had money. So we had a little Datsun B210, little blue car. We went in the old neighborhood where I grew up in. I knew all the ins and outs and found this little street and kind of did a few things on top of the car. Again, no real penetration at this point going on. Again, I don't know where these guys, I guess they grow them like that in Camden. [Laughter] But again, you know, little quickies and so forth, and so we messed maybe one or two times during that summer and during the fall and all that.

And I had that job from like July to February and then they called me at Winthrop [College], said they had an opening up there and they wanted me. So here was my chance to get back to Rock Hill. I got back to Rock Hill and I started working at Winthrop and forgot all about that what was going on in Camden. And so I had my own little apartment. I had a two-bedroom apartment. Didn't have a roommate. And you know got back in the swing of things and met this guy who I knew was family [i.e., gay]. And then we didn't call it "family." I knew he was "in the life," that's what we used to say then. And we kind of just messed around from time to time. It was penetration on both parts. That's the first person that I had penetrated. That's the first person that I had actually was able to penetrate, for him to penetrate me and go all the way, 'cause his size wasn't a big issue. So that kind of happened and then, lo and behold, I ran into the guy who I just had to have. Remember the one I said I had to have and I gave him money for the concert? And of course those feelings came back up. So again I had money now so I could, you know . . .

Well, I get him over to my apartment. I go pick him up. I go pick him up. I tell him I will give him whatever, fifty dollars or whatever it was, if he would screw me. So I go and I pick him up off campus 'cause he never graduated. Never to this day, he has never graduated. But he was still up there. Remember within a year after I graduated I was back there working. And he probably should have been a senior by then, but like I said, he just never . . . just a loser. But anyway I go pick him up. I'll never forget it. I go pick him up, bring him there, and he's sitting here trying to screw me. No grease, no nothing. [Laughter] You know, just trying to force it! And it was HURTIN'! I'm saying, "No. No." And of course he gets up and says, "Well, Motherfucker just pay me. Just give me my money." And I said, "I'm not going to give you any . . . I'm not going to give you" . . . I think it was fifty dollars I was going to give him. I said, "Here's a twenty. Nothing really happened." I said, "You didn't do . . ." "Oh, you just couldn't take it," and all this kind of stuff. Anyway, I'm tipsy now and I drive him back to campus and he gets out and calls me a mother-fucker and all this stuff.

So this was like on a Friday or Saturday night. And so then on Monday, I'm at work. Now remember I work at Winthrop. He comes by my office. And the way my office was, in front of my office is a receptionist. My boss's office is right there so we all were in a suite together. So he comes in and asks the receptionist if he can come see me. So he comes in there and says, "Mother-fucker you give me the rest of my money." Real calm and all. And I said, "I'm not gonna give you no more money. That's it." "You said this much." And I said, "I did. But nothing really happened." So he kind of like walked out. But he was real cool. He didn't go off. I thought, "Oh God this is a lesson here I need to learn too." Man! So needless to say, we never ever . . . That was as close as I got.

A LAY IS A TERRIBLE THING TO WASTE: HOMOSEX AT HISTORICALLY BLACK COLLEGES AND UNIVERSITIES (HBCUS)

While the first historically black college was founded in 1837 in the North (Cheyney University in Pennsylvania), the majority of HBCUs are located in the South. My home state of North Carolina, for instance, boasts eleven HBCUs, second only to Alabama, which has fourteen. These institutions emerged to educate first the handful of freed blacks in antebellum America and then emancipated blacks following the Civil War who were barred from white institutions because of Jim Crow.

More than a few of the narrators attended HBCUs and speak of their alma maters with great pride and loyalty. More to the point here, all of these HBCU alums speak of homosex on their campuses as not only common, but in some cases encouraged. I have to say, I was a bit surprised when this theme emerged across the narratives. My surprise stems from what I had always experienced as a thinly veiled conservatism on black college campuses, especially with regard to homosexuality or gender nonconformity. Imagine my shock, then, when I learned about basketball stars sleeping with their male roommates, as in the case of "Lamar." Or, drag queen homecoming queens, college professors "keeping" young male students, and nine-man orgies, as told by "D.C."

I do not mean to suggest that all HBCUs are open to homosexuality. In fact, events that have occurred in recent history would suggest that many of these schools still foster an intolerant climate for their gay and lesbian students. The example that immediately comes to mind is an incident at Atlanta's Morehouse College—a college, incidentally, that has the reputation among black gays of being a "sissy" school—in which one student attacked another student with a baseball bat because he was looking at him in the shower. What these narratives do suggest, however, is that regardless of an institution's attitude toward homosexuality, gay men create their own communities within a larger black student body. Sometimes they are incorporated into the fabric of student life at an HBCU, and sometimes they are cordoned off into their own discrete and discreet organizations.

From the narratives presented here, one gets the impression that these institutions were much more tolerant during the 1950s and 1960s than they are today. The stories from Bob, "D.C." and "Lamar," for instance, all speak of an open acceptance of homosexuality and homosex, while the narratives of younger men like Ted and Timothy, both of whom attended college in the 1980s, suggest that things were more clandestine. "R. Dioneaux" (see Chapter 5) was even more explicit about his feelings about historically black colleges: "So my advice to my gay brothers and sisters who are going to school, 'Don't go to a HBUC. Ever.'" The one exception to the conservatism that these narrators speak of in the 1980s is Fred-Rick's narrative (see Chapter 5) that explains how the gay men on his campus had their own sorority modeled on black sororities like Delta Sigma Theta and Alpha Kappa Alpha. And in 2005, some students at North Carolina Central University in Durham created the Gay, Lesbian, and Bisexual Student Alliance, the first such organization at any of the HBCUs in North Carolina.

Whatever the political climate, homosex was and is being had on these campuses—and plenty of it. As sexual agents, black gay men on southern historically black college campuses are thriving—openly and secretly—and signalling that not only is a mind a terrible thing to waste, so is an opportunity to have sex.

....

BOB (B. 1940, BAXLEY, GA.)

Talk about your time at Morris Brown.

Oh, that was interesting. I had roommates who were all straight. There were two football fellows who had an attraction for me. And one of them cut hair. And I never had a relationship with him, but he cut my hair one night and he got very aroused and came in his pants. And then the other one was shoved in a closet. My roommate was gone somewhere and he came to my room and locked the door and shoved me in a closet and I didn't know. I was very naïve. I kind of thought I was being murdered or something. But there was no penetration, none of that. He wanted to feel on me and touch me. And I had never kissed a man then, I mean, never was active, I'd never do that. And he wanted to do that and forced that on me and I got sick, because I didn't really want to do that and I was like "ooh, ooh." It was my first time ever, ever having kissed a man. Like oh. It was not something I wanted to do, and so it was repulsive at the time. And so that was my experience, except when I was taking a class in sociology. And there was a man who had been in the military. I don't remember his name now. We were taught managing family; that was the class. And he wanted to go back to my dormitory because he didn't live on campus, to take a shower or something like that. That was his pretense. I didn't know he was gay. We had had this discussion about premarital sex or something like that. This was back in the '60s and so it was very much ahead of its time to talk about those issues. But the professor was very, very open-minded. He had three Ph.D.'s, and he was also a Ph.D. in music. And he's also a sociologist, and he was also an anthropologist. A brilliant man, Dr. Robinson.

And so the question was raised, I never shall forget it, "Why not have sex before you get married?" And so the girls would say, "That's crazy," in the class. And so this young man said, "Well, you don't buy shoes unless you try them on." That was the conversation. And then, of course, we all started talking about that whole issue of the morality of that and the risk of pregnancy and STDs and what's the religious connotation—my friends were Methodist school and so they had all these morals and stuff like that. And so that was very interesting. And so he wanted to go back to my dormitory to take a shower because he didn't want to go back to where he lived. And so he came back to my room. And he didn't touch me at all. And he just stood there and I was looking out the window and he started beating off. Ahh.

And then, of course, there was another person who's now dead who didn't live on campus. But he would come to the dormitory to see one of his fraternity brothers. And I studied late at night. My habit was always to study late at night and take a shower at two or three in the morning. And I would go to the shower, and he would always be in the shower at two in the morning, waiting for me to come down there, because he knew what my pattern was. And then he invited me from time to time to come to his basement room at this little rooming house. And I would go there sometimes and we would have these encounters.

"D.C." (B. 1951, SHREVEPORT, LA.)

Going back to your time at Southern [University], what was the social climate like at Southern? Did you have lots of friends? Were there other gay people at Southern?

I didn't associate with a lot of gay people per se. In fact, I didn't really associate with gay people at all. I wasn't closeted, but I mean I was an athlete. I ran track and some other things. And my gayness was a private matter. Now don't get me wrong. I had numerous gay experiences. I mean plenty. In fact, there wasn't a sport that we had there that I didn't have an athlete that I was having sex with. [Laughter] Seriously. Serious as a heart attack. And it was all good. It was all good. I was student mascot. I traveled with the football team. There were many that were my bedmates. I mean sometimes it got a little complicated because folks would want to fight over me.

In those instances, when you would travel with the football team, how does one approach . . . you know . . . Is it eye contact?

You're talking about the gay part?

Yes. For instance, how do you know that some football player is attracted to you? I mean, he doesn't come to you and just say it. I mean, how does that happen?

Well, let me tell you like this. There were some that were very aggressive. At the time, they did not have like football dormitories at the football fields. And I recall, in my sophomore year, this person who was the captain. I mean, he just liked to be rough with people and then take over. And he used to wrestle them in there and in the process of wrestling, he'd say, "Put my dick in your mouth," you know. I mean this is not just he and I in the room wrestling. I mean other people are there. And hell, he would do it, you know. He was just that kind of a nut. And I remember in my senior year, I remember there was one that I mean I was just attracted to. I looked up and he looked back at me, and one night he came out of the shower and I went in his room and we just got it on. And it was so freaky I guess you'd say, because it was like, hell, he was like, "What took you so long?" And I mean this was a big lineman guy. I mean he was as sweet as he could be.

And were these guys who were known as straight?

Uhm hmm.

Did they have girlfriends?

Yeah. The whole nine yards. Even in my freshman year I had a roommate football player, and we were lovers. So much so to the point that the dormitory we lived in was very small and narrow, but he decided that we put our beds together. We slept together every night. Yeah. And then there was another football player, a friend of his and mine, that started trying to be jealous of us, and hell he started trying to spend the night with us too.

[Laughter] Did he ever succeed?

Oh yeah. We romped in the sack too, you know. [Sighs] If I thought about the number of athletes I had at Southern, or just on the football team, golly . . . I'd have to be doing some counting. I'd have to really think back, because there were a lot of them.

Now in your opinion, and maybe you've followed these people after they left Southern . . . was that something that just happened then, while they were in school and that didn't happen after they left Southern? Or did some of them eventually . . . ?

Some didn't. Some did continue. In fact, at the Bayou Classic I saw one who was . . . I mean he's as big as it gets. And he went on to become All-Pro, Pro Bowl, and all this kind of stuff. But he's still on the down low if you want to say . . . [Laughter] I mean it's quite a few of them. I don't see a lot of them for whatever reason. But you know it could still be done, in other words. Put it to you like that. But like I say, it wasn't just football. It was track, tennis, golf, swim team. Oh those swimmers. Wow! Lord hammercy. They're something else. [Laughter]

What was the sort of general climate for gay people at Southern, or were there any people who were more outwardly gay?

Ooh Lord, yes. Oh. Oh my. Oh Lord, when I came to Southern as a freshman, I got shocked. I mean, at the football game, they had this queen, this person and her court. Every game. She would almost wait until the band, Southern's band was noticed for whatever. The band makes its entrance on the south end. She comes in the north end. She gets the boys' attention. And after the game, the band would play for her and you should see it, all the guys would be out drooling and wanting to get some of that.

And this was a gay man?

Gay. Just as gay as could be. [Laughter] Oh and if you really want to hear something, the worst thing that I think happened was—which year was it?— it was around my junior or sophomore year. The girls at Southern put an article in the school paper, protesting their lack of . . . let's just put it like this, "getting some dick." Because they said the teachers, the gay teachers were doing it on one end, and in the dormitories at night the gay students was having it. They actually put that in the paper. But, then the gay students formed them an organization called JUGGA, Just Us Gay Girls Association. And they marched on the campus. Oh yeah, there was a lot of stuff. Let me tell you something, it was so gay in my collegiate days until you know, you couldn't believe. You wouldn't believe it.

And this would have been in the '60s?

It was '69 through '73. And it was almost like if a guy basically looked at you and you felt you wanted him, you probably could have had him. It was just that way. But like I said, for my situation, I wasn't open with mine. I guess you know a lot of the time, maybe that's why they didn't mind doing it, you know. They played the little game for a minute, but it's who plays it best. And I remember playing games with a guy that was on the golf team. He said, "You want it, you gotta do this." So I said, "No I can't do that." He said, "Yes you can if you want it." I mean it was like a little courtship. And I knew that eventually I was going to get it. And he knew eventually he was going to give it to me because he wanted it as much as I did.

The thing about it is, that really gets me, and now that I'm older and understand everything, is that . . . I don't want to say that guys are less . . . so-called straight guys "gay," but it's hard not to. But there's a lot of times they want experience. And they try to lead you to believe that you're making them do this. And it was just cute the way I had to do mine 'cause I was an athlete with them; I was a mascot with them. I was in the mix of them all the time, you know. And I guess they felt comfortable with me. But they felt comfortable with some of those other ones too. They had some of the queens in my dormitory my senior year paying them to leave them alone. And then they had some in the dormitory that cooked for them. They'd come down to get their meals and they got whatever else they wanted too. [Laughter] When I think of it, there were a lot of things that happened at Southern. Oh goodness gracious. Oh my goodness. Unh unh. Oh man.

It's quite fascinating.

And a certain fraternity, which I won't say, they were just, shit, they were just full of them. Well, I can't say . . . Now that I think about it, I could say it about several of them. All of them. Shit. I think I had more in this particular one, though, than I did in the others. [Laughter] I mean I was turning them out just like I don't know what. We used to go and rent a little motel room right off the campus there and just have a ball. Just have a ball. [Laughter] And the strange thing about it is, most people would be surprised as to the people who were doing it, and they were totally clueless. And I'm not the kind that talks. I do my thing, I usually just try to keep it to myself, you know. There was a lot of stuff though, man. When I got to Southern, my freshman year, I got hooked up, I was going with one of the faculty members. I was going with one, but I was having sex with about three or four of them. Or five. I don't know. I was. Shit, oh yeah!

Men?

Yeah. My background, I was very poor. I mean I didn't have much shit. This faculty person that I hooked up with, I don't know, they just loved me. And they just took me in and just bought me everything. I mean I would basically every weekend, spend the weekend out at the house. And eventually I took two of my football player friends—hell, we all three were in bed; all four were in bed together. And this lasted throughout my whole college career. I was with this person all this time. Oh Lord, I had all the clothes I wanted. I had all the money I wanted. I had liquor in my room. You name it, I had it. Summertime, they would go up and work at various places around the country. Fly me out there. California. Flew me to Yonkers. Well, they was working in Yonkers and flew me to New York, twice. Two years. I mean I had one that I met through some faculty member, and they secretly got in touch with me and I liked him too, I must say. [Sly laugh] They didn't want me to catch a bus from here to New Orleans, so he got me a ticket to fly from Baton Rouge to New Orleans. And I thought that was really crazy, but I still was impressed with that, you know, that they cared that much about me to fly me. [Laughter] There's so many things that happened, it's hard to try to remember all the stuff. I mean, well, it's not hard to remember, it's just sort of hard to encapsulate it, you know.

Right. Do you think that that experience that you had was an experience that a lot of people were having at HBCUs?

Oh yeah. Because I knew a lot of the guys that, you know, had connections. I mean, I used to see them get picked up and this, that, and the other. Sometimes we had parties and I'd see them there, and all this kind of stuff. A lot of guys, at that time, if they did something, or whatever, you know, shit, they did it. It wasn't like a lot of them, some of them, they try to, "Oh don't believe that, I didn't do nothing." They weren't like that. So yeah it was heavy. I'd have to say it was heavy. In fact, my best friend now, who came to Southern as a teacher, when he came, he came and he called folks from wherever he was from and told them, said, "This is the boringest place. There's nothing going on, especially in the gay world, gay life, whatever." And then he met me. [Laughter] And once he met me, I inundated him. He happened to have a house right there by the university in Southern Heights or whatever you call it there. And guys, students didn't have cars like they have today. So that was a good walking distance from the campus, and they walked. They walked. The house stayed full. Yes, yes. IN FACT, I wasn't gonna say this, but in one day, I had nine athletes. [. . .] And I only had the ninth one because he was supposed to be all of that. And they had all his buddies, this track team out there and they were daring me that I couldn't *handle* him. And so I said,

"Shit, why not? One more won't hurt." [Laughter] And he was supposed to have me hollering and I said, "He ain't shit." I said, "That's supposed to be hurting me right there? After eight already, what can you do?" [Laughter] Oh you know, that's just one of the things. It was a lot of sex going on at Southern, yes indeed.

· · · · · · · ·

"LAMAR" (B. 1945, JACKSONVILLE, FLA.)

Where did you go to college and what was that experience like?

It was so enlightened. I went to undergraduate school at Knoxville College in Knoxville, Tennessee, which was a HBC. And it had a dual degree program with the University of Tennessee, also at Knoxville. Now, keep in mind I told you I had that first sexual experience when I graduated from high school that night. I didn't have another sexual experience, and I went away to college. [. . .] I had fairly good grades, but no one in my immediate family had ever been to college. I chose a college which was the farthest away that would pay for my tuition. And I went to school at a time when black was beautiful. So, I mean, my family definitely wouldn't have had the money, but when I went to this program, you know, I had a scholarship so I didn't have to worry about that. [. . .] I got there a day later than the freshmen were supposed to arrive. So when I got to Knoxville, to college, the freshman dorm was full. So, they put me into the athletic dorm, because the athletic dorm, the athletes were there waiting for football season, and then they were going to make adjustments when the other classmen, the sophomores or juniors came or whatever. But I never left that building. [Laughter]

And my roommate at the time was a junior, and he was the star basketball player. And he played football also, but he was the star basketball player, and I was in his room as a young freshman. Keep in mind I, as you can see, I'm very small and I was just, I was seventeen years old. And I think he was closer to twenty-four, twenty-five because he had been to service, he had been in the service and come back. So he was a little older, much older than I was, and much older, and older than the average student. And so I was in that dormitory. And I think about the second or third night of my freshman experience, you know, I woke up he was getting into bed with me. Now, we had never had any kinds of conversations or anything like that. So nothing was spoken. He just assumed from my presence that I was gay, that I would be accepting, and he was gorgeous. He was just handsome.

Now did he date women?

Yes. He dated women; he was a Kappa. He was one of the biggest guys on the campus. I mean he was a superlative. He had the prettiest girl on campus. Obviously, he was worldly. And his girlfriend, her daddy was a physician of prominence from Nashville.

So this thing about the DL, that's old . . .

Oh that's always been old because now, when I say this I don't want you to laugh or, because I do it differently, I'm not attracted to effeminate men. You know, I have lots of friends, you look at them and you know both of them are gay. Are you following? Now, that's not my attraction. I'm attracted to very physical, what I would call a straight man. But I say that with some hesitation because if they were straight they wouldn't be with me. But, are you following? But that is my attraction. And every man I've loved has been that way.

Were there other people on campus that you knew that were gay?

Oh yeah. When I went away to college now, this was a whole new world. My best friend going through high school, he was gay. Birds of a feather attract one another. And in hindsight, now when we were on our way to college and came back to town, he was having sex all through high school from the time he was in fifth or sixth grade. But now I wasn't. I was a good girl. [Laughter]

But did you know anything about that when it was going on? Or you found out later?

I found out later. Some of the things I knew was happening, but I was not doing any of that. But now, when I went away to college, again birds of a feather, I met so many other kids that were gay and who had been gay most of their lives. And who were certainly not virgin or who just, you know. I had a lot of catching up to do. And I made up for lost time, so to speak. But I got around other folk and they really helped me, and to let me know I was not [the only one], because I was not isolated. These were kids from Birmingham, South Carolina, Louisville, New York, I mean who just, their way of life and all was so different.

Was there a sense of community, like was there some kind of underground network or something?

No. I think when you live on a small black campus every day, people know. You see these folk every day at breakfast, lunch, dinner. You go to classes with them. You just know. And people just kind of knew. And all of us gay kids, we kind of just gravitated to one another. And I can remember it was just so wonderful to me because I had never had that opportunity as a child. And some of the friends had plenty of resources. Keeping in mind I came from a family with limited resources. And we would go out. See, I had never been to a gay bar.

There were gay bars?

Oh there were gay bars. We would go out, there would be house parties. We would have parties in the dormitory rooms. You know, back in those days, most of the kids at the college were poor. I mean this was not More-house or some school. But, you know, we would get a couple quarts of beer and have a party. Just have wonderful times. And the girls had curfews back in those days, you know. The girls had to be in at eleven, and if a guy was out with a girl dating and on the campus kissing and hugging and got aroused and all, she had to go in. And then the guys would come back to the dormi-tories and there we were. [Laughter] And so, I mean, it was just, it was really a utopia when I kind of look back on it.

. . . .

STANLEY (B. 1950, PORT ARTHUR, TEX.)

I was not out at Dillard. However, I knew a lot of gays at Dillard. I was actually very close friends with a guy who was gay at Dillard, who was very out. But he was so sophisticated that people never really bothered him. Now, there were gays there who were not quite as sophisticated. And when I say, "sophisticated" I mean—John [last name] was his name. He had grown up in Gary, Indiana. He knew the Jackson Five. He was very into music, you know. Very into all of that stuff. He was a theater major like I was, and so that's how we were close. And we were good, good friends. And sometimes I wasn't sure that John was gay. He might have been bisexual, but I can't say that for sure. Because there was a woman that he was good friends with and close to. But I don't think they had anything sexually going on.

Anyway, then there were the gays. And they were the loud ones. They were the militant ones. They were the ones who wore the crazy hairdos and, you know, big Afros and they would, you know, just shoot you down in the middle of the school, middle of the campus and call you names. "Oh girl, quit looking at me like that" and that kind of thing, you know. And those were the ones I often wanted to be around, but was scared to be around because they would out me. And not only would they out me, but anybody else who saw me with them would out me. And then they would say, "Oh he's got to be gay. He's messing with them." And so I stayed away from them for that reason. I was scared of them. And I was scared even to go by their rooms, you know. And scared when they called my name. And just, you know, I was so homophobic. But you know when I go back and think about that, you know, I was just really scared. And part of it was because I had friends who were not gay, and I guess I always felt like, if they found out that I was gay, then they wouldn't be my friends. And so I think that was a big part of it. Another part was that I had some small political aspirations at Dillard Uni-versity. I wanted to be in student government and things like that, and I figured if I were gay, probably people would not vote for me, you know, wouldn't want me to serve as NSGA or anything and like that. And I did win for like parliamentarian for SGA like two or three times and, you know, I was in a lot of organizations on campus. I even joined a fraternity, Alpha Phi Omega, which is a service fraternity. I was part of a charter group and so it wasn't established already so it wasn't like we could be scrutinized real carefully by guys who were already there and know who were the macho guys and who were not the macho guys. So it was kind of that thing too. And so I was not out. But, I had my first real gay experiences in college at Dillard University. My last year, my senior year.

I had a roommate named Brewster. He was a huge guy. He was not gay, as I knew, you know. He might have been bisexual, but I wasn't sure. And we were close. We were very close. We were in totally different fields. And he was considered macho by everybody on campus. It was kind of neat to be with this guy. And I didn't have the hots for him or anything like that. But we were just close friends. And we ate a lot. We'd go and buy chicken and donuts and stuff like that. And we were very friendly, and it was a very open room in the dorm. And I can remember we had all kinds of people in and out of our room at night, visiting. And I can remember this one guy visiting one night, and I was really turned on by him. And I realized that he was probably gay. And one day he invited me to his room. And he took out some gay magazines and showed them to me. Guys doing all kinds of things. And we sort of masturbated each other. And he ejaculated and I hadn't. And as was the case with me, I decided, "Well, that's finished. That's over," you know. I didn't ejaculate and maybe I can't. And even at one point, it was in the back of my mind that I might be impotent. I don't know what I thought. I called it that, but it was like in the back of my mind, it was like, "I can't ejaculate. There's something wrong with my body that I can't ejaculate." But when I said I was finished, he said, "No you're not." He said, "You haven't ejaculated yet so you're not through." And I said, "Yes I am" and he said, "No, you're not." And he continued to masturbate me. And eventually I ejaculated. And it was wild. It was crazy. [Laughter] And you know what happened to me after that was that I went back again and again and again to this guy, to do the same thing to me. And it was like a new toy, you know. I couldn't get it up I was hounding him all the time. He would say, you know, "Look, you've got to stop. You've got to cool down." And I just wanted it again and again and again. And never penetration. I had never been penetrated until I met Bill four years ago. Always afraid of that experience.

But that's what happened to me. Now, in the meantime, I had met a guy at church. I used to go to a church in New Orleans, near the campus, near the university. And when I went to that church, there was a preacher who sat in the pulpit every Sunday. He was not the pastor, but he was just an associate minister. And he eyed me one Sunday and I knew he was. I knew he was just gunning for me. And when church was over, I did what I normally did, and that was I was going to walk back from church to campus, to Dillard. Well, he followed me in his car and asked if I wanted a ride, and I said, "Yes." And I got in, and I probably knew what he was after at that point. And he brought me around, sort of around the back of the campus where you could park and kiss. And he played with me through my pants. I played with him through his pants. And you know, it was a real turn-on for me. And then I visited him a couple of times at his house. And I guess we had oral sex. But that's about it. And sort of masturbation and played around.

In general, do you think Dillard was accepting then of homosexuality? Or what was the general atmosphere toward gays at Dillard?

I think Dillard was accepting. I think it was okay. I just didn't know and was afraid, probably of being ostracized. But those guys were not really ostracized. If anything, a lot of people liked them, the gay guys that were really out. And not only that, I found myself being jealous of them because they always had straight guys who went to their rooms. Now, whether or not they had sex with those straight guys, I don't know. But the straight guys liked to go down there and kid with them and play with them. And who knows what else was going on. You know, I kind of think stuff was going on. Even now, I think stuff was going on, but nobody would talk about it, you know. But I used to wonder why so many straight guys were going down there. And then I'd say to myself, "Well, they're having all the fun 'cause they're out." And the guys knew they were out. So the guys knew who they could approach if they wanted to have sex with gay guys. But me, they didn't know so I would never get any takers. I would just be left out in the cold. And that kind of pissed me off. That made me upset quite a bit.

. . . .

TED

Like a few other narrators, Ted loves to talk. I may have asked him ten questions during the entire interview, since, in answering one question, he would get caught up in his stories and end up covering most of the territory of his life I was going to inquire about.

Although he now lives in Atlanta, he was born in Yazoo City, Mississippi, in 1961, the third of five children. According to Ted, his hometown "was named after Yazoo Indians that sort of settled the town, years ago . . . of course, centuries ago. And it's just about thirty-five miles north of Jackson,

Mississippi, which is the capital of Mississippi. It's a town of about 15,000 people." Because the town was small, Ted says that the community helped raise him and his siblings after his parents divorced. The interview took place at Ted's home on November 3, 2004.

My girlfriend from high school, she went to Mississippi State, so we'd still talk on the phone, but I was not involved with any girls on my campus at all. And so now this was a whole new environment. I'm hanging out with all these guys that are like me, you know. And we're going to these little parties of other students that had apartments off campus. We would go to their houses or apartments and interact with each other. It was almost like a playground, basically, because you'd have all these guys that looked like you, about the same age, and they were all experiencing this new lifestyle for some of us.

Now, I was going to say, were they sex parties?

It was not a sex party. It was like a bunch of friends that everyone knew each other and sort of got together and we would just play games like Monopoly and those type things. Like for instance, some of the guys there were dating each other, you know? And then it would always lead to those two guys probably getting together at this place. And then there may be somebody there that was cute, that you sort of was attracted to, that you were sort of like engaged with. But it was never anything like a group thing. It was more so where you sort of splintered off and you were with whoever you thought was attractive or whatever. And that's how I sort of became a little bit experienced with this, was doing that type of thing. [. . .] This group of guys were all guys that were either in the band or—one of the guys was a mascot for [laughter], he was the school mascot. These were like the popular people that you would not think would be doing this. So that all of them were sort of intriguing to me in knowing that, you know, "Oh the tiger. He's gay, you know." [Laughter] "I've had a sexual experience with him." You know, that type of thing. And it was like a fun thing.

And this was at Jackson State?

It was Jackson State in Jackson. And even when I decided to go to Jackson State, I did have some family members and other people asking me, "Well, why you gonna go to Jackson State?" Because Jackson State was known to have a lot of gay people . . .

Really?

Yes. It was known for that. It has been known for that for years. You know, even way before I went. Because I went in 1980, and it had always had this reputation for having a lot of gay people. And I guess because it's in the capital city, the largest city in Mississippi, so this is where you're going to have most of those type of activities and more liberal people, in Jackson.

Even though it was an HBCU?

Oh yes. Yes, if you ask anyone. You know, out of all the HBCUs in Mississippi, and there are three of them—Alcorn and Mississippi Valley are the other two— which school has the gay reputation, they would all say Jackson State. I mean, it was just known for that. And that's one of the questions that my girlfriend asked me before I went off to school. Because I had a scholarship to go to another HBCU and I said, "No, I'm not going there; it's in the country. I don't want to go to the country." And you know, it [Jackson State] had that reputation, to be a fast school, to be a school that's very liberal and a lot of gay people were there. But I wanted to go because I knew other people that had gone there, not because of the gay thing. I knew I wanted to be in the largest city. And then I knew more about that school. I was attracted to the school.

. . . .

TIMOTHY (B. 1965, DURHAM, N.C.)

I lived off campus. There was, of course, a student union [at North Carolina Central University]. And we would go in the student union and I met some other, as we were referred to, Durhamites, people from Durham. We would just hang out. And I befriended people through organizations such as the dance group. I was in the dance group on campus. And we would just sit around chatting, talking, and that's when my first lover used to approach me in the student union. "Hey what's up? How you doing? I'm So-and-So, I live in such and such a hall." You know, introduced himself basically. Said, "Come by and see me sometime." I said, "Okay, sure."

Prior to that though, there was this guy, I don't know how I met Eric. He basically wanted to take me up under his wing. Because he said [. . .] he read me. And I was like, "What do you mean you read me?" Anyway, he was someone on campus that kind of kept to himself, and lots of the group of friends that became my gay friends didn't associate with him because basically he was kind of a loner. I guess he chose to be. We became friends, had some classes together, things of that nature, but we didn't really become close, close. But everything I learned, I basically learned from my partner and his friends and in my relationship with him. But on my campus there was no gay organization. So it was, you know, it was an enjoyable time.

So how did you all socialize? In people's homes, or?

No. Mostly going out. I was underage at the time, but I would borrow a friend's ID to get into clubs. There was this guy named, older man named Jeff Smith, he would have—you know Jeff Smith?

I interviewed him.

Did you really?

Uh huh. He's the eighty-six-year-old I interviewed.

Okay. Gosh, that is wonderful. He would have, like, maybe two or three parties a year. Those were the only house parties I knew about. Just going to the clubs, hanging around the dorm, that's basically it. That was just, the only lifestyle that I knew. In terms of the gay lifestyle.

What was the climate at Central for being gay?

I mean, no one was out then apparently. No. Unt un. Even when I lived on campus one year, lots of the gay men wanted to stay on the top floor, and they used to call that, you know, the gay floor, the gay wing, or something like that. Because the rooms up there were bigger and they were on the very top floor so they had like the little eaves or dormers, whatever. So they were just cuter rooms, so everybody tried to get on that floor. But it was, it was definitely negative. I did not want to come out to anybody, except for just my network of friends. And we would even kind of watch how we behaved in public settings such as the cafeteria or the library, things of that nature. We would try to keep on the DL so to speak.

Going back to Jeff Smith, what were those parties like? And how did you find out about them?

Just word of mouth. You know, I probably was taken there by my partner at the time. But when I got there, it was just enlightening because just seeing so many black men from other parts of the state just interacting. It was kinda cool, it was cool, it was exciting for me.

DOIN' AND TELLIN': HOMOSEX IN THE MILITARY

No one is surprised to hear that homosexuality exists in the military. If that were not the case, the controversial military policy of "Don't Ask, Don't Tell," the compromise legislation passed under the Clinton administration that allows gays and lesbians to serve in the armed forces as along as they are not open about their sexual orientation, would not exist. The stories told by the men in *Sweet Tea*, therefore, confirm what is common knowledge, but they also add nuanced ways of thinking about *how* queer communities thrive in the military. Indeed, from the stories of Jeff Smith and the Countess Vivian (see Chapter 7), who served during World War II,[4] through Harold, who served between World War II and the Korean War, and Bob, who served in Vietnam, to Jaime, who served in the 1980s, these narratives provide us with a fifty-year history of homosexual activity in the armed forces that helps explain the coping strategies of gay men in the military. And, like the men who attended HBCUs, the narrators who are veterans also explain how homosex was not always clandestine or even condemned by those in power—especially since, according to some of these men, those higher-ranking officers were sometimes engaging in homosex themselves.

· · · · · · · ·

BOB (B. 1940, BAXLEY, GA.)

I'd been in the military. And that's when—to tell you the truth, that's when most of my experiences occurred, in the military.

What branch of the military?

I was active Air Force.

This was in the '60s?

In the '60s. But by then, I had been through college. And I had worked for a medical school in New Jersey, so I had experience doing research. And so when I went to the military—during the Vietnam War I was drafted, so then I joined the Air Force to get out of the draft. So then I took what they call a bypass test, and I went straight to the laboratory and I became a medical laboratory technician. It turns out that one of their commanders, who was a young white man, came to the lab for something one day, and I drew his blood because he was anemic, and he asked me—this was my first experience in the military—he asked me, "Well, what should I eat to make my blood better?" I said, "Well, you know, you really should be talking with your physician about that." He said, "Well, I will take you out to dinner, if you like. And then we could have something. And in about three or four weeks, I'll come back for my other lab report and maybe that will be a little bit better." And I said okay. So it was out to dinner, all right. So that was quite a thing that happened there. That was my first experience in the military. That happened early on; within two months of my assignment there, I became involved with this person.

Oh, so it developed into a relationship?

It was not a love relationship; it was a sexual thing.

Did it open the door for you to be exposed to other Air Force men who were gay?

Yes, uh huh, yeah, um hmm.

So where did you hang out?

Well, there was a club that you went to.

Where were you based?

I was in Texas, near San Antonio. And there were clubs. And then certain nights of the week, you went. And, of course, the clubs were raided so you had to have IDs, you had your fake IDs, and you knew how to get your ID to show that you had a civilian ID. [. . .] You're asked for your ID. If you show your military ID, then of course you were busted. So you left your military ID someplace. So that was interesting. And then the lesbians went. And so whenever the MPs came in, the alarm would sound. Word was passed and so the boys would start dancing with the girls. And vice versa.

What would be the signal?

It was—oh, somebody would just know, yeah. And the person at the door would pass the word, you know, but even the plainclothesmen would show up and they would know who they were because they'd been there before or whatever. So people would know, you know, you're not a regular.

And they were coming to raid?

They were coming just to bust, to raid. But the MPs had to be in uniform, they could not come as plainclothesmen, unless you were what they called OSI, Officer's Special Investigation, and they only got involved when a person got really busted, and then it had to go to court-martial or something like that.

Did anyone ever get thrown out?

Oh, yes.

Oh, really?

Um hmm, um hmm, um hmm. I'm in touch with a person who lives in Florida, Miami, now, was thrown out because he was busted. And I almost had a relationship with his commander. [Laughter] He would come to my door. I lived in the barracks and he would come to my barracks two o'clock in the morning. I had a private room. And knock on my window and I would— and he lived off base in a very small apartment and I would get up and go to his apartment with him and we'd carry on and then he'd bring me back to the base the next morning.

. . . .

HAROLD (B. 1936, ST. LOUIS, MO.)

Now, it was a different Army than what we have today, with the "Don't Ask, Don't Tell." It was all undercover. And I think it would have been the same way in a cavalry division or in an armory division. Men get really tight, okay?

In the company that I was in in Seoul, Korea, the 8th U.S. Army Headquarters, there were men from all over the U.S. There was a core of about five of us that were chummy. We did things together. I couldn't stand Army food. And by this time, I couldn't live on Mr. Goodbars. [Chuckle] But they had clubs where you could buy your meals, and I didn't go to the mess hall to eat 'cause I hated that stuff. So, we would meet after work and we'd go to these clubs and we would have steak of whatever the thing was. And again, there were two other New Englanders and another fellow from Chicago. And we knew that we were. But you didn't talk about it.

Okay now, two buddies and myself, we went on a pilgrimage with a group to see ruins in Korea. South Korea. And we stayed away from the Army base and we slept together in these houses, Korean homes that the heat was in the floors. And that didn't work for me. [Laughter] Plus, they didn't have enough blankets and what not. So, I slept next to the person that I was with, which is no different than what you do with a soldier if you're sleeping in a tent and one of you is cold in extreme conditions. That was the extent of sexual involvement on my part because it was this fear that you would be thrown out and dishonorably discharged if anybody caught you in the act of that. Now many of them went to Japan on what they call "R and R." And they would go with their best buddies. And it goes without saying that that was what they were doing. I mean, they took a trip together, okay?

Uhm hmm. So "best buddy" was just a code word for their sexual partner?

Yes. Uhm hmm. "Main squeeze" at the time, or "my stuff" or whatever. Yes. And it was all sorts of little code words and actions.

Do you remember any of them?

No, let me think for a second. No. I don't. It was the person that you were the closest to that you did things together, and nobody questioned it, especially when you're in a foreign country that was still under the siege of war. But see they considered the North Koreans could come over that border any time. So we had weapons and then we had a key to the armory, where we just took the ammo right out because we didn't know when we had to go. So, no.

I was chummy with a guy who, in our section, was the Jewish chaplain's assistant. And he was responsible for everything Jewish. And during the holy days of the Jewish religion, they would receive things like wine and gefilte fish. Well, he made the mistake and instead of getting twelve bottles of Jewish wine, he got twelve cases. And he couldn't send it back. And so quietly he was saying that we could have parties. And he would drink too much. And we were always trying to save him because when he drank, he got a little outward, you know, and he started with, "Oh, I love you" and this sort of thing, and everybody knew, "Well he's just drunk." Okay? [Chuckle] [. . .] We picked him up to take him back to the room and we had him and we were carrying him upstairs by the hand, and all of a sudden there was this "bink" [erection] in your shoulder, you know. [Chuckle] And it was that kind of thing.

Then we went to a lot of mountain retreats, and they were places of natural beauty as well as like health spas. And in the Oriental culture, both

Harold at Fort Lee, Virginia, 1959. Courtesy of the narrator.

Harold with two students at Seoul National University, where he taught English and American history, Seoul, Korea, 1961. Courtesy of the narrator.

Korean and Japan, nudity is not a no-no. So we were up in one of these health spas once and we're all bouncing around. And as soon as we come out of the water, there was, "Okay we're supposed to be . . ." [chuckle] that kind of thing. But I can't remember any specific words, but you just knew by the closeness of two people.

. . . .

JAIME (B. 1961, COVINGTON, KY.)

When I first went in the military, I went in right before my twenty-first birthday, and I was really skeptical. I was really naïve in the sense that gay, straight, or whatever, everybody was horny, they was having sex. And I honestly thought that it was like some really big conspiracy that everybody knew, or the powers that be knew I was gay, [that] they were just sending agents to hit on me to try to attack. I thought that was something that the military did because I was getting propositioned for sex so much.

In the military?

God, yes.

What branch were you in?

Air Force. I mean from day one. Basic training. You know, I'm thinking, oh my God, somebody knows. Because it was like everywhere I turned people were hitting on me. And see growing up in Covington what I didn't get into, I was always hit on and followed around, like if I would be walking around by myself, older men in the community, you know, ride up on me and say little things. Or different people's parents, fathers that I knew trying to hit on me, you know what I mean. It was all so weird for me, so I just thought that people in general were just freaks. Honestly, this is what I felt. I knew that I was attracted to men, but I think because of the fact that the way I saw other people reacting to it, it was like, my God, if this is such a bad thing, why is everybody doing it? I just could not understand that. When I first got into the military, I thought okay, I'm going to take a breather back from this because in the military I won't have to be worried about sexuality and all that because I'm going to be training, learning my job and this, that, and the other. It's like okay, here we go again. [. . .] And I will never forget because I had a training instructor, a Mexican by the name of Ray [last name]. I will never forget this man because he was fine as shit. He was so damn fine. And, I mean, I kind of understand people's fascination with men in uniform because he was one of those guys, about 6′3″, slender build, nice, you know, everything was in place. I always had drill instructors [whose] belt buckles were always lined up right, their shoes were always shined until you see your face, everything. Name tags were right and everything was always perfect.

Hair slicked back, dark, black hair, just as fine as shit. So I'm down in this, I had to pull duty on my baby flight, and they're in class all day.

So I go down here and I'm standing there and I'm reading my book, it's called Uniform Code of Military Justice, reading all the laws and the rules of the military and how to wear your uniform so when you're not, when you're on duty you're supposed to be studying this book at all times. Well, Sergeant [last name] would be in the office because he would march his flight to whatever class they had to be in, then he would come back and take care of any administrative paperwork he was doing. So it's just me and him in this big old dorm by ourselves. So I'm standing guard. So he calls me, he's like, "Airman [last name]" and I'm like okay. So I go in there. He asked me if I knew how to type. I'm like, okay, this is a weird question, why would somebody want to ask me if I knew how to type? So, I said, "Sir, yes sir, I do know how to type," which I was lying. I was about thirty, thirty-five words a minute at that point. But I figured if he don't know how to type at all he ain't going to know that I don't know how to type, so I, "Yes sir, I know how to type." So he told me that he needed me to type up these index cards. You know, there's fifty-two men in the flight, and I get to type up these index cards with, I guess, all this little information on each individual on each of the cards, file it away, blah, blah, blah, blah. So he told me if you type up these cards for me then you can kind of relax, you don't have to read your book. However, if the master sergeant comes to the door you have to jump up and get back to your position or whatever. Okay, fine. So I'm sitting there pecking on this little typewriter, the next thing I know I look over and Sergeant Luna's got his shirt off, he's down to a t-shirt and his little fatigues. I'm thinking okay, it's getting a little hot in here. I mean he would literally undress down to his, he had on boxers, the shorts because he said it was so hot in there. And for like a whole week I would come down, I'd be standing guard and then he would call me in, ask me to do some more typing, and I would do some typing and then he would get hot and start taking his clothes off. I mean I never acted on it, but I'm thinking they even got agents trying to spot, they're trying to get me coming in the door.

[. . .] I get to Biloxi, Mississippi. All right, to go back two weeks, there was a guy, I'll never forget, his name was Johnny [last name] from Los Angeles, California. [. . .] So I was pulling guard in his dorm. But I always noticed he was always staring at me. [. . .] Well, we found out we were going to the same place, Biloxi, Mississippi. And we found out we were going to the same job. Well, he told me, he said, "I'm going to be coming to Mississippi. I'll be looking forward to seeing you when I get there." And I'm talking street-rough hard, streets of Los Angeles–type guy, and you know I'm not used to this because I just wasn't. So sure enough, two weeks later he gets there and he told me he wanted me to try to get in a room with me, but we couldn't change room assignment. [. . .] So like in formation one day one of my friends that I did know to be gay, me and him were talking about going to the Ebony Fashion Fair [hardy laughter], in formation, because it was coming to Mississippi, right. If that wasn't a clue. So he spoke up and said, "You know, you all mind if I go with you?" So me and Mark kind of looked at each other, and I'm like, "Okay." So he wound up going with us, which even that was kind of weird.

[. . .] But it was this one guy from Birmingham, Alabama, who, you know, God forbid. I always made it a policy in the military to never hit on anybody myself, but God this man was looking so good, he was looking so good. And I never would let myself act on it. But here I am. We have what they call the day room, which is a big open room with a TV and a whole bunch of couches and sitting in there, it was a pod or whatever—sort of like a dorm situation in college, but it was a military base. About two o'clock in the morning and I'm just out there by myself up under cover on the couch watching TV. I'm the only one in the TV room. So Wade, which was what the common name of [. . .] uh [first name] Wade, we used to call him. Everybody used their last name. He comes into the room.

This is the guy from L.A.?

No, this is the guy from Birmingham. But I was leading up to why I never really connected with the guy from L.A. in Mississippi because I was already kind of looking at this guy from Birmingham. I figured if anything was going to happen, I would rather it happen between him first. And we were, you know, we was just kind of doing that little dance. Well, he came and got up under the blanket, under the cover with me. I'm thinking okay we up in the dorm and anybody could walk in at any time and he's like wanting to cuddle up under me. So I'm like, you know, sitting there, and he said, "You don't mind, it's a little cool in here. I just wanted to get up under the covers you know." Okay. So this is how we started off.

To make a long story short, my birthday was eventually when we did the deed because he had gotten in trouble at school and he had a whole bunch of homework to do and that night he told me, he said, "I'm going to take you out and celebrate your birthday." This was a Thursday night, and we had curfew about eleven o'clock. So he said after they come by and do a bed check, we're going to sneak out. Now me, I'm straight Joe Blow military, always following the rules and everything. But I'm thinking, okay if I'm going to get some of this man I'm a go ahead and get dressed tonight.

So needless to say, what we did was we went down the fire door, we put a rock in the door to hold the door open, climbed over the fence—I mean had we got caught we would have been in big trouble. We jumped across train tracks, went down, we went to this apartment complex that wasn't far from our base, and we sat in the laundry room and I helped him with all his homework. He had to write so many Morse characters so many times because he kept messing up or something like that. He had like a thousand of them to do, so I did half and he did half. So he said, "Okay, we're going to go celebrate your birthday now." It was about one, two o'clock in the morning. We get us a case of beer and we go to the beach and we start drinking the beer. So once we drink up the beer and we're all drunk, we're going to go to the peepshows, because at any military base you're going to find peepshows and titty bars and all that kind of stuff. So we go to this one movie house in particular, there's this black queen in there and she's trying to hit on us, and I'm thinking to myself okay, this is my birthday, and this queen thinks she's going to get this man as hard as I've worked on him, she's got another thought coming. So Wade tells me, he says, "This guy wants to know if we want to come out to his house and hang out." See, we couldn't go back to the base until that morning at six o'clock, we couldn't go back on the base and we were getting kind of tired and we kind of needed some place to bum around. He said, "Well, this guy wants to know if we want to come back and have some drinks at his house," and I'm thinking oh my God, this queen is a hot mess, but we ain't got enough to do, we'll go back to his house, have a few drinks, this is my birthday, don't worry about it.

Well, I had gotten up to go use the restroom and I come back and the guy had gone to move his car from the driveway into the garage and Wade told me, he said, "Well, this guy said he wants to do something, but what do you think?" And I'm thinking, first of all she's not going to get the goods before I do. [Laughter] At this point it's a competition. So I said, "Well, Wade what do you think?" He's like, "Well, I don't know." He said, "Would you do her?" And I said, "Well, I mean, if you want to, you do what you gotta do." So I'm thinking okay, that's why I didn't say yeah because I'm going to miss my opportunity, so what I did, I just worked the script to my advantage. I said, "Let me get the ball rolling, I know what to do." So when he came back in I told the guy, I said, "Look." I pulled him aside and I said, "That right there, that's my birthday present, so if you're going to do anything," I said, "I'll give you some dick, but as far as him doing anything, that's going to be me by myself." So I went in and did the business with him, took me a shower and then I put him out of his own bedroom. I said, "Can I use your room for a minute? I've been waiting for about three months for this." [Laughter] So needless to say, that was my first experience on my birthday in some other guy's house.

But wait a minute, but before that time, you and Wade had never had any conversation about what was up?

No, but he had just threw me hints. And I figured it was my birthday, if it was going to be wrong, then we were both drunk, you know, in the military that was a common thing, you could always blame the alcohol. But from that point on we started messing around. So that's why I never hooked up with Johnny, the guy from L.A. And then I was in Mississippi from October of '82 to, I think it was April of '83.

Were there any codes or signals that people used to indicate that they were gay? Or, you know, clothing, wearing it a certain way. I mean anything that clued people?

Well, now there was a guy on my base, and I'll never forget his name was Keith. You know how the Europeans like to carry the man purses? Keith carried a clutch. And I mean, in full uniform there's a man bag up under his arm. [Gets up and walks like Keith holding the bag under his arm.] He walked across the base so everybody, you know, everybody pretty much knew, you know, in that regard. [Laughter]

And that's before "Don't Ask, Don't Tell"?

That's before "Don't Ask, Don't Tell." Honestly, everybody knew he was. It was just no question. But, he did his job, nobody said anything. And I mean I had even had friends that had gotten found out or told on by a partner. Because that's all it takes in the military, somebody call your commander and say that person's gay. And they'll start investigating you. But other than that, it was basically—I would say as far as people finding out somebody was gay, but knowing somebody was going to mess around, it was pretty much "Ooh, I'm going to go out and get drunk tonight, ain't no telling what I might do." So a lot of the guys used that thing. However, my best friend, and my best friend to this day, who lives in Washington, D.C., now, he's actually retired from the military about two years ago, we always laugh about the fact that when I first got to Oklahoma, all my friends were straight. I didn't go out. I thought okay I'm trapped in this little cornfield somewhere, I know there's got to be a gay bar somewhere, because that was your release. Probably within an hour, you try to find somewhere within an hour where on the weekend you can go and get your hotel room, kick up, do your thing, come back to the base and not have to be worried with it.

Well, my friend Larry, I always tell him, "I didn't know about you, and I didn't know about Tony," he was my friend that passed away, I said, "but Sheila gave you up," because I knew she was a card-carrying dyke. And not only that, on Friday I would go to the NCO [noncommissioned officers'] club and I'd be sitting there by myself having drinks, you know, with nowhere to go, nothing to do. Well, it got to the point where I was noticing that like every Friday evening about a certain time [. . .] I was noticing them kids coming in like clockwork. And I said only queens could be in that big of a hurry to be going somewhere. Because they just had the look of determination on their face, like I just knew they were going out. So that's how I met my best friend. One day I sat right there by that window and said, "Damn it, if there's some barge going on, then I'm going out tonight." I [started] with Eric, pulled him to the side and said, "Look, I don't mean to be rude, I don't mean to be forward, but if I'm wrong let me know," I said, "But, I've been noticing ya'll coming in here, I know ya'll going out somewhere and I just want ya'll to know that wherever ya'll are going tonight, I'm going with you and I don't care where it is." And they just kind of looked at me like, "okay." And from that point on we were best of friends. So we started going out, that's where they were going, right out to the gay bar. And it was weird because the one bar we went to, it was a mixture of black, white, big lesbians off the farm in cowboy boots. It was called Rumors and it was an hour away from our base and you go there, some night you go there on Saturdays, you're going to kick your heels up and they might have straw in the middle of the floor having square dance there. You sit right in there, drink your beer because you were out, you were open, you know. Plus all of them fine Army boys, the ones that like sneak out there, so you did have, get a little release from that. It pretty much, I think it's kind of the same in the general population. You know as far as, what I was saying earlier about your own neighborhood. Everybody can kind of, pretty much comes at it the same way, just as far as people that you look at and say I'm sure they're gay as opposed to somebody that you think will mess around because to me it's kind of two different things, especially in the military. I mean there's a lot of guys that messed around, but that didn't necessarily mean they were gay. They were just horny freaky dogs who would mess around with anybody.

"IS HE SICK?": HIV/AIDS

In 2004, many stories about the increased HIV infection rate among African American males at HBCUs in the South appeared in the media. These stories coincided with the media frenzy around the "Down Low" (DL) phenomenon, whereby black men who have sex with other men, but who don't identify as gay, were being seen as the culprit for the spread of HIV among black women. Given that blacks comprise a majority of new cases of HIV infections among women, men on the DL were seen as a natural source of contagion.

J. L. King, a self-professed "expert" on the phenomenon and "recovering" DL brother, wrote a book entitled *On the Down Low: A Journey into the Lives of "Straight" Black Men who Sleep with Men*, which purported to expose the DL "lifestyle" and provide women with a "guide" for how to detect whether their man is on the DL. King's book was a financial success, due in part to his appearance on the *Oprah Winfrey Show*. King's appearance on that show is relevant to the discussion of black men of the South and HIV only inasmuch as one of the other guests on that episode was a young, black gay man by the name of Jonathan Perry, who is HIV-positive and attends Johnson C. Smith University, an HBCU located in Charlotte, North Carolina. Perry's appearance on *Oprah*, alongside J. L. King, was a welcome antidote to what I believed to be a blame game for the spread of HIV/AIDS and the equation of homosexuality with HIV. Indeed, Perry and Phil Wilson, the director of the Black AIDS Institute, provided the voices of clarity on the show because they focused on the need for men and women to take responsibility for their sexuality and on the need for more honest discussions about sexuality in black communities.

Perry also represents the face of HIV/AIDS in the South. It is not just a disease affecting and infecting older men, but also one having an impact on a younger generation. In 2004, for example, researchers in North Carolina released the results of a study conducted on infection rates among college students between 2000 and 2003. Of newly infected male college students, 73 out of 84 were black, "representing 20 percent of the state's new HIV infections among 18- to 30-year-olds."[5] But this trend is indicative of a larger picture of infection rates among black southerners. As one newspaper story summarized the situation: "While AIDS has declined or leveled off elsewhere in the U.S., cases are rising in the South, according to a report last year by the Southern AIDS Coalition, which is made of health officials in 14 states. Forty percent of the people estimated to be living with AIDS reside in the South, and an estimated 46 percent of new cases occur in the region, according to figures from several sources, including the CDC."[6] Again, part of the reason for the rise in HIV infection rates among southern blacks could be the general complicity of silence around black sexuality. Rather than being open and frank about safe sex and HIV/AIDS prevention, black southerners tend to remain silent about issues of (homo)sexuality or to speak about them in stereotypical euphemisms accorded other health issues (like "sugar" for diabetes or "high blood" for hypertension), using "sick" to signal someone who has AIDS. "R. Dioneaux" (see Chapter 5) is particularly articulate about this latter point.

I did not ask any of the men I interviewed whether they were infected with HIV. Instead, I questioned them about how the disease has impacted their lives and if they thought it was more of a problem in the South. It was in the context of that questioning that a few narrators revealed that they were HIV-positive. None of the narrators, however, suggested that HIV had not had an impact on their lives. Of course, the older men had lost friends, family members, and lovers. Others have been living with the disease for over twenty years. Younger narrators discuss the significance of living in the age of HIV such that they have never experienced sex without a condom, while others admit to some "slip ups." There are also narrators who consider themselves activists in the fight against HIV/AIDS, like Duncan Teague.

HIV/AIDS continues to shape the way homosex is practiced in the South, especially among black gay men. That is the case whether they embody the DL brother or the flamboyant drag queen—and every identity performance in between. Ultimately, these stories of sex, protection, and contagion provide an intricate glimpse into the complexities of southern sexuality across gender, class, and sexual orientation.

· · · · · · · ·

"WB"

"WB" was born in Henrico County, Virginia, in 1948. He resides in a small town in southwest Virginia. The interview took place in Charlottesville on August 12, 2005.

Well, I was blessed in the sense of I knew about it early on, before it was even called AIDS. A buddy of mine from college, this is very interesting, he was a gay man; he was white. But he went out to New York to live because he thought he could live his life as a gay man more freely. And we were best friends, very good friends. And I would sometimes come up to New York to visit him and he lived in Soho and I would go and visit him and things like that, and so he often talked to me about what was going on in the gay community and stuff like that. And it was in the late '70s that I got a call from him in which he said, "You know, there's something—there's this disease going on up here." He says, "There's something going on in the gay community." He says, "People are getting this sickness and they're calling it GRID, gay-related"; that was the first name that they were using. And they said, "The doctors think maybe it's from promiscuity, that people are having sex with too many people so they're saying to people that they need to limit the number of their sexual contacts. And they think it might have something to do with poppers." There were these early theories. And that was the early part of when the epidemic was sort of beginning to surface, and people were dying. And then it began to come in the papers. And I kept abreast of that and read about it. And I think this was one of the reasons why I was able to sort of be involved in the AIDS support group here.

But I say I was blessed in the sense that it—you asked how it affected my life. It affected my life in this sense, that it made me more careful and it made me shun at a time when people were talking sexual liberation and things like that. It was a time when I said I don't know how sexually liberated or how promiscuous I should be and maybe I need to be real careful. If I'm going to be sexual with somebody, I have to be safe, especially as soon as things started saying, you have to be really careful about the exchange of bodily fluids, things like that. And limit your number of partners and things like that. So that was that personal effect on me. It was also an effect on me socially because I was not in the mainstream of gay culture, because I've never been in the mainstream of gay culture in the sense of, oh, you know, some gay people, all of their friends are gay, they spend all of their spare time with other gay men. They do everything with other gay people. That was never the case in my life, as you can tell. It's never been exclusively with other black people. It's never been exclusively with church people. It's never been—that's just the way I work, you know. And so it's effect on me was not the same effect as in the early stages of the disease, when so many people lost so many of their best friends.

Now, I did lose some friends to it. Again, you know, this thing about one of the early friends that I lost was a married man who never came out to me, but I knew and he knew, you know; we remained friends after his divorce and things like that. And I even met one of his partners and he was raising his kids because his wife had just sort of left him. But when he was dying, I knew what he was dying—I knew that it was. But I had other gay friends who lost so many of their close friends in the epidemic, especially people in New York and things like that. The guy who was director of this center, the guy who was director of this operation, he was very much involved in the HIV/AIDS thing. He's no longer here. But, you know, we worked together here on grounds. I went to NIH, National Institute of Health, did training for people in working with college students and things like that. And I participated in those trainings and things like that. That was fairly later, much later, after the epidemic. But the way in which it affected my life was, I was looking at it as one would observe a train wreck and trying to stay out of the wreck myself personally. And also though, trying to warn people that I loved, especially female relatives. I told them, it's black women who are really in danger. And I remember saying that to my sister very early, my mother and my sister, very early. I said, "There's something going around." I said, "Sex can kill you."

[Laughter] And I told them that. I was spared, in some ways, by the fact that I didn't lose a lot of people in the epidemic. It was partly an artifact of who my friends were. [. . .] It's a sad thing to talk about. The AIDS epidemic is a real tragedy. [. . .] The thing that was more tragic was when black people said, "Oh, that's a white thing, for gay white men," you know. And it kept them from really educating themselves and they remained ignorant about it. And this is another thing that's caused—ignorance, I think, is really—it's been a danger to black people, to black men and black women, because of this ignorance about it and these misconceptions about what AIDS was and who could get it and things like that, instead of understanding that it was the spread of a virus, and how you get the virus, and what you have to do to keep from getting the virus, you know. And that ignorance continues to wreak havoc on the black community. And now with so many men who are engaged with the low-down culture that they talk about, who then spread the virus to their—the women they love is very sad. So it affects my life in terms of just the sadness of ignorance. I think that's the thing that's affected me most, ignorance. Ignorance about what homosexuality is and who is homosexual and why people are homosexual. And then ignorance about other things, too, you know, this unscientific way of looking at things, you know, and sort of seeing it as some kind of punishment by God instead of understanding sort of a more natural explanation of just what's going on with people.

. . . .

DAN (B. 1943, DURHAM, N.C.)

I've lost a lot of friends. I mean it was unbelievable that this was going on. I mean, one night when we first became aware that there was something happening in the gay community, it was like the late '70s or so. And to this day I have no proof, it's just my gut feeling, I still think it was something that was man-made that got out of control. Because when originally people started getting sick, most of the people that I knew were heavy users of amyl nitrate poppers. And they were getting sick, and so I always thought that it was something that was being tested that got out of hand. And I thought that was the way it was introduced into the gay community. And then of course, it started spreading. 'Cause I mean, God, men have been fucking men for three thousand years.

And you were living in San Francisco?

Yeah. It was. And you know, there was this gay community about an hour drive outside of San Francisco, the Russian River where gays started going to buy second homes and stuff life that. And I mean, within three years that place, it was like a ghost town.

Do you think that HIV/AIDS is more of a problem in the South than it is in other places right now?

You know, it seems, it's hard to tell by just what you read. I know it's still a major problem on the West Coast. I know it's a major problem in the black community in the South. I know it's becoming a major problem among heterosexual women. So I think it's not even a lack of education anymore, it's a lack, I think what it is is young people especially, are thinking, it's not going to happen to me.

. . . .

"D.C." (B. 1951, SHREVEPORT, LA.)

What has been the impact of HIV and AIDS on your life?

Oh Lord. Humungous! It has taken the ultimate pleasure out of sex for me. And what I mean by that is that there's nothing better than skin-to-skin sex. It's just nothing like it. And to go back a little, in my little earlier time, before that animal [HIV] was born, when I was going to clubs, the clubs closed at two o'clock. I'd tell them, "Just because the club closed doesn't mean the party has to stop." Everybody used to go to my house. And we'd go to my house. We'd have drinks. And after we'd have a round or two of drinks, I'd then say, "Okay it's time to take your clothes off and let's have an orgy." And I'd say, "If anybody here don't want to do it, get out now because the light stays off and we're going to have a ball." And I miss that. I went to the bathhouse a few times, and I know they still have them but because of that animal, I haven't been. Oh gosh, I couldn't tell you the last time, it's been fifteen years or better. When I first went there and I experienced that experience, I enjoyed that and that was another situation that was skin-to-skin. Basically, when I came up as a kid, the only sexual problems that I ever remember encountering and hearing about was gonorrhea and syphilis. And they pretty much took care of that. I mean, if you get gonorrhea, they go to the health unit and they shoot you in the ass, both sides, and you have seventy-two hours and you're back in business. And that's another thing that really spooks me as hell. How and where did all these damned diseases and knots and chlamydia and all these . . . Where did all these things come from? I mean people didn't just start having anal sex and sucking on things and all that shit. They've been doing that since mankind. And all of a sudden in the '80s or whatever, here comes this animal, you know. It's wiping people out. And that's why I believe that AIDS is a man-made, created disease. And there were some things that used to advertise. I remember them on the *Question of the Day*,[7] talking about the King Alfred Plan.[8] [. . .] And I believe a lot of those things about that. But I get so angry, I don't even like to think about it.

Because I feel like whoever that jackass that did this, oh my goodness, whoever did that [. . .] they messed up a lot of people's lives. And if it was meant to genocide a certain race or whatever, I think that the person who tried to do it is really sick as hell. And I wish that they could soon find some kind of cure for that because the way I see it, the way that people are having sex now, especially in this town, they are not even paying attention to safe sex. They just go about their business and do it. It's like, "Well, if I get burned, I'm burned." And I guess that's why we're like the second in the nation right now, in the city of Baton Rouge.

Really?

Yes, we are the second-fastest-growing city in the nation with cases of AIDS, HIV/AIDS.

Did you lose a lot of friends to AIDS? That you know of?

[. . .] The answer to the question is yes. [. . .] We lost a lot of people in our club to AIDS. But the thing about it is, it's more young people who've gone than otherwise. And to me that the young people just don't think, they don't care, they just go and they do, you know. But the majority of those young people that I'm talking about were people that were from here who went to Atlanta and got the bug and came home to die. Yeah. [. . .] If I hear somebody say they're coming back from Atlanta, moving back home, I start setting my watch. I set the watch timetable, to see how long they're going to be around, because that's been the pattern. And I guess you could kind of say it's like they are not leaving "Hotlanta," you know. They're not coming to slow little Baton Rouge just because they love Mama Dearest or Daddy Dearest or whatever, or home cooking or something like that. That's not the reason. They're coming home because they're sick and they're going to need somebody to take care of them.

· · · · · · · ·

"DLB"

"DLB" was born in Washington, D.C., in 1960, the eldest of three children. The interview took place in his home on May 7, 2005.

It's been probably a very big impact on my life because whole groups of friends of mine have died, way too numerous to count. Friends of mine are just gone, and it all happened in very short periods of time. It just flashed over my mind twenty, thirty people that were close to me, they're just gone and, so it's been a real big impact. Not as much of an impact probably now because people are not dying in droves like they were. People are living longer. So it's a big impact.

When you first learned about HIV and AIDS, how did that influence your sexual activity?

Well, I don't know; I should also say that I'm HIV-positive. And when I first found out, I was in denial about it, so I didn't change anything. I just changed now.

Did you feel that you didn't have enough information at the time?

Everybody was dying. There wasn't any information to have had at the time. They were just dying, just going away, there was nothing to do. No information to have. It was coming slowly.

How old were you when HIV/AIDS started?

I guess that had to be like in the mid '80s. Right? Early '80s. Then so I was twenty. Early twenties. And I can remember definitely twenty-five years old to maybe thirty just slews of people just going, you know, with obvious pain.

Do you think HIV and AIDS is more of an issue in the South than in other regions?

I know when I lived further south that information wasn't getting there. And so I would have to say that it's probably a lot bigger in the South than it's believed. Places like New York, California, they've been getting information a while, and then probably on a larger scale. So the information doesn't seem to be trickling down to people in the South, so it's probably bigger than people know in the South.

Since learning that you are positive, have you been a part of any educational programs to teach people about HIV?

No. No, I can't say that I've been, no. I just try to keep myself educated and do the things that I need to do. It's been a very personal thing. I haven't gone out and been active. Well, actually I'm on a board of an organization here that have a group that does research and outreach and what not. So I do get to go over there and in my community [I'm an] actual board member, and I do go in and give my opinion about things they can be doing, especially in the mental health department.

How would you describe your feelings about the life choices that you've made in light of being gay?

Once again, I haven't had a bad life.

No regrets?

No regrets. I went through a drug addiction thing for a few years, and that had a lot to do with me finding out my HIV status. I didn't care anymore. It was a death sentence to me at that time, and I thought that well, I know I'm not going to be here much longer, everybody else around me is dying. My turn is coming; I'm no better than anybody else. You know, that's where my mindset was, I believe. Because there was no reason for me to even do drugs, I never did before, growing up. I got hung up in drugs at age thirty. Never got hung up. It just wasn't something that was done. I wasn't raised like that and didn't have a lot of friends who were doing drugs. That's just how I handled that when I found out about my status. And I did that for about five or six years. And then finally it was like okay, that's enough of that.

What clicked?

It was God's intervention. One hundred percent God's intervention. One hundred percent. Nothing else, nothing else that got me to stop getting high and to stop doing drugs. It's been about ten years now. It was just nothing else, it was just one day I was just taking something that whisked me off to de-tox, okay, and from that day on I have not felt the need to get high off anything. I was never a cigarette smoker. I was never a drinker. I went straight to getting high. Straight to the big stuff. No in-between, no lead-up. Like I said, I think maybe about four or five years I was getting high and then it's just God's intervention. I can't say it was anything that I did except be willing.

· · · · · · · ·

DUNCAN TEAGUE (B. 1960S, KANSAS CITY, MO.)

How much tape you got left? [Chuckle] I don't want to be disrespectful to you in your educational and everything in this project, but that question is almost unfair, because it's a whole other area. There's all these faces that I don't have time to name. I'll just name one, Crawford, who moved to Atlanta about the same time I did and helped me write an article that helped me start my career as an activist. Helped me write an article that shook up the black gay community in such a way that they started attacking me, actually, which was fine. *Now* it's fine. It wasn't then. But you know, it said something about us and what we could do. It shook up things. And then behind the scene, he was involved with Black and White Men Together, and he's a writer, and we were such good friends that we would stare at the phone and go, "Crawford's gonna call" and within two or three minutes, the phone would ring. Or I'd go, "I need Crawford to call me." And the phone would ring. We were connected. And he ain't here. That's the impact of AIDS on my life. 'Cause that would be a twenty-something year friendship now. And multiply that by a hundred. And that's what AIDS has done to my life. So I don't know who I would be because I would be different if Crawford was here.

I moved here to get involved in black theater, not to do AIDS education, not to become a black gay activist. I was going to be a leader in the theater, honey. Y'all gonna pay to see me. And I was going to take this to New York and do my show and go around the world and have dinner with Diana Ross.

That's what I was going to do. And then we had to have this fucking epidemic. Yeah, there are conversations that I would have never had with my parents and never been hurt, mortally wounded, by my peers, had we not had AIDS. And some of what we face and that hurt our own community around this whole business about being out and black and gay and lesbian and what have you. It's about people's fear of losing their loved ones. And they didn't have any language for it, and they didn't have any way of dealing with it, and they didn't want to know because we already lost, you know, Big Mama to heart trouble or breast cancer or something else like that that we weren't talking about, and now we've got this thing and it's killing white fags and you want us to talk about it? No! And so what would the community have been like if we had never had—can you imagine the Broadway shows we'd have had without AIDS? That I would have been star of? [Chuckle] And the fashions and the . . . ? I mean we would be wearing different clothes. If Willie Smith was still alive? Child, please. I know I'd have lots of Willie Wear now. At least I'd be able to afford some now.

Do you think it's become more of a problem here in the South? Infection rates?

Hmmm. I mean the reality is that it is because of the numbers. But a problem is a problem when you accept that it's a problem. So I guess it ain't a problem for most of them, because they ain't accepted that it's a problem. Although it is a problem. How do you like that one? I'd love to see that in print. [Laughter] But anyway, do you know what I mean?

· · · · · · · ·

"D. BERRY" (B. 1960, MEMPHIS, TENN.)

Well, since I have it—HIV, that is—I do what I have to do to stay healthy and take my medicine. I eat right. I don't exercise as much as I need to 'cause I sit on my fat ass and get fat. But other than that, I'm not down about it. I'm not depressed about it. I'm not concerned about it. I usually take my meds. I go to work. I know I need to exercise to help strengthen my body. And you know, I've been undetectable now for, oh, about ten years. It don't faze me. But I'm very careful about sex and other people. The married man that I see, he is . . .

He's positive?

Umm hmm. And the other guy that I was seeing, he is. [. . .] And if it's somebody that I feel I can trust, that keeps hounding me about it, and we sit down and we talk and they say, okay, and then we go on. But just far as being just out and about and having sex with people, it's not as frequent as it used to be. But now, sometimes I do have some one-night encounters, but I'm very careful about it.

How long have you been HIV-positive?

I found out about eleven or twelve years ago.

How did you find out?

I went and had a test.

Were you having symptoms? Or did you get sick or did you routinely get check-ups?

I was always kind of a overweight person. Not overweight, I feel like I'm overweight, but I think it's more weight than I need to be. So I took dance class for a long time and stayed slim; then after I didn't, I picked up some weight and I started dieting. And after I started dieting, I noticed that the weight is coming off real fast and I said, just let me go see what's going on. And that's when I found out I was [HIV-positive].

Did you go through a depression when you first found out?

For a very brief time. Like when I did with rehab. You know, I went through the crack stage. See, it was a two-year period, but not total two years I was doing it. I'd start doing it and then I'd stop. And once I got the education of what drugs was and why I was using, why I wanted to use them, and after I got the education and stayed up on the education of HIV and the research and all this stuff, I wasn't in depression long. And then I know some people that have been long, much longer than I have. And are still living, doing fine.

Which came first, the drug addiction or the HIV?

The drug addiction.

Do you think that awareness about HIV/AIDS is less in the South than it is in other places?

I can only speak about here because I don't go nowhere. I don't go nowhere else. I think it's less; people are not really listening. They don't think it can happen to them. Young folks just don't care. Period. Period. I don't think that it's being discussed enough. I really don't. 'Cause like, for instance, on TV, you very seldom hear about it. You know, every now and then in a magazine, they have an article about HIV medicine. They have some few pages in there, like in *Ebony* they have a few, in *Jet* they have a few. And that's basically it. Look like to me, when you get a STD and you go there, that's when you hear about it. But it's like there's nobody like really just talking about it, telling people nothing. I know they're not. And it's like two Sundays ago, I went walking at Barry Park, and there these hookers be walking, and this attractive boy walked by and I said, "Umm, he was good looking." And I walked around. Then I came back, I didn't see him. And I said, "Let me go behind this abandoned house." And I looked in there and he's screwing this hooker —without a condom. So I went back out. When I got through walking, went back around, however we came across each other's paths, and I asked him what was his name. He said, "You don't need to know my name." I said, "You having sex with that hooker without a condom." I said, "What about the ones she had sex with all night last night and then you do it?" I said, "You need to put some condoms on." And he just kind of looked at me, and I just walked off. But they don't seem to care, 'cause it seem like now—a lotta guys that wanna talk to me or approach me for sex, they're mainly young guys. And some of the ones that I went there with, I just kind of sit back and I'm gonna see. You put a condom there, they be like, look at it like it's a foreign object, but I make them use 'em.

Really?

They don't. They do not. [. . .] I just look at 'em and shake my head. It's just something else.

Do you think it's because they feel that they're invincible, that it can't happen to them or . . . ?

I think, from the ones that have talked to me, they think it's a gay thing, that it can only happen to gay men. It seemed to be discussed like that. To me, they still have it under the realm of HIV is a gay thing, instead of saying that it's an STD.

So even though they're engaging in gay sex . . .

Umm hmm.

That doesn't make any sense.

They don't. Baby, they do not have 'em. They do not tote 'em, you don't see them, they obviously need to do something.

· · · · · · · ·

ED (B. 1952, NEW ORLEANS, LA.)

I [. . .] received my diagnosis of HIV in 1996. So I was almost dead at that time, but I have come back to life. I had a viral level of two-and-a-half million, and a viral level of anything over 400 is considered, you know, anything in the thousands is bad. High viral level and a low T-cell count. The T-cells, you've got to have, the normal person has 800 T-cells. In '96, I had twenty-four. I was walking dead. I had lost fifty pounds. I was a skeleton. I was working at Xavier. The president of the university, Dr. Norman Francis, saw me. And I was tired all the time. I would fall asleep. I would sit at my desk and just fall asleep from general fatigue of the illness. And then he told the head of the library to have me go and see the campus nurse. And she put me in touch with a task force, and then I became case-managed and I was able to get medication and care. I've been on the cocktail since then. But in actuality, I knew that I had this illness for ten years before that. I was anonymously tested, and I tested positive. I lived in denial for ten years, and I was asymptomatic. And I absolutely refused, I said, "AIDS will not get me. I will not accept it." So there's something to be said about the power of the mind and physical ailments.

But there's even more that can be said about the power of the spirit and the power of God in physical ailments. And as the Countess [Countess Vivian, another narrator] once told me, when I really confided in her about my illness, "Well, Sweetie, we all gotta die with something." [Laughter] And I looked at her and I said, "Well, you know what? You are right. We're all going to go with something, whatever it is. Cancer or whatever. AIDS or whatever it is. We're going to die of something. We all die." Even Jesus had to die.

[. . .] Someone once told me I lead a charmed life. And I guess I do. I mean I've been able to live through all of this so far. They've changed my medication like about five different times. I've actually become resistant to certain medicines I can't even take anymore. But the ones I'm on now caused me to bounce back up. Actually, you're looking at somebody who had lost about seventy pounds in the past year and a half and then gained about fifteen of them back over the holidays. [Chuckle] And the new medicine is—I'm happy to report that right now I'm undetectable.

But I'm just grateful for my life. And I don't know why I'm the way I am, but I do know that I'd like to do what is God's will. And if this is my personal cross to bear, then I guess I'll have to bear it. But when I was younger, I couldn't see it this way. And I wouldn't see it this way. To me, it's almost like a miracle that I'm still living. Because so many of my friends have died. People I've known. People who've been my lovers have died, you know. And so I'm just grateful for life and I appreciate my life. And I try to live my life in a way that I have something to give back as well as learn every day. You know like I had thoughts about whether I should do the interview, but then I said, "For the sake of history and the sake of education and knowledge," which I certainly agree with wholeheartedly. That I might be . . . my words are going to be valuable to somebody, you know, somebody else that has a similar situation or who may need some direction in how to look at a certain thing a certain way. And I've gone down certain roads already, that other people have yet to travel. And maybe I could inspire somebody, help somebody. And there's something good about being able to confess and bare your soul and to just put it out there and not feel ashamed about it. Because you have a clear conscience once you've done that. The kids have an expression about, it's not this, but it is similar to "I ain't mad atcha." But it's something like, you said what you had to say and have nothing to hide and all of this, you know. What you see is what you get.

[. . .] I think, to a certain degree, black people don't want to admit a lot of stuff. And I know when AIDS hit really big in the '80s, they were saying that the black churches need to take up the mantle and try to have it be out and educate the populace and stuff. And unfortunately, it was affecting so many people, everybody had somebody that they knew or were related to that had the disease or had died from it or was sick with it. And I have lived in the North and the South, and I must say that I think the South has a different way of looking at it, and I think what it is is that they would rather not admit that it exists. Meaning homosexuality.

· · · · · · · ·

HAROLD (B. 1936, ST. LOUIS, MO.)

Well, first of all, for fifteen, twenty years, it [AIDS] has taken many people that I knew. It did not affect me because it was not difficult for me to say, "Well, here is the cause and I'm not going to be a part of it." And I would have done this whether I had a partner or not. Because it's just like saying, "Well, if you run through the cold water and you get to the other side and it's freezing, you're probably going to catch a cold," or probably not. But I did not indulge in the practices that would put me in that situation, even though many people I know did.

Do you think it's more of a problem in the South than in other places?

No, Patrick, I think it's more of a problem in urban settings versus geographics. I don't know of any statistics or studies. No, I think it's more in the cities. And it could be southern cities, but I think it's more prevalent in urban settings because I think there is more activity. And it doesn't have to be approved by the law; it can be undercover. But there's more activity. And people are less prone to stop and think. Whereas in a small town, they don't have that many contacts. Remember how narcotics, dope, marijuana—it took a while for it to get into the rural areas and the small towns, but it made it. And because you didn't have that many people as you do in the city who are buying it and shooting it up. And I think the same thing happened with AIDS. But the person who introduced my partner and I died of AIDS. His partner died of AIDS. There was a while when African American gay men were producing literature as well as gay literature. It exploded. All of a sudden, AIDS wiped out all of those who . . . Okay? Melvin Dixon, who I knew well, died of AIDS. There was another fellow, Steven Corbett, a beautiful writer who had a real future. AIDS. Marlon Riggs, the fellow in San Francisco who was a moviemaker and had a great mind, produced a few things but some great stuff. Dead of AIDS. And sometimes you know, you've heard the line, "How I got over." I don't realize how I got through all of this that has hap-

pened in my life, and perhaps still to a degree, healthy and here. But I'm
thankful that my lust did not take over. And I considered myself the most
lustful person of all. [Chuckle] But that scared me. And I decided then that I
was not going to do that. Not only would I endanger myself, but I'd endanger
somebody else. And I don't have that right to take somebody else's life. And
do you know that all of the people that I knew who were partners who
became victims of AIDS and died, took their partners with them. And it's
really sad. I had two neighbors down the way. A great lawyer, promising
lawyer; and somewhere along the line he and his partner were in lust. And
one dies, and then the other dies. [. . .] That was more traumatic than the
death of my father, who was the first death of someone close to me, that
makes for lasting trauma. But AIDS really is something. Yes.

. . . .

JAIME (B. 1961, COVINGTON, KY.)

Well, to be perfectly honest with you, I got sick; I had HIV, and I got sick in
'97. It's kind of weird because before I got sick and you kind of hear people
say, you know, it changed my life for the better, and I never could understand
what they really meant by that, you know. But now that I do because I think if
I hadn't gotten sick when I did, I probably wouldn't have moved back home
first of all. And I probably wouldn't have had those last few years that I had to
reconnect with my mother and help out with her and then be there for that
whole process of her getting sick and dying and that whole thing, and just
kind of reconnected with my family again.

Have you lost a lot of friends?

Two of my closest friends. I mean there have been a lot of people that I've
known, but as far as my friends, there's been two people that were really
close to me.

*Do you think that HIV and AIDS is more of an issue in the South in terms of
people being educated about how the disease is spread and so on and so
forth? Or do you just think it's, you can't, that it's no different in the South
than it is in other places?*

For me personally, I don't think it's any different. I mean, you know, just
take someone like myself. I did my share of playing around, and I can almost
pinpoint the time when I actually got infected. I'm not for sure, but I'm
pretty sure because that particular person that I was seeing at the time is no
longer around. I mean I was well aware. I knew what the risks were, and the
sad thing about it is the person that I think infected me, I got infected using
contraceptives. You know, you try to be as well informed as you can, but

sometimes things happen beyond your control and it's the way it is. But I think in general we still kind of tend to take the "it'll never happen to me" kind of approach. And that can't be a good thing.

Are you a part of any HIV, AIDS prevention organization or groups or anything?

No, and I'll tell you why. As I said I first got sick in 1997, and all of my family, my partner, everybody that I know and love and cares about me knows what the deal is. But when I first came home, I tried to reach out to an organization, the Northern Kentucky AIDS Volunteers. And it was really weird because I signed on and I had a caseworker from there who was good friends with a woman in Covington that I knew which, as I said, I don't make no excuses for who I am, what I am and, what's wrong with me, because I'm not one of them people that sit around and pine about, woe is me. But on the other hand, it was like I knew that I hadn't shared that information with nobody but this woman at this agency, and then all of a sudden people were just walking up to me commenting about my HIV status. And, in general, it was some of the same people that would just assume you be a fag and not really care and just trying to be nosy. So that kind of scarred me as far as getting involved in that sense. For me it's still just a personal struggle for me. It's no different than my diabetes or high blood pressure and all that. I don't go around screaming that to everybody. You might see it sometimes if my blood sugar gets down and I'm woozy, looking like a drunk out on the street. I knew some guys that would rather say that they were intravenous drug users than say that they got sick the way that they really got sick. To me that's kind of sad because, as I said earlier, I have sisters. I love women, and I hate the fact that a lot of our black women are being infected by men who for whatever reason have not been able to be honest about who they were. Had they been able to in the first place, a lot of them women would not have gotten infected. I won't say that they wouldn't have. At least they would have known up front what they were dealing with. And to me that's kind of a sad statement in our community, where once again you've got the black churches saying they want to help, but if you can't be honest about everything across the board, it makes no sense to sit up there and be hypocritical and lie, saying that you really want to help your community. I think that's all a big lie.

. . . .

"KEVIN" (B. 1981, MEMPHIS, TENN.)

What was been the impact of HIV and AIDS on your life?

None, praise God. But no, I've been tested, so it's like I praise God because the tests come back negative. HIV and AIDS have scared me to the point of where you really want to be careful. And I'm about to say something that I even saw myself saying, but I used to have this fear that one day I was going to go to the doctor and they were going to tell me that I have HIV and then I just wanted to die. But one time I went to the doctor, it wasn't HIV that they told me I had, and it wasn't even AIDS, it was an STD that somebody else gave me and I was like shocked. Because I was like, I'm not nasty. I'm like, a STD? You know, so I'm like, oh my God. And I think what brought up from the fact that I'm like, this guy had it in his mouth. I was like, uh. I was like, what have you been doing? I come to find out he's messing with this chick who had chlamydia. I know that was a lot of information. But [. . .] this is what pisses me off about the down low brother. You're down low and you're not telling anybody and you're thinking these little sexual escapades are okay. But now all of these black women are dying because you're taking your little down low dick back over here to this woman who has no clue, and you're infecting her.

It's like when you cheat, it's like you're trying to make sure that you don't have any evidence, so a lot of times they're not going to use condoms. And then a lot of times they're messing with guys who are more than likely already infected, because sometimes you can be infected and you don't know. Then you have a lot of black people, they aren't getting tested. Then that goes back to a lot of people in church are dying, a lot of women are dying, and then you have a lot of black men, gay men that are infecting. Now these women aren't gay, so where are they getting it from? And because the church is not willing to get the information, because you have a lot of churches that are so crazy they just fail to realize you have plenty of people out here who are having sex, but they don't want to deal with that. They're just thinking, oh no. Not everybody is holy, Sweetie; you cannot tell me everybody in this church is not doing something. When you have six teenagers pregnant, none of them are married, but they're all coming from houses to where they have parents who are married. I mean, come on, they're learning and they're seeing some things somewhere and they're able to explore it and talk about it somewhere else, other than here. So that's when it gets down to where that freedom is broken. I've even heard stories of a lot of people even contracting that disease because they continue to go after they've had other STDs and you get to a point to where your system is so shot anything is possible. I think what pisses me off the most is the fact that a lot of people don't care.

I remember reading this one story about this guy, once he found out he had AIDS he wanted to start spreading it around. Sometimes I've thought about, like some people who do that, they still use condoms but they put holes in condoms and go and have sex. I'm like, what? I mean, I reported this one guy to the health department after I found out he did that. I mean, he didn't do it with me, praise God, but I'm like, oh my God. Once we sent him to the health department, they actually ended up arresting him. I mean because you're walking around here, you're killing people. Attempted murder. And I'm grateful when I go and get tested and it says negative.

I know this one guy. I hope I don't cry. We're standing in the gas station, the line was so long, and this guy was just talking and before I knew it we're in this conversation and really laughing, he knows a cousin of mine. From there we just exchanged numbers and talked. Basically, we talked on the phone, and one day he came up to my job carrying flowers and I was like getting embarrassed. I was like shocked and happy, but embarrassed all at the same time, like oh my God a man is bringing me like three dozen white roses. I'm like, what? And this was not Valentine's Day, this was just out of the blue. And I remember we talked after that because he then wanted to have a relationship with me, and I said, "Well, I have to be honest with you, I don't want a relationship with somebody who has AIDS." I said, "Granted, your life is not over, but I'm at a point now. I'm trying to live and I don't want that to be cut off and I don't want to always have that fear." And at that point that was one of my biggest fears. And I told him that, and I said, "Well, just because we're not in a relationship does not mean we don't have a relationship, we just don't have a sexual relationship. We have a good friendship." After that, we talked a couple of times after that, but I knew he was not fine with that. He tried to keep up his guard, but after that he ended up in the hospital like a few months later. And then he passed. The way he got it is he was raped by a black man going to the club. And see I already didn't go to clubs and things like that, so it was like all this did was to help me to build up such blocks and boundaries even within the gay community. It's like, okay, some things I do not want to be associated with. You just don't know what you're going to run into, so you just have to be careful. But not always be on your guard to be so paranoid. I know when it comes down to AIDS and HIV or any other STD, it's like I try to make sure I'm like totally careful. And if that means going without sex, fine.

But the guy I even got an STD from, my first and only and preferably the last, was a guy that I refused to have sex with for three years. I knew he liked me. I did. But it was like, something was always like in the pit of my stomach, like don't mess with him. Like don't mess with him. And it was like the one time he catches me off guard, and it was just for sex and it was horrible. I felt so violated I didn't know what to do. And now I really feel like I was dying because even though it was just chlamydia, I felt like I was really dying. I felt so hurt. I felt so violated. I'm like I've been trying to stay on point, and when I finally let my guard down, this is what happens. So that's motivation on not to be a 'ho. Great motivation on not to be a 'ho. I'm like if that's what it's going to be, that's what STDs and HIV and AIDS, if that's what that motivation does, keeps me from, or keeps me wanting to be in something monogamous versus being so promiscuous, then fine. I can deal with that. But it's like it annoys me that you have a lot of people that don't give a damn, and they just go out here and they just, you know, spread it around like it's just Christmas cheer or something.

· · · · · · · ·

KENT (B. 1967, BEREA, N.C.)

As I mentioned earlier, I lost a brother. I mean that's the closest thing that's happened to me. I've watched every stage of his weakness, his going down, his health just leaving him. Obviously, it was a painful thing. My mom was in denial. I had to deal with her because again she didn't quite understand everything. To deal with this meant her having to deal with his being gay again. And as you know, for a long time—and even today, there's no separating one from the other in a lot of people's minds. The first thing I did was to educate myself. And I knew a lot anyway, having lost friends to HIV/AIDS. We both had mutual friends. And those were painful. And seeing your own brother, it does something. I don't know. For me, it inspired me to research. And like I said, I learned. What I didn't know, I learned. And I tried to learn more and more and more so that I could inform my family, so that I could inform my mom and break it down to her to let her know what we're dealing with, and so that I could talk with my brother. Because I needed to educate myself to know the different stages that he would go through. The times when he would be sort of "Okay, I'm happy today." And then the times when, toward the end, when he would totally withdraw. I needed to be prepared for that. So if anything, it motivated me. And today even, I visit a couple of the area hospitals on certain days during the week. I visit the AIDS wards and the cancer wards in honor of my brother and my father. And I just visit and I just talk with the people. And a lot of times, that's all they want is just somebody to talk to and listen to. So it's made me very socially aware.

Has it changed the way you feel about dating? The things that you do?

Oh yes, definitely. Definitely. You know it is true, education is the key. It's funny, there's something that someone in college said to me. Actually, a gay man that we both know. Not you. And he said, "You don't have to do anything that you don't want to do." And I've never forgotten. He said, "AIDS is real." And that was at a stage when we really didn't know anything, as much about it as we do now. But then again, I've always been the type person who—I did what I wanted to do. If I didn't feel comfortable doing something, then I wasn't going to do it. And at the same time, I'm the type who never can impose my will on anyone else either. I'm a civil person, you know?

Do you think it's a bigger problem in the South?

Uhm hmm. I heard that report, too. I don't know when that report came out. Right now I'm thinking of a situation of a good friend of mine. He dated this guy. The guy was married, but my friend didn't know the guy was married. And the guy not only stepped out on my friend but his wife, and contracted AIDS and brought AIDS back to his wife. And they have children. So now they both deal with this issue. We heard a lot obviously, earlier this year, of the "down low" phenomenon. Quite honestly, a lot of people think it's new and it really isn't. There's nothing new of the idea, they just stuck a label on it. And that's probably why you see more cases are emerging probably in the South now. People have to deal with it now. And quite honestly, it's not just a gay disease. It never really has been just a gay disease. And now that situations like what I just described are happening, people are forced to deal with it in the South now.

· · · · · · · ·

MICHAEL (B. 1968, RALEIGH, N.C.)

My first experience of HIV and AIDS was my uncle. I found out my uncle was HIV-positive when I was in the tenth grade. And at that time, nobody really knew what that meant. And then to find out that he had been HIV for so many years because you knew about it in D.C. but you didn't know about it in North Carolina, but he could trace his diagnosis back to whatever. And seemingly, he was one of the first individuals to be HIV-positive. And as I said, he only died maybe three years ago. But he was never symptomatic up until maybe five years ago. I'm sorry, my college best friend, he passed at twenty-two, twenty-three, something like that. But I, I couldn't put a face on it. You know, I didn't see the spiraling that you go through because he moved away and moved to Atlanta. And then when he came back, he was so far gone that he didn't have visitors. And he was so vain, he was cremated before I could even get down there to see the body. You know, his mom called and said he passed like this morning. He was [laughter] cremated before I could get there that afternoon.

But I did have this friend of a friend. We were in college and we were all around. We were saying, "God, your hair is so pretty." And one of my friends said, "What kind of perm do you have in your hair?" And he said, "Bitch, this is not a perm, this is my hair." [Laughter] And in hindsight, I realize that the medicine did that, you know, because I didn't know anything. And to see friends that I've had who have become ill over the years, I didn't really see the effects of it, other than, you know, they got slender, their face was shrunken in, and that kind of thing. But I didn't really get it until my uncle became ill, because he moved back from D.C. and stayed with my parents.

[Sighs] And actually, I think people have been worse. I'm sure there have been people that have been, much worse than my uncle. He became slim, couldn't keep food on his stomach, but he didn't have lesions everywhere. If I see people with lesions and these types of things, but I think how it affected me, it made me want to do something. But it also made me fearful in terms of wanting to do what I wanted to do because I didn't know what other people would think about me. Since he has passed, I've wanted to do it even with friends, and I never do, and I don't understand why the hell I don't do it. Because really I'm not afraid to do it. But I just don't want to be character- ized as being fixated on that. And I say I'm going to volunteer but then I keep saying if I volunteer at some hospice or some organization, I'm going to run into all these gay people and they're going to see me on the street and holler my name out when I'm with my co-workers. So those things, even though very shallow, prohibit me or at least play the role of me being active in that arena, which goes back to why I'm not active in terms of organizations that deal with gay issues.

Do you think HIV is more of a problem in the South?

I think HIV is a problem everywhere, but in particular in the South, I think it's difficult for people to ask the tough questions prior to being intimate with someone. I think people are more fearful of asking questions about do you have AIDS, as well as to confronting that issue. Oh, I even forgot about that person, one of my—another one of my friends passed. You know or you think you know but you never ask. And in particular this one person I'm speaking about, I'd known he was sick forever, and then someone even confirmed he was and I never, ever even mentioned it to him. I mean, even when I was standing there watching him die, I never said nothing. And I think it's just a stigma or shame about asking, because in the South you don't ask a lot of stuff, you just don't. It's rude or offensive. So I think in contrast, people in general just have to learn to protect themselves and to do as much as possible to lower risk behaviors.

. . . .

JONATHAN S. (B. 1983, WARRENTON, N.C.)

People here as a whole have become aware of gay culture, but only in a negative light, in the fact that there's such a high rate of HIV in the black people in this state, college students in this state. Because of this whole issue where men don't identify as gay, so they don't feel the need to use protection when they have sex. At our Black Student Movement meeting—I wasn't there, but I heard about it—[laughter] what was brought up, the issue of men being gay and not telling anybody and practicing unsafe sex. And the oddest thing to me is that these people are in there talking about it, but they don't realize that it's the men in that room that are doing that. There's still this sense in this black community that it's them out there, but they don't realize that it's us in here. [. . .] I'm like how can all these people be so oblivious? I'm like, do you not realize that what you're saying applies to half the males in this room and you're talking to them, like, telling them to go tell your friends? I don't know, that's always interesting to me, and it will always be interesting to me. Like I said, in high school, I didn't understand how they couldn't see that. They're just so oblivious to it.

What has been the impact of HIV and AIDS on your life?

I think it makes you definitely a little bit—not a little, it makes you a lot—more cautious with who you will have sex. I know like if I knew that a person had sex with a lot of other men, especially these freshmen and sophomores now that I would not put it past them if they didn't use protection—I probably wouldn't mess with them.

. . . .

"ROB" (B. 1965, EDEN, N.C.)

My brother who passed away in '95, he was HIV-positive. He was gay. I have a nephew who was older than I am, my oldest sister's son, was gay. He passed away of AIDS as well, in '91. And so, for me, there has always been this tremendous, as there is with everyone else I'm sure, this tremendous burden of homosexuality, and being gay, and you know, this is what will happen to you if you don't straighten up and fly right. And I think that, for me, has been another endurance test. How long can I last, how long am I gonna be here to sort of carry this torch that now has been passed to me? Now I'm far more settled with who I am than I was five years ago, or even ten years ago, of course. But with that burden comes tremendous responsibility about what it means to be a responsible gay person, sexually speaking. Because I know what pain AIDS and all that brings, to those you love, to your associates, to your friends, to your family. And I think that those, having lived through those experiences, with my nephew and watching him grow so emaciated, and watching my brother, who for my brother, was a very, very short period of time, from diagnosis to his demise, it was a little over a year. He was diagnosed in the spring of '94, and in the fall of '95 he passed away. And I talked to him about it, before he passed away, and before his health had declined, and, he thinks he knows the person from whom he was infected. One experience, when he was in his twenties.

My nephew's experience was much more prolonged. He was diagnosed in '88, and he passed away in '91, and just all kinds of illnesses beset him, and just watching the toll it took on my sister, and our family, was devastating. The scariest thing about it, and I was in my mid-twenties when my nephew came out to us, and watching my family's reaction was interesting, because there was almost no reaction. Even though we had grown up with parents who taught tolerance, and all this, there was tolerance but, you could tell, okay something's not quite sitting right, something's under the surface that's not quite fully accepting my nephew's lifestyle. And my nephew told my brother, who is the one who passed away of AIDS as well. He told my brother, and I remember my brother telling me, just in tears, long before he was diagnosed. This was in 1990. My nephew had said, there's more, there's more. And we all kept going, there's more, never would say anything else. So my brother took that and knew what my nephew was talking about because I think, to this day, and I never asked my brother and he never told me, I think they either had a sexual experience with the same person, who may have been carrying the virus. I don't know, but my nephew knew that my brother was in fact, somehow. I don't know how. And so my brother fought that and fought that and fought that, and was never tested for the three, four years after that. And then in '94 finally was tested, and he was positive. It was a very obviously difficult time.

But interestingly enough my family banded together and remained together, and remains together today, living and working through that. My brother and I would go up every single weekend, from '89, from 1989 until July of 1991, when my nephew passed away, every weekend, for those two years, to help take care of my nephew. And it wasn't until the last year that he became absolutely bed-ridden, and that's when we decided, gosh there are ten of us, we need to rotate shifts and weekends, and you have this weekend. And so, as it was, we would all congregate there to assist and do whatever. And having the repeat performance with my brother, of course we'd learned quite a lot from having dealt with my nephew in terms of care and what to do, and the signs, and those kinds of things, that are sort of harbingers of what's to come.

· · · · · · · ·

RODERICK (B. 1974, BATON ROUGE, LA.)

I have an aunt, my mother's older sister, who actually lost two sons to AIDS. Definitely one of them was gay. We called him Junior. And he actually did prison time, too. But I mean he was gay before he went to prison. It's not like he got turned out in jail.

My older brother's HIV-positive. He's been positive for ten years. Thank God he has not had a hospitalization. [. . .] In fact, this just happened recently. My mom calls me at work. I was going to take her shopping for Christmas. We were going to have a shopping day. "I've got to cancel the date because I'm here in the emergency room with your brother," blah, blah, blah. And of course I'm like, "Why are you telling me this?" And I'm up for grabbing my shit and leaving work for a trip to the hospital. But it was basically, you know, maybe some medication had changed and he had a bad reaction and he just had some issues. And he's doing all right. And we've known for ten years. He may have found out, he may have had it longer than that, but we found out ten years ago. But that's been devastating. And a conscious decision was made by my family, my immediate family, to not tell a soul. It was not because we all sat together at the table in a Cosby moment and said whatever. That was my brother's wishes, and my mother kind of threw her hands in the air or whatever. I know she has confided in other people, probably some people. I have confided in other people. And I don't give a fuck. I'm like this is part of letting people know that this is real for me by telling them, "Yes I live this every day. It's not in my body but it's in my brother's body. And so I too live with it every day."

I have lost two cousins, like I said. My aunt has lost two sons to it. There's some paranoia attached to it too. AIDS has got me crazy. But the paranoia, I guess, is that, you know, I believe in karma. I believe in some of these superstitions. I believe in all that other shit. So I'm like I don't want history to repeat itself. And my mother, she's like, "Okay, I've got two sons too." So for me, it also makes me more aware and makes me more careful and more cautious. I had my test done just last December or November or whatever it was. The lady was like, "I want you to just relax." I said, "I'm going to be okay." She said, "Do you use condoms consistently?" I said, "Yes, but I've had a lot of partners. I've had a LOT of partners, especially since I moved back to Baton Rouge and there's nothing else to do but that." But still, you have to be careful because condoms are not 100 percent effective and that's just the fact of the matter. So that's a lesson, even more motivation for like, you know, it's time to be a one-man man and that also helps curb my Internet chatting. Because I did a lot of that when I moved back. And it's sort of like . . . whatever. So it has an effect.

I've lost friends. I lost a very dear friend, you know. Barry. In 2003. That was devastating because, although I saw my cousin . . . the first . . . seeing my cousin years ago. But that memory, you know, it's still fresh. I can see him right now in his hospital bed, my friend, Barry. I can see him right now. I was warned before I got there, and I got there and I thought it truly was like skin on a skeleton. You know? And bloody mouth because the lungs were mush. Barely coherent while he was awake. There was a moment when he did wake up and he said little funny things, you know, and we were like, "Okay he's here." So we had that one little precious, last moment with him before he was gone. And that's devastating, you know. And of course I know there were problems and this and that. It was devastating. And I have lots of emotions when it comes to HIV and AIDS. The anger comes from the ignorance out there. The lack of willingness of people to talk about it, especially in the black church. People are so willing to condemn gays and lesbians and not realize that they are the ones that to blame for this.

. . . .

TIM'M (B. 1972; RAISED IN TAYLOR, ARK.)

I met this white guy when I first moved to D.C., and one of the first questions he asked me was [was] I HIV-positive? And I said, "Well, yeah, I happen to be HIV-positive." And he said to me, "Well, yeah I usually assume when I meet black guys that they're HIV-positive." And I was taken aback, obviously, by that comment. But then I thought, "You know what? That's probably not that uncommon a perspective among a lot of white gay guys." You know? Given the stats and given the way that gay black men are pathologized in the media. It's probably not that uncommon that they kind of say to themselves, "Well, you know most . . ." In their minds, most black gay men are HIV-positive. Because the stats almost maybe appear that way. And it just so happens that I am in that statistical category, but then in my life, most of the men that I know are HIV-negative. At least that I'm aware of. So there's a kind of contradiction between the reality as being the way people see it.

You talked about your HIV status. This question, you've answered some of it. What has been the impact of HIV on your life?

Testing positive gave me a lot of courage to find, to actually move out of the space of sort of cordial, like "let's not ruffle any feathers." Prior to HIV, I was a good southern black gay boy. Like, I was out in the gay world, but I was not out in the straight world to a certain extent. I wasn't out back home. So I was willing to go back home and just kind of be silent about stuff just to kind of keep the peace. And I remember that testing HIV-positive was, for me, it sort of brought about this urgency of living an authentic life, which to me goes back to the things that I was told by my grandmother. You know, "to thine own self be true." And feeling like, you know, I want them and those hugs and kisses and "I love you's" that I experienced as a kid, and I said to myself, "You know, I want them to really know who they love when they say, 'I love you.'" Like in the fullness of who I am and who I've become and not the seventeen-year-old boy who left home, who liked school and is smart and bright. "I want you to know the fullness of who you're saying you love. And I want to know you more fully."

And it's interesting how my own war on visibly coming out, since HIV, has also created opportunities for other siblings of mine, not gay, to come out of some of their sexual problems. I guess it was like the punishment of their erotophobic southern culture, you know. A sister with a baby by two different men. A lot of shame around that. And being able to say, "You have some beautiful kids. You are a single mother. How can we celebrate that? How can the others of us support you in that?" And it's not this dirty secret that we can't talk about, you know. So yeah, just in a number of ways, that truth telling has enabled other family members of mine to really get to know each other genuinely in some ways that we just hadn't done before and some ways that we hadn't explored. And I think HIV forced them in a sense that my initial diagnosis wasn't very great, you know. I had 192 T-cells, which is a full-blown AIDS status. And you know, 37,000 viral. And was told by the first set of physicians that I needed to get on something really fast or else my future looked really grim. And I remember my doctor. I remember specifically how gray he was. He was shaking. So I wasn't so scared when I found out I was HIV-positive. But after he came in there shaking and talking about what my stats were, I really got concerned, and I started to think then about the kind of legacy I wanted to leave. And the story that I wanted to tell that maybe nobody else would. If I don't tell it, who will? And I almost felt like once I took the challenge to tell the story, I've been given more time.

So now I don't write with the same level of urgency that I did in that first couple of years when I was not so sure. Because I really do expect to be around for a while. But I'm happy for the wheels that it started turning. And I can honestly say I probably wouldn't be doing the activist work and the creative performance thing that I'm doing if I weren't HIV-positive. In this really tragic way sometimes—"beautifully tragic" maybe is one way to put it. You know, HIV outed black gay men. HIV continues to out black gay men because unfortunately sometimes we don't respond to some of the death and dying that's happening, especially in the South. You know, when people die and it's called disgusting. You know, when people's partners kind of like are ignored.

I want to be buried in Taylor [Arkansas] next to my grandparents, because I also want like all my friends and loved ones to be there. I want there to be an affirmation of who I am in my fullness. And I think that provided an example and a window for other people. You know? And I get a lot of responses from southern boys, younger southern boys who say, "Thank you." And I think something I've articulated in my writing that stays true to my southern roots. The way that I spell some words. I sometimes do phonetic spellings of words because I'm like, "No, they say SOU-the-REN. They don't say SOU-thern . . . southerner." And so I may spell it a certain way because I want to kind of honor that voice, that tongue that the people where I'm from speak. And I think there's a way that HIV . . . and I think faced with death sort of gave me life.

....
TONY (B. 1961, MEMPHIS, TENN.)

As I mentioned, I had chronic hepatitis, and I thought I had HIV—or that I was HIV-infected at the time. And so it forces a whole reexamination. That's when I felt more shame than I think when I did about trying to just be gay in the beginning. HIV and my sexuality became inextricably linked. And so I had more shame around that than I did just around being gay by itself. Because even though I knew it wasn't a gay disease in my heart, I felt like it was. And in some ways at that younger age, I had to grapple with God is punishing us. God is punishing me, I didn't know if I had AIDS or not, but I thought I did. And, you know, this is me reaping what I sowed; this is some type of bizarre punishment. So I did have to go through a whole reassessment of what that meant over the years. But because I thought I was HIV-positive, I became very concerned about making sure that people knew everything that they could know about that disease and about hepatitis B, because I figured if I was teaching people about the spread of HIV, if they practiced these things, they were also going to save themselves from other diseases, including hepatitis B, which I knew I had that for sure. I found out like a little later that I did, when the tests finally came out and I actually did have it, I found out I was HIV-negative and have remained so. But it set me on this path of education as an individual, just talking to people, but also as a real educator, as a volunteer for AIDS organizations, and ultimately I worked in AIDS and prevention in D.C., San Francisco, and New Orleans, because it was important for me. I knew white people weren't going to help us; we had to help ourselves, and I wanted to be part of that. I wanted to save other young black men from the suffering that could come from having that disease or the other diseases one can get in a sexually transmitted way. And that became my focus for a long time.

And that's where my most sense of community came from; it was working with other men and women on that issue. Now, the other side of that then is losing all my friends to HIV. And the fact that I'm still here, I used to have guilt about it and you've heard of that, how this guilt of the positive people—the negative people, some of whom become positive so they don't feel like they don't belong, or some who do other things. But I felt like I didn't get it for some reason, I don't know what it was, but that had something to do with my divine purpose, so I damn well better fulfill it, whatever that purpose was. And at the time I thought that was education. But all the deaths of my friends, I've never taken it well; I've never handled it well. It's like I was never around when people would die, because I moved around so much, so I'd always hear about it after the fact. And the void hasn't really been filled because they just were dying off like flies.

And the only time a friend of mine died who I was around, who is a friend of mine not in the South, though, I lived across the street from him, and I remember the last time he went to the hospital, I took him. And he couldn't really walk at that point. His legs couldn't really fully function anymore; they couldn't bend fully. And so he had to crawl around most of the time. And his skin was dark and crispy and black and hard. I tried to massage, and I didn't know if he could even feel anything. And he said, "That feels good." I said, "Do you feel anything?" I felt like it was just a big, charred piece of flesh. But I carried him in my arms out of the house and put him in the car, took him to the hospital. Got a wheelchair, got him up in there. Stayed with him. He screamed and hollered, screamed and hollered, screamed and hollered. He was afraid of needles. And I'm like, "Girl, you've been positive for how long and you—you better get over it." And then I got him up in there, and then I had to go to Chicago. Now, don't you know he went and died while I was in Chicago? And I was so angry with him. I was like, now, you know you could have waited one more day. Because I heard about it while I was in Chicago, and I was devastated. It's like this is the one person I am trying—that I am with during this time and I'd lived the closest to him of all the friends he had, physically I was right across the street. I had to say I probably went numb for a long time after that. I couldn't cry at his funeral. I couldn't respond. I just couldn't believe it. And it was really difficult for me.

And then the next friend, who actually had been a lover of mine, he died in New York, and I wasn't there either, but I did make it in time for the funeral. And I think it was the first time I was ever able to actually express my grief for the loss of a friend with HIV in my community, so we could share that grief together. I have not had the benefit of being able to do that like some people do, because I'm usually in California and they're in New York, or I'm here and they're in Kansas City and I'm just hearing about it and trying to have my own personal process. But I think it's important to grieve as a community and I'm glad I had the opportunity. But it has shaped a lot of who I am. A lot of people thought I was weird in the early days because I was promoting this message of safer sex before it was popular to talk about it. And it made me just an outsider really, but no regrets. I felt like I was good at it. It helped me hone my teaching skills for later.

trannies, transvestites, and drag queens, oh my! transitioning the south

5 Given the supposed provincialism of the South, it is perhaps the last place one might expect to find a thriving trans (i.e., transsexual, transgender, transvestite) or even drag culture, especially in black communities. And yet, I remember many a flamboyant "queen" or preoperative transgendered person from my childhood. Although I did not have the terminology at the time, I knew that these "men" were different in that they often wore women's clothing, makeup, and wigs, and carried themselves as if they were members of a bourgeois aristocracy, even though they were just as poor as the rest of us. As renowned drag performer RuPaul reminds us: "Some of the most unforgettable women in the world are men"[1] And, as some of the narrators have suggested in their stories about gay men in their communities during their childhood, no one ever physically or verbally attacked these men; rather, they were incorporated in the community, along with the rest of the cast of characters in the neighborhood. In my experience, if disparaging things were said, at least when I was in earshot, they were said behind closed doors; or they may have been communicated in stereotypically black southern ways of signifying: rolling eyes, sucking teeth, pursing lips, and verbal indirection. But then again, these were adult privileges of ridicule. Children, at least in my neighborhood—and especially in my household—were chastised for poking fun at anyone for their "indifference," to use narrator Chaz's term for his transgenderism.

The fact that some of the most famous gay men of the South have been visibly gender-nonconformist also belies the belief that the South is necessarily inhospitable to those who embrace a trans or drag identity. Notable among such trans celebrities is The Lady Chablis, a self-identified preoperative transgender and female impersonator born and raised in Savannah, Georgia, who became famous playing herself in the Clint Eastwood film *Midnight in the Garden of Good and Evil*, based on the best-selling book by John Berendt. And while

RuPaul was not born in the South, he got his start as a drag performer on the Atlanta circuit. Arguably, some of the most entertaining drag performances can be found in the South.

The narrators in this chapter share provocative stories of coming to terms not only with their same-sex attraction, but also with their feelings of gender and sexual nonconformity in relation to their race and within the context of gay communities. Nonetheless, three of the four narrators have fully worked through their gender-nonconformity issues and speak passionately about their transition across gender and societal thresholds. While some embrace the "trans" or "drag" identity label, others choose to remain in a liminal state when it comes to "an" identity. Indeed, as "R. Dioneaux" proclaims in his narrative, the most important label for him is simply "human."

Regarding labels, however, it is important to note the distinctions that the narrators themselves make among gay, transgenderism, transvestism, and drag. Chaz, for instance, does not identify as gay but as a preoperative transgender person. For the most part, Chaz/Chastity lives as a woman, except on Sundays, when "he" occasionally dresses as a man to sing in the tenor section of the church choir. While "transgender" has become somewhat of an umbrella term,[2] the way Chaz/Chastity employs the term seems to be more in keeping with Virginia Prince's definition of transgender as "somebody who lives full time in the gender opposite to their anatomy" but who has not "transed the sex barrier."[3] As Chaz/Chastity will explain below, the desire to have the surgery to transition biologically to a woman waned for him because the psychological, emotional, and outward transitions have all taken place and that seems to be enough. Like The Lady Chablis, Chaz/Chastity prayed for guidance about the decision and received a similar answer. The Lady Chablis writes: "I kept on praying on it, and one day, all of the sex-change issues came into some kind of focus: I really didn't want an operation, didn't need one. It wasn't the answer. I was just as legitimate as a woman who'd kept her candy, if I believed with all my heart and soul that I was one. An operation could only allow my full-length mirror to tell me what I already knew and felt inside, but it wasn't gonna make those feelings and that knowledge any stronger. Just more anatomic'ly correct."[4] Further, Chaz/Chastity explains that since she had already paid the emotional cost of coming to terms with her identity, the financial cost is simply not worth it.

"R. Dioneaux," on the other hand, is still questioning his identity with regard to transgenderism. Unlike Chaz, he outwardly lives and dresses as male. Psychologically and emotionally, however, he feels that he may be transgender. Literally living in that liminal space between gay and transgender has made clear for R. Dioneaux the politics of authenticity within all of these groups. According to him, he even felt oppressed at a transgender conference because he was, ironically, interpreted as a female-to-male trans-sexual rather than a (questioning) male-to-female transgendered person. Moreover, he says that this same gathering failed to address issues that speak to the intersection of race and class. "To encompass all trans persons," according to Richard M. Juang, "a robust transgender politics of recognition should address the discriminations and prejudices targeted not only against gender but against racial and ethnic differences."[5] Unfortunately, this was not the case at the conference R. Dioneaux attended.

"Mademoiselle Grégoire" (the stage name for narrator Greg T.) embodies and embraces several gender-nonconformity categories. He fashions himself as a gay, transvestite, drag queen. In other words, his "sexual" identity is homosexual, his gender affinity is femininity expressed through cross-dressing, and he sometimes performs as a drag queen in pageants. Greg is very clear about the distinctions among these identity categories, however, and is adamant about not being transgendered. As he puts it, "I like being a man."

Fred-Rick identifies as a "gay" man with a "drag" past. Once a preacher–turned drag queen, Fred-Rick no longer performs drag, but embraces that part of his life history. Admittedly, he still expresses some ambivalence about his affinity for performing drag and even about being transgender. He says that during the time when he was performing, he was "confused" about what it all meant—a confusion that he still seems to carry with him. Currently, his only "drag" is that of an English teacher and an occasional impersonation of Maya Angelou that is dead on.

It was an honor to hear these narrators' stories. Their conspicuous presence in their communities speaks to the elasticity of acceptance the South sometimes affords even its most dissident citizens. This is not to romanticize their place in these communities, for surely they suffer from homophobia, transphobia, and gender discrimination at the hands of their fellow southerners. Nonetheless, their presence in these spaces complicates the myopic view of the South as intolerant of difference, and also provides a more complicated portrait of southern black sexuality. These "men" are brave, and they are fierce. Here are their stories.

• • • • • • • •

CHAZ/CHASTITY

As noted in the Introduction, Chaz lives in my hometown of Hickory, North Carolina. I did not know Chaz as a child, partly because he grew up in a neighboring town and partly because no one ever mentioned that there was

a transgendered person in our community. My first sighting of Chaz was
when I visited my home church several years ago. He was singing in the tenor
section of the mass choir. He was dressed in a three-piece suit, his hair was
permed and fiercely coiffed, his eyebrows were arched, and I could see the
slightest evidence of foundation. Although I had "clocked" Chaz as being
"family," at that time, I had no idea that he was also "Chastity." Chastity
introduced herself to me at, of all places, my brother and sister-in-law's
annual Christmas party in 2003. I was astonished to see that no one else
attending the party batted an eye at Chastity's presence. It turned out that
not only was Chaz/Chastity a welcomed guest, but also my sister-in-law's
hairstylist.

Chastity and I spoke at great length at that party. She was wearing
leather pants, a satin blouse, and cowboy boots. Her face was "beat back
into her temples," as the children would say. Or, in other words, her
makeup was subtle but flawless: perfectly arched eyebrows, foundation that
blended in with her skin tone, just a hint of blush and eye shadow, and an
understated lip gloss. She was a marvel to me—not only because of her
confidence and comfortableness in her own skin, but also because she was
the first trans person that I had ever encountered in my hometown and in a
predominately heterosexual context, let alone in the presence of my family.
During our conversation that evening I revealed that I was living in Chicago
and about to begin doing research on a book on black gay men of the South.
Chaz told me that she would gladly be a part of the book and looked forward
to me coming back home so that we could visit.

The interview took place on September 27, 2004, in my sister's kitchen.
As noted earlier, Chaz and I had already been out and about town, sharing
lunch and running errands for my mother. I was greatly inspired by Chaz's
story. His life is one of courage that speaks to the resilience of the human
spirit.

I was born on July 28th, the year 1969, here in Catawba County, North
Carolina. It was a happy childhood. My brother and I are only eleven months
and twenty-three days apart, and so a lot of people thought that we were
twins, because our mom dressed us alike, and we were both in bottles and
diapers at the same time. But, it was a good childhood. Both my mother and
father are factory workers. They are both fifty-nine, and have been working in
factories for all of my life. I attempted to work in a factory for like a month,
but it just did not suit me.

My parents played the most dominant role [in my upbringing], because
my mother and father were very strict, in my upbringing, and it was some-

Chaz at his salon in Hickory, North Carolina. Courtesy of the narrator.

what frowned upon for my brother and I to frequent other relatives' or friends' homes. I knew both my grandmothers as a child, just lost them maybe twenty years ago. And yes, my grandmothers did play a very great role in my life. As a matter of fact, they were my caretakers when my mom and father had to go to work. Up until the time for me to go to school.

My first year of kindergarten I went to school at Shuford Elementary School in Conover, North Carolina. First grade, I attended Central, here in Hickory, and then second grade we moved back to Conover, where I attended Shuford again, and then Newton Conover Middle, and Newton Conover High. I was very introverted as a child. Did not have a lot of friends—a lot of times because of my indifference, "indifference" meaning, my sexual orientation. I knew at a very early age that I was different from the other kids. The majority of my friends, quote/unquote, were females, and a lot of times we would play games, or do things that little girls did, even though I was not a girl.

So you didn't have any close friends in high school either?

[. . .] Not really. I was still somewhat to myself. I did have one friend, at the time, his name was Michael [last name], and Michael and I were very close throughout all of our years at school, from elementary up through high school, but it was because he and I both shared this same lifestyle, the same tastes.

Was the town segregated, when you were growing up?

No, but of course there was always innuendos of racial prejudice, things like that, but I really didn't get into it either way because I didn't really have a lot of white friends, or black. And if I had to say so, the majority of the people who treated me fairly were Caucasians.

Was your community at all black?

Yes, I lived in a predominantly black neighborhood. Very much working class. I would say that 95 percent probably were factory laborers.

How would you describe the influence of church and religion on your childhood?

Church and religion played a very dominant role in my childhood because from my earliest memory, my mom always took my brother and I to church. Always. That was expected. You did not go and get up on a Sunday morning and not go to church. And you were there for that whole day from Sunday school, sometimes they didn't even feed after morning service, and then you'd stay for evening service.

Was church something you enjoyed?

I did. I truly did, up until I was in my, I'd say rebellious teens, and decided that I no longer wanted my mom to be able just to dictate to me my goings

Chaz in first grade, 1976. Courtesy of the narrator.

and comings, especially as far as church. Because, who wants to sit in church all day on Sunday when all your friends, or your peers, are out doing the other things like movies, going to the malls, things such as that?

What kind of things were going on in church?

Well, I was raised in the Fire Baptized Holiness faith, and so they're raised Pentecostal, predominantly. They would have a lot of organizations and auxiliaries in the church. They were active with the youth, like doing different speaking engagements, or like, oratorical presentations, or going to different churches and singing, and fellowshipping with one another, things like that.

So, did you sing in the choir?

Yes. It was very nice, because I have a very creative nature, and singing in the choir allowed me just to express my creativity. And I could be somewhat flamboyant with the guise of being spiritual.

Were there other children who enjoyed singing in the choir just as much as you did?

Yes, because we made it fun. I mean you gotta remember that we were all Pentecostal children, so we all had friends that were, quote/unquote lived secular lives, and this was our outlet, this was our way of having fun.

When did you first become aware of your same-sex orientation? And did you tell anyone?

To become aware, and to know what it was, I would have to say in my early teens, but I've always had a very effeminate nature, from my earliest memory, even like being, three or four years old, playing with my cousins, and, different neighbors and things. In the South we had these games called, Mama and Daddy, and playing church, and so rather than taking on a male's role, in the Mama/Daddy situation, or in the church situation, I was always one who took on the gender or the genre of a female. In the Mama and Daddy situation, I was always either like the auntie, or the grandma, or in the church situation I was one of the praise leaders for the testimony service. [. . .] And I could remember my mother at Christmas and birthdays, she would always do her best to get my brother and I really nice gifts, and if we ever were like, interacting with our other cousins, especially my female cousins, and I would see that they had been purchased dolls, I sort of resented the fact that I got a truck, as opposed to a doll. Especially when I went to play with the toys, I was not going to play with my brother or my other boy cousins. I wanted to play with the girls. My truck and their dolls just did not mix.

Did you tell anybody about these feelings that you were having?

I think I was more so expressive in the physical sense as opposed to verbal. I would act out the way that I wanted to be perceived, or the way that I felt that I was, or the way things were. Like I said, my cousins had dolls, and I would like to play with their dolls and style their hair and make clothes, things like that, and play with them, interact with them. I did not want to play with my brother. I did not want to play with his stupid trucks. I did not want to ride bikes, or anything like that because it was a boy's bike, and it just did not behoove me to do so.

Did you have intimate physical or sexual experiences while growing up?

I did. I distinctly remember what was a repressed memory that just came back to me, maybe three years ago. Upon my going to school here in Hickory for that one year, I was in the first grade, and my mother had started a second job, to where she wouldn't, we would get off the bus, there was no one at home to pick us up, or to let us into the house. And so my mother inquired of one of the neighbors as to whether or not she would allow my brother and I to wait at her home until she got off that evening. And so, in doing so, the lady had older sons, and one of her sons molested me.

Have you talked to him since that time?

No. No contact.

How would you describe the influence of Southern culture on your childhood, on your ability to recognize and come to terms with your sexual orientation?

Most southerners in my opinion, in my observation, are very genteel people, very cordial. You really don't meet a lot of strangers. When people come to your home, they're guests, and so I've always had that type of nature about myself, to where I want to be very hospitable to people, and to not really make any enemies or ruffle any feathers, so to speak. I've always tried to be one that got along and persevered to be the go-between of people. You know if people were ever in an argument or they were ever in a disagreement, I like to be the one to try to mediate, and try to bring peace within the situation. And I think a lot of that has played a major role in my life. I don't care for altercations, or being in situations where there's a lot of violence or animosity, or ill feelings towards people or situations. I try and stay clear of that. That's why I've always been somewhat a loner and just kind of off to myself. I'm like, "Don't fight me."

Is there any particular theory explaining the cause of homosexuality that you subscribe to?

Well, I can only speak for my own self. I don't know that the molestation that took place early in my life, or the, the interactions with quote/unquote other family members, who were doing exploratory things, as far as sex, were contributing factors. I really, deeply feel that before I was even created, or formed in my mother's womb, that these traits, these ideals, these desires, were already inside me. Now, what prompted them to bring them to fruition, is plausible for a, possibly other theories, or, or, reasons, for which I'm not really known. But, for the most of my life, I've always been Chaz. I was born Charles Kenneth Danner Jr., but I always felt like I wasn't born the right person. I don't feel that God made any mistakes, mind you, but I just feel like I've always been different, for whatever reasons.

To what extent have you come out to your parents and other family members?

One hundred percent. I have nothing to hide. I feel that when you, when you feel a need to hide something, a lot of the basis for that is because you are embarrassed, for a lack of better words, by the choices that you've made. I've no embarrassment, or any, any type of, remorse, or, or, regrets, for better word. As far as the choices I've made, about my sexuality, or the way that I choose to live my life, I treat people with very much respect, and I, that's all I ask for in return.

My parents and family members first learned of my orientation when I was in beauty school, which was around the year 1989, 1990. I just came out and told them, and not only did I tell them, but I started acting out, more rebelliously, as far as the way I would choose to wear my hair. I started wearing makeup and adorning more effeminate attire so that I could be identified as such. Kind of up in your face. [. . .] Some of them were very angry. Some felt that I was, in a quote/unquote state of confusion, or that this was a phase for me, or that I was struggling to find myself or to fit in. What they really didn't realize was that I already knew and had embraced these feelings for a long time prior to that, but just didn't know how to go about acting it out.

How would you describe your current relationship with your parents and other family members?

I have a good rapport with my family. My parents, I love them, unconditionally. I'm very appreciative of all of my mom and my dad have done to further me along in life, be it the way that they've backed me financially, all the way through, my rearing, upbringing, to the emotional and parental type of things that they instilled in me. As far as, extended family, I love them but I love them from a distance, and that is primarily my choice. I don't have a lot of patience or time to rationalize with them as far as what my life choices are, and how they affect their life. I feel that it's really irrelevant to the situation, as far as how I live my life, and how I love them.

Did you ever consider moving out of the South?

I did, but because of the way that I was raised, you have to understand my mother always told us, she went and worked two jobs so that my brother and

I could have the things that we needed, and some of what we wanted, and for that reason, of her going to work, two jobs, she worked to provide a roof over our heads, as well as food in our mouths, and clothes on our backs, and beds, nice clean beds for us to sleep in. Therefore, there was no need, or rationale for us to spend the night, or to go on sleepovers with other family members or friends. Therefore, I think my mom always wanted to keep me close at hand, to where she could see me, and I think really in her mind, keep me out of harm's way.

So that's why you haven't considered moving away from the South?

Prior to now, the options have become more tangible, shall I say, within the past two to three years, more so than in the past. I've become very complacent with being here because this is all I've ever known, and as far as I was concerned, you know, I knew that there were other choices, and other opportunities, but I just did not feel that they were open to me.

Do you feel that there was something about being in this environment that made you feel that you didn't have other opportunities, that you were stuck here? Was there something about being in this particular area and within the particular mindset of these people, that you internalized that and felt that you couldn't go somewhere else or do other things?

Well, if you can hear me, most people always revolve back to that which is familiar to them, and this is all I've ever known. To go elsewhere, or to step out and launch into the deep, so to speak, would have been too far outside of my comfort zone. But staying here in the South, especially so close to my mother, was a way . . . yes, I live my life as vicariously as I chose, but only within the parameters that I always could go back home, because home was a safe place; it was a haven, you understand. You know, regardless of what people saw, I thought of me out in the world, or in the streets. I could always find some refuge if I could get back home.

Why do you continue to live in this area of the country?

I continue to live in this area because I've become established as a stylist and makeup artist. I have a great deal of clientele that have been, some of them have been with me eighteen years or more. And so, because of that, there again becoming complacent, and I really like the salon in which I work at. The people I've worked with for a very, very . . . we're all on the same page, so to speak, as far as our goals in life, as well as our abilities as far as stylists, and makeup artists. And it's just, I've made this my home.

How did you become interested in becoming a hairstylist?

Believe it or not, at the age of twelve, I had a great auntie that asked me to help her with her hair on the weekends. And, one saga led to another as far as me helping her to set it at night. [. . .] Being that I was only twelve, you know, I could read directions on a box and follow the directions enough to get you by, but not enough so to where I felt secure in picking up a pair of shears and giving you a nice cut. And so, from that, I met different stylists and continued to pursue that venue. Even up until the time when I graduated from high school and enrolled myself into beauty school, and the rest is, shall we say, history.

So how long have you been doing hair?

Collectively? Professionally, I would say, I became licensed in '91, and this is, so it's been thirteen years professionally, but collectively about twenty.

Describe your clientele: is it mostly women? is it mostly black women?

Predominantly black women, but [. . .] the type of school that I went to was a university of cosmetic arts that their main focus was training you on the ability to do all textures of hair. We are [a] very aggressive and progressive salon. We are known as one of the most elite salons in the Southeast. We just acquired Paul Mitchell products in our salon, and we are one of his signature salons. So it's very prestigious working there, and, so the opportunity I feel I would not have had, had I not have made the move to Hickory. Prior to working in Hickory I worked in Newton for nine years at the same salon. At that same salon, I started working there as a preoperative transsexual, so, like I said, you know, I've stayed in this area, and this area has become home to me because the people are somewhat over the shock factor, they're just waiting for what's next.

Talk a little about your psychological transformation in terms of being a preop transsexual. How did that come about? How did you realize that, you know, you really were trapped in the wrong body, or if you felt you were trapped in the wrong body?

For the longest time, I always knew that there was something different about me. I knew that when I would disrobe, that I was, quote/unquote a male. My mother never hesitated to remind me that she had two sons, but I was always very effeminate in my nature. And I had really suppressed those feelings, because the way that I was raised in church, you know, you really were not supposed to be sexually active until you know, you were grown and married, and what have you. And so, of course, that's not to say that I did not have affections, or attractions towards men then, but because of the way that I was raised, I was really afraid, because of my mother, to, enact upon that. It was only until I joined beauty school, enrolled in beauty school and met two entertainers that were quote/unquote drag queens, not female impersonators but drag queens.

What's the difference between a drag queen and a female impersonator?

Well, a drag queen is, a quote/unquote man who dresses in an effeminate way, but it is more so for the theatrical aspect of it, or for the entertainment

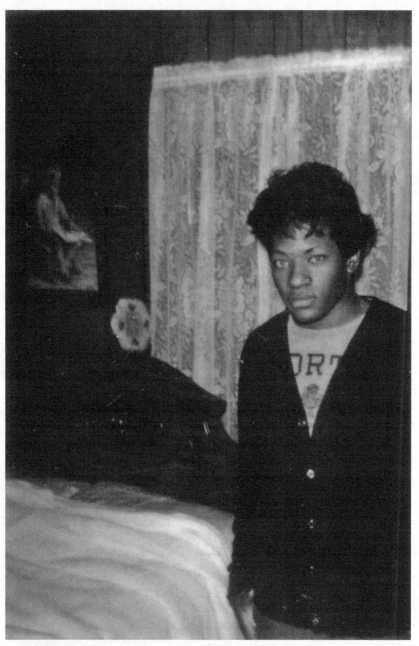

Chaz, age sixteen, beginning to transition to "Chastity."
Courtesy of the narrator.

factor of it. A female impersonator is one who also is a male, but conditions their body, or conditions their look, to emulate femininity in its most, in its truest essence. To pay compliment to what it's like to be effeminate, or a woman, as opposed to make mockery of it.

And so, upon meeting these two gentlemen in this school, they introduced me to the gay life. Well, I didn't even know that there was such a thing as a gay club. They took me to the club, and I entered into a talent show, and they put me in quote/unquote drag, but the drag was just not enough for me. I felt like it, there had to have been more to it. And, there was one particular morning, I was watching [. . .] *Donahue*, and he was interviewing a woman named Caroline Cossey, and her stage name was "Tula," and she was from London, England, and she was one of the world's first transgendered people. And she was a supermodel, and a beautiful one at that. And I was so intrigued by the show that I watched the transcription, the credits, and then I went to the yellow pages here in my town and found a sexual therapist. Upon finding them, I made, scheduled an appointment and went to see him. He [. . .] diagnosed me as a preoperative transsexual, saying that I had more female chromosomes in my anatomy than male, and that through medication and surgery, he could make my body match the way that my mind was. But part of that process was that you were to be subjected to living as a female, or to live out the gender reassignment for at least a year, the minimum of a year, and during that time you were evaluated mentally, physically, and emotionally, to make sure that you were truly transgender. I did that for five years. For five years I worked, lived, slept, breathed, ate, as a female here in Hickory.

I would go to church only when the churches would have choir anniversaries. A choir anniversary is where the church celebrates being together [. . .] for a year, and they're consecutive. And I [. . .] loved being there. I was raised in a church. I love gospel music, and it was one of the only times that I felt, quote/unquote secure, or safe to go, and not to be judged, or not to be ostracized, or overly criticized, because of my indifference. Because when I went, I went in high drag. High drag is when you are really, really just, to the nines, so to speak. As far as your hair, your makeup, everything is, no detail was left undone, unaddressed. I had very lavishly sculpted nails and the pedicures, and then, the custom-tailored suits, and very nicely coiffed wigs, and hair pieces, and, makeup, that looked like it was airbrushed on.

What was the reaction of people in church?

I don't know, but it's something about the black race, that blacks are always able to call you out, especially the children. So, when I would enter a building, or enter a room, be it church or the mall, or a store, convenience store, even a doctor's office, a lot of the people, especially the children were able, they would see something but they weren't sure what they were seeing. Because here is this, five-foot, eleven woman, very statuesque, large feet, large hands, but very immaculately dressed, and very polished. It was just almost too good to be true. No natural woman would look that good and pays that particular amount of attention to detail.

So would they say things, or just look?

Most times they would look. Sometimes you would hear them whispering or snickering amongst themselves. Snickering meaning laughing, or because it was something that they didn't understand.

And did you work in full drag too?

Definitely.

So you did hair in full drag?

In full, baby. Sometimes my skirts were so short, I could not bend over to pick up the combs. And I worked in a salon that was also a barbershop. The only thing that separated us was a wall, a partition, and a lot of times the men from the barbershop would come in just to see what I was wearing that particular day.

Did they think you were a woman?

Some did that were not from the area, or just did not know. But a lot of times, because of the mentality of the people, they would say, "Oh, that's not a woman. That's not a woman," you know. Or people would tell them, you know that's not really a girl, you know. And they would call you out, so to speak.

What would they say?

Well, exactly that. That's Charles, or that's Chaz, you know, he's not a woman, you know, he just dresses like that. But that was because they didn't understand. And so, little by little I started to educate my clients, and whoever would give it, give me the time of the day to let them know the difference, that this was not, I was not a cross-dresser, I was not a sissy, nor a faggot.

And did it make a difference?

To some, yes, because everyone does not want to be in the box. Everyone does not want to continue on the path of being insecure and being ignorant, because knowledge is power. And the only way that something can harm you or threaten you, is when you're unsure or unaware of exactly how it works, or why it works, why it even exists.

And apparently they kept coming, even people who didn't know? They kept coming to you because you were a fierce stylist?

Definitely. And, the fact that I wore makeup, and carried myself as a female, I think in a lot of ways gave them that much more insurance that I was going to make them look their best, because I paid particular attention to detail, and was always considered a perfectionist. [. . .] I would not misrepresent my clients. I would always tell them, "I'm not going to give you a hairstyle that I would be uncomfortable wearing."

Well, after the fifth year, during the course of that time, I had met many people in the gay lifestyle. And, [. . .] a lot of the quote/unquote entertainers at the club who I had began to befriend, would tell me that, "After you have your surgery girl, you're not going to have any time or place for us." Because in the gay community they saw transgendered people almost as a totally different lifestyle, because then you're no longer considered just, quote/unquote, a man or a woman.

You've crossed over.

Yes. Yes. And you've not crossed over to the straight side; it's in a world totally unique to yourself.

And so, because of that you decided not to go through with it?

Well, no, because of that, and then, as I said, this stress with my mother, because my mother did not accept that whatsoever; she and I fought like cats and dogs, literally, physically and mentally, because of my decision and my indifference. And so, I had had a really bad dream one night. And in the dream, I saw this SUV pull up into my driveway, and out of the SUV stepped my brother. Well, no sooner than he stepped out of the SUV, there were like hundreds of people who surrounded him, and they brutally beat him to death, in my driveway. In the dream, I recall running to my mother and to my father to try to awake them from their sleep but they would not awaken. I went to the doors and to the windows, beating, pounding upon them, and it was to no avail; I could not get them to open. I recall awaking from the dream, and my hand was still on the telephone's receiver, where I was evidently trying to dial 911 for help, because my brother was lying there, on my driveway in a pool of blood, and there was nothing I could do to save him. And so, the dream shook me up so bad, and it was so intense, that I could not go back to sleep. So, I was a nervous wreck, to say the least, and I called my godsister and she told me she was going to come over, and while I was waiting for her to come over, a very dear friend of mine at the time was Glenda McCorkle, and she was one of my only friends that I had that was quote/unquote very spiritual and in the church. She was saved, and she would always witness to me when she would come to get her hair done, and things like that, but she was not overbearing with it. And she called me that weekend before and asked me, could I do her hair, and I told her I was too busy. But really, the reason why I wouldn't do her hair was because in the lifestyle that I was living, I had acquired an addiction to marijuana, and the addiction was so much so to where I was—my marijuana habit probably ran me anywhere from three to five hundred dollars a week. I ran tabs with the supplier. And I was really angry that particular weekend, because I could not find my drug of choice. And, it was my party drug, it was what helped me to be me, you know, it was what helped me to say, to hell with what people thought about me, or, damn, so, to what they said. But, I was adamant that I had to have it. Well, I went for like three days without it, and this, the third day was the night that I had this dream. And so when Glenda called me that morning, I wanted to tell her desperately about the dream. And so, I told her, "Just come on down to my home and I'll cut and style your hair there at my home."

And so, upon me telling her the dream . . . I couldn't even get the dream out without weeping just profusely, because it was really, really horrifying. And Glenda did nothing but sit there the whole time, very quietly, a lot like you are now, and just listening very intently to every syllable that I was saying. And then, I asked her did she know what the dream represented, or what it meant? And she convinced me that the dream was not my brother in actuality, but that it was me, and that the people that was, that were kicking and beating him so profusely in the dream were not people, but actually, my inner demons. And that it was just a matter of time before something very, very violent or terrible would happen, and that God was asking me to allow Him to shield me from that.

And so, I didn't really know how to take everything that she was saying because, you know, I was spiritual, but not to the level in which she was. And all I asked her—she was going to noonday prayer that day, because it was Wednesday—I said, "Well, when you go to prayer, would you remember me and my family in prayer?" Well, she said that the Lord directed her to pray for me before she left. And in doing so, this overwhelming feeling came over me, and I accepted Christ, right there in my kitchen. Well, I went through with that, and Glenda was my mentor, and I was living life [. . .] through her eyes. I really didn't know what it was like to be quote/unquote saved from my sins, and I was trying to appease her and appease my family, because my mother, my mom was just happy that I was no longer wearing dresses. She was happy that people were no longer talking about her son, the one that wore the dresses, and that thought he was a woman.

So you were wearing suits, and pants again?

Yes. [. . .] The night that I had a dream, I was in my bedroom, in Victoria's Secrets. I didn't even have men's undergarments, let alone shoes, or clothing, nothing, nothing that pertained to a man, did I possess. I mean, my God, for the past, the five years prior to that, I ate, slept, and drank what it

Chaz in a suit donned to appease his mother. Courtesy of the narrator.

was like to be a woman. I was flown to Los Angeles, California, to be on a talk show called *The Other Side*, because there was a topic for this particular show, "Can a psychic help me to decide?" And the psychic was Patricia Michelle, and she was, at that time, known as a world-renowned psychic. And, one of the questions that I asked her was, if I would ever go through with the surgery, and after having the surgery, would I truly find happiness. And what happiness to me was at that time was to find a very good mate, a soul mate, and to have the quote/unquote natural life. You know, my idea was [. . .] to have the surgery, to go out and marry, if technology [. . .] would not have allowed us to have children, then to have been able to adopt, to join a church, to go to the PTA, and to have the beautiful home with the picket fence, and the little dog. That was my ideal life. Needless to say, that is no longer the subject matter. My ideal life now is just to be content, to be happy within the skin that I'm in. I've finally learned to embrace everything that makes me who I am. All of my indifferences, all of my attributes, all of my qualities, as well as my faults, and to realize that God has made no mistakes in making me, that his words said, I was fearfully and wonderfully made. Who am I to say anything different? But because of that, keeping that in retrospect to the way that society treats you because of your indifference, I'm at a level of maturity where I no longer am overly concerned about what people say or think about me, or my lifestyle, or my life choices, for that matter. I feel that the most important person in my life is me. If I'm not happy, if I'm not well, if I'm not content, then anything else is irrelevant. And then, once I've established that happiness, being content with who I am, and with where I am at, then I can appreciate others, and add to the quality of their lives.

And so, now you're at a point where you are fully embracing who you are, but you have decided to remain preop?

Exactly. And what has brought me to that decision more so than anything, was because I felt that once the doctors would have done the reassignment, meaning that, the physical reconstructing of my body, the only thing that they would not have been able to tamper with was my essence, who I am as a person, you know. Yes, Charles would have been no more, but "Chastity" has always been and always will be. "Chastity," I do believe was here before Charles was. And, the one thing that the surgery would not have changed was that very fact. And why should I put myself at the risk of losing my life on a surgeon's table to appease others? And would it truly have appeased them? Like I said, I had to become comfortable with the skin that I was in, and realizing and knowing that a physical change was not going to change who I was mentally. [. . .] It may soften the blow for you to say, "Well, shit, at least she looks like a woman now. She's got natural looking breasts, and she's got a vagina, and she has soft smooth skin, or long flowing hair." But does that truly constitute being a woman? Or does a penis and facial hair and a muscular build or physique truly constitute masculinity? And the only one that can decide that is yourself. And I had to learn to be content with whom God had birthed me to be, and he gives us free reign over our lives as far as the choices that we make, and how we govern ourselves, and enact upon our lives. So, I can be whomever I choose to be. I can put on the most elaborate ball gowns, the most coiffed coiffures, and be every bit of Chastity that I dare to be, but it doesn't change the fact of who I am to Him. Or the type of friend that I can be to others, or the son, or the child, even more so that I am to my parents.

So are you performing again as well?

I am. I just recently started back performing approximately three months ago, and I love it. Like I said, the reason why I'd gotten away from it was because of me going into the church and trying to live amongst the church's stereotypes of what a Christian should be, rather than seeking a personal relationship with the Savior, which is truly what Christianity is all about. And knowing that, His greatest commandment was that we love one another, but you can't love someone else until you first learn to love yourself. And being that I've embraced that, yes it's allowed me to embrace my effeminate nature. And the character that I'd most like to impersonate is Patti Labelle, and a lot of my family and friends, and quote fans, have all said that I favor her a great deal. A future goal of mine is to possibly one day land a job working at the La Cage [a female impersonation cabaret at the Riviera Hotel in Las Vegas], and I think that that would be a great honor, to be able to perform before Patti.

What is your favorite song of hers to perform?

My favorite song is "You Are My Friend," because the lyrics of the song says that "you are my friend / I never knew until then / that my friend / I see your love / and it helps me make it knowing that people like you care / the thought of you, helps me carry on / when I feel all hope is gone / I see the world with brand new eyes / because your love has made me realize / my future looks brighter to me / all because you are my friend." And, if I were to dedicate that to anyone, it would be to Christ, because Christ has truly shown me that, in spite of all the negativity in life, in spite of all the obstacles that I've had to face, and the challenges, is that, of everything that has come and gone in my life, He's the only thing that has remained constant and consistent. I can depend on Him like I can depend on the air that I breathe, on my next breath. He is the only one that's never left me, never forsook me, never judged me.

Chastity performing "You Are My Friend." Courtesy of the narrator.

Wow, that was a powerful story. So, at this point, you feel free?

Very much free. Oprah had a talent show called, "Pop Star, Pop Idol," and the winner of that was Lechelle Griffith, and she wrote a song called "I'm Free." And, I do that number in some of my shows as well, because it's a personal testament for me. And, when I'm lip-synching, because I do all lip synch, when I'm lip-synching that song, it's like I'm touching into my spirit, and making that connection helps me to connect with my audience, and all the people. I can truly understand. It's almost like it was Lechelle, or whoever penned that song, were hiding in my dreams, read my thoughts, you know. Or living my life through a mirrored image.

You've touched on this a little bit. What role does religion, church, play in your life now?

It plays a very dominant role because I feel that I can do nothing unless God enables me to do so. The next breath that I take is all due to Him. He is my source.

And so you still sing in the choir . . . ?

I still sing in the choir. I go to church when it is conducive for me to do so. Being that I've started back entertaining, a lot of times I'm in Charlotte or out of town on the weekends, so it's not conducive for me to attend church every Sunday as I used to. I don't attend Bible study any longer, because of my work schedule, but my relationship with Christ is exactly that: it is mine. It is very intimate, and it is one that He and I understand.

So, since you've been back entertaining, do you go in drag again to church, or . . . ?

No, because they are two separate lifestyles for me. Chastity is quote/unquote almost like an alter ego. She is very much a part of me, but she is someone whom I choose not to share with the entire world. Because I have no points to prove, you understand? Chastity is, for a lack of better terms, like my recreation. She gratifies me as far as my artistic sense. Chastity has charisma, she has spunk, and Chastity does not go to church. Chastity believes in God, she loves the Lord, but that's about the extent of Chastity.

But, Charles goes to church?

Charles goes to church. Charles loves the Lord as well. Charles is very tolerant. [. . .] And when I say tolerant, meaning, I tolerate anyone's beliefs, whether they be good or bad, right or wrong. It's simply to acknowledge that you have a belief in something, you understand. And I value that. Now, it may not suit or fit me, but I like to think that I'm able to distinguish and to separate myself from my needs, my beliefs, and your own, you understand. Because what struck me may not work for you, but who am I to judge you for that?

So when you go to church you wear a suit?

Yes.

What about your face?

My face? I wear a little bit of enhancement today because I just chose to, but normally I don't. I do enhance my brows, and I keep my hair done in a coiffed way, because I'm a stylist. It's a direct reflection of my work.

How do you account for church people accepting gay people as long as they, you know, are not out about it?

That it's just a key, as you mentioned in our earlier conversation. I think as far as the church, you've got more that are at a rate of tolerance, than acceptance. And, that is a long time coming. It's still not where it should be, and not where it's going, but so many people I feel are homophobic, or have issues with the gay lifestyle, because they have a fear of that which they don't understand. Fear begets anger.

Is there a place in the church for gay people to sort of be themselves? Is the choir the only place?

Until the church comes up, and when I say, when they come up, until the church takes on the true mind of Christ, and let go of their doctrines, let go of their protocol, let go of their own insecurities and mentalities, until they take on the mind of Christ, and follow the commands of God that the greatest command of all was that you love thy neighbors as you love thyself, until then, no. I don't see there being other avenues. I mean, who's gonna want someone who is openly gay watching their heterosexual children? You know, gay people are always stigmatized, and labeled as being pedophiles, and child molesters, or dealing with pornography, or being immoral, when that's really not true. You know, you've got a lot of these people who do these horrible things to children, its not because they're gay. Yes, they may sleep with someone of the same sex, but it's bigger than that. There are larger demons that they're fighting, facing. People need to be able to see the truth for what it is.

You were saying earlier that when you were singing in the choir as a child something about going to radar because it was being interpreted as being the spirit, but it was actually about being gay; does that happen now, where there's certain codes or something that, you know, one group of people are reading it one way, but people in the know are reading it another?

Oh yes. We say all the time, well she's just a big ole sissy, referring to a guy that's in the choir, or possibly the director, or you know, someone who's very flamboyant as far as the choir's movements, because in black choirs a lot of times there's a lot of emotion in the song, not just in the way that the song is sung, but in the way that you move to the song. Because from the beginning

Chaz "giving face." Courtesy of the narrator.

of time, you know, African Americans, Africans have evolved, or incorporated music with spirituality and dance. Also, all those play major roles in worship. So yes, even now when I'm observing some youth choirs, you can see the traits, especially with some little boys. [. . .] Sometimes I'm observing youth choirs, you can see the little boy that's got the tambourine. He's just going on, and I mean, very much on time with the beating, and just more into it than the other kids, that a lot of the times it's because of his artistic nature, and through time, you'll be able to see that I was right.

There again, hitting on being raised in the church, you know, a lot of quote/unquote men who are in the church, especially if you're active like in the choir or in the music ministry of the church, you find a lot of homosexuals in the church. And, there, too, I believe this because they are allowed to be expressive, you know, because I've found that gay people are very articulate; they're artistic, and especially in the black church, gospel music is so full of energy and so full of spirit, that it's easy to get caught up, so to speak, in the spirit and, you know, it's acceptable, until you start crossing the lines. Crossing the lines being, openly gay, in a quote/unquote heterosexual church, you know, and flaunting your sexuality, or the fact that you like to sleep with men. Because according to men's standards and the way that the Bible is versed, homosexuality is known to God as an abomination, you know, and so that is very much frowned upon. And when you are very flamboyant, when you are very showy with your mannerisms and with your beliefs in church, that's when you begin to cross that line.

Do you think that the church is a place for folks to meet other people?

As far as gay men, like joining the church to hook up, or . . . I do know that it does go on. I'm not in a position as to whether I could make a values statement as to whether it's good or bad or right or wrong. I know I've never found anyone. And I've not often considered myself to be the most attractive man, but I'm certainly not the least either, and for whatever that's worth, I've not been able to have an encounter such as that. But, I just feel like people are people, and wherever you meet someone, you know, I would love to meet someone in the church. Hopefully, they would be sincere, being that they were there, you know, and that, and that their lives are based upon morals and principles, you know. But, it's really hard to say.

Do you have a partner?

No.

Are you looking for one?

I'm looking for a soul mate, as I was when I went on the talk show. But they are very few and far between. And I feel a lot of it is attributed because of my surroundings. A lot of people, especially really close friends, tell me well,

"Chaz, if you're ever going to find anyone, you're not going to find them here." I'm just ignorant enough to believe that, you know, nothing happens by chance. I'm not just still here for no reason. So, I don't know if the love of my life is abroad, or if they are right up underneath my nose, but I do feel that God will show me when He feels it's time. Now, I don't have the patience of Job, but I try to be content and continue to wait it out, because as the adage says, "good things come to those who wait," and I'm still waiting for mine.

What are you looking for?

I'm looking for someone who has compassion, someone who is sensitive to my needs as well as their own, someone who is not afraid to try new and different things, and to march to the beat of their own drum, not always overly concerned about what other people are going to think, or say. Someone whom, when I've had a bad day at work I can come home and they can almost just look in my eyes and know the whole story. Or someone whom, very appreciative of the things I do for them, such as when I cook their favorite meal, or run their bath, or sing their favorite song to them at night before they retire, or the way that I choose to arrange his cabinets, you know, as far as his clothing and things like that. You know, someone who is a "just because" person. You know, I love you just because, or I did this just because.

Do you feel a sense of community among other black gay men?

I do. It's not very strong here because gay, especially black gay men, a lot of the times can be very facetious, very catty, kinda like the analogy to the crabs in the barrel. You know, you have to be able to pick and choose your friends just as well as you pick and choose your fights, so to speak. Everyone does not have your best interests at heart, and a lot of times, their motives are questionable, as far as why they are befriending you, and what is it that you expect to get out of the relationships. Are you in it totally for this gratification of befriending someone? Or are your motives otherwise, you know? And a lot of times I feel that that is why [. . .] I kinda stay to myself because I don't like cliques. I like to march to the beat of my own drum, so to speak, and I don't appreciate conformity, having to conform to everyone's wishes. I mean, of course, in any civilized race, you gotta have structure, and a way to go about doing things, but with that all in stride, I still have my own unique individual self, and march to the beat of my own drum. And to find people who can appreciate that, and respect that, is far and in between.

Do you find them among your co-performers? Or is it worse?

As far as I can see, with my co-performers, it is about the same way. You got a lot that hold you in high esteem and high regard that look up to you.

I'm considered somewhat a "lady" as opposed to, a "get it" girl. A "get it" girl is like, a club 'ho, you know, somebody that, they go to the club looking for dates and are very promiscuous. You know, they dress very provocatively. [. . .] These girls are a different level; this is slutty. Like the girls that you see working the streets, you know. I'm not perceived that way. I'm perceived more so as a lady, like a southern lady, you know, very genteel, very, very, very elegant, because that's the way I carry myself. Yeah, so I can wear, a, Patti Labelle's known for showing her legs and wearing a cleavage, but she's still one of the most sought after in the highly respected, highly regarded, you know, entertainers in the world, very much respected, and known by millions of people. Even people who possibly never buy her music know who she is and what she stands for.

So is there a hierarchy?

There is. And, I don't necessarily see myself as being better than, or at least I don't attempt to be, or to make other people feel less than, should I say, but I do try to live my life to where people will think well of me and respect me, as I want to be respected—that they would know that they couldn't just come up to me any kind of way, and approach me with just any kind of conversation, or with any type of situation that would cause me embarrassment, or cause me to feel belittled, or to feel, in any way, inadequate.

What has been the impact of HIV/AIDS on your life?

The impact has been that I had an uncle that died from AIDS back in '93? A lot of my family said I look like him, and he was a dear, dear, sweet man, precious, and he loved the Lord. And my Uncle Norman, he was very, very, very spiritual but very intellectual too. He was. I mean, he was like a walking computer. He could retain, read and retain things, and quote routes and everything. I mean, he was just a phenomenal man. Phenomenal.

And of course, being in the entertainment industry, I've lost a lot of quote entertainers, and people whom I've befriended that I've started out with that are no longer here because of this dreaded disease. And I feel it's just like anything else in life. You know, it's happened, and it's happened for a reason, and it's for reasons that are, in which, beyond my control. The only way that I can control it is to take care of myself, and to be responsible and aware of the people that coexist with me, or that I befriend, or that I choose to date, to know their status and to know what their views are on it. Because you've got a lot of people, it's like Russian roulette, you know; they know the risk, they know the game, and they still take those chances, meaning, you know, unprotected sex, or being very promiscuous.

Do you feel it's more of a problem here in the South?

Only because of these—I attribute a lot of it to, quote/unquote the down low syndrome. You got a lot of people that want to do things, but they don't want anyone else to know about it. I really believe that that has a lot to do with why I've not found a mate as well, because people couldn't just look at me and know my orientation, you understand, there's nothing that I'm trying to hide from you, which I perpetrate. And so, maybe they feel that they would be, seem guilty by association, you know. But, yeah, I really do believe it is a problem here.

What are your best memories of growing up in the South?

My grandmother. My grandmother was one of the most phenomenal women that God has ever blessed His earth with, and that is true in my opinion. Both of them, well, I also had a godmother, who was like a grandmother. I called her grandma. Those three women established a foundation and a basis of my life in which I will never forget. They taught me what it was like to love myself, because they loved me unconditionally. They taught me what it was about to be good to people and to be kind to people. It costs nothing to be kind, considerate, and compassionate to people, and toward what they're going through. How to fend for myself, to keep a clean house, and keep a good meal on the table, and just about being good people, and [. . .] taking pride in the simple things of life, things that so many people, for whatever reasons, take for granted, like family, and fellowship with friends, and with, with your higher power.

What are your worst memories of growing up in the South?

My worst memories are the stigmatisms and stereotypes of being labeled faggot, sissy, punk, and the hurt that it caused me throughout my life. Being told that you can't do something because of your orientation, or because of the color of your skin. Being told how far you are allowed to go in life. Only God charts out my destiny; only God holds my future. So therefore, only God can judge me.

How would you describe the influence that your southern upbringing has had on your character, the quality of your life?

It has taught me compassion. It has made me truly appreciate the sacrifices that were made on my behalf. It has made me less likely to take things for granted, or people. And it has made me very appreciative of growing up. One thing that is a positive about growing up in a small town is that if the people truly know you, and truly care about you, they truly love you. And I feel that that is something that you don't encounter or interact with in the city. Because in the city, you're a million faces, going a million places, you know, everybody's got their own motives, their own, you know, itinerary, so to speak, you know, their own life to live, and you are just the, really a figment in a lot of them's imaginations, you know, you don't even really exist. You know some of them are sitting right beside you in the subway, or on the airplane, or wherever. Or if you are in a busy metropolitan area, like a mall or whatever, or even if you are in church, you're just a number, or a face. But in the South, people are more connected, and they take time to get to know you.

How do you feel about life choices you've made in light of being gay?

I feel that I've been very cautious as far as the places I would go, the people I would befriend, and the things that I would do or say, because of being gay and living in the South. You have to be able to live with yourself. There was this saying, "To thine own self be true," you know. You have to be true to yourself and you have to be able [. . .] to sleep at night. You know, I have to have a good conscience about myself, about the way that I've treated others, and about the impact that I leave on someone's life. I want to know that I've done nothing to harm you, physically, mentally, or otherwise, that I've added to the quality of your life, more so than taken from it. And hopefully from those life choices, that I've been able to let someone know that being gay is not all bad, that they're just people too, that being gay possibly is their choice, maybe it's their birthright, maybe it was just a cruel joke played on them by their higher power, I don't know. But they're still people. If you cut them, they bleed. If you suffocate them, they won't breathe. If you don't feed them, they'll die of starvation. If you allow them to live, they'll flourish, just like you.

Is there anything you would like to add?

I'd just like to thank you for considering me for the interview. I've always had a lot of things in my mind to say, about the way that my life has went, and the way it's going, or the things that have transpired in my life, but I never had a format, or a genre, in order to express that. And I thank God that He is established within you the desire, the will, the determination, to make this happen. I wish you the best of luck in all your endeavors, definitely, most definitely, with this book, and that, I pray that this book is able to change lives. Every life [. . .] every hand that picks it up, that that life be transformed, that that mind be renewed.

· · · · · · · ·

"R. DIONEAUX"

I was introduced to R. Dioneaux (a pseudonym that he went to great lengths to devise) through a mutual friend in Washington, D.C. He holds a Ph.D. in African American history and taught for several years before going on disability. His knowledge of African American history informs his outlook on life, especially regarding racism, classism, homophobia, regionalism, and transphobia. He also is familiar with several languages—Latin, French, and Spanish among them—as his narrative attests.

R. Dioneaux did not disclose his disability to me, but makes veiled references to it in his narrative. What he does discuss, however, is his emerging feelings of being transgender and the difficulty of being on "a fellowship from the government" (his euphemism for receiving government aid) while working through this gender transformation. Rather than wallow in self-pity, R. Dioneaux sees each challenge as an opportunity to learn and to grow.

R. Dioneaux speaks very rapidly and sometimes in a free associative manner that makes it difficult to follow him. But it's worth the effort, as his wit and political commentary on many topics is biting and insightful. The evening of the interview, he seemed to be in rare form. The interview took place on August 17, 2005, at his home in Tampa, Florida.

I was born in the panhandle of Florida in 1963.

And how would you describe your childhood?

I'm still trying to figure that out. When you have a mother that is the daughter of an AME minister, I think that says it all. A very conservative, working-class neighborhood. Youngest of four. [. . .] My father taught me that no matter if you live in a box, make that box look so elegant that some-one would want to live there. My mother taught me the universe is mine as much as everybody else's. And so, with all the minutiae of religion and everything else that goes on with the African American community, some-how I managed to wind up being me.

Did you have chores?

Who didn't? [. . .] I'm a child of the South. Yes. I mean I'm like, "Who didn't?" I mean, Saturday morning was, "You will mow the lawn. You will do this. You will do that." I can't imagine life without a regimen. Even during the week, there was a regimen. I guess I can't almost even imagine the question. I guess I should ask, "Who didn't have chores?" Of course. In the whole neighborhood, you could hear the buzz of the lawnmowers and the clipping of the hedges. There was no such thing as a lawn service. It was called "Get up!" And if he was in a good mood, my father would say, "And do the next-door neighbor or do Miss Sadie's down the street." So that was just the thing to do. There was no playtime until that was done.

And what was your neighborhood like?

It was and still is an African American neighborhood. But it had an inter-esting mixture of people in the African Diaspora. We had folk from the

Caribbean. We had a couple of people from Africa, but most of the folk were from the South. Some from the North. Some were in the military. It was not unusual to see someone with an Asian wife. That was not uncommon. It was not uncommon to have a Haitian neighbor three streets away. It was not unusual to see somebody from the Gullah Islands. Some people call it "Geechee," but I prefer the formal term "Gullah." It wasn't unusual to have an Afro-Cubana, you know, down the street. It was not unusual at all to have a Jamaican and somebody from Barbados, somebody from Trinidad, someone from Dominica, the Cayman Islands, Nevis Island. I had nutmeg from Grenada. I mean from somebody from Grenada. You name it, it was there.

What did your parents do for work?

My father was a laborer and my mother was a teacher assistant.

Besides your parents, were there any other adults that played a significant role in your upbringing?

In an African American community, that's a given. I mean as someone who attended church—something I repudiate to this day—but of course anyone who was in your church was part of the neighborhood. And all of the upper-echelon people were a part of the community. It really was the Miss Sadie down the street [who] knew your business. It still was the proverbial Miss Sadie [who] knew what you were doing before you thought about doing it. That was always the case. It was [. . .] the light rule. Not traffic light, but it was the streetlight rule. When the streetlights were on, you were in the house. That was a given. And if it was the summer months, the lights would not come on because they were operated by the sun. Then you had longer to play. But when the lights were on, you were inside the house or you were on your way or Miss Sadie saw who it was with the light and said, "You're not home yet." That was, you know, we didn't need a curfew. We did the streetlight rule. You may not have heard of that before, but if you haven't heard about it, trust me. When the streetlight came on, you were in the house.

And that was understood?

Oh! And adhered to, strictly. [Chuckle] Very strictly understood and adhered to.

Do you remember where you went to elementary, middle, and high school?

Interesting question because of my age. I'm early forties. There was still the Mecklenburg case in '71. And I say that because my first year of school was '69. So the first two years, I had gone to a segregated school. I'm old enough to remember segregation. And then in third grade, it was, "Oh, we're going to this white school." And it was a major culture shock. For the white kids as well as the black. I mean it was the first time I really saw poor white kids. I never thought white people were poor. I didn't know. It was one street, and if I name it, everybody would know it, so I'm not going to. There was one street that looked like a row of shanty houses, and I knew that this was where the cows lived. And I saw somebody coming out of it and I'm thinking they're milking the cows. No, somebody lived there. And it was a bus in front of us and this woman, this girl goes in. I remember her name was Ruth. And she would get on the bus with the same dress on *every single day*. And, of course, the smell of the cows after they had their hay. And trust me, we knew they ate. We saw the fruits of their eating on the ground and we smelled it on the wind. And as punishment, the bus driver made us roll the windows down if we were bad. [Laughter]

I also knew that there were poor whites when we would go to Busch Gardens. That's when, you know, at the end of the year teachers would get burnt out and they were like, "field trip, field trip. We need to learn about animals." No, the truth was . . . and now that I'm on the other side of the podium I understood what happened. It was like, "films and we'll go to Busch Gardens." And that's when it was like one dollar or two dollars to go. Everybody wanted to go on the brewery tour. At that time, Busch Gardens actually had a brewery. I didn't realize why the adults were so eager to go there until I saw at the end how many red-faced folk was sitting there, sampling the goods. And the other reason was that they couldn't get rid of us, so we would go.

What was really heartbreaking for me was hearing those kids say, "I would like to go with the rest of you but we can't afford it." You know, being African American in the South, you've just been told, "You're poor. You're this." I didn't realize how quote rich unquote I had it. I mean no, I did not come from J. Paul Getty background. No, my last name was not Johnson as in publishing. No, my last name was not King, as in Martin Luther King Jr. But I had three square meals a day. And you know sometimes you never know what you don't have until you see it in somebody else's home. But I didn't miss most of that. But I heard this kid say, and 'cause most of the kids are going out and for some reason I was tagging along in back and I heard him say, "I can't afford this." And the teacher said, "Just bring the permission slip and we'll take care of it." And so at that time I learned a lot about class consciousness and that, even then, no matter how poor you were, just as in antebellum—and I do mean antebellum days—no matter how poor you were, even in the 16- or the 1700s, after the U.S. became the U.S., you would hear this argument, "But you're white and we'll take care of you." And that white skin will help you through. No matter if you don't own land, you can't vote, you can't do this, but we'll take care of you. And I wonder aloud if that was an African American kid, (a) would that kid have done that? You know, would have told the teacher that? Or (b) what would have happened? I'm sure there were kids that couldn't do it, but somehow somebody scraped up the money and said, "I'll be dang if I'm gonna tell."

And this was school in the early days of integration, so it was parents open the door to the kids and making sure, "You're going to be dressed to the nines. You're going to have this. You're going to do that. You're going to prove you're just as good as" and this, this, and that. I mean there was this sense of, you know, "You're not going to let these folks do this." And there was the culture shock in the lunchroom where there're certain foods and we were like, "unh, unh, unh." They capitulated and actually gave us chocolate milk. That was revolutionary. They actually had to cook some things because we didn't know the word "rare" meant something that you didn't get often. But the hamburgers were rare! And we went back and said—I was just one of those types. I would walk back to the lunchroom with the plate and say, in a nice way like, "What is this?" And they said, "Is it not warm enough?" I said, "It's not cooked enough." And then everybody else followed suit. And I didn't realize then how much of a rebel I was then. "This isn't cooked. It's still got blood in it." And then, you know, eventually they learned, and we gave a little and this and that, and so it took 'em about two years. So third, fourth, and fifth grade, I went to a white elementary school.

Then the school I'd gone to the first two years became what is called sixth-grade center. And what they did in the South was that they transferred or transformed all the neighborhood schools into either sixth-grade centers or maybe junior high schools, at best. And so the sixth-grade center was in my neighborhood, so that was the only other year in which I had a neighborhood school experience. But you know, it's interesting you mention that. It brought back some interesting memories. I look at the place now and I'm going, "It wasn't all that." But at the time it was state of the art. I mean, you saw a difference in supplies, this and that, and you saw new books. I'm going, "What is this?" A desk and the idea of changing classes. You have your tray. You move your stuff around. And I mean a TV in every room. Color TV, *at that*. Anyway. You know, "What is this?" And it was interesting.

But I did well. And there was still a sense, even then, of African American students couldn't possibly do well. And I was one of those anomalies. [They would ask] "You know how to do that?" And I'm like, "Yeah." "How?" Like, "Well, it's called studying." It's not that difficult a concept. Many of the teachers already had an expectation that African American students in general could not do well. They were not used to them, particularly the African American males, they were not used to at all. The only ones they were used to were the ones they saw on TV and the six o'clock news. And so they realized that these little puppies were going to grow up to those dogs that we learned to hate. That's what they saw. And it was obvious. Fortunately, there were a few African American teachers that were transferred to the schools to try to make integration go down a little more smoothly. But it took a while.

What role did religion play in your upbringing?

I cannot imagine any African American home where religion doesn't play a role—whether you've gone to church or not. As my role as an historian, and I always tell people, "If you really want to understand African American culture, you have to see the workings—the good, the bad, and the ugly—of the black church." And notice I use the word "black" as a political construct as opposed to an ethnic designation. And so I believe that the black church is paramount in the African American community. I mean, you cannot escape it. I wish we could! [Laughter] My uncle said, and I concur, that the only legitimate theater in the African American community is the black church. And I think we're full of it, and it sometimes reminds me of a diaper that needs changing. And often. And for the very same reason.

Did you enjoy church as a child?

It was theatrical. It was interesting. I mean, I loved the cap and gown then. I love the cap and gown now. I loved of all the gowns in town, even then. I enjoyed the pageantry. It was another socialization. It was another social environment. And there were some good memories of it. But even then, I questioned some of it. I mean there was the pews where certain families were supposed to sit. There was the rule of the first lady getting to wear the largest hat, except where Women's Day, where the guest speaker, you know, gets to wear the largest hat. And then of course Easter Sunday, where all bets are off. It would become just *laisson faire* and it's, you know, it's on. And of course there's what you call your "silk stocking" churches where certain families, certain leading black families would go to *those* churches. And the more quote "proper" you become, the less primitive you become. So you go from primitive whatever to Primitive Baptist, and you drop the "Primitive." Then it's Baptist. And then there's AME. And then it was AME and CME, which now means Christian, but originally it meant *Colored* Methodist Episcopal Church. Because the colored folk went to that church and the Africans Diaspora folk went to AME. We've done a number on ourselves. And then you had certain African American churches where they'd put a comb with thin toothes, if you couldn't get your hair through it, you couldn't go to the church. There were some churches which had stained glass in the windows. If you were darker than the stained glass, you could not enter that church. So the churches themselves acted as a caste system within the community.

How many churches were in your community? Black churches.

Well, that depended on who you ask. Well they all were gonna be black 'cause it's in the community. But that depended on who you asked. How many churches? How many churches? How many institutions or how many break-offs? I mean because when I was there, it was only about maybe two or three. Now, depending on what's happening in someone's home on a given Wednesday, I honestly can say I don't know. I really don't know because there's always someone meeting in somebody's auditorium or somebody's schoolhouses. When I say "schoolhouses," I mean school auditorium. I honestly don't know.

Church is not an institution which I particularly enjoy. I eschew the black church. I do my best to divest myself from any affiliation with any religion whatsoever. It's my credo that there is no monopoly on stupidity in any religion. And there's no monopoly of wisdom. Because I have found that a careful survey of history will reveal that when someone's rights are taken away; when someone is subjugated and when genocide occurs; when someone's land is taken away; when people are hurt, abused, wounded; when acquisition of land is taken, the first thing you will hear is "in the name of God" or "God told me I could do it." And I cannot tell you how many times whatever you want to call that divine thing in the sky or wherever, that has always been the rationale behind doing it. And I learned a long time ago that, for my well-being, to eschew religion. Now, that is not to say I do not have my own providential moral compass, but it is mine. It belongs to me. If I want to be entertained, I might enter a church. But I haven't found that notion to be so entertained in that manner, so I don't do it.

Why do you think there's so many black gay men in the church, especially in the choir?

That's a question I would love to have to ask them because I will not tolerate being castigated and then asked to sing a solo. I can't. I can't be castigated and then say, "Oh please. I'll usher." I cannot do that. I think that there's a very schizophrenic relationship. There's a nod, nod, wink, wink, as if to say, "Now you know what I am but I'm really working on it and give me one more week. I'm really working on it." And it's almost a way of atonement, like "I know that you don't like what I'm doing but listen to me sing. I know you don't like what I'm doing but I'm tithing. I know you don't like what I'm doing but if I can . . . give me just a little more time and I'll help you out. Give me just a little more time and I promise I'll marry Miss So-and-So down the street. Give me just a little more time." And I think it's a very unhealthy game. It's almost like bribery. "You let me in. You let me be a part of the community and I will grant you this service." And I come from a different cloth. I say, "If you don't like my packaging but want my gifts, you should be granted neither." So, no tango idea. I have no idea. I think it's foolish. In fact, I would say the congruous question, "What would happen if every gay, lesbian, transsexual, or bisexual person did not show up in church?" And that includes the minister. And they'd find out that, you know, the lights turned off and the tithing and the building fund and all that didn't reach the goal. I wonder what would happen then. So to me there's a lot of self-hatred. I mean there's this sense of, again, "I feel guilty about what I'm doing." It's very Catholic, if you will. "I'm going to do it and then I'm going to ask for mercy. And then I'm going to read these ten verses." And instead of reading ten verses and rubbing the rosary . . . And we're assuming there's no such thing as black Catholics, right? Like St. Augustine and all the black popes in antiquity. Beyond that, of course, I do believe there's a sense of atonement. And you said "black men." I assume also lesbians, also. Same thing. And also there's no alternative. I mean MCC. Metropolitan Community Church is not exactly welcoming with open arms, either. Because the greater gay community's just as racist as the general African American community is homophobic. So you're in a very tenuous zone there.

When did you first realize you had a same-sex attraction, and what was your reaction to that realization?

That's like asking, "How do you know that which you know you don't know how you know but you know that you know what you know but you don't know how?" Hmmmph. Some would say, "Since conception." And see I'm still going through a process. Because that use of the word "gay" . . . Right now I have to ask myself the next question, "Well am I transgender or not?" So it's even another question. So that's a closet within a closet within a closet within a closet. And so, ooh! Instinctively, you know that there's something you're not supposed to say or think about, or articulate. And I would say probably since four or five. There's always that intangible, for whatever reason. And I could always blame it on a lot of things. "You know you were a very bright student." And of course African American men aren't supposed to be bright, so that was the reason. Or "You didn't do sports." Well, I did sports. "Well, you didn't do . . ." well, I did that. "Well, you were in a gifted class." Well, I did that. And so each rung I always had an excuse, but there's always that "it" factor.

Did you discuss these feelings with anyone?

Not particularly. I mean, I was always the neighborhood sissy, and thank goodness I learned how to fight early because I did it often. I mean, the only thing I had going for me was that I was fairly smart. I can't tell you the times the dean would say, "We know we could suspend you for this but you're so bright." [Laughter] When you're the only African American male in the geometry class in ninth grade, you can afford a few fights on campus. And that was the only thing really, "But you're so bright." I still remember one dean, if I look back, I would swear she was a lesbian, trying to give me life lessons. And you know I had a fight on the bus again and I was swinging somebody else's crutch and somebody whistled at me as I walked. Some things never change. And I took this crutch and I said, "You wanna whistle?" And I started swinging it all over the bus and folks were ducking. I was sitting on the bus and—they didn't send the dean of boys, interestingly enough— they sent her. Miss [last name]. And they sent her on the bus . . . and you're going to have to scratch her name out. "Miss F.," okay? She got on the bus and she's gonna speak to me. And the bus driver had known me for a long, long, long time. So they had deliberated my fate and said, "Okay, we'll write you a pass to class." YES! An excused pass to class, okay? And she said, "You know what, instead of getting in fights, you're very bright. What you need to do is show them how bright you are such that, instead of fighting, set the curve. And they'll beg you to help them with their homework." It worked! I made them beg. I made them pay. You didn't have to tell me about tutoring. I learned divide economics. My services, my goods. And I have this, you know, this talent. And I had this commodity and I knew how to package it. "You need me to pass. Call me a name, you flunk. Piss me off, I'll raise the score." And it wasn't good enough just to get a hundred. I had to get the extra credit points. So I would set the curve at a hundred and five. And I would look at them and I'd say, "Now suffer. Call me faggot now. Please, call me sissy now. Come on! Oh, please do." And that's what I mean. "Call me that. I'm gonna take home an A." So folks found out it was better to be my friend and get a C. Folks used to *beg* to sit by me during exam time. Though they thought they could cheat so I had a deal with one teacher. I said, "I'm going to write all the wrong answers to the problems and then I'm going to correct the answers," until folks were nice. And then in high school it was the same thing. I can- not tell you how many folk I helped through high school. All roads to a diploma led through me. And this is not grandiose. I am serious. Those folk would be, "Could you help me with this term paper?" And it's so sad. Now it's the second generation of them coming in and asking me, "Can you help my boy with his term paper?" I say, "Boy, some things never change." So they learned. It was so much fun to do that. And she [the dean] taught me. She said, "Use your brains." She said, "It's easy to fight, but find 'em another way." I remember that. She said, "Eventually, somebody's gonna throw you out of school. And you're too talented for that, so do this for us." So that's what happened. That's how I got revenge.

When did you first act on these feelings?

There's two answers to that. One was involuntary. And that also happened to be church related. Let's just say it was another "Catholic" experience. So we will rephrase the question and say, "When was the first *voluntary* experience?" I was probably about fifteen, sixteen. There were some precocious teenagers at my high school. We'll just leave it at that.

And these were sort of your experimenting?

Oh well, that's what you call it? Yeah. That's a good word for it.

And after these encounters, did you talk about what had happened?

No, we *knew* what happened. There was no need for discussion. I mean there was no colloquium. I mean there was no need. There was no need at all.

Were there other people in your community that the community saw as gay? And how did they treat those people?

That's interesting because the African American community does not hate gay people. We hate those who we think are gay. We don't ostracize gay folk. We never have. And if they're rich enough, we'll make excuses for them. And if they have children, we'll make excuses for them. The only reason you have this very racist, sexist notion of the down low brother—and I will explain that—is because of HIV. In fact, we invented—well, it's not invented—it's called a "closeted person." That's been going on since, hmmm, way back when. But we all but told folk, "Be in the closet. We don't care what you do, just get married, have some children, adopt if necessary." It sounds like we're talking about a Supreme Court justice nominee. But we invented that. And I will state this. I always hear Oprah say, "Well, why not be honest?" Well, [what] incentive is there to be honest? There *is* no incentive of being honest. Zero.

I love to tell this. First of all, and let's go back. It's racist because we assume only African American men are down low brothers. That they're the only ones that are cheating on women with other men. That's racist and stupid. Obviously, it can't be just black men with all the white men who want big black dick. Obviously, THAT'S NOT THE CASE! They don't want to see you on Sunday or what else through the week, but on Saturday you are the latest rage. You are IT! You are the IT girl or the IT boy, or whatever. But it's also sexist because we assume that women do not marry to hide their sexual identity. And as far as the issue of HIV, I cannot tell you how many sisters have told brothers, "Why you wearing a condom? You must be a punk." Take ownership. You want to talk about why I can't trust this man? My worldview is assume everybody's HIV-positive and conduct yourself accordingly. Conduct yourself accordingly. I mean, nobody's telling you not to use condoms. "Well, he doesn't act as this way." Well, why would he? Because I would then have said, you're going to ostracize this person if they do this or that, so they do exactly as you say. "Well we don't mind you being gay, just don't be the flaming guy." So you give them what they want. And you're mad about it? I mean you're the lie that the liar produced. Don't get mad that the person evolved to the lie that you told them to produce. If you don't want a dog, don't raise a puppy. You want the truth, then you start the truth at the beginning. So you know this idea of the down low brothers causing AIDS. No. No one told you to spread your legs and have unprotected sex. Nobody made you do that. Unless in a case of rape, nobody made you do that. Nobody. And sisters need to take ownership. I would love to speak to them. In fact, I have. I said, "Why have so many of you told brothers who were willing to be responsible . . . heterosexual brothers and told them, 'If you use a condom that's proof that you're a punk'?" And a few of the brother that I know said, "Well, you know I can go somewhere else." Number one, I can't afford a child now. Number two, I don't know what you have. And number three, maybe I'll just get some baby oil and call it a day. And they have said that. Where are those comments on *Oprah*? Where's that? Where is that written? I don't hear that. Where is the part about, "Well, I'll make a deal with you. I'll be honest about who I am if you don't fire me the next year from that HBCU [for] not being married in my thirties." You can't have it both ways. And the African American community is going to have to decide, "Do we really want to be honest about these issues or not?" And right now, while we're being academically dishonest about this issue, a lot of people are dying. And that's the tragedy, you know. If lying means death . . . You know, ACT-UP says, "silence means, equals death." I think lying equals death for the African American community. And we have been involved with this vicious, understood lie among each other and it's time to start telling the truth. And if we're going to hate quote faggots, then don't be surprised if, by social evolution, that these faggots are going to mimic what you say should be a successful brother. I don't understand why that would not be the case. I really can't understand that. I mean I would love to ask them, "What do you expect?" This is what you want. This is what you're saying is acceptable. The person's giving you what you claim you want, and you're upset about it. And then you don't take responsibility for your own bodies and then you blame the other party. I have a problem with that. I have a major 'tude about that. Again, nobody told you gay your legs. And I'm saying wide-open unprotected sex. Nobody. And that's what men, women, dogs, cats, rats, I'm like, as far as I'm concerned, every time I enter a sexual relationship, that is potentially Russian roulette if I'm unprotected. Being protected is not 100 percent, but I know I have 0 percent chance if I don't use protection. Sorry. And I think it's a *sin* for the black church not to have an AIDS ministry since the cases of AIDS are so high in our community. It is a sin. Everybody wanna talk about Christ and deities and all that. But I happen to have read that book—that sixty-six volume book a few times. Yes, I actually read it. It just doesn't sit on a desk and collect dust and have everybody's birth certificates in it. I actually read it. A few times. And I remember that deity said, "Feed my sheep. If you love me, feed my sheep. Take care of my sheep." It also said in Matthew 25:40, "Whatsoever you do to the least of these, you do unto Me." So that person that's singing in the choir that might have purple spots on in two years or three years later, is still a part of—not *a parti*—the African American community. And we are going to have to be very honest. I mean we can't even call it AIDS. We call it "the ninja." Oh yeah, usually the term for AIDS, "the ninja." Or they'll say, "Oooh, he's siiiick. He's siiiiiiiick." And you can tell by the voice inflection, like you know what it is. I mean I'm almost waiting for somebody to say, "He has R-O-L-A-I-D-S." I'm *waiting* for that to come out, but I mean that is what we have here. A lot of dishonesty.

Is there any particular theory about homosexuality that you subscribe to?

I call it the "apple pie, peach pie," and I'll explain that. I believe that there's orientation. And I believe that every person knows their orientation. I believe that, in a given world, that everybody will gravitate toward—if they like pie—that apple pie is pretty, or peach pie, or both if that's what one so chooses. I believe that in this world we have been told that the only pie that is acceptable to eat is that peach pie. And I think people will eat that peach pie to survive. To get a job. To stay in better relationships. To be in the family will. To go to certain churches. To move up in social rankings. You'll eat that peach pie. You may be dreaming apple. You may be praying about apple. You may be lusting apple. But you're eating peach. And if all the apple pies went away, you will eat that peach pie because you need food to survive. You'll eat it. You won't like it. You'll eat it. But I've got news for you: If you even just sniff some apple pie, if somebody in the room says, "There's an apple pie in that bakery over there," it will be like, Miss Russell sang the song first, but Oleta Adams took it over, "Get There." You will use an airplane. You will use a camel. You will use whatever. You will *get* to that apple pie. And I think there's a lot of folk who get . . . a lot of unhappy folk who been eating that peach pie, but their orientation says, "apple." So there's this week's preference and orientation. You may *prefer* something else, but you'll accept peach. If the only thing there is peach pie, believe me, you'll eat it. But, if you had your choice, without recrimination—now notice how I said that—if there were no recrimination. If you didn't have to worry about getting your head bashed in like that poor guy at Morehouse College a couple years ago, but yet you don't see civil rights leaders there talking about hate crimes—ooh, interesting. Interesting. I mean, we have Matthew Shepard. We talk about that. But you didn't hear about one brother hitting another brother because he *thought* he was looking at him in the shower. Umm hmmm. Umm hmmm. Um hmmm. And this is in Atlanta, so this is the gay Mecca for black folk, so they say. And you wonder about living in Tampa. Hmmm. So my advice to my gay brothers and sisters who are going to school, "Don't go to a HBUC. Ever." But anyway, I believe that, without recrimination, folks will go toward apple pie. I believe that about issues of transgender. If in a perfect world people would go toward their orientation, I think that inner gut—some people call it a consciousness, some people call it their inner spirit, you know, whatever you want to call it. I don't care about the nomenclature. I don't care about the parlance. I don't care about the language, the lingo, the parlance, the slang. Whatever it is inside you that says, you are you. I think that it's a pretty good guide. It'll tell ya.

You said that you're currently trying to work through your own sexuality. Did you ever identify as gay and then felt that you were making a transition?

It seems like the prevailing wisdom is that in ten or fifteen years that's what you do because a very occidental worldview is, "It's all about the destination." It's all about the destination. Here's Point A. Here's Point B. We only care about "Here's Point A. How do we get to Point B?" The oriental worldview is about the journey. And the mistake people have made is that, "Well, you're gonna get a man anyway, so what's the difference if you're going as a man or woman?" Well, the journey makes a complete difference. How you get there is just as important and, in my case, more important. So it's enough of a closet to say "gay." And then you're like, "Something's not quite right here. Something's not fitting here." You know. The journey's not correct. And then you're feeling, "Well, you may have to review this." And the average age for someone to find this out, go figure, is around late thirties, forties. Many times after they have families and children and this and that. And finally, you know, you're sneaking out and that's not enough. And there are even organizations that are given conferences. One in Atlanta called "Southern Comfort," which will be happening this September. And it's the largest transgender conference in the world. Now, go figure. I'd gone there last year in search of answers. And I've come to find out that in any group, in any oppressed group, there're oppressors. I can tell you that I was oppressed, even there, because I was thought of—and you're gonna love this. If you notice in that picture [points to a picture on an end table] I have a full beard, salt and pepper, and I'm unnaturally bald, and so I had salt-and-pepper hair, perfectly cut, great. You can't get barbers here in Tampa. You have to go to

Atlanta. I didn't think I was that good-looking. I walked out of that shop and going, "Hmm, I might even date me." [Laughter] And I walked in and the beard was just too well shaved. And I was dressed in too masculine clothes to be anything but a female-to-male transgender person. I even had folk ask me who did my surgery. And my answer was, "Providence." And they said, "Is that the name of the physician or the town in which, you know, the capital city of Rhode Island in which you had it done. And so, I knew what it felt like to be a female-to-male transgender. Only ones who knew better were the female-to-male transgenders themselves, who knew that I was a biological male and the people who worked there.

The other problem was there were more blacks *serving* the food than *eating* it. There were only a few blacks. And being segregated at a table alone in a city where I could throw a rock and hit Martin Luther King Jr.'s tomb was very disconcerting to me. Here I am looking for answers. I'm a newcomer. So I wasn't in the "kiss my ass" group (another mistake). I'm of African descent. I was a de facto female-to-male transgender. And these male-to-female transvestites, transgender folk were telling these individuals, "You're not really *men*." Which begs the question, "Are you really *women*?" And so I came to the conclusion, after the conference, that I was quite disenchanted with the conference itself and one of the leaders of the conference called my home, had the temerity to call my home. And I remember telling her this comment that I think everybody, I said, "You know what's so pathetic? You want your dicks cut off but you want to maintain your white boy privileges. *Damn* you."

[. . .] And I mean you know that whole thing was only upset because people were looking at me, wanting to see how great of a job my plastic surgeon had done. I was taken aback because this one woman took learning how to live 24/7 just a little too far. Because she was in the bathroom and she stood up better than I did. And I had years of practice. I should tell you the rule of thumb was, you had to go to the bathroom where you were dressed. I was a little taken aback by that 'cause I'm like, "No, if I were a biological woman I don't care if you thought this gold lamé dress didn't make your butt look fat, *you* don't need to be here." They should have said, "Well, go to the second floor and mezzanine." They should have had some bathroom designated for that. That's my own person opinion, but the hotel seemed to be cool about that. Besides, I think the majority of the people there were for this conference. So whatever way you were dressed, that's the bathroom to which you would go. And so this person who had not quite crossed over the burning sands, [laughter] decided to show that, "Hey, I'm just as much a man as anybody else." Stood right up. Now they left her alone. But they were looking to me and I mean I wore a scoop neck t-shirt and they were looking for scars from a mastectomy and I'm like, "You've got to be kidding." I didn't go to the pool party 'cause I knew what they were . . . I thought that they would realize. "Are you sure you're not a . . . ?" "I'll let you figure it out." I said, "Since we supposedly accept differences, I'll let you figure it out for yourself." I had already written an e-mail telling them "I'm coming in without makeup, without the mascara, without the wig. I'm coming in looking for answers." I really didn't care. I had more answers from films and some of the movies. Actually, some of the films they showed in the different workshops actually answered some questions. And ironically they spoke about the same issue about the hierarchy of "Who's the most transgendered of us all?"

Being transgender does not cost a penny. How you feel inside does not cost a penny. Your not feeling that you are in the right vessel doesn't cost a penny. What costs the money is to augment that which you feel. And it is up to you to decide do you really need this or not. [. . .] From speaking with some elders of mine and people that I've met along the way that have done all the paperwork, lived the 24/7, did this, did that, got all the body parts and everything removed or augmented, and were still unhappy. So I'm doing the exact opposite. I'm working from the inside out. Because apparently pain is going to be there. And if ten years from now I decide I don't want to battle the pain, fine with me. As it stands now, it's difficult just to find even a support group because some had said, "If you don't wear a dress or this or that, we feel uncomfortable with you." And I'm like, "You know what? Being some-what of a darker hue of the human spectrum, I know what it is to be myself and not change for folks, so get over it." And so if you see the intersection of all these different issues, and if you hear this constant theme of a pox on your house, yes, you are hearing that. That is not your imagination.

To what extent have you discussed your sexuality with your family?

It is a truly "don't ask, don't tell." And when it is discussed it is not quite good, so we don't ask, we don't tell. I'm quite the gentleman in this. If I can't say nothing nice, I won't say anything at all. So I will speak well of my mother and I will leave everybody else alone. It's unfair to discuss them in that they're not here to respond. I may not be given that same courtesy, but that's their ethos. This is mine. So I will not discuss them. I know that in many ways I'm a persona non grata. Other than perhaps having paper hanging behind the door, behind my name—Ph.D. Other than that, that's probably the only talisman I may have. And quite frankly, that's their loss.

Shift gears just a little bit. Have you ever lived out of the South? And if you
haven't, have you seriously considered moving out of the South?

Visited, yes. And the only problem is it's too cold—*casa mucho frío*. Min-neapolis would be very nice, but after you pull off that hat your ears freeze, okay? I mean it may be great for Mary Tyler Moore but you know. And Minneapolis is considered one of the fifteen best places in the U.S. to live. It's one of the best kept secrets. Juneau, Alaska, would not be bad. But too cold! Too cold. That's the only problem with it for me is weather. I think I would enjoy some aspects of northern living; but in many ways, there is no hiding place. The South is just a bit more honest. I mean we didn't overturn school buses in Tupelo, Mississippi. We did that in Boston. The South is just more honest. That's the *only* difference. It's more in your face. It's there. Honest. Because if that was not the case, why is there this repatriation of African Americans to the South? I mean there are many economic reasons, but I think there's more to it than that.

So do you feel that the South provides a better life for most gays of color?

I think urban progressive areas provide that. I could make the argument that a Miami would be far better than here. I've taught in the greater Miami area as a college professor, so I know a bit about that. New Orleans, I taught there. D.C. It's below the Mason-Dixon line. I hate to tell folks D.C. is in the South. I hate to tell them that. It's in the upper South, but it's still the South. If they learned their history, they'd realize the capitol moved to the South so that the National Bank would be built. That was the old wives' tale. They built a little swamp called the Potomac. [Laughter] And swampy things have been happening there ever since. [Laughter] They call it a tidewater. I call it a swamp. If you don't believe me, go there now. It's a swamp. Go to National [airport]. I refuse to call it by its other name [it was renamed Ronald Reagan National Airport in 1998]. Go to National where you fly over the *swamp*. And I lived in New Orleans. I know about *swamps*. Then there's Atlanta. Then there's Charlotte. There's the Research Triangle area. So it's either urban areas or areas of higher learning, the Research Triangle in North Carolina. Those areas, yeah. But small rural towns, whether you're in Wyoming, which is the least-populated state I'm sure. We know about Wyoming and Matthew Shepard and all that, no, not a good idea. Again the case of the hate crime where a person is accused of being gay and he gets his head smashed in by another Morehouse student and you don't hear much of that. It wasn't sexy. We heard a lot about a lot of things, but we didn't hear that. We didn't hear that. Why?

Is there much interaction between the black gay community and the white gay community here where you live?

As opposed to anywhere else? I would say, as others have said and I'm sure you've heard this before, unless it's a very sexy issue, unless it's a hot-button issue, unless you need a couple of black drag queens for color commentary, no. It is just as segregated as the general community.

Where do people socialize?

That's a good question. Since I only moved here a few months ago, I do not know. I mean there are certain watering holes I will not go. There are certain mangrove swamps I will not go. I did say "mangrove swamps," didn't I? Did I say "mangrove swamps"? [Laughter] I did say "mangrove swamps"; sorry about that. I'm sure they are, but I am apart, detached from the gay community for several reasons. Gays tend not to like people who think they're transgender. I mean, I'm sort of tired of the pecking order. Right now I'm taking a sabbatical from both the African American community and the gay community. I'm just a bit bored. Someone asked me, "Who are you?" "I am a human being." That's the first thing I say. "I'm a human being." And you know, politically speaking, I don't go to the "rah-rah" rallies. Now, of course I am no fool. I understand what my appearance is has a large bearing on how I want to be treated out there. So I do not sing the song, "It don't matter if you're black or white." Sorry Michael. No, no, no. I'm not that quixotic. So I'm very well aware that when I walk in a store, more than likely somebody's going to be following me. Although I may have more money in my pocket than they'll make in ten days, I know someone's going to follow me. And that's just a given. But having said that, I don't buy into the "You must join us because we're this" or "You must join this rally." I'm like, "No, I don't." I don't deal with that. I believe my best activism is one person at a time. It is. For instance, once someone come into this [house], once I open this door, I don't let pejorative words, ugly ad hominems. By definition ad hominem's ugly, but I don't allow certain words to be used in my home. I have kicked people out of this home for uttering such words. It can range anything from "faggot" to "kike." Out! Out! I mean like, "Out, out damned spot, out!" You get one chance. One strike. Out. I tell them, "When you learn, come back." But I don't allow it. I don't allow that spirit in my home. So if I hear a pejorative joke, I simply say, "That's not funny." And I snap it at that point. I nip it in the bud. Go ahead Barney Fife—nip it, nip it, nip it in the bud then. I don't wait ten days later when "What type of comeback?" Uhn uh. I don't wait. I'm like, "That's inappropriate. No, I won't tolerate it." Or "You can say that, just don't do it when I'm here. Don't do it when I'm around." That's my activism. I don't have to sit there in a march and wave rainbow flags around, and I don't have to wear red, black, and green and have my hand in a fist and go this and that. I don't believe in just mere affectation. If I study African history or African Diaspora history, it's because I enjoyed it. Not to become myself. It is because I am. And whereas as you say you're in Africana studies yourself, I believe that it is as much of a discipline as any other study, as Judaic studies, women's studies . . . . I don't make any apologies for that.

However, I don't think the dashiki makes one—or kente cloth or, let's see, what else?—dreadlocks, or listening to rap is going to make me any more black or any more African American than if I listen to Tchaikovsky, Chopin, or Schubert, I'm not any less or any more black than I am.

It's interesting how we describe African Americans. We put them in a corner. Or Condoleeza, whose name comes from *con dolcezza*, meaning "with sweetness," a musical score term. And for all those folk who talk about weird names, her mother got it from reading a musical score. Oprah got her name because her parents read the Book of Ruth and could not pronounce Ruth's sister-in-law's name correctly. Instead of O-R-P-A-H, as it is in the Book of Ruth, it's O-P-R-A-H as we see it today. Never saw illiteracy worth a billion dollars, did you? But yet you hear people say, "It's because you have that messed-up Shequita name." Go ahead Bill Cosby. That's the reason why you failed. So Condoleeza, Shaquille O'Neil, "Oprah" instead of "Orpah." They're all failures because of their messed-up names. Meanwhile, my real name is dramatic, Teutonic in origin, and I'm still being treated like . . . Because at the end of the day, somebody's gonna see my face. And guess what? No possum block [in New Zealand, a block of bush allocated to a licensed opossum trapper] here. [Laughter]

Where did you go to undergrad?

Oooh! Rumor has it there's this University of South Florida that has a Tampa campus. You know, you could look at the wall and read all of those. You could turn around and read it for yourself, but no, you want me to tell you. Okay. University of South Florida.

And what was that experience like?

[Makes a growling noise for a minute] Young, dumb, full of cum, but I managed to do just enough work to get to graduate school. Just enough. Did juuuuuuuust good enough on the GRE. Just enough. I had other things on my mind. I was exploring. I had a great time. I still wonder how much more fun I could have had, and I thought, you know what? I felt like Templeton the Rat in *Charlotte's Web*. It was a feast. Glut, glut, glut glut. [Laughter]

Was the campus open to gay people?

It was more laissez-faire. Because it is a commuter campus, it was more concerned about, "Can you do your work?" whatever. I mean there was all these subcommunities. I mean it was not like the University of Florida, and it was definitely not like University of Miami, where, if you want to see the student cars, you look where the old cars are, look across and see the nice cars and that's the student car lot. It had a different feel to it. And now you have to remember that now there's the football team there and so it has changed its whole mentality. And fraternity row now, that did not exist. I remember this campus opened in like 1956, so it is very much a twentieth-century construct. I mean it does not have the history as a UF or FSU. It doesn't have the money yet. It doesn't have the rich kids, but I didn't have good enough grades to go to certain schools in Miami, like "University of" [clears his throat] and so, that's the difference.

Was there a large black student population when you were there?

I told you there was a football team there, so that should answer that question. There did not exist a football team there. Therefore, the answer should be obvious. And in fact it was so pathetic that there was this one class, an African American history class, and it had the largest number of, the largest concentration of African American students on campus. And it was a majority African Diaspora class, and the professor at that time was an African American and still is. He's still living. And so when they wanted to show a shot of, or a cameo appearance of African Americans on, or African Diaspora people at USF, they always shoot the same picture. And we could point, "Oh, that's you. That's you. They're gonna show you digging in your nose." It was the same footage over and over and over again. It was just this running joke. And whatever you call that African history month or black history month. "They're gonna show that damned footage again." And it was the same footage over and over. I mean and the good news was that African Americans were there; the bad news was that was the largest concentration. In class. Now I'm not talking about step shows. You know, usually there's people other than students. But other than step shows and things of that type, as far as in class, that was by far the largest concentration of black folk. And you had about forty students. And, yes. They were so hungry for knowledge. And to consider that I, later on, would get a Ph.D. in history and one of my subareas was African American history, and to find out I made it in the classroom, but I certainly was not in the top ten. Let me say that again. I have a Ph.D. I made an A. I had like a ninety-six average and I was probably in thirteenth place. And I mean students were so hungry for knowledge about themselves. And I graduated in '87 around age twenty-three, and there was an appreciation for this knowledge. And the teacher was quite charismatic. But in addendum to that, it was just an appreciation. Something I have not seen. I've never seen a class of students that bright, ever. I think the most proud I was as an African American student on that campus was when the professor was late, apparently he was stuck on one of the bridges coming from St. Pete's [Petersburg] to Tampa. And there was a presentation one of the students put together. He was an artist. And he was showing African Americans during the [Harlem] renaissance. He showed his own art pieces. And the professor walked in in the middle of the class. And we could have done anything we wanted. And after you know fifteen minutes of understood professorial privilege of being late, he was about thirty-five, forty minutes late. No one left. I mean there was such a respect for the professor. And in fact, I think we showed an encore performance to him because he saw the rest of it. And it was like one of those three-hour classes where you have the one-hour in one day but we had two hours that day. And we sat through our break time and saw the rest of it. And he came in. I think he was more impressed that we stayed. No, let me rephrase that. I'm not so sure if he was that impressed or the professionalism of person that did the presentation. He was the class clown, but when it came to what he could offer as far as African American art, it was like he had command performance. And no matter what the attitudes toward people . . . no matter if you were in this group or that group, love, hate, whatever, we were all one. We all felt like whatever was done, whatever good, bad, ugly, whatever, feuds what have you, it was nobody knew about it. When that door closed, it was like we could knock-down-drag-out fight. It stayed there. What was said there stayed there. It was like Vegas. And I think the professor was really touched by that. And that was the moment that . . . that's when I knew I wanted to teach. I saw that and said, "This person can have that much effect on folks." And again, the people in there were so bright. If you made anything lower than a B, that's because you worked hard at messing up. And I think people really worked very hard to do well. The majority of student aid, it wasn't given to them. And I'm so tired of people thinking—à la Cornel West—that if a student does well in the African American studies, African American history class, oh it's because the professor felt sorry for that student. Unh unh. Sometimes, even in banking, you do not garner an interest unless you have a principal. People do not take interest in something until they find it interesting. And sometimes speaking about oneself is the first time that they heard about themselves on their own terms. And I was very proud of that class. That was probably one of the few things I actually enjoyed about the experience of USF. That classroom. And that really changed my mind about what I wanted to do.

You mentioned the step shows. There was black Greek life there?

That's what you call it? If that's what you call it. If that's what you want to call it. Yes, it existed. Yes. I heard the mating calls. The skee-wee and this and that and the other. Yeah, it existed. And it exists today. And of course the Q's [Omega Psi Phi Fraternity] as usual would get kicked off campus and kicked back on campus, go underground. I mean, as Q's do all over the country, so yes, very much so.

Did you know any other out black gay students at the time?

Depends on what you mean by "out." Out as ostracized? Or out?

Out.

Someone told me the best way to be in the closet, is to be out of the closet. They existed, but I was a bit jealous because they had a better veneer than I did. I was very jealous. And in a way, I'm still very jealous.

Do you feel like you took the brunt of the being ostracized?

The only advantage I had was brains. And I parlayed that talisman to the hilt. The only thing I had going for me, so I thought, was brains. So I thought. I've come to find out there was a lot more to me than met the eye, but I thought that was the one thing I knew I had. And so it was myself versus the book. Myself versus the exam. And so in that respect I was far more focused on my schoolwork because I felt like I had nothing else.

What are your political perspectives regarding issues facing gays and lesbians in this country?

I try not to look at issues politically. I try to do what is in the Constitution, Article I, Section 8. The "necessary and proper" clause. That's underneath what Congress is supposed to declare war. I know. Go figure. You wouldn't know that by the actions of today, but Congress declared war, not the president. [Clears his throat] But there is a necessary and proper clause. I try to look at each issue, one issue at a time. Is it a necessary and is it proper? And if it doesn't pass muster on both of those levels, then I won't do it. If it doesn't pass the level of "is it necessary?" If it doesn't pass the level of what we di-lemma, if you will, no. But if it's necessary and proper, I will do it. I don't do things because it is a *black* cause. I do it because it's the right thing to do. I don't do things because it's a *gay* cause. What is more noble? Doing something that is self-seeking or doing it because it's the right thing to do? We need to de-romanticize movements and realize that there were a whole bunch of people, not our color but were our kind. And there were a lot of people our color that sat on their rusty butts and did absolutely nothing. If you listen today, everybody was with King on that fateful day in '63, talking about "I have a dream." In reality, most folks wished he had stayed home. The irony was that the coordinator of that march was Bayard Rustin, who was gay. But nobody wants to talk about that. So the best compliment that black folk can give gay folk is [whispering] "We just don't talk about it." Again, we'll take their trinkets. We'll take their gifts. But we won't embrace those gifts with the packaging that this is also a gay person. So no, I don't embrace gay issues simply because they're gay issues. I will look at an issue and see if it's necessary and proper, if it grants due process to an individual or individuals. That's it. I am the type who'll say, "Yes, the Klan has every right to be foolish and have their first amendment right." I believe that. In fact, I like it because I like knowing who my enemy is. Please speak. Please do it without the hood. I want to see you. The only way I can know what my enemy feels like is to listen to them. So hey, I don't cherry pick my issues like that. I don't. And for communities in which I feel have not served me well, why would I? And that includes the transgender community. Why would I?

What has been the impact of HIV and AIDS on your life?

Other than folks that I loved and care about who've died, other than seeing how a community, the African American community, can self-destruct by denial and lack of education. In addition to the legacy of the Tuskegee Experiments [in which, in the 1930s, scientists studied the effects of syphilis on 400 black men, without treating them for the disease or telling them they had it] and the possibility of similar experiments being done on foster children, even as of today in New York City foster care system where the majority of those kids are African Diaspora children or Latino children. Black and brown children being de facto experimented on. And heavy allegations that that is happening. And these are some kids who are allegedly HIV and some of the drugs are being used on them. So it's all about judgment and Nuremberg, right?

When HIV, AIDS came into the scene, how old were you and how did that affect you?

High school. Just high school. It didn't at the time. You gotta remember that in high school you're invincible. I mean so you would be reading about this disease, I mean keep in mind that the rainbow flag was formed in '78 so, in my early college years, you *heard* about it but it was always somewhere else. It was a New York disease. It was a Frisco disease. I didn't think about white males. But it was New York. It was Frisco. It didn't hit home until I saw some people. And then when I moved eventually to Miami and New Orleans, it did [. . .] hit home.

Do you think that currently it's more of an issue in the South?

There are some things you don't discuss over dinner. I don't know if it's an issue. I mean, let me rephrase that. It is an issue. The question is, "What are we going to do about it?" I mean because when you say, "Is it an issue?" implicitly the question says, "Is it an issue of interest?" And I think, to me, that's a better question. "Is it an issue of interest?" I think I said earlier, in response to one of your questions, is that I think every "institution" that calls itself a temple, a church, a mosque, a synagogue, what have you for African American or African Diaspora people, should have an AIDS ministry. And I will state again that the only reason that the down low brother, the closeted brother, is getting interested is because of, "Now we've got it. Oh my gosh, HIV. HIV. HIV. HIV." I would hate to think that it would take a disease for people to realize there are gay folk in the community. I do not want to have a discussion dealing with gays and African Americans and necessarily mirror HIV. I mean that's a very ugly trap, to always discuss gay life and HIV. I am not saying that that is not a part of it. But it's a part of intravenous drug users. It's a part of heterosexual sex. To the credit of *The Young and the Restless*, they showed a heterosexual couple, you know, where the guy tips out on his wife and he could have contracted the virus from his strumpet. You know, to the credit of *The Young and the Restless*, they showed that; they didn't go the easy route and show him as a down low brother. And so why do we have to always put up the poster child for AIDS as that? We didn't show about the drug users. We didn't show about your using, having drugs at a party and you're having an orgy—heterosexual orgy—and we're not talking about how AIDS is spread. We're not talking about that. I mean we're not having that discussion. I believe that you cannot be so myopic as to just point and say, "Now if you just don't deal with the faggots, you'll be okay." Because that's the message the African American community is putting out there. We're not talking about all the other permutation combinations of which one can contract the AIDS virus. I mean, you know, or HIV virus. We have *not* done that. And I think it's a disservice to always speak of African American gay life and gay and lesbians and transgender, bisexual life as simply, "Do you have AIDS or not?" I'm tired of a gay person dying and the first they say, "Did he die of the ninja?" [Laughter] You know, I'm like, "No the person had a heart attack. Their arteries clogged up." [Laughter] The person was ninety-seven. That person died of old age. "Oh it must have been that AIDS." Yeah. I pine for the day in which we can have an open and honest discussion about gay life, without HIV being the top billing.

What are your best memories of growing up in the South?

Oh God. The beach. Disney World. Summer vacation. The old tourist attractions like Cypress Gardens, Bok Tower, Key West, Old Key West. Going to Ybor City when it was Ybor City and not a very bad imitation of rue Bonbon. A very bad imitation. Being able to see the different flora and fauna. Driving through the Everglades. Being nude at Haulover Beach and seeing a European and nobody really caring. Being alone on a beach. Going to St. AuGUstine—most people pronounce it St. AUgustine as in the story—and walking through history. Going to Eatonville Festival and although I know that's still romanticized, it's still fun to think of Zora [Neale Hurston] talking about this place. And when you see it in real life, she romanticizes a lot. Hmmmmm. Talk about dust tracks on a road! Anyway. [Laughter] But not just touristy Florida but La Florida [pronounced with Spanish accent]. Seeing the other Florida. Tubing down the Ichetucknee. Walking through Apalachicola National Forest while getting your mind clear of writing a dissertation. Looking for stalactites and stalagmites in the cavern near Mariana. The Redneck Riviera at Panama City Beach. Going to St. Andrews State Park, one of the best beaches, I think, in the world. There's so much to see in Florida. And that is not advertising. What I do is, I list where all the tourists go, and I go the other places. Going to Tarpon Springs when the tourist season's off. And going to off-the-beaten-path restaurants and getting real Greek authentic food, not the one from the well-known touristy spots. Getting a real Cuban sandwich in Tampa. Smelling a *real* Cuban cigar that tastes all like real Cuban coffee. Very strong, very pungent, very different from the café au lait that you would get at Café du Monde in New Orleans. And again, just driving through the South, really smelling magnolias. Seeing the mansions. Looking at the majesty of the South. Looking at the pageantry. The difference between the black Mardi Gras with the Tchoupatoulis Indians—that's spelled with a "t" by the way—and seeing the beaded costumes in which they would probably work on 365 days a year, just for that grand moment. There is so much to the South. I think people talk about the South being slow. I think the reason why we do things slowly is because we appreciate it for so long we want that moment to last as long as we can. We don't have to rush through life because we enjoy it so much.

What are your worst memories of growing up in the South?

The provincialism of it. Knowing that there was a world out there. Knowing that the seasons did change [laughter] but you could not tell by the leaves. Either they were green or they were brown. [Laughter] There was nothing in between. Well, the rest of northern Florida is a little different and, keep in mind when we lived in Tallahassee, we called it southern Georgia because within fifteen minutes you were in Georgia. And if you ever have the time, there's the best barbecue place just north of the border, called J.B.'s on, we called it Thomasville Road. I'll have to show it to you one of these days.

It's still blatantly prejudiced. It's still blatantly bigoted, and it's sad because there's so much to see. But again, I prefer the South. I prefer the honesty of the South. Although it stings, although it hurts, it's at least honest. It's that bumblebee that says, "I'm going to sting you." As opposed to the stealth bumblebee in the North that you don't see but you still feel. Because I have always been told that power is rarely seen, rarely heard but always felt. Same way with bigotry. At least in the South they're either stupid or honest. I haven't quite figured out which one it is. To show you, "Yes I'm a bigot." I like that.

*How would you describe the influence that your southern upbringing has
had on your character?*

My southern rearing. We call it rearing. See you raise cane or you raise
hell. Christ raised from the dead . . . rose . . . He raised Himself. But you *rear*
children. Ummm. I never understood why, but, you know. How did it affect
my ethos, is that what you're asking? The literature. Reading Faulkner. Reading Zora. Listening to the slow cadence. Being able to see issues very clear. I
mean there's that clear dividing line of race. There's nothing nebulous about
it. Nothing cloudy. It's very clear. And that has shaped who I am. I like clarity
in what I do. I also understand the role of the mask. Whether it's the Mardi
Gras mask or the one you put on at work. Or you put on one for survival,
where you know that you must drink this brand of scotch to gain tenure. It's
not about *what* you know. It's not about how well you teach. It's not about
job performance. And although people talk about affirmative action and
quotas. It really is about, "Can you join the club?" And there's something
very honest about that. You still have the guts to say, "No women. And Tiger,
we'll let you in only because . . ."—and Tiger's not a member—"as long as you
win, you can come." They're very honest. Again, I like the honesty. I've been
quoted as saying, "It is far more noble to be hated honestly than loved
conditionally." It is far more noble to be hated honestly than loved conditionally. I think that's the South.

*How would you describe your current feelings about being, although you
don't really embrace this identity, but for lack of a better term, your current
feelings about being a black gay man?*

I am a human being who is gay. Who is black. I am a human being who is
black. I am a human being who, at the moment, is male. At least the shell
says that. The vessel says that. The driver's license says that. I put the emphasis on, "I am a human being who is . . ." The noun is more important
than the adjective, for me. The adjectives describe aspects of me and I am
proud of those, but at the end of the day, it is the noun that drives the
sentence. The noun and the verb. The adjectives are just that. Adjuncts. They
describe the noun. They do not make the noun. And the most important
aspect is I am a human being, uniquely and divinely made by my providential moral compass. That's the most important thing I can say about myself.

*How do you feel about the life choices that you've made thus far in your life?
Any regrets?*

It is the fool who claims that one does not have regrets because that
means that the person has not learned. I would hope that I have learned.
Some things I have done, I probably would have done differently, knowing certain aspects about myself. There are some things, which I will not

reveal here, but there were medical conditions that I did not know that were affecting me until fairly recent. And it's easy to look back and say, "Oh, that's why." I'd rather not do that. I'd rather say, "Eureka! I found it!" and then move on.

. . . .

FRED-RICK

Fred-Rick is yet another one of the contacts I made through my friend Curt. He was quite willing to be interviewed for Sweet Tea *and not under the condition of anonymity. A year after the interview, however, he changed his mind and actually threatened to pull his story from the book. His change of heart had less to do with being ashamed of being gay and more to do with him not wanting to jeopardize his position as a college English instructor. His fear was prompted by a scandal at his university (a historically black college) in which a gay colleague embarrassed the university at an extracurricular event at another university. Fred-Rick worried that his narrative might raise a few eyebrows and create a hostile environment at his college, or, worse, lead to his dismissal. After we had several conversations, he decided to remain in the book if I could guarantee anonymity. Then, the following year, he contacted me yet again to say that he wanted me to use his real name after all because he had had a "revelation" in consciousness and that he refused to be ashamed of who he is. He also decided to legally change the spelling of his name from "Fredrick" to "Fred-Rick."*

I am happy that Fred-Rick agreed to let me include his narrative because it is one of the more unusual stories in Sweet Tea. *Fred-Rick was, at one time, a practicing preacher and a drag queen, who kept these two worlds separate. Members of his church had no idea that he had another life as a drag performer. He stopped performing drag years before he gave up his life as a preacher, but he still revels at the memory of sneaking out of his house with a friend as a preadolescent to perform drag at the gay bar in his hometown.*

Fred-Rick was born in 1967 in Winston Salem, North Carolina. The interview took place in Raleigh on October 30, 2004.

I would describe my childhood as adventurous. I had a lot of freedoms. I was born in a, I guess you would call a lower-middle-class family, the youngest of five. And so grew up in a modest house. My grandfather said the house was on two lots. [Laughter] So I had plenty of room to run with neighbors. And I just remember being all over the neighborhood, climbing trees, playing in the creek, just adventurous in that way, I guess.

What did your parents do for work?

My mother, she wore a light blue collar. She was a blue-collar worker. Her collar was very light blue. And my father was a blue-collar worker, and his collar was dark blue. He worked at R. J. Reynolds Tobacco Company. And let me see. I can't think of his title. He made cigarettes, but I don't know what that was. My mother was in administration, in the housekeeping department at Wake Forest University Baptist Medical Center. She was the first black female to have that kind of administrative position. And the first black person, so she made history at the hospital.

When did she start working there?

She started working at the hospital I think in 1950, maybe '51, '52. And my father worked at R. J. Reynolds at the same time, so.

Besides your parents, were there any other adults that played a significant role in your upbringing?

Oh, yes. My maternal grandmother and my paternal grandparents. My paternal grandfather was, what do you say, he owned real estate in our area. So he rented houses and he retired from R. J. Reynolds. My grandmother worked at R. J. Reynolds. So they made pretty good money to be born—I think my paternal grandmother was born in 1912. So I guess growing up, you know, during that time to come to Winston-Salem from where they were from, they did really well for themselves.

And so you spent a lot of time with them?

I did spend some time with them, especially Sundays, my father's parents, that was big for us because my mother, of course, she worked. She had to work because of her job responsibilities. So my grandparents, my father's parents, would come by every Sunday morning and take us to Sunday school. My grandmother was my first Sunday school teacher in primary class. And her brother was the pastor of the church. And so spent Sundays with them. My mother's mother, I would see her quite often, too. I compared them to country living and city living. [Laughter] Even though my mother's mother lived closer to me, I could walk to her house, not even a mile away, maybe just at a mile, I could walk to her house. She was born in 1900 in Fort Valley, Georgia. And she was a very earthy, spiritual woman. She died in 1988; she lived eighty-eight years. And [I] loved spending time with her, loved it. My father's parents, sometimes it was a drain. [Laughter] We couldn't put our elbows on the table when we ate. And we had to use the right fork and all of those things. So they forced etiquette on us.

Describe some of your friendships or talk about some of your friendships in elementary and middle school, high school. Did you have a lot of friends?

I have always had people that I could consider friends, you know, I'm an easygoing person. I like to think I am. And extroverted, I like to think I am. So growing up, in elementary school I loved to entertain people. I loved it. Actually, one of my favorite stories to tell, when I was going to kindergarten, I think they call it daycare now, but we called it kindergarten back then, Miss Cook's kindergarten. I remember getting out of the station wagon, walking up the hill to my house. It was about this time of the year, the fall. And I slipped and fell on some leaves. Didn't get hurt. So all the kids in the station wagon, they laughed. And so I loved it. So I fell again. And so I think I did that about five or six times. And so that stands out in my mind as, you know, being an entertainer. And so I think that's how I've made friends over the years. Not willfully or wanting to entertain people, but just having that part of myself. I have a good friend, we're still friends today, we became friends in the fifth grade. And so some people, of course, you know, you forget over time, and they'll remember me. And now that I'm teaching, I am even teaching people that I went to school with who are now just coming back to school and they remember me and have little kind of things to say about me, different phases of growing up.

What would you say were the racial politics of the town?

From what I remember, I don't remember, I'm sure maybe my older siblings probably could tell you some things, but I don't really remember people being overly racist, not overly racist. Of course, there was segregation until the laws were passed. But I remember going to town with my mother as a child and my maternal grandmother, and I knew they would always dress up to go to town. I couldn't figure that out. Why do we have to dress up to go downtown? And my mother would wear a dress or skirt, always have the gloves on, so they shopped with gloves on. And I was maybe five or six years old. I distinctly remember that. And I think it was a part of because we're black, we have to, you know, meet the white standard. And so I remember my mother and my maternal grandmother shopping in stores, but a lot of black people couldn't afford to shop there, but I don't remember them being mistreated in any way. I don't know if I answered your question. So it was just some things—like a postcard town to me, it's kind of strange.

What would you say was your family's attitudes and beliefs about—when you were growing up—about people that were different from you, whether regarding religion or race or sexuality?

I don't remember hearing my mother ever saying anything negative about any person. And my father, either. I don't remember them really being judgmental or critical people. I think my mother was that way because her mother was open to all people. I'm sure you're familiar with the Jehovah Witness movement. And a lot of people are aggravated [laughter] when they come to their door. But I remember being a child and my mother's sister didn't want to let them in. And my grandmother went to the door and she told them, she told my aunt, she said, "Don't ever do that again. I told you about this." And I'm thinking to myself, I'm a kid and I'm thinking, oh, she's still scolding her, you know, this was the way my mind ran at the time. But anyway, my grandmother said, "Don't ever turn anyone away from your door." She lived by that and she raised her children by that. And so my mother, she raised us by that, as well. So if they had prejudices, I hardly ever heard them. I hardly ever heard them, you know. And maybe I think the only time, as far as gay people are concerned, I can remember once or twice maybe them having something negative to say, simply because I was dealing with my own sexuality. And I'll talk about that at some point.

What about gender roles? Did your parents follow traditional gender roles, where your father was sort of the breadwinner and did the outside work and your mother was in charge of the housecleaning and the cooking?

It's very interesting, very, very interesting. I can remember, now my father was visually impaired for most of my life. He lost his sight when I was maybe six years old, so he had to retire from his beloved job that he had already worked for 25 years at that time. But he was still a young man. And so he went totally blind from the time I think I was maybe four-and-a-half to six years old. But he would bring the groceries home, literally, every Friday. That was his role in our household. My mother cooked, of course. He could cook; he would cook sometimes. But she cooked every meal or, you know, of course she was away during the day. But even when he became ill, she would make sure that his lunch was there and everything. He didn't do outside work. We had someone to cut our grass.

Oh, so the kids weren't responsible for it?

No. [Laughter] And I'll tell you, it was a funny story. Again, I'm the youngest of five: two older brothers, two sisters, and myself. And I remember maybe I was fourteen years old and he [Fred-Rick's father] bought a lawn-mower. And I'm thinking, who in the heck is he buying this lawnmower for? I know he's not [laughter] buying this lawnmower for me. Well, he did buy it for me. I don't know what kind of lessons he was trying to teach me. But I think I cut the grass twice, and I absolutely hated it. And his father came over one day because he was collecting the rent from the people across the street. And he went into the house and he said, "Why is he [Fred-Rick] out there cutting that grass?" because I went in with him. Because actually, the lawn— just holding onto it hurt my hands. [Laughter] And I'm not spoiled, trust me, I'm not. I'm not a brat; I'm not a snob. But that bothered me, just holding on, the vibration of the lawnmower, I hated it. And so the insides of my—between my thumb and finger here swelled up. And I don't know if that was a sign from the universe saying you're not cut out for manual work or what, I don't know. Anyway, my grandfather told my father, "You never had to do this, so why in the world do you have him doing this? Hire somebody to do this again." So I never had to cut the grass again, never had to cut the grass. My mother loved flowers, so she had a flower garden in the front and back. And so I would get out there and mess around with her, you know. I think I was in the way most of the time. [Laughter]

What role did church and religion play in your upbringing?

Oh, my goodness. Again? I may as well had been born in the church, right on the altar. Really. My paternal grandmother, she was a stickler for church. And her brothers, I think there were maybe six of them, all but two were pastors. And so the church that we went to at the time, her brother was the pastor of that church. And so we were in church all day on Sundays. So I know that story, you know, being in church from sunup to sundown. I know that.

Was it Pentecostal?

It was Baptist.

Okay. Um hmm. What was your participation?

I sang a lot. I was in church plays. And so I think around the age of seven or eight, we then started to going to my mother's family church, a Baptist church. And so I continued to attend that church until a few years ago.

Did you enjoy going to church?

I loved it. I loved it. And they used to always tell me growing up, "You going to be a preacher when you grow up." I would hear that a lot, you know, "Be a preacher when you grow up." And I became one, I did. I became one, in the traditional role. I'm not one in the traditional role anymore. Thank God for freedom. [Laughter] Yeah. So church was a big part of my life. It really was. But with that, I saw a lot of hypocrisy. I think I probably learned more about deviance from church people than I did from quote/unquote worldly people, yeah.

Interesting. When did you first become aware of your same-sex orientation? And what was your reaction to that realization?

For me, I think it was probably early in childhood. Just really early in childhood. I could identify with girls more than I could with boys, as weird as that may sound. Inwardly, I could. I was attracted to boys, crushes, more crushes on boys than girls. Maybe five or six years old, maybe five or six years old, yeah.

Did you tell anybody?

No, I didn't tell anybody. My mother said I was always just a very colorful child, you know, just always, just always. I think I had, and not to sound stereotypical, but I think I had drama in my blood, theater in my blood as a child. Because I would get out in the backyard with a stick, you know, just singing, it was my microphone, you know, or, you know, just make my own plays, you know, a lot of creative play, you know, where I was the star of the show. And I liked playing the girl part, you know. Even with my friends growing up and, of course, you know, the Super Friends were really big back then. And, of course, you know, Wonder Woman was my favorite. So I could identify. And so I continued to identify. Strangely enough, the little boys kind of liked me for that, yeah. So, you know, so that kind of validated me at that time, you know. Yeah.

Did you know other people in your community growing up that were gay?

Yes, I did. I had a really good friend at that time. I'll just call him "T." And this was at the intermediate school. I was in the sixth grade; he was in the fifth grade. And his mother was a lesbian, open lesbian. And she had a live-in lover. And so a lot of things that I kind of wanted to know about, he clued me in on, you know, other guys in the neighborhood that we called "trade," who were our age, and this is when I'm, you know, I think twelve, thirteen years old. So there was—there were people starting to come out, not like they do now, it was still secretive, but everybody knew who each other was. So T was the closest person to me at that time that I could confide in and we could talk. And we were really interested in what adult gay people were doing and what that lifestyle was like, yeah.

Were you sexually active when you were a child?

I was not, in the sense of experience. I'm thinking about innocence and experience. Innocently, maybe a kiss, a peck, a touch. That was sex to me. [Laughter] What some people call, what is it, bumping and grinding. That was going all the way as a child.

How do you think your southern upbringing, southern culture, affected your ability to come to terms with, or even recognize, your same-sex orientation?

That is a really good question. I remember being in the first grade, where I caught the bus to go to school. There was a very deep hill. And I loved running down that street. I'd love running down that hill with my arms wide open, and just screaming to the top of my lungs. The kids would do that. But when I did it, it felt girlie to me, that felt really good. That felt really, really good. And so I'm thinking, now that you ask me that question, that in the South girls were allowed to be girls. They didn't have to be tough, they could be feminine. And so that appealed to me. I'm seeing that now, that that appealed to me, that it was okay to be feminine, effeminate. And I'll probably talk to you at some point about this whole role issue stuff amongst gay people. And I can get into it because I still hold onto those southern values that even in relationships that it's okay to have roles. I'm not going to bash those, you know. I think it's a beautiful thing to celebrate one's femininity or masculinity. And to me, southern is soft. It's soft, and so I see myself running down that hill. [Laughter] I still see myself running down that hill. That's soft. That was southern, just being able to be free, you know, like Scarlett O'Hara [laughter], you know, before the war. Yeah. Innocent. Just really innocent and soft.

Is there a particular theory of homosexuality that you subscribe to?

Yes. Having been dogmatic, growing up in the church, being bashed at times by clergy, even after becoming a clergyperson myself, it's dysfunctional as being gay is to church folk, they just don't get it. I just think that there is no limit on creation. I think that we are born gay, we are born straight, we are born bisexual, we are born transgender, you know. You come here that way, you know, and of course I would love the world to open up and see it that way, too. But from what I understand, there are some Polynesian cultures that accept gay people, that this is the way God made you, you know, there's male, there's female, there's heterosexual, and there's homosexual. It's just as real to me as I guess straight people accepting their own sexuality. So my theory is that whatever the sexuality, I think people can be born that way, you know, even if they say, "Oh, I was forty years old before I had my first gay experience." Well, you know, perhaps you *did* choose but maybe it was just lying dormant all that time. So that's my theory.

Okay. To what extent are you out to your parents, family members?

Well, my parents are deceased. My mother passed away in 1996 and my father passed away in 2002. My siblings, we don't talk about it. We don't talk about it. And the reason I don't talk about it with them is because they're in their comfort zones. I act the same around everybody. So, I mean [. . .] a person would have to be a real ignorant person. I don't mean that in a negative way, you know, just real clueless not to know.

So you think they know?

Oh, I know they do. I mean, because I've heard from other family members that—I have a cousin, he's also gay. And I'm sure they assume about him but, oh, he has told me some stories that, you know, how large families are, and I have a very large family, so the word has gotten back to me that they know some of my activities or they assume. But, you know, I think they think they're protecting me or they're being polite or something like that. But for my parents, of course, you know, mothers always know. I tell this to even my friends now when we have conversations about family and coming out to family, you know, I see a lot of white people doing that. And, you know, I just think it's just so nice that they can, you know. For some reason, being gay and black is so, you know, still taboo. It's just really sad. But back when I was doing drag, I went through that whole phase; it was a fun phase for me. I was really young. I'll talk about that, too, I hope.

And I remember sometimes between changing from ladies clothes at T's house, to rush home before curfew, I didn't get all of the foundation off, so the foundation would be inside my collar. And so my mother washed my clothes. Even when I was still in college, she still washed them; she was a good lady. And she came to me one day and she said, "How in the world did this makeup get inside your collar?" And I said, "Oh, Mom, you know how it is, you know how the girls kiss you. And sometimes their makeup rubs off on you." She said, "Oh, so they're kissing you inside your collar?" So she had her ways of letting me know that she knew what was going on. And I think she had some sense that her secretary was a gay man, a white gay man. And I later found out that she confided in him about some things and he opened up, he opened up to her. And she would always talk about him, not in a negative way; she loved him very much. And I think she would bring him up and his lifestyle up to let me know that she really didn't have a problem with it. But again, there's this dogmatism, this spiritual thing going on in the family. I remember once, I thought my mother had to work that day, but she took a half a day. And I wore her coat to school, a beautiful swing coat. [Laughter] I was in the tenth grade. And when I came home, she was standing in the doorway, waiting for me to come home. And she came out on the porch, she said, "Hmm, now if you want to be a girl, we can go shopping and I can buy you all the girl clothes you want. But please don't wear my clothes." So I had to contend with those things. And I think the most negative thing my father ever said, and it did hurt me because I didn't even know what I was going through at that time with the whole drag thing, you know, that's a very confusing area for me still, the transgender thing. I don't know how the conversation came up. I know how. I would miss my curfew during the week, which was like at eight o'clock. I had strict parents. And this time of the year [fall] it gets dark really early. And I just got tired of lying, you know, just really saying, "I'm at T's house." I really wasn't supposed to be with him because he was really out and everybody knew it and, you know the old saying, "birds of a feather flock together." So I would have to say something else like, you know, "I was here, or I was here, I was here." And my father said when I came in the house one day, "Do you need help? Professional help?" And my mother laid into him and she said, "No, he doesn't need help."

He said that without saying specifically whatever you needed help for or with?

I'm trying to see. To me, they had had a conversation or someone had had a conversation. But I knew what he meant, as far as him trying to understand what is *this* child going through, you know, he's my youngest child. I've never had to deal with this before. So that was the most negative thing he ever said, you know, and I think I was maybe fifteen years old. It hurt me. I didn't cry because I was still confused myself; it's a very complex thing. That's what people don't know, you know, that this is something that you have to deal with. You're trying to figure out, who am I? You know, it's very complex.

But my mother, I'll never forget, one time I was in college and I had done drag again. And I'm not referring to drag as if it's some horrible drug that you slip in and out of. I was doing it for fun. I was doing it because I could get away with it. It was just fun. And my college friends wanted to see how I looked. And I had had some cocktails, too. And so when I came home, I had taken off the hair, and all of that, but I still had some makeup on. It was about four in the morning, no curfew at this time, of course, I'm almost out of school. But my mother was still working; it was before she became ill. And instead of her following the rules that we were raised on to knock [knocks on the table beside him] upon the door before entering, I was using the bathroom, sitting on the toilet, and she just came and opened the door. And I'm sitting there with eyeliner on. I'm sitting there with still blush on and foundation, not a whole lot, but just enough. And I think she talked for a whole probably seven or eight minutes about what we were going to do the next day, you know. "And when I get off work, I want you to take me to so-and-so." And you know what I did? I just kept my head down the whole time. I just kept my head down the whole time because she wanted to see how is he coming in here when he's coming in late, you know, because I would spend time in the bathroom getting all this stuff off. But she got me that time but she didn't say anything negative, she didn't.

She died of cancer in 1996. And her last chemotherapy treatment I think was in the winter, late winter. And my older sister had said something negative about somebody being gay. And my mother brought it up to me. And we had pulled up in the driveway. She said, "You know, what that young man does is his business." And she looked me in my eye as I turned the car off. And she patted me on the knee and she said, "What you do is your business." So even though we did not have a healthy dialogue about it, she wanted me to know that, "You're okay," you know and that what you do is your business. So she kind of gave me, you know, her okay. I didn't *need* her approval, but she wanted me to know, you know. And then something else she said. She was really getting ill at that time. I was cooking for her and someone called for me. And my sister answered the phone. And I said, "Well, tell him I'll call him back," because girls never called, maybe one or two. And so I asked her, I said, "Well, who is it?" before I said tell them I'll call them back. And then my mother, she yelled to the kitchen, she said, "Oh, it's nobody but your boyfriend." And she laughed hysterically. So she wanted me to know as she was dying, you know, that was her way of letting me know, "I know who you are, you know, you are my child. And your lifestyle is okay with me," you know. And her sister is the same way. I know for sure because again this cousin of mine who is also gay came back and told me some negative things that some other cousins were saying. And my mother's sister stood up for me and she said, "Don't talk about him like that. He's a member of this family. And he's all right." Now, that made me feel good. She has no clue I know that she stood up for me. So, you know, they have their own way of saying that, "I love you," that "You're okay." And I think for some African American families, or families period, who don't talk about it but give you these nods that you're okay, that's their way of saying, you know, that "I don't judge you. I love you for who you are." And so back to my siblings and other family members, we don't talk about it. We just grew up with this, "I'm not going to bring up your lifestyle out of respect." That was a long way around to answer your question.

So do you identify as gay? Or do you use that term or do you use some other term?

I am gay. But the strangest thing, I don't have this longing to be in a relationship. That may be strange. I don't. Not yet. My life is really full. It really is. I think I went through crushes. I've been in love. But I identify myself as gay. But what people think of as gay, I don't live that lifestyle because I'm not into men, if that makes any sense. If I see a handsome man, attractive man, he's a handsome man, he's an attractive man. I don't fit the stereotype of, "Oh, I got to have him," or "I got to have a man," you know. Maybe I'm the Oprah of gay men. I don't mind the term "gay," doesn't bother me one bit. At work, I'm just like I am now. One or two co-workers and I have talked about it. They asked me, I told them yeah. I'm waiting on my family, you know, if they ask me, I'll tell them anything they want to know. And so that's why I agreed to even have this interview. I have nothing to hide. But "gay" doesn't bother me one bit, the term. So I identify myself as gay. And who knows, maybe one day I might have a ring on my finger, I don't know. I just may get there. I may get there.

Did you go to college?

Yes. I attended Winston-Salem State University. Have a B.A. in English and a minor in speech communication. Attended North Carolina A&T State

University for graduate school. I have an M.A. in English and African American literature.

Why did you choose to stay in the South to go to school? And specifically to historically black universities?

Well, black educators in my school system were great in steering black students to HBCUs. Winston-Salem State, my God, to me that was like Harvard because my neighbors, many of them, again they were educators. And they had gone to Winston-Salem State, that's what it was at one time. And so growing up hearing how wonderful Winston-Salem State was, I wanted to be a part of that, I really did. I got applications from all over the place, you know, in the mail, you know, come here, come, you know, you know, and I didn't go because I felt like they were into me for—because I was black, you know, they just wanted to meet their quota. Plus my SAT scores weren't fabulous, so I'm thinking how in the world would I get accepted to your school, so I know you want me because I'm black. But I'm so glad I went to an HBCU, I really am. I really am.

What was that experience like? Did you have a lot of gay friends?

Oh, yes. Oh, yes. Oh, my goodness. When I got to college, and I didn't stay on campus.

Not even your freshman year?

No, school was ten minutes driving distance. And so my mother didn't have a driver's license, so I had to take her to work. So, I was the chauffeur. So her response when I wanted to stay on campus, "Well, you can stay on campus, but" she kind of threw a guilt trip on me, "you've got to still come and take me to work." And so I'm thinking, well, if I got to do this. So she didn't have a problem with me hanging out over there; sometimes I would be over there until 5:00 A.M., you know, just having wonderful conversations, all the stuff that you do in college. I just didn't spend a complete night on campus. But I was in on, you know, the pizza parties at 2:00 A.M., the study sessions, you know, the philosophical discussions sitting in the hallway. I didn't miss any of that in the dormitories. But gay people, what is it, "gaydar"? They have a way of knowing who each other is, you know, even those who don't fit the stereotype, were not effeminate, you know, you kind of figure them out. And so that's what we did my freshman year. And the great thing about Winston-Salem State was, of course, if you were effeminate then, of course, you had to belong to the gay sorority, which, of course, patterned itself after the black female sororities. And so that's a whole underground culture that a lot of people don't know about. And this is across the country. So the Delta Sigma Theta Sorority has a lot of gay men who consider themselves Deltas too, even though they did not pledge Delta

Sigma Theta, you know, it's a woman's sorority. But there's something about Delta that appeals to a certain gay men or AKA. And, of course, AKA was it for me. And yeah, interesting, it was quite interesting, that whole experience. So my gay friends, you know, we just hung out. We identified with what we thought was, I don't know how to say it—was fabulous, you know. And so those sororities were fabulous to us. And so we just made our own underground culture. Even at the other HBCUs, we had friends and sorority sisters. So, you know, isn't that something?

What was the reaction of your heterosexual classmates to—I mean, because apparently if you were effeminate and flamboyant did they ostracize you?

I never did, I never got that. Let me tell you why. Because at nineteen years old, I entered the ministry. So on campus, even though people assumed I was gay, they didn't bother me because I was a preacher boy, as well. So, you know, if you're a preacher boy, you're okay, you know, you'll grow out of that, you know, so that was—so nobody bothered me. And I didn't see that a lot at Winston-Salem State. If you were around people, you know, respected you, we respected each other. The football players, they would tease you but it wasn't malicious, you know, they would tease you the way an older brother would tease a younger brother, you know. It wasn't mean. They would pick you up and swing you around, because they just knew.

You probably enjoyed it.

[Laughter] You're right. I loved the attention. I loved to get the time. A very masculine guy who was a classmate of mine kept me from getting in my car for fifteen whole minutes. That was the highlight of my month. [Laughter] You know, every time I would go to reach for, you know, the door, he would block me, you know. So that kind of teasing. So I don't know if they were interested in, you know, more than friendship, but no, I didn't see that. I think that some people were probably verbally abused. I remember this white gay guy coming to our school and living in the dormitory. And they gave him hell. And there were a lot of us, black gay guys. I mean, I could tell you at least fifteen people, you know, that we were all there at the same time. And they didn't bother us. You know, we were Rams, too, you know, and so we were in the choir or band, cheerleading, you know, honor students, so all over the place, tutors, you know, so.

So you were just integrated like . . .

Integrated like everybody else. And that made me feel good because I kind of saw what society could be like. That once I'm out of my parents' house, once I'm on my own, I won't have to worry about the crap that you go through as a teenager when you're trying to figure this whole thing out. So to get to college and to be embraced by faculty, staff, and students, that was fabulous, yeah.

Talk about how you came to be a minister.

I was very involved in church. I mean, extremely. In the Baptist Church, of course, you know, you have to be called, you know, you feel that there's a calling. And one of my favorite writers is James Baldwin, because he went through the same thing. And so I can identify with what he went through. I felt like I had this calling, you know, that on that pulpit is where I was supposed to be in life, preaching, reaching people, you know, to get born again. Now, in the Baptist Church, too, you have to understand what that means, which is you become a new preacher on the inside. No matter what your lifestyle is, no matter what your addictions are, if you're alcoholic, prostitute, homosexual, didn't matter, once you get saved, you're changed on the inside, and eventually your outside is going to catch up. [Laughter] So I jumped into that head first.

How old were you?

Nineteen. Eighteen when I really felt the calling. Kind of felt something as a child. I was a very spiritual child. And so I started counseling with my pastor to go into the ministry. And he was really a good counselor, you know, he told me the truth about it. He said it's no cakewalk, that you give your all and these same people will spit in your face. So if they did it to Jesus, they're going to do it to you. So you have to go into it knowing that you're doing this because you feel like this is what you're called to do. You're not doing it for the people, you're not doing it for attention, or any of those things. And so when I first started, I was somewhat of a novelty, because I was nineteen years old. And I had friends, I met friends later on who started preaching even younger than nineteen. So you kind of become, I don't know, not a freak but an oddity, you know, oh, this young guy is preaching. Now that I'm thirty-seven years old and I look back on it, I now realize, okay, I was just entertaining those people. Because adults who know they're adults, it doesn't matter what any preacher says, they're going to do what they want to do and they're going to live how they want to live. So I don't know if I made a difference or not, you know. Sometimes I see people at the supermarket from back in those days and they will tell me, "I remember when you preached so-and-so. That changed my life. I will never forget it." Now, that makes me feel good. But as sincere as I was, I was not happy simply because I know who I was. And so the same Bible that I preached out of to save people was the same Bible that bashed people, that bashed me. And so that's dysfunctional. And so I thank God [for] college, because without it, I don't think I ever would have studied developmental psychology and sociology and all the other "ologies" where you really get into what we are as a human being. So that freed me from traditional ministry. I'm still a minister, but now my ministry is for the upliftment of humanity, all of us.

How long did you preach?

In that setting, from nineteen until about thirty-one, thirty-two. Then I left the Baptist Church. Big mistake. It's like the mafia: you leave, you're out for good, you know. Because there was a network going on. You stay with us and we will keep you busy on Sundays. So you go from church to church, you know, you're in the loop, you know, you're in the in crowd. Go to another denomination, they don't want to have anything else to do with you at all. So I stopped getting calls. I went to a Pentecostal church, because I wanted to see a different side of life. And some things were better but some things were worse. The thing that was the same was the bashing. Not of just gay people, but everybody, you know. What's amazing to me about "church folk," this is what I call them, I was a "church folk," too, is the same God that lifts us up is the same God that will whack you over the head if you do wrong. That is dysfunctional. And so I finally learned that either love is going to do what love does or it's not. And so I can't serve the God that gets back at people or punishes you because you didn't do thus and so. So I preached seriously until around thirty years old.

So tell me about this drag experience. How did you get into drag?

Okay. Again, my good friend, T [laughter], and my good friend, Ian, his name—he's what we call trade. Ian was maybe five years older than T and I. And he would tell us about these clubs that he was going to. And I think he was seventeen, eighteen years old. And about these drag queens. And so we started learning these terms: "trade," "drag queen," "read." So-and-So got read, or I'm going to read So-and-So. All of these gay terms. That was exciting, you know. Here I am in the seventh grade, on my way to the seventh grade, twelve years old, the summer of 1979. And T's mother's lover said, "If you guys really want to know what's going on in the club, I'm going to take you. But don't tell your mother." So I asked my mother could I spend the night. And that was real big because she was so overprotective, but she let me spend the night. So we went out in full drag. Twelve years old.

Who made you up?

We made ourselves up. We looked at the *Ebony* magazines. We looked at the models in the magazines. That was my standard of beauty as a drag queen. Not a white woman with blonde hair and blue eyes, but a beautiful African American woman wearing Eunice Johnson's Fashion Fair cosmetics. And so we got really good at it. We practiced after school until we got really good at it. And so we went out. We walked to the club downtown, a club called Rox Lounge on the corner of 9th and Patterson Avenue. It has been torn down. And now, the clubs were segregated at that time, in 1979. Not by law, but by choice. And they were liquor houses, you know, I'm sure you're familiar with those terms. And just all kind of little dives to go into, speak-easies or whatever you want to call them. But Rox was a place like that. And it had a potbelly stove in the center of the club. And the bar was a card table with liquor on it. And there was a person actually playing 45s and albums. And back then, you didn't dance, unless someone came and asked you to dance, you see. Now, this was a southern thing. And I loved that. I loved that kind of etiquette. I loved it. I don't do too well nowadays, so I got to catch up. I got a lot of catching up to do, but I'm getting there with the hip-hop generation. I'm going to get them figured out sooner or later. But anyway, twelve years old, we looked like adults, we looked like young ladies, you know. Nobody was going to card you back then anyway. And we made ourselves up, as I said. But I stole my sister's clothes out of the closet. Yeah, I did that. And I know she knows because I found out from this same cousin. I love this cousin because he helped me to see things from the other side. That she was running back to these other cousins saying, "He's been wearing my clothes. He's been going to clubs. So-and-so and so-and-so." So I know, you know, that's how I knew my family knew what was going on.

And I must admit, we looked pretty good, you know, because the little thing we wanted to go for was to look *real*, you know, wanted to look real. And I think perhaps I went through a phase maybe where I wanted to be a woman, but it didn't last very long. I mean, it was very short. But as I continued to do drag, I was thankful that I was a man. Even doing drag, it became fun, so we did it for entertainment reasons. We didn't do it at that time because we wanted to be women or I was a woman trapped in a man's body. I didn't feel that, you know, not at all.

Sadly, T turned to prostitution. That goes hand in hand sometimes when you start so early. And so he didn't even finish high school, you know, so his story is tragic in that he's still out there prostituting. And now even prostituting for crack cocaine. So I hardly ever see him, you know, we just live two different lives, you know. So that's how I started, you know, into that whole thing. And let me tell you this. We had the option of being a drag queen, being a butch queen, or being trade. And I knew I wasn't going to be trade. [Laughter] I knew that. No way. Me? Trade? Unh uh, no. A butch queen was a gay man that wasn't a drag queen, but then you had drag queens. So the gay black culture in 1979 in the South was very black-and-white, you know. It wasn't all this diversity that there is now. And so that's why I chose drag, because I went to the road that best suited me at that time, which was to be a drag queen.

And how long did you do drag?

I did drag maybe four or five times a year. Because remember now, in my other life I was a church boy. So you can't be in the club and in the church, too. So, you know, I lived like five different lives. I had to be a good boy at home. Had to be a good boy at school and church. Then there was the whole gay issue. So I had all of these people to please, but I felt good being able to dress up in drag.

When did you stop performing drag?

It was probably in high school, because I did it once in college simply because my friends had heard through the grapevine, "Oh, we heard that you were just a fierce drag queen. That you couldn't be, you know, clocked, you know," which means that no one could tell that you were a man dressed up as a woman. And so they begged me for months and months. And so I finally did it for them. And they couldn't believe it, you know.

Did you have a drag name?

Yes, Paris. Paris Maldavia Van Buren. [Laughter] Yes, yes. I came up with that name at twelve years old. So that shows you how creative I was. And so Paris was such a beautiful name to me because, you know, in mythology, Paris is a man. But it's such a feminine name, you know. And then Maldavia, that just sounds so grand. And Van Buren, of course, you know that's the infidel. So Paris Maldavia Van Buren, that was my drag name.

Have you ever seriously considered moving out of the South?

Yes. [Laughter] I have. You just don't know. I have considered living in New Zealand. I have considered living in Australia. In Toronto. In Paris. Anywhere but here. And I think education will be the way for me, because I'm starting to hone in on what I want to get my Ph.D. in. And I think that once I go to get that Ph.D. and secure it, I won't come back to live in the South.

Why?

I've done the South. Been there, done that. You know, *lovely.* I mean, I am so fortunate and blessed to have been raised in the kind of family that I was raised in. It wasn't perfect—no family is perfect. And there was some dys-functions. But as far as the South is concerned, I've just done it. I want to do something different. You know, I have a lot of friends who moved to Atlanta who are in love with Atlanta. I'm not ruling out Atlanta. But it's just like a larger Winston-Salem to me, you know. It's just seven times larger, you know. So I want to see what the North is like or the West Coast is like or the Northwest Coast.

Do you think there are other regions in the country that provide a better life for black gay men?

I do think so. I really do think so. My first job out of college, I was a professional storyteller. I toured for six months with a company in Asheville, North Carolina. Did stories for elementary, middle schools, high schools, colleges, and teacher workshops. And so I went on a twenty-one-state tour. So I had an opportunity to see a lot of parts of the country. I saw mostly the midwestern states. And there are just some places where gay men, period, and gay women, period, don't have to look over their shoulders. You know, we're still discriminated against. We're not the norm. Something is wrong with us. This is what heterosexual society thinks. And, of course, I think the same of them. [Laughter] There's something wrong with them. Simply because they don't get it. So, you know, I pity them the way they pity me. But to answer your question, I know that there are places. I have seen places where gay people are just totally free to be themselves. And that's wonderful. And I want to experience being in that culture twenty-four hours a day. Because when I look at the gay lifestyle, I don't see what some people would consider the dark side. I see the good. I see the unification. I see the uplifting. I see the humanism, the common good. I don't see the back alleys. I don't see the bookstores. I choose not to. I'm not ignoring it, but I think a lot of gay people live on that dark side simply because they don't know they have a choice. You know, that you can be gay and you can have a fabulous, clean life, you know. And if you're into having sex with men for the fun of it, so be it. And if you're into having sex in alleyways, that's okay, too, but you don't have to. A lot of gay people just don't know that they don't have to live that way. They come out of the closet and go straight into the bookstores and they think that's what being gay is, and it's not. And there are plenty of cities where people don't live that way. And, you know, they have very nice, supportive cultures, yeah. So I want to experience that.

How would you describe your attitudes about intimate relationships with men? And let me sort of expand that question. Do you think southern culture is more conducive to establishing intimacy between men or not? And when I say intimacy, I don't mean sexual intimacy, but friendships and close emotional bonds, that kind of . . .

One thing I do like about southern culture is that we're touchy-feely. I like that. It's a shame when we can look to the animal kingdom and see how touchy-feely they are and humans, we're standoffish. But in the South, you can touch somebody's hand or shoulder or their knee and that's really nice. I really like that. I just wish that we could see more of it. I think that gay people everywhere think more about what others are thinking of them. If I could just put my idea into their heads, I think maybe it would do some good. What I mean by that is if I could tell them and they really get it, it doesn't matter what other people think, it's what you think, you know, go on and be your touchy-feely self, be your intimate self, it's okay, you know. But I think that's a part of southern living, being able to cozy up to others in intimate relationships, friendships. I have friends that I'm very intimate with; we can sit on the couch and we can just sit and just—as close as possible, nothing sexual at all. I have one good friend, I will massage his feet, he just loves for me to massage his feet, and it's nothing sexual there. We're good buddies, you know, we're just real good buddies. And so I love that. I think that's a human thing and that we're a bit too mechanical in our society.

How would you describe your involvement in the gay community?

In Winston-Salem, I would say that I am involved in a very small group. We have a small group that we call the monthly potluck of upwardly mobile gay black men. It's somewhat selective, not snobbish, but selective in that these are gay black men who are white-collar workers and professionals in every area of professionals, from doctors, attorneys, professors, other areas of education. And so I'm involved in that potluck but it is more of a support group than anything else. So as far as activism, I'm not into activism, not at this time. But I really have some ideas up my sleeve. I really do want to help gay people, period. What I really want to do is to help them to see their worth, if I can uplift some kind of way. So at some point I may write a book or poetry. I love writing. I don't know if I told you that. And I may just dedicate a book of poems or short stories that yell these themes that you are lovable. That you can take the personal responsibility to love yourself. You don't have to find validation in any other person, place, thing, event, or idea. That's why I say the Oprah thing, you know, I love her and I love what she has done for humanity. But I want to do that for gay people at some point, so. The university may help me do that. So that will be my contribution to the cause. But as far as parades and gay rights, specifically so, no. I'm not involved. But I am interested in human rights, you see, because I can represent the gay person. I can represent the minority. Those two things I know well. I'm a double minority. At some point I will get there. So that's the extent of my involvement in a support group. But we just call it the potluck.

So you feel a sense of community among black gay men where you live?

I do. I certainly do. And something I'm very proud of—not to brag or boast, now this is a southern thing, humbleness, got to be humble—is that I don't look over my shoulder when I'm around gay people. Another term that we didn't mean, Judas, as in the friend of Jesus who pretty much stabbed him in the back. Or the Judas goat that leads innocent sheep to the slaughter, that gay people can be Judas. I'm not a Judas person, and I'm so glad I'm not a Judas person, I really am. And so there are gay black people who mirror all parts of black society. You have poverty-stricken gay black people. You have gay blacks who are struggling to make ends meet. You have gay blacks who are wealthy, who don't worry about anything. And then you have gay black people like us who are doing all right. So when I am in a large group of people, perhaps at a club, because that's where you're going to find everybody usually, or some kind of celebratory event, I can go to the person who arrived in the taxi cab simply because they don't have a car or who came on the train or came on a bus to the club and give them a hug and know that I'm well loved by them and accepted by them. And I accept them and I can turn right around and hug the person who came in the limousine, that I don't see myself as one because I have a good education and really try hard to represent what that means, I don't worry about trying to fit a certain stereotype. I refuse to be a snob.

So what am I saying? What I'm saying is I can go to the person, the gay black person, who is just basically poverty-stricken and be well respected by them and the person who arrived in the limousine. And I'm proud of that, that I don't look down on them and that's not a self-righteous statement. That's the truth. I'm so happy that I don't look down on people. Because in the gay black society, just like society, there are real snobs. People apply how they walk and talk and what they're wearing and what they're driving; it's sickening, to me.

Do you see much interaction between the white gay community and the black gay community?

Now, in Winston-Salem there is a club called Odyssey. And there is a white side and a black side. In Winston-Salem now. But at least we're in the same club. [Laughter] Where in large cities, the clubs are segregated, you see, in large southern cities, like Atlanta. Oh, my goodness, there may be seven gay clubs and bars there that are black. Black-owned, and the patrons are black. And then you have white clubs in these cities, and you have one or two blacks who go there because, for whatever reason, they don't feel comfortable in the black clubs. And I won't go into that, especially those who feel like they're too good, or they're into white men only. Yeah, that's a trip. [Laughter] That's a trip. But in Winston-Salem there's a black side of the club and there's a white side. And you'll see white folk on the black side, you'll see black folk on the white side. But we're under one roof. And so it's not blatant separatism, it's not segregation. It's based on the music. See, there's this hardcore, this new house music, I don't know what you call it, rave music. That's on the white side of the club. And black folk just don't get into that. So we like our house music that has rhythm to it, that has a gospel beat. And our R&B mixed in with it. So that's why there's a black side and the white side. [. . .] It's about the music. Just about the music. You'll see people going on each other's side. But, you hardly ever see the black people going over to the white side because they can't tolerate the music. It's not the people.

Okay. What role does religion or church play in your life currently?

Ooh, boy, I love that question. Church plays in my life now, it's the foundation; it was a good foundation for me, very good foundation. I'm not active in the church anymore. And I doubt if I ever will be, even a gay church. And I'm for gay churches. I have such a personal relationship with God that the church would have to catch up, to be honest with you. Because God really does love me unconditionally, and I know that. So I don't see why I should go to church unless I'm going to contribute in some way. You know, I see if I'm there I need to be contributing. I need to help in some way because I'm not going there to take. Because I can give so much and what I've been giving has been multiplied. And so I've learned from the church. I've come down that path and so I'm thankful. So at this time, for me, religion, church, those are very interpersonal or intrapersonal, that's what I should say. It's an intra-personal experience for me now.

Why do you think so many black gay men are in the church, particularly the church choir?

You know what? This is a fact: many gay people are very talented. And so, we try to go where we feel we can be used or we can be welcome. A lot of gay people, black gay people, are into the church, I guess for many different reasons. But that choir, I think it's because they just feel that this is something I can do. Some of them are on the treadmill, that dysfunction treadmill. You know you're going to go in every Sunday and the preacher is going to beat the crap out of you verbally. But you're a part of the abusive cycle. They don't see that. So what am I saying? For a lot of gay people, just like a lot of straight people, church is an addiction. It's not a necessity. They don't know they're addicted. It's a drug. It was a drug for me, until God showed up and helped me to see. Because I didn't have a relationship with God, I had a relationship with the church. That's what I had a relationship with.

Do you think the church is a place for men to meet other men?

I'm sure they do. I know they do. I have seen it myself. I will not go to church to meet other men, but I know it does happen. I know it does happen. And I don't like it. [Laughter] But, of course, you could fill this whole house up with things I don't like, because I'm a utopian-thinking kind of person. And so I like for motives to be pure and as sincere as possible. And to go to church to meet a man? Oh my goodness, that's totally wicked. Now, that's wicked. If there is a devil, the devil is in that. Going to a church to meet a man. All these men out here, you can meet a man at the stoplight, but to go to church to meet a man, no, I hope not.

But that works both ways, right? If straight women are doing the same thing.

Oh, yes, of course. Of course. And that's the thing about black gay culture that I wish everybody knew, we're just gay, but we're just as human as everybody else. And so there is the dark side to the heterosexual club. They have their pornography. They have their whips and chains and the things that they're into. But for gay people, it's factual and some is stereotypical and blown out of proportion, as well. Sometimes we get a little bad rap.

What has been the impact of HIV and AIDS on your life?

Oh, my goodness, I have lost so many friends. I'm thankful that I'm HIV-negative. But that's by the grace of God. Now, we talked about being Judas. When a lot of gay black men in my community started getting sick, with full-blown AIDS, the Judas queens talked about them. That bothered me. I'll never forget, I was at a party one time, and this one Judas queen was just going on and on about, "Yeah, I knew So-and-So was going to get it, blah, blah, blah, blah, blah." And I told everybody standing right there in that circle, "The same trade that she slept with, you slept with, too. If you didn't, you slept with his cousin." You see, there's only so much trade around here. So to tear somebody down because they got HIV, that was horrible to me. But I have lost some good friends. And so the same men that they slept with, I probably slept with, but I was fortunate. I was fortunate.

So you were coming of age right around the time that we were learning about AIDS?

And see, that's the thing about it. And I still need to deal with this whole southern thing, with my southern ways, my southern belle ways, my AKA ways, being a number one fan of the Alpha Kappa Alpha sorority. Even as a young man, as a teenager, gay young person, I didn't want to be seen as a whore. I didn't want to be seen as a slut. I didn't want to be seen that way. So my standard was no. No, unh unh, I'll flirt with you. I'll tease you, but I'm not going all the way with you. And I think that's why I'm still here, because I didn't go all the way. And so as arrogant as some of those southern ways could be at that time, I'm not that way anymore, as far as having all these high standards and Victorian ways, because you will be lonely, it saved my life. Um hmm, yeah, it saved my life.

Do you think that HIV and AIDS is more of a problem here in the South because of what you were talking about earlier, this whole notion of sexuality just not being talked about?

I think that the virus doesn't discriminate, of course. But I think in the South, people just don't want to even go there, even those who are infected. I had friends who were infected who were in denial. Even up until their dying day. It's a shame. And some of us have a way of making shame, you see. But the sad part about it is when we let somebody else's belief system become our own, because this is a shame for them or it's horrible, then we take that onto ourselves, too. Yeah, this is horrible. I must be a bad person because this happened to me. Yeah, that's sad.

What are your best memories of growing up in the South?

Ooh, boy. Playing outside as a child. I loved to play. And again, a lot of my play was creative play. But I had good neighborhood friends. We played all the games, freeze tag, kickball. But just to climb the trees; I had a lot of trees in the yard growing up. I just loved getting to the top of the tree and looking out. And now I can look back and see, yeah, I think I was a spiritual child. Sometimes I would just sit and just look at the sky, look at the clouds, as a child. And I just think and meditate. Going to the community center, the recreation center, which was like right up the street from our house. I didn't even know that there were poor people, just a few streets over. Had no clue. I just thought that's where they lived. I didn't know they were poor. I didn't know what poor was. But all of us came together in the summertime. Learned how to swim when I was six years old. So the morning part of the day would be some kind of recreational activity, swimming lessons and all of that. [In] the afternoon [we] would go to museums. And this was paid for by the parks and recreation department. So I loved the summertime. Because all of the kids in the community could go to their nearest recreation center, and the government, oh, boy, there was no problem funding programs back then. And so our parents were happy to send us because they knew that that was an extension of our education. So I didn't spend summers watching television growing up. I was active at the recreation center. And so that was a fond memory, too, arts and crafts. I think one of my fondest memories again were my neighbors who were educators, who would invite me over for arts and crafts or to read a book or to teach me to play piano. That was nice. I had a nice childhood in that regard.

How would you describe the influence of southern culture on your character?

Again, it's that southern etiquette, you see. And that shaped my character. Manners. Having good manners. Growing up to be taught to say, "yes, ma'am," and "no, ma'am." I can remember being five years old and my father plainly telling me, "You have to say 'sir' to me. Your brothers and your sisters say it. You say it, too. And you call your mother 'ma'am' when she calls you." So having good manners, that was really important in my house. Having to say, "good morning," oh, my goodness, I hated it. Because sometimes I didn't feel like saying "good morning." But if I didn't say "good morning,' my father would chew into me. Now, what's good about that? So there is even dysfunction in southern hospitality, you see. Am I being nice to you because this is what we do, or am I being nice to you simply because this is what the culture calls for? But when it's genuine, it's nice. So those things have shaped my character. I'm a very polite person. Even in e-mails, I try to be polite. I really do, because of that, because of those things that were taught. I think one psychologist calls it "shadow beliefs," growing up under the same umbrella or shadow that your parents grew up. But when it's sincere, it's nice. It's nice to be on time for work, and to open the door for people, and to say, "please" and "thank you." But now, what bothers me about the whole southern culture as I look at it on shaping my character and the characters of other people is this: They borrowed these same things from Europeans. And the Europeans borrowed it from somebody else. And nobody is an original. Now, that bothers me. So, I'm coming into this phase in my life where I really want to be me, more of me every day, and less of something else that I've been shaped by.

How would you describe your current feelings about being a black gay man?

I'm loving it more and more every day, the older I get. The older I get, the more I love me. And that means I love my race, I love my culture, I love my sexuality. Even though I'm not involved in a relationship, I still love my sexuality, because this is who I was born to be. So, I mean, I have on my screen saver, G-U-D, the number 2, the letter B, and ME. Good to be me. So that's my mantra. It's good to be me. I'm happy for you, love you, but it's good to be me. And I need to continue to do this because I have had low self-esteem in the past. And so the older I get and the more I accept me, the higher my self-esteem becomes. And so I'm just thinking right now, hey, I got the best life on the planet. I really do. Despite the fact that there are things I want to accomplish there. There's always room in the bank for more money, in the bank account. There's always another kind of car you may want. That used to bother me, but it doesn't bother me anymore. So I'm just happy with me being me. Whatever that means today.

How do you feel about the life choices that you've made in light of being black and gay?

I think I spent a lot of time caring what other people thought about me. The disease to please, that hindered me. And so now I'm playing catch-up.

So I'm really playing catch-up. So I'm just at this point now where, I'm just going to keep evolving, and just keep going towards the light. As New Age as that sounds, I mean every word of it. But I got a lot of catching up to do because I spent so much time in the darkness, in fear. I'm like either you're going to love me or you're not going to love me. And that's why I don't mind my real name being in this book. Who am I running away from? Not a runaway, that's so unnecessary.

Anything you'd like to add?

I think again I just want to really emphasize to all gay people that we have to take personal responsibility in uplifting ourselves and each other and stop worrying about the other culture. You know, if they love us, that's fine. But if they keep being the a-holes that they can be sometimes, move on. We have each other and that's good enough. Yeah, that's it.

· · · · · · · ·

"MADEMOISELLE GRÉGOIRE"/GREG

I've known Greg for close to ten years. We met at a National Communication Association convention when we were both graduate students. Even then, Greg was always the talk of the convention because of either his over-the-top outfits or his confrontation with a speaker or panelist. Being provocative is his primary occupation.

When I traveled to New Orleans on May 10, 2005, to conduct the interview with Greg, I had no idea how adventurous it was going to be. I arrived at his home near the Garden District and landed in the middle of a confrontation between him and his stepfather about where I had chosen to park the car. I was also surprised to discover that we wouldn't be conducting the interview at Greg's home. He asked me to take him to run several errands—to the post office, to a café to check his e-mail, etc.—before sitting down for the interview. After the errands, however, he wanted to stop by the Society Page, a black gay club on Rampart Street in the French Quarter, for a drink. I was beginning to feel that the interview was not going to happen, as it was approaching 10 P.M. and I had a 7:30 A.M. flight out the next morning. Finally, at around 11 P.M., we left the Society Page and walked up to the Bourbon Street Pub—a highly inhospitable place for an interview because of the loud music. Nonetheless, we sat outside on the balcony that overlooks Bourbon Street and had the interview.

Greg is as grand as his stage name. As he notes in his narrative, he enunciates every syllable in a word, owing, he says, to his very strict Catholic school education and his experience as a forensics and debate coach. In fact, he has taught speech and debate at several high schools and universities around the country, and his students have, according to him, placed very well in regional and national competitions. He recently took a job in China teaching English. I would bet all the "tea" in China that he's turning Beijing inside out.

I was born in New Orleans, Louisiana, on April the 14th, 1956. My grandmother raised me. I went to Catholic school for eight years. I went to the Sisters of the Blessed Sacrament, who own and operate Xavier University. A very genteel, very pristine Catholic childhood. Khaki pants, khaki shirt. Altar boy. The whole thing. You know, the nine yards. Black tie. I was very arts-oriented, very cultured in arts and theater, drama, music, opera, things of that nature. I truly enjoyed the Catholic school education. It was great. It laid a strong foundation in my academic career, especially discipline-wise because the nuns were strong disciplinarians. Having a strong foundation in public speaking and oratory. Language arts. Things of that sort.

And what was your neighborhood like?

Well, I grew up in the Third Ward of New Orleans, which is a Third Ward Calliope housing project on Martin Luther King and Galvez. And very quiet. Of course, thirty years ago, living in a housing project was the most modern thing you could live in, you know, and we had all of the modern facilities. So it had not gone by the wayside like we know them today. Thirty years ago, they were just lovely apartments. And my grandmother had it furnished in French Provincial style, with the plastic covers and all of that. You couldn't sit on certain furniture and all of that. So you know it was very decorative, very ornate, that kind of thing. You know like grandmothers do. Very doily. Very ornate kind of living.

Do you have siblings?

Yes, I'm the oldest [and have] three sisters.

Oh wow! And were you close to your sisters growing up?

Definitely. Always close. Very close. My grandmother raised me, and my grandmother raised a sister, my sister after me. And my mother raised the two younger girls. You know, for financial purposes. And it went well. And the two younger girls went to Catholic school as well. And so it was really good because we were able to kind of divvy up the economics between my grandmother and my mother. So it worked well. And it was small enough for just us four. And large enough for us to have a family-oriented type of environment. Big on holidays. Big on birthdays. Even today. I just celebrated my birthday April 14th, and all my sisters were at the house and we had ice cream and cake and my sister made me a dinner. My sister from Houston called in and my sisters that are here had their children and things there. So it was nice.

Did you know your father?

Oh yes. My father left New Orleans and went out to California in the '60s in the military. And he and I have kind of kept in contact on and off over the years. However, I was raised by my mother's people. And so we communicate and, he was someone that was in my life. He was not estranged. But being the very feminine type and kind of gay young man that I was at that time, I always gravitated to my grandmother and my mother, because they have all of the lovely things. All of the beautiful stuff. And I always loved beautiful things. So I always gravitated towards them and my sisters because they always liked nice stuff, so I tend to gravitate toward the girls as opposed to my dad and his people.

Were your grandmother and your mother born in New Orleans, or did they migrate from other places?

My family is originally Haitian from Haiti. My great-great-grandmother was from Haiti. Her name was Tess in French, which is Theresa in English. My mother was Theresa. And my grandmother, Sophia. They were from St. James, Louisiana. And they migrated from St. James, Louisiana, to New Orleans, groups of sisters, back in the 1930s and '40s, and took careers here. My grandmother worked as a domestic for two rich millionaire Jews that worked at Tulane. And then my grandmother's sisters, they all were seamstresses, and they sewed and they patched. They were very decorative women. So I probably inherited that kind of artistic flair from them. Very church women. Done up to the nines, with the gloves and the hats, the purses, the shoes to match, all of the regalia. In fact when my grandmother died in 1989, she had clothes, hats, and shoes in the closet with tags still on them.

And what did your mother do for work?

My mother, in the beginning stages of her career, she was a teacher. She was very much involved in physical education. And she coached girls' sports. Volleyball, softball, a lot of girls' sports. And she was a track star when I was a kid. In fact, she was going to try out for the 1956 Olympics but was not able to try out in '56 because she was pregnant with me. [Laughter] And so she had issues with that. So you know she could have probably been another Wilma Rudolph because she was quite a talented athletic star. Unfortunately, she died very young, in 1980; she died at fifty-three. I guess of a broken heart. The man that she was living with at the time was rather strung out, and addicted, and things of that nature. And they moved all around the city and, unfortunately, she didn't have any peace. But she died at fifty-three and she's at peace now, I'm sure. So she found peace.

You grew up in New Orleans in the '50s. Was it segregated then?

Oh yes. I was born in 1956, so, when I grew up it was basically, of my knowledge, was in the '60s actually. Of course the '60s was a very segregated South. And I remember, everything was very "colored" or "Negro." I can still remember some things, some signs, vaguely, about "colored" and "Negro" areas. And then I definitely remember in theaters where, African Americans were relegated to sitting in the balconies and the white folks sat down on the floor, to their unfortunate situation because the blacks, of course, would hurl things down on the floor. Popcorn, etc. So it was an interesting time. But I never thought I was poor because I had everything. I never went to bed hungry. My grandmother provided everything. My grandmother and my mother were a team. When my grandmother didn't have, my mother picked up the slack. When my mother didn't have, my grandmother picked up the slack. They were a tag team for four children, and they did exceedingly well. All my sisters are professionals. Of course, I'm a teacher, a university professor. And my sister after me is a youth minister in the Catholic Church. My sister after her owns her own business in child development. And my youngest sister is a paralegal in Houston. So we did very well.

Do you have any friends from your childhood that you're still in touch with?

I see, periodically, some of my childhood friends. One thing about academia, you kind of go different roads. And it's such a really intense kind of profession that you're always embroiled in doing things. Sometimes, you'll see people. A lot of times I see people that I grew up with or that I know from the past, during Mardi Gras or Essence Festival, things of that nature. And we kind of talk and hang out or something of that nature during that time. But a lot of times, the career in academia keeps you very busy. Sometimes I come out on the weekend; sometimes I'm busy grading papers. I try to make some time for some leisure because, of course, all work and no play makes Johnny a very dull, dull gay boy. I am not a dull gay boy. I like to be flamboyant. I like to be fiery. I love fire and music, that kind of thing. So I try to make time to indulge myself.

What role did church play in your upbringing?

Oh a lot. Very into gospel music. I'm one of the original Gospel Soul Children of New Orleans. I got my gospel musical training from the great Albert Sylvester Hadley. And Albert Hadley was a great gospel musician back in the '70s. I joined the choir back in 1974 and traveled all over the country with the Gospel Soul Children. And I was also a soloist and also a narrator for the choir. And then moved on to college. My undergrad is Morehouse, and I did my master's at Southern [University] in Baton Rouge and trying to get ready to go defend this Ph.D. at Florida State in the next week or so. A busy task.

So you enjoyed church?

I really did. I learned how to play the piano and I learned gospel music in church. In fact, I have some theater performances that I do. When I was an assistant professor of humanities at Livingstone College in North Carolina, I had a production of *God's Trombones*, gospel music and dance, theater and song. So I like James Weldon Johnson and of course I did his work when I was a student, competing in speech and dramatic arts. I took first in the city of New Orleans, fourth in the state of Louisiana, and sixth in the nation, with "The Judgment Day" by James Weldon Johnson. And so I love the *God's Trombones*. It's one of my favorite pieces. At my mother's funeral, I recited. At the wake services, I did "Go Down Death," which is a beautiful piece talking about Sister Caroline. And of course I changed it, with poetic license, and said "Sister Theresa," which was my mother's name. So I love gospel music. I love the church. And the gospel music ministry was very strong and very powerful for me. And to this day, I'm a very strong gospel music fan. I love gospel singing.

You were raised Catholic?

Originally raised Catholic. You know, however, Catholics now are some of the biggest holy rollers. And you can see when they sing their gospel in churches. You know, they do a lot of gospel music in Catholic churches now. When I was in Catholic churches, they had the seminarians and they were doing the guitars, the high masses and [. . .] the Latin and all of that. Then they moved from Latin and the guitar masses to the gospel music. So I was able to actually be involved in some gospel singing in Catholic church from having a strong background with the Gospel Soul Children. In fact, I went to one of the original National Offices of Black Catholics in the late '70s at Rensselaer Poly-Tech University in Rensselaer, Indiana [it is actually located in Troy, New York]. And we did lots of wonderful music there, and we've had our National Office of Black Catholics here in New Orleans, where we perform some of the great music of the Edwin Hawkins Singers and Father Clarence Joseph Rivers and Grayson Brown and a lot of great liturgists, musical liturgists in the Catholic Church. So I've been involved in the Catholic Church in music since I'd say like the late '70s. I'm not very active now because I'm so embroiled, in getting this Ph.D. and this dissertation, which is the "big D" word.

When did you first become aware of your same-sex orientation, and what was your reaction to that realization?

When I was a little bitty boy, probably about six or seven years old. And I always had an affinity for boys. And it just was a natural thing for me. You know I had a very good childhood and a very strong childhood, with Mother and Grandmother and my sisters. And being the only male, of course all of them spoiled me rotten. And even to today. So you know without any hard knocks. For a little while, we had a little rift where we weren't speaking, but you know everybody got over everybody and we moved on and we realized that this is my life and I was paying the cost to be the boss and hey, I was going to play my tune and I was going to be my own pied piper and march to the beat of my own drummer. And so once my family realized it, they attempted to understand. And then of course I reached out and started embroiling myself in female impersonation and the art of cross-dressing and illusion and transvestism, and that took my being gay to a whole other level. Pure drama. Lots of theater. Lots of makeup. Lots of eyelashes and all of that kind of carrying on. So I love it. I love the gay lifestyle. It's a beautiful lifestyle. And if you look at it and look [at] it in a good way, it's very liberating and very freeing. In fact, the paper that I'm going to do in Boston at the National Communications Association is going to talk about the liberation and the mental health policy of transvestitism and drag and cross-dressing; how it's so liberating. How it's so freeing. And it gives one a self-assured policy of mental health because it's very freeing. It's very liberating. You know it's a situation where you can be yourself, do *you*. You don't have to be bottled up. You can move outside of the box and do your thing. So I'm looking forward to doing that paper in Boston.

When did you begin cross-dressing and doing drag and all that?

Well, I had an affinity for drag when I was in college at Morehouse in the late '70s. I'm in love with the great music of Sylvester. And of course I've performed Sylvester's music at several National Communications Association conferences, my "Divas to the Dance Floor." And of course you were at one of the panels we had in Atlanta. And I always loved Sylvester's music. I always loved his art and his performance style. And he was always such a great mentor to me. And I started getting very embroiled in drag in the late '70s, early '80s when I was a student at Morehouse. And then when I graduated Morehouse, I went to New York City and got really involved in it, traveling in the Northeast and performing and things of that nature. Clubs and shows and pageants and, all of that. You know, it's a wonderful life, being able to travel to the different clubs and shows and pageants. It gives you a lot to look forward to. Lots of hope. Lots of opportunities. It's very liberating. You know, it's very freeing. And it takes you to a level of awareness, where you really get attuned to yourself and know who you are, both internally and externally. Because you know when you put on the makeup and the eyelashes and all of that, you have to really know your face as a canvas to be a beautiful queen. And since I consider myself a legendary diva and a lot of other people do, as well. So a lovely queen has to stay beautiful, when you put on the makeup and all of that, so drag was always a liberating thing for me. And when I went to college at Morehouse, we used to experiment in the bathrooms, perm each other's hair on the weekends. We used to have fun in the dorms, in each other's rooms. We'd have little parties.

At Morehouse?

Oh yes, indeed. In our own little private rooms. And some friends of mine, we were all members of the Morehouse College Glee Club. And of course the great singing organization of the school. And I was on speech and debate team and all of that. And you know we'd just get together as a group, and we would do *us*. We would focus on us as a group of gay men, and it was always so interesting. You know we'd have the disco music and we'd dance and we'd perform and we'd swing out and have our cocktails and wonderful things to smoke back in those days. You know it was just such a liberating time. A very, very freeing and liberating time. And one thing I love about being gay, especially the time period that I've had the opportunity to come along . . . You know because so many people before me, such as Sylvester and Lady Bunny and the Queens from Stonewall and all of that, they paved the way for me to come out and I did in the late '70s. I finished college in 1978 so I was a disco baby. And that was a very freeing period. Donna Summer, Sylvester, "Dance with me in the disco heat"[6] and all of that. You know, the Weather Girls and all of that. So the late '70s and early '80s of the disco era was a great period to come out.

Talk more about what it was like being gay at a historically black college, men's college. Did you find people accepting, or did you have problems there?

It was very interesting. My grandmother used to tell me this as a young child. You get more bees with honey than with vinegar. So I always used my good looks, my great speech abilities, the swing of my hips, and the command of my flamboyance and my "gayism" and all of that, as a calling card to be able to have all entrée, to be able to succeed as a novelty and to go through the hallowed halls of academia with success. And at Morehouse, it was that way. I had a reputation of being a national champion in speech and debate. Forensics and speech and dramatic arts is my life. I've been doing it for thirty-some years now and I was on the speech and debate team at Morehouse and in the glee club. So I always took the arts very, very seriously and embroiled myself around the arts and people associated with the arts. And I always found that, at the historically black colleges, when you have a persona, when you have an elegance, when you have . . . when you're gay and have flamboyance and you use it to your advantage, you use it as a positive, as a plus rather than as a negative, you can achieve and succeed. So I've always believed that you get more bees with honey than with vinegar. I've always believed in being a charmer and being able to use what I have as an entrée, as my forte. You know, as Glenn Close says in *Dangerous Liaisons*, she believed that she wanted to win. And that's what I've always felt. That you use what you have as a calling card to give you carte blanche, to have access and to have doors open for you. And therefore you get more bees with honey than with vinegar. So you want to have doors open for you rather than have doors slam.

And are you still in touch with some of the other folks who were doing drag back at Morehouse, today?

I had several friends of mine that used to perform back in the day. Unfortunately, they're no longer with us. They have passed on. Many of them have passed on.

Is there any particular theory about homosexuality that you believe?

My biggest theory is that homosexuality is not a mental disorder and should not be classified as such. And the time that I was coming out, in the late '70s, it was removed off of the American psychiatric lists, as being a mental disorder. So for me, that's one of the most freeing and liberating forms of theory that there is.

And do you identify as gay, or do you identify as trans, or . . . ?

I identify as a gay man that is a transvestite. You know, I'm a gay man that loves women's clothing. I love the feel of beautiful silk, of gorgeous fabrics. I love the look of beautiful eye makeup, of gorgeous hair, of beautiful makeup, and things of that sort. Which is something that I inherited from, growing up as the oldest male with a mother, grandmother, and three sisters. And so I identify with gay men. I identify with cross-dressers as well. I'm not interested in changing my sex. I like being a man. But I have a lot of friends that are transsies, that have changed over. And they're beautiful people.

When you were growing up, did you know other people in your neighborhood who were gay or that people said were gay? And if so, how were they treated in the community?

Well one thing about growing up when I came along, we didn't have all of this homophobia. You know, when you were a gay man coming up in the '60s and '70s, you're always seen as a very big novelty. A big novelty item. Somebody that's *someone.* Somebody that's *somebody* in the gay community. And Sylvester talks about that a lot. You know, that when he came out of Los Angeles and went on to beauty school and went into the churches and played gospel music and things of that nature. Or when you were a gay man, back in those days, African American gay men were very novel. You know, when they came through, the trumpets blared. You know, the red carpets came out. They were just grand, ultra, very grand in anything. The way they dressed. The way they lived. The way they spoke. The way they just lived life with a great zest and a very great zeal. Unfortunately a lot of white friends of mine, they have horror stories that they have to tell as being young and gay and coming out. But back in the day when I came out, because I'm forty-nine now, society has changed immensely now. The young kids nowadays are extremely homophobic. But even the young kids nowadays, they have their own forms of creative expression. As a teacher, I work with these young students every day and they have their bounce music. And they get into their bounce music and they [mimicking the rhythm of the music] bounce-uh, they bounce-uh, they bounce. They're bouncing to this and bouncing to that. They're bounce to bounce and all of that. And they have their great bounce celebrities and all of that. And then before that, we had the voguing and all of that. And when I came along, it was the sophisticated sissies and the disco and all of that. So the kids now, they have a lot more homophobia against them, but they seem to do very well. They seem to battle it well. They seem to have a strong concept of themselves. And I'm just so glad that, as a harbinger and as a mentor and a leader, I can be there to show them what gay is all about; what being gay-educated is all about; what being educated, gay, and grand is all about. It's all about being gay, educated, and the grand diva. And so a lot of my children, a lot of the students learn that. And they push forward. They push forward. We have a lot of opportunities coming up. A lot of things were very new to us, back in the late '70s, early '80s. However, I think society is changing. You know it's getting for the better. We're opening a lot more doors. As gay people, we're everywhere. We're queer and we're here. You know we have a lot of doors and a lot of opportunities out here. Society has become very politically correct and very politically accepting of us, as gay people. So therefore, since society has become increasingly accepting of us, and then we bring to the table lots of education, experience, backgrounds, and things of that nature, and then when you bring credentials to the table, you cannot be denied, regardless of your sexual orientation.

Have you ever seriously considered moving out of the South?

Well I have. The South is my home and I have been back and forth. I lived up north in Ohio, Michigan, New York. I've been out west. Colorado. And down South is where I'm born and raised. New Orleans. And once I get the Ph.D., make me an offer I can't refuse and I will be there at the drop of a hat, because education nowadays has also become a business. And it's a situation where you no longer teach in the same district for thirty years, like our predecessors. You look around and search around for opportunities that can come your way. And so I'm looking for greater opportunity all the time. And so hey, if I find the opportunity that can give me the best deal, once I get my Ph.D., I'm there.

So you're not necessarily tied to the South?

Oh no. One thing about academia, you cannot be tied anywhere. Academia is such a ethno-*graphic*, in light of what we're doing [the interview], it's a very ethno-graphic type of profession where you have to be ready to roll. You know you have to be almost like a roving reporter, ready to go to where the opportunities come and where you can have the biggest advantage, you see, and have a great department and a great team of scholars, pushing your kind of research and the kind of academia that you bring to the table and that you bring to the forefront, in a place where you can really call home when you get your Ph.D. and be able to seek tenure in that particular territory. So that's what I'm looking forward to doing. I'm ready.

Do you think there are other regions in the country, outside of the South, that provide a better life for black gay men?

Oh I would think so. I would think so. The North has always been very progressive. The West Coast has always been very progressive. And surprisingly, when I was teaching in Ohio, the Midwest is very progressive as far as African American men are concerned. The South has areas and territories that are very progressive. You have Atlanta, New Orleans, Miami, Houston, Dallas. The major cities are very progressive as far as African American gay men are concerned. So it just depends on, you know, the person, where they want to be, and the opportunity and how the opportunity strikes and at what particular time. You know, timing is everything. Opportunity is everything. Personally, I won't rule out opportunity in the South. If I can get a beautiful gig in some of those Atlanta universities or Miami or Dallas or any of those places, I tell you I'm there. But I think that, as gay men, we should be able to cast our eggs everywhere. Not put our eggs all in one basket. I would not want to put all of my eggs in the South, as one basket. But I want to be able to seek myself out internationally. I've also thought about toying with the idea this year of maybe going abroad, to China, to teach English you know in some of the Chinese universities because they're looking for professors there. I'd like to try out international territories, and not just be embroiled in one particular area.

Do you think that the South is more homophobic than other places?

Not really. Not really. The South has opened up immensely in a lot of areas as far as sexual orientation. As far as gender is concerned. I mean we're right here on Bourbon Street at the Bourbon Parade on Bourbon and St. Anne and just looking off the balcony, you can see a plethora of people; different races and cultures and nationalities and things of that nature here in New Orleans. So I'd say that the South is opening up a lot as far as being gay is concerned. I think that homophobia is a state of mind. It's only homophobia if you *allow* it to become that. It's a rhetorical referent that can oppress if you allow that rhetorical referent to oppress you. You see? Like when I'm working within the Harlem Renaissance, these artists of the Harlem Renaissance who are artists and activists, they did not *allow* reference of race to oppress them. So they used their art to become activists. And I think that's what a lot of gay people are doing now. They're using their sexual orientation to become politically aware and to become very actively involved in the community. And you know once you go over that hurdle and stamp out that oppression, then you can succeed.

Do you currently have a partner?

No, I've always been a single number. I've always been single. I've had the opportunity. I've been proposed to many a time. I've had many a caller. However, I've always relegated myself to being single. I have fancied myself as a Mademoiselle. I'm forty-nine and still a "Miss." I like being a spinster schoolteacher, a bon vivant Mademoiselle about town. You can do your thing. You have no ties, no restrictions. You can do your thing and fly your wings around, flap your wings and be a butterfly. Free. Liberating. And you know you don't have to answer to any man. Because I don't want to have to do like Celie did in *The Color Purple.*

Is there much interaction between the black gay community and the white gay community here?

I think there is. A lot more than in the past. We have lots of krewes. We have carnival clubs. We have African American carnival clubs and krewes that are very interacting with the mainstream community. And that's a very important thing because at one point in time, historically, we didn't have that. And just a lot to keep things in tap. And we have an African American organization here called The Brotherhood, which is very involved in community-based activities. And we have a paper here, a mainstream gay paper, which is *The Ambush*. And in *The Ambush* we have lots of African American–oriented types of articles, and also in *The Southern Voice*, which is published outside of Atlanta. We have lots of African American articles in *The Southern Voice* as well, so there is a strong Southern voice for African American culture and being gay. We have a lot of strong issues and a lot of strong agendas as African American gay men. And we're being heard.

How would you describe your involvement in the gay community?

Very active. I love being active. I love traveling. I love going to Chicago to the Miss Continental Pageant. To the Miss Continental Plus. Miss Continental is on Labor Day. Miss Continental Plus is usually around Easter. And I love going to the Circuit parties and things of that nature.

So you participate in the pageants?

Oh yes. I have performed. And I love traveling around and being in the Circuit pageant and being in the Circuit Club and stuff like that. I like going to the Circuit and performing. In fact, in Chicago, I did Jennifer Holliday on her "And I'm Telling You I'm Not Going" from *Dreamgirls* when it was a house mix. And I was in Chicago at the time at the Miss Continental Plus. And I got on the stage, honey, and I just worked them over. And of course, all the boys in the audience had ripped off their shirts and everything, at Circuit Club over on Halsted. So it's just a wonderful, wonderful kind of performance. A lot of performance can be impromptu, extemporaneous on how I feel. And a lot of times I'll go out, according to how I feel, strike up the band and do a performance. And then sometimes I'll get on the list and be a special guest or something. The last pageant that I [did] was the Miss Florida pageant in 1992. I've been so busy I haven't really been involved in pageants as far as performing in them. But as far as going to the Circuit parties and the Circuit Club—oh I love to go to those and just really whip up the Circuit and just perform. You know and just tear down the house in the club.

What's your stage name?

Mademoiselle Grégoire. [Laughter] That's my stage name. When I came on as a young little kid on this corner with all my girlfriends back in the day, Miss Tasha Richard [pronounced Ri-shard] and Miss Erica Wells and those girls, they're no longer alive today, but they used to go, "Miss Gregory" this and "Miss Gregory" that. So I've changed my name from "Miss Gregory" to French, which is Mademoiselle Grégoire. Clever. Enchanté. [Laughter] And of course I love Eartha Kitt, and all of that kind of French action. And Josephine Baker and all of those people. So it was very fitting and very apropos for me as a Creole goddess [laughter] of New Orleans, a Creole fashion plate.

Have you ever won a pageant?

Oh yes. I've got lots of bar pageants. I've got lots of those. I've never gotten a major title because I've never really had the opportunity. Because of so much being involved in academia. If I pursued it 24/7, I'm sure I would have swiped a lot of pageants. But I don't have the opportunity to get involved in it

24/7. It's more like a hobby for me. It's more like something like a release when I'm teaching all week and maybe I'll go out on the weekend, something of that nature. Just a little fun. So I've not been involved 24/7. It's more of a hobby.

Can you share or think of a time when you went out in drag and you just sort of wrecked the place because they weren't expecting it, for you to show up in drag?

Oh yeah. That time I was telling you about, when I went to Circuit in Chicago, I wrecked the place. I broke the house and wrecked the place. When the National Communication Association [met] in Seattle, we went to [a gay bar called] Neighbors [. . .] a group of us. And I was like one of the only African American queens in the place. And honey, I *wrecked* the house! [Laughter] I met a *gorgeous* little island man. Of course we went back to the Renaissance Hotel and made beautiful music. [Laughter]

What about instances where it wasn't a gay environment? It was straight and people weren't expecting you to show up?

Oh yeah. You know when I did the drag performances at the NCA, at the National Communications Association. We have all of those so-called heterosexuals at our communications conference and honey, I come through there in drag and wrecked the house. No shame in my game.

Do those people ever say anything to you, or do they just look?

Some of them just look, and then I have them come up to me and, of course, they'll come up to me and give me praise. You know, how wonderful I look and things of that nature. You know, how well the conference paper was. You know, things of that nature. So I look forward to the adulation. You get lots of that. I like going to NCA. I like the novelty of it. You know, I'm one of the only drag queens, I guess, that performs in drag these days there. Which is a wonderful thing because that means not any of the bitches can't touch me. [Laughter] They're too scared to come out with their makeup and their wigs. I love it. So "Divas to the Dance Floor," get your shit together girls for Boston! I'm telling you now, whores. Get your shit together for Boston, girl. Get your hair, your makeup, your eyelashes, girl. Get your fierce, beaded dress, honey, and be ready to go to Jacques'. [Laughter] That's a fabulous club in Boston. Okay, see I'm ready already, honey. I know my places to go.

Do you feel a sense of community among black gay men here in New Orleans?

Yeah, there's a lot of community. I mean where we just were, talking over at Society Page, they have their association. They have The Window. They try to get people involved and all of that. They have a brotherhood through The Window.

How would you describe your political perspectives with regard to issues facing gay people?

Very Democratic. Very right-wing [a misstatement for left-wing] liberal. And looking for a Democratic administration to take over soon. [Laughter] The Republican girls have had it enough. It's time for those bitches to click up their heels and get on their broomsticks and fly out of the hutch. [Laughter] Okay?

What role does religion play in your life, currently?

Oh, I'm a very spiritual person. I love to listen to gospel music. I love the Bible. I love prayer. I am a very spiritual person. I believe in it. And I believe in the spirits. I believe there's a higher being because when you go into transforming yourself into drag, you have to call upon spirituality to give you the power, to give you the strength, the power and the *knowledge* to transform yourself. You know it's not easy. It's like being a chameleon. It's very difficult. So you have to call upon the spiritual realm to give you that guidance so you can have that stroke of mascara here or that sweep of eye shadow there or that swoop of lipstick there, that turn of lip liner there, that scoop of blush there, the whole costuming. You really have to call upon your internal forms of spirituality to give yourself a higher calling. Which is in itself, as I will say in Boston, "very free and very liberating" and which provides for the transvestite a self-assured policy of mental health because of the freeing aspect; because of the butterfly syndrome. The rainbow. All of the signs and symbols of "gaydom." The rainbow. We have a gorgeous rainbow flag there [pointing to a flag hanging outside a bar across the street]. You know, transcending the rainbow. The butterfly and the wings and all of that.

Why do you think there are so many black gay men in the church, especially in the choir?

Because music is very, very important in our lives. We have to have music. We have to have music to calm us, to give us peace, to give us understanding. We call upon the power of music to give us a purpose, a raison d'être, a reason to be, a rationalization, to make some sense of the madness. You know to be able to put what being gay is all about and put it into perspective. And the music does that. It soothes. It calms. It gives you understanding. It gives you perspective.

What has been the impact of HIV and AIDS on your life?

Oh Lord. A lot of queens, I know a lot of drag queens that have gone on. A lot of the good sisters here from New Orleans have passed on. A lot of girls that I know nationally, who were performers and things, have unfortunately passed on. It's played a major role, not only in the role of female impersonation, but also in academia, as a gay man. A lot of gay boys in academia have passed on too.

Do you think it's more of an issue here in the South?

No. It's everywhere. It's a beast, and we should hopefully be able to kill it in this millennium. God willing.

What are your best memories of growing up in the South?

The food. And the hot men. The hot men and the food, yeah.

What are your worst memories?

[Pauses to think] I guess being misunderstood. You know. That's not a good thing. Everyone wants people to understand them. So coming up, sometimes you're misunderstood where you're trying to do things. Being involved in academia and being involved in drag and this, that, and the other. People tend to have their labels and things of that nature. But you have to be strong and hold out. And I've always believed, honey, that if the bitch is not paying my rent and giving me no money and I'm keeping a roof over my head, honey, I'm not worried about it. You know I tend to have a focus. I have a strong concept. And then I'm Aries. High self-esteem. You know an Aries is really focused. So I have a strong concept of self.

What has been the influence of your southern upbringing on your character?

It's interesting how I can lapse into my mannerisms of speech. You know, I have a very interesting form of diction where I enunciate and pronounce very articulately because of going to Catholic schools, and the nuns, and the recitation, and all of that. And then I can lapse into my lazy southern kind of accent. And I just love the laid-back feel of the Big Easy and the southern mentality of, kind of take your time to do whatever you want to do. You know, not be in the hustle and bustle. A lot of girlfriends I have in the Northeast, they kind of hustle and bustle a lot. I love hustle and bustle every now and then. But I love the kind of flow. The kind of smooth little rhythm of the South. You've got to get that when you can, honey. You know, the girls have a perennial kind of little CP time ["colored people's time," black slang meaning perpetually late].

How do you feel about the life choices that you've made in light of being gay?

Oh. Je ne regreton. I have no regrets. No regrets. I would do it again.

And what are your current feelings about being a black gay man?

All I can do is get bigger and better. Bigger and better, move up. You know just like the Jeffersons. Bigger and better. Up to the big, big, big, big. Deluxe this. Deluxe that. Bigger and better.

Anything you'd like to add?

I would just like to say that, to all of the African American gay men wherever you are, North, South, East or West, how they say, like my students say, "Do you." You know. Be proud of who you are. Do you. Be free. Be liberated. Don't let anyone hold you down or let anybody hold you back. Tear down the mountains. Scream and shout. Do your thing. And be liberated. Be free. And then you'll have a good form of mental health. You'll have a good self-assured policy of mental health. And do come and see me in Boston. Plug, plug, plug. When I do my grand drag performance, "Divas to the Dance floor, Part 5," bitches! [Laughter]

sweet magnolias
love and relationships

6

From the perspective of many conservatives, all gay people are promiscuous. The truth of the matter is, of course, *some* of us are promiscuous. And promiscuity is a legitimate expression of sexuality for all sexual beings. The rhetoric of *gay* promiscuity, however, has often been a tool used by a homophobic society to justify institutionalized discrimination. The irony, of course, is that when gays and lesbians have expressed a desire to be in "legally" binding committed relationships (i.e., marriage), they have usually been told that they are immoral for coveting and wanting to debase an institution that is designed solely for one man and one woman. This irony was quite poignant as I sat in the homes of some of the men I interviewed, who had been in relationships for over 40 years, or as I listened to narrators who felt liberated by being single and promiscuous or by being single and celibate. I conducted these interviews between 2004 and 2006, when opposition to gay marriage was at the top of the Religious Right's agenda and had been front and center in the reelection campaign of George W. Bush. And while a number of the narrators in *Sweet Tea* also opposed gay marriage for a variety of reasons, all of them believed that gay people should have the same rights and protection under the law as heterosexuals.

Notwithstanding the political backlash against homosexuals, the stories collected in this chapter exemplify the courage and resilience of people loving each other against a host of obstacles—whether they be race, class, family dramas, or sexual politics. Indeed, the stories are romantic in the sense that they are about people sharing their lives with one another, but not in the sense of their relationships being idyllic or being something that they did not have to work at. Although the stories told by Freddie and Harold of the forty years they have spent with their partners are awe inspiring, what is compelling to me is not the number of years involved, but these men's sheer will to stay together *in spite of* the difficulties they faced in society, within their families, and with each other. The beauty of these relationships, then, the sweet scent of the magnolia, stems from the steadfastness of their commitment to building and sustaining a life together.

There are also stories of loss and longing. More than a few men have lost their partners to AIDS, other health problems, or other men. The loss of a loved one is never easy, but these men demonstrate the various ways in which we deal with grief. Sometimes we remain stuck in that place of mourning, while other times we heal and move on, as did Bob and Dan, both of whom were in relationships for over twenty years before losing their partners. Coincidentally, both of these men lived with their partners in the San Francisco Bay Area, and both original partners were white, while their current partners are black. Given the great racial divide in this country, especially in the South, I find it quite remarkable that the model for cross-racial unity, or at least one model as manifested in this book, takes the form of gay relationships. Three of the long-term relationships in this chapter are interracial. Transgressing both sexual and racial taboos, these couples managed to stay together, embodying what I would call a pedagogy of love. That is, a way to learn and teach each other how to love beyond racial difference—no easy feat in a context where homosexuality is an abomination and "dating outside the race" is paramount to treason.

I wanted to include not just stories of men in relationships, but also stories of men who are in search of a companion or who are content being single. These narratives are also important in exemplifying the diversity of black gay southern life with regard to intimacy and desire. They also speak to these men's humanity, as they, like most of us, are in search of companionship and desire to be desired in a way that connects them to another person.

. . . .

BOB (B. 1940, BAXLEY, GA.)
And you've been talking about a partner that you had for twenty years.
When and where did you meet him?
Well, now that's interesting. I was at Emory University—no, I was in the military, we met, in '68. And a chance meeting in a little bar. And it was in August of 1968. And I had never really—I mean, I had had a relationship with a white person before and not had any racial experience—I mean, it was this thing about, I mean, I had never had any therapy yet, but I've gone to therapy since then, so I know what my issues were. But I had started having that relationship with the base commander, who was a white guy, in the military. So when Al came to Texas, he was white, and I thought, "I'm not going to do this. This is really insane." So, he asked me if I would go to his hotel. And I

said, "No, I won't do that." It was in the Y and the Y was hot, it was not air-conditioned, and so I said, "Well, you know, there's a hotel—the Y is hot, I'm sure it's not air-conditioned so let's go to dinner." And so we talked about an hour. So I went to his hotel and we started a relationship. And I gave him a false ID, false name, false everything. But the next day, I did agree to see him. And then he was leaving, going back to California that Sunday, and then I did go to see him the next day and we had dinner and stuff like that. So then I didn't make contact with him for a year because I was getting ready to get out of the Air Force in '69, and I came to Emory University. And then when I was at Emory, I ran across his telephone number, and I called him just to say hello. He said, "Oh, I've been praying to the Virgin Mary, saying the rosary. And can I come? What are you doing?" That was on a Thursday. "Can I come to Atlanta? I could come tomorrow. I've been thinking about you. I can't get you out of my mind," dah, dah, dah. And I said, "Well, yeah, I suppose. I mean, I'm a student now." He said, "I'll be in Atlanta. I'll come to Atlanta tomorrow." So he got a plane and came to Atlanta the next day. And the rest is history. And so he said, "I just want to know—I just want to see if the feeling is the same as I had when I was with you in August of '68, because I can't get you out of my mind. It's just like you're just always there." And so he came to Atlanta and I was a student. And I came down to the hotel.

What year of college was it?

I was a nursing student. I'm a nurse practitioner. But I had gotten out of undergraduate school at Morris Brown College in '63. But by then, I was in nursing school at Emory and after having been in the Air Force. So he came to Atlanta, and then I met him. And he said, "Oh"—I walked through the door and he said, "I can't believe it." He said, "It's like I've never, ever forgotten you. You're just as I remembered you would be." And so then every two weeks, he would come to Atlanta.

Every two weeks, from California?

Um hmm, every two weeks. And write to me every day. And then once a week, every Wednesday evening he would call at a certain time. He would call. And then I would go to California on my breaks, on my school breaks. Because he was an only child, and he was an architect and his family had money and stuff, so. And he had issues too, because, you know, after years of therapy, you realize that we all have issues, and he really didn't like white people because he felt that they were—and he was also of German heritage and he didn't like that part of his heritage because that was, you know, his father was German and escaped out of Germany, but not Jewish. They were Lutheran or something and his mother was Irish Catholic, and so that was his history, so the dynamics were very, very strange. But we'd been together twenty-seven years, a long time.

When did you leave Atlanta and move to California?

Directly from Emory. Well, when I graduated Emory in '72. [Laughter] I would go to California at break times. And so it was kind of expected that when I graduated, I would come to live with him. He'd asked me if I would do it and I said I don't—I was studying anesthesia and I would have to go to Georgia Baptist for an internship. And then he was saying, "Well, you know, California has more opportunities and you could—if your first love is pediatrics, why don't you come to California and study pediatrics and go to University of San Francisco and get your practitioner," dah, dah, dah. And so I said, "uh." So for graduation, he sent me a one-way ticket. [Laughter] So I went to California in '72, in March of '72.

And did you go to school?

I went to the Methodist Center in San Francisco for the practitioner part. So I did the practitioner part, and then I went there. And he had gone to the University of California at Berkeley and he really wanted me to go there, too, because that was kind of prestigious; I mean, everybody was going to University of California at Berkeley, so then I thought, well, but by then I was working and had a really good job and I was—and I liked what I was doing and I was—but then I got accepted into the School of Public Health, so that took eighteen months to go back to school to get the MPH. And he supported me in that, because I only worked—I think I worked one day a week in the hospital. But I mean, I wrote all my papers, but then he typed them, and that's before computers. And he was very good in English, in grammar, so he typed all of my papers, proofed them and typed them. It was very interesting because I would—Berkeley was known for either writing papers or flunking. If you write your papers, because the professors use your papers to do their research, so you research all this stuff and they just took them. So, I would have one paper in my head. I would be writing one paper while I'm thinking about the other paper that I need to sort of organize. And then he would be typing a paper for me. And then I would be in the library and he would—and I would know to meet him at a certain place, at a certain time, and he would drop a paper off for me to turn in to one of my professors, and I would give him the other manuscript for him to start typing on. And he typed all my papers for me, every single one, and there were tons of papers, and I got all A's. [Laughter] A-pluses. It was wonderful. And when I graduated, he sent for my mother to come out for the graduation. My mother came for the graduation from UC-Berkeley, which was wonderful. And we went shopping for me, a new suit and stuff like that. And we had a housekeeper who is now ninety years old, who's still very much alive and knew the whole story and loved me and loved him and so.

What was the first meeting like between your mother and your partner?

Oh, it was very cordial. Although my mother had been in contact with white people, she had never been in intimate contact with them; she was in a more subservient role. And this was an equal role. And, as a matter of fact, I was the one who was actually the more dominant part of the relationship. I was actually in charge of everything, I ran the house and, you know, my position. And my therapist said that I was a trophy. [Laughter] Because if you think about it back in the '70s, the civil rights movement had just come into vogue, and in Berkeley it was the in thing to have these interracial meetings. And you really weren't considered to be in the upper crust unless you had people from different ethnic groups in your home. And if you had black friends and, you know, you went to the opera and the symphony and to the ballet. And I was always dressed impeccably. I was very attractive and I was in that age group, I guess. And his friends, many of them were black; of course they were professionals. And many of them were white, and some of them were Jewish. And they all had an attraction for me, and he knew that and I knew that but it was like, "this is mine, don't, you can't touch." And so—and for him, that was a sexual turn-on, in hindsight and now that I've gone through my counseling, I knew that was—I mean, I didn't know it at the time, but I put it all together, so—because it was like, "Why don't you wear those pants tonight? Those really look good on you." And I was running five miles a day. I was also in the military reserves at the same time. So I was running and keeping my body together.

Mother came out to visit. And we were sitting on our deck in '75. And Al said, "You know, we should send for your mother and your father to come out." I said, "Oh, we can't do that." I said, "that's ridiculous." I didn't think anything else about it. [. . .] About a week later, I got this telephone call back from my father. He said, "We got these tickets to come to California and the date." And so I said, "What do you mean?" He said, "Well, didn't you know we were coming?" I said, "No." So I asked—he said, "Oh, it was supposed to have been a surprise." I said, "Oh, shit, you can't do this to me." So that's when they came, that's when my mother and I had the conversation. But my father never asked. But it was very cordial. We gave a very formal party for them. The credit cards, he said [to my mother], "Here's the credit card. Go down to I. Magnum's. Find you a dress that you want." And we invited a very diverse group of people to come, blacks and whites and Jews and Indians and Asians, because the neighborhood was very mixed, to come to the champagne reception. And a pianist was there to play classical music. And it was all catered and it was very nice. And I have pictures from that event. My father was in a tuxedo and my mother was in a long gown and it was wonderful, um hmm, yeah. And so it was—that was her first exposure to equal. And my mother is not a person who is educated beyond I think tenth grade maybe. And so she's a little bit shy in terms of her abilities. She has a lot of mother wit, and people love her because she's so warm. But that day I believe she really, really felt equal to anybody else. We took her to the opera, she'd never been to the opera before. And we took her to the finest restaurants in San Francisco and on the boat rides and, you know, all this kind of stuff. So then we took her to Europe after my father had died. But then I took him, the white man, to south Georgia in '81.

How did that go?

Poorly. My mother—well, actually for us, for the family it was fine because I was going to go home that Christmas because my father had been not that well, and so he had been in the hospital eleven times that year. He was very fragile, cardiac fragile, so—and respiratory fragile also. So Al said, "Well, I guess we really should go because, you know, you may not see your father alive next Christmas." And I said, "Al, that's a bunch of bull, you can't say that, I can't face that now." He said, "We're going to go." So he called my mother and said, "I'm going to come with Bob for Christmas." And my mother said, "Fine, come on." Well, now ain't no white folks ever been to any black folks' house then. Well, the whole town was abuzz. They all came to visit, to borrow sugar, to see what, you know. And we were downtown shopping and doing stuff. And it was the talk of the town that Bob was coming home with this white man, and that's his person and they're sleeping together in the same—and his mother's allowing them to stay in the same room, in the old bedroom. And we did stay in the same room, but it was twin beds. And so we didn't violate my mother's house because we knew we just wouldn't do that, because he [Al] was very, very, very upstanding in terms of his morals and stuff, so.

Did you ever meet his?

His mother? I have met his mother. His father died early, but his mother was alive when I went to live with him. And I've been a nurse. I took care of her for a year and a half—well, no, I got there in '72 and she died in '73, Easter Sunday '73, she died. But she died and I was her—I took care of her.

So he died when you were still in California. And then how long did you stay out there after he passed away?

Oh, Lord, he died in '89 and I left there in 2004.

"BRIAN"

I have known Brian for over twenty years. We met when I was still an
undergraduate. The third of four children, Brian was born in Virginia in
1962 and raised on a military base for most of his younger years. His father
was a chaplain. While he has had many same-sex encounters and even
relationships, he doesn't necessarily identify as "gay." "Bisexual" might be a
more appropriate term, although he disavows most identity labels. As he
recounts below, he was married to a woman for many years, and they have
two children together.

The interview took place on August 18, 2004, in the Research Triangle in
North Carolina.

You've answered this indirectly, a number of times: were you ever married?
What motivated your decision to get married?

I think it was still the mythology of the way things are supposed to be. We
had similar backgrounds. I mean, it's almost as if you were gonna lay out a
contract, there were so many things that would have been perfect about it.
And the way with those similar backgrounds, both of us were rebellious
against those strictures in particular ways. So yeah, I'm different enough for
her, she's different enough for me. As we started living our lives, we started
living those expectations, and how those things worked and didn't work. I
knew from an early age that I always wanted children, and I achieved that. I
was very specific that I wanted boys. Which I achieved, and which is freaking
me out because now that I am at my age now I would like a little girl, and
that's a role, you know, to be a little girl's daddy. Not my baby's daddy, but a
little girl's daddy, and to treat her specific ways, as I think that father's give
little girls, either by attention or inattention. I would have liked to experience that, but that wasn't happening with this particular woman that I had
married.

And also the, the first relationship that I had [with a man], it was more
than once or twice, it spanned years. I remember having a conversation with
this gentleman that, when we grow up, you'll have your wife, I'll have my
wife, and we'll still see each other in particular ways. Hindsight looking, I'm
still basing it on intimacy, so basing it on the idea that sexuality goes away,
you know, that you're hot and randy for a while, and then after a while, it's
not the fucking, it's the intimacy that's important, in which case, sex can be
boring. Tab A into slot B. But if you can make those connections, and that's, I
think, what I was trying to foresee, in which case it was still based on being
married and having close, intimate male friends. Because my ex-wife knew

of this gentleman, and was slightly, I perceived her being uncomfortable. I didn't invite him to my wedding. I was invited to his, and my wife and I went to his wedding, and just various instances where all of our lies have crossed and uncrossed, is just another tangled tale. [Laughter]

But it's like be thankful for what you ask for, especially when you get it, but also be careful with what you ask for. I wanted to be married, I wanted to have children, all these things that I wanted, I'm getting. And part of that is the learning how to dream about something, want something, and then walk toward it, and then you—either one, you'll get it, or the journey will get you there to something that is appealing. Inasmuch as I never put sexuality there, or same-sex sexuality, or gayness, or however you wanna describe it, I'd never put that as a destination, as a target for me to walk towards. In which case it's never been completely defined. It's been defined by history, it's been defined by my actions and my behavior, but it's, it's been amorphous, inasmuch as I'm not scared of it. I know what I like, so there's no self-doubt or self-loathing, "Oh, I'm doing this," that doesn't enter into what I'm doing—or what I'm doing, how I'm living, how I'm feeling. But it's also not something that I'm gonna shout from a mountaintop. I don't foresee having a very public ceremony, as beautiful as those are. I don't see myself doing that, and then part of me is like wondering, is that where self-loathing and self-doubt comes in too?

Since being separated, there are a couple of gentlemen that I've known that has entered my consciousness. It's like, "Oh my gosh. I could do this." I could set up house. I could start living a public life in particular ways. And how is that? And what is that? And is it with this particular guy, or this particular relationship? And then having been married as long as I was, what kind of things am I comfortable with, what kind of things am I not? Hopefully that answered your question.

Do you think that now that you've been married, and to a woman, and divorced, that you could see yourself with a same-sex partner long term? Are you open to that?

I'm open to that. I don't know what all of that means, but I'm open to that. And part of it is, it's the intimacy, it's the closeness, it's the companionship. Not necessarily the sex, but it's tied to the sex, and understanding, or beginning to understand, how that's been tied to gender, with me, all along. So, you know, if I do end up in a same-sex partnership, is this the lost father, the lost brother, the lost uncle, the lost cousin? Are these all of these men in one? [. . .] And then understanding now from the vantage point of age, what that love would be. How to ask for it, how to elicit it, through things that, you know whether it's a physical or emotional or, you know, my facial experience. You know, if I look at you this way, send love back. I understand how all of that kind of works, you know, it's not a game, but there is this particular interchange, and I've learned that from being married in particular ways. So yeah, that type of maintenance. Sex is one thing: it's lust. Attraction is one thing: that's lust. But connection and companionship, that takes a whole lot more work than, "Hey let's go have coffee," especially over time, and especially if you live with this person in the house every day. I mean, yeah, you can wow me in the sheets, but, "Damn baby, why you want to leave your shit all over the place?" That's to me, something that's missing from discourses, particularly with same-sex partnership and marriage discourses, that it gets down to the level of human beings living with each other in connection, not necessarily what's in the bedroom. And I'm not sure where there's totally separate apart, or whether there's a congruent or intertwined thing that goes on. See I don't care about the political stuff; this relationship will last with the maintenance of day-to-day stuff. It's like that for heterosexuals, it will be like that for gay folks. But it's the realization of that, you know. This political thing is show, it's like the passing of a law, and all of the civil rights legislation, okay; the laws are in the books, but the shit's still happening on the streets. The same thing will happen within partnerships, because for me, sex is somewhat ephemeral, it's the relationship and the connection, which has to happen for a long time. I haven't necessarily found it enough satisfying over time, but that, for me, that's a goal destination.

· · · · · · · ·

DAN (B. 1943, DURHAM, N.C.)

I stayed in New York from '64; I moved in '70. [. . .] I left because I wanted to be in a relationship. I wanted the *Ozzie and Harriet* thing. *Father Knows Best*, you know. I wanted to be in a committed relationship. And I just said, you know, this is not happening, and I had a very good job and I had lots of friends, and I played at a great church. All of that was going, but there was that missing element. The parties were fantastic, you know, you were young and you were crazy, we did the Fire Island thing. It was just I wanted stability in my life, and so I thought maybe if I moved to a smaller place, I would find that.

So where did you go?

I moved to San Juan [Puerto Rico]. I was a bartender, I played in a nightclub, I worked as a waiter. [. . .] It was a three-year vacation.

Did you find love?

I did. That third year.

And then, so you were there for three years, you found love, and then you . . .

Well, he was from California, so we met in the club that I worked in, and we just hit it off, I mean it was intense. In fact, he was supposed to have left two days later, and he ended up staying an extra week and a half. And we wrote to each other for about a month and decided, hey, let's give it a try. I packed up, put my stuff in storage, and moved to California. [. . .] He lived in Oakland, and so I moved to Oakland in '73. And we were together for twenty-five years.

Wow. What did you do while you were there? What did you do for work?

In California? I first started working as a recreational specialist in music, working with retarded children. I did that, and then I decided, you know, hey, there's something different. And so we opened a disco in San Francisco. And so I started a catering business, and then I got into real estate.

Tell me about the disco.

Oh, well that was fabulous. I mean, it was predominantly black, it was—

It was in Oakland?

No, it was in San Francisco. I don't know if you know the cartography there. There's Berkeley, Oakland, and San Francisco, so it was twenty minutes across the water. And, at that time I mean you know, San Francisco was, had become the mecca for gay people from all over the country. And there was some discos, but there was nothing really elegant and upscale for blacks. And so my lover and I decided, hey, let's buck the trend, and so we opened a disco. And it was fabulous, absolutely fabulous. It was called "Different Strokes." I mean, the opening was televised. It was great, you know, just very, very nice. And we did that for, I think, I guess we opened that in '76?

Oh so right in the middle of the disco era?

Oh it was right in there, yes. I mean we had the Two Tons [of Fun] were there, Sylvester, you name them they came to Different Strokes if they were in San Francisco, so I mean it was the place to go.

So you had live performance too?

Yeah, yeah. It was the place to be and to be seen, so it was quite nice. And then of course, you know, AIDS reared it's ugly head, and between that and just burning out, we, I think we sold it in '82 or '83.

Is it still there now?

No, when I sold it, it became a Asian fusion disco.

Why do you continue to live in this area of the country now?

Now? Well, obviously, I met someone after my friend of so many years died, and he works here, and my family's here, and we have a very stable, good life here. I'm doing the things I enjoy doing.

Do you think that there are other regions in the country that are better for black gay men?

If I were single, I would not live here. Because I mean even though people in the circles where I run are very, very accepting and tolerant and all that sort of thing, I think as a single, gay person, black or white, this is not the area where you can easily meet people. And so if I weren't in a long-term relationship, no I would not live here.

And so do you think that the difficulty of meeting other people is because of the southern culture?

I don't think so much of it as southern culture, as a lack of social activities, you know? You know, like where we normally meet people, they don't exist here. Not only just for gay people, but you know, for heterosexuals. [. . .]

Did [your first partner] ever meet you family? And how did that go?

Oh yes. Oh, it was wonderful. My grandmother absolutely adored him. [. . .] I brought him home, and the first day she's, you know how people in the South do, she had cooked all this stuff, and Richard loved to eat. And he sat there and he ate and he ate, and she said to him, "I've never seen a white man eat that much food in my life." And that just did it, they just became—he and my father became, actually became really close friends. My father talked more with him, was more open, than we ever did, because they had more things in common. My father loved baseball, and that, you know, [laughter] that was not my thing.

And your mother?

Oh my mother just thought he was really great. In fact, when we decided to move back here, he came out before I did, because I was, I needed to close my business up and that sort of thing. And so he stayed with some other friends of mine, but he ate dinner with my parents for the month that until I got out here. It was a very close relationship.

And did you meet his?

Yeah, oh yeah. No, I didn't meet his parents, his parents were dead when I came out, but Richard had two daughters, and I met them when they came of age. And we still to this day, we still have a very, very close relationship. Richard and their mother are dead, and so I'm the only link that they have to their childhood.

He had been married before?

Yeah.

And how did he pass away?

He had a heart attack.

And how long ago was this?

Oh, God. Richard died in 1998.

Oh I'm sorry, not that long ago. And so at that point you decided to move back to . . .

No, we were living in Durham when he died. When he retired, we moved to Durham. He had never lived anyplace else, he wanted to experience something different so we looked all over and decided, well, you know, we know some people here and the cost of living is, we could live well here, and so we moved to Durham in 1992.

What was that like, moving back here after being away for all those years?

It was bizarre. I mean, I, not in a million years would I have ever thought that I'd have been back, back here. But you know, once we made the transition and got here and got settled, we lived in a fantastic neighborhood, and had a great house. We lived in Duke Park. And had gotten this great old house, and remodeled it. Wonderful neighborhood for Durham, I mean, the problem is there are three neighborhoods in Durham that I think are really great for an interracial couple, or liberal couple, I mean whatever you want to call it. I mean people just want to be themselves and not have hang-ups and stuff like that, and that area was one with great neighbors, great friends. A lot of gay couples, and so you know we just, we lucked out, as we always do, you know. And, it was, it was, it was a good move, and he really enjoyed, you know, the environment.

So did you feel like you moved back into a community since this neighborhood was so great? Then there were other gay people, there were open people?

Oh yeah, yeah. In fact I, I told the realtor before we got, you know, I just put my cards on the table. I said hey, you know, we're a gay couple, we're interracial, I wanna move into a neighborhood, I don't want people flipping out, burning crosses and putting on, you know, and he, it was funny, he sent me all this information from Durham. You know, the *Front Page* [the local gay paper], I think at that time there was a gay bar in Durham, and stuff like that, so. We knew that it was not as repressive as Jesse Helms would have wanted us to believe. [Laughter]

How would you describe, in general, your attitudes about intimate relationships with men?

They can be as good as you make them. [Laughter] Or as bad as you make them. Mine, of course, my relationship with Richard, of course, was just a very positive experience. Which is the reason I, after he died, I wanted to be in another relationship.

What did you look for in a man?

I wanted someone who was basically a good person. And that's all. You know, I mean, it didn't matter, you know, what color he was. I wanted someone my age because you know I, you know I'm not into a teeny-bopper kind of thing. And, and you know, I lucked up, I've been very lucky, you know I've found exactly that.

How did you meet your current partner?

I put an ad in the paper and he responded.

So did you go on many dates with a number of people before you landed . . .

I went on three other dates. [. . .] They weren't what I was looking for; probably I wasn't what they were looking for.

And long have you been with Leonard?

It was four years in August.

And do you see yourself being together forever, or . . . ?

I do.

. . . .

"D.C." (B. 1951, SHREVEPORT, LA.)

Were you ever married?

No. I attempted to get married at thirty-five. And I don't know why, because that's something I had written down in my book, my high school book. I said I would not marry until I was thirty-five because I felt that it would take me that long to acquire some things. I did not want to live like I lived as a kid coming up, not having nothing, not having this, not having that. I mean, I didn't have everything I needed, and I don't have it now. But at least I could've lived a better life than I did as a child. And the crazy-ass girl that I was going to marry, she ran me away real quickly when she started telling me all what I was not going to be able to do and what I was going to have to do. And she said I couldn't have the fellas over and all this kind of stuff. She was going to move here and she was going to take and change my house and do this and I said, "Baby, wait a minute baby. I've been doing by myself for all these years and you're going to come in and make all these changes on me like that?" I said, "I don't think so." I said, "So we really need to talk about this marriage thing." [Laughter]

And I'll tell you another reason I was going to marry her too, by the way. She's gay herself. And actually, she's my son's mama. And we talked about it years before that, and she even told me something about her gay experiences, how she had her first piece and all this other stuff, so I felt comfortable marrying her. Now, probably just to marry a regular so-called straight girl, no, I probably would never even consider it. No. But again, with her, that didn't even work out.

Do you currently have a partner?

At age fifty-three, I just fell in love with a guy. Everything else has been just "wham bam, thank you ma'am" or whatever. And this love thing-bug, hit me in mid-November, well about Christmas. The bug's dead. [. . .] I had heard people say how it feels you know to have your heart broken. And I didn't know until then. It was like an elephant standing on my chest. [. . .] I left town for a few days, and then I came back. It still wasn't right. I left for five more. I'm all right now because I have control of it. And because of that, *I*, that's a personal pronoun, I will not allow myself to fall in love with another guy again in my life.

And to answer your question, I have three guys right now. They all are my significant other. And I pretty much play them like roulette. Whichever one I feel I want. Feel this one today, whatever. However, they don't have that same calendar. [. . .]

Do they know about each other?

Not really. Two of them know about each other. There's one I've been with since '83. Oh that's nothing. I had another one, a married guy, I had been with him for thirty-some years. I mean, I like consistency. And I mean, this guy that's married, well he's incarcerated now. But when I met him, I think I was about a senior in college. And it's been since then. And that's another thing. His mom and his dad love the hell out of me.

They know what's going on?

Hell yeah. Do they know? Yes. In fact, they would call me and tell me, "[D.C.] come and get him." He's in and out of jail sometimes. When he gets out of jail, they don't worry about where he is. They *know* where he is. Mom says, "[D.C.], is my son over there?" I say, "Yeah, he's laying over here."

Does the wife know about it?

The wife caught us in the act once upon a time. She was nosing around and stuff. She was pregnant at the time, by the way. So she came to my backyard and we were in my bedroom but I had my bathroom window open and all, and she's looking in and she saw us in the act. She called me on the telephone and told me she did see us doing what we were doing, told me the position we were in and everything. And she said, "I want to let you know I was there because I left a can outside your bedroom window." And I went out there and it was out there. But even after that, she, the wife, on too many occasions, called and told me, "Come get him and keep him." Because he beats her. Okay? And she knows that that's a relief, you know, to have him with me. [. . .] And he'll come here and make his love, get his little pressure—he calls it getting his pressure off—and all this kind of stuff. And act just as nice. You wouldn't believe he was cut out like that. And I have him around long enough, I get tired of him and send him on back. But she knows what we're doing. It's no secret about him and I or what we are to each other.

Does he consider himself bisexual?

Yeah. I find a lot of guys who have been to jail and mess around, they have this thing that they've got to have them a woman and a boy. They'll tell you that. They need to have the two to make it. Why, I don't know. I guess what they got used to when they was in jail, or what they had before they went out or whatever, but they will tell you, "I gotta have a boy and a girl."

Are all three of your friends your contemporaries? Are they younger or older?

All except one. One is younger. That's the one I fell in love with. And I fell because I fell for a lot of jailbird jargon lines. When summertime came and I was able to go and visit him, I'd visit him every week and oh boy, the sweet nothings that they were saying to me. They penetrated like gosh [sound effect, Phewphewphew]. I bought it, hook, line, and sinker. And then all these great things that we were gonna do and have and whatever when he got out, and this kind of thing. And none of that happened. And I was just totally, you know . . .

So, he was incarcerated when you met?

Oh no, no, no. I met him about five years ago.

Okay. Then he became incarcerated?

Yeah.

And then when he got out, he went somewhere else?

Well, he really didn't. But he didn't come directly here. Well, he said that he had family to deal with and this and that, and I said, "But that's . . . family didn't get your ass out." So I felt that family could have waited. Because if it had not been for me, family still would be waiting. But like I said, he's young and he's not, and he's not all that bright, so I understand him a lot more now, but it's not enough understanding to make me even want to think about loving him. That's just something for others, not me. I don't want to love no guy, no gay person, period. And I guess I'll grow old and die like that.

· · · · · · · ·

DUNCAN TEAGUE (B. 1960S, KANSAS CITY, MO.)

When and where did you meet your current partner?

David? Eleven years ago. More than eleven now. My good friend and a play daughter of mine, who's a Quaker, knew that my long-distance relationship was like about to end. And she was trying to get me to meet this friend of hers who is a Quaker. And he was also in a long-distance relationship that I guess she didn't like because she kept trying to get me to meet him. And I didn't trust her taste in men. Because she didn't like men. She didn't even see them walking down the street, so you know, I didn't know.

So we did actually meet casually at some event. But I didn't notice him because I was noticing this guy with a cowboy hat on, because I thought he was kind of cute. I'm so glad I didn't make that mistake! But anyway. It turned out that my relationship did end because of the distance. He was transferred to Hemet, California, and that was too far away to maintain the relationship the way I wanted it. And so I found myself single. And it is Thanksgiving, and I have decided I'm going to get dressed and I'm going to the Quaker Thanksgiving dinner, and I think I might meet somebody, but we'll see. And lo and behold I looked across the room and I saw him. And I said, "Who is that?" And I asked my friend, Brooke, my play daughter, "Who is that?" And she hit me. And she said, "That's the doctor I've been trying to introduce you to for months. So I don't understand why you don't . . ." She was mad! And David noticed me. And I think he was clerk of the meeting at the time. It's sort of like a minister of the Quakers. They don't really have ministers. And so he had to do a lot of hobnobbing. But we sort of made a connection. And to be a little more subtle, because you know when you're playing for long term, which I was, you don't put everything on the table at once. So I said, "Why don't you come over to the house afterwards for tea . . ." and something or other, I don't know, ". . . with your friends?" Keep it subtle. So Brooke and Ian and Euclid and David came over.

And David's very shy. And I thought because they were Quakers, you know, and they don't say much and I knew that they weren't going to say much. Ian and Brooke and then Euclid talked and talked, and talked and talked and talked and talked. And drank up all my tea. And ate up everything. And David could hardly get a word in. And then at some point, after he'd been there a while and we had actually made a date (he [David] tells me to be sure and say that [i.e., that they made a date]) he got up and left! And they continued to sit there and talk and eat and drink up all my stuff and eat up all my stuff. But we went out on a date and that was the start of it.

Is he from the South?

No, he is from Salt Lake City, Utah.

And was that a source of tension, him not being a southerner?

No! Really I consider myself more of a midwesterner. And westerners or midwesterners and I get along very well. I have been charmed out of my right mind by southerners, and they were gorgeous and they were crazy as they could be. [Laughter]

Have you met his parents or other family members?

No. David is a few years older than me. And he is the youngest child of some folks who were older when they started having children. And so by the time we met, his mother was in her eighties and she was a very staunch, at that point, elderly Mormon woman. And his father had already been deceased. His father died in the late '70s, I think. So, he made the decision never to come out to her. And I didn't like it at first. Actually, it was a real bone of contention between us because I thought she knew. And I still believe she knows. Whether she ever wanted them to know she knew, because this woman was a teenager in the '20s and had worked to keep her family together in the '30s during the Depression. And lived to be ninety-something. I know she wasn't stupid. Now maybe she never wanted to know, but I think she knew. She didn't know about me. But I think she knew.

And has he met your parents?

He has met my stepmother. My parents did not want to meet him. When we got married last year, I sent invitations to every member of my, all the people I named. And they made their own reasons for not being here. They gave me excuses. But they got the invitations, so they can't ever say that I didn't invite them. And it was the event of the season. [Laughter] It was a small wedding with three hundred people. [Laughter]

Where did it take place?

Here in Atlanta.

Where did you go for your honeymoon?

We're still working it, honey. I had to pay for that wedding. No, we took a family vacation, which was really beautiful, this past summer to the Oregon coast because his cousin, who was in the ceremony—I'll show you the website—his cousin who was in the ceremony is very cool. And her and her husband and David's brother and his sister-in-law are also . . . were all at the wedding. And they invited us out. And so this summer we spent almost a week, or a week and some change, in Portland and Eugene and the Oregon coast. And so I got to see a crane and a tidal pool at sunrise and seals on the rocks below the condo.

Do you find it difficult being in an interracial relationship in the South?

No. I don't. 'Cause it ain't nobody's business. [Laughter] And I've been in many interracial relationships, ever since I came out. I've also been in relationships with other black men. Relationships are hard. It don't matter what color they are. It's about, "Is it the right one?"

How do you feel about the life choices you've made in light of being a black gay man?

My next-door neighbor, who shall remain nameless, is a Mexican American. His father, I think, is first generation, but I'm not sure. His wife is a white lady from the South. They have two beautiful children. And they have been very dear to me and David. But they just broke up. She moved to an apartment with the two children, Saturday and Sunday. And so I was comforting a straight man who is coming to terms with what he is going to have to do to get his family back or to get his life in order so that he can be happy [. . .] And whatever I've done, I've never ended up in that predicament. And I came home to my lover of eleven years and I've never been so fucking grateful in my life, that I don't have that level of hurt and sense of needing to do something about my life to get it together. At least at this particular point in time, I am so happy with at least the current decisions I've made. Ummm, and I think the big one around staying with David, going back to be with David, living with David, marrying David, all in opposition to all the stuff that I was taught and brought up to believe, and establishing a home with David, a home that we have welcomed family into. I've had cousins here. I've had my stepmother here. And they love him. Yeah. I can't say I'm proud of every decision, but at least by some miracle—and I do mean it's a miracle because we weren't always saints and we were very popular and pretty, younger—I made some kind of decisions that have allowed me to be negative of HIV, but yet still involved in the epidemic because my status has not prevented me from being affected and infected in other ways. Some folks say I might be crazy 'cause of it, but, you know. [Laughter] And I might say that some days. And I think the big decision early on, around going ahead and being black and gay, not being something else, but being black and gay and going on from there, was the big one that I'm most proud of. I have not suffered through a so-called marriage to a *woman*. Now, we won't go into some other things, but to a woman. [. . .] I've loved men. And as fully as I possibly could. And I feel like I've been blessed because of that. I've loved women as a gay man, not as a straight man but as a gay man. And I feel like I've been rewarded for that. And I've lived a *full* life. If this tape gets struck by lightning right now and I accidentally get struck too, 'cause it would be an accident, you know the memorial service is going to be humungous. And I've accomplished a few things in this skin. And not just black and gay but, you know, if you need to print in there "kind of sissified" and "a little soft around the edge" and, you know, "occasionally a vicious Miss Thing," yes. Yeah. And sometimes in drag. Sometimes *pretty* in drag. Not just in drag. Yeah. Wow, I hadn't thought about that one. I'm glad you asked that. And took my sense of faith, whatever that is this week, with me, too. I'm glad I hung onto some of that. And questioned it. I don't need to be strangled by anything. So no, I no regrets. I am black. I am gay. I am the South. MISS South.

Final question—

[Interrupting] Uh oh! Yes, I was a virgin when I met David.

....

FREDDIE (B. 1944, MADISON, GA.)

Well you heard me mention earlier that I dumped the shoplifters. [Laughter] I met another person through the same guy, Billy [last name]. His name was Leroy, and I think Billy introduced us for the purpose of us having sex. But we never did. We became friends. And he lived in a community called Dixie Hills, and I would visit him. He was a very bright guy. He had dropped out of Morris Brown College and [went] to work, I think to help his parents out. But also was just going wild. [. . .]

I was visiting him and another friend was visiting him. He said, "Do either of you have any money?" And I said, "Well, I've got a little money. I've got a few dollars." So I remember he borrowed three dollars from me to buy some cubed steak and I think some cabbage and rice or something that he wanted to fix for a dinner guest. And then he started to try and walk us to the bus stop, trying to get us to go home. So I said, "We're not ready to go home." And so he said, "Well, okay bitches, since y'all won't go home, when my dinner guest comes and I offer you some dinner, you have to say no because I want there to be seconds if my guest wants seconds." [Laughter] So I looked, I said, "There is no way I will not see who's going to eat my cubed steak that I can't have any of." So in walked [my partner, also named Leroy]—almost forty years ago now, because it was in January or February, I think it was, it was early about this time of year—and to eat my cubed steak.

And immediately I felt some kind of connection. Well, I thought he was a handsome little man. Leroy's 5′7″. I'm 5′10″. I thought he was the nicest little man and we started chatting, and they brought me home. And they went on out to wherever they were going. But I needed to read *The Coming of Age in Samoa* by Margaret Mead, because I was in college. And Leroy, *my* Leroy, gave me his phone number to call him to remind him to give the book to the other Leroy. So when I called him, we talked, it seemed like a couple of hours. I remember I called him three days in a row because he said, "Call me tomorrow. Call me tomorrow." So after the third day, I said I really think I like him. And so being the decent person that I am, I called my friend Leroy and I said, "Leroy, I need to ask you something." He said, "What is it?" I said, "Are you serious about that little man?" I think I said "that little man." He said, "You mean Leroy?" I said, "Yeah." He said, "You like him?" I said, "Well, I called him and we talked and I do think I like him. But I just want to know what your intentions are because I would never want to go behind your back and do anything like that." And he said, "Well honey, if you can get him, get him." [Laughter]

So I kind of knew. I kind of sort of already had him; I kind of had the feeling. So I continued to wean myself away from the other Leroy. I was doing that anyway, and unfortunately he had—this will tell you what segregation can do around here. He worked at a hospital and had insulted a nurse. I think he told her to take the job and stick it up her ass, and he was convicted of whatever archaic law is on the books in Georgia, and he had to go to prison. But I was dumping him anyway.

And my partner and I continued to interact, and here we are. The other Leroy I think hated me until he died because when he said, "If you can get him, get him." Because what he said was essentially, "You know me, I'm just a whore. I let him out the front door and pulled a piece of trade in the back door. But if you can get him, get him." But I don't think he meant that. Obviously, he didn't. He should have just said, "Well, I do like him. Hands off." But he didn't say that. I never felt guilty about it because I think that, if it had been me, if I had been interested, I would have said, "Well, I really am interested in him and you should leave him alone." You know, I always believed in being honest, and he wasn't. And I kind of sort of got, I didn't get reacquainted with him, but I certainly did see him. He worked in lighting at Home Depot. And I think he never, ever forgave me.

And [you and your partner have] been together for forty years?

On February 1st. February 1st we also designate as our anniversary.

And is he from the South as well?

From Jackson, Mississippi. Well, maybe not Jackson, but probably the metropolitan Jackson, Mississippi, area. I think he might have been born in some other little place. He says Jackson, Mississippi, so it's Jackson, Mississippi.

So did you ever meet his family?

Bits of them have come through Atlanta. I have never agreed to go to Mississippi with him because his family members don't seem to have kind of what I call good upbringing. I mean, it's not uncommon for them to just show up at the front door without calling first. And so I kind of didn't think that I would be comfortable in . . . sort of surrounded by them. But bits of them have come through here and I know I'm kind of a legend in the family because I've had to speak up a couple of times. Because I mentioned earlier that I kind of always after meeting someone I kind of establish Leroy as an entity. He doesn't always do that.

So one of them was here once, talking about all this stuff and speaking in the singular . . . 'cause they call him Jack. "Jack, what are you gonna do with all this stuff?" And I've heard that . . . experienced that scenario many times, where he allowed them to speak in the singular. And so on this occasion, I said, "Did you know? I've got a scoop for you. All this stuff is not his." I said, "Look at me. I exist. We moved here together. What you see is *our* stuff. Some of it's his. When it's between us, some of it's his, some of it's mine. But when it gets to *you*, it's ours." I said, "You people have come here for years and ignored my very existence. We moved into this house together and we have been acquiring this stuff since before we moved into this house. So what you see is *our* stuff. And that particular item you were just talking about is mine. I bought that." [Laughter] I said, "But it is our stuff. And *we* will decide what's going to happen to it. *He* will not. *We* will." You know, I said, "I don't understand that. I'm here but you can totally ignore my existence and speak in the singular as if everything is his. It is not."

That didn't go over too well.

Didn't go over well at all. Well, they should have looked. We were visiting California. We had a good friend in San Francisco several years ago. Leroy has two sisters in Oakland. And one of them was sort of having lunch with us. I don't remember specific things that she did, but it was almost like she was trying to antagonize me. And at some point she said, "You know, you are deceiving. You seem like you're one way, but you're really quite different." And I said, "No, that's not the case, my dear." I said, "You have *assigned* a way of being to me, without getting to know me." I said, "Because I'm soft-spoken and I'm small or whatever." Because I was much thinner then. I said, "You have done what a lot of people"—I never did say, "what a lot of people do with gay people"—I said, "You have done what a lot of people do. You have decided how I am without getting to know how I am. You set yourself up. Other people have done it. You've done it." I said, "You have not *allowed* yourself to get to know how I am, and I don't fit the mold you made for me. That's just the case." And she said, "Oh!" And I said, "You've done yourself a disservice." So, she sort of looked.

What have been some of the challenges, or maybe there haven't been any, of being a black gay couple living here in the South?

You know, I'm sure there should have been some, but I must admit that I have not noticed them. Because what I think is that, if you kind of go about your business in an open kind of a respectful manner, that people will kind of respond to you in kind. Most of our friends, I would say that most of our friends are not gay. We don't choose—I certainly don't choose—we don't choose our friends based on sexual preference. With me being an artist, I have met a lot of people through showing and selling my work. And many of them have become friends. I would say most of the friends we have would have, in fact, been my friends—that I brought them into our situation. But

I've not noticed a lot of challenges. Like earlier on I mentioned that I think I have a bit of wisdom.

When Leroy was teaching school, he would have taken me with him to PTA meetings if I would have gone. When Leroy's father and stepmother came to visit, their bedroom was next to our bedroom. We didn't make any explanation. We went to bed. Sometimes had sex with them in the next room. [Laughter] Didn't make any explanation. And I said to him, "What will they think?" He said, "This is my house. If they don't like it, they have to leave." And it's experiences like that with him that kind of solidify my love for Leroy because I'm sure you probably—well, maybe you don't—but I certainly know of horror stories where when family members come, couples . . . and I've even seen people move out. One of the partners will move out of the house. If I had ever moved out, I would never have come back. I really wouldn't have. So that's been our position. And Leroy's father one day said to me—I forgot his exact words, but he kind of in a sense said that he kind of knew what was going on and that it wasn't that . . . it was our lives or . . . he didn't care what people did or something. In his own inept way, he kind of sanctioned our relationship.

And one of Leroy's half brothers did the same thing. This guy was obviously homophobic, until his wife's—his stepson turned out to be confused or was sort of pretending to be gay for a while. I don't know. I think the guy was just confused. [Laughter] But I think what brought it all home for him, Leroy's half brother, his biological son was involved in a credit card scam and is in prison for several years. And I think he was so heartbroken by what his biological son did and all of the hope and expectation he put in him, and I think that kind of softened him in a way. So several years ago, he called and said he wanted to come and take us to dinner. And his wife said to me that, "This is his way of saying to you and Leroy that he's accepted your relationship." Because [. . .] whenever his family would visit, I was always prepared to ask him to leave because I expected him to insult me any moment. Because I could just feel this something from him. But this particular time, he came and took us out to dinner. We had a lovely time. And his wife said to me, she pulled [me] to the side and said, "Well this is his way of kind of saying that you're all okay with him. He kind of accepts you." And I'd gotten rumors from . . . Leroy has a niece who's gay and if someone hears this tape they just have to know, I'm not going to call her name. But she was here in Atlanta for a while and had a partner and she's kind of given little reports of bits of family discussions about me, among family members. But for us in general, like I said, most of our friends are straight, and we have really good friends.

"G.C." (B. 1958, ALBEMARLE COUNTY, VA.)

I met my partner thirteen, well, yeah, just about thirteen years ago. Really interesting, it was alumni weekend for the University of Virginia. I was one of the faculty advisers, chapter advisers for my fraternity with this chapter here at the University of Virginia, and there was a big steeplechase race earlier that day [that] everybody goes to known as Fox Field. Went to that. Went back to the fraternity house for this party to chaperone, also to greet all of the other alumni, Phi Gammas from all over the country that would be there. And I knew all of the guys in the house, which we all knew who were the regulars and who weren't, and all at once we're downstairs, there was a band playing, someone watching the door. We had a station out for everybody to watch out, and Dan comes in, I didn't know who he was, along with two others. [. . .] I was like, wow, he looks like a fricking geek because he had on this like fishing hat that you would put tackle on and he had on these round glasses. He was like a preppy geek, but something very much caught my eye, and I just remember looking at him while I was shaking his hand, "yeah it was good seeing, you know, hope you had a good time." And then I remember thinking, I hope I see this person again. That was it. I hope I see this person again. In the back of my mind it was nothing about sex, but just seemed interesting because I didn't get a chance to talk to him in depth like I did the others.

But wouldn't you know how fate works; three days later I happened to be in a restaurant at a board of directors meeting for a non-charity group that I work with, and two of the three guys happened to walk into the restaurant. One happened to be Dan, and the other one was the chitter-chatter that had been talking to me. The chitter-chatter sees me, walks over and goes, "Hey, remember me? I was the guy who was at the party." I said, "Yeah, I remember." I said, "You know, I'm just about finished up with this meeting, so if you'll be around, I'll come talk to you in a second." He goes, "And by the way, remember Dan? That's Dan over there at the bar; he was with us too." And I look over and Dan looks and waves, we wave, and always in the back of my head it was like, ka-ching. I hope he stays and not leaves before I finish this meeting. So anyway, fast forward, we finish up the meeting, I go over to the bar where he's at, introduce myself. And he's like, "Yeah, I remember you. Pull up a chair and have a beer with me." So I pulled up a chair and we chat and have a beer, and now he appears to have had quite a few beers prior to me sitting down. In fact, I think he had maybe had a whole beer to himself, maybe two prior to me sitting down. But it was one of those cheap night things. So we chatted and we chatted, and I won't go into the details of the conversation, but it ended up that he outed himself and had commented on my legs and that he liked my legs and that he would go for me. Needless to say, I was speechless and I looked at him, and it was like the cat that had just swallowed the canary because he was like, his expression was "oh shit, I am going to get my ass kicked. What did I just say to this big guy?" And he looks at me and tucks his head. Well, I knew then that I had the upper hand and I just looked at him and said, okay [G.C.], what do you say, you are attracted to him. How do you handle this? Do you just play it off or what? And I thought, well go for it. And I just looked at him and I said, "It's okay," and I put my hand on his shoulder, and I said, "Yeah, I go for you too." And he looked at me and he smiled, he goes, "Oh gosh." I said, "It's okay."

Well, needless to say, that was the first night we met, and we've been together ever since. Literally. Literally. We left the restaurant and went for a nice long drive and talked and talked and talked and consummated the night. The funny part about it, or the good part about it, was at the end of the night he said, "I'm going to give you my phone number, but only if you're going to call me. Only if you promise to call me." And I said, "I will. I will call you." I said, "I'm going to give you my number. The best place to catch me would be at my office tomorrow." So we exchanged numbers, but before he let me have it he goes, "What time are you going to call?" I said, "I'll call you at eleven o'clock." He said, "You better call." I said, "I will call you at eleven o'clock." Like the television commercial, I'm in my office, I'm prancing. I'm jumping up and down. I'm contemplating, do I call this number, do I not? It's probably not the real number, it's probably a fake. I go to the phone. I dial the number, the line is busy. I hang up and I walk around and one of my office mates are looking at me like, is everything okay with you over there? And no one in the office have a clue, they have no idea. I said, "Yeah." And this young lady goes, "Are you sure?" She looks at me and she goes, "I know that look." I said, "What look?" And she goes, "Uh huh." She walks away. True southern lady with that drawl. [Mimicks her drawl] "Uh huh." So I pick the phone up again to dial it, this time it rings, but then I hang it up anyway because I'm thinking, oh gosh it's not right. So call three, I pick it up and all at once there's Dan's voice on the phone. He goes, "Hello." And I said, "Yeah, may I speak with Dan?" He goes, "This is Dan." And I said, "This is [G.C.]." And his voice was like, "Oh thanks. Gosh, I'm glad you called, you actually called." I said, "Yeah." And he's like, "When can I see you?" And I said, "Today?" He goes, "Can I come by your office?" I said, "Come on by." So he met me for lunch, and then we walked down and had lunch and talked, and he says he was working nights. He goes, "I'm going to fix dinner for you. When you get off work come by my place. I'll have dinner and then you can drive me to work." Well, from then on each day we were together, it was either for lunch or dinner or something. I had a house-sitting business, so he would come over to my house when he got off work and that was in April. In August on the day of his birthday, August 12th, which would be tomorrow, we moved in our first apartment together. And that's the way it's been.

Have you found it difficult being an interracial gay couple in the South?

Actually, no we haven't. We have not encountered what some of our other interracial couple friends have encountered, or have seen. Maybe not blatantly or to our face. We have had some comments from a family member of an acquaintance of ours, a mother who we know is kind of on the jaded side who made a comment to Dan, was like, oh well it must be tough for you being gay in a racial relationship too. What did your family say? To his family, not so much what my family would say, but was his. And the one thing you'll notice in the South it's always more of what the white families will say. And you would think that you would hear more adversity from black families than you do white. But it's always the white side. But other than that, no. No we haven't.

But we had a situation with Dan when he was coming out to his family, how his grandparents tried to use that against him because they weren't exactly proud of him being gay. So they used it, oh it's bad enough you being gay, but you're with a black guy. You know at first, even though they had already met me the year before as his roommate, not as his partner. But he stood his ground, and he told them, "It's like well, if that's the way it is, if I'm not welcome, if he's not welcome I'm not welcome." They got over that real quickly. But it was more so because they were more upset with him being gay, not so much about him being with a black person. Again my family has been out and spent time with their family there in Washington State, and his family has been out and spent time with my family here in Virginia. They all call each other for birthdays, this kind of thing. You know, my parents, oh we talked to Dan's grandmother this morning; she had a birthday. We're like, "What?" "Yeah, oh yeah we called Dan's father." Or Dan's father would call and say, "Oh, I talked to [G.C.'s] parents last night, called and checked up on them, see how his sister was doing" and blah, blah, so. They have a good connection.

. . . .

HAROLD (B. 1936, ST. LOUIS, MO.)

Now, I also have to tell you that, thirty-nine years ago, I met my partner. My partner went home with me to St. Louis for holidays, Christmas mainly. So my family knew that I was living with another man. And my mother instructed me by saying, "No matter what you do, you make sure you self-respect and respect others." And we had a deal. If I couldn't introduce them to my mother, then I can't take them home. And it worked. Because it made me look at people rather than just for the excitement of their physical being. Do I want to be involved with this person? Can I take this person home? Because she told me, "If you can't bring your friends home, there's something wrong. If you're ashamed of them or say, 'No I can't take you home,' then it's not maybe." And she was right. She liked him genuinely and he was . . . well, he has principles. And I think that when she saw this, then she knew that perhaps my life wouldn't be as hectic as [laughter] if you didn't have a partner. Okay? And she always said, "Well, you better listen to Harold." And by the way, his first name is Harold also.

Is he a southerner as well?

No, Pennsylvania.

So it wasn't a conflict with him being a northerner when you took him home for the first time?

Well only when my sister tried to serve him chitlins. [Laughter] No, because guess what? From the very first time we met, we talked about ourselves and our families. So there would be no hiding, no shielding or anything. And I have to tell you that my partner is white. Okay, now this was another freaky thing that was thrown in there, okay? [. . .] But we went at Christmas and we assembled my nephew's toys. He rode our backs, we took him hiking, we threw him into snow dumps, we did all these kinds of things. When he calls me now, he says, "Hey Unc, where is Harold?" That's the first thing he says, okay? So I don't think that there was the first-time fear of difference. And even my sister forgave him for not eating chitlins, okay? [Laughter] 'Cause I didn't like them, okay? But we had a really good time.

Where did you meet?

We met in Providence, Rhode Island, where I lived. And it was the summer of 1965, and a mutual friend of ours was coming to visit and I had not seen him. We had been romantic when I was a soldier. And by this time, I'm out of the Army. And so he was planning a summer vacation and he said, "Can I bring a friend? I think you'll like him." And he brought him. And I did. That was in August of '65. And then we ended the summer vacation, and we corresponded until Christmas of '65. I went home for Christmas to St. Louis, and on the way back, I cut that short out there and stopped here in Washington, where he lived. And we spent some time together again. By the time January rolls around, I can't live without him. So I moved to Washington, D.C. We lived in an apartment for a year and a half. And I didn't like apartment living at all. I mean, you want to see daylight, you've got to throw on your coat and go somewhere, you know? So we decided that we would buy a

Harold and his partner, Harold, in their home in Washington, D.C.
Courtesy of the narrator.

house. And we talked about it, and we thought we would never be able to do it. It would take forever, but we still wanted to do it. Plus he had caught some flack because the apartment building that he lived in, they didn't want blacks in there. And he promised her that if she insisted on that, then he was going to take her to court and have her sued for unfair housing segregation in the city, which was illegal then. So that quit that. And it was funny because the woman who owned the apartment building belonged to the same church that I did. A Catholic. She knew it because she saw me go to Mass. Plus some other tenants who lived in that building, because it was very close to the building of the church. [. . .]

When we first moved to this house and we'd be walking, the police would follow us. One time, I got off the bus at the corner to come home, and the police was parked there and they called me over and they said, "Show me some ID. What are you doing up here?" And I said, "I live in this block." And he said, "You live in this block?" And I said, "Yes." So I take out my ID and I take out a little thing that has my address. And he did not believe me, and he walked with me until I got to the house, put the key in the door, and I said, "See ya."

When did you buy this house?

Thirty-seven years ago.

And was it mostly white?

It was a mostly white neighborhood. And then right after that, it changed. Then it becomes totally black. [. . .] They sold out like mad and left or rented or whatever they could do to get away, okay? Then within our own group, the gay population . . . many were a little unsettled.

Because of the interracial thing?

Because of the interracial thing, okay? Now Patrick—may I call you Patrick?

Yes.

Really, people were people to me and still are. I don't care about your skin color or your age or whatever. If I like you, I like you. Or if we can see the possibility of being friends, you know that's it. I don't care. But many of them, we don't know whether or not there was a dislike of the two races or just the jealousy part. But I have to tell you, I didn't pay any attention to anybody. Okay? Most of the time it was wrong, but I just went headlong into anything. So it was like, "Hey I don't care." Because I didn't feel that way. And I still don't. I think that man and his work cannot be judged by his color. I don't care what happened to my ancestors. I can't change that. But I can certainly change the time in which I live. And if you hate, it not only destroys you but everything, you know? Now there are a lot of people I don't like, but this has to do with their beliefs, their actions, not their color.

Harold and Harold on the Potomac River, 1968. Courtesy of the narrator.

Was most of the animosity coming from your black friends or your white friends? Or both?

Okay. I didn't have that many white friends. So I had more black friends. Or beginnings of black friends, in this city. And this is a unique thing about Washington, D.C., because it has a large African American population. In other cities, I knew both blacks and whites. But I would strongly say it was basically from African Americans that I met. I remember someone telling me, "Oh I didn't know you dealt in snow." And I had no idea what the hell he was talking about, okay? But I have to tell you, Patrick, I loved my partner from the very beginning. I didn't know it would last this long. I trust him emphatically. I think he knows more of my weaknesses and accepts them than anybody. And I didn't find that with anybody else, whatever their color may have been or their religious beliefs. And we just got word a dear friend died on the first. And the strange thing is, now that we've reached a point where all these people that we knew in that small period between thirty-five years and fifty years are dead or dying. But I'll let you ask me any more questions.

Did you meet his family?

Yes.

How did that go?

It went well. There were a few little kinks, but his immediate family—his mother and his sisters, their families—I was treated as a friend, honestly. His sister still sends me a birthday card with a present. His sister who is in southern California with her family, has lemon trees. She still sends me huge homegrown lemons that look like oranges. And I love that. When we would go to California to visit his mother, when she was alive, his three nieces, his sister's children, lived nearby. Well they lived very near Disneyland and Knott's Berry Farm. And as soon as their school was out, there were three girls, and the youngest one would say, "Do you want to go to Knott's Berry Farm?" [. . .] He would say, "No more amusement parks. I'm sick of them." So I'd go with her to Knott's Berry Farm. And she had some of her little high school friends who works there, and they'd give us free rides and this sort of thing. [. . .] She is now married and the mother of three children. I'm remembered at Christmas and my birthday. When she writes a note, she asks my good health, am I okay? His brother's children, who are much older and pretty close to my age, they're very, very warm and cordial. She sends me notes telling me, "I love you, Hal," and I don't think people wouldn't say this if they didn't mean it. Not at this stage of my life, you know. No, we had a lot of . . . we had good times because we sort of just . . . you know, "That's your problem." Now at work, it was a different thing.

My partner is in the same profession as yourself. He was employed by the State of Maryland and taught at the University of Maryland. It was quite obvious that he was gay, but he was good at his job. And he worked very, very hard. But in ways that they could do it, they could slow down his advancement to another rank or even more pay. But he stayed there and persevered for thirty-seven years and retired. He had his seventy-sixth birthday last Friday. He had students that he had in his early teaching career calling him from California to wish him a happy birthday. And we talk about this. See we stayed away from each other's . . . I don't know how you do it, but you have parties at work, don't you?

Umm hmm.

Okay, well his secretary would insist that I come out. Okay, he was the faculty adviser for Sigma Tao Delta and every year he'd get new members and that. But he really got the enrollment up and whatever. And they always wanted to do something for him. And they would give him these T-shirts. And he really hates T-shirts, okay? So I would find him with all these sweatshirts and T-shirts and say, "What are you doing with those T-shirts?" He said, "I'm not wearing that." Because we've got a joke. I'm an avid baseball freak. I love baseball. And you know, we just got a baseball team here after thirty-some years, okay? So I'm going to ballgames. And my joke to him was, "You wanna go to the ballgame?" "No!" Because when I first met him, you know how you're all glazed over with love? Well, he went to a ballgame, and I knew it was by mistake because he was grading papers and reading. So I figured, "I'm not going to buy a ticket for you anymore. If you're going to go to the ballgame, you can't grade papers." So he said, "I won't go." So this year, when we found out it was going to be a team, his sister sent me a birthday present of money to buy a ticket for the opening game. Okay? So I said, "Last chance, if you want to go, you've got to tell me." He said, "No I don't want to go." Okay. So I love baseball so much that I go on my own. I just love the spectator aspect of watching a baseball game. And I was denied it for the years that we didn't have a team here. Well, I went to Baltimore a couple times, but that was a trip. For this, I just go get on a bus or the subway and I'm at the ballpark.

What is left of relatives and friends is still a warmth, and they consider us for who we are. Not what they think we are. Because, once again, I think we both try to carry ourselves the way that my parents said, "Respect for yourself and respect for others, and eventually people will respect you for what you are." [. . .]

Sometimes I stop and think about all the turmoil of being black in America. Being black and gay in America. And it has not been as traumatic as it

Harold and Harold on the beach in Santa Monica, California, 1974.
Courtesy of the narrator.

sounds. And I'm not sugarcoating this either. It happened and you move on. I also have to tell you that now I feel much more confident in who I am. A black man. A black gay man. And with that in mind, I don't feel as torn up inside as I was when I was young. But that had to do with achievement. And the fear of not achieving. Maybe because I was a black man, and at that time, it really was a struggle. Even if you were good. Even if you were qualified. People found a way to keep you out of it. But I fought through it. Let's say I was successful. And I went on to the next thing. Well, because I am retired, I should have a peace of mind. But now I feel really at ease. So much so that the idea of retirement doesn't . . . You just quit work. [Laughter] You know, that's what everybody wanted to do. [. . .]

So okay, the opportunity to take courses in subjects that I had not enough of or didn't have at all. I took a course in understanding poetry. I took a course in art appreciation. And I really was interested in American art/African American art, and that's a big skip to get through. But because of the Smithsonian and all the outreach programs or whatever . . . and also you don't have to pay as a senior citizen to partake of a lot of these courses. So I took a course in understanding literature. But the reason I took the poetry course was because I knew nothing about poetry. And I wanted to. I want to know why is it that I can't read this and get something out of it as I would read a novel and get something out of it. Something was there. I think I've improved a little bit on the understanding of poetry. But these are things that I wanted to do. When I was a kid, we had music appreciation but it stopped at a certain point. And then you'd pick up on whatever you wanted to. It can be jazz or popular culture music, whatever. But I was always fascinated by the creation of musical composition. And then I thought, when I had all these turmoils in my life, my partner would say to me, "Well read this" or "Listen to this." When I was at home, mourning the death of my mother, he said, "Read *Long Day's Journey into Night* while you're there." And I thought, "Well" . . . And I did. And all of a sudden, I didn't forget my mother had died but I started to think about something else. [. . .]

So this is that ease that I was telling you about, life becoming quite pleasant. I have some control of my time. And I still really feel that I should not waste it by looking at dumb-dumb stuff on TV. [Laughter] So since about 1969, I have been reading and amassing a collection of African American writers. I was told to start with what was happening then, but when I moved here, I moved here on the train with my bags. And I didn't have very many clothes. I had records and books. And I remember the ride from Boston to Washington, D.C., to begin. I read *In Cold Blood*. And it's that kind of thing. So I guess that I can say that, with the help of my partner, who was an English teacher, I have my own instructor right at home. We could discuss things. We could talk about things. He could help me analyze plays, that kind of thing. Not analyzing in the sense that everything I'm reading I'm analyzing, but there comes times when there are certain questions that a person who has a critical eye for a subject . . . especially as a teacher, which you know this quite well, can pinpoint certain things that may, you may have missed. It doesn't mean that you didn't know it, but still it could bring it out. So he has really helped me with this collection. I have all of the James Baldwin works. I had a chance to meet him. Ralph Ellison. Had a chance to meet him. I had correspondence with Ralph Ellison and his wife before his death. And that's been an interesting thing. It's so bad now that things are in boxes because I don't have any more bookshelf space. [Laughter] And I guess you know this too.

. . . .
"LAMAR" (B. 1945, JACKSONVILLE, FLA.)
When and where did you meet your current partner?

Well, I was in Atlanta. I was out of graduate school. I, one of my dearest friends was dating a guy and I was looking at the guy's yearbook and I saw this picture, I said, "Oh he is so handsome." And he said, "This is a friend of mine." I say, "Oh really." He said, "Yeah." I said, "I'd like to meet him." He said, "Okay. I'll bring him by one day." You know how the girls always, everybody's their friend, they'll meet him. Anyway, maybe two or three weeks he brought them by my house and we met and we kind of chitchatted and we exchanged telephone numbers. That was in May. Then he called me around June. And by this time I had just adopted my son, who was about three years old. And he called and he came over and we started, you know, just kind of seeing each other. And then one thing led to the next.

How long have you been together?

Twenty-two years.

Have they been good years?

Yeah. They've been very good years. And I say they've been very good years, but again, this was a guy who I still say he thinks he's straight after all these years. He's not been married. He has a daughter. He still dates women kind of off and on because I won't permit it. But he seems to think, and I don't know whether this is in his mind or he has to justify, but after all these years, you know, he wanted to be married, could certainly be married because he's extremely handsome, has a lot of things on the ball.

So do you live together?

Yeah, we live together. We're not together now only because he's out of town. His company established another business out of state and he's working that business. But he comes home, five or six times a year. I go where he is five, six times. But he is gonna come back next year because he's tired of being away from town. But we've lived together all these years.

So how does that work if he's still dating women?

Well, when I say dating women—he thinks he wants to date women. Because I won't allow it, you know.

And he's from the South as well?

Yes.

Was that a big deal for you, that you wanted another southerner as a partner?

No. I just think I'm in Atlanta and he was in Atlanta. But again, I think in the black community, especially in the South, guys have to justify, you know, they always want to have a front. Because early on in our relationship he was real concerned about his mother knowing we were living together or his straight friends and all of this. You know.

But you all have worked that out now?

I never had the issue. I always thought it was his issue, you know. He was literally not locked in and he could have left any time he wanted to. He didn't leave. But in the South it's so difficult for black men to be gay or to express their sexuality. Because people go crazy. Just as the election, I don't know whether you know. Gay or straight marriage. I find it repressive. And the one thing I do like about the current generation, my children and all, their friends, they don't get hung up as we do. They are more into as long as it makes you happy, whereas we have to be concerned about other folk[s'] happiness rather than our own happiness, you know. The mere fact that I'm gay, I know, why would people be concerned about who I'm with or what I'm doing in my own home, taking care of myself. They're just issues.

· · · · · · · ·

PATRICK (B. 1966, VIDALIA, GA.)

How, when, and where did you meet your partner?

My current partner? Fourteen years ago, March 1990, I was the public relations coordinator for the African American Lesbian and Gay Alliance, which was one of the first social and political organizations for gay and lesbian—black—African American gay and lesbians, and we were quite politically active. I'm very, very proud of the work that we did. But it was during that time that we met.

And has he met your parents?

Oh, yeah. Oh, yeah.

And what was their reaction to him?

There is no reaction. I mean, it sounds anticlimactic, doesn't it? [Laughter] But there is no—there was no reaction. I told you my brother wanted to know one thing—was he black—and after that, it was cool. You have to understand. My brother is twenty-eight years old. My brother met my partner for the first time when he was thirteen. So for half my brother's life, that's all that—that's the partner that he has known his brother to have. There are things, even today, as a grown man, that my brother will call up and tell my partner, because he's—he doesn't wanna tell his big brother. Because he knows that his part—my partner will come and will relay the message or . . .

Soften the blow? [Laughter]

Soften the blow. Exactly, exactly. I arranged the first meeting very purposely. I did not take my partner home; I had my mother and my little brother to come to our home. And they had spoken to him on the phone, they had heard all about him, but the first time they actually saw him was actually in our home. And it went very well. I mean, in a matter of minutes, everybody was just everybody.

And have you met his parents?

Oh, yes.

And his family?

His mother. His father died when he was a teenager.

And did that go well?

Oh, very well. Yeah.

So your families are very integrated?

Um hmm, fairly, yeah, yeah. Again, there's no drama. [Laughter] There's no drama. It sounds like a boring life, doesn't it?

No, not at all.

You know, just this past week, my partner needed to go and take care of some things for his mother, and my mother was about to undergo surgery, and she was just completely worried, you know, how are things turning out up there, how are things going, did he take care of everything? She was asking these questions right up until the time they moved into the surgery suite. So that's—we are a family.

· · · · · · · ·

ROOSEVELT

Roosevelt and I met through his current partner, Tom, whom I dated many years ago. He is one of several narrators who have been married and have a child. He was born in 1966 in Washington, D.C. The interview took place on October 6, 2004, in Arlington, Virginia.

Were you ever married?

Yes.

And explain how that happened, how that occurred.

The marriage? I had broken up with the first guy that I was dating, and I decided I would try the straight way.

Did you feel like, pressured from society or something to do that?

No, it was pressure from myself, because I had never tried it. I did try, you know, but never to the extent to, going all the way, marriage and all the rest, and that's what, what it primarily happened.

So was this someone you met in high school?

No, I met him in elementary school.

No, the wife.

Oh my wife! I met her, let's see, in the eleventh grade, yeah.

And then you dated for a while?

Mmm hmm, but we met through family, it wasn't through school.

Oh, okay. So her family was a friend of your family?

Mmm hmm.

And how long did the marriage last?

Ten years.

And were they a good ten years?

The first six years were, but there were complications with it.

Did you have any children?

One.

And, how old is your child, now?

Fourteen.

And are you out to your child?

Yes.

And what has that been like, being gay and a parent, and having an ex-wife?

It's been quite an experience that no one could ever understand, because, one thing, I'm very outspoken, when it comes down to that, and I don't let, I don't hide the truth of who I am, or what I want to be. I don't allow, worldly thoughts, that's what I call them, to dictate my life. One thing, before I got married I disclosed to her that I was gay.

Really?

Yes I did.

And she married you anyway?

She married me anyway because I told her I was trying to change, because of what happened. It was a bad experience with the guy, and you know, and I was like, well, this is not the way it's supposed to be, and this is the torture, this is the punishment that God had imposed on me, because of me living this lifestyle, so I'll try it the other way. But, that was trading the devil in for the witch. [Laughs]

Why do you think that she agreed to marry you even though you had come out to her?

Because of the things she went through of her own, and her own life, and we both were in need of certain, we gave each other certain things, at the beginning. I gave up a lot to get married, I really did. That's, it was very different, I can tell you that, because a lot, my family knew, everybody knew, that I was, gay, and when I started dating her it was, it blew everything out of, well it made my grandmother very happy, but she was very sad, because she didn't want me to marry her. She felt it should be someone else.

Were you in love with her?

Yes.

And what are you, what's your relationship with her now?

Oh we don't talk. We don't. We talk very little, because of how she thinks. Her mother and father, they had a very strange relationship, where my family was, we stuck together, they did not. They stuck together when they had to, but not, other than that, no. I remember when we got married, my grand-mother lit into her father and mother about the wedding, because they didn't want to do anything, and she was like, this is your child, don't you want your child to be happy. And as far as the marriage goes, you know, this is her day, this is her day, and his day, it's not your day, and you shouldn't, you know, they didn't give her anything, and what it was, was I gave her everything, I spoiled her, I really did. And because of that, that was part of the breakdown of the marriage, too, or why everything didn't work out, because I kept giving but she didn't give back in return.

While you were married to her, were you still having feelings for men?

No. They all were, they, they disappeared. And until, she started, well, after I decided we weren't, that the marriage was ending, and I realized that I really put in my mind it was ended that's when I decided I would go ahead and go back into the life.

And who has custody of your child?

She does now.

Did you have custody at one point?

Yes I did. I have custody until this year, April of this year.

And why did you switch custody?

To end the pain that my daughter was going through from her mother, because her mother was telling her that, by me having a partner, it created big tension in the relationship of, my daughter and her mother. Had nothing to do with me, and the reason why is because, it seems that I was doing everything better than her mother, her mother felt slighted, especially by the people that knew her when they found out I had custody of her. Well how can that be, he's a gay man, and, and, where I thought it was this, my whole idea is to raise the child, had nothing to do with what no one else think, it's to make sure she has what she needs, and to guide her to get to adulthood. I tell you, her mother's way of thinking is really screwed up, it really is. And then what her mother did is she played a lot of games that, that my daughter's going to regret later, because of, trying to prove something. And that's not what rearing a child is about, to me.

. . . .

TONY (B. 1961, MEMPHIS, TENN.)

Do you currently have a partner?

Umm, sore subject. I can answer other questions, honey. This is one we don't like to tell. I talk about it a lot, but I don't have to talk about it on tape because that's scary, see. I don't actually. I don't.

Are you looking for one?

Um hmm.

What are you looking for in a partner?

It's changed. It's funny you should ask, because I wrote it down the other day. I was trying to articulate what I'm looking for now, and I was really looking at how different that may have been from what I was looking for ten years ago or five years ago. You know, for fifteen years I would have told you, first of all, he has to be black because I just hated seeing my black brothers, my intelligent, beautiful black brothers dating these white men. I just could not tolerate it. And that is so wrong for me, Mr., you know, Rainbow Coalition and multicultural world and all this bullshit, but they all said they couldn't find decent black men, and I thought that was a cop-out and thought that was bullshit and they just didn't care enough to find one. And I was going to be different.

Fifteen years after I made that pronouncement, I threw it out the window. So he doesn't have to be black, and that's new for me to say. He does need to be really honest and really concerned about communication, interpersonal communication. He must, he must love people. I can't date somebody who's a recluse and, you know, I've met plenty of those. He must love people. He must love children. In fact, he must want to have children. If he doesn't have any already that I can assist him in raising, then he must be interested in having some. Because I meet so many gay men who are like [makes "poof" sound], "Yeah, I like children, somebody else's." Uh oh, bye, go. He must have some appreciation for the beauty of the world. I mean, the world is a horrible place, but it's also very beautiful. And I had this conversation with a man yesterday. We were talking about men in our lives, you know, where he had this boyfriend who he tries to do fun, little romantic things with him. The guy's not responsive to that. Or I had a boyfriend where I would try to encourage him to do something new or to think of something new and he couldn't because he's not—he doesn't think that way. Or the boyfriend I had where I say, "Oh, my God, isn't the moon beautiful?" And he said, "It's all right. It's just the moon." No. So they've got to—and you'd think you could find men like that easily, but you really can't. They have to appreciate the beauty of the world. And in that comes a certain kind of sensitivity, I think, that goes with it. They have to—this is going to sound weird to you, but they have to be in a twelve-step program. Just flat out, that's all I'm—that's the truth, they have to be. And I can explain that further, if you like. And then the last part is they—I'm not dating some man who is a Baptist or a Catholic or a Church of God in Christ person. They don't have to belong to Religious Science, but at this point if they're not along into some sort of new-thought religion or their own brand of spirituality which they do on their own, then I can't be bothered. They have to be a spiritual person and believe in a creator, whatever they want to call that creator, but I'm not interested in dating someone who has strong ties to some mainline religion that is homophobic. You know, because though he may not be homophobic, the fact that he tolerates this in this religion that he belongs to, I can't have that. And so that's what I look for. He can be anywhere from fifty-five to thirty-five. He can be anywhere from 5′2″ to 6′10″. He can be a garbage man. He could be a corporate executive. I don't care. Those things are not important to me. He cannot smoke. So that's what I'm looking for.

Have you been in a long-term relationship?

Child, well, I've tried, you know. I've had a spotty history, let's just be clear about that. I've tried, you know. Only now can I look back and see all the men that I've tried to go out with, most of whom were not right for me and were destined for failure as relationships. But the last one, the one I mentioned that my father watched football with, we tried on and off for eight years. There were some off times. There were a year and two months or this and that, nine months where we weren't together. That happened several times in the eight-year period, we weren't together the whole time. But finally called it quits. So that would be the longest one. And everything prior to that had been very, you know, short, six months, nine months. I learned a lot from that relationship. And I think that did shape a lot of what I'm telling you today. I think I'm clearer now, who I was then, I was basing things on emotion and not really on what I really want, you know. So I think it brought a sense of clarity. Because we did go to couples' counseling and we did go to individual therapy. And though it didn't help the relationship, I think it ultimately helped each of us sort of—he was like me in terms of he wasn't dealing with his own baggage and probably didn't believe he had any baggage. When anything went wrong, it was his fault, not my fault, you know. But I think with each other, we were forced to reconcile that, no, we have our own baggage that is contributing. So I felt like I was late in coming to that sort of self-awareness. And it was painful, the relationship was painful, but it was also very beautiful. I wouldn't change anything, I would do it again, you know. But I think it's made me more ready for this next level of the type of relationship I'm looking for with this new type of man that I have to find, that I'm looking for.

· · · · · · · ·

"ALEX" (B. 1967, GREENWOOD, S.C.)

Do you currently have a partner or boyfriend or lover?

No. I've been trying to date, but for some reason or another, I don't know. I told somebody just the other day, I'm just not dating material. I just think that I'm going to grow old and I'm just going to be alone. Not alone. But I won't be with someone. You know, every guy that I've ever dated . . . and this is something I've been trying to work on myself. I mean I've been looking at me because obviously I contributed to half of the situations, if not more. And being able to take that responsibility and knowing that, you know, that I share in that responsibility of the success or the unsuccessfulness of the relationship. I'm very aggressive. I'm an aggressive/passive person. The passive side of me, people like. The aggressive side of me, people are intimidated by. And I've been trying to figure out why and how to balance it. And every time I try to change it, it still comes back to the same thing. You can't . . . What's the word I'm looking for? People react and respond based on their own beliefs, insecurities . . . How people respond to you has nothing, typically, to do with you. It's more so to do with them. And so it took me a minute to realize, you know, I can't take on that responsibility. You either like me or you don't. You either like me being direct or you don't. Of course I can curtail it a little bit. You know we all can curtail it.

Like I met this guy a couple of weeks ago. He actually approached me. A very attractive guy. Tall, kind of a debonair type, you know. Wavy hair. Sort of a Cuban, Puerto Rican looking fellow. And I'm attracted to lighter-skinned men, typically. I like men in general, but you know I am attracted to lighter-skinned men for whatever reason, I don't know. Maybe it's because I grew up around all the white folks. [Laughter] But I don't date . . . I'm not dating anybody white, and I never have. But he told me right up front, you know, he's a workaholic. He's career driven. He's very direct. He's very dominant, and he's controlling. I said, "Okay. I don't have a problem with that, at all." And I think he's having an issue with someone who is . . . because he's talked about his past relationships . . . And his past relationships have been more . . . He's been in control. I don't have a problem with giving you control, you know, but you also have to realize too that I have a career. I'm just as driven and just as focused as you. I'm independent, so I don't need you for anything other than, you know, your companionship. You know, those kinds of things. So don't tell me that, you know, you're looking for someone of that caliber and then when you find someone of that caliber it's like, you know, well, "Am I really looking for someone of that caliber?" You know. So need-less to say, he's kind of backed off from me a little bit and . . . Which is fine. And there are two ways that I look at it. He's backed off because he feels that he doesn't have control, and by backing off he puts me in a position of feeling insecure, to where I'm becoming submissive to him and I'm going to chase after him. Well he got the wrong one. [Laughter] I mean now, granted I'll call sporadically. But I'm not going to hound you. I'm not going to make comments about, "Oh why are you working so late?" I'm not going to make comments about, you know, "Why didn't you call me until now? I haven't heard from you in two to three days." I'm not going to make a comment . . . Like for example this past weekend. He calls me on Sunday morning, "Oh you're on your way from church?" "Yeah I am." And "How was church?" And we talk about church and what have you, and I told him what the message was all about and what have you. And it's all about him. So he says, "Well I wonder . . . I was thinking about doing a movie this afternoon." I said, "Okay, that's good. Well what did you want to go see?" Well, "I want to go see X, X, and X." So I said, "Well you know what? I would like to go see one of those movies." And he says, "Well what are your plans?" I said, "Well I really don't have any plans." Leaving it open. "Well I'm going to lay back down. Take a nap and I'll give you a call a little bit later." "Okay fine." No call. Well I didn't call either. Because I figure, you know, it was on you. You said you were going to call. I didn't say I was going to call. And if I had said, "Okay, well I'll call you later" or if he had said, "Well give me a ring later on" and I agreed to it, then I would have followed up. But I wasn't following up on your . . . What's the word I'm looking for? On your . . .

Promise to call?

Right. Exactly. And so I'm sure that probably threw him for a loop. And I'm not here to play games with people. I told him just like I've told any other man that I've ever dated, that if you want to play games, I'll play a game with you. [Laughter] I will. And I will play to win. But I'm playing the game on your rules, not mine. So when I do win, you can't look at me and say well, you know, I manipulated the situation. No, you make the rules and I'll play the game. Bottom line. [Laughter] I mean, that's how I kind of live my life.

# of legends and young'uns
black gay men across generations

7

The title of this chapter riffs off the by now famous "Legends Ball" hosted by Oprah Winfrey in honor of black women actresses, dancers, poets, writers, activists, and singers who paved the way for her and other "young'uns" who came after. While Oprah's celebration was in honor of mostly self-identified heterosexual black women, this chapter pays homage to two forefathers whose lives stand as examples for how to live and die with dignity and respect. They, too, are "legendary," but more in the black gay ballroom sense than the Hollywood rags-to-riches sense.[1] Like Oprah, however, I am invested in paying homage to my forbears. Don Clark's sentiment about older gay men's history rings true for me, as I'm sure it does for others of my generation and those younger: "Now we wake to our aging and search for our elders, our ancestors, living and dead. We want to hear their tales and touch their scars. We want to know the path they followed. The beauty of youth and the beauty of age are ready to meet."[2]

George Eagerson (aka "Countess Vivian"), who is now in his 90s, and Jeff Smith, who died in 2005, came of age in the 1920s and 1930s and lived into the new millennium. Their South was by marked by Jim Crow, the Depression, World War II, McCarthyism, the civil rights movement, the HIV/AIDS epidemic, and our contemporary debates on gay marriage. Coincidentally, both also survived colon cancer. All of this shaped who Jeff was and who the Countess is in the world, how they negotiated their (homo)sexuality within the context of specific times and events. Their lives span some five generations of southern black gay life, cutting across any one identity and demonstrating how race, gender, sexuality, and class are always pivoting around the other.

But how do the lives of their generation of black gay men differ from those of gay blacks coming into their manhood contemporarily? Astonishingly, not much has changed. Two of the youngest narrators in *Sweet Tea* reveal lives that are fraught with more angst than either Countess Vivian or Jeff recount. Stephen and Joe, ages twenty-two and twenty, respectively, have overcome seemingly insurmountable obstacles to succeed in life. While they have not experienced publicly sanctioned Jim Crow laws or segregation, as did the Countess and Jeff, they have experienced overt racism and de facto segregation, especially in their school systems. The poverty that the two forefathers speak of was tempered by a sense of cooperative responsibility and sharing within their black communities, while the two young'uns have had to cope with homelessness and rely on the kindness of white philan-thropists. One of the legends and one of the young'uns lost his mother at an early age, both to horrific events. HIV/AIDS affected all of their lives in ways that converge and diverge across a spectrum of people and personal circumstances.

These four men's lives span over ninety years of southern black gay his-tory. The legends' lives and the young'uns' lives overlap during only the last twenty-four years; yet these men's perspectives on life, love, politics, and personal struggle give us a glimpse into how black queer southerners have employed the same strategies of survival and pleasure-making across time and space. And yet, these transgenerational commonalities notwithstand-ing, as James T. Sears suggests, "Across the five Southern generations of this century are distinct generational personalities and individual histories that become most apparent in the contrast to one another."[3] Whatever their common bonds, each of these four narrators expresses his own personal attitudes and beliefs about his life circumstances viewed from the perspec-tive of his position in society and history.

. . . .

"COUNTESS VIVIAN"

Countess Vivian is the oldest person I interviewed. Ninety-three at the time of the interview, he was unbelievably agile and lucid. Before Hurricane Katrina, he lived alone on St. Anne Street in the French Quarter, just one block from where St. Anne intersects Bourbon Street, marking the divide between the "straight" and "gay" ends of Bourbon Street. Since Katrina, I have not been able to reach the Countess, but I have seen a newspaper photograph of him, indicating that he survived the storm.

Ed, one of the narrators in this book, who lives in New Orleans, introduced me to the Countess and accompanied me to the interview. Ed suggested that I take the Countess a bottle of sherry, as it is a ritual for him to have an afternoon glass of sherry during "tea time." Upon meeting him, I immediately fell in love with the Countess. When we arrived at his home and he opened the door, he said, "Hey, Sweetie, come on in," acting as if he had known me all of my life. During the visit he referred to me alternately as "baby," "honey," "chile," and "sugar," in the endearing tone that many southern black women use when speaking to those younger than themselves. His home was a typical "shotgun" house, with only three rooms and a hallway through the center of the house, down which you could see to the back door. Scattered throughout the living room were pictures of a younger Countess, including a picture of him in the Army. Before the interview began, he showed me many of these pictures and introduced me to his family members, including his mother, via their photos.

The interview took place on January 22, 2005, just a week before Mardi Gras, or what the Countess referred to as carnival. He was expecting guests from out of town, which, apparently, was a tradition. He told me off tape that he used to have lots of parties at his home, especially during the Mardi Gras season.

I was born here in New Orleans in 1912. November the 12th, 1912.

And you've lived here all your life?

All my life. Well, we were poor. We lived in a great big old house—two stories.

Here in the French Quarter?

Oh no. Lord no. We lived on what was called the Seventh Ward. In the beginning when I was still like that [gestures to how tall he was as a child], we were on Marais Street. It's further back this way, where the project is today. And as we grew up to about, say, like ten, twelve years old, we moved to what's called the Seventh Ward, and it was down on North Derbigny Street below what's called Esplanade here. And we stayed there for many, many, many years. And then, after I decided I wanted to be [. . .] grown, then I left home and I moved to this area where the project is today—of course the project wasn't there at that time. And stayed there for quite some time. Then I moved uptown. Then I got schooled in the practical nursing. Then I worked at Charity [Hospital] for a couple of years. And then from Charity the war started in '41 or '42. And from there I went to the Army and I stayed in the Army about three years. And then I came back here. And then I went to . . . I lived . . . my mother was still living on Derbigny Street and I stayed halfway there and halfway [in my own place]. I had an apartment up on what's called South Rampart Street. And of course, then my mother took sick, then I went back to stay with her completely. And then we were living on Laharpe Street, between Derbigny and Roman. That was in the '60s, because she died in '61; no, she died in '60. And I stayed there after she died. I stayed there until 1978. Then I moved here. And I've been living here since 1978, since October.

Countess Vivian in the doorway of his home on St. Anne Street in the French Quarter, January 2005. Photo by the author.

What was it like as a child growing up in New Orleans in the 1910s and 1920s?

Well, it wasn't like it is today, I can tell you that. [Laughter] Because, well, everything was segregated and, of course, things were a little cheaper 'cause you could go to the store and buy, take a nickel and get what we called at that time half rice and half beans—two things for five cents. And you could buy almost everything you wanted with just a little of nothing. And there were many things that you could go to the store and buy. And not only buy, but get stuff for free. You go to the market [and get] like fish head, 'cause we would make what was called court bouillon. That's stewed, stew the head, fish heads, with a red gravy and throw that on top of rice. Of course you have to be careful of the bones, etc. But it came out real good and it was filling. And almost everything you wanted at that time was really cheap, cheap, cheap, cheap.

And before I got into nursing I worked in a boardinghouse. They took care of students from Tulane, up way, way, way up St. Charles Street. You know where that's at. And they also took care of students from Loyola. And, well, in any given boardinghouse, the students would live, and they would also have their meals there, three meals a day. We worked there from sunup to sundown. [. . .] Well, they'd call you half a day Sunday, but you know good and well if you serve your dinner at one o'clock on a Sunday—because we didn't serve it 'til after one o'clock dinner, that was it, no more meals that day—if you serve the dinner at one o'clock, and after you get allllll your tables all cleaned up and everything straightened up, you have to wash the dishes. You have to wash dishes too because the cooks at that time, most of them that worked in those boardinghouses, even at that way, way, way long time ago, they didn't wash no pots. They didn't wash no dishes. All they did was cook. Well, after you get all that done, if you was a slow person, well, you know what time you was gonna get out of there. It sure wouldn't be no half a day.

Right. But you only got paid for half a day.

Yeah, you got paid for half a day. And [. . .] to begin with you wasn't making nothing. Because some places wasn't paying but five dollars a week and I'm telling these people today where they're making all kinds of money today, and they don't appreciate it. And we was making five dollars a week. Coffee was seven cents. And if I lived way downtown and then had to wake up in the morning and then have seven cents, well I took myself up the road and walked all the way to Broadway—well I shouldn't just say St. Charles because it wasn't really St. Charles. I didn't work on the corner of St. Charles, you know we worked two or three blocks from St. Charles and walked over and worked all day—well, I'd have seven cents to come back home. Well, it was sort of like primitive, but then too, those were the times at that time. Those were the things that was going on at that time. Nobody was making nothing. And if you had a job working, say like, getting twelve dollars a week, there were some jobs that were paying that much. Like certain people that worked in tailor shops, because we had many, many, many tailor shops. Many, many men at that time had their clothes tailored, and they wore all kinds of monograms: monogrammed buckles, monogrammed rings and monogrammed, everything you look at had monograms. On their suspenders and all that had big old monogrammed things on it.

Black folk?

Yeah, black folk [. . .] especially the guys that were called pimps. [Laughter] And then you had these people that was, because just like *now, then* they was doing the same thing: selling dope. And they were selling, there was people that sold dope and things; and riding around in big pretty cars and everything.

What years were this, in the '20s or the '30s?

Way in the, way, way, way, way back in the '20s and the '30s and coming into the '40s. And if they were making money selling whatever they were selling, then they could afford all these things.

And then, like these women that hustled—you see, when they closed the district, it was over here where this project is—not this one, I'm talking about the one over here by the graveyard. You know this graveyard right over here? Well, from Iberville and Basin to St. Louis Street and from Basin to Robertson, going back, was the red light district. Well, during the second war, no but during the first war, the government closed them down. So that meant all the hustling women left, you know, because they still had some of the big houses that remained, but eventually [they] all closed and they just paraded them all out 'cause a lot of those women that did the hustling, they came over on this side. And those women, if they hustled, well they would have what I call pimps. And then the people would come for them, would come and the women would take care of the men. And that's the reason why they would be dressing so well and with all kinds of diamonds on their fingers and everything. Of course, everything was much, much, much, much cheaper then than it is today. So they could afford all of that.

What did your parents do for work?

Well, my mother, she took in washing. My father, he died way, way a long, when I was a little child. And I don't know too much about him. But my mother, she did work. She worked. And she took in washing and she did housework. She would get up at four o'clock in the morning, and her house would be clean; her house that we lived in would be cleaned from front to back before she left. And the front, I mean, the sidewalk was swept and everything. In the house we slept on mattresses with moss [claps his hands together] in them. And we had a big slit in the middle of the mattress and you'd put your hand all in there and raise all of that old moss up and get it smooth, you know. And chinnnnnnches, you ain't never seen a chinch. It's a little bug. It's a bug. And it sucks blood. Honey, a million of them and you just be killing chinches like nobody's business. [Laughter] And the more you kill . . . we'd pour oil on them because we had kerosene lamps, pour oil on them and that didn't do no good. Next morning after you done kill God knows how many, the next morning you get up and they done ate, ate, ate and sucked all your blood. [Laughter] You'd have a million more to kill.

They would come from the moss?

They came from somewhere and they were in the mattress, and they might have came from the moss but must have multiplied like I don't know what, because like I say, they'd be all in the cracks of the mattresses, all in the corners and everything. And you'd be squeezing chinches, squeezin' 'em and squeezin' 'em, smashin' them you know. Next morning you had the same thing. [Laughter] But we got through that. We had grates in the house, like this thing here [points to the grate over the heating vent]. And we had burned coal and we'd burn wood. And you had to pick up the ashes every day and we stoked the fire to keep it going all night. And we had kerosene light because we didn't have no electric light. We had wood stove. Well, at that time a whole lot of people didn't have no electric lights 'cause the electric lights really and truly didn't come into being until way, way, way, way later, you know, for everybody. There were many people that had electric, but the poor people didn't have it. And we had these kerosene lamps. And we used to have to clean the lamp globes every day to keep them, because they get all smoky. And naturally we had to wash, we had to iron, we had to scrub. We sold rags, we sold bottles, we sold scraps, we sold everything, papers. We sold everything that we could get our hands on to make a little money. All that's gone. Today, you don't have to do it. Peoples coming up today have it really good. They don't have all that to do. And even if they had it to do, you got these people that came behind us, they wouldn't even think of doing nothing like that. Ooooooh. You tell them something like go sell some paper, or go sell some bottles or something, and sell some rags. Lorrrrrrd no. Uh unh. [Laughter] But we did all right, you know.

And then, like I said, after my mother died, I stayed in the house almost twenty years. After she left. After she died. And then I moved over here, and I been here ever since.

Did you have any brothers or sisters?

I had three brothers. All of them are dead. All of them were younger than me. And I had one sister, but she died when we were children. And the other boys, they died—the last one died about, now he's been dead about six, seven, eight years. And my youngest brother, the one right behind me, he died in 1961 because his house blew up and he got burned and he lasted maybe about two, three days. And my oldest brother, he died in about 1970. He used to drink, drink, drink, drink, drink, and ran into I don't know what. I guess the drink must have hurried his life away, because he died. And in fact all of my people are dead: my mother, brothers, sisters, everybody's gone. I'm the only one left. 'Course now, I have a lot of nieces and nephews, but that's just like not having anybody because I don't ever see them unless they need a favor. And then there they are. They'll call you up and this, that, and the other. And then they want to borrow something. And then when they borrow it, they don't ever bring it back.

Are they still here in New Orleans?

Yeah, they all live in New Orleans. Scattered around this town. But I don't really know exactly where they stay at because, you know, like I don't keep up with them. I just don't have no kin people.

Do you remember where you went to elementary school or grade school or high school?

Oh boy, chile, I can't remember all that. Uh unh. When I was in grade school, oh it must have been, really and truly I can't remember. There are many things I just don't remember. [. . .] I went uptown yesterday, and I was on a bus, and got on a bus. [A] person that I've known for God knows how many years, and was setting right next to him and didn't even recognize him until way later after we had rolled for several blocks. Because he had called me as I was passing, because I was going to sit on another seat. And his half was vacant so I sat there, and we talking and he knows my name and all that. And I was wondering to myself, now who is [he]? I can't place him. And then it came to me, way, way, way down the line who he was. There are just, you know, some things I can remember, and many things I just don't.

You said you went to nursing school?

Yeah. It was like a private school. It was really like a small college, you know. And they taught practical nurses. You see, long ago, when I went to nursing school, we didn't have to have, like the practicals today are licensed. So you just learned a little something and then you walked on out the door. [Laughter] And you, of course, you could do as well as some of the other people did. In fact, sometimes some of those did better than some of the regulars did. But it wasn't like getting a degree or anything like that. Just a little piece of paper saying that you did this, that, and the other.

Did you work in a hospital?

Uh huh. I worked at Charity for two or three years before I went in the Army. [. . .] There, I did orthopedic. And when I went in the Army, well I was doing, not orthopedics, but I was still in the medics . . . 'cause I didn't do no fighting. I was in the medics and we were attached to the 96th engineers. Unlike these soldiers today, those engineers they build roads, carry shovel picks, poles, rifles, they build bridges, they build houses, they did everything. And we were attached to them, and we took care of the sick and the wounded and things like that.

Where were you stationed in the Army?

Well, from here we went to California. It was six months training in Abilene, Texas. And then from there we went to Millinet Bay. Really we began [. . .] in the Southwest Pacific. We went to Millinet Bay. We went to little islands. Little islands, little islands, little islands. And then we went all the way up to the Philippines. [. . .] We were up there because they were fighting the Japanese in the part of the Army I was with. Now, my youngest brother, he was also in the Army, but he was in the European part because they were fighting the Germans. And the part I was in [was in] the South Pacific. Like I say, we was always on a boat. [. . .] The black people at that time didn't have the privileges that they have today in the Army. And of course they tell me that it's not all that much better. [Chuckle] But then, too, it was really, really bad then because the blacks were always to themselves, only we had white officers. The chaplain, he was black. But all of our officers were white and everybody else was black, and we had the worst, the worst, the worst, the worst, like throwing away stuff we would get.

In terms of food?

No, in terms of the facilities for living over there. I never forget when we arrived in Abilene [for] our training. Even though you was in the medics, you had to learn how to do this, do that, drill and all that other kind of stuff. And we were in the worst, worst, worst black barracks. With those big old potbelly stoves, you know, burning coal. And all those white folks were all in the big nice and shiny new barracks and all that other kind of stuff. But we made it. [. . .] I said I was determined to go in there and do what I had to do and come on out. But there were many of us that didn't want to be in it [the Army]. And they was in it, and before you knew it they was out. Because they'd always do something. [Laughter] They would always do something.

Countess Vivian in a World War II Army photo. Courtesy of the narrator.

So they were trying to get in trouble so they'd get thrown out?

Well of course, they didn't want to be in it. [. . .] You can't hardly blame them. [. . .] When we first got to Abilene, Texas, it was in all of them old [. . .] black dirty barracks with these big old potbelly stoves burning coal. And we were right next door to a cesspool and a greeeaaat big old thing. When I first started, I thought it was a little lake, you know. And then the next two, three, four days or something like that, then I found out that it was a cesspool. Right there, right by us. But no white folks. They were somewhere else. All on the same base, but way, way, way off from us.

Did you go to church when you were a kid?

Well, of course I was a Christian. Went to church. Well, when I went to Catholic school and we had to go to church every morning. Nothing like these children today; we went to mass *every* morning before we went to class. And I used to, long ago, I'd go to church quite often. Of course, I don't go to church that much now. But once, occasionally, I try to get there, but that doesn't mean I don't do no little praying or anything. I do that every morning. I was [raised] Christian Catholic.

When did you say you got out of the Army?

I got out early '46. I meant to say in early March of '46. And I immediately started work for the Veterans Administration around the end, I'd say like around the 25th or the 26th of March in '46. And I stayed there for thirty-two years and six months and some odd days.

Was there a gay community here in New Orleans in the '20s and '30s?

Ooh, I hope to tell you, but at that time I did not know or realize that they had white sissies, [laughter] 'cause all the ones that I ever saw were over on that side of the track, because the railroad tracks used to run all the way over to Canal Street, the Southern Railroad. Right across beyond Rampart there. [. . .] Just like they have lesbians today, they have many, many, many black lesbians—all black on that side. Just like I said, I didn't know because we didn't see any white gay people 'cause everything was segregated. And over here, the only time you would come over here [in the French Quarter] would be if you was *working*. You couldn't bum or you couldn't this or you couldn't do that. You could come over here and scrub the floor and clean the toilet and things like that, but you couldn't say I'm going to go hang in a bar and buy me a drink or something like that. You couldn't do that. But you could have in your own areas on the other side of the tracks.

And so there were lots of black gay bars?

Oh yeah, I hope to tell you, there was a whole lot of them. Not as many as they got as white bars, but there were many, many, many black bars. 'Cause I was young and all those older children, well I knew of them, saw them, they'd be all in the bar because most of them used to drink wine. And during Prohibition they had a place where they would go, and they used to make the wine. But it was really, really, really good. I don't know what they was making it with, but it was really, really good. [Laughter] It'd be ice-cold, and just one glass of it would make you kind of dizzy. [Laughter] It was really good. And that's the, all the blacks would be all up in the bars together and the gay bars would have all their people. Of course, you could go in almost any place. But [. . .] just like they have gay bars, white gay bars today and black gay bars, there were black gay bars then. And, of course, the only difference was the black stayed in their place, the whites stayed in their place.

What was going on in the bars? Was there music or were they just sort of sit-around bars or did people dance?

They had pianos. Put a nickel in the piano and it'd play a tune and you could dance. Then, that was before the music boxes came. And you could dance if you wanted to. Some places had, we used to call them funky butt places. [Laughter] They had, because the ballrooms at that time they had sawdust all on the floor and everything else, you see. And they would have maybe two, three little pieces of music, they have a drum and a horn or something like that, and you'd go back there and you'd dance like nobody's business.

How did people find out about the bars, or you just knew?

Oh they just knew. They just knew.

Were there signs outside?

Not during Prohibition, there wasn't no sign because it wasn't allowed. The bars weren't allowed. That came after. After Prohibition the bars were open. But during Prohibition they had what was called at that time speak-easies. And all you had to do was know somebody where the speakeasy was, because it would be just like a little club; they give you a little card or something like that and you belong to the club, let you in the place. Just like during elections time, in those days the bars were supposed to close up. Black. But what they would do, they'd put a sheet or something up over the liquor [laughter] and you couldn't see what's behind it, but they would be right open and be selling you liquor underneath the counter.

So, you know, sometimes, I'll think back and I say times were really hard, hard, hard, hard for many blacks at that time. But then, too, we made it; the things were cheaper. And [. . .] *then*, it was not like here *now* that people are being shot and every day you got one, two, three gone. You didn't hear of all that shooting. If people got a little fuss, fight or something like that, and it was over. Today if you just bump up against somebody they just want to shoot you.

[. . . .]

Were there drag queens back then?

Yeah, [. . .] we did have a couple of them, not a couple of them, more than a couple of them because they used to hustle too in dresses, like Julia Pimpay. These peoples died way years ago. In fact all these people I've mentioned, they've all died long, long ago. Like Julia Pimpay and several others that used to dress, put on dresses and dance and hustle at night. They wouldn't have nothing in the room but the bed and the one chair. And that one chair would be like that door right there [points to the door dividing his living room and bedroom], and the bed maybe be way over that way somewhere, because the rooms were big, bigger at that time—wasn't no little small room; the houses had very large rooms you see. And you have somebody in that room right there and we used to call them "creepers" [laughter]. See like they [would] get a trick, they would creep in the door, creep to come in the door, and while the man that you'd be going with, he is busy and they go in his pocket and steal his money. That went on for God knows how long because that's why they didn't have nothing in the room, because if it gets too big a haul, then they have to get out of there right because the people would go get the police and then many, many, many times the person that got robbed wouldn't even go get the police because they would be ashamed to go and tell the police that they were up there with these black . . . if they didn't know he was a sissy; they thought it was a woman. And even if it was a real woman they didn't want people to know that they was in there, you know, with these blacks. Because at that time blacks and whites wasn't close. Of course, they're not all that close now. But then, too, they were further apart than we are today.

So sometimes these were white men picking up these tricks?

Well, not sometimes, always. Always white, no black men, honey. No black men. And women. Even the black women that hustled, they didn't fool around with them black guys.

Because they didn't have any money?

That's right. That's right. You go where the money is. [Laughter] Not fooling around and wasting your damn time with those blacks. Because a lot of the black guys, like I said, they were pimps. The women would hustle and they'd give them the money and they'd be dressing and looking like little princes and all that stuff.

When did you first realize that you were gay?

Oh Lord, chile, must have been a little baby child like that. [Laughter] Right away. Right away. I don't know what caused it; it just come right on just like that. [. . .] When I was going to school I had a nice little young girl that she was, well, you know, we were supposed to be friend and boy, boyfriend and all like that. But I never, you know I didn't, she was nice and everything else, but I never did have no feelings for like these boys today they want to go to bed and all that. I never did. All I'd want is like some boy or something like that. And then I kind of knew that I was quite different than the rest of the guys. Because all of them didn't want no boy; they'd be looking for little girls. But still, I don't know, it just came. I guess it's just like they say, it's born in you. [. . .] I don't think anybody makes you do it. [. . .] If it's not in you to be that way, you're not gonna be. That's the way I look at it.

Were there other kids in your neighborhood growing up that you knew that were gay or felt the same?

Just one or two, that's all. Just one or two. And they all dead too. They died when they were young. In my block where I lived at they had one, one that I was sort of like raised up with. And he died when he was young. And then another guy that I knew that was young in my, sort of like when I was coming up, he died too.

What about in the Army, did you know other gay people in the Army?

Oh Lord, they had God knows how many of them. Like I said, when you go down there to the canteen, oh now I wish you'd see them. [Laughter] [. . .] There was a group that wanted to go home. They had their hats, those little caps that we used to wear, fixed all kinds of ways on their head and everything else, child. And you could tell that they were, of course, like me. I knew them. I had been with them for God knows how long out of the Army. And I knew as soon as I looked at 'em. I could tell, I'd say, "Oh Lord, there's another girl." [Laughter] Hooooney, they did e-very-thing. And everybody in the place knew that they were, you know. Because they wanted to leave. And then it wasn't like it is *now*. Because *now*, if you act like a girl or something like that, they gonna put you out right away. And *then* they didn't do that. You had to really do something really drastic, you know, for them to say, "Well, we're gonna discharge you," or discharge you. But it's altogether different today. Because they did just like Clinton said, "don't ask, don't tell," and all that. But me, myself, I didn't have any problem within the Army. None whatsoever.

Have you ever had a boyfriend or a partner?

In the Army?

No, just in your life.

Oh Lord, honey. God knows how many. [Laughter]

What was the longest relationship you had?

Maybe about two or three years. One. And then like, because I was a person that never like this one, that one or the other. I like *one* person. And we would stay together something like that. Some of the people that I've gone with, they're already dead, too. And they, we would stay until we break up or something like that. And after that wears off, [you] go get somebody else. I had many friends that wanted to have six and seven and eight and all like that. Friends of mine, before they went to bed at night, they would have their two and three men. But I don't see what they could get out of it, you know, 'cause it looked to me if you done had one, you don't really need no more. Lord no, uh unh, they'd be working like nobody's business. [Laughter]

How did you get the name "Countess Vivian"?

Well, I can't say. I can't remember. My name was Vivian or they nickname Vivian way long, long, long ago when I was young, young, young. And some of them sissies . . . the older people give me that name, Vivian. And then down the line somebody put that other attachment to it, "The Countess." And so, of course nobody calls me that today—just one or two people that remember me from way, way, way long ago. But younger people I've known, you know, they don't know nothing about me, my nickname being Vivian. 'Cause it really and truly don't matter that much, but people forget and people don't know and you don't act and you don't go telling. Then too, the life that I live today is not like one that I had way on back because I don't entertain no more or anything like that. And then I don't go nowhere. Just to the grocer or something like that and then go somewhere else. I used to be in the ball-room all the time, 'cause I'd get in there and you never could get me out.

In the ballroom you say?

In the bar, uh huh. Yeah, I like to go sit in the bar. Listen to the music. And drink. I used to drink whiskey. Scotch. I like scotch and milk. And I loved that. But I stopped drinking it, and I started drinking beer. Now I drink wine and sherry and beer.

When you entertained, was it at this house?

Here. And after my mother died, and even before my mother died, if I would have a party or something like that, I didn't have to wash the dishes and this that because no sooner something was dirty she'd be done cleaned it. [Laughter] [She] did all that. But not as much; when she was living I didn't do all that much entertaining, but like I did after she died. Because down there I'd have so many people in that whole, because it was a large house and we had a great big like a driveway and a great big ol' yard. They had people all in the yard and everywhere else. And then here, you would have so many people you couldn't hardly get in here. Like especially during carnival time. And we'd be playing cards and we'd be drinking, we'd be cooking and doing a little of everything. And, of course, nowadays all the people that come, used to come for carnival, got three or four that still come for carnival, but all that other group that used to come from St. Louis and all over the place, they all

Countess Vivian in his living room, 2005. Photo by the author.

dead. [. . .] Even the ones that live here in town a little further down and back and all that, they don't come anymore because they can't get around. And there's some that'll say, "Well, we'll just stay home and drink our little wine and play cards."

So most of the friends that you had are passed away now?

Most of them, of course. [. . .] I have about two people. They're older people that I still keep up with. We don't go out like we used to long ago. And they can't hardly walk, walking with canes and all that other kind of stuff. Course me, I ought to have a cane too, but I don't have one. [Laughter] Because I kind of do a little bit better. And then I don't go, hardly go anywhere. Like I said, I go to the grocery or something. Maybe sometimes I go around the corner. When I say, "around the corner," it's one of them bars that I used to like. I could go around there and sit and talk to the guys that own the place, but he is no longer there, so I don't go around there no more. But when my little group come, I always go with them because they like, they be going, going, going, going.

So you have visitors come in town?

Yeah, one of them coming on the first. But this one here [a man who was sitting in the kitchen during the interview],[4] that's here now, I don't go with him because he works right next door there. He cleans up and he's waiting to get his apartment. And he's always full [i.e., drunk], so by the time they get over here he gets over, finishes work around two and instead of him leaving, he sits right there at the counter. And I say they ought to be glad he's working there because he could take the little salary in one hand [and] give it back to them in the other hand. [Laughter] They making money off of *him* as far as I can tell.

So you've been pretty healthy?

Yeah. Of course in '83 I developed cancer of the colon. And I had an operation. And then I had therapy, radiation therapy for about six or eight weeks. And I was told at that time that if I would live five years I would be doing alright. Well I done lived . . . [Laughter]

Twenty something years passed then.

I done this since '83. So I guess I'll keep on going. [Laughter]

So you enjoy life.

That's right, honey. Don't let them set me in that chair, holding my hand, twiddling my thumbs because that's not gonna help at all. And set to worry about this or worry about that. You know, I just don't let things worry me. And I don't have too many aches. Just sometimes I get stiff and things like that. But after I start walking or something like that, moving about it's all gone. The only medications that I do now is take a few aspirins sometimes.

Countess Vivian celebrating Mardi Gras at a local bar on Bourbon Street, 2002. Courtesy of the narrator.

And I keep my Alka-Seltzer. And to keep my beauty up, I uses Oil of Olay. That's right, child.

It's working.

It sure is. I hope to tell you. Because I know people that's way, way, way, way, way younger than me [who] look woooorse than me. So I say I'm blessed. And I have a couple of teeth if I wanted to put them in my mouth, but I don't wear them. Unh uh.

Have you ever seriously thought about moving out of the South?

Out of the South? No, no, no. One time, years back, when I first went to New York I would say that. Of course my mother was living at that time, and I was sort of like, even though I had all my other brothers living, I sort of like felt that I had to stay here because she was mostly dependent on me. So I didn't ever move. But other than that I have never wanted to go nowhere else to live. But I've been many places, but I never wanted to, say, move out of the South to go somewhere else to live.

What are your best memories about growing up in the South?

Nothing but that we was poor. And everything was segregated when I was coming up. Everything. That's the one thing that's most vivid in my mind. The hard times that we had.

What do you think about HIV and AIDS around today? Because y'all didn't have to worry about that.

Never give it a thought. At that time we didn't worry about that. But it's just like people at that time were dying with pneumonia, and that's just a form of pneumonia. Of course they're just calling it something else today. But me, myself I never give it a thought because after all, if you're doing this, that, and the other, then you might have to worry about it, and I don't be doing all those things, so I don't have to worry about that. And I hardly ever give it a thought. Of course I know many, many people that, had two, three friends that died with it, and you got other people that's coming up and that's got it, things like that. But I never give too much a thought about that.

So you didn't lose any friends or anybody from it?

Yeah two or three of them. Uh huh. Some of them were large, big healthy-looking people, and then they just droop, got thin and lost weight and some of them just couldn't raise up, they couldn't use the bed pan, couldn't even use the urinal. And then they eventually died.

The only thing you had to worry about was what, syphilis and gonorrhea and things like that?

Well, long ago you did. Not only you had to worry about syphilis, you had to worry about gonorrhea, and that was maybe the two main things that you'd worry about catching it from somebody else. But then, too, if you were careful, you wouldn't catch anything. But if you were not careful, just like the things today, like gonorrhea and a whole lot of these things that they had way back then, they had been eradicated, supposedly. And today well you don't have to worry about that. All you have to worry about the hive thing. Or whatever they're calling it. When I was in the Army, I developed malaria. Of course we were back there in the jungles all the time and the mosquitoes biting and all that other kind of stuff. I caught malaria, but I got over that. And since that time I have nothing to really worry me. And like I said, I had the cancer, and they did the operation and then my radiation therapy. And they kind of arrested all of that.

Do you think it's a better time for black gay people now or back when you were coming up?

Oh much better.

Now?

Now, much better. A hundred times better. Of course, it's not really perfect, but then, too, it's much, much, much, much better now than it was back then.

How did you know if somebody was gay when you were little? How could you tell if somebody was gay?

Well, most times you could tell by their mannerism. And just looking at them. Because me, I could just look at somebody going down the street and tell whether they're one way or the other, you know. Because the way they walk or the way they talk or the way they swing their hands and different things like that. You can tell, you almost can tell. Okay, women I've met maybe, you've got people that wouldn't be able to tell that somebody is gay if they just see them passing the door or something like that. But for some reason I don't know, me, I can tell them right off just looking at them. [Laughter] [. . .]

Did you know your grandparents? Your grandmother or your grandfather?

Now let me think. The first person I went to the funeral, went to the wake with was my grandmother. And that's been so long ago. She was the first person I think that, the first funeral that we went to—that I went to, because we were little bitty children then. But she died, and all the rest of them started dying and been dying one after time ever since and they all gone now.

But you didn't really know her?

Uh unh. Not really. Not really.

But she lived here in New Orleans?

All my people lived here; nobody lived out of town. The only one that lived and died out of town was one of my brothers. And he lived, he was born and raised here, and he was married two times. He married here and then he married, he divorced his first wife, and then he married again and they moved to Seattle, Washington. And then they stayed together Lord knows about almost forty or fifty years together—the second wife. And then the both of them is dead now.

What were things like here in the '60's during the civil rights movement?

We was out there; we were fighting. When they started integrating the schools and it started downtown here at two little schools on North Rampart or St. Claude, I think, St. Claude. And there was fighting and everything else. Because the whites didn't want the blacks in the school. But we didn't have, considering some areas, we didn't have that much, many problems. Like some of the places they beating them up, beating the blacks up and all like that, they didn't do too much of that here in New Orleans. But they had problems, you know, they had problems. And then after, eventually it all died down.

Was there a lot of tension between the blacks and Creoles, people who consider themselves Creole?

Unt unh. The only thing with the Creoles, those people that were called Creole they all were white—not white, but almost white. And they had their own clubs—some of them, not all of them. And some of the clubs [. . .], one place down there, I guess it's still down there, was called the Autocrats and that was just, if you wasn't white, you had to be just like white and they didn't take skins like this [pointing to his arm] in their big club. Of course, today they tell they're looking for everybody, because everything has changed today. And they had a big beautiful place down there. I think the building is still down there. I don't know if the club is still going on. Because you could go up there and gamble, and they had this bar and everything, socializing and everything else. But it was for all light-colored people. But all that changed. Because you don't, you got a whole lot of these people that call themselves Creole, but they're not like the one way, way, way long ago, you know the quadroons and all that other kind of light, light, light-colored people. You got them around, but you can hardly see them like you used to see them. Lots and lots of them were especially down there in the Seventh Ward where all the Creoles were supposed to be living. They all gone.

So you like to cook?

I can tell you the truth. I don't like to do nothing now. [Laughter] I don't feel like doing no-thing, I don't feel like getting up in the morning. Feel like getting up in the morning. Yeah, I used to cook. I used to cook all the time. Like I said, we had company all the time. I'd be cooking, cooking, cooking, cooking. Cooking and washing dishes.

What's the one thing you would like to do before you die?

Oh no, what would that be? Maybe go on one of those big boats for a cruise somewhere. And I do want to go to New York one more time before I die. Now, I've been there about six, oh maybe about twelve, fourteen, or fifteen years, times. Not all in one year, but a year at a time because there was one time I had a friend and he died about two years ago, he was going up there almost every year for about six years in a row. I would like to go on a boat, on one of those big cruises. A greeeat big ol' boat like I saw in New York. I ain't never seen none of them down here. Greeeeeeeeat BIG ol' boats. You know, it was four and five and six decks high. That would be nice.

Where would you like to cruise to?

Well, wherever the boat and wherever they had some gambling on it, pinball machines or something. Not no pinball machines, them . . . slot machines. Where I had enough money to sit down and play the slot machines, or either sit down and play at a card table and play poker, because I like to play poker, and I like to play pitty-pat. Now we sometimes, we have a little group that we come over here and we play pitty-pat because that group, they don't know how to play poker. Then I had two, three, four, five others that like to play poker. We'd do that sometime, we don't do that often like we used to long ago. But we'd do it once in a while.

And what do you want to do in New York?

Just walk around look at the sights, like I usually do. Go sit in the bar room.

Final question I have to ask you. Do you like sweet tea?

Oh yeah, I drink it sometimes. Occasionally. Not much. No I drink mostly coffee. Occasionally, I have tea, but occasionally I drink it. Sometime I'm sitting there watching the TV or sometime and I feel like eating little crackers, because I always keep Ritz and jelly and things, little cheese or something and make my little things. And then I come get me a cup of tea and I sit there and drink it and eat. But not often. My main drink is coffee. Now, I drink maybe about four, five, six cups of coffee a day. And you know something? It puts me to sleep. [Laughter] A lot of people drink coffee and it keep them awoke. And no sooner do I drink a cup of coffee, I could be sitting in my little chair over there [. . .] I don't sit there to go to sleep because I'm watching the TV and I go right to sleep. And it don't make me nervous or anything like that.

. . . .

JEFF SMITH

Jeff Smith features prominently in the history of the black gay community in Durham, North Carolina—thanks mostly to the parties that he held at his home from the early 1950s to the late 1990s. More than one narrator in this book mentions Jeff's home as a place where he was first introduced to other gays in the community. Some of them never knew Jeff's name, but remember that "this older man used to throw parties" and that when you entered Jeff's home, you would find him seated at the door, expecting a kiss before you could enter. Folks who attended these parties came from as far away as Charlotte—the parties were just that "legendary." In 2003 this same community came together to honor Jeff for his years of providing a sense of community through these gatherings. They threw him a big party and awarded him with a plaque.

I found out about Jeff through Carlton Rutherford, who was a graduate student at Duke University at the time. He told me that if I wanted to interview Jeff, I should do it soon because he was showing signs of senility. Carlton spoke with Jeff on somewhat of a regular basis and agreed to set up a meeting with him. He and another acquaintance took me to see Jeff to introduce us and to help Jeff feel comfortable talking to me. About thirty minutes into our visit, Carlton and his friend left me alone with Jeff to conduct the interview.

Of all of the interviews I conducted for Sweet Tea, *this was the most challenging, as it was not long after my introduction to Jeff that I recognized he was losing some of his cognitive skills. He would often repeat things over and over again as well as jump from one topic to the next. Thus, my interaction with him was less an interview in the strict sense of the word, and more a conversation that allowed him to speak on whatever came to mind. Still, there were moments of real lucidity, especially when he talked about his time in the military and growing up on a farm.*

Jeff was born in Northampton County, North Carolina, in 1918. The interview took place on August 18, 2004, at his home. I had planned to travel back to Durham later to do a follow-up interview, but, unfortunately, Jeff passed away before I could make that trip. He died on April 6, 2005. He was eighty-six.

I was reared by my grandmother. See, I was already with my grandparents. At five, I went to stay with them. My grandfather would come and pick me up to take corn to have it ground or wherever he was going to shop, he'd pick me up and take me. Then I got so I'd stay all night. Then, soon, I just left my parents and just started living with my grandparents. So, my grandmother said that she was going to send me to college because I wasn't cut out for the farm. I tell people I had more headaches and stomachaches than anybody. [Laughter] Anything to keep from working in that field. She had me plowing one time and I tied that mule up to a tree and I went and got under a shade tree and went to sleep until it was time to go back home. Sometime she'd ask me, "You got much more to do?" I'd say, "Oh, I finished it off." [Laughter] I just did not like farming. Just did not. So, my grandmother said that she was going to send me on to school. And see, the thing about it, my grandparents, neither one of them finished school. My grandmother, she could solve a problem. And my youngest uncle, he could figure it out in his head sometime quicker than he could figure it out on paper. See they learned, they learned how to do those things. Yeah, a lot of these people couldn't read and write, but they learned how to do all those things.

We had a nice farm. We had apple trees, pears, grapes, cherries, you name it. We had ducks, geese, chickens—the worse things were those ol' ducks. [Laughter] Yeah, duck's a trip. Geese we couldn't eat. But we had all of that stuff.

My grandmother used to drive sometime. It was amazing to see a woman driving a T-model Ford. And my grandfather had this buggy he carried to get corn ground into meal. That's what people used to do back in those days. Every time he'd go somewhere to go shopping, he'd carry me in the buggy. And I'd ride in the foot of the buggy, 'cause he was chubby, so it took a while to steer. [Laughter] Yeah, my grandfather was chubby. So, yeah, I left from staying with my parents. It so happened that my mother was accidentally shot. A guy was shootin' at my father and killed my mother. What happened, the guy was running from the house and shootin' back and Mama was cookin', and like most people do, she ignored the argument. So, she came around the corner looking to see what was going on, and he was shootin' back and hit her. She didn't live but about thirty minutes 'cause they couldn't get a car to get her to the hospital.

Where were you living then?

I was living in Northampton County then—across the river from Roanoke Rapids.

That's where you were born?

Yeah. I was born and reared there. I went to school down at Garysburg because at that time that was the county school for blacks. See, you had black schools and white schools then.

Do you have any brothers and sisters?

It was five of us by my father's first wife. I'm the only one living now. And my father was married a second time, and I have a half sister and a half brother. I don't know where they are. We didn't grow up together. I was already living at my grandpa's when my father married the second time. His wife, my stepmother was nice to me when I did go there, but never did spend no time there and all that stuff. And so all of them are dead now. All my whole brothers and sisters is dead.

What were some of things you did as a child?

We played ball and run track. We'd get it at school too. I was good on the track running. I wasn't fast starting off, but I would kind of pick up speed. The further I had to run, the faster I got. I was never one of these that could jump right in. Some of these start off fast and then get tired and slow down. But I start off kind of slow, you know, and gradually pick up speed.

So you're more of a distance runner than you are a sprinter?

Yeah. We used to do that in high school. But I didn't ever play any football or basketball or anything like that. Well, they didn't have no football when I was in high school. In fact, they didn't even have intramural. See, for one things the schools were so far apart they didn't want to develop them, 'cause Elizabeth City, Fayetteville, and Winston-Salem. See, all of those were teachers colleges. That was the three black ones.

This would have been in the '30s?

Well, starting in the '40s, I guess. Yeah, now they off into other things now. Computer science is something all the schools trying to teach now. One thing, it's the computer age.

So where did you go to college?

Elizabeth City [State University]—first one. And then I went to [North Carolina] Central and then I went to New York University.

What did you study?

Well, I got a degree in administration and supervision. Then I got one in something called management—it was a lot of things it was called. And now management covers all those things. Then I went out to Duke and took a course out there. Management. I took that at Duke. Got a A— out of the course.

Did you know John Hope Franklin?

Yeah, I knew him. I knew him when he was at Central. I think he ended up at Duke, I believe, before he died.

He's not dead. He's just retired.

Oh, he's just retired. Where's he living now?

He's still in Durham. He taught at Duke for a while.

Yeah, I knew about that.

[. . . .]

So you went to college before you went into the service?

Yes. Yeah, they let me finish college, and then I had to go the next day. Well, they would take you out of high school, but they wanted you to get the most education that you could get, 'cause see you were more valuable to them. So they just deferred me going in until I finished college. And so, the next day I had to report. When you first go in, it's called in zone training and then they break you down after you finish that and then you go into . . . see I come back into engineering after I had finished the basic training. And we build the roads . . . so then I looked around . . . they had me go to school, so I went to be a supply sergeant. So I went and took that, supply sergeant school. That's all I could deal with then, you know, order your clothes. Like you pull off all your clothes each week, all your dirty ones and turn 'em in and we take 'em and send 'em to the laundry and have 'em washed and get 'em back on Saturday and give 'em back to you. All of 'em was like that, you had to have somewhere for them to wash. Now, overseas—if you were over there in combat—what you do is you had to go to a portable, like a trailer or something. They'd take you there and they'd have clothes there. What'd you do is you'd pull off the dirty ones and you take a bath and then you'd tell 'em your size and they give you some clean ones. You didn't know how many people wore them same clothes, see? [Laughter] But they were clean! 'Cause they didn't care if they fit you no way.

So were you a sergeant?

Yeah, I made staff sergeant. They offered to send me off to officer training school, but I didn't want to be no officer. I didn't like no Army, to tell you the truth. I mean, I got along all right. But, I'm glad I went 'cause I got to get to Europe, England, France, Germany, Luxembourg, Belgium, all of those countries. [. . .]

I was in there three and half years. If I had been married I could have come out earlier. See, if you were married and had children . . . the more dependents you had the quicker they would get rid of you. If you didn't have any they'd keep 'til the last one could leave. 'Cause see I had no dependents, so I had to stay. [. . .] That's where I started smoking. We said we were smoking our troubles away. Yeah, we started smoking before the war was over. And they give you the cigarettes anyway. Everywhere you go in the Army they would give you cigarettes. I told people, I said, "Shoot. I should sue the government, because I didn't smoke until they gave 'em to me." They'd give you a whole carton when you report to duty. I'd give 'em away then. But we were over there in the Philippines and it was hot and everything. Brookins from Brooklyn [a friend], we started to smoking. Smoking our troubles away. But I don't regret it. A lot of people say I just burn up cigarettes. See, I don't inhale, you know. [Laughter] I don't blow the smoke out of my nose. [Laughter]

And I used to love to write. I used to help people write theses. I used to make a lot of money helping people write theses. And I helped a guy over at North Carolina Central. A black guy over there that was a schoolteacher. Of course, I did his dissertation for him—I did. You heard of a light-skinned guy over at Central? Yeah, I helped him. I helped a lot of them. I could make good money doin' that. Sometimes I'd be writing and I say, "Well, let me find two or three more pages to add to this. Let add a few more pages until I find something else to do." [Laughter] I did. Keep on adding. And Dr. Rose Butler Brown, she'd fling a scarf. She'd try to be so proper. She'd tell me, [mocking her proper voice] "Mr. Smith, this is pro-duc-tion." So she'd make all who were writing for her to bring their rough copy in and then get it typed. 'Cause if they had it typed up, she probably knew that somebody else did it. [. . .] Yeah, I could make some money. I told the people, "This is my fourth home I bought." I started back there. That's where I got a lot of my money from. I worked on a lot of people stuff.

I had a record shop in Durham years ago. I sold a lot of gospel. Gospel was a big seller. Jazz—a lot of white people come to buy the jazz. It was over there off of Fayetteville [Street]. I used to make good money. The only problem I had over there, I had a lot of break-ins at night. So I just tired of it. About one or two o'clock, the police would call. Had a break-in. They'd stay there 'til we get there. Sometimes they'd be done broke out a whole window or something. You'd have to stay there and call them to come to fix the window. So, I got rid of that. I got a lot of music here, out there in the garage. I be selling it. CDs and cassettes and all that stuff. I still got a lot of it. I had the store about five or six years. It was called the Record Shop. [Laughter] *The* Record Shop. [. . .] But you sell a lot of gospel. Black people like that gospel. And all of 'em like the blues, too. And then you had your jazz. A lot of whites come and buy jazz. And some of 'em would buy that popular stuff too.

I understand that you used to have a lot of parties for black gay men in the community.

I had parties. I made good money, too. I would furnish whiskey. This lady that had a whiskey house, she told me what to do. She said, "Always have food. Keep 'em eatin' and that'll keep 'em from gettin' drunk quick. They'll eat more." I had food. I did have food. And they didn't get drunk. See, most people get drunk because they don't eat. If you keep your stomach full, you'll can drink a lot—'fore you fall out. [Laughter]

Sometimes I had parties every weekend. And on a holiday weekend, I might have one on Friday night and one on a Saturday night, too. But you see, you didn't have this crack and stuff. I wouldn't try to have one now. It's a different kind of person now. See, along then you didn't have to worry about all this fighting and stuff. I wouldn't try to have one now. I mean, I wouldn't mind having just a little, about a half a dozen people or something like that. But back then, anybody that come along could come in.

Is this when you were living on Cornwallis [Road]?

Uh huh.

How long did you live over there?

Quite a while. I guess about ten years I stayed out there. I moved from there to Craig Road. And I left there. I didn't stay there too long. I was living in a split-level. Then I moved out here. It's mostly white, but they don't bother me and I don't bother them. This white lady over here [points toward his neighbor's house], we talk a lot. And it's a black family in front of me now, but I haven't met them. It's quite a few of them because they [have] five cars over there. But I've seen the little boys. They've come over here asking if I had anything for them to do. [. . .]

So people danced at your parties?

Yeah, that's what they were for. [Laughter] It was for dancing. My DJ was really good. He lived with me. He didn't have anything else to do. So, he would mix music. Sometimes he might take some of my albums, and sometimes he might put it on a CD or put it on a tape and play it. [. . .] He moved to Chapel Hill and he and I had an apartment together. He caught AIDS some kinda way. He asked me was I afraid of him. I said no. When he moved over there I said, "We ain't havin' no sex." I said, "You got this AIDS over here." I went to the hospital, and it was so sad. He had a bad case of it, too. And all that corruption would be running out of his mouth and nose. He couldn't talk. He had to write out everything. It was really sad. The nurse called me and wanted me to come there. And he had his mother to come, grandmother. So we all got there about the same time. So, he'd write out on a piece of paper what he wanted to say to me. He could hear you. But at the same time, his mouth would be full of that stuff. It was really sad. He passed away, and [I] gave them five hundred dollars on the funeral. 'Cause when I was taking him back one day to Chapel Hill he was saying, I guess he knowed he was gonna die. 'Cause his mama was paying for the car and the house, so I kept that in mind. So, when he passed, I gave five hundred dollars. Back in that day, five hundred was good. So, I gave her that. I offered to give her his clothes. I don't know if she was afraid of them or not, but it didn't bother me. 'Cause, you know, if you wash 'em.

Have you lost a lot of friends to AIDS?

I know two or three people who died.

I guess you didn't have to worry about it back when you were coming up, huh?

Well, no, not then. But I could have gotten it because I was participating in sex. [Laughter] I have this truck driver I've been knowing since I was in the house over on Cornwallis. He was driving a truck back then, and I remember he used to bring me some bananas from Florida and they'd be green. I had never seen green bananas. I didn't know. I said, "What am I going to do with these green bananas?" He said, "Hang 'em up. They'll turn yellow." But I didn't know. And he brought me a big stalk. And he still driving trucks. He come by here to see me here sometimes. He's the onliest friend I got. [Laughter] Yeah, he got me way back there when I was on Cornwallis Road. We started having sex then and still having sex. Somebody said, "Do you still cut the mustard?" I said, "Do you wanna find out?" [Laughter] He's married and got children. His daughter married a little fellow—a cute little fellow. He called me. I had this whole side of the house cleaned up, and he did that for me. He was gonna do some other work, but he hadn't called me. But I think he wanted to get into something. Really cute. But he hasn't called.

So you still got it?

Yeah. This truck driver, he's still stopping by. And this one that's coming by, he married his [i.e., the truck driver's] daughter.

He married his daughter?

See, the one I was going with, he got married and had children. And so this guy who came to do some electrical work—that's how I met him. But he called me one night, but he never did get here. I think he was getting into something. I think he found out something was going on. But he hadn't called back in a while. But the one who's a truck driver, he pulls two trailers behind this big truck. He parks it out here on the road when he comes in. It's so long. He'll back it when he get ready to leave. He hasn't been by here in two or three weeks. I don't call him 'cause see, he's married.

I done had so many friends. The truck driver—that started way back there when I was on Cornwallis Road. We started having sex back then. But he's married now and got children. But this fellow that's married to his daughter, I called him and he ain't never got back to me. I think he's messing around too. He's a cute little fellow. Kinda short.

Back in the '40s and '50s, how did you know that men were interested in other men?

You'd find out. You just meet people. You haven't had any trouble finding anybody have you? [Laughter] I mean, people know.

[Long pause] I gave up driving, but I plan to get me one more car. I told people that I was going to get me a convertible. I don't care what they say. I've always wanted one, and I'm get this convertible. You know? That'll be my last car, I tell 'em. I don't know whether it'll be white or red or what. I think it's going to be a Ford. I'm going to look at the convertibles of all makes. See, I'll get him and we'll go and look at 'em. 'Cause see, the one that does my driving, I'll get his input on it too, 'cause I wouldn't want him to drive something he didn't like, you know. When I have the opportunity for us to agree on it together, 'cause he'll be drivin' it—well, he's not my only driver, I have one or two other drivers. I have friend from Rocky Mount who comes up and drives me.

I've been in Durham County hospital. I had colon cancer. They had to cut my stomach open and cut out some of my intestines. But the doctor told me, he said, "You don't have to worry about it." He said, "You cut out more than half of it you still have more than you can eat." Well, if you eat hog guts and all of that stuff you know about what people got in their stomach. [Laughter] They took it all out. Lucky. Well, you see, one thing, I like flowers, growing plants and gardening. I don't have a garden. I gotta get a fence put up first. But I've got flowers out in front. When come back in the summer you'll see a lot of flowers. Yeah, I just like growing stuff. You see those pots over there. They're filled up on the side and everywhere. I got some vines running.

This is my fourth and last home. But I've been looking at rest homes, just in case I have to go to one. But I haven't been to too many that I like. Most of them got whites in 'em. [. . .] But I've been to about two that had quite a few blacks. And some of 'em got mostly wheelchair patients. But some don't have. There is different kinds you can find. I'm not quite in a wheelchair yet. Well, see, I still work out in the yard. I like flowers. I like to see plants grow and bloom.

· · · · · · · ·

STEPHEN

My interview with Stephen stayed with me for days afterward. I was moved not only by the content of his life, but also by the passion and conviction with which he rendered it. I could see why he has been so successful as an actor. He has a presence and a voice that would, I imagine, be quite commanding on the stage.

I met Stephen through Marsha Houston, my colleague who teaches at the University of Alabama, who taught Stephen. She knew that he would have a compelling story to share. His life has been full of ups and downs for someone his age. Like other narrators, he has struggled with reconciling his spirituality with his sexuality, with issues around masculinity, and with negotiating family demands on his time and his own desire to be a successful actor. Regarding the latter, I can say that he is on his way, as he was cast in a show in New York shortly after he graduated from college.

The interview took place on November 5, 2004, on the campus of the University of Alabama, three days after the presidential election. Some people around the university were still smarting not only from the election, but also from some of the legislation passed at the state level that maintained racist language in the state constitution. Stephen makes several references to the election and to the constitutional amendments in his narrative.

I was born in Atlanta, Georgia, on January 7, 1982. My childhood was pretty much both typical and atypical. I guess, pretty much the setting was a single-parent home, but despite that, [we] still had a strong sense of family. And, I don't know, most of my family is from here in Tuscaloosa or from Mobile, so we were really centralized and close by. I have two half sisters, one older and one younger.

What did your mom do for work?

It varied a lot of times. [. . .] When I was growing up, she was a nurse's aid. And, a lot of the time, she would work in retirement homes, situations like that. She went back to school and became a master cosme . . . what is it? A hairdresser, you know, the big three-dollar word that I can't pronounce. She went back to school. She's in school right now to get her business degree to fully run her own shop that she has now.

Besides your mother, were there any other adults that played a significant role in your upbringing?

My family—it was touch-and-go a lot of times [. . .] my mom, she is the most consistent in my life. There would be short periods where my dad would be in and out. The women in my family played a big, big part in my life and how I was raised, my grandmother and my great-aunt. [. . .] It went from being just going to church with these people to these people actually being a part of your family.

You say you were born in Atlanta?

Oh, I stayed in Atlanta long enough to get my social security number, but I lived in Tuscaloosa.

Oh, I see. So, you were raised here.

Right. I was raised in Tuscaloosa. Yeah. I went to Crestmont Elementary for a couple of years. Then we moved. I want to say it was my fourth-grade year. And, I went to Crestmont . . . no, Northington, that's the city school here. And I stayed there until the fifth grade. Then, my sixth-grade year, I went to live with my father in Jackson, Mississippi, for a year and a half. Yeah. It was a weird situation there. But, I went to live with him for a year and a half. I came back and started Tuscaloosa Middle School, and I stayed in the city school system until I graduated from Central [High School] in 2000.

Were any of your schools—elementary, middle school, high school—
segregated, or were they all integrated?

They are all integrated. [. . .] But it's not like that anymore. [. . .] Unless it was private, there was only one school. So, I went to middle schools and high schools where everybody, the rich people and the poor people in Tuscaloosa, went to school together. I want to say seventh, eighth, and ninth, and tenth grade, I pretty much hung out with the people that I came from, or the people that were part of my background who I've known for most of my life, all that I lived here in Tuscaloosa. I don't know. It was weird because, like I said before, it was just everybody together. And, because of that, I guess I am more tolerant of other people and just different things because I haven't been like so closeted for all of my life.

Do you have some special memories of friendships from elementary, middle
school, high school, people that you befriended then and are still close to
now?

Yeah. Quite a bit, actually, just because people who are from Tuscaloosa tend to stay here. So, I'm in college now with people I've known for ten years. Yeah. This girl named Allison, who I have known since, I want to say the fourth or fifth grade, and we've gone to school together since then. The whole gay thing didn't really start to play a part in my life until eleventh or twelfth grade. I guess more than anything that's so related to your book is the black issue. That played a big part from an early standpoint.

What do you mean by that, being black in the South, in Tuscaloosa, or . . . ?

Well, the thing about it, there's this interesting dynamic. Tuscaloosa is really segregated. It's really segregated. But, the way the school system was set up until recently, everybody went to school together. And, so within these schools, you have teachers and principals who really fought hard to let you know that although it's not what we say out loud, this is the way things are. And, although it goes unspoken, you still need to know your place. I've been called just about every racial slur from teachers. And this is early on. I recall in the fifth grade . . . God, I was a runt until my eleventh-grade year, and so I was the small, pudgy kid in elementary school. And so, I remember at this one point where this white guy was like a bully of our class, and he started picking a fight with a guy who was even smaller than me after school one day. And, it got to the point where I intervened, and the guy and I got into a confrontation. [. . .] We got into a fight. We both beat on each other a good bit. But the next day at school, he had bruises on his back. I was taken out of class by the principal, and I was brought into her office. And, she was like, "What do you have to say for yourself?" I was like, "Well, he was picking on one of my friends, and I intervened, and he hit me, and a fight ensued." Well, she was like, "That's not what he said." She said, "He said he was waiting for his mom to come pick him up, and you instigated a fight." I was like, "Well, if you want, there was a playground full of people there, and anybody can tell you what happened." I mean, the guy was known for being a bully. She didn't want to hear it. She was like, "I don't want to ask anybody anything," because she picked him up, turned him around, pulled up the back of his shirt, and showed the welt marks on his back. And, she was like, "Do you have any?" And, I was like, "I don't know." So, she picked me up, and she lifted up my shirt, too. She was like, "No, you don't have any. You don't have any because your people are like animals." And, it's so funny. At this point, it's stuck in my head from early on that although we say something, how we really think is not exactly the same. And, it stuck with me for so long then. The kid wasn't punished. He was sent back to class. I spent two weeks in an in-school suspension. An in-school suspension is the situation where you go to school, but you're contained in a room with other kids that are behavior problems. I don't know.

And, this was in the '90s?

I was in the fifth grade, so let's see . . . seven plus the four now, eleven . . . yeah. Uh-hum. It was. And, it was so funny. And, situations like that had continued in my life for a long time, and I would be told by my family as well, because it was on both sides, it was from white people saying that I think you're inferior, and black people in my family being like, "Don't trust white people." I have relatives that . . . my great-aunt, specifically, "I have relatives that were slaves. I don't trust them. I work with them. They love me, but I don't trust them any farther than I can throw them." [. . .] So, you have this dynamic, but what was really interesting is that in eleventh grade, I got involved in theater. And, what was so amazing about the theater program was that it was ran by this white woman, and because it was Central, and because everybody went to school together, all these people were in this class together. And, it was different from any other classes because what Central did to try to segregate the school from what it was, they had accelerated programs within the school. Like, IB [international baccalaureate] and AP [advance placement] classes, and [. . .] they were 98 percent white. And so, the regular classes were the rest of the school, which were black people. And, what was so odd was that this theater class was the first time it was an even amount of people, even amount of people from all over the social spectrum, people's racial spectrum, and we would be cast in these shows where we would be together all the time. Like, we would have rehearsals, and we would be in rehearsals from 6:00 to 10:00 in addition from being in classes together. So, what was so odd is that I got in this situation with these people that were completely different from me, but it grew into some family situation. And, it was the first time that it honestly did not matter. It was the first time in my life where I honestly did feel like just because I was poor, or just because I was black, that it really didn't matter. We would have plays, and there would be blind casting. We did a show called, "The Children of Eden," which caused *such* an uproar in Tuscaloosa because "The Children of Eden" was the first three books of the Bible. You have Adam and Eve, and Noah and his wife. Well, my best friend, who was black, got cast as Adam, where this girl named Ty, who was white, got cast as Eve. I got cast as Noah, and my friend Allison Wilkes was cast as Noah's wife. Adam and Eve were supposed to kiss in the show. I still remember it to this day being a big deal. But, the teacher . . . it was so funny, just being such a champion for, "It doesn't matter. It doesn't matter." And this was evident through it all because this play was set up along the lines of it being this big family, Adam and Eve and their family. And, Adam was black; Eve was white. And their children were black and white and Asian, and I see pictures of it now. [. . .] I am so thankful that the situation happened at that point in my life with me about to go to college, me about to pursue a career. Because, it honestly broke down a lot of things that were instilled in me by teachers and my family. To this day, I still keep in contact with that teacher. She was the first person not related to me to actually be compassionate in a way that I thought was true, that was genuine, to the fact that this woman would do things for me, and nobody would see it. Do you know what I mean? [. . .] I was like seventeen, eighteen, didn't have my license, didn't have a car, didn't have money to get a car, and I didn't think it was important. One day, during rehearsal, she was like, "I need you to go to Kinkos for me to run off some copies of the program." And, I was like, "Well, I don't have a license." She was like, "Do you have a job?" I was like, "Yeah." She was like, "Why don't you have your license?" I was like, "It's not that big of a deal." For the next three weeks, this woman taught me how to drive and took me to go take my driver's test and paid for it all. And, it wasn't a way like, "I'm gonna do this for you," and it wasn't along the lines of "I'm gonna tell other people that I'm doing this for you." And she honestly called me her son, and I honestly believed her.

There was this point in my life at home that I was really pulling away from my family just because of those things I was taught and me really coming to terms of being gay, 'cause I think that's when it was at the point when I couldn't ignore it anymore. But, I started to pull away from my family and was being embraced by this woman. And, at first, I was like, "Okay. She's being real nice. What does she want from me?" I don't know. I guess it was so amazing because, for me, I couldn't understand it, and it was one of the first times where I felt that someone loves me, and they don't have to. It was so amazing. And, it got to the point, too, that she honestly changed my life because I got into theater by mistake. I actually enrolled in like PE or something. PE was full. I got in that class. The first day of class, she was like, "Okay. We're gonna stand up and give introductions," and I stood up, and I gave my name. I was being a smart-ass. I was like, "My name is Stephen. I'm in here by accident. Hopefully, I can get my schedule changed." Then, I sat down. That was the end of it. And, I went up to her after the end of the class, and I was like, "What do I need to do to get my schedule changed?" She was like, "I don't think I'm gonna let you out of the class." She was like, "There is something about your voice that reminds me so much of Sidney Poitier, your presence." And, I was like, "Here we go again. White people thinking black folks look alike." I had no idea who he was. No idea. And, so I was in this class bitter, bitter in this class. And, she went even further. In the first play they did that semester, she cast me in that show. And, it was like, "I don't think you understand. I don't want to be in this class let alone be in this play." Well, she made me do it. And, I fell in love with it. And, I've been doing it ever since. And so it was something that I just fell into, and it came so natural. It was just this outlet that just felt so great. And she was like, "Well, I'm gonna take a group of people to Lincoln, Nebraska, for this International Thespian Festival. There will be schools there, and you will audition for colleges." I was like, "Oh, okay." For one, I had no plans after high school. College was definitely not one. It just seemed like something that wasn't obtainable for me. And so, I was like, I really don't understand exactly what she's doing. But, I went with it along the lines of, if this works, if I go and audition for these colleges here, and I fall on my face, then I know I just need to get a job after high school and be done with this theater stuff. I went to Lincoln, Nebraska, and there was like thirty-three schools there. And, out of the thirty-three there, twenty-three called me back. And, out of that, fifteen offered me some type of scholarship there. This was amazing to me. This is a little boy from Tuscaloosa, Alabama, for who theater was a mistake. Me being involved with all of these people was a mistake, and it was so odd, but I guess I needed to pursue this. And, so she *pushed*. She *campaigned*. She made me get an application and scholarship things, made sure that I was getting for the ACT and the SATs. This is the woman who got me into school. She got me into school just because she believed.

How was your family reacting to her influencing your life?

Well, that's the thing. That's what is so interesting. I got involved with theater in high school, and also got involved with it in the community. And, I started getting really involved in it. And, what was so stressing and taxing on my family was that because I was in rehearsals at night, I couldn't work. And, in addition to that, I needed rides back and forth to rehearsals. And, it got to the point where my mom . . . I mean, I understand the pressure on her now, but then, I didn't understand it at all. She was like, "You don't have a future in this. This is not something that is stable." And, "You're around all these white people, and they cannot be trusted. You need to quit running up behind these white people because we are the people that truly love you." And, it was so odd that it honestly got to the point to where all the money that I would get, I would save for cab fare to my rehearsals. To this day, I don't understand why it meant so much to me as it did, other than it being an outlet, an escape from everything that was going on, 'cause it was really rough. There is a type of situation that we really don't talk about issues in our family. There are so many family secrets, and you just found them out in real intense situations, these family secrets.

'Cause I never understood why I went to live with my dad. I didn't know him that well. And, so I had spent the summer with him my fourth-grade year, and that was odd because that was an entire summer with the man I barely knew. And, then the next year, I went to live with him for a year. And, I didn't understand it. And, it was conflicting. We fought a lot. And, I didn't understand it. He was pretty well off, I mean, middle class. His wife was a doctor. And he was a doctor's assistant. So, they were well off. And, I was brought from being from this poor background to this situation. I'm forced to, like, be a part of this situation that I don't know these people. I have a stepbrother now? A stepmom? A father? And, it was so hard. And, it was so funny. And, at that point, when I was in Mississippi, I stayed in trouble. My grades remained impeccable, but I stayed in trouble, stayed acting out. And then it got to the point to where he and I just kept butting heads, kept butting heads. And, I was like, "Why don't you just let me go home? Why don't you just let me go home?" 'Cause, I honestly felt that I was messing up this picture that they were trying to make. "Why don't you just let me go home?" And, he was like, "Your mom is homeless. That's why you're here."

Where were your other siblings?

My oldest sister went to live with her grandmother, and my younger sister lived with my mom in a shelter. And, from early on, there was this resentment because, for one, I wasn't told. And, for two, I didn't know why my mom chose to give me up. So, I harbored all these feelings with me, never spoke of it, never spoke of it. Because, eventually, I did come back to live with my mom. Never spoke about it. She never knew that I found out why I was living with him. By that time, she had gotten back on her feet. But, it was to the point to where, I guess, me looking for a family was so important because I honestly felt like I really wasn't wanted by my family. And it was just along those lines until about eleventh- and twelfth-grade year when I really, really started to pull away from my family 'cause she didn't want me to go away for school. And, she tried really hard to keep me from going.

So, your mom didn't think that going to college would provide a better life for you?

I just don't think she wanted me to leave Tuscaloosa. She never pushed for college, but she was completely against me going to somewhere far off. Ms. Raymond pushed for me to go to NYU, really pushed for me, set up applications. Her husband, who was at that point an English professor here at the university, helped me with my essay. And, I had no idea about the prestige of the school until right before I went to audition. And they were considered the number two theater school next to Yale for undergraduate and graduate work in theater. And, [I] got in. This was a $42,000 school a year, and I got in. I got $36,000 in scholarships. And, I was going to New York after high school, going to New York to go to school, to pursue my dream and all of that. It was so funny because my mom kept doing little small things to slow down the process. And it got to the point that it was about two or three weeks before I was supposed to leave, and I realized that, I don't have a dorm assignment. So, I called. I called NYU, and they were like, "Well, we have you classified as an off-campus student." I had three weeks to find an affordable apartment in New York. So, it fell through. Now, at this point, me and my best friend Brandon both applied to this school, and we both got in. And so, we were going up to New York together. We were gonna be brothers. We were gonna be the black Ben Affleck and Matt Damon. [Laughter] You know what I mean? And, it fell through. So, it felt like I had let down her [Ms. Raymond], like I let down him [Mr. Raymond], because I didn't get there. Well, I just sat there feeling . . . really, really for a long time during that period, for those three weeks, really defeated. And, she was like, "Well, that didn't work. I'm gonna get you into the University of Alabama." She did. Two days before school started, I got a full ride to the University of Alabama. I got into their Accelerated Liberal Arts Program, called the Blunt Undergraduate Initiative. I got into the theater program on a scholarship.

And, I guess at that point, it was the first time that I was able to truly deal with myself as a gay man. It was weird because just always growing up so close to my family, so deeply rooted in the church, we were always told that being gay is a sin. It's a demon that needs to be cast out. It's a sickness. It's an illness. And, I struggled. I struggled. I'm from a family where we went to church four to five times a week, and you would go there to these places. At one point, we were raised Baptist, but later on, Full Gospel. It wasn't Full Gospel, it was a newer denomination, but it was along the lines that we tried to believe in the Bible in its entirety. Some people try to like, well, we believe in this part of it, and we only believe in that part. It was just an incorporation of the whole Bible. It was an emphasis on the entire book.

Well, it got to the point in growing up . . . I had these feelings since I could remember. It had always been along the lines of I was just wired differently, just was wired differently. Growing up, being around my sisters, I was really, really effeminate, and would get beat up a lot because of that. So, what I did was I decided that I would look at the other boys that were considered normal, and I would tailor my behaviors to that. And, it got to the point to where I got really good at it, really good. And it was to the point to where it wasn't even an issue anymore. It was to the point that it stressed our family out so much growing up. I vividly remember my mom saying, "Don't you grow up to be no faggot." I *vividly* remember hearing that. And, you're getting beat up at school 'cause you are a faggot, you're a little girl, you're a little sissy, and she was like, "Everybody is telling you this is wrong." So, I was gonna fix it. I'm gonna fix it. I'm not gonna hang around my sisters as much anymore. I'm gonna change. I'm gonna change who I am. And so, I got to college, and I was known as the only straight guy in the theater department. [Laughter] I became really good at it, became really, really good at it.

When you say, "really good at it," what is the "it"?

At passing, you know what I mean?

Acting masculine?

Right. Right.

Which entailed what? The way you walked? The way you talked?

Exactly. That's the thing. 'Cause, I was raised around my sisters, and it was my mom, my two sisters, and me. Women ran the house pretty much. So, it was everything done on that level. So, my closest friends were my sisters, and we were always together, and we all acted alike. And, so this entire point where I felt that I was being punished for being this way. 'Cause, at one point in my life it was fine. It wasn't a big deal. But, I felt like I was getting punished for this. And my sister got older, and she was like, "Quit hanging around me and my friends." And, so from every angle, I was being told, "You've got it wrong." So, I fixed it. I fixed what I thought people thought that was wrong about me and what I thought was wrong. It was so funny because I would have girlfriends, and treated them awesome, treated them awesome. [. . .] It makes me now wonder because I'm still looked on as being straight acting, masculine, although I'm out. And, sometimes, it makes me wonder how much of this is really me, and how much of it is something that I've changed myself to fit in? Because, there was nothing when I got to college, nobody knew. There was nothing. There were some gay men that are in the closet, and it's like, "Sister, who you kidding?" You know what I mean? It's like, come on. Right? And, it's like, you're gay, and it's not a big deal, but you are clearly a gay man. And, that's fine. But, there wasn't that pressure at all. Me coming out was solely something that I thought I had to do myself because I was exhausted. And, it got to the point to where when I got to college, and I had pulled away from my family and my church completely—I stopped going to my church. Although I went to the University of Alabama, I saw my family Thanksgiving and Christmas. It was because right before I got to college, the pressure was so much. It was so much all the time. And, it got to the point to where I really wanted to kill myself because of how deeply rooted I was in the church. I wanted to die rather than to continue to displease the God that I loved so much. Since I can't stop these feelings that I've been told are wrong, I would really prefer to die and to be able to say I'm going to heaven than to continue to live this way and to go to hell because of this. And, it got to the point where I struggled, and I hated myself for it. In college, I pulled away from all these things, pulled away from what I've been taught, and the people around my life, and really to look for who I was. And, it got to the point to where I made the realization I believe in the God who is all knowing. I believe in a God that doesn't make mistakes. I believe in a God that has created me. I believe that I'm not a mistake. I believe that this is the way that I was created. I didn't choose it. Who would choose it? It was just beyond me. It was beyond me, and it would frustrate me so much being in the closet early on, and here there are people like, "It's a choice. It's a lifestyle change." It's like you really don't understand my struggle. I've tried that. I've tried that. I read up on ex-gay therapies. I have tried to be what you thought Stephen should be, and I'm exhausted. I was headed for destruction. I was either gonna have to come to terms with this, 'cause it was something that I was ignoring for a long time, ignoring this fight within myself, that was killing me. And, it got to the point to where it was like, "No. No. From now on, what I believe is gonna be something that I find to be true for me and who Stephen is, not something that I've been fed since I was smaller."

So, I started to examine the relationship I had with my family, 'cause it is so easy to be loved for something that you're not, than to be hated for something that you are. You know what I mean? It's so easy. So, I started to examine that. I started to examine my relationship with God, and my Christian faith, 'cause when I got to college, I started to read about all these other people who weren't like me, who weren't black, who weren't Christian, and I started to read Mahatma Gandhi. And it was so odd because we hailed Martin Luther King for being THE man. Well, Gandhi would have been Martin Luther King's man. And, so I read about all the things that he did, how he took on the British army, how he freed his people nonviolently, and then he died. So, I started to think. I believed something to where if you only believe in Jesus Christ, you can only go to heaven if you believe in Jesus Christ. And, I started to sit with myself. And, I was like, "So what people are telling me is that Mahatma Gandhi is going to hell?" And, so everything . . . everything about everything I ever believed in, I started to reevaluate. You're telling me God hates me because of a way that me made me? Mahatma Gandhi is in hell? It was so liberating. It was so liberating to be like, "No. No."

And, it was so great because in terms of performance, the only way that you can truly be effective as a performer and effective in telling a story is for you to be comfortable with yourself because you have to assume somebody else while you are on the stage. And, the only way that you can get some kind of understanding of another person is for you to have an understanding of yourself. So, as I started to move toward this point where I truly started to come into myself, theater became something that took on this world that . . . I'm at a university where they don't cast black people in roles. I was a lead in the first all-black production at the University of Alabama. And, so all these doors are opening, all these things because I think that it's completely related to me being more and more comfortable with who I am. And, I know for the longest time, I just fell in so many pits because I tried to be what other people thought.

It's so funny. [. . .] I guess the first time where I honestly stopped to think about it was about seventeen years old, sixteen, had a girlfriend. And [I] really wasn't interested in physical anything with her. I really wasn't. But, this is something that both of our families approved of. She was about two or three years older than me, two years, three years older than me. And, it was a situation where we were close, but it was mostly like two friends [rather] than boyfriend and girlfriend. And, the sex thing was always an issue. Sex was always an issue until finally, I thought, "Well, for me to prove myself as a man, we need to have sex." It was the first time I had sex. I fathered my son. And, although he is something that motivates me, someone . . . when I get exhausted, or when I really start to like, "What am I working towards," he motivates me past those moments. But, it's one of the earliest moments where I was like, "You came to this point being something that you're not."

What's your relationship with your son now?

He may be one of the only people in my family that I've come out to. Early on, the relationship between our two families was really strained by it [the pregnancy]. It was really strained.

Even though they were the ones that were pushing you to be together?

Well, here's the deal. Here's the deal. Here's what is so crazy about it. When my girlfriend found out that we were actually pregnant, she called me 'cause we had broken up. She called me, and she was like, "Well, I'm pregnant." I flipped out. This is, yet again, something else that is confusing everything. Gay men don't have kids. And, so I go to my mom. And, her first reaction was to really tear me down. "You done threw your whole life away. You are so stupid. I can't believe you did this. How do you know it's yours? How do you know?" I was like, "I know." "You don't know. We're gonna get tested before we do anything. They think we got some money. That's what it is. They think we got money, and they just trying to get money from us." So, she calls their family and says, "We need to get a test done." That really um . . . hurt her and angered her family. So, they fought. And, we were stuck in between this thing. And, what was so odd about it, it got to the point to where she refused to take the test. And so, my mom was like, "Well, there you have it. We know it's not yours." Six months later, she's married, and moving to Texas. She [his mother] was like, "See?"

My freshman year in college, I get subpoenaed into court to prove paternity. And, it is so funny, this thing that . . . [laughter] it's really involved . . .

Did something happen with her and her husband that he . . . I mean, how do you go from her not wanting to test, to her getting married and moving to Texas, and you getting subpoenaed to court?

Well, here's the thing. This is what was so interesting about it. She was under the mindset that if me and my family didn't want to have anything to do with my son, then she would be fine. So, she went and married this guy who was in the Army. They applied for insurance. Well, for you to get insurance by the Army, all information about the kids that you have who are gonna be covered are gonna be on there, and like all that information has to be given. Well, for them to get health care, that [the child's paternity] had to be for certain, and it wasn't. So, this is something she didn't want to do. [. . .] My mom told me to forget about it. So, my freshman year, I'm subpoenaed because of this, and it got to the point where we took the test, and it was something she knew. It was something that I knew. [. . .] But it got to the point where I was in school, working two jobs, and paying child support. When my son was in town, he was with me and my family, my mom, and my sisters. [. . .] I was so blessed because her family was so understanding even after all of that. They were like, "You do the best that you can until you graduate." This was right before I got my first professional job doing theater in college, and this was about two years ago, and I was having to leave for the summer. So, the night before I had to leave, I spent all day with Ledarius. We were riding in the car, and I explained to him who I was. I was like, "The same way that your mom loves her husband, I feel the same way about other men. I don't even know if you can understand this yet." He was four at the time. "I don't know if you understand this or not. If you do, let's talk about it. If you're not comfortable with it, that's fine too. More than likely, you'll probably be angry because you don't completely understand it, but come to me with that anger. Let's talk about it." And, that was that. It was surreal. It was like, here I am coming out to my son, the only person in my family that I've truly, truly come out to. My mom, we will have arguments, and it will be thrown in my face.

So, she knows?

Well, I think all moms know. You know what I mean? I honestly believe that one of the closest people on this earth right now is me and my mom. And, the first summer of my freshman year, I went to live with my mom for the summer. I lived in a dorm, and then the summer, I went to live with my mom. I was hanging out with my friends, and one of them was gay, but the other ones were girls. And, we got into this argument. [. . .] We had just been arguing back and forth, back and forth, back and forth. And it was so odd because I'm the child that is never disrespectful who, even if I think mom is wrong, "Yes, ma'am," and that's the end of it. Well, it was just one issue that I felt so passionate about, and we were going back and forth, and she was like, "Oh, yeah, don't think I [don't] know that you're having sex with men." And, we both stopped because I think she couldn't believe that she had said it, and I couldn't believe that she had said it. We both just stopped. And, I was like, "Do you honestly think I care what you think about me at this point?" And, so that was our conversation about that. That was the only time that we truly talked about that. And, um . . . [laughter] that was the most in-depth that it had gone.

So, you're not out to your sisters or anybody else in your family?

No.

Do you remember the first time you had a same-sex experience, and what was your reaction to that?

Well, my thing was that it was something that was always in the back of my head, something that was always in the back of my head. And, I thought about it, and thought about it until this guy came in our choir. He was from Louisiana. He was a white guy, the only white guy in this all-black choir. This was in high school. And, he had some people over to his house, and a lot of people stayed, but most went. I ended up staying, too. And, it was actually one of the first times I ended up drinking too. He pulled out these porn magazines, and we started looking through them. But they were straight porn. They were straight porn. But, in the back, they had these ads for this gay stuff, these gay hotlines, you know what I mean? So, we were flipping through them, flipping through them, and then I stopped and looked at it. He was like, "Do you want to do that?" I was like, "Man. Yeah." [Laughter] I said, "Okay." And that night, we did. Both of us were really, really drunk. [. . .] I know now that it pretty much had little to nothing to do with him. It was me for the first time coming to terms with myself, and it felt right 'cause I had been forcing myself to be intimate with women. And I could. I mean, on some level I found women attractive, but it felt more like a chore than anything. And, I was like, "So, I guess sex *is* great. Sex doesn't have to be the boring thing." I don't know. It wasn't wonderful by any stretch of the imagination, but . . .

Did you talk about it afterwards?

Yeah. It was so odd, because this was a point that I'm really, really good at playing my role, but this guy, this guy is a queen. And, so after it happened, I found out it was his first time, too. And so, I called him the day after it happened, and he says, "I'm not gay." He tells me that he's not gay. And, I don't know. That set me back a couple of years, too. So, I was like I really don't know what's going on. So, although it happened late in high school, I put that part of myself in a little box 'cause I couldn't really figure it out. After that night, I had figured this out. I figured it out. I like men, and men like me. [Laughter] And, the next day, it was not really necessarily being that.

So, he was at your high school, so you saw him on a daily basis?

Yeah.

But, after that next day, when he said he was not gay, you didn't talk about it anymore?

It was never something that we talked about again until after I had gotten to the university. I got to the university, and just because people from Tuscaloosa tend to stay in Tuscaloosa . . . he wasn't going to the university, but he was here, and I would see him around. He had gotten to that point, too, where he was more comfortable with it. And, so we talked about it.

So, you think he freaked out?

Yeah. Yeah. I don't know. The first time. Because my freshman year, when I first got here, I discovered the Internet, and I was part of those dumb freshmen that was like buck wild. And, it was so funny, this gay thing took off from me trying to find myself, me trying to find meaning in the shit I was doing, existing on the down low. Until, what was so odd, the first real relationship I was in, this guy that was about three years older than me. I was at this party, still in the closet. I knew that he was gay. I started to hang out. We started to hang out. And, it grew into this relationship. And, he was the first time that I fell in love with a man. And, that's when I truly think that I truly believe for myself that it wasn't a defect in me, and it wasn't a demon. 'Cause, this was truly the first time that I fell in love with a man, and it was the first time that I had truly been in love with a person period. That was all the evidence that I needed because I would tell some people that I was bisexual, but this was it. I knew. Because I had been in relationships with women all my life, and I had been in this relationship with him, and it was so odd. It was so odd, because I knew that we were the exact opposite, but I also knew that there was some commonality in us because he was actively involved in high school. When he would tell people he was gay in high school, people didn't believe it because he was straight acting. He was an activist, out to his family, the whole nine. And, he pretty much dragged me out of the closet. Pretty much. That next spring, I started to come out to my friends. They were like, "Oh, we knew." I was like, "Okay."

Was he white or black?

He was black.

And, out to his family?

That got me.

From Tuscaloosa?

No, he was from Birmingham, about forty-five minutes north of here. And, it is the largest city here in Alabama, but he was out. And, I don't think that he understands the role that he played in my life, by him being out, and him being so okay with himself, and this being who he is and not necessarily a choice or just truly just being a part of him . . . and, the fact that it was a part of him and not something that encompasses his entire life, it really was. I am so fortunate that he was so positive in that situation, so fortunate that the first real healthy situation I had was with somebody that had their head on their shoulders, who had denounced the whole down low thing. And, I did, too. I was like, "No. Why am I hiding? I'm not some subcitizen." Because, the thing about it, the thing about the down low, it lets you exist on this thing that, okay, for one, you're perpetuating this belief that what you're doing is wrong. And, also because you are on the down low, whatever relationship you have with anybody is not on the same conventional ideas that define a relationship. You don't have to be monogamous. You don't have to be safe, and that scared the hell out of me because although I was a part of this thing for this short amount of time, it was like, "God, there was a period when I was involved in this." And, I don't know. It just [got] to the point where I had made up my mind that I wouldn't live this way anymore. I wouldn't. And, I don't know.

Growing up, were there other people in your community that were gay, and that people knew were gay?

Early on. Early on. I had never met them. I had never seen them. But, I always heard about them: sissy Mickey and sissy Greg. That was their names. Now, I couldn't point sissy Mickey, I couldn't point them out anywhere, but that's how everybody knew them. The girls were going to get their hair done, the guys were known sometimes to go on over there and getting favors done.

Was this a couple that lived together?

No. These were two men that actually fought when they would come in contact with each other. I had never seen them before. This was just some myth, some mythical creatures [laughter] that . . . and they would just interest me because everybody knew them. Everybody knew that they may be sissies, but don't fuck with them because they will cut you. [Laughter] Because they are crazy. You know what I mean? And, they just took on this like larger than life thing to me being like not even truly dealing with these feelings I had inside myself. I was just intrigued. I was just intrigued the way they could sort of be integrated and sort of not.

So, to this day, you still haven't met them?

I have no idea who they are. [Laughter] No idea. I have no idea who sissy Mick is or who sissy Greg is. [Laughter] But that was their names, and they were two project queens. [Laughter] It's true. It's true.

Do you identify as gay, or does that term not have any resonance with you. Are there other terms like "queer," "same-gender-loving," or does "gay" do it for you?

[. . .] Let me say something first. When I first came out, my biggest thing was not that people were going to judge me for who I was, because at that point, I was actually proud of who I became to be. But, I was so upset that I would be labeled as the other things that came along with gay as part of the down low, or as a part of these people who truly . . . these two-dimensional people, who, because this is the South, and there is no big gay community, they get their definition from watching TV. So, you have these two-dimensional people walking around just as confused as the day is long. And for a long time, that kept me in the closet a long time in college. That kept me in the closet a long time, just because it got to the point to where I was afraid of it. I ignored it, and then I started to come to terms with it. And I wanted to come out, but I didn't want to be associated with that. I didn't want to be known as "the gay guy Stephen." I wanted to be known as Stephen, the guy who happens to be black and who happens to be gay. And, I hate that. People are giving me compliments in the theater like, "You are just one talented African American actor." Now, what the fuck is that supposed to mean? It's like what is that about? It just really burned me up because I was proud of being black. I was proud of being gay, but they are parts of who I am as a person. So, a lot of times I refer to myself as being queer.

[. . .] There was this big movement in the past five years for women to take back the word "bitch." I started to take back the words "fag" and "queer" and "sissy." I do to some of my friends who are going off to college, and I'm just now getting back in contact with them, so they know Stephen as a straight guy, not knowing Stephen for being around him for four years and then getting back in contact with him, and then he is a gay guy who refers to himself as fag sometimes. And it kind of unsettles people, but it really is because it's like I think the only way words hurt is the definition that we assign to those words, the power that we give those words.

Did you ever seriously consider moving out of the South, or do you want to move out of the South?

Yeah, just along the lines of me wanting to do theater and just being an actor and a singer and a dancer. I know that I have to. But, there were some times when I regretted living in the South, but there were a lot of times where I'm really thankful just because now I was able to learn the lessons that I needed to learn here in Tuscaloosa, and I have learned them and can take them to Atlanta, or San Francisco, or New York. I truly thank God that the thing in New York fell through when it did because I can't imagine trying to find myself, who I am in that city, just 'cause I was so confused. I had so much stuff to combat. I had so many negative things in my head that I'd been programmed that I had to sift through and sift out. I'm really glad that I came from this town that I was forced to find out who Stephen was as a person before I had to find out who Stephen was as a gay person. Does that make sense? So, in that case, yeah, I'm glad that I was raised in the South, but now that I feel that I have so much of a grasp on it I know that it's about that time. It's about that time to leave.

So, you think that there are other places, other regions in the country that would provide a better life for a black gay man?

Yeah. It was so funny . . . [Laughter] A boyfriend that I had for a short stint while I was in college, his name was Jordan, and he had an uncle who lived in Atlanta. Well, at this point, I had seen big groups of gay people on TV, and I had read about these portions of town that are all-gay, but not here in Tuscaloosa. We went to Atlanta, and now I'm just, in general I'm not a very big public affection person, but I don't have anything against it. But, we got out of the car in a part of Atlanta that was, I want to say it was the red district. I don't think it was that, but it was a part of Atlanta where the stores and the business are gay friendly.

Midtown.

Yeah. So, his uncle was taking us out to eat, and his uncle was gay as well. And, his uncle had taken us out to eat. And, as soon as we got out of the car, he grabbed my hand and we started walking toward the restaurant. I was like, "Jordan, what are you doing?" He was like, "It's cool." "It's cool." [It] was the first time I honestly got to see, again, that, wait a minute, maybe this is okay. Maybe . . . maybe I'm not this thing people try to create me out to be. It was one of the first instances when I knew that I had to get out of the South. I just had to get out of the South because the thing about it, it's just subdued racism now, and it's just blatant homophobia. [. . .] I have to get out. I have to get out.

Do you think the South is more homophobic than other places?

Hummm . . . I don't know. I can't really accurately say that either way just 'cause, I mean, I've traveled quite a bit, but I haven't lived in places to actually appreciate the true, like racial climate of a place. Yeah.

Do you currently have a boyfriend?

I do.

How, when, and where did you meet?

It's funny, actually recently. I was at this big theater conference in Charlotte, North Carolina. We were there, and it was so funny because I had just sworn off men. It's like, "I'm exhausted. I'm tired." I was like, "I'm *tired* of these *tired* southern men. I'm so sick of it. I'd rather be by myself." So, I'm heading up to Charlotte, and I go, and I see this guy. And, this guy is like just stunning. I was like, "Wow. Out of my league. Completely ignore him and walk away. Go do the rest of my stuff." And, we started to hang out. And, ah . . . we started to hang out and talk, and before I knew it, we had spent that entire day just hanging out and going to auditions. [. . .] The companies there were calling people back, and we had actually started to get acquainted to each other because we were being called back for the same parts. And, it was so odd. And, it was like, "Hey, you again." He was like, "Hey, you, see you later more than likely at another call back." And, we started to hang out. And, it ended up to where we had spent all day together, and we had spent all that night together up talking and just walking through Charlotte and seeing all these places. And, my thing is sometimes, I'm really forward in just conversations like this, but when it comes to men, if like if I have a crush on somebody, I'm kind of soft-spoken. So it was like, "I really like him." So, we were getting ready to say bye that night, and um . . . I wanted to kiss him so bad, and I reach over, and I hug him, and I kiss him on the cheek. And, I'm like, "UGH, what are you doing?" And, I get out of the car, and I just stand there on the sidewalk beating myself up as I'm waving as he drives off. And, so I text message him. I was like, "I just want to say that I think you're really beautiful, and I'm sort of kicking myself that I didn't kiss you. I hope I will see you again sometime. Be blessed." And, he calls me back. And, he was like, "Why didn't you kiss me?" And, I was like, "I have no idea." And, so we go, and we walk through Charlotte, and we spend the night together, and it was to the point to where the next morning, I woke up, and I was like, "What the hell is this?" And, he was like, "I have no idea." And, he was like, "Well, this is 'see you later.' This is not 'goodbye.'" I was like, "Okay." And, I told him, "You call me when you get to where you're going safely." Because I thought, this way I would know for sure if it was just me in this situation, or if it was just him. And so, he calls me. And, he's from St. Louis. He's from St. Louis, and we started this dialogue back and forth. And, we're talking and talking on the phone. It's a little awkward at first. He was like, "I'm coming down because I have . . . I'm going to Valdosta, Georgia. I got a job working there, and if you don't mind, I could stop by and see you a couple days before I leave because I have to go through Birmingham to get to Atlanta, 'cause I have some people in Atlanta." I was like, "Yeah. Yeah. I would like that." And, so, he came. He called me, and he was like, "I'm not taking the job in Valdosta." I was like, "Oh, man. He's not gonna come. God. Doggone. I thought this was the guy." I was like, "Oh, that makes me sad." He was like, "Why?" I was like, "Well, you can't come and see me now." He was like, "I can still come. I can still come to see you." And, he did, and that solidified it for me then. It really solidified it for me there. It's the first time in a long time to where it was like this person is amazing. But what's also great about that is that they think I'm amazing, too. [Laughter] And, I'm after Thanksgiving going up to Lancaster, Pennsylvania, to see him 'cause he has a job up there. Doing dinner theater. Yep, he's doing dinner theater up there. And, it's to the point now to where it's like, I have lucked out. I wasn't supposed to go to Charlotte. I went. I had just . . . [laughter] damned all men. And, he comes in my life when I stop looking.

Has he met any of your friends? Has he met your family?

He met my friends, not my family. He came down here, and he stayed for three days. And, I was in rehearsal for a show, and of course I had classes. So, the bit of it, we were actually away from each other. But, the thing about it, he has been out of school for two years, and he has spent those two years working. So, this was the first time in like two years that he actually got to sit and chill. And, so he did. Him and my roommate got along together great and took him out when he was here. He would hang with my friends. He thought it was odd that I didn't have more gay friends than I did. [Laughter]

How would you describe intimate relationships among black gay men here— and this is sort of a two-part question—do you think southern culture makes intimate relationships between black gay men easier, or do you think it inhibits . . . and, maybe I should take the gay out, but do you think it provides a conducive space for men to be intimate with one another, or do you think it inhibits it?

Aside from the South, there are stigmas that, as a black man, I have to fight against just because, I don't know, people see you as an object. They see you as your dick. And, it's so hard to work against that. Being southern, I think, it's exaggerated here. It's to the point that, I know black men who won't date any other race because of that simple fact. But, I have found that just with the people I've come in contact with, a mindset that comes along with people who say, "I only date black men," or people who say, "I only date white men." It's just some mindset that I've dealt with them to a certain extent, and it was like there is a part of me that really doesn't agree with that. So, it's so interesting that it's one of the things I ask about people just in passing, "Have you dated somebody of another race?" And, it's always so interesting. I've found this reoccurring pattern in the people who say, "I date outside my race. I mean, for me it's about the person and not the bag that they come in." You know what I mean? And, I don't know. I found that. I mean, just being in the South and knowing you could be physically harmed by doing things out in the public. You quickly find places where it's okay. You quickly find places that it's okay. So, it makes it a little difficult, but when you do find those places where it's accepted, it's okay. But, a lot of people are programmed here to think a certain way. A lot of people are programmed, and so it's hard to find a person who has broken out of that mold. And, so it's so hard because you either compromise, or you go without. You decide to be by yourself.

How can you tell if somebody is gay?

How can I tell? For me, it's really intuitive. [. . .] I think it's because early on, when I watched people and knew what to put on to make myself acceptable, I can spot the people who are doing the same. And, it's so funny, too, because [laughter] closet cases are drawn to me for some reason. I don't know what it is, but I am cursed with the closet cases. [Laughter] It's hard to explain. There are some cases to where like, oh, the way that person talks, or the way . . . especially if they're attracted to you. That person just held eye contact a little longer than what is normal, most people wouldn't even pick up on it, but things are subtle. Because, I mean, you kind of have to be covert in the South. But, for me, it's just this list of things. It's this list of things that I see. And, it's like people will tell me, "He is not gay, Stephen. You think everybody is gay." And, I'm like, "Watch. Watch." And, sure enough . . . And, it's so funny, too. You get people in parties, and they get drunk, and all of a sudden these straight men . . . it's like wait a minute, man. And, even if I think that you're gay, and you tell me that you're straight, I'll file you in my mental Rolodex as straight. So, it really bothers me. It really just takes me aback when people say something, and then they act completely against it. But, I don't know. Along those lines, it's a lot of really small things, a lot of really small things.

How would you describe your involvement in the gay community?

My involvement? What's odd is that there is an all-black college here, and the all-black college has a disproportionately high number of gay men there.

Here in Tuscaloosa?

Yeah. Stillman College. The thing about it is . . . there is this huge population of gay people and nobody is out. A *huge* number of gay people; nobody's out. I'm from here. I know a lot of people. A lot of people that were going to school with me, and because I'm in theater and perform a lot, people tend to see me 'cause there's not a lot of black men in the theater department, and I've been blessed with [being] consistently cast, so I'm always up in front of people, always in the newspaper. And, being from here, just having a lot of people know who I am because of how long I've been here. And, it's so odd, because I've had a friend that came to me who said . . . 'cause he was dating on of these closet cases from Stillman, and he was saying how . . . he was like, "You have really shaken up a lot of people here." I was like, "What do you mean?" He was like, "It was on the lines of, you're out, and you don't have to be." And, I think what he meant by that was just along the lines that people didn't assume that I was gay. I had become really good at playing the masculine thing, but I don't know. It had something to do with me being at peace with myself more so than anything. So, I don't know. I was real proud about that though. Really proud about it.

So, people are looking up to you as a role model?

Right. Right.

Sort of giving them permission to say it's okay.

Right. And, it's just along the lines of not having to. You know what I mean? So, I don't know.

Do you feel a sense of community among black gay men here?

Most people in the university, gay men here, are men who play on the DL or in the closet. There are very few that are out. But, the ones that are out, we know each other. We know the ones in the closet [laughter] who play.

[Laughter] I don't know. There's a great power with saying, "I'm out in the open," because everybody else who is also gay, but in the closet, they all think, "Oh my God. He's gonna out everybody." [Laughter] And, there are some people who do that, but that's not necessarily my bag. You take your journey in the time that it takes you to take that journey. You know what I mean?

What do you think their fear is based on?

That judgment. You are not a man. You are not a man. You really need Jesus in your life. You need that demon case out of you. You need to be healed. It's just all the statements that are associated with it. And, especially in the arts, especially in the arts, [. . .] although, the arts do seem to be the most progressive aspect of our society, it's pretty homophobic. It's pretty homophobic, too.

How would you describe your political perspectives with regard to gay and lesbian issues?

Well, here's my thing, especially with the recent election, Jesus help us all. Lord have mercy. What are we gonna do? But, just along the lines, especially with the issue of the gay marriage thing, I think the government should never be in the position to where they are enforcing the churches to recognize anything. I feel very strongly that the government should not mandate how the church runs. And, I also feel that the church should not mandate how the government is run. And, so in saying that, I don't necessarily think that government should mandate the churches to recognize gay marriages. But, when it comes down to rights and liberties how married, straight couples are given different things from the government, such as tax breaks and different things like that. I think that if two men come together, and they are given a civil union, which is something that has nothing to do with the church, this is something that is more so on a legal aspect of things. Because [people] who have been disowned by their families, who get in these relationships with their partners, and they die, and their partners who have been with this person as family for years and years, have no say in hospital treatment, no say in the property that they shared together, have no say in anything, and I think that it has nothing to do with what you think is right as something religious. You have your opinions. Your opinions don't bother me until they start to infringe on my rights. That's the problem. So, I do believe strongly in civil unions, and I don't think that government should mandate gay marriages and make the churches recognize them. But, on matters of legality, I don't know. That's where I stand about it.

What role does the church and religion play in your life currently?

It got to the point to where I have truly backed away from organized religion. [. . .] I feel as if the relationship I have with God now is more so based on just that, a relationship and not customs. I have been just disappointed by a lot of people in the churches, different things that they have done and different ways that they have conducted themselves, and them always saying, "God is love. God is inclusion. God is unconditional." But, then they go and say the very opposite. [. . .] I'm in the process of coming to terms with religion, 'cause I still have to resolve myself. I feel as though I am a Christian. I also feel as if, if you live your life a certain way, if you exist on . . . 'cause, basically, the principles in all major religions are the same, and I guess I'm trying to resolve myself with being a Christian and with the simple point that if you are not a Christian, specifically a Christian, you're damned to hell. I'm really trying to resolve that within myself. Because, I mean, it's something I believe. I believe in God. I believe in Jesus Christ. I just have issues with damning people. I really do.

Why do you think so many black gay men remain in the church, and specifically in the choir?

Right. [Laughter] It's a level of acceptability. And, I say this just because the choir of the church, gay people being accepted, and I think it's so funny because it's the same terms of how black people were accepted. For one, there was that level where we're not mixing at all. We don't want to see that. Then, it got to the point that, well we only accept blacks as being comical or making fun of themselves. And, then it got to the point, well, we only accept black people if they are really experienced or really talented at what they do. And, I think a lot of the things, a lot of the progression that we've done has been through the arts. A lot of the performers have broken down doors and done different things, like Sidney Poitier, and Dorothy Dandridge, and all these people who have done this, who have crossed over. And, I just think that is, we're just on that part of acceptability. I think that a lot of people think that they still fit in. [. . .] If people think that you're gay, I think more so than anything, they would be less to accept you as a minister, but more so accepting you being in the choir because it's just that. Look now at TV, we can only see gay people as comical, as stereotypical, much like the minstrel shows. And, I think that we're just along that journey of progression, of acceptability. I really do. I think it's to the point to where it's gonna have to grow from us being that level of, okay, we're going to become characters, we're gonna do this, and we're going to be seen as two-dimensional to where it's honestly gonna be that we're gonna really have to stand firm as a community and say who we are and stand firm on that. Because, it's different than the civil rights, in that black people can't really hide that they're black. But, gay men have that out. And, I think that we have to shut that door. It's like, you're out of the closet. As a group, we need you to progress because we're gonna have to do it together either way. I don't know. I just think that we're just at that point of progression.

What are your best memories of growing up in the South?

Best memories, um . . . my family—best and worst part of my childhood [laughter], truth be told. Because we're so centralized, because we've been here for so long, having times with, like Thanksgiving and Christmas are huge in our family, not necessarily because of all the things that you get, it was more so everybody in the family is together. It's the only time that it's this big, 'cause we really don't have like family reunions, per se, but like Thanksgiving and Christmas, everybody comes together. Everybody cooks, and . . . I don't know. It keeps rooting me back in who I am. It keeps rooting me back because a lot of times, how I want to de-emphasize the fact that I'm black or de-emphasize the fact that I'm gay, I also need to realize, wait a minute, that is a part of who I am too. You know what I mean? So, I don't know. My family.

And your worst memory? Your family?

[Laughter] Yeah. [Long pause] My household, I guess. It was a little rocky than what I would have preferred. It wasn't as stable as what . . . and, that's why I honestly feel that if, although my family is really important to me, I'm not as close with them just because mentally I never associated that with a place that was a constant, that was a place that was stable. You know what I mean?

Yeah. What has been the affect of HIV/AIDS on your life?

It makes you really put everything in perspective. It really makes you take a step back and look at all the trivial things in your life. I have never met anybody with HIV or AIDS, that I know of, 'cause, a lot of people go undiagnosed. Just the thing with constantly realizing over and over again this is real. This is here. This is now. And, it's affecting the work that I do and the performance pieces that I choose, that it's really important that this stays in people's faces, that they don't just think that this is something that is in the big city, that they don't think of it as something, the boogeyman, something that really doesn't exist although everybody talks about it. It has to be real. You know what I mean? And, so I think that's reflective in my art, because it's really important to me. It's really important to my community, the black community, and the gay community. It's that important. And, it's really bothering me, and I think that's why when I had that first positive relationship with the first guy that I dated, that's why it was so potent for me when I finally did take a step back from it. It was like, this is real, people are dying down low. They are existing in this lifestyle because of fear, and they are dying. And, I don't know. It's real in my life, and I try to be responsible and safe, and I try to be vocal, and I try to use my art to, "Get off your butt. Do something about this. Listen. Look at these people who are real," to do something to impact people, to move people, to really take notice 'cause I mean, it's our modern day epidemic.

Do you think it's more of a problem here in the South currently?

Yes. The numbers might not reflect it, but I think the way that we're set up mentally, because we don't talk about this entire portion of our population. And, if we don't address it, how can we address the issues that are prevalent in that population? If we, as black people, don't embrace our brothers and sisters who are gay, how can we embrace any of these problems? There are people who feel alone. There are people who feel alone, and there are people who are acting out, and people who are compromising themselves because they are looking for something, looking for something outside of themselves, something that they haven't gotten, something that fills this void. I think when we win it here, that's when we'll win it numberswise. But, if it's something that we won't even address . . . you know what I mean? I guess that more than anything bothers me, 'cause sometimes it can just get discouraging.

How would you describe the influence that your southern upbringing had on your character?

I guess on a superficial level, you learn how to say real mean things nicely. [Laughter] I have learned from my grandmother and other people in church, you can say anything about anybody as long as you put a "Bless they heart," at the end of it. [Laughter] "Lord, that girl is trash, bless her heart." And, that's all right. [Laughter] But, seriously, I guess more so than anything, a strong tradition. A strong tradition, something that I really am proud of the South for, and [. . .] how tightly we hold onto tradition. Because I feel that I'm not only Stephen, but I'm at one point going to be a part of a tradition, it's important for me how I mold that tradition, what that tradition is, 'cause I'm gonna be a part of that. You know what I mean? [. . .] Me, a black gay man out of the South. I'm responsible. And, it's so funny, too, because a teacher, a while ago, was talking about Sidney Poitier, and so I just started researching him, looking at his old movies, and reading his biography, and there was one thing that he said. He was like, there were points that movie roles came up to him and where he couldn't do it, him and his family are hungry, and he would not take these movie parts because of how they depicted black people during civil rights. Also, it's different now that it's not that big of an issue for a black person to take a role of a villain. At that point, he couldn't do that. He could not do that just because he felt responsible to an entire race of people. And, so I was like, well, what's good for Sidney, is good for me. You know what I mean? So, I guess that really molded who I am.

How would you describe your current feelings about being a black gay man?

Because of a lot of things that just recently happened with this election specifically on a nationwide level, and on a statewide level, I'm feeling a little displaced. Because, I don't know if you know about this, but in addition to the presidential elections, we also had these state elections where there were all these amendments to add things and take things out of the constitution. Well, one of the amendments that was up for debate was this Amendment Two. And Amendment Two during the election was to repeal segregationist language out of the state constitution. That's been there since 1901.

Really?

Really. This amendment was to repeal that language. This amendment was also supposed to take out the things about poll tax that was supposed to be discouraged by people who vote. It was also supposed to take out the line in there saying that everyone is not entitled to an education. It was supposed to repeal all of this. That amendment died. Half the people in Alabama thought that the segregationist language in our constitution was not that bad. The poll taxes, although they can't enforce it . . . this is *half* the people who voted. So, we can't blame it on the ignorant rednecks. You know what I mean? These are registered voters. These are registered voters who are potential jurors. And, it makes me take a step back. It's like, I've always believed that there is a universal truth, and then in that universal truth, a universal right. It's laughable to me that it's 2004, and we're voting to take racial language off our state constitution. It is laughable. And, the fact that it passed. It did not pass because the state was split in half. And, then [. . .] we're voting in a presidential election not because of the policy of that person, but because the religious morals that this person has. It just makes me take a step back and wonder, like I said, I've always thought that there was a universal truth, and that there was a universal right. And, I thought and I believed in that universal right. You know what I mean? But, it's sort of a kick in the face when what you hold to be true is the minority of the country. You know what I mean? So, I guess that right now, I have a feeling of displacement, of like, okay, you said we progressed as a state, but we still have this on our constitution. And, you're okay with this?

· · · · · · · ·

JOE

Joe's story is heartbreaking and hopeful at the same time. As his narrative reveals, he has made it through quite a few challenges for someone his age. I met him through Stanley, another narrator in Sweet Tea, *who teaches at Nichols State in Thibodeaux, Louisiana, where Joe was a student.*

Although Joe is quite soft-spoken, he is quite outspoken and involved in the gay and lesbian student organizations on his campus. Despite his involvement with gay and lesbian political groups, his views on certain issues, like gay marriage, I found to be surprisingly conservative. It was also the first time in an interview that I felt compelled to push a narrator on his views—not out of judgment as much as for clarification on what seemed to be illogical rationales. The interview took place on May 10, 2005, on the campus of Nichols State.

I was born in New Orleans, December 17th, 1984. My childhood was unstable, rough. My mother was a crack addict who turned prostitute. And so my sister and I, my mom, would kind of go from pillar to post, really unstable. My grandmother is an alcoholic, so at times when my mother couldn't take care of my sister and I, she'd dump us at my grandmother's. And it was just this terrible, horrible cycle. That would just about describe it. Just rough, hard, just trying to deal with my mom and her addiction and then my own personal stuff. I have dyslexia, so dealing with that and at the same time knowing that I wanted to be a Christian man, whatever that was supposed to mean. And just juggling a lot of that stuff.

I moved out of my grandmother's house the sixth grade and moved into a children's home. But that was only after the sixth grade; I tried to commit suicide.

You?

Yeah. [Laughter] So I think it was really more of a cry for attention because things weren't like they should be. I didn't have the normal family, so yeah.

So you were in a children's home at the age of twelve?

Yeah.

And how long did you stay there?

Five years, up until actually last year.[5]

What was that like?

A roller coaster. Finally stability in my life, so that was nice. A time for a lot of inner healing. And a time for a lot of exploration. [Laughter] I know that's terrible but I finally was able to go to a private school so I could get help with my dyslexia. My mother died from complications of AIDS my last year at the boys' home. My first boyfriend was there. And actually contrary to what most people think, this place wasn't—it wasn't at all a scary place for a young gay kid to live. We were a family. It was a nice, quiet, familylike atmosphere. The only difference is you have thirty brothers. If I could go back and relive all of it, I would. It's actually on Carrolton Avenue, but I don't want to give the place a bad name. [Laughter]

Besides your mother, your grandmother was responsible for some of your upbringing?

Yeah. My aunts and my grandmother for my younger years were mainly responsible. This is a long story actually. My uncles played basketball at a local church. And they were invited to go to dinner and stuff like that and they drug my sister and I along. And I kind of stuck around. So people from my parish really kind of got involved in my life. I guess you could say I'm adopted, in a way. I met my adoptive family at my church. And we've been connected throughout all of the stuff that happened. And they were really there to provide a lot of financial support, a lot of pulling strings to get me into schools, and making sure that life was sort of okay. But yeah, they were really just there to provide financial support and emotional support, as well. I think I actually came out to my rector, which is the head priest, at my church. He was the first person I came out to, so that was quite weird. So just to show you just how close we all were and how much they actually supported me. But they were the first few people that I ever told that I was gay.

So what happened to your sister when you went to the home?

My sister, she's kind of the rebellious kid. She didn't want to experience all of the great things that I ended up [experiencing]. She chose to stick with my mom and my aunts. And she's actually dropped out of school and she's only seventeen. She'll probably end up being pregnant because she's living with this random guy. We lost contact with each other and we don't talk very much. And it's more because she hates me because I'm making something of myself, or at least trying to. So her life has just really been a shit hole. She hasn't been able to do much. Life really hasn't changed much for her, positively at least.

Where did you go to elementary school?

[. . .] I actually went to several different schools. I started off by going to a public school that was in St. Thomas Projects. You know where that is? It's a housing development in New Orleans. But it's Laurel Elementary. And it was rough there.

Why was it rough?

Mainly because I was labeled as being emotionally disturbed because I was acting out in school and everything. But it was really just because they weren't teaching me how to read or write. So it was rough just because I was, battling with this—you know, I'm not stupid but you people are saying that I'm stupid, so you put me in these classrooms where I can't learn anything. [. . .] I wasn't being fed the way that a child is supposed to be fed, educationalwise.

Did you have friends?

I did have friends. They were all the wrong people. [Laughter] Gosh, not very many, though. They were all girls, but I guess that's typical. [Laughter] That's very typical for a gay guy anyway. I didn't really have much of a social life, though. I stayed inside most of the time. Outside playing hopscotch on the playground or jumping rope better than any of the other girls could. Or talking with the teachers because I was always more mature than the other kids were. In grammar school, at least, I didn't have a lot of friends, just a few here and there. None that I really remember, though. Like I couldn't tell you their names or say oh, I knew So-and-So. I take that back. There was this one girl, and it just dawned on me. I had the biggest crush on her in grammar school. And it turns out that she's actually a lesbian now. [Laughter]

And when you went to the home, did they provide your education there, or were you sent to school away from the home?

I was actually sent to a Catholic high school, De LaSalle. It's the only coed Catholic high school in the city. The boys' home and my church members paid for my education there. I had a lot of friends there. But unfortunately, I knew too much about myself that I didn't really—my freshman year was really a battle between keeping hush-hush who you are because I'm at this private school where I'm constantly being told that, "Oh, you can't be gay, you can't be gay" or, "I'm sorry, it's okay to be gay here. You just can't practice." Okay, that doesn't make any sense. But I think that's when my life started to change, that eighth-grade, ninth-grade year. Things started to get better for me. High school was hard but a lot of life lessons learned.

Were you in contact with your mother during this time?

No. No, by then I basically cut her off totally. She was kind of in her final stages. And I didn't really talk to her very much. I only heard from her or anyone in my family when they needed something. And as far as like, getting my Social Security number so that they could get money and things like that. Other than that, I really have no contact with them. My family was the boys' home and my church members and my friends from high school. There was nothing. I think I may have saw my mother three or four times my five years at the boys' home. Talked to her maybe even once on the phone. There was really not much contact at all, but that was by choice, by *my* choice, not by hers. I just didn't make an effort to see her anymore because it was too hard to watch someone spiral like that. It's hard to love somebody when they're constantly screwing up and they let you down, so.

Do you know your father?

No. I don't. I just knew the man's name. [Laughter] That's about it. He hasn't bothered to contact me; I haven't bothered to contact him.

But he knows that you're in the world?

Yeah, he knows that I'm here. He knows that I'm here. I think my sister is friends with like our like stepsister. But I haven't met the girl. My ties have been really severed with my family. We have no contact at all.

Was your neighborhood segregated?

The neighborhood I lived in since I was in the projects for most of the time was pretty segregated. There were maybe three white people who lived in the whole neighborhood. But they were all nuns and priests and stuff like that who were missionaries in the area. And when my family moved from uptown to the New Orleans East, that area, things were still pretty segregated. In fact, my grammar schools and things like that were either all black or all white. I went to St. George's. I think [that] was the time that I was around different types of people.

What would you say are the racial politics in New Orleans?

If you're black and uneducated, there's no hope. If you're black and educated, you have a slim chance of making it. And even being a part of a family that's pretty white, people still—like I'll give you an example. When I went to St. George's—it's a fairly affluent school. And the kids would invite me to their bar mitzvahs and things like that. And I'd show up and their grandmothers would hand me their coats and ask me to get these drinks and things like that for them. And I'm like, "No, I'm here for the party," you know. And that still happens to me when my dad will take me to architecture parties and things like that or introduce me to people from Tulane, professors and things like that. And he introduces me as his son and they're all just like, "What?" [Laughter]

You said your dad?

My dad, my adopted family.

Oh, okay.

No, not my biological father. My family that I've created. [Laughter] Even in our own house, after I moved out of the boys' home into my adopted family's house, my dad was the president of the Tulane Alumni Association. And I'm in my De LaSalle uniform and, very Catholic, preppy, kid. And we're all out chitchatting. And one of the guys, one of these big business guys in the city walks up to me and he's like, "Well, what are you doing here? Why are you here? What's the deal with you?" And I'm like, "This is my house. This is my family. What are you doing in *my* house?" [Laughter] And then to have my adoptive mother walk over and, to introduce me. They were just like, "Oh, my goodness. Well, I'm so sorry. I didn't know. You know, I thought you just, wandered in." So there's definitely racial tension.

Is your adoptive family white?

Yeah, *very* white. [Laughter] A lot of my friends are now white. And when I go out with them, they get stares and things like that. And now that I'm at Nichols, I'm even noticing it a lot more. I was actually out with a couple of friends last night. And one of the guys had asked me about my family and I told him. And he just was amazed. He was like, "I can't believe it. My family would never, ever have a black person in our house. They would be crushed if I told them that you were one of my good friends."

Even as a guest?

Even as a guest. I've been told by people who go to school here who I'm friends with that if I went into their neighborhoods, too late at night that I may as well stay locked in my car, or call the cops immediately, because you won't make it out alive. Or sitting in church and having a little girl or a little boy stare you in the face because they've never seen a black person before.

Are these people from rural parts of Louisiana?

Yeah, these are rural parts of Louisiana. I mean, in the city it's still pretty bad. In fact, my uncles and I went to a Mardi Gras parade. This when I was actually with my family, my biological family. We were in the white side of town, and these guys, these—they were hicks, but anyway they yelled out across the street, "Go home, niggers, we don't want you here." And, I'm this young kid going, "What?" You know, I thought this was just like, a place for all of us to hang out. I mean, this was in Chalmette. I don't know if you know anything about Chalmette, but it's the boonies of New Orleans. And, I mean, there's definitely racial tension. But it's getting better, it's getting better.

What was it or what is it like being the adoptee of a white family? And how did that come about?

Adoptee of a white family. [Laughter] The way that it all happened was that, like I said before, I started going to this all-white parish, to the Episcopal church, a very, very wealthy parish. And my adoptive mother was the children's liturgy coordinator, and she just kind of met me and fell in love with me. [Laughter] And so since then, we've been close. They're helping me pay for college and things like that. It's hard in the sense that even when I lived with my family, I was never black enough because I was always around these white people when I went to church and things like that. So it causes a lot of confusion. For the longest time I lived in two different worlds. On one level, I was loved and cared for by these people. But then when we did things outside, we were always stared at or looked at differently. It's like, where do you fit in? And even now sometimes I wonder about that. You know, I don't fully connect with all the black guys on campus because I'm not black enough. I've even been told by one of my professors that I needed to get in touch with my own culture because I was too far removed. So, confusion and pain. I don't know if I'm describing that the way that I want to. Am I making any sense?

Um hmm. So when you're not living here, you live with your adoptive family?

Yeah, in New Orleans. They have three kids of their own. Older. My eldest brother is a student at Tulane Law School. My youngest brother is at Georgetown. And my sister just graduated from Middlesex, is a teacher at our local church, at the church school.

And you get along with them?

I do. For the most part they accept me. It took a while for them to actually, okay, well, this guy is going to be around for a while. Yeah, I mean, we get along really well. But just like with any family, we always bicker about who's getting what. "You're getting more than I am"; everyone wants their fair share. But, I mean, as far as a family goes, I think we're pretty normal. We've got our problems but we're pretty normal.

What role did religion play in your upbringing?

[Deep sigh] A serious one. It's probably been one of the reasons why I've hurt so much. I was raised by my biological family to be Southern Baptist. And well, I need not say any more about that. [Laughter] So, that was always tough. But then I converted when I met my adopted family.

Before you go on, so I do want you to actually say more about church. Did you not enjoy church?

Oh, I hated church. I hated going—I loved going to church, I hated the people in church. Does that make any sense? I've always had a strong relationship with God. I'm probably as gay as you're going to get and as faithful as you're going to get, together. I was always told, you can't do these things, you can't feel this way, you can't be gay, that's just not—that's not right. You know, the Bible clearly says that it's wrong. And to hear that and then on the inside know that, well, if God is love and God is all love, then how can God hate? And if I'm created in his likeness and image and God doesn't make mistakes, then why do I wake up every morning or I walk down the street and I see a beautiful guy and I go, wow, he's gorgeous. Why do I have these feelings? If they're not from God, then where are they from? So I kind of rejected church itself for a long time. But never rejected God. Rejecting the Baptist Church's teachings and things like that, but always being faithful to God in my own way. Things got better after I converted. I'm now Episcopal. And we've got our own issues, gay bishops and the church splitting and everything. But for the most part, I've found it to be a welcoming, loving place. I don't feel pressure to, confess that I'm gay and that I'm going to hell, and ask to God to save me. I don't feel like that. I don't feel as guilty as I would have if I would have stuck with my family's denomination. I probably would be on my knees every fifteen, twenty minutes, but anyway so, I'm actually in discernment to join a religious community, New York. So I'll be a Benedictine monk, hopefully. So, I mean, religion has always been something dear to my heart.

When was the first time you became aware of your sexual orientation? And what was your reaction to that realization?

I would say I actually first came to realize it when my mother—my mother's boyfriend at the time was a DL man, they call it, but a pedophile anyway. And I was actually sexually abused by him. And I've come to realize that I think he took advantage of me because I was always that little swishy-walking little boy. So, in a sense, I've always known. But I came to realize it after the abuse stopped.

When did it start, and how old were you?

Gosh, I don't remember exactly, it's all a blur. I'm in therapy for it, but it's okay. [Laughter] But I want to maybe say like nine or so. Yeah. Even before all of that happened, my uncles were always afraid that I would be this little queer. It's like I was always forced to go play football and stuff like that. I always found it to be more comfortable to be in the house cooking and cleaning and things like that. But after the abuse is when I really realized that this is really who I am. My reaction to it was to shut up about it. To not tell anyone because it wasn't safe for me to do so. To keep it all to myself, write it down, draw pictures, but never, ever say anything. But it was always hard because my—I shouldn't say it was hard but, well, my mother, her boyfriend, we were homeless for a while. And they would take us, my sister and I, walking through the [French] Quarter. And I always found myself drawn to St. Anne Street. [Laughter] Being around all the gay people, it's like, "Whoa, you people are fun." But it was just originally just not to say anything, because I couldn't. It just wasn't a safe environment. Nobody in my neighborhood would understand. I was afraid of being labeled, the fag, the AIDS-carrying queer, things like that.

So you said that you were homeless for a while?

Yeah. I'm sorry, you're finding out all of these different things about me. And you're just like, "Oh." My mother, because of her addiction and everything, we lost our house, our apartment, when we lived in the St. Thomas housing development. We lost the apartment because she couldn't pay rent, because she was smoking and she obviously wasn't making much money being a prostitute, so we were out on the street. Actually slept under a bridge. I'll never forget that night. It was cold, but anyway. Having to rely on other people to provide for us. My mother had the sense enough to, after like two weeks of going from homeless shelter to homeless shelter, to give my sister and myself to my grandmother, and trying to get her to provide for us. And every now and then, she'd come back and she'd screw up again and so we'd be out on the streets again. So it was just this cycle. I don't know how else to describe it.

So how old were you when this happened?

It would have to be sometime after the abuse, so eight, nine, somewhere around there. That's when all of that drama took place.

Was your mother's boyfriend's abuse of you the first time you'd ever—?

Had a gay experience?

Yeah.

Yeah. Which is terrible because no one should have something like that taken away from them. But that was my first, very first gay sexual experience.

Did you know—at that time did you know what was happening?

I knew that it was something that shouldn't—that a grown man shouldn't be doing to a boy. I knew that it was something that adults did. But, I knew what was happening. I knew what was happening.

And at what point did you tell anyone?

Didn't tell anyone. No one still knows about it. It's just, well, there are a few people who know about it, like my therapist, my priest, things like that. But my family still has no clue, not even my adopted family, has any clue that any of that had—has ever occurred.

Did he threaten you if you told?

Yeah, but they were empty, and I knew that. It's just I was more ashamed. I felt like I was responsible for it, it was my fault. If I didn't stay inside and I went outside with the boys and played football, this wouldn't happen. This guy wouldn't have come into my mother's life and, pimped her out, if I would have stopped doing what, if I would have said something. I think what keeps me from telling my biological family now is the fact that I don't want to put them through that. I feel like they've gone through enough with my mom and my aunts and my uncles. They don't need that extra load. And part of me feels like my mother knew what was going on but she didn't know what to do. And I wouldn't want them to blame her for it, seeing how's she dead now, but anyway. Life is already tough for them, without that extra garbage. And I'm dealing with it, so it's not anything for them.

So at what point did you experience same-sex sex where you initiated it?

Let's say my freshman year of high school. It was my first boyfriend. [Whispering] Miguel, Miguel, Miguel. [Laughter] It was actually really strange because when I was admitted to the home, I was very honest with the coordinator who let me in and everything. I'm just like, "Well, I'm gay, I just wanted you to know that." And he was like, "Okay, you just can't have sex with any of the guys over here." And sure enough, anyway. [Laughter] But I'd always had this crush on him. He's this beautiful, handsome, sweet, intelligent guy. And from the moment I set eyes on him; it was even funnier because he actually was the person who took me on my tour of the home. [Laughter] And just one evening, like two years had passed, he actually said, "I've always felt this way about you," yadda, yadda, yadda. And next thing I knew, we were having sex. And we dated for a while after that.

Did other people know that you were dating, or you kept it a secret?

We were supposed to keep it a secret, but everybody knew. [Laughter] And the reason I know that is because the boys would poke fun. Of course, they would only say things behind our backs and then it would get back to us. And, of course, because we were the two bigger guys, that was always kind of squelched. But I think the guys just didn't know what to make of it; the boys all knew. Because, we'd always be together. When we were upset with each other, it's like it was obvious [laughter]. And the adults knew to a certain extent. They would always watch us, closely. But I guess when you're in love with somebody, you always find a way around the loopholes. Like at one point, they stopped us from taking showers together, because we had shower time. And, they would assign him a shower time and they would assign me a shower time. And we weren't supposed to break it, but I guess you always make things happen that you want to.

Is there any particular theory about homosexuality that you believe?

I believe that we're all on this line, this spectrum. And on one end, you have very gay and on the other end you have very straight, but nobody's ever on total opposite ends of that. I think that we're all in the middle. Some people [are] more gay than others, but everybody is lopped in the middle. One of my lesbian friends and I were talking at dinner. And this is just interesting, but you couldn't prove it, but we were thinking that maybe gay men are—how did it go? That the reason gay men are gay is because they didn't have the vaginal passageway when their moms gave birth to them. But that was just something that was really funny. But the one thing I really believe [laughter] is that homosexuality and heterosexuality are all on the spectrum and no one's totally either/or.

How would you describe the influence of your southern upbringing on your ability to come to terms with or even recognize your sexual orientation? In other words, do you think growing up in the South made you more naïve about such things?

I do think it made me a little bit more afraid. It made me feel dirty, feeling, like having cooking oil dripped all over you and that nastiness, because it wasn't something that was accepted. You didn't see it. I've always felt like if I've had to keep something a secret, then—or I should say the things in my neighborhood that were kept secret were bad things. And because I wasn't able to say this is who I am, this is how I feel, then I guess that was a bad thing to feel attracted to men. I think if I lived up North, I wouldn't think like that because I'd see more gay couples freely together.

To what extent have you come out to your parents? And what was their reaction?

I told my biological mother in a therapy session. And she nearly shit a brick. She thought it was her fault, and I was going to go to hell. And, of course, I'm thinking in the back of my head, well, if I'm going to hell, you're going to be right there with me because you're a big whore. [Laughter] Anyway, that it was her fault. That I was going to hell. That she'd never have grandkids. At first she was like, "Just don't tell anybody. You can't tell your grandmother about this. This is wrong." And the week after I told her that, I attempted suicide. [. . .] I think that and a number of other stresses, going to this private school but still living in the ghetto, living in two different worlds. Knowing that I was gay. Not being black enough. Just really kind of overwhelming. I tried to cut myself. But that night was actually the night that I told my whole family, and my Aunt Nicole tried to beat the snot out of me. She tried to beat the gayness out of me. Of course, my grandmother, the sweet woman she is, talked her out of it. She was going to open up a can of whoop ass on me, but anyway. My uncles didn't want anything to do with me; they didn't understand it. My sister, she just really didn't care. She thought it was just kind of nasty, but she didn't really totally get it. My grandmother just didn't want to talk about it. And to this day, it's not something that's talked about a whole lot with them, when I do see them. My adopted family, everybody knows. My father thought that maybe I was too young and I didn't understand. He felt like maybe I should just give being straight a chance. But my mom was—her response to him was, "He's been dealing with it longer than you have." [Laughter] So they all know, and they're very accepting and loving. In fact, they on my like eighteenth birthday, Miguel went to dinner with us, and they knew that I was dating him and they were just like okay. [. . .] But just like you don't talk about your sister being straight, they don't talk about me being gay. But it's not something that they're ashamed of at all either. Because, they'll take me to the gay and lesbian community center in New Orleans.

The people at my church all know. And everybody's—they're either comfortable with it or they're not and they don't say anything. I mean, that's really about it. It's not celebrated, but it's not frowned on by anyone. I think if I chose to get married to some guy, then they would be sitting at the church. If I decided to get married to a woman, they'd probably say, "Well, what's up with this?" you know. [Laughter] But still be there. So they're supportive.

Did you ever seriously consider or have you ever seriously considered moving out of the South?

Yeah. I want to move up North someplace, Boston, New York, South Carolina, North Carolina, but that's not really—that's still south but it's north enough that it's still kind of liberal.

So you think that there are other places outside of the South that provide a better life for black gay men?

Yeah. I think people aren't as ignorant. Everywhere, every place has its skeletons, but I'd feel more comfortable in a different environment. And I've thought maybe that I need to move to Texas, then that's okay, but I seriously doubt that. But I think other states up North provide a better nurturing environment.

Do you think the South is more homophobic than other places?

Rural south. The cities, not so much. I think that's changed. But I wouldn't say I have a pride march in Thibodeaux.

What about New Orleans?

Certain places in New Orleans. I think that in the South that there's a stigma around gay men as being pedophiles, as being really promiscuous and things like that. And I just find that up North you don't have that. I mean, to an extent. But most gay people up North are—they're educated men and women who have jobs and are CEOs and are normal people, whatever that's supposed to mean, but they're not afraid to go to work and have the picture of their partner, in their cubicle or their office for fear of losing their jobs. I just think that there's just ignorance in the South. [. . .]

So you're not currently in a relationship?

No.

Are you looking to be in one?

No.

No? Why?

Because I'm trying to discern my vocation to live a religious life, and I understand what that means. And I don't think I could totally do that if I was in a relationship with someone. And if I chose to go into a monastic life, then it would be wrong for me to enter into a relationship with someone and then say, "Well, I can't be with you anymore because I'm going to move away to go to New York and be a monk now." I'm not really looking for a relationship with anyone right now. Now, I do feel lonely. [Laughter] But I'm dealing with that. I'm not really looking to be in a hookup type of a relationship or an emotional relationship or anything. I'm just kind of happy flying solo.

So you're considering going into the monastery?

Yeah. My order, I don't know if I should say this, well, my order is Benedictine Community. They're the Order of Holy Cross. And most of the brothers are gay, but all celibate, at least they're supposed to be. Some people mess up on that, but let's just hope I don't do that. They're not priests, they're not pedophiles or anything. But I want to join this community and do some missionary work and things like that.

So you don't feel that you'll miss having sexual relationships?

I know that I will. But with anything, there comes sacrifice. And if this really is something that I really want to do for God, then something has to give. And that's not because I feel that my being gay is wrong or immoral. It's just that if any man was going to commit himself to something like this, he should commit himself to being celibate and open to whatever God wants to put him. A relationship would only put strain on that. I couldn't fully give myself to something because I'd be preoccupied with, well, is my partner okay and whatever. I can fully give myself to those who I serve if I'm celibate.

Do you feel a sense of community among other black gay men here?

No. [Laughter] No, no. They're all closeted. And are too ashamed to come out and say this is who they are.

So there are no openly gay—?

There are very few. There are very few. I'm probably, when you think of openly black gay men on this campus, you will probably hear my name, at least now, I don't know about years past, but at least now. I'm the president of the GSA here on campus. Gay Straight Alliance. And we only have four black members of like fifty members. And two of those girls are lesbians. And I think the other guy is bisexual. And then there's me. And that's it. The white gay men on this campus have it much better, much more of a community going on. And that's just because the whole DL thing, people want to, I don't know [laughter], I don't know. But there's no community at all. There's nobody here I could turn to and ask for support that is black and gay.

Do you feel animosity from other black students toward you?

Yeah, I've heard girls tell me, "Why waste yourself like that? You have so much to give. And all the good black men are either married or gay." [Laughter] And they're upset. I get it more from the girls than I do from the guys. Just because of the ratio between black men and women. You're either in jail, married, or gay. And everybody else in between is just, there's not anybody suitable, there are not enough bachelors, and women get pissed. [Laughter] In fact, I mean, they're even upset with the football players who have white girlfriends. So there is some of that. One of my tutors has been trying to hook me up with this girl forever, and she knows that I'm totally gay and she still would—she's like, "You know, I don't understand. I don't get it. She's beautiful. You're great. Why don't you get with her?" And I always hear the religion card, "You're going to hell. Why don't you get it?" [Laughter]

How can you tell if somebody is gay?

Umm. How do I tell if someone is gay? There's always that, I see you on the street, you see me. We walk past each other and you turn back and you look at me. There's the clothes that some gay men wear. This is just on this campus, I'm just talking. And some in New Orleans. There's the tight, revealing clothes. There's the preppy Abercrombie guys who I found that every single one of them that I've met that's been black has been gay. It's just the attitude. I just find that black gay men have just this, I don't know, there's just this presence. And the way they talk and the way they walk. I don't really know how to describe that. The guy who you never see, the guy who's got a bunch of girlfriends and isn't dating any one of them, any of them. The guy who won't let you in too close because he's got this tough outer shell. Or the guy who has to be really macho; overly macho guys are really funny to watch. That's how I tell. I have bad gaydar, though, or at least it's gotten worse.

How would you describe your involvement in the gay community?

I am very, very much so involved. But I'd like to be the gay person that people meet, who isn't—who doesn't fit the stereotypes, who doesn't give us a bad name. I'd like to do the bridge-building sort of things, between the straight world and the gay world, the person who helps to wipe away the bad stigmas that are placed on us.

So you said you're the president of the GSA? How did that come about? And what are some of the things that you've done as the president?

Our campus has had a GSA before, but they've always fizzled out. And we just recently, just last semester actually, got started up again. And we're doing community service things, AIDS walks, breast cancer awareness, things that affect gay people as well as straight people. Habitat for Humanity. Helping to raise money for elevators for our handicapped students. We're really just doing positive things for the community that affect us all. So that people that surround this campus won't see gay people as being these terrible immoral people. We actually had a protest on campus since the start of our organization, the Westboro Baptist Church, Fred Phelps, came here three weeks before the semester ended to protest the organization. And that actually kind of helped to put a spotlight on us, so that we could get a bit of a boost. So we could show the world, the community around here that we weren't these people that the Phelps people said that we were. And the response from the community, campus community, was great. There were straight people who showed up in drag and with their signs, "go home" and things like that. That was great. But I see myself as being more of a proactive bridge-builder.

How would you describe your political perspectives with regard to issues facing gays and lesbians?

I'm opposed to the word "marriage" being used for gay couples. And the reason for that is because marriage is a sacrament that's done in a church setting. But I'm also opposed to the word "marriage" being given to people who are married—who are together and committed to each other outside of a religious ceremony. Until the church or churches themselves recognize gays and lesbians and their relationships as being blessed by God, the word "marriage" shouldn't be used to describe those relationships. But I do believe that we deserve the same rights that heterosexuals do as far as the government is concerned. But those again shouldn't—the state shouldn't be recognizing marriages, period. Everyone should have a civil union because marriage has nothing to do with the state. Adoption, I believe that gays and lesbians should have the right to adopt, although it does create for some very sticky situations because different states have different laws. But I think that we can be good parents just like anybody else. Those are the only issues I can think of right now. But the one that I'm really passionate about is the word "marriage." That upsets me.

So you were in support of the Louisiana amendment to the constitution?

This is a really hard one for me because I believe that it should have gone through, that states should have recognized it, but just the word "marriage" for me, that's—because it has different meaning. So I was in support of it, but at the same time just kind of like, well, I have to make up my mind but I'm really not for—if you eliminate this one word, I'll be okay with it.

So you were saying that if the church changes the meaning of marriage to accommodate same-sex couples, then you would be fine?

Um hmm.

And what would that process be for the church to change what that means?

For the Episcopal Church, we're already doing that. We have already made accommodations in our *Book of Common Prayer* and functions related to that which recognize the blessing of same-sex unions.

And call it marriage?

We are calling it marriage. But just because what we're doing, we shouldn't force the Baptists to do it. But those unions that are recognized by the Episcopal Church as being marriages are marriages. But a Catholic couple that is gay and living together and their church doesn't call that a marriage, then it's not a marriage. For me it's a gay union. Now, I believe that those relationships can be blessed by God, but if their church doesn't recognize it as being a marriage, then it's not a marriage because it's not recognized. [Laughter]

Why are you giving so much weight to the institution of churches as opposed to the authority of God? Or do you see a distinction between those?

Well, I believe that God—I do believe that God does bless, does bring a man and a man together, I totally believe that. But [. . .] there's just the technicality there. Because "marriage" is a word that we use to describe a particular group of committed people. That's my only quarrel, it's just that it's not a marriage because the church says it's not a marriage. But that doesn't mean that it's not blessed by God. Does that make any sense? It's just that there's a sacramental difference there for me. But it just can't be a marriage because the church doesn't say it's a marriage, but God can bless it. Am I making any sense?

I'm just trying to sort of understand the leaps that you're making from it's not a marriage because the church doesn't say it is so, yet God—.

Right, God—because we as humans use different words to describe different things. And until the definition is changed by churches, then it can't—you can't call an apple an orange. [Laughter] It just isn't there. Maybe that was a bad example. [Laughter] I can't describe it more than I think I already have. Until different priests and religious leaders can bless unions and things like that, I am totally for that. But until that whole group, until the Baptists, the Southern Baptist Convention defines two people being together, two homosexual people being together, a marriage just isn't a marriage, it's just the word. That's my only thing, it's just the word. Because we define it as this. Until we open the door to let this group of people in, these people aren't that. These people are married, but these people are blessed and are together but they can't be a marriage because we haven't said that it's such.

Why is the power of redefinition given to heterosexuals when there are homosexuals who are part of those bodies, the Baptists, the Methodists?

Well, in the Episcopal Church it's just we've already done that. I mean, we've come together and have prayed about it and said God can bring two people of the same sex together. As far as other faiths are concerned, I kind of am opposed to a bunch of old men making decisions for 10,000 people or, a whole religion, I'm opposed to that, whereas in the Episcopal Church we all come together and say, what do we believe as a body? But until those old men do that, then that isn't a marriage for those people. If you're Episcopal and you and your partner decided to marry in the Episcopal Church, then that's a marriage because it's recognized by our church.

Why do you think there are so many black gay men in the church and especially in the choir?

Because gay men have love for music and art and beautiful things. [Laughter] And I think it's the one place where we can actually be ourselves. In a place where it isn't always welcome. And it saddens me when I see a black gay man go to church and I know that his preacher hates him but is gladly going to use him to play the organ. It saddens me but I guess that's how the cookie crumbles.

Do you think it's a place for people to meet other people? Hook up?

I think like anything it's a place where people can meet. I think you just have to be very careful about things like that. But just like heterosexuals meet and it's like, "Oh, wow, I'm in love with the choir director. Oh, he's so great." Wonderful. But you just have to be careful. I just have trouble with just people being promiscuous. Sex without commitment, that's my thing. If you're committed and you're willing to really give yourself to this other person, and using sex for the way God intended it to be, to be a gift, go for it.

What has been the impact of HIV and AIDS on your life?

I lost my mother to it. It's been a real awakening to see her the last few, you know, the last few days of her life to see her digress so much.

When did she pass away?

March of '03, '04, I'm not sure. Yeah—no, no—, '03. It's made me look at sex differently. I don't know.

Besides your mother, have you lost any friends?

No, I haven't lost any friends to AIDS.

Do you think it's more of an issue here in the South?

No. Oh, God, no. It's a worldwide problem. But I think in the South we just—people are just afraid to talk about it. I think that's the real difference. There needs to be more education. I did some work with NO AIDS, and I handed out condoms and stuff like that. And it just breaks my heart to know that people willingly put themselves in situations where they just need to get off, so they put it in the hole and pray to God that somebody doesn't bite it off, you know. But it's something that we as a society need to deal with and stop running away from it and really face it and show people the reality of it all. But I guess that can only happen when it happens to them, when something like that hits close to home

What are your best memories of growing up in the South?

Best memories? Riding in a Mardi Gras parade. Yeah. But I guess that would be my best memory of growing up in New Orleans, but the South. Going fishing and hunting with my friends. Being out in the heat. Just seeing the hospitality. Just visiting with my friends and hunting and things like that.

What are your worst memories?

That would be Louisiana—but just seeing how our government is so crappy, and our education system, how much it sucks. Just how unfair things are. But they're getting better. But the diversity—not diversity—the division between rich and poor people, it's really obvious here. Yeah.

How would you describe the influence of your southern upbringing on your character?

Being real with myself. I think because I've grown up here that I'm more honest with myself. And to just fight through it. And it's not the end, to not sit back and give up. You have to fight for it.

How would you describe your current feelings about being a black gay man?

I don't know. I'm happy with the way I am. I just wish other people could be there.

And how do you feel about the life choices that you've made in light of being gay?

I really don't regret anything because it's all worked out for the good. There have been some hard things but they've all worked out for the good—every single one of them.

epilogue
why this story now?

The news of both deaths arrived via voicemail. The first message was left on May 20, 2004. My partner and I had just
returned home from running errands when I noticed that
there was a message waiting. "Rob," one of the narrators in
this book, had called to ask if I had heard from Curt, a mutual
friend of ours, a former student of mine from the University of
North Carolina at Chapel Hill, and a future Ph.D. student in
the Department of Performance Studies at Northwestern University, where I teach. I had indeed spoken with Curt just
a week before. He was making plans for his move to Chicago from Durham, North Carolina, and wanted to know if he
could stay with me on one of his apartment-hunting trips over
the summer. But the message was odd. Why would Rob, who
spoke with Curt almost daily, contact me in Chicago to ascer-
tain if I had spoken to him? The message was cryptic and did
not sit well with me. I immediately returned the call to inquire
further. Curt was missing, and a body had been found in his
apartment but had not yet been identified. Through the myr-
iad of questions I began to ask—When was the last time someone saw him? Has he been to work? Have you called one of his
brothers? Wasn't he hosting an event at Duke this week?—the
horror of the unspoken began to settle on the two friends on
the phone—the one asking questions and the one with no
answers.

Two days passed before the official word came: the body
found in the apartment was indeed Curt's. Among the various
rumors and hearsay was the story that he was found naked,
bound and gagged, in the hallway outside his bedroom, and
that he had been stabbed over twenty-two times—three of the
stab wounds proving to be fatal. The suspect, an "acquaintance" according to the newspapers,[1] stole a van that Curt
had rented to transport items to an event at Duke University,
where he worked as a minority graduate student recruiter. The
authorities found the van not too far from town and eventually
arrested the assailant after a co-worker tipped the police off

that he had been holding several electronic items in his locker and was selling them at a local pawn shop. None of us wanted to believe that Curt had lost his life over a television set and a DVD player. What we all thought, but never voiced, was that it was a trick gone bad. That's the only thing that could ever explain the *how* of it. The *why* was still lodged somewhere between our willful denial and silent tears, Curt's final moments (Was he afraid? Did he feel any pain? How long was he alive?), and the closed-mouthed convicted murderer's indignation.

The second voicemail came almost two years later on March 16, 2006. This time, however, the voice on the other end was female, the daughter of a former colleague and friend. Her mother had told her to get in touch with me to share the news that Dean, a student at Southern Methodist University and one of the narrators in this book, had been brutally murdered in his Dallas apartment. The daughter was sorry to break the news to me in a voicemail message, but she thought I should know.

The similarities of the murders were uncanny. Like Curt, Dean had been found bound and gagged, and there was no sign of forced entry. Instead of being stabbed, however, Dean was shot in the back of the head. Like Curt's murderer, the assailant was thought to be an "acquaintance" of the victim, and it's believed that he actually called 911 to report that the murder had taken place. Was this a moment of compassion? Regret? I imagined Dean's body lying face down near the place where I had sat in his tiny, one-bedroom apartment in January 2005 to record his story, a story filled with ambivalence about his sexuality, which manifested in various networks of "virtual" meetings, encounters, and, yes, danger. As a flood of emotions consumed my by now immobile body, Curt's face ghosted my reflection in the television on my kitchen counter. Then, an inaudible wail surfaced just beneath my slightly parted lips. Not again, I thought. Not again.

I close this book with the stories of Curt's and Dean's deaths because they are powerful reminders that the South is still a place where hate flourishes and manifests itself in senseless violence. And while we may never know if either of these men's deaths resulted from homophobia (internalized by both the victims and the assailants), the brutality of the murders is ghosted by the lynchings of black men because whites feared their sexuality. The South is still a site where cultural and social transgression may render one silenced, physically harmed, or worse.

These brutal murders also remind us of black gay southerners' unrelenting resilience and bravery. Viewed as backward, closeted, uninformed, and apolitical by "liberated" and "unencumbered" gay northerners, these southern, to-the-manner-born queers rallied around their fallen brothers. One week after Curt's death, his friends and colleagues organized not one, but two memorial services—one held at Duke Memorial Chapel on Duke University's campus, and another at the church to which Curt belonged. His closest friends—two of whom are narrators in this book—also approached Duke University about starting a scholarship in Curt's honor. These friends have held fund-raisers to generate money for the scholarship. At Southern Methodist University in Dallas, scores of Dean's professors and fellow students, along with family members, held a memorial service in his honor. The students planned the service not only to honor Dean, but also to shift the focus away from the news coverage that suggested that Dean was a closeted homosexual who was murdered by a "trick."[2] In the wake of these tragedies, then, black queer communities availed themselves of an opportunity to take a stand and remind their heterosexual brothers and sisters that gays, lesbians, and transgendered people are a part of the community and deserve to be treated with respect and dignity, without fear of violent attack; they also reminded the "city sissies" that the "country" ladies of the southern tier are a force to be reckoned with.

The men who dared to share their life histories with me reminded me that there is power in storytelling. That power manifests itself in the affirmation of the "I" and the "eye," the "I" who tells, and the "eye" who witnesses. My "eye" to "I" encounter with the men of *Sweet Tea* has implicated us all in the making of history—the history of what it means to live in the South as black gay men. If nothing else, this book demonstrates that there is no master narrative of southern black gay experience. And yet, there is a note of commonality that rings through these narratives that exemplify the roots and routes of the South.

Traveling back to my roots and driving over thousands of routes to the narrators' homes made me realize how important it is to get these stories into the world. Certainly, the world has changed since my days of growing up in North Carolina, but my forty years of life changes pale in comparison to the changes that the Countess Vivian has witnessed over the past ninety something years. No more time should pass before these stories are told. Jeff Smith's light has dimmed, but I am proud and honored that he was able to share a piece of his life before he died. Curt's and Dean's deaths were not in vain if these stories help someone who is struggling with being a black gay southerner find inspiration in the words or experiences of one of the narrators. As I earlier noted, Michel de Certeau asserts, "What the map cuts up, the story cuts across." Not only does the larger story told here cut across borders, boundaries, and Bibles; it also preserves and sustains. Sometimes our stories, our expression of our experiences, are the only thing that we have to hold on to. And in the midst of story are reverie and revelation, confirmation and condemnation, affirmation and atrophy. Ultimately, it's the will to tell that's important.

Marlon Riggs critiqued the homophobia of the black community in much of his work. One memorable line from his film *Tongues Untied* is "I cannot go home as who I am." After the experience I have had researching and writing *Sweet Tea*, I would have to alter Riggs's slogan slightly to suggest that "I cannot go home as who I *was*," for I have truly been changed by this experience—and for the better. I do not wish to idealize these men or to romanticize my experience, because they are not innocent subjects and not all of my experiences in the field were easy or pleasant. But the exchange that occurred between us was about more than just me pulling out a tape recorder and gathering stories. Rather, it was about the preservation of the undocumented lives of men who have contributed, and continue to contribute, to the maintenance of black southern life. After this book, no one will be able to say otherwise. In this way, we, the men and I, were "blessed" that I had the resources and motivation and that they had the courage, goodwill, and wit, to share with one another. I hope this will not be the final word and it will spawn more books on other aspects of the black queer South: black lesbians, the history of black gay bars and clubs, and the history of black queer organizations, for example. *Sweet Tea* only begins to mine the multiple and rich histories waiting to be let loose and shared with the rest of the world.

These life stories dance at the zenith of dusk and dawn, spinning new tales in the light of the moon and sun. They are my brothers' stories, tucked beneath the "Amens" and "Hallelujahs" lifting us to Jesus and condemning us to sit with Satan. They are my fathers' stories, moaned and hummed in that half-sung, half-sobbed chorus coaxed from the mouths of our pleasured partners. They are my sons' stories, rich in red delta soil and baked in mud pies fresh from Easy Bake ovens. They are my granddaddies' stories, hot with the lash of "faggot" inscribed on the back of Miss Thing's too-cute-to-resist ham-wide ass. They are my great-granddaddies' stories, and the stories from as far back as my black queer paternal lineage will allow my mind to imagine. The circle must be unbroken.

appendix
black gay vernacular terms

. . . .

With any slang, origins are difficult to trace. Therefore, the vernacular terms that I collected from the narrators of *Sweet Tea* are not all peculiar to the South or to black gay men. Many of them are a part of general gay parlance or even popular culture. Some of the terms, however, are specific to a narrator's community of friends and family. "Kevin," one of the youngest narrators I interviewed, got it right when he said: "Gay people are some of the wittiest people I know. Because when you think about it, any time that you're expressing something that's totally against the norm in any way, that requires you to be yourself. If this is how you feel, you're free in that regard. You're so free to where you're just creative. [. . .] Gay people use a lot of metaphors. We talk in a lot of allegories. So with that, the terms and the phrases are endless." Indeed, terms and phrases are created daily, and some of them never circulate beyond their spontaneous creation. Others, however, take hold and take on a life of their own.

While the narrators cannot take full credit for many of these terms, each certainly puts a southern spin on them. As I discussed in the introduction, southern ways of speaking facilitate the passive-aggressive ethos of southern gentility. Anthony "First Lady" Hardaway put it this way: "Northern gays will cut you. Southern gays, we'll cut you, but we're going to do it sweet. You may not know that you're cut until later on, but it's sweet. You know what I mean? So we try to do the southern, polite thing when we cut, and say certain things." Thus, the "sweetness" of *how* the words are said sometimes literally "sugar coats" the significance of *what* is said.

But if some of this terminology resonates elsewhere as well, some of these words, terms, and phrases arise out of the sheer creative spirit and playfulness of black queer southern life. I have presented the definitions of these terms in the narrators' own words.

GLOSSARY

Alice

"The cops . . . It's like here you have this masculine sort of state, federal-driven entity that can sort of lock you down, but you refer to it as 'Alice.' It's almost this biting way of, like inverting its masculinity and making it a supremely . . . not only feminine but, like little-girl feminine, like *Alice in Wonderland*'s Alice." (Tim'm)

Bear

"Big, hairy man. Straight acting. Masculine." (Stephen)

Beat; Beating one's face

"Referring to someone's face being made up." (Tim'm)

" 'Beat.' To say that one is beat means that one is dolled up, you know, with maybe makeup or a nice facial or a very nice outfit, you know, ensemble. So to say, 'Oh, child, you're so beat,' means that, you know, that you are really, really following through, you're really shining." (Fred-Rick)

" 'Beating one's face'. That's more so of a drag queen term. That's like applying the makeup, putting on the makeup or doing whatever it takes to look fabulous. . . . Or for any man, gay man, like you know, 'Beating my face' is like making sure I have it together. I'm well groomed." (Roderick)

"Someone's face will be beat out, just really flawless, really polished, maybe some makeup, eyebrows plucked, just really in order, really, no blemishes, just really beat. And beat is also sort of, you know, you're, you're very current, very, very current, very fresh, like very just, really put together." (Shomari)

"That's hot; that means it's really good." (Anthony "First Lady" Hardaway)

Bird

"Dick." (Charles)

Butch queen

"A butch queen's a black gay man who performs masculinity, you know, on a sliding scale, like it's not like you have to be a certain, you know you have to, if you wear boy clothes, and you gay, you're a butch queen." (Shomari)

Butt munch

"Oh, that's a bottom." (Joe)

The children
  "Meaning gay." ("C.C.")
  "Gay folks." (Sean)
Clocked
  "You've been clocked. You've indicated in some way that you get down."
    (Albert)
  " 'Clock' is like, to detect. If I'm clocking you I'm detecting that you're
    gay," or "to detect" (Charles)
  "If you're trying to figure out if somebody's gay or not, you clocking
    them." ("DLB")
  "You know, if I knew he was gay, 'I clocked him.' " (John)
  " 'Clock' means to learn something about somebody." (Kenyatta)
  "Clocking is, you know, you're figuring out somebody's gay, you know."
    (Roderick)
  " 'Clock' is like, you know, if a fish or say if a drag girl is trying to pass as
    a real fish. You know 'She can't be clocked,' you know, meaning that
    they can't tell that she's a real man. You know, 'Oh girl, she can't be
    clocked, Honey.' Meaning that she's a pure fish, you know. She's a
    real woman. She's passing as a real woman." (Mademoiselle Grégoire)
Clutching your pearls
  "You know like, 'How dare you say something like that?' " ("Larry J.")
Coins
  "Money." (Sean)
Come into my yard
  " 'Come into my yard' means that you're all up in my mud, you're all up
    in my tea, my grill, so you want to play. 'Oh, girl, she out in my yard.'
    'Come on, girl, come up in my yard.' That could be it's all up in my
    business. You're trying to find out if I'm with somebody. You're trying
    to find out if I'm a top or a bottom. That's what that means, and all of
    that." (Anthony "First Lady" Hardaway)
Cunt
  "A boy who's really feminine." (Shomari)
Dinge queen
  "A white guy that prefers black guys." (John)
Dish
  "Dish, dishing the dirt, pouring the tea, it's the same thing, it's dishing the
    dirt for me; it was about somebody's business, but it was gossip." (Tony)
DL or down low
  "That's someone who has an interest in [the] same sex but is not—it's
    not openly known that they have that interest or they are living that

lifestyle. That's straight men who have quote/unquote gay tendencies as a form of release or just getting off with other guys." ("Rich")

"And so the DL, the down low term. The DL, in my understanding, is a person who has interest in the same sex but does not want people to know it. And may be married, may be divorced, and may even be in a relationship with a same sex, but is under this title, pseudo title, to keep anonymity, so." (Dean)

"Closeted . . . masculine." (Charles)

"Somebody that I would say that is conservative with their actions." ("D.C.")

"A man who's basically thought of as straight, who's having sex with another man." (Freddie)

"DL guys, some of them are not able to deal with it and still call it something, but some of them know who they are but they just still keep it under the radar so that other people don't find out." (Jaime)

"DL men are the guys that gay men and women want." (Joe)

"DL means that you are gay but you don't want nobody to know about it." ("Larry J.")

"Someone who actively pursues a man in private but openly gives off the persona that they are completely heterosexual." ("Alex")

Done

"Someone whose face is done up." (Tim'm)

Douching

"Keeping one's anus clean." (Roderick)

Drop pearls

"And dropping a pearl meant sort of signaling to someone that you were one of Judy's friends . . . And that meant he was gay or something like that." ("WB")

Dyking

"Dyking is when two bottoms are together and one's trying to be the top or something. But 'dyking' was definitely one of the expressions for all lesbian women." (Roderick)

Extra

"Just like too much." (Jonathan S.)

Fag hag

"Fag hag. Fruit fly. Those things are all the same, along the same lines as a woman who pretty much draw gay men towards her." (Stephen)

Femme queens

"They're wearing girl clothes." (Shomari)

Fish

"A derogatory term that refers to women." (Roderick)

Fishy

"That's womanish. Or that could be like when a drag queen aspires to look 'fishy' or look . . . Because that's supposed to be how a woman is supposed to look." (Roderick)

Getting down

"Getting down indicates that you're a part of the family, you know, have interest, or have likings in same sex, the same sex." (Albert)

Gil

"Don't say 'girl,' they say 'gil.' The 'R' is silent. Okay he's a 'gil,' which is gonna mean he's feminine. We don't use the word bottom and top. He's a gil. That means he's what? He's a bottom." ("Larry J.")

Honey-boo

"A response to a, something that we think is silly or that doesn't make sense." (Jeryl)

Honey boom

" 'Honey boom' is something like don't try to comfort me—honey boom. Like you're giving, like I caught that but the bomb's back on you. You thought you got me but you didn't." (Timothy)

Hot talent

" 'Hot talent' means that whatever you did, you really worked it over; that's hot talent. That means that you fixed a meal, "Ooh, honey, this is hot talent." (Anthony "First Lady" Hardaway)

Husband

" 'Husband' does mean you're a man. My piece is the one that I'm probably with and screwing but he's not the main person." (Anthony "First Lady" Hardaway)

In the life

"It's a gay black man who he is doing gay black things, you know." (Keanan)

"That means you're living it. You're gay and you're right in the gay lifestyle." (Stanley)

Judy

"As in 'You are Judies,' You're friends." (Charles)

"The elite gay black men." (Keanan)

" 'Judy' is like, 'We're friends, we're buddies, we're Judies.' . . . I think it comes from Judy Garland." (Ed)

Judy Justice

"The police." (Ed)

The lick

"'The lick'; we say that a lot in Memphis. 'Girl, that was the lick.' The lick means it was good." (Anthony "First Lady" Hardaway)

Maggie

"The police." (Ed)

Miss Thing

"That's someone that acts like a woman." (Kevin W.)

Mister Man

"The real hunky, beefy, beefy guy." ("G.C.")

Moose

"A nice ass." (Charles)

Morphodite or morphodice

"The corruption of the word hermaphrodite . . . a gay person." (Ed)

Pay it

"Pay it no mind . . . don't pay it no attention . . . let's move on." (Charles)

Peppermint twist

"'Peppermint twist,' that's just a little, oh he is so sweet, boy I could eat him like a peppermint stick." ("G.C.")

Pickle-popper

"Penis." (Ted)

Plucked

"Upset . . . annoyed." (Charles)

Polly Pureheart

"Somebody who's trying to be sweet and innocent." (Charles)

Pouring tea

"Pouring people's business . . . gossiping, and sharing business, and whatever that is, good, bad news, it's always been. You know I can hear my friends saying, 'Ooh child, let me get my teacup, so we can share this little bit of dirt.'" (Bryant)

"As in 'information.' As in pouring. As in granting the information or spilling the 'tea,' as in telling tales." ("R. Dioneaux")

"Telling secrets." (Freddie)

"You want to get someone's tea, well, you want to find out what's up with him." (Keanan)

"I got some tea . . . I got some gossip, basically." (Ken)

"That's the goods . . . the gossip, the dirt." (Roderick)

Preserves in a biscuit

"Sometimes some of the older ones say, 'Child, you don't want me to put some of these preserves in a biscuit.' That means he don't want me to fix his plate. He don't want none of this because it's going to be over, that's what that means. And we say that sometimes amongst each other. You don't want me to put some of these preserves in a biscuit, because it's going to be on." (Anthony "First Lady" Hardaway)

Press

"Oh, to 'press,' that is the most recent that I've found out. When you press, it means to, to persevere, or to go through. You're gonna take this book, and press, because, you know, when you get it to the publisher, they're gonna, it's gonna blow up, you know, and in order to achieve your goals, you have to press. Or, 'Girl you get on the stage, and you press,' you know, in that evening gown. Girl, she pressed. That is the most, that's the newest term that I've become familiar with." (Chaz/Chastity)

Pull a date

"Try to seduce some unassuming . . . heterosexual boy that might think you're a woman or whatever." (Charles)

Read

" 'I'm gonna read you' . . . it might have meant 'I'm going to curse you out' or 'I'm going to tell the truth on you.' " (Freddie)

"He got read, which means told off or called out or put in his place." (Fred-Rick)

" 'Reading.' You know how the children get together, comically? A very comical thing where gay men get together and 'read' or say something like signifying or as an African American term called 'the dozens.' You know where you tell 'your mama' jokes and things of that nature. Or who's the grandest queen? You know. So you'll be trying to 'read' the girl's outfits or her hair or her makeup or something of that nature." (Mademoiselle Grégoire)

Saint

"In the South, in the black gay village, we call each other saints sometimes. 'Hey, Saint, what you doing, Saint?' 'Well, Saint, how are you?' And we say that because we were raised with that." (Anthony "First Lady" Hardaway)

Salt

"Salt was sort of like the southern form of 'shade.' Sometimes people would just go 'Ch-ch-ch.' They would make that sound like the saltshaker. Like if you went to somebody and they were kind of like short with you, you'd go, 'Oooh, ch-ch-ch, salt.' " (Tim'm)

Shade

"I'm a say you something but it's more subtle." (Charles)

" 'Shade' is you just look at the person like, "You're not even worthy of telling you off." ("R. Dioneaux")

"When you distance yourself from somebody you're throwing shade, you know, you don't want to be bothered." ("DLB")

"To be somewhat closed or short with someone else." (Roderick)

"It would mean that somebody was giving you attitude or treating you badly." (Tony)

Sisters

"Definitely your tried-and-true Judies." (Tim'm)

Snow queen

"A black guy that prefers white men." (John)

"A black guy that's all into—that's only into dating white men or—well, I can't really say Latinos but, you know, only dating outside of his race and predominantly he's dating white guys." (Keanan)

"A snow queen is a black gay male that hangs out with all white people maybe." ("KG")

"Black folk who liked white men." ("Lamar")

"A black guy who likes white guys exclusively." (Kevin W.)

Spilling tea

" 'Pouring the tea,' you know, that's somebody who's really telling what's going on. 'Spilling the tea' is just blabbing, and just throwing it everywhere no matter where you are." ("Kevin")

Star

"The old, old gay term for gay men were stars." (Michael)

Stunt queen

"And then there were the 'stunt queens.' You know 'stunt girls' are the girls that go to pageants and steal gowns and things. Or go to department stores and steal gowns for pageants and all of that. Those are like 'stunt queens.' " (Mademoiselle Grégoire)

Tea

" 'He's tea' or 'She's tea' . . . That meant that that person is gay or that woman is lesbian or whatever." (Roderick)

"What's the truth, what's happening." (Shomari)

"Gossip." (Stanley)

Temple

" 'The temple' is the club. Are you going to the temple? Girl, I'll be there. That's the club." (Anthony "First Lady" Hardaway)

Trade, rough trade

"Back in the day, 'trade' meant trick, meant somebody sold his body for money, but I think that's, like now it's more general, just to refer to a heterosexual man that would have sex with a man but not because he wants to." (Charles)

"Maybe there was an exchange of something other than sex with the
   person you call trade." (Freddie)

" 'Trade' is like say a guy that is into the gay lifestyle, that deals with gays,
   that has sexual contact with half-gays, you know? He's trade."
   (Gerome)

"Just guys that will mess around for whatever reason, but don't
   necessarily put a label on what they do or who they are." (Jaime)

"That's the feminine gay guy." (Joe)

" 'Trade' is more so more out than somebody who's down low." ("Kevin")

"In my mind it was [. . .] maybe thuggish looking guy, standing on the
   corner, you know, waiting to be picked up." (Kenneth)

"What that word means now is that a lot of the gang members that you
   have that are maybe gay, they may trade sex to other men in return
   for, like, monetary gifts or other things like that." (Jonathan S.)

" 'Trade' is somebody who knocks at the door, you know you going to
   have." ("OKC")

" 'Trade' just means somebody who is available for the evening." ("Rich")

" 'Trade' can be like a thugged out kind of guy." (Roderick)

" 'Trade,' when I first learned it, it was about somebody who was not
   identified as being gay and who presented themselves as straight, but
   you got him to sleep with you, so you pulled some trade and so you
   slept with a man who was not really gay or who did not present
   himself as such, and that was considered like a really big thing like,
   you know, getting the prize. But then as people, as I heard people use
   it over the years when I was younger, it also meant just somebody who
   was not, you know, even if they didn't say the word rough trade, it
   meant rough trade, just somebody who was actually gay but who was
   not like you, you know, who was uneducated, you know, boy from the
   streets, even if he were gay identified, he could still be called trade
   because he was rough trade. So that had two meanings." (Tony)

"Someone who sees themselves as heterosexual and tend to be a kind of
   rougher guy, you know, maybe on the make for money, you know,
   from a gay guy, wants something out of a gay guy usually." (Henry)

" 'Trade' was really a bisexual guy, you know, who was very masculine."
   (Fred-Rick)

"Sexual favors in exchange for something." (Angelo)

"A rough trade, I think, is simply the kind of trade we're talking about.
   But what makes him rough is he's masculine, you see. And that was a
   term used a lot in the Harlem Renaissance, um hmm, rough trade,
   yes." (Fred-Rick)

Trade piece

"Someone that you may sleep with but may not necessarily . . . Let's say not sleep with. That you may hang out with and have sexual desires for and may ultimately sleep with but it would only be for just that one time or a two-time type deal." ("Alex")

Trendy

"The trendy gay kids were the gay kids who shopped at thrift stores and sort of had what we would call now sort of bohemian." (Tim'm)

Twink

"Small, a really feminine gay man." (Stephen)

Up in them

"Being up in drag." (Charles)

Vexed

"[. . .] honey she vexed me, you know, and that's to say that, you know someone, tried to embarrass you, or, or they tried to, pull something over on you, or they tried to be shady, with you. Honey, I was vexed." (Chaz/Chastity)

What's the Tea?

"What's up, or what's going on." (Charles)

Whore of Babylon

"That means she is, whoo, don't try to stop her, she's in her own world. She's the Whore of Babylon. They're actually talking about a man. She is the whore." (Anthony "First Lady" Hardaway)

Working

" 'Working.' Working somebody is when you don't know if they're gay or straight or not, but you're trying to. That's working. You're trying to work your magic or work it so you can find out the deal and even, better yet, get a hookup out of it, you know." (Roderick)

notes

. . . .

INTRODUCTION

1. The Lady Chablis, *Hiding My Candy*, 55.
2. Daniel, *Standing at the Crossroads*, 66.
3. This and the other names in the quotation are pseudonyms.
4. As John Howard argues in *Carryin' On in the Lesbian and Gay South*, the phrase "carryin' on" has multiple meanings in southern parlance, but often among gays and lesbians refers to "stepping over some perceived line of propriety" (*Carryin' On in the Lesbian and Gay South*, 2).
5. Sears, *Rebels, Rubyfruit, and Rhinestones*, 4.
6. Beemyn, "Introduction," 1.
7. McRuer, "A Visitation of Difference," 222.
8. Smith, "Queering the South," 381.
9. Ibid., 380.
10. Whittier, "Race and Gay Community in Southern Town," 73.
11. Hurston, *Mules and Men*, 2.
12. Howard, "Place and Movement in Gay American History," 213.
13. Painter, *Creating Black Americans*, iv (emphasis in original).
14. See Conquergood, "Performance Studies," 149.
15. Madison, "The Dialogic Performative in Critical Ethnography," 323.
16. Howard, *Men Like That*, 5.
17. For more on the ethics and responsibility of the ethnographer, see Madison, *Critical Ethnography*, 5–8.
18. See Geertz, "Thinking as a Moral Act."
19. Benjamin, *Illuminations*, 87.
20. Langellier and Peterson, *Storytelling in Daily Life*, 4.
21. Certeau, *The Practice of Everyday Life*, 129.
22. I do not wish to imply here that there is "inherent" danger in meeting men on the Internet. Indeed, I met my current partner online. I also do not wish to appear prudish about sexual "hookups" or "tricks" garnered through chat rooms. For the purpose of researching this book, however, I believed that contacting subjects online would not have been the most productive way to obtain subjects. One downside to this, however, is that the sample of narrators is skewed toward those with a college education.
23. In his latest novel, E. Lynn Harris actually dramatizes what happens when all the gays of a church in Atlanta decide to walk out. See *I Say A Little Prayer*.
24. See Phillips and Lewis, "A Hunt for Middle Ground."
25. Howard, *Men Like That*, 299.
26. Smith, "Queering the South," 381.
27. Beam, "Brother to Brother," 231

28. This is a vernacular phrase among black gay men meaning that a person's makeup is applied very well and very heavily. See the Appendix.

29. See Hemphill, "Loyalty."

30. Howard, *Men Like That*, 27.

31. The Lady Chablis, *Hiding My Candy*, 25.

32. For more on the history of tearooms, see Edelman, "Tearoom and Sympathies" and "Men's Room"; Humphreys, *Tearoom Trade*; and Chauncey, *Gay New York*, 195–201.

33. Mintz, *Sweetness and Power*, 139.

34. Quoted in ibid., 141.

35. Quoted in ibid., 142.

36. While there have been numerous theories of the origin of the term and what behavior constitutes "camp," many white gay scholars have traced the aesthetic back to Oscar Wilde.

37. See <http://whatscookingamerica.net/History/IcedTeaHistory.htm>, accessed on March 24, 2006.

38. See ibid.

39. Wat, *The Making of a Gay Asian Community*, 6.

CHAPTER 1

1. See Johnson, *Appropriating Blackness*, 249–52.

2. The Lady Chablis, *Hiding My Candy*, 52–53.

3. See, for examples, Nero, "Why Are Gay Ghettos White?"

4. I can't help but make the association of this negative term for blighted black neighborhoods with the gay vernacular term "bottom," which refers to one's sexual position (i.e., on the bottom and therefore the one being penetrated), although in the case of the latter, it is definitely not considered an unpleasant or displeasing "destination."

5. West, *Race Matters*, 11–20.

6. Du Bois quoted in Boyd, *The Story of Durham*, 277.

7. Auburn Avenue, also known as "Sweet Auburn," was designated a national historic landmark in 1976. Like the Hayti community in Durham, Sweet Auburn was an economic center for African Americans during Jim Crow and was home to the Atlanta Life Insurance Company, the second-largest black insurance company in the United States. It was also Martin Luther King Jr.'s birth home, and it boasted both the *Atlanta Daily World*, the nation's first black-owned daily newspaper, and the Rucker Building, Atlanta's first black-owned office building. Like many inner-city neighborhoods, it fell into disrepair in the late twentieth century and became a haven for crime and poverty. Currently, it is being gentrified with encouragement from the city of Atlanta through the Historic District Development Corporation.

8. It's interesting to note that the devastating effects of Hurricane Betsy were just a prelude to those of Katrina in 2005. The images of mayhem that Ed recounts are eerily similar to those the world witnessed after Katrina. It is also ironic that

where Ed lived at the time of this interview—the Ninth Ward—is the very place that suffered the greatest destruction from Katrina.

9. A spreader is a garment factory worker who spreads spools of fabric out on larger cutting tables and cuts out patterns to make garments.

10. For a discussion of black homophobia from different perspectives, see McBride, "Can the Queen Speak?"; hooks, "Homophobia in Black Communities"; and Ross, "Some Glances at the Black Fag."

CHAPTER 2

1. While Eve Kosofsky Sedgwick was the first queer theorist to theorize "the closet" as a term, her failure to consider the racial implications of the coming out process has prompted black queer theorists like Ross to rethink the applicability of the closet to racialized sexuality. See Sedgwick, *Epistemology of the Closet*, and Ross, "Beyond the Closet as Raceless Paradigm."

CHAPTER 3

1. Lincoln and Mamiya, *The Black Church in the African American Experience*, 8.
2. Howard, *Men Like That*, 55.
3. Hurston, *Their Eyes Were Watching God*, 183.
4. In the African American folk church tradition, many preachers relate stories about how they were "called" to preach, thus the "call story."
5. The style of singing that Roderick is mimicking is known as "raising up" a hymn, a style in the black folk church tradition derived from slave church services. Typically, a leader—the preacher or a deacon—begins the hymn with a rapid succession of words from the first line of the hymn, in what is known as the "call." The congregation then repeats the line, but in an exaggeratedly drawn out style—the "response."

CHAPTER 4

1. See Major, *From Juba to Jive*, 195.
2. McCune, "Doin' the Down Low, Remixin' the Closet."
3. Howard, *Men Like That*, xviii.
4. For more on homosexuality in the military during World War II, see Bérubé, *Coming Out Under Fire*.
5. "Black Colleges Seek to Stem HIV Cases: Stepping Up Safe-Sex Education After Spike in Infections," MSNBC, March 22, 2004, <http://www.msnbc.msn.com/id/4556054/>, accessed September 28, 2006.
6. Glanton, "Emerging Face of HIV."
7. The *Question of the Day* was a talk show hosted by Genevieve Stewart that aired on KQXL FM in Baton Rouge in the late 1980s and early 1990s. Listeners could call in to discuss various "questions" posed by the host.
8. The King Alfred Plan was an alleged FBI plan to contain black communities in large cities in the event of racial unrest. Its goal was to neutralize black militant groups such as the Student Nonviolent Coordinating Committee, the Southern

Christian Leadership Conference, the Revolutionary Action Movement, and the Nation of Islam.

CHAPTER 5

1. RuPaul, *Lettin' It All Hang Out*, 140.
2. See Currah, "Gender Pluralisms under the Transgender Umbrella."
3. Quoted in Feinberg, *Transgender Warrior*, x.
4. The Lady Chablis, *Hiding My Candy*, 101.
5. Juang, "Transgendering the Politics of Recognition," 243.
6. This is a line from singer Sylvester's song "Dance (Disco Heat)."

CHAPTER 7

1. On ballroom legends, see the movie *Paris Is Burning* (1990).
2. Clark, "Introduction," 8.
3. Sears, *Lonely Hunters*, 10.
4. Apparently, the Countess allows men who are down on their luck to board with him from time to time.
5. He is obviously mistaken about the dates and number of years he resided in the children's home, as the years don't add up.

EPILOGUE

1. Aisling Swift, "Murders Put Gay Community on Alert," *The Independent Weekly*, June 9, 2004, <http://www.indyweek.com/gyrobase/Content?oid=oid%3A21875>; "Duke Man Charged With Murder of Duke Employee," WRAL.com, June 4, 2004, <http://www.wral.com/news/local/story/111441/>, both accessed on January 9, 2005.
2. The only coverage of Dean's murder was on the local television news. Coverage of the story was brief and connected the murder to another "gay bashing" that had occurred just a week prior. This was particularly distressing for Dean's family, who did not know that he was gay.

bibliography

Bailey, Marlon M. "Queering the African Diaspora: On Ballroom Cultural Performance and Black Queer 'World-Making.' " Ph.D. dissertation, University of California, Berkeley, 2005.

Beam, Joseph. "Brother to Brother: Words from the Heart." In *In the Life: A Black Gay Anthology*, 230–42. Boston: Alyson Publications, 1986.

Beemyn, Brett. "Introduction." In *Creating a Place for Ourselves: Lesbian, Gay, and Bisexual Community Histories*, 1–7. New York: Routledge, 1997.

Benjamin, Walter. *Illuminations*. Edited by Hannah Arendt. Translated by H. Zohn. New York: Schocken, 1969.

Bérubé, Allan. *Coming Out Under Fire: The History of Gay Men and Women in World War Two*. New York: Free Press, 2000.

Boyd, William K. *The Story of Durham: City of the New South*. Durham, N.C.: Duke University Press, 1925.

Certeau, Michel de. *The Practice of Everyday Life*. Translated by Steven F. Rendall. Berkeley: University of California Press, 1984.

Chauncey, George. *Gay New York: Gender, Urban Culture, and the Making of the Gay Male World, 1890–1940*. New York: Basic Books, 1994.

Clark, Don. "Introduction." In *Quiet Fire: Memoirs of Older Gay Men*, by Keith Vacha, 7–8. Trumansburg, N.Y.: The Crossing Press, 1985.

Conquergood, Dwight. "Performance Studies: Interventions and Radical Research." *TDR* 46.2 (Summer 2002): 145–56.

Currah, Paisley. "Gender Pluralisms under the Transgender Umbrella." In *Transgender Rights*, edited by Paisley Currah, Richard M. Juang, and Shannon Price Minter, 3–31. Minneapolis: University of Minnesota Press, 2006.

Daniel, Pete. *Standing at the Crossroads: Southern Life in the Twentieth Century*. Baltimore: Johns Hopkins University Press, 1996.

Edelman, Lee. "Men's Room." In *Stud: Architectures of Masculinity*, edited by Joel Sanders, 152–61. New York: Princeton Architectural Press, 1996.

——. "Tearoom and Sympathies or The Epistemology of the Water Closet." In *The Lesbian and Gay Studies Reader*, edited by Henry Abelove, Michèle Aina Barale, and David M. Halperin, 553–57. New York: Routledge, 1993.

Feinberg, Leslie. *Transgender Warrior*. Boston: Beacon, 1996.

Geertz, Clifford. "Thinking as a Moral Act: Ethical Dimensions of Anthropological Fieldwork in the New States." *Antioch Review* 28 (1968): 139–58.

Glanton, Dahleen. "Emerging Face of HIV: Fear of Discovery Adds to Burden." *Chicago Tribune Online*, March 30, 2004,<http://chicagotribune.com/news/local/chi-0403280353>; accessed March 30, 2004.

Harris, E. Lynn. *I Say a Little Prayer*. New York: Doubleday, 2006.

Hemphill, Essex. "Loyalty." In *Ceremonies*, 69–71. San Francisco: Cleis, 1992; revised edition, 2000.

hooks, bell. "Homophobia in Black Communities." In *Talking Back: Thinking Feminist, Thinking Black*, 120–26. Boston: South End Press, 1989.

Howard, John. *Carryin' On in the Lesbian and Gay South*. New York: New York University Press, 1997.

——. *Men Like That: A Southern Queer History*. Chicago: University of Chicago Press, 1999.

——. "Place and Movement in Gay American History: A Case from the Post–World War II South." In *Creating a Place for Ourselves: Lesbian, Gay, and Bisexual Community Histories*, edited by Brett Beemyn, 211–25. New York: Routledge, 1997.

Humphreys, Laud. *Tearoom Trade: Impersonal Sex in Public Places*. Revised and enlarged edition. New York: Aldine de Gruyter, 1975.

Hurston, Zora Neale. *Mules and Men*. New York: Harper and Row, 1990.

——. *Their Eyes Were Watching God*. New York: Harper and Row, 1990.

Johnson, E. Patrick. *Appropriating Blackness: Performance and the Politics of Authenticity*. Durham, N.C.: Duke University Press, 2003.

Juang, Richard M. "Transgendering the Politics of Recognition." In *Transgender Rights*, edited by Paisley Currah, Richard M. Juang, and Shannon Price Minter, 242–61. Minneapolis: University of Minnesota Press, 2006.

Langellier, Kristin M., and Eric E. Peterson. *Storytelling in Daily Life: Performing Narrative*. Philadelphia: Temple University Press, 2004.

Lincoln, C. Eric, and Lawrence H. Mamiya. *The Black Church in the African American Experience*. Durham, N.C.: Duke University Press, 1990.

Madison, D. Soyini. *Critical Ethnography: Method, Ethics, and Performance*. Thousand Oaks, Calif.: Sage Publications, 2005.

——. "The Dialogic Performative in Critical Ethnography." *Text and Performance Quarterly* 26.4 (October 2006): 320–24.

Major, Clarence. *From Juba to Jive: A Dictionary of African American Slang*. New York: Penguin, 1994.

McBride, Dwight. "Can the Queen Speak?: Racial Essentialism, Sexuality and the Problem of Authority." *Callaloo* 21.2 (Spring 1998): 363–79.

McCune, Jeffrey Q. "Doin' the Down Low, Remixin' the Closet: Black Masculinity and Sexuality." Ph.D. dissertation, Northwestern University, 2006.

McRuer, Robert. "A Visitation of Difference: Randall Kenan and Black Queer Theory." In *Critical Essays: Gay and Lesbian Writers of Color*, edited by Emmanuel S. Nelson, 221–32. New York: Harrington Park Press, 1993.

Mintz, Sidney. *Sweetness and Power: The Place of Sugar in Modern History*. New York: Penguin, 1986.

Nero, Charles. "Why Are Gay Ghettos White?" In *Black Queer Studies: A Critical Anthology*, edited by E. Patrick Johnson and Mae Henderson, 228–48. Durham, N.C.: Duke University Press, 2005.

Painter, Nell Irvin. *Creating Black Americans: African-American History and Its Meanings, 1619 to the Present*. New York: Oxford University Press, 2005.

Paris Is Burning. Directed by Jennie Livingston. Off-White Productions, 1990.

Phillips, Frank, and Raphael Lewis. "A Hunt for Middle Ground: Travaglini Voices

Confidence on a Marriage Accord Today." *Boston Globe*, March 11, 2004, <http://www.boston.com/news/local/articles/2004/03/11/a_hunt_for_middle_ground/>; accessed May 9, 2006.

Ross, Marlon B. "Beyond the Closet as Raceless Paradigm." In *Black Queer Studies: A Critical Anthology*, edited by E. Patrick Johnson and Mae Henderson, 162–89. Durham, N.C.: Duke University Press, 2003.

——. "Some Glances at the Black Fag: Race, Same-Sex Desire, and Cultural Belonging." In *African American Literary Theory*, edited by Winston Napier, 498–522. New York: New York University Press, 2000.

RuPaul. *Lettin' It All Hang Out: An Autobiography*. New York: Hyperion, 1995.

Sears, James T. *Lonely Hunters: An Oral History of Lesbian and Gay Southern Life, 1948–1968*. New York: Westview, 1997.

——. *Rebels, Rubyfruit, and Rhinestones: Queering Space in the Stonewall South*. New Brunswick, N.J.: Rutgers University Press, 2001.

Sedgwick, Eve Kosofsky. *Epistemology of the Closet*. Berkeley: University of California Press, 1990.

Smith, Donna Jo. "Queering the South: Constructions of Southern/Queer Identity." In *Carryin' On in the Lesbian and Gay South*, edited by John Howard, 370–85. New York: New York University Press, 1997.

The Lady Chablis. *Hiding My Candy*. New York: Pocket Books, 1996.

Wat, Eric C. *The Making of a Gay Asian Community: An Oral History of Pre-AIDS Los Angeles*. Lanham, Md.: Rowman and Littlefield, 2002.

West, Cornel. *Race Matters*. Boston: Beacon, 1993.

Whittier, David Knapp. "Race and Gay Community in Southern Town." In *Out in the South*, edited by Carlos L. Dews and Carolyn Leste Law, 72–94. Philadelphia: Temple University Press, 2001.

index of narrators

. . . .

Note: Names appearing in quotes are pseudonyms.

index